EDGE WORK

EdgeWork Books began like this: A room full of writers—women, most in their 50s. Some had written bestsellers, some were poets. Most of them were therapists, or teachers of some kind. And all of them, once they started comparing notes, were worried about the shape and direction of the publishing industry. More and more, the really hot books were being turned down as "brilliant but too literary," "too feminist," "too unusual" to compete for market share. If this was happening to them, at the peak of successful careers, what was happening to the voices of emerging women writers? Who was encouraging, publishing, distributing, and marketing their best work?

EdgeWork Books began when this room full of women said, "We've got to have viable alternatives to the New York publishing machine," and one of them responded "Well, if not us, then who?"

So that's us. We're trying to be the press we've been waiting for. We want to be part of the decentralization and democratization of the publishing industry—the structures that support it, the people who run it, and the work it produces. We publish well-written books with fresh artistic vision and, through our Web site, we offer, as possible, supportive writing classes, individual writing consultation, coaching, editing, and open forums.

But something else has happened along the way. As we gathered allies, we found not just writers, but filmmakers, playwrights, musicians, painters, cartoonists all facing the same challenges. We became a group of women of many ages with a striking cultural and racial diversity. EdgeWork Books turned out to be the heart of something larger. Please come join us—we look forward to meeting you online.

www.edgework.com

SING,

FEMINIST VISIONS

WHISPER,

FOR A

SHOUT,

JUST WORLD

PRAY!

M. JACQUI ALEXANDER,
LISA ALBRECHT,
SHARON DAY, AND
MAB SEGREST, EDITORS

EDGE
WORK

Cover and book design: Sarah Chesnutt
Copyediting (where copyright allowed): Jennifer Woodhull and Nancy Adess
Coordination: Dorothy Abbott and Tracy Gary, with Annie Holmes and Nancy Adess
Wood sculpture and cover photo by Sharon Marie Day
All other photographs © Margaret Randall
"Introduction" © 2003 M. Jacqui Alexander, Lisa Albrecht, Sharon Day, and Mab Segrest

Library of Congress Cataloging-in-Publication Data

Sing, whisper, shout, pray! : feminist visions for a just world / M.
Jacqui Alexander ... [et al.].
    p. cm.
Includes bibliographical references and index.
  ISBN 1-931223-07-6 (Paperback : alk. paper)
  1. Social justice. 2. Women—Social conditions—Cross-cultural
studies. 3. Women—Economic conditions—Cross-cultural studies. 4.
Feminism—Cross-cultural studies. I. Alexander, M. Jacqui.
HM671.S567 2002
305.42—dc21

                              2002151596

Printed in Canada.

2   4   6   8   9   7   5   3   1

WE, THE WOMYN OF THE WORLD, STAND!

We stand here and here and here and here.
We stand with hope
We stand with dignity
We stand to love whomever we please!

We, the womyn of the world, stand
We stand here and here and here and here.

We stand for peace
We stand for justice
We stand for honorable reconciliations for every conflict in our world.

We stand for our mothers
We stand with our daughters
We stand for the streams and rivers and oceans
for clean water everywhere.

We, the womyn of the world, stand!
We stand here and here and here and here.
We stand to give birth
We stand to mourn
We stand for those who cannot stand.

We stand in New York City
We stand in Afghanistan
We stand
We stand
We stand

We stand in Jerusalem
We stand in Chiapas
We stand
We stand
We stand

We stand at Yucca Mountain
We stand at the Borders
We stand
We stand
We stand

We stand to sing, whisper, shout and pray for a just world.

Nagamoo Mahingen
Sharon M. Day
2002

Contents

II: STILL IN THE BELLY OF THE BEAST: COLONIZATION AND RESISTANCE

III: THE MYTHOLOGY OF RACE,
THE REALITY OF RACISM

IV: STRATEGIES FROM THE FIELD

V: SPEAKING (ABOUT) SILENCE

VI: SPIRITS OF VISION, SPIRITS OF CHANGE

Acknowledgments

During the years 1987 through 1993, when we initially began working on this book, many women helped us. We thank Barbara Smith for originally proposing the idea for the book, and Lillien Waller and Mattie Richardson at Kitchen Table Press, with whom we worked. We also thank Sally Gordon, who initially typed the manuscript.

During the many years of this project, we have had profound support and encouragement from communities of women all across this country. As we traveled to each of our home cities to have marathon editorial meetings, we met women over many dinners. In Durham, we met with African-American and Latina women: Ashaki Binta, Christina Davis-McCoy, Leah Wise and Carmenza Salgado. In Minneapolis/St. Paul, we met with Indian women: Jo-Anne Stately, Shelley McIntyre, Laura Waterman Wittstock; and with white women: Emma Hixson, Ann Viitala, and Cynthia Turnure. In Oakland, we met with Chrystos, Cherríe Moraga, Nellie Wong, Merle Woo, and Opal Palmer Adisa. Norma Alarcon was part of our collective for about two years, from 1988 to 1990. We thank her for the insights she brought us.

We also remember the women and men who attended our workshop in Iowa City in April, 1989 at the conference, Parallels and Intersections: A Conference on Racism. In June, 1990, we gathered at the National Women's Studies annual conference in Minneapolis. We remember a meeting we had there with Audre Lorde, Mitsuye Yamada, Nellie Wong, Papusa Molina, and Merle Woo. So many extraordinary women have supported us.

We also thank the women in Boston for helping us to believe that we were on the home stretch in June of 1991, and that that would be our last meeting. (We didn't want to admit it then, but it couldn't have been further from the truth!)

Almost from the book's inception, there were a small group of women who acted as a kind of advisory group for us; they believed in the integrity and importance of this book and made critical suggestions about content, or what they saw as crucial developments taking shape within communities in struggle. Among these women are Nellie Wong, Beth Brant, Audre Lorde, Adrienne Rich, Elly Bulkin, Suzanne Pharr, Cherríe Moraga, Ruth Frankenberg, Gloria Joseph, Merle Woo, Papusa Molina, Nancy Bereano, Gloria Anzaldúa, Chandra Talpade Mohanty, Judith McDaniel, Minnie Bruce Pratt, Rose Brewer, and Margaret Randall. We also thank Ann Viitalia for the valuable legal advice you've given us.

Between 1987 and 1993, more than a hundred women submitted essays out of a faith in the vision of this anthology. Some of your discussions are not printed on these pages but we have benefited enormously from your insights.

And there were women who helped with financial resources. Beth Brant, Meridel LeSueur, and Margaret Randall gave a benefit reading for us in the Twin Cities, and Margaret donated one of her photographs for a raffle; bell hooks did a benefit reading that was hosted at New Words Bookstore in Cambridge, and books donated by South End Press were raffled there. Minnie Bruce Pratt gave a benefit reading in Durham. In Durham, Boston, and Oakland, women opened their homes to us during our editorial meetings: thanks to Helen Lange, Eleanor Holland, Leah Wise, Ashaki Binta, Marcia Still, Barbara Herbert, and Lucha Corpi.

In January, 2001, Kim Chernin contacted us about the possibility of publishing our manuscript with EdgeWork Books, a feminist publisher. Dorothy Abbott suggested to them that they contact us about the anthology that had never come out. It's without question for us that we would have never finished this book without the work of Dorothy Abbott. Thank you for your commitment to our book, to us, and to feminist and multiracial social justice movements. Thank you. Tremendous thanks also to Tracy Gary, whose belief in the book and efforts to see it come to light have sustained the process. To everyone at EdgeWork Books, thank you for believing that our book is important, and for making this book happen.

Jacqui Alexander is grateful to all who have been placed on her path to teach her the distinction between truth and illusion. The journey is neverending.

Sharon Day would like to thank my daughters biological and otherwise, Suzanne and Melissa, Terra and Tara, and my grandson Kirby, who helps me to see the world through fresh eyes. And Carmen Suarez and Ann Viitala for your assistance, support and love.

Mab Segrest would like to thank Barb Culbertson, who sustains me, and to our daughter Annie, who keeps me on my toes.

Lisa Albrecht would never have been able to do this work without the loving support of her partner, Pat Rouse. She also wants to thank the many wonderful friends in her life who have loved and challenged her, especially, Rose Brewer, Ellen O'Neill, Sharon Jaffe, Bonita Hampton, and all the folks at Project South.

➤€   ➤€   ➤€

EdgeWork would also like to thank our angels and friends, without whom this book, in its current incarnation, and EdgeWork itself, would not be possible: Kim Chernin, Constance Spheeris, Gen Vaughn, Margot Duxler, Tobey Hiller, Renate Stendhal, Martha Easter-Wells, Nancy Schaub, G.N.,

Michele McGeoy, Léonie Walker, Katharine, Lisa, and Peggy Keon, Laurie Emrick, Trish Houck, Cathy Rafael, Kaylin Koch, Ruth Ann Harnish, Margaret Foster, Melissa Kohner, C.B., Margaret S., Diana Barrett, Lekhas Singh, Peggy Newell, Elaine Dallman, Dorothy Abbott, Liz Colton, Tracy Gary, and our anonymous investors and donors.

Edgework's consulting editorial and production team is honored to be part of this important project: Nancy Adess, Annie Holmes, Annie Kriel, Jennifer Woodhull, Sarah Chesnutt, Barbara Brust of Lucile Design, Claire Kirch, and Cynthia Frank and the CypressPress staff.

We offer this book as a tool for bridgebuilding and changemaking.

Introduction

*There are no new ideas still waiting in the wings to save us as women,
as human. There are only old and forgotten ones, new combinations,
extrapolations and recognitions from within ourselves—along with the
renewed courage to try them out.*

—Audre Lorde

We finish editing this manuscript a month after terrorist attacks on the
World Trade Center and the Pentagon on September 11, 2001, and in the
midst of U.S. bombing of Afghanistan. A new New World Order lurches
into partial view, midhusbanded again by generals and oilmen and obscured
more than explicated by television journalists who have become almost completely complicit with their corporate owners and sponsors. This week, as
bombs still fall, our grief is for all the people bombed and bleeding and
grieving themselves, in Manhattan or Washington DC, after terrorists turned
commercial airlines into incendiary devices; and in Kabul or Jalalabad as the
United States military retaliates and Afghani refugees mass at the borders of
Pakistan. Basta! It's déjà vu all over again; and this anthology, rolling again,
seeks to gather it all in.

A large part of this work, personally and collectively, has its roots in our
experiences of the 1980s, when the New Right seized control of the federal
administration and the courts, and had begun a systematic dismantling of the
gains of progressive struggles of the 1960s. With the rationale of "rolling back
big government," the Right worked to reverse these gains while at the same
time expanding and solidifying the relationship between government and big
business. It blamed "single-parent households," feminism, and lesbian and
gay communities for the decline of the heterosexual family and a growing
cultural crisis that was itself brought on by the abdication of state responsibility for what happened to people. The Reagan administration had
reactionary America "riding tall" again.

These aggressive developments manifested themselves across the culture of
the late 1980s, as: reversals of civil-rights protections by the Supreme Court;
the election of neo-Nazi David Duke to the Louisiana legislature; the nazifi-
cation of the Klan; the daily increase of racist, sexist, homophobic, and
anti-Semitic violence; the forced pauperization of larger sections of the population in central cities, particularly women and children of color, which
bred a deep sense of despair that would make them easy targets for a drug

economy; "homelessness" as a huge, growing institution; cutbacks in health care services, simultaneously with the callous ignoring of the AIDS epidemic; a massive assault on abortion and women's reproductive freedom; and successive military interventions in Grenada and Panama. Racism was on the rise; it manifested itself on the streets, in the courts, in state and federal budgets, in the popular media, on college campuses, in the voting booth— in short, everywhere we looked.

In the early 1970s, faced with rising competition and falling profits, corporate decision-makers decided to deindustrialize the United States, rather than retool industries and increase productivity. They sent unionized factories and jobs to Third World countries for cheaper wages and more degraded working conditions, or they automated. In these poor countries, tax benefits with which neocolonial governments lured "maquiladora" factories were not returned to their people, least of all to women, whose labor was exploited as they were recruited into these global corporate networks in larger and larger numbers. In the United States, a parallel shift towards lower-paying and nonunionized service jobs "feminized" the work force. Less pay, more hours, less job stability, poorer working conditions: this growing, "silent depression" made white people susceptible to the scapegoating campaigns (against "reverse discrimination," "special rights," and "welfare queens") that the New Right began to perfect in the 1970s, and that go on today.

We understand that policies of "structural adjustment" that the International Monetary Fund and the World Bank forced on Third World nations were the international equivalent of the New Right domestic policies we had been tracking. In order to refinance huge and growing loans, the increasingly corrupt governments of poor countries for decades had agreed to cut wages, undercut labor standards, privatize formerly national resources, and cut social programs such as health care or education, paving the way for increasingly huge multinational corporations to have free access to their economies.

Whether "Reagonomics"—or later, "Clintonomics"—at home or "structural adjustment" abroad, these programs increased the burden of work for women who, as caretakers, provide a range of social services, and pushed them into poverty. Structural adjustment not only reinforced the structural inequality in the world order, but it also bred authoritarian and militarist governments internationally and a "prison-industrial complex" at home. The deepening poverty and alienation of globalization's "McWorld" and the continuing Israeli occupation of Palestine have also bred militant fundamentalist movements, such as those allegedly behind the attacks on the Pentagon and the World Trade Center.

Mab writes: Responses to September 11 have made clear, once again, that element in the U.S. (read: White?) psyche that resists global knowledge, empathy, or memory—that leaves us as a democratic voting public so dangerously deluded as to the sources of the global dangers we now face and leaves us equally misguided, I believe, in how to respond. Our leaders can now make tragically oversimplified arguments (so clearly belied by our own foreign policy) because of thirty years of careful propaganda and political work by the Right that has constantly rerouted conversations about class and power, race and power, gender and power, sexuality and power, into different narratives of "reverse discrimination" or "special rights" or "right to life." It is as if causes and effects have been so scrambled and distorted, the radar over our causal fields so jammed, that events come to us, quite literally this time, out of the blue and crashing into national consciousness.

I accepted the call to work on this book as a way to sort through my own questions about feminist, lesbian-gay, and antiracist movements after four intensive years of organizing against Klan and neo-Nazi movements in North Carolina. As a white person, I respect the imperative for autonomous organizing by people of color. So I generally jump at opportunities where people of color have decided that it is necessary and strategic to work interracially with whites, because those occasions offer me huge opportunities to learn and grow. (I was born and raised in the segregated South, and when I was thirteen George Wallace sent two hundred armed men to keep me from going to school with thirteen black children with whom I might have become friends.) I also wanted our collective work to contradict the despair that many white feminists carry about the difficulty of doing interracial work.

My essay that appears here, "On Being White and Other Lies," grew out of rich collective discussions, including our need to understand the relationship between racism and anti-Semitism, as well as my own desire to assimilate what I was learning about the different trajectories and struggles of people of color into a larger analysis of U.S. history and the history of my own family. (This introduction also brings its contents up to date.) My second book, *Memoir of a Race Traitor*, published by South End in 1994, was greatly shaped by my collaboration with Jacqui, Lisa, and Sharon on this anthology.

We intend this book to contribute to a growing transnational feminist movement. The events on and subsequent to September 11 are our threshold to the twenty-first century, which we are on the verge of making even bloodier than the twentieth. Carolyn Forche, fresh from the wounded ground of El Salvador's civil war, got it right twenty years ago: It is either the beginning or the end/Of the world, and the choice is ourselves/Or nothing. It is time, again and as always, in Forche's words, to go after all that is lost, to shape a postmodernity in which humaneness and justice and democracy are more than ironic doublespeak. We have faith that the tremendous courage and experience of the women whose writings we collect in this anthology will help us move forward, to help build intentional and international communities of hope, movements that will undermine the politics of fear, repression, violence, and cynicism by imagining and creating different possibilities.

It is time to say to the multinationals: Share the profits of modernity with all the communities and the continents that capitalism has sucked dry.

It is time to say to the patriarchs: Women will shape a future beyond your control; to the homophobes, there are many ways to love and we will use them all.

It is time to say to the racists: We are finally dismantling the legacies of slavery and colonialism, and together we will repair the damage they have done.

It is time to say to all the warmongers: You cannot have this century. Stand down.

⇒← ⇒← ⇒←

Like it or not, we are inscribed in this global system, and different ones of us benefit in different ways from it. We rely literally, not metaphorically, on millions of people (mostly women) in different parts of the world to reproduce our daily lives, in spite of the masculinist state rhetoric about U.S. superiority and U.S. might. In a not-so-paradoxical, yet inescapable way, it is U.S. might that props up that production, whether it is of bananas, of clothing, or of oil. Militarization and masculinity work hand in hand to secure our consuming interests. Are our hands clean?

Blood-soaked fields fill the landscapes of too many countries throughout the southern hemisphere. Where are the blood-soaked fields of the U.S.? There is, of course, the most recent devastation, whose acronym bears the symbol of national emergency—911. Blood from these urban fields, now charred, has been folded into all manner of things, indistinguishable from one another. Some of it still smolders from anguished resistance, months later; some of it, shorn of its luster, is pasted on slabs of concrete for miles in different directions, the permanent coat of testimony to that emergency. So much blood spilled.

Yet, no rivers of red grief carry the tale. They have been replaced by talking heads who believe that democracy means having as many talking heads as possible, not having as many interpretations of reality as possible. We know this since the media seem capable of telling mostly one story, the state's story. You will not hear the stories of other blood-soaked fields from these talking heads. Stories from the "the belly of the beast" whose national emergency began more than 500 years ago with the onset of colonization.

We have not heard from these talking heads that sweatshops in New York (and perhaps others in Los Angeles and Chicago) have suspended the usual production of garments and now turn out American flags by the millions. All throughout the fashion district between Twenty-Third and Thirty-Eighth Streets, between Seventh and Eighth Avenues in New York City (whose trendsetters compete for the most tasteful design of stars and stripes), immigrant Filipina and Dominican women now sew American flags to satisfy the state-made demands of this hypernationalist (read: war thirsty) emergency, stitching together the symbols of an ostensibly seamless nation to bind a country to which they do not belong. How must it feel to sew alienation with one's own hands—alienation donned as patriotism? Immigrant men, who weeks before sold incense, charcoal, and books as part of the informal economy, have now been drawn into this necessary economy, while still marginalized. They sell flags at bargain rates. Are my hands clean?

Jacqui writes: Fields do not ordinarily require blood; it is not a necessary ingredient to make things grow. In fact, we can argue quite the opposite, that the spilling of blood makes certain growth difficult, especially when that spillage remains unexamined, which seems to be the current requirement. George Bush has asked God to bless America, to sanctify American blood as it spills Afghani blood, as it single-mindedly externalizes terror, refusing to examine the sources of terror within.

Blood is a powerful signifier. While it looks the same everywhere, it has been used to color all kinds of privilege and hierarchy, especially racial hierarchy. Just one drop was all that was needed to mark one "race" superior, the other inferior. In this new moment of terror, supposedly "foreign"-born blood is easily distinguishable from "American" blood. "Foreign"-born bodies can now be detained, without question (those that have not fallen casualty to the backlash), without cause, as part of Operation Freedom in order to protect "American" bodies in their homeland.

No one can identify lesbian and gay blood in the rubble of New York and Washington yet agencies disbursing monies to grieving families seem determined to distinguish between good heterosexual blood and bad lesbian and gay blood, since domestic partners who never officially declared their domesticity cannot claim their loved ones without proof of marriage. Do we die a different kind of death as lesbians and gay men? As bisexual and transgender? As two-spirit people? In the midst of Operation Freedom abroad, the Alliance for Marriage, a coalition of religious and political leaders, is attempting to slip by Congress a constitutional amendment that denies legal recognition of gay relationships and deprives lesbian and gay families of fundamental protections. Some freedoms are simply not worth protecting, especially when it comes down to blood—lesbian and gay blood—the perennial threat to good familial, patriotic blood, which one would think is in short supply in this emergency.

I don't know anyone for whom this is not a time of profound dislocation; anyone for whom the symbol of outside devastation has not had internal company in the form of displacement, terror, *dis*ease of some kind, manifesting itself in insomnia, nightmares—when sleep does manage to prevail—difficulty concentrating, and forgetting, which is not an inconsequential sign since cultural amnesia is part of what fuels a national search for a foreign enemy; anyone for whom the usual preoccupations of daily living have not now been dwarfed in relation to the sheer scale of this collective trauma.

Where were you on 9/11? As numbness collected itself as a protective shroud on shoulders all over the globe, I was in self-imposed quarantine, assembling my dossier for review. At a moment of collapse and devastation, when the symbols of capitalist security crumble, I clutched different symbols: the symbols of a promise, on which no one can really deliver: security—the very condition the national security state also promises in the midst of collapse. As I wrote my statement for candidacy, I had to demonstrate the uniqueness of my scholarship, the ways in which it differed, excelled beyond the contributions of others, the specialness of my ideas; I was to speak as if my achievements belonged only to me, as if they were all my doing, unassisted. Collective projects such as these carry little weight within the logic of individual academic merit. Tenure and promotion, then, is the academy's reward for finding security in separation.

It was a hard price to be paying on that day of self-imposed isolation, but it was a necessary and ultimately an insignificant price. Necessary, because sometimes we have to be pushed against a wall on roller skates to realize that although we teach freedom and talk about freedom, we still need to learn how to free ourselves completely. And to know that no human being has the capacity to confer on another the discipline of freedom, as Howard Thurman puts it. Insignificant, because ultimately it paled when compared to the scale of loss that the world suffered on that very day. Still the *costs* of our living were being reshuffled in massive ways, and the cards that kept appearing on the top of the deck were asking me: How have you applied the sacred promise to use healing as the antidote to oppression? What have you done to reverse the mad belief in separate thoughts and separate bodies that lead separate lives and go their separate ways? How can there be permanent security in separation of any kind?

⊰⊱   ⊰⊱   ⊰⊱

We always intended that this book further the dismantling of racism in the United States and globally. Among us, the question of the relationship between anti-Semitism and racism led us to a more complex understanding of the dynamics of race and of racism. Should anti-Semitism be defined as a form of racism within the scope of this anthology? This was the question that, earliest on, provoked the most disagreement and tension among us. Many Jewish feminists whose work we respected said, "Of course." Some were surprised that we had posed the question. Adrienne Rich wrote to us: "I think that there needs to be more underlining that anti-Semitism is part of racism. You don't withdraw energy from one to oppose the other. The situation of Jews as largely white-skinned people in the U.S. tends to make us forget that millions of us have been persecuted and killed on grounds of race….In North America the majority of Jews who are white participate in white skin privilege on a daily basis; yet in the mythic mind, we are also seen as 'dark' and as racial outsiders."

This mythic "darkness" had practical, political implications, however. Barbara Smith cautioned: "There has been considerable confusion in the women's movement about whether North American Jewish women are women of color and whether anti-Semitism and racism as they are practiced in North America are interchangeable; I don't want this book to contribute to that confusion." In our internal discussions Jacqui had argued for us not to make "an a priori decision that anti-Semitism is a form of racism before placing anti-Semitism in a historical, material context and clarifying the links between what we see in the contemporary United States, for example, to that history." Mab's essay, "On Being White," began out of this urgency to historicize the concept of race.

Lisa writes: For me, *Sing, Whisper, Shout, Pray!* mirrors the work of building a multiracial movement for social justice. It takes an extraordinary lifelong commitment of hard work, a willingness to hold ourselves accountable to each other, and a deep spirit of generosity and love. I thank Jacqui, Sharon, and Mab for sharing this journey with me. I have grown so much as a result of working with all of you.

For the past sixteen years, I've been a professor at the University of Minnesota. I teach in General College, which is a last remnant of the days of open admissions. Now, rather than accepting all students, General College is a transfer college where "at-risk" students have an opportunity to work on their skills, so they will no longer be "at risk." On a limited basis, I also teach in the women's studies department. The reason that I don't teach regularly in women's studies has to do with the corporatization of the academy and the insular barriers of departments and disciplines. Women's studies has to "buy" my labor, so General College is reimbursed for giving up my labor. Everything is bought and sold: knowledge, teachers, and students. Higher education in this country is about the reproduction of the social order. It is not a place where books like this one are taken seriously, or where social-justice activism is encouraged or rewarded.

During the 1980s, feminist and multicultural education were marginally accepted in the academy, but only after they were stripped of their activist roots. Today, multicultural education is mostly a buffet of melting-pot voices, with little attention given to seriously dismantling white supremacy. Feminist education and women's studies do acknowledge power and privilege, but only on a limited basis.

I am very weary of my white women's studies colleagues around the U.S. who write inaccessible theory about gender, race, and class, but do not hire women of color in more than token positions ("one is enough in my department..."). These same white women, hiding behind the safety of institutional elitism and the relative security of their positions, rarely do political work outside the academy and rarely encourage their women's studies departments to do activist movement work. They also rarely have very many people in their lives who reflect the "theory" they write about.

I am also tired of my white male colleagues who embrace "cultural diversity" by using work of people like Gloria Anzaldúa, Toni Morrison, and Paula Gunn Allen, but talk about their work obtusely, in postmodernist jargon, and rarely address their own white male privilege and power. And of course, these men are the ones who get the promotions and raises.

The hypocrisies embedded within higher education have driven me further and further to its margins, even though I love my work in the classroom doing social-justice education in all the courses I teach. As I've moved away from the academy, I've continued to do education as an activist. The work of Paulo Freire has had a profound effect on me. Twentieth-century movements for social justice had deep connections to popular education, both internationally and in this country. Popular education is political education for all people. It involves understanding who we are in the world, what visions we have for justice, and how to develop strategies to make change. This, to me, is what education needs to be about in the twenty-first century.

As the "Jewish white woman" editor, I've also felt the particular burden of making sure that this book addressed two critical issues: 1) the relationship between racism and anti-Semitism; and 2) the Israeli-Palestinian conflict.

For me, this dialogue pushed me to move beyond the kind of defensiveness that occurs when someone feels she has to speak for all of her people. In looking back at my notes and journal entries of these discussions, I wrote:

I wanted to storm out of the room after I raised my voice, remembering not only my family history but also that the annihilation of Jews was a result of racist ideology that named Jews as a race, and not merely a religious minority....But I cannot storm out; I also have to constantly acknowledge that many U.S. Jewish women have moved up the racial hierarchy by stepping on people of color and using their labor, while simultaneously ignoring white privilege as they articulated "otherness" from white Christian people.... Finally, and intricately connected to our group's understanding of racism and anti-Semitism, is the need for me, as a Jew, to speak and act against Israeli occupation of Palestine. It is not a separate issue. Israeli Jews cannot stand on the backs of Palestinians and expect non-Jews globally to stand up in the fight against anti-Semitism. U.S. Jews are implicated as well; it is U.S. tax dollars, over $6 billion yearly, that help to finance Israeli settlements all over Gaza and the West Bank.

It was Matthew Lyons's essay, "Parasites and Pioneers," that gave us the kind of detailed, careful historical analysis we needed to understand anti-Semitism and its relationship to racism. I thank Matthew for his willingness to seriously engage our questions about the relationships among white supremacy, male supremacy, and anti-Semitism.

Also during these years, and directly as a result of my work on this book, I have moved from silence to action as a Jew regarding my stance on the Palestinian-Israeli conflict. I no longer avert my eyes when I see the repressive conditions in which Palestinian people live, imposed on them not only by the Israeli government, but by the U.S. government's military and financial support of the occupation. I have also had to spend a great deal of time sorting through the relationship between racism and anti-Semitism, something I'd certainly thought about, but not in the ways in which I was pushed by my coeditors. Again, I go back to Barbara's initial letter to all of us. She envisioned a multiracial collective of women, imagining a Jew as one of the editors, given the historical presence of Jews and feminist Jews in leadership in both progressive and women's movements in the U.S. And here I was, the "typical" Jew: I'd done lots of progressive, feminist, and lesbian/gay organizing, but had not really integrated how being a Jew was tied in. I honestly thank my coeditors (all non-Jews), as well as two of the Jewish contributors, Matthew Lyons and Sharon Jaffe, for being the impetus for my own growth.

Now that we've crossed the threshold of the new millennium, I want to have hope that my grandbabies will see a new century in their lives—where there will be clean air to breathe, equal distribution of wealth globally, and a genuine multiracial, just community. With the stolen presidency of George

W., and September 11th etched into the fabric of our beings, it is increasingly clear to me that the only way we will have a future is through our communal actions. Two thousand years ago, Rabbi Hillel said, "If I am not for myself, who will be for me? If I am only for myself, what am I? And if not now, when?" Now is the time.

>€   >€   >€

Sharon writes: Boozhoo, Nagamoo Mahingen Indishnikaz. Wahbahzhizhi indodem. Anshinabe Ojibwe equay indow. Ahpahding M'de.

Greetings, Singing Wolf is my name. I was born into the Marten clan, I am an Ojibwe woman, first-degree M'de.

This morning as I was drinking my coffee, I reread Berta I. Perea's piece on the Colombian drug war. The sky is gray and cloudy. I feel a need to burn sage as sadness washes over me, a kind of cumulative sadness. There is so much pain in the world. As my grandson Kirby says, "so many haters." Berta's article reminds me that the drug import/export industry is a tool of capitalism that fuels the economy. Before drugs it was alcohol that devastated my community. It anesthetizes us so we do not know who we are. We become lost to our families, to our traditions, and to our land. In the place of traditions and family come the bootleggers, pushers, gangs, social service agencies, corrupt police, and corrupt governments. We endure unemployment, homelessness, and violence in our communities, whether it be the reservations, barrios, inner cities, or rural farms.

We have the largest number of prisons in the history of this country. These prisons are filled with our men and women. Our young people. Our young join the military to get away or to finance higher education; in the process they will fight brown-skinned people in this hemisphere as well as in Afghanistan and other parts of the Middle East. We have brown-skinned people who think like white people—Colin Powell and Bush's right hand, Condoleezza Rice, are cases in point. It is the same around the world: We cannot drink the water in our rivers and streams because dumping of chemicals from factories, farm pesticides, and acid rain have poisoned them. The rivers and streams have been diverted, the earth has been plowed up, the forests continue to be clear-cut, people are displaced along with habitats for animals. Our ecosystems are destroyed.

This summer while I was on a reserve in Canada, a water truck delivered water. On this reserve, they cannot dig a well, because the water is poisoned from the chemicals used by the farmers for generations. The farmers are white folks who have leased the land. In Minnesota, land of ten thousand lakes, we cannot eat more than one walleye a month because of the high levels of mercury in the fish, and the state warns pregnant women to eat only one fish per year. Today, a gallon of water costs as much as a gallon of gas.

Ingrid Washinawatuk El-Issa, Flying Eagle Woman, was born July 31, 1957, and died March 4, 1999 at the hands of warmongers in Colombia. Ingrid worked for peace and justice all of her life. She was invited by the Uwa people in Colombia to visit with them. They were building schools and devising strategies to keep the oil companies from drilling on their lands. They were prepared to commit mass suicide if the oil companies continued to plunder their land. They gave her tobacco. She was afraid to go, she told me so, yet she went because she thought she could help and, upon returning home, educate us about what was happening there.

When I think about Ingrid, I still cry. I remember her at ceremonies; once she was on Moon Hill, where women are mostly quiet and reflective. I looked back and laughed to see Ingrid dancing her heart out up there on Moon Hill. That was the way she was.

There are times when the Nokomis, the grandmother of us all, sits in the heavens and covers her eyes with clouds, because it is too painful to observe what we humans do to each other and to the earth. Sometimes we need to cry, grieve, and mourn for those who have left us and for the pain we feel. But then we must rise up, like the Nokomis, plant one foot in front of the other, care for our children, our elders, this earth, and our rivers and lakes. We need to practice sustainable development. Take what we need and leave the rest. Take what we need and leave some for reseeding so what we take can be replenished.

Today, I will go and pick apples with my long-time friend, State Representative Karen Clark. She and her partner operate an organic apple orchard. They plant trees from this orchard in south Minneapolis, at places like Manidoowahdak Odena, a housing complex for Native People living with HIV, and at day-care centers. This planting of trees will allow folks in these neighborhoods to enjoy apples that they might not otherwise be able to afford.

Art Owens of the Prairie Island Dakota Reservation in Minnesota has worked tirelessly for twelve years to bring the buffalo back to the Dakota land. A nuclear power plant sits one mile from the Dakota community and on the banks of the Mississippi River. Art says, we must go backwards to being Indian again if we are to go forward. The buffalo are our brothers, the sustainers of life. They take what we cannot handle and give us what we need.

I am grateful for people like Art Owens; Lillian Rice, respected elder and my adopted mother; Edward Benton-Benai, fifth-degree M'de teacher; and for all the people who continue these ways, who speak to people about love, who can shed tears, then rise up and continue to teach us the languages, the songs, and the ceremonies. This is sustainable development.

I do not know the ceremonies of the people in the East, but I know they have them. I do not know the ceremonies of the people in the Middle East, but I know they have them. I do not know the ceremonies for the people from the West, but they must have them. As Valdina Pinto states so eloquently, if you do not know the ceremonies, find a place, a spot to sit quietly and meditate; even if we do not remember, the earth remembers.

Since September 11, we have been building a M'de-style ceremonial teaching lodge adjacent to Fort Smelling. One hundred and fifty years ago, the United States government imprisoned sixteen hundred Dakota people just below the fort. The students learned the mathematical equations to construct sketches to scale and then to determine the amount of materials needed to construct the lodge. They learned the origin story of the lodge and the spiritual framework of the Anishinabe people; they learned about native architecture and science. Building this lodge with young people from the Native Arts High School and holding our first ceremony for the victims and families of 9/11 and the Dakota women and children who died at the fort was the most important thing I could think to do. This is sustainable development.

My ancestors, the Ojibwe People, once lived on the eastern seaboard. Through prophesies that came to them from seven grandmothers and grandfathers, they were told to move west until they came to a place where food grows on the water. They settled in small bands in Minnesota, Michigan, Wisconsin, North Dakota, and Canada—where food (mahnomen/wild rice) grows on the water. A megis shell appeared to them to lead the way. They were instructed to remember the seventh generation yet to come, and to practice the ceremonies, sing the songs, and care for each other. They were told that in the seventh generation, great changes would occur. The People would have to make a decision to move towards the light and great healing or continue the path towards darkness and destruction.

We need to actively engage in transforming our societies. Make connections between our peoples. Ingrid's megis shell is still in Colombia. The night she was killed, the Uwa elders said, a shell appeared to them and they knew she was on her journey to the other world.

The ozone layer keeps getting thinner, the spiritual people are becoming ill as they absorb the negative energy continuously released into the atmosphere. We need to speak to the silence, understand what strategies have worked, develop new ones, and dream.

The old people say, if you want peace, you must be love.

Nahconidanah…all my relations.

Section I, "The Color of Violence," begins with prose written by Suheir Hammad ten days after the 9/11 attack on the World Trade Center. "Fire in the city air and I feared for my sister's life...and now I fear for the rest of us." Suheir expresses what we all feel, fear for the rest of us and our children and succeeding generations. The fabric of our lives has changed as we struggle to make sense of this violent act, perhaps surpassed only by the enormity of people killed within a dense space and happening before our eyes via television.

Violence is all around us. This section provides an analysis of how racism and sexism are embedded in societal, governmental, and capitalistic policies that harbor and cultivate violence; policies that value profits over people, the land, the water, and our very existence in the long term. The essays examine U.S. foreign and domestic policies, exploitation of women workers, welfare reform, and the prison-industrial complex. Cherríe Moraga's article, "A Xicanadyke Codex of Changing Consciousness," describes the manifestation of violence in our lives as mothers, lovers, and community members, and our responsibility to act.

"Lurching through These Frightening Days" moves us into the terrain of the second section, "Still in the Belly of the Beast." This section reads like a geography lesson; no matter where we are situated on this globe, we are still in the belly of the beast. Hawai'i, Vieques, Palestine, the West Bank, Akwesasne, the South, Big Mountain, Cincinnati, a women's studies classroom. We are still learning the art of espirit de lucha: the spirit of struggle and resistance to move ourselves to justice and liberation.

Section III, "The Mythology of Race, the Reality of Racism," includes discussions of skin color, language, blood quantum, citizenship, nation status, anti-Semitism, the vestiges of forced removal and relocation/slavery/immigration, "Crossing the Bridges of Pain," and the U.S. war on people of color/the "war on drugs."

"Strategies from the Field," Section IV, begins with Becky Thompson's "Multiracial Feminism," which documents how multiracial feminisms have emerged locally and globally. In this section of the book, the writers discuss various strategies employed by women globally as we work for social justice. Audre Lorde's words close this section as she wrote, "I am a Black, feminist, lesbian, warrior, poet doing my work and a piece of my work is asking you how are you doing yours?"

Section V is entitled "Speaking (About) Silence." The women in this section write from very personal perspectives that transform the way they act in the world. The particulars they write about—incest, adoption, sexuality, poverty, racism, segregation—move them into activism in their communities. And with the activism comes a sense of emergency and urgency that we as editors have shared since the beginning of our agreement to edit this book.

"Spirits of Vision, Spirits of Change," the sixth section, brings us full circle as we read the words of women who inspire us with their visions of mothering, nurturing, and caring for our children, the land, and the water in a spiritual way that is connected to the earth and rooted in our cultural ways. Thanks to Winona LaDuke, Beth Brant, Merle Woo, Cherríe Moraga, and Valdina Pinto for your work and your words of wisdom. May we be inspired to action and more action.

This book was begun in 1987, completed the first time in 1993, and revised in 2000–2002. It has been an amazing journey. We thank Barbara Smith for inviting us to put forth a work that would complement the classic *This Bridge Called My Back: Writings by Radical Women of Color.* We hope to honor all the women around the country who spoke to us of their experiences, hopes, and struggles. *Sing, Whisper, Shout, Pray! Feminist Visions for a Just World* contains about half of the original articles; we thank those early contributors and we thank those writers who submitted new articles, prose, and poetry for this book.

We believe all these voices resound with the brilliance, eloquence, passion, love, and tenacity whence they came. Migwetch, thank you, and blessings to all of the women who wrote, rewrote, revised, and sometimes sent something entirely new to us for inclusion. We are indebted to you. It is our voices that will sing/whisper/shout/pray a revolution into existence. A revolution without violence, a revolution that has no generals or arms, except arms that will till the soil, arms that will nurture an infant and endure until there are peace and justice in this world.

I: THE COLOR OF VIOLENCE

first writing since

SUHEIR HAMMAD

1.
there have been no words.
i have not written one word.
no poetry in the ashes south of canal street.
no prose in the refrigerated trucks driving debris and dna.
not one word.

today is a week, and seven is of heavens, gods, science.
evident out my kitchen window is an abstract reality.
sky where once was steel.
smoke where once was flesh.

fire in the city air and i feared for my sister's life in a way never
before. and then, and now, i fear for the rest of us.

first, please god, let it be a mistake, the pilot's heart failed, the
plane's engine died.
then please god, let it be a nightmare, wake me now.
please god, after the second plane, please, don't let it be anyone
who looks like my brothers.

i do not know how bad a life has to break in order to kill.
i have never been so hungry that i willed hunger
i have never been so angry as to want to control a gun over a pen.
not really.
even as a woman, as a palestinian, as a broken human being.
never this broken.

more than ever, i believe there is no difference.
the most privileged nation, most americans do not know the difference
between indians, afghanis, syrians, muslims, sikhs, hindus.
more than ever, there is no difference.

2.
thank you korea for *kimchi* and *bibim bob,* and corn tea and the
genteel smiles of the wait staff at wonjo the smiles never revealing
the heat of the food or how tired they must be working long midtown

shifts. thank you korea, for the belly craving that brought me into
the city late the night before and diverted my daily train ride into
the world trade center.

there are plenty of thank yous in ny right now. thank you for my
lazy procrastinating late ass. thank you to the germs that had me
call in sick. thank you, my attitude, you had me fired the week
before. thank you for the train that never came, the rude nyer who
stole my cab going downtown. thank you for the sense my mama
        gave me
to run. thank you for my legs, my eyes, my life.

3.
the dead are called lost and their families hold up shaky
printouts in front of us through screens smoked up.

we are looking for iris, mother of three. please call with any
information. we are searching for priti, last seen on the 103rd
floor. she was talking to her husband on the phone and the line
went. please help us find george, also known as adel. his family is
waiting for him with his favorite meal. i am looking for my son, who
was delivering coffee. i am looking for my sister girl, she started
her job on monday.

i am looking for peace. i am looking for mercy. i am looking for
evidence of compassion. any evidence of life. i am looking for
life.

4.
ricardo on the radio said in his accent thick as yucca, "i will
feel so much better when the first bombs drop over there. and my
friends feel the same way."

on my block, a woman was crying in a car parked and stranded in hurt.
i offered comfort, extended a hand she did not see before she said,
"we're gonna burn them so bad, i swear, so bad." my hand went to my
head and my head went to the numbers within it of the dead iraqi
children, the dead in nicaragua. the dead in rwanda who had to vie
with fake sport wrestling for america's attention.

yet when people sent emails saying, this was bound to happen, let's
not forget u.s. transgressions, for half a second i felt resentful.
hold up with that, cause i live here, these are my friends and fam,
and it could have been me in those buildings, and we're not bad
people, do not support america's bullying. can i just have a half
second to feel bad?

if i can find through this exhaust people who were left behind to
mourn and to resist mass murder, i might be all right.

thank you to the woman who saw me brinking my cool and blinking
    back
tears. she opened her arms before she asked "do you want a hug?" a
big white woman, and her embrace was the kind only people with the
warmth of flesh can offer. i wasn't about to say no to any comfort.
"my brother's in the navy," i said. "and we're arabs." "wow, you
got double trouble." word.

5.
one more person ask me if i knew the hijackers.
one more motherfucker ask me what navy my brother is in.
one more person assume no arabs or muslims were killed.
one more person assume they know me, or that i represent a people.
or that a people represent an evil. or that evil is as simple as a
flag and words on a page.

we did not vilify all white men when mcveigh bombed oklahoma.
america did not give out his family's addresses or where he went to
church. or blame the bible or pat robertson.

and when the networks air footage of palestinians dancing in the
street, there is no apology that hungry children are bribed with
sweets that turn their teeth brown. that correspondents edit images.
that archives are there to facilitate lazy and inaccurate
journalism.

and when we talk about holy books and hooded men and death, why
    do we
never mention the kkk?

if there are any people on earth who understand how new york is feeling right now, they are in the west bank and the gaza strip.

6.
today it is ten days. last night bush waged war on a man once openly funded by the
cia. i do not know who is responsible. read too many books, know too many people to believe what i am told. i don't give a fuck about bin laden. his vision of the world does not include me or those i love. and petitions have been going around for years trying to get the u.s. sponsored taliban out of power. shit is complicated, and i don't know what to think.

but i know for sure who will pay.

in the world, it will be women, mostly colored and poor. women will have to bury children, and support themselves through grief. "either you are with us, or with the terrorists"—meaning keep your people under control and your resistance censored. meaning we got the loot and the nukes.

in america, it will be those amongst us who refuse blanket attacks on the shivering. those of us who work toward social justice, in support of civil liberties, in opposition to hateful foreign policies.

i have never felt less american and more new yorker, particularly brooklyn, than these past days. the stars and stripes on all these cars and apartment windows represent the dead as citizens first, not family members, not lovers.

i feel like my skin is real thin, and that my eyes are only going to get darker. the future holds little light.

my baby brother is a man now, and on alert, and praying five times a day that the orders he will take in a few days' time are righteous and will not weigh his soul down from the afterlife he deserves.

both my brothers—my heart stops when i try to pray—not a beat to disturb my fear. one a rock god, the other a sergeant, and both

palestinian, practicing muslim, gentle men. both born in brooklyn
and their faces are of the archetypal arab man, all eyelashes and
nose and beautiful color and stubborn hair.

what will their lives be like now?

over there is over here.

7.
all day, across the river, the smell of burning rubber and limbs
floats through. the sirens have stopped now. the advertisers are
back on the air. the rescue workers are traumatized. the skyline is
brought back to human size. no longer taunting the gods with its
height.

i have not cried at all while writing this. i cried when i saw those
buildings collapse on themselves like a broken heart. i have never
owned pain that needs to spread like that. and i cry daily that my
brothers return to our mother safe and whole.

there is no poetry in this. there are causes and effects. there are
symbols and ideologies. mad conspiracy here, and information we will
never know. there is death here, and there are promises of more.

there is life here. anyone reading this is breathing, maybe hurting,
but breathing for sure. and if there is any light to come, it will
shine from the eyes of those who look for peace and justice after the
rubble and rhetoric are cleared and the phoenix has risen.

affirm life.
affirm life.
we got to carry each other now.
you are either with life, or against it.
affirm life.

The Night the Lights Went Out in Durban: Report from the United Nations World Conference against Racism

LINDA BURNHAM

The following speech was delivered on October 21, 2001 at the Women of Color Resource Center's 3rd Annual Sisters of Fire Awards and Report back from the U.N. World Conference Against Racism. The Sisters of Fire Award for Courage and Conscience was presented to Congresswoman Barbara Lee, whose speech to Congress on September 14, 2001 follows.

That light of outrage is the light of history
springing upon us when we're least prepared. [1]

And oh, how unprepared we were for September 11th.

In many ways, the United Nations World Conference Against Racism seems like a lifetime ago. Those of us who participated in the conference did so in the hopes that we could help create new conditions, new understandings, and new strategies for the struggle against racism. That we could help move the international community another step forward in its fitful efforts to eradicate racism, ethnic conflict, and xenophobia. Our time in South Africa was intense and we came home intending to work together to evaluate what was gained and what was lost, and to share our rich experiences with all of you here at home. Instead, we, along with the rest of the world, were overtaken by the horrific, unconscionable acts of nineteen desperate and murderous men. The light of history did indeed spring upon us when we were least prepared, and the shape of the world shifted dramatically on that September morning.

The U.N. conference was rapidly overshadowed, relegated to a dim, possibly irrelevant, pre-September 11th past. For our delegation, part of the struggle to find our bearings in the these deeply unsettling times has been to cull some of the lessons of Durban and link them, as best we can, to current circumstances. If it was about anything, Durban was about how the past bears down upon the present, about how unevenly the weight of history is borne. The battle over reparations was central. It widened out from compensatory measures for descendants of the African slave trade in the Americas—an issue that made its way in from the outer margins of political discourse due principally to the dogged persistence of African American activists in the U.S.—to include the full legacy of colonialism in Africa, Asia, Latin America, the Middle East, the Caribbean, and the islands of the Pacific.

The yawning, ever-widening gap between the nations of the North and the nations of the South raised the question of debt relief: Who owes what to whom, and why? In Durban the question was asked: Having been robbed for centuries, are not the nations of the South due restitution from their assailants? Can the appetite for gobbling up the wealth of other nations and peoples to support the ill-gotten prosperity of North America and Europe ever be curbed? And the answer from the North: The U.S., fattened on the land, lives, and liberty of conquered nations and enslaved peoples, said no—not today, not tomorrow, not in this millennium. What is on offer is not compensation, restitution, reparations, and heartfelt regrets, but new forms of global plunder. And Belgium, head of the European Union, its hands still damp and sticky with the blood of the Congo, said No, we don't want to talk about it. The legacy of colonialism is not relevant to our discussion of current-day racism and we won't have it mentioned in the final document.

This was not simple recalcitrance. It was willful, shameful denial of the past in the service of preserving racist, profoundly unequal relations between nations and peoples in the present and far into the future. The U.S. and Israel, unprepared to face the horrendous consequences of past or present policy, turned on their heels and walked out. The conference was convened in South Africa, making us guests of the people whose recent triumph over a most egregious form of twentieth century racialism we all celebrate. It was not lost on many of us that the U.S. and Israel had also stood arm in arm—until the bitter end—in providing support and encouragement to the terrorists of the apartheid state.

What has this to do with September 11th and its aftermath? The U.S. impulse to "rule and rule without end, forever and ever"[2] is not an impulse to dominance simply for its own sake, but dominance for the sake of the protection of wealth—wealth already stolen and wealth anticipated. If that dominance requires alliance with unsavory despots, corrupt regimes, and fanatical reactionaries, so be it.

The deal struck with the Taliban, through Pakistan and the CIA, must have seemed like a thousand others made round the world: We will turn a blind eye to the imposition of repressive, theocratic decrees. We will turn a deaf ear to the torment of girls, women, and homosexuals. We will ensure that the American public remains comfortably ignorant of the bargain struck and its terrible toll on the suffering Afghan people. And in exchange, with the abundance of armaments our taxpayers provide, you will keep at bay any and all forces viewed as hostile to U.S. interests in the region. Though the details may differ, such deals are operative worldwide, backed by massive military presence on every continent and all the seas. But this deal turned sour as fundamentalist tyrants, encouraged, armed, and emboldened for fifteen years, developed their own fearsome agenda.

The Soviet Union was brought to its knees in part due to its defeat in Afghanistan. But the U.S. had only twelve short years to revel in the downfall of its enemy and enjoy the pleasures of capitalism triumphant. And then the fundamentalist fanaticism and patriarchal warlordism it had so generously subsidized turned round to seize it by the neck.

An aside that is not beside the point: As those jets screeched towards the World Trade Center and the Pentagon, some people in the Americas commemorated another September 11th, twenty-eight years ago. On that day in 1973, U.S.-trained military commanders, under the leadership of Augusto Pinochet—yet to be brought to justice for his crimes against humanity— toppled the democratically elected president of Chile, Salvador Allende. The U.S. could not abide the tenure of a socialist reformer who put the interests of his people before the interests of corporate America—as it could not abide Lumumba in Congo or Arbenz in Guatemala or Sandino in Nicaragua or Bishop in Grenada. And what the U.S. cannot abide, it attempts to destroy.

Ruth Manorama, a fierce advocate for the rights of India's Dalits, spoke with passion at a Women of Color Resource Center workshop in Durban. The Dalits were a huge presence at the U.N. Conference, insisting that thousands of years of caste discrimination be brought to an end. Ruth and other Dalit leaders reminded us that while religion may bring solace, comfort, and a moral compass to some, it can be, at the very same time, an instrument of repression and degradation for others. Those others may be coreligionists, those of other faiths, or secularists. And often enough it is women who suffer. Millions of crimes against women are committed each day in the name of religion, custom, and tradition. Religious fundamentalism—whether Christian, Islamic, Judaic, or Hindu—constitutes a mortal threat to women.

If the events of September 11th represented an awful, imaginative leap towards previously unimaginable terror, the response represented a massive failure of the imagination—a fallback to the military option and a reckless willingness to join in the spiral of violence. Apparently not a moment's thought was given to alternatives. To working within the framework of international law. To using the mechanisms of the United Nations. To accepting the authority of the International Criminal Court. To convening an international tribunal to consider right action.

Instead, with a consensus built on fear, racism, and heightened xenophobia, we descend into war without borders and without end. New "terrorist havens" are added to the potential hit list on a regular basis—Iran, Indonesia, Malaysia, the Philippines. And the national security state institutes measures constricting civil liberties that we will all live to regret.

And now anthrax. I think we need no further proof that Fortress America is not a viable strategy. Neither the gated communities of the upper classes, nor the Star Wars missile defense shield, nor the ominous Office of Homeland Security can protect us from the consequences of a world overflowing with men, women, and children whose fate, from cradle to grave, is grinding poverty, crushing labor, and crippling disease. Let us remember that within two weeks of the Twin Towers tragedy the airline industry had managed to squeeze $15 billion out of the sides of the federal budget. The insurance industry is in line to get its share and others line up at the trough—the very same trough that can't provide funds for women on welfare or free medical care for seniors on fixed incomes.

Fifteen billion dollars. Could the U.S. not survive the demise of one or two of our multiple airline carriers? What if that $15 billion were devoted to eliminating infant and maternal mortality worldwide? Or to AIDS treatment and prevention? Or to water, sanitation, and electrification? Or to eliminating school fees, raising teachers' salaries, building schools, and buying books and computers? To the education of the girls of Afghanistan? Or to adequate housing for the homeless and those who find shelter in shanty towns, favelas, and migrant shacks around the world? What if that $15 billion and another $15 billion after that were devoted to finding a truly just solution to the unending crisis in the Middle East?

Dream on, girl. Is that what you say? Well, we must dream on because the dream of endless greed, aggression, and world dominance has been revealed for the appalling nightmare it always was. The fortress has been breached. And it will be breached again and again as long as we have a hand in feeding the desperation, alienation, and disillusionment that stoke the myriad forms of murderous male rage. Either we walk out of the fortress together into the sunlight of our creation, or we shall be tethered together deep in the shadows, vulnerable and permanently afraid.

Our time in Durban did give us hope, despite the actions of the U.S. government and others who refused to honestly engage the struggle against racism. We marched through the streets with thousands upon thousands of energized, organized, politically conscious South Africans determined to hold their government accountable to their needs. We met with incredible women in Durban and in Johannesburg—women who are leaders in their communities and nations, leading the fight for the rights of girls and women, for the rights of racial, ethnic, and religious minorities. Our hopes were raised and our vision expanded in intense exchanges of experiences and strategies with dedicated activists from around the world whose lives are committed to the struggle for justice. So Durban was both an encounter with the ugly face of racist resistance and a source of sorely needed optimism.

I got an e-mail from a friend the other day. The subject line read: "Trying to wrap my soul around all this," and my friend talked about how profoundly unsettled she has been over the past weeks. I think that this is true for most of us. If our souls are not slipping towards despair, they are restless and agitated. It is time, then, to turn to whatever it takes to steady your soul and keep your spirit in touch with the generosity of our planet and with all that is creative and transformative in the human species. Hug your children, your grandchildren, or your neighbor's children and promise them a future. Dig in the earth and plant some bulbs as a token of faith in the coming of spring. Turn to the musicians, poets, and artists who restore your optimism in the ultimate capacity of humankind to coevolve in peace. Learn from the spiritual leaders whose lives are dedicated to being, seeking, and teaching peace. For you will need steady souls and buoyant spirits in the difficult days ahead.

And, as you draw on sources of strength and inspiration, remember Barbara Lee's courage. Remember the heart it took to stand up and say, "I must vote my conscience." Remember the backbone it took to resist the craven consensus of 421 of her colleagues. Remember that each of us must struggle, as she did, to live up to the true definition of a patriot: "A patriot is one who wrestles for the soul of her country as she wrestles for her own being. A patriot is a citizen trying to wake from the burnt-out dream of innocence…to remember her true country."[3]

Stand for peace as Barbara Lee did, as though the future of the planet depended upon it. For indeed, it surely does.

© 2001 by Linda Burnham.

NOTES

[1] Adrienne Rich, "Through Corralitos Under Rolls of Cloud," in *An Atlas of the Difficult World, Poems 1988-1991*. New York: Norton, 1991.

[2] W.E.B. DuBois, in the speech, *"I Take My Stand,"* in *W.E.B. DuBois Speaks: Speeches and Addresses, 1920-1963*, Philip S. Foner, ed. New York: Pathfinder, 1970.

[3] Adrienne Rich, from the poem, "An Atlas of the Difficult World," in *An Atlas of the Difficult World, Poems 1988-1991*. New York: Norton, 1991.

I've Seen This War Before: To the House of Representatives, 14 September 2001

BARBARA LEE

Democratic Congresswoman Barbara Lee, representing California's Ninth District, cast the sole dissenting vote against Senate Joint Resolution 23: Authorization for Use of Military Force. The resolution was passed on September 15, 2001, and signed into law by President George W. Bush three days later.

Mr. Speaker, I rise today with a heavy heart, one that is filled with sorrow for the families and loved ones who were killed and injured in New York, Virginia, and Pennsylvania. Only the most foolish or the most callous would not understand the grief that has gripped the American people and millions around the world.

This unspeakable attack on the United States has forced me to rely on my moral compass, my conscience, and my God for direction.

September 11 changed the world. Our deepest fears now haunt us. Yet I am convinced that military action will not prevent further acts of international terrorism against the United States.

I know that this use-of-force resolution will pass, although we all know that the president can wage war even without this resolution. However difficult this vote may be, some of us must urge the use of restraint. There must be some of us who say, let's step back for a moment and think through the implications of our actions today—let us more fully understand their consequences.

We are not dealing with a conventional war. We cannot respond in a conventional manner. I do not want to see this spiral out of control. This crisis involves issues of national security, foreign policy, public safety, intelligence gathering, economics, and murder. Our response must be equally multifaceted.

We must not rush to judgment. Far too many innocent people have already died. Our country is in mourning. If we rush to launch a counterattack, we run too great a risk that women, children, and other noncombatants will be caught in the crossfire.

Nor can we let our justified anger over these outrageous acts by vicious murderers inflame prejudice against all Arab Americans, Muslims, Southeast Asians, and any other people because of their race, religion, or ethnicity.

Finally, we must be careful not to embark on an open-ended war with neither an exit strategy nor a focused target. We cannot repeat past mistakes.

In 1964, Congress gave President Lyndon Johnson the power to "take all necessary measures" to repel attacks and prevent further aggression.[1] In so doing, this house abandoned its own constitutional responsibilities and launched our country into years of undeclared war in Vietnam.

At that time, Senator Wayne Morse, one of two lonely votes against the Tonkin Gulf Resolution, declared, "I believe that history will record that we have made a grave mistake in subverting and circumventing the Constitution of the United States . . . I believe that within the next century, future generations will look with dismay and great disappointment upon a congress which is now about to make such a historic mistake."

Senator Morse was correct, and I fear we make the same mistake today. And I fear the consequences. I have agonized over this vote. But I came to grips with it in the very painful yet beautiful memorial service today at the National Cathedral. As a member of the clergy so eloquently said, "As we act, let us not become the evil that we deplore."

NOTE

[1] Gulf of Tonkin Resolution of 1964, 78th Congress, JH RES 1145.

Phantom Towers: Feminist Reflections on the Battle between Global Capitalism and Fundamentalist Terrorism

ROSALIND P. PETCHESKY

This paper was first presented at Hunter College Political Science Department Teach-In, September 25, 2001

These are trying times, hard times to know where we are from one day to the next. The attack on the World Trade Center has left many kinds of damage in its wake, not the least of which is a gaping ethical and political confusion in the minds of many Americans who identify in some way as "progressive"— meaning, antiracist, feminist, democratic (small d), antiwar. While we have a responsibility to those who died in the disaster and their loved ones, and to ourselves, to mourn, it is urgent that we also begin the work of thinking through what kind of world we are now living in and what it demands of us. And we have to do this, even while we know our understanding at this time can only be very tentative and may well be invalidated a year or even a month or a week from now by events we can't foresee or information now hidden from us.

So I want to try to draw a picture or a kind of mapping of the global power dynamics as I see them at this moment, including their gendered and racialized dimensions. I want to ask whether there is some alternative, more humane, and peaceable way out of the two unacceptable polarities now being presented to us: the permanent war machine (or permanent security state) and the regime of holy terror.

Let me make very clear that, when I question whether we are presently facing a confrontation between global capitalism and an Islamist-fundamentalist brand of fascism, I do not mean to imply their equivalence. If, in fact, the attacks of September 11, 2001 were the work of bin-Laden's al-Qaida network or something related and even larger—and for the moment I think we can assume this as a real possibility—then most of us in this room are *structurally positioned* in a way that gives us little choice about our identities. (For the Muslim Americans and Arab Americans among us, who are both opposed to terrorism and terrified to walk in our streets, the moral dilemma must be, I imagine, much more agonizing.) As an American, a woman, a feminist, and a Jew, I have to recognize that the bin-Ladens of the world hate me and would like me dead; or, if they had power over me, would make my life a living hell. I have to wish them—these "perpetrators," "terrorists," whatever they are—apprehended, annulled, so I can breathe in some kind of peace. This is quite different from living at the very center of global capitalism—which is more like living in a very dysfunctional family that fills you with shame and anger for its arrogance, greed, and insensitivity but is, like it or not, your home and gives you both immense privileges and immense responsibilities.

Nor, however, do I succumb to the temptation of casting our current dilemma in the simplistic, Manichean terms of cosmic Good vs. Evil. Currently this comes in two opposed but mirror-image versions: the narrative, advanced not only by the terrorists and their sympathizers but also by many on the left in the U.S. and around the globe, that blames U.S. cultural imperialism and economic hegemony for the "chickens coming home to roost," versus the patriotic, right-wing version that casts U.S. democracy and freedom as the innocent targets of Islamist madness. Both these stories erase all the complexities that we must try to factor into a different, more inclusive ethical and political vision. The Manichean, apocalyptic rhetorics that echoed back and forth between Bush and bin-Laden in the aftermath of the attacks—the pseudo-Islamic and the pseudo-Christian, the *jihad* and the crusade—both lie.

So, while I do not see terrorist networks and global capitalism as equivalents or the same, I do see some striking and disturbing parallels between them. I picture them as the phantom Twin Towers arising in the smoke clouds of the old—fraternal twins, not identical, locked in a battle over wealth, imperial aggrandizement, and the meanings of masculinity. It is a battle that could well end in a stalemate, an interminable cycle of violence that neither can win because of their failure to see the Other clearly. Feminist analysts and activists from many countries—whose voices have been inaudible thus far in the present crisis—have a lot of experience to draw from in making this double critique. Whether in the U.N. or national settings, we have been challenging the gender-biased and racialized dimensions of *both* neoliberal capitalism and various fundamentalisms for years, trying to steer a path between their double menace. The difference now is that they parade on the world stage in their most extreme and violent forms. I see six areas where their posturing overlaps.

1. Wealth—Little needs to be said about the U.S. as the world's wealthiest country, nor about the ways in which wealth accumulation is the holy grail, not only of our political system (think of the difficulty we have even in reforming campaign finance laws), but of our national ethos. We are the headquarters of the corporate and financial mega-empires that dominate global capitalism and influence the policies of the international financial institutions (IMF, World Bank, WTO) that are its main governing bodies. This reality resonates around the globe in the symbolic pantheon of what the U.S. stands for—from the McDonald's and Kentucky Fried Chicken ads sported by protestors in Genoa and Rawalpindi to the WTC towers themselves. Acquisitiveness, whether individual or corporate, also lurks very closely behind the values that Bush and Rumsfeld mean when they say our "freedoms" and our "way of life" are being attacked and must be defended fiercely. (Why, as I'm writing this, do unsolicited messages about Wall Street investment opportunities or low fares to the Bahamas come spewing out of my fax machine?)

Wealth is also a driving force behind the al-Qaida network, whose principals are mainly the beneficiaries of upper-middle-class or elite financing and education. bin-Laden himself derives much of his power and influence from his family's vast fortune, and the cells of Arab-Afghan fighters in the 1980s war against the Soviets were bankrolled not only by the Pakistani secret police and the CIA—$3 billion worth, writes Katha Pollitt in *The Nation,* "more money and expertise than for any other cause in CIA history"[1]—but also by Saudi oil money. More important than this, though, are the values behind the terrorist organizations, which include—as bin-Laden made clear in his famous 1998 interview—defending the "honor" and "property" of Muslims everywhere and "[fighting] the governments that are bent on attacking our religion and on stealing our wealth."[2] Political scientist Paul Amar, in a recent talk at Hunter College, rightly urges us not to confuse these wealthy networks—whose nepotism and ties to oil interests eerily resemble those of the Bush family—with impoverished and resistant social movements throughout the Middle East and Asia.[3] There is no evidence that economic justice or equality figure anywhere in the terrorist program.

2. Imperialist nationalism—The Bush administration's initial reaction to the attacks exhibited the behavior of a superpower that knows no limits, that issues ultimatums under the cover of "seeking cooperation." "Every nation in every region has a decision to make," pronounced Bush in his speech to the nation that was really a speech to the world. "Either you are with us or you are with the terrorists…. This is the world's fight, this is civilization's fight"—the U.S., then, becoming the leader and spokesman of "civilization," relegating not only the terrorists but also those who refuse to join the fight to the ranks of the uncivilized. To the Taliban and to every other regime that "harbors terrorists," he was the sheriff stonewalling the cattle rustlers: "Hand over all the terrorists or you will share in their fate." And a few days later we read "the American announcement that it *would* use Saudi Arabia as a headquarters for air operations against Afghanistan." As the war campaign progresses, its aims seem more openly imperialist: "Washington wants to offer [the small, also fundamentalist, drug-dealing *mujahedeen* mostly routed by the Taliban] a role in governing Afghanistan after the conflict," according to *The New York Times,* as if this were "Washington's" official role. Further, it and its allies are courting the octogenarian, long-forgotten Afghan king (now exiled in Italy) to join in a military operation to oust the Taliban and set up—what? A kind of puppet government?

Nothing here about internationally monitored elections, nothing about the U.N., nor any concept of the millions of Afghan people—within the country or in exile—as anything but voiceless, downtrodden victims and refugees.

Clearly, this offensive involves far more than rooting out and punishing terrorists. Though I don't want to reduce the situation to crude economism, one can't help wondering how it relates to the longstanding determination of the U.S. to keep a dominant foothold in the gulf region and to maintain control over oil supplies. At least one faction of the Bush team, clamoring to go after Saddam Hussein as well, is clearly in this mindset.[4] And let's not forget Pakistan and its concessions to U.S. demands for cooperation in return for lifting of U.S. economic sanctions—and now, the assurance of a sizable IMF loan. In the tradition of neo-imperial power, the U.S. does not need to dominate countries politically or militarily to get the concessions it wants; its economic influence backed up by the capacity for military annihilation is sufficient. And, spurred by popular rage over the WTC attacks, all this is wrapped in the outpouring of nationalist patriotism and flag-waving that now envelops the American landscape.

Though lacking the actual imperial power of the U.S., the bin-Laden forces mimic its imperial aspirations. If we ask, What are the terrorists seeking? we need to recognize their world view as an extreme and vicious form of nationalism—a kind of fascism, I would argue, because of its reliance on terror to achieve its ends. In this respect, their goals, like those of the U.S., go beyond mere punishment. Amar says the whole history of Arab and Islamic nationalism has been one that transcended the colonially imposed boundaries of the nation-state, one that was always transnational and pan-Arabic, or pan-Muslim, in form. Although the terrorists have no social base or legitimacy in laying claim to this tradition, they clearly seek to usurp it. This seems evident in bin-Laden's language invoking "the Arab nation," "the Arab peninsula," and a "brotherhood" reaching from Eastern Europe to Turkey and Albania, to the entire Middle East, South Asia, and Kashmir.[5] Their mission is to drive out "the infidels" and their Muslim supporters from something that looks like a third of the globe. Provoking the U.S. to bomb Afghanistan and/or attempt ousting the Taliban would likely destabilize Pakistan and possibly catapult it into the hands of Taliban-like extremists, who would then control nuclear weapons—a big step towards their perverted and hijacked version of the pan-Muslim dream.

3. *Pseudo-Religion*—As many others have commented, the "clash of religions" or "clash of cultures" interpretation of the current scenario is utterly specious. What we have instead is an appropriation of religious symbolism and discourse for predominantly political purposes, and to justify permanent war and violence. So bin-Laden declares a jihad, or holy war, against the U.S., its

civilians as well as its soldiers; and Bush declares a crusade against the terrorists and all who harbor or support them. bin-Laden declares himself the "servant of Allah fighting for the sake of the religion of Allah"[6] and to protect Islam's holy mosques, while Bush declares Washington the promoter of "infinite justice" and predicts certain victory, because "God is not neutral." (The Pentagon changed the "Operation Infinite Justice" label to "Operation Enduring Freedom" after Muslim Americans objected and three Christian clergymen warned that "infinite" presumed divinity, the "sin of pride.")

But we have to question the authenticity of this religious discourse on both sides, however sincere its proponents. A "Statement from Scholars of the Islamic Religion," circulated after the attacks, firmly denounces terrorism—the wanton killing of innocent civilians—as contrary to *Sh'aria* law. And Bush's adoption of this apocalyptic discourse can only be seen as substituting a conservative, right-wing form of legitimization for the neoliberal internationalist discourse that conservatives reject. In either case, it is worth quoting the always-wise Eduardo Galeano, writing in Mexico's *La Jornada*: "In the struggle of Good against Evil, it's always the people who get killed."[7]

4. Militarism—Both the Bush administration and the bin-Laden forces adopt the methods of war and violence to achieve their ends, but in very different ways. U.S. militarism is of the ultra-high-tech variety that seeks to terrorize by the sheer might, volume, and technological virtuosity of our armaments. Of course, as the history of Vietnam and the survival of Saddam Hussein attest, this is an illusion of the highest order (remember the "smart bombs" in the Gulf War that headed for soda machines?).

But our military technology is also a vast and insatiable industry for which profit, not strategy, is the driving rationale. As Jack Blum, a critic of U.S. foreign policy, pointed out in the *Sacramento Bee*, "the national defense game is a systems and money operation" that has little, if any, relevance to terrorism.[8] Missiles were designed to counter hostile states with their own fixed territories and weapons arsenals, not terrorists who sneak around the globe and whose "weapons of mass destruction" are human bodies and hijacked planes; nor the famously impervious terrain and piles of rubble that constitute Afghanistan. Even George W., in one of his most sensible comments to date, remarked that we'd know better than to aim "a $2 billion cruise missile at a $10 empty tent." And yet four days after the attack, the Democrats in Congress piled madness atop madness and withdrew their opposition to Bush's costly and destructive "missile shield," voting to restore $1.3 billion in spending authority for this misconceived and dangerous project. And the armaments companies quickly started lining up to receive their big orders for the impending next war—the war, we are told, that will last a long time, maybe the rest of our lives. U.S. militarism is not about rationality—not even about fighting terrorism—but about profits.

The war mania and rallying-around-the-flag exhibited by the American people express desire, not for military profits, but for something else, something harder for feminist and antiwar dissidents to understand. Maybe it's just the need to vent anger and feel avenged, or the more deep-rooted one to experience some sense of community and higher purpose in a society where we are so atomized and isolated from one another and the world. On September 25, Barbara Kingsolver wrote in the *San Francisco Chronicle* that she and her husband reluctantly sent their five-year-old daughter to school dressed in red, white, and blue like the other kids because they didn't want to let jingoists and censors "steal the flag from us." Their little girl probably echoed the longings of many less reflective grownups when she said that wearing the colors of the flag "means we're a country; just people all together."

The militarism of the terrorists is of a very different nature—based on the mythic figure of the Bedouin warrior, or the Ikhwan fighters of the early twentieth century who enabled Ibn Saud to consolidate his dynastic state. Their hallmark is individual courage and ferocity in battle. Malise Ruthven's *Islam in the World* quotes one Arab witness who described them, foreshadowing reports of Soviet veterans from the 1980s Afghan war, as "utterly fearless of death, not caring how many fall, advancing rank upon rank with only one desire—the defeat and annihilation of the enemy."[10]

Of course, this image too, like every hypernationalist ideology, is rooted in a mythic golden past and has little to do with how real terrorists in the twenty-first century are recruited, trained, and paid off. And, like high-tech militarism, terrorist low-tech militarism is also based in an illusion: that millions of believers will rise up, obey the *fatwa,* and defeat the infidel. It's an illusion because it grossly underestimates the most powerful weapon in global capitalism's arsenal—not "infinite justice" or even nukes, but infinite Nikes and CDs. And it also underestimates the local power of feminism, which the fundamentalists mistakenly confuse with the West. Iran today, in all its internal contradictions, shows the resilience and globalized/localized variety of both youth cultures and women's movements.

5. *Masculinism*—Militarism, nationalism, and colonialism as terrains of power have always been, in large part, contests over the meanings of manhood. Feminist political scientist Cynthia Enloe remarks that "men's sense of their own masculinity, often tenuous, is as much a factor in international politics as is the flow of oil, cables, and military hardware."[11] In the case of bin-Laden's Taliban patrons, the form and excessiveness of the misogyny that goes hand in hand with state terrorism and extreme fundamentalism have been graphically

documented. Just go to the Web site of the Revolutionary Association of the Women of Afghanistan (RAWA), www.rawa.org, to view more photos of atrocities against women (and men) for sexual offenses, dress code offenses, and other forms of deviance than you'll be able to stomach.

According to John Burns, writing in the *New York Times Magazine* in 1990, Gulbuddin Hekmatyar, the "rebel" leader in the Afghan war who received "the lion's share of American money and weapons"—and was not a Taliban—"dispatched followers [during his student movement days] to throw vials of acid into the faces of women students who refused to wear veils."[12]

In the case of transnational terrorists and bin-Laden himself, their model of manliness is that of the Islamic "brotherhood," the band of brothers bonded together in an agonistic commitment to fighting the enemy to the death. The CIA Pakistani Saudi–backed camps and training schools set up to support the "freedom fighters" (who later became "terrorists") in the anti-Soviet war were breeding grounds not only of a worldwide terrorist network but also of its masculinist, misogynist culture. bin-Laden clearly sees himself as a patriarchal tribal chief whose duty is to provide for and protect, not only his own retinue, wives, and many children, but also his whole network of lieutenants and recruits and their families. He is the legendary Arabic counterpart of the Godfather.

In contrast to this, can we say that the U.S. as standard-bearer of global capitalism is "gender neutral"? Don't we have a woman—indeed an African American woman—at the helm of our National Security Council, the president's right hand in designing the permanent war machine? Despite reported "gender gaps" in polls about war, we know that women are not inherently more peace-loving than men. Remember all those suburban housewives with their yellow ribbons in Midwestern airports and shopping malls during the Gulf War? Global capitalist masculinism is alive and well, but concealed in its Eurocentric, racist guise of "rescuing" downtrodden Afghan women from the misogynist regime it helped bring to power. Feminists around the world, who have tried for so long to call attention to the plight of women and girls in Afghanistan, cannot feel consoled by the prospect of U.S. warplanes and U.S.–backed guerrilla chiefs coming to "save our Afghan sisters." Meanwhile, the U.S. will send single mothers who signed up for the National Guard when welfare ended to fight and die in its holy war; U.S. media remain silent about the activism and self-determination of groups like RAWA, Refugee Women in Development, and NEGAR, a French group of information and support for Afghan women; and the U.S. military establishment refuses accountability before the new International Criminal Court for the acts of rape and sexual assault committed by its soldiers stationed across the globe. Masculinism and misogyny take many forms, not always the most visible.

6. Racism—Of course, what I have named fascist fundamentalism, or transnational terrorism, is also saturated in racism, but of a very specific, focused kind—which is anti-Semitism. The WTC towers symbolized not only American capitalism, not only finance capitalism, but, for the terrorists, *Jewish* finance capitalism. We can see this in the reported misreporting of the September 11 attacks in Arabic language newspapers in the Middle East as probably the work of the Israelis; their erroneous allegation that not a single person among the dead and missing was Jewish, so Jews must have had advance warning, etc. In his 1998 interview, bin-Laden constantly refers to "Jews," not Israelis, in his accusations about plans to take over the whole Arab peninsula. He asserts that "the Americans and the Jews . . . represent the spearhead with which the members of our religion have been slaughtered. Any effort directed against America and the Jews yields positive and direct results."[13] And finally, he rewrites history and collapses the diversity of Muslims in a warning to "Western governments" to sever their ties to Jews: "The enmity between us and the Jews goes far back in time and is deep rooted. There is no question that war between the two of us is inevitable. For this reason it is not in the interest of Western governments to expose the interests of their people to all kinds of retaliation for almost nothing."[14] (I cringe to realize I am part of the "nothing.")

U.S. racism is much more diffuse but just as insidious; the pervasive racism and ethnocentrism that fester under the American skin always boil to the surface at times of national crisis. As Sumitha Reddy put it in a recent teach-in, the targeting of Sikhs and other Indians, Arabs, and even Latinos and African Americans in the wave of violent and abusive acts throughout the country since the disaster signals an enlargement of the "zone of distrust" in American racism beyond the usual black-white focus.[15] Women who wear headscarves or saris are particularly vulnerable to harassment, but Arab and Indian men of all ages are the ones being murdered. The state pretends to abhor such incidents and threatens their full prosecution. But this is the same state that made the so-called Anti-Terrorism Act, passed in 1995 after the Oklahoma City bombing (an act committed by native white Christian terrorists), a pretext for rounding up and deporting immigrants of all kinds; and that is now once again waiving the civil liberties of immigrants in its zealous antiterrorist manhunt. Each day the *New York Times* publishes its rogues' gallery of police photos of the suspects, so reminiscent of those eugenic photographs of "criminal types" of an earlier era and imprinting upon readers' minds a certain set of facial characteristics they should now fear and blame. Racial profiling becomes a national pastime.

⋙⋘ ⋙⋘ ⋙⋘

If we look only at terrorist tactics and the world's revulsion against them, then we might conclude rather optimistically that thuggery will never win out in the end. But we ignore the context in which terrorism operates at our peril, and that context includes not only racism and Eurocentrism but many forms of social injustice. In thinking through a moral position on this crisis, we have to distinguish between *immediate causes* and *necessary conditions*. Neither the United States (as a state) nor the corporate and financial power structure that the World Trade Centers symbolized *caused* the horrors of September 11. Without question, the outrageous, heinous murder, maiming, and orphaning of so many innocent people—who were every race, ethnicity, color, class, age, gender, and some sixty-odd nationalities—deserve some kind of just redress. On the other hand, the *conditions* in which transnational terrorism thrives, gains recruits, and lays claim to moral legitimacy include many for which the U.S. and its corporate/financial interests are directly responsible, even if they don't for a minute excuse the attacks.

It is often asked lately, Why does the Third World hate us so much? Put another way, Why do so many people, including my own friends in Asia, Africa, Latin America, and the Middle East, express so much ambivalence about what happened, both lamenting an unforgivable criminal act and at the same time taking some satisfaction that Americans are finally suffering too? We make a fatal mistake if we attribute these mixed feelings only to envy or resentment of our wealth and freedoms and ignore a historical context of aggression, injustice, and inequality. Consider the following facts.

- The United States is still the only country in the world to have actually *used* the most infamous weapons of mass destruction in the nuclear bombing of innocent civilians—in Hiroshima and Nagasaki.

- The U.S. persists to this day in bombing Iraq, destroying the lives and food supplies of hundreds of thousands of civilian adults and children there. We bombed Belgrade—a dense capital city—for eighty straight days during the war in Kosovo and supported bombing that killed untold civilians in El Salvador in the 1980s. In the name of fighting communism, our CIA and military training apparatus sponsored paramilitary massacres, assassinations, tortures, and disappearances in many Latin American and Central American countries in Operation Condor and the like in the 1970s, and has supported corrupt, authoritarian regimes in the Middle East, Southeast Asia, and elsewhere—the Shah of Iran, Suharto in Indonesia, the Saudi dynasty, and let's not forget the Taliban regime itself. September 11 is also the date of the coup against the democratically elected Allende government in Chile and the beginning of the twenty-five-year Pinochet dictatorship, again thanks to U.S. support. Yes, a long history of state terrorism.

- In the Middle East, which is the microcosm of the current conflagration, billions in annual U.S. military aid and the Bush administration's refusal to pressure the Sharon government are the *sine qua non* of continued Israeli government policies of attacks on villages, demolition of homes, destruction of olive orchards, restrictions on travel, continual human rights abuses of Palestinians and even Arab citizens, assassination of political leaders, building of roads, and enlarging of settlements—all of which exacerbate Palestinian despair and suicide bombings. The U.S. thereby contributes to deepening the illegal occupation and "Bantustanizing" of the Palestinian territories, and thus perpetuating hostilities.

- Despite its pretense to uphold women's rights, the U.S. is one of only about two dozen countries that have failed to ratify the U.N. Convention on the Elimination of All Forms of Discrimination Against Women, and the only country in the world (as of April 2002, when Somalia finally agreed to sign) that refuses to sign the U.N. Convention on the Rights of the Child. It is the most vocal opponent of the statute establishing an International Criminal Court as well as of the treaties banning land mines and germ warfare; a principal subverter of a new multilateral treaty to combat illegal small arms trafficking; and the sole country in the world to threaten an unprecedented space-based defense system and imminent violation of the ABM treaty. So who is the "outlaw," the "rogue state"?

- The U.S. is the only major industrialized country to refuse to sign the final Kyoto Protocol on Global Climate Change, despite compromises in that document designed to meet U.S. objections. Meanwhile, a new global scientific study shows that the countries whose productivity will benefit most from climate change are Canada, Russia, and the U.S., while the biggest losers will be the countries that have contributed least to global climate change—i.e., most of Africa.

- As even the World Bank and the United Nations Development Programme attest, two decades of globalization have resulted in enlarging rather than shrinking the gaps between rich and poor, both within countries and among countries. The benefits of global market liberalization and integration have accrued disproportionately to wealthy Americans and Europeans (as well as small elites in the Third World). Despite the presumed democratizing effects of the

Internet, a middle-class American "needs to save a month's salary to buy a computer; a Bangladeshi must save all his wages for eight years to do so."[16] And despite its constant trumpeting of "free-trade" rhetoric, the U.S. remains a persistent defender of protectionist policies for its farmers and steel and textile manufacturers. Meanwhile small producers throughout Asia, Africa, and the Caribbean—a great many of whom are women—are squeezed out by U.S. imports and relegated to the informal economy or sweatshop labor for multinationals.

• The G-8 countries, of which the U.S. is the senior partner, dominate decision-making in the IMF and the World Bank, whose structural adjustments and conditions for loans and debt relief help to keep many poor countries and their citizens locked in poverty.

• In the aftermath of the September 11 attacks, the U.S. Congress was able to come up with an immediate $40 billion for "anti-terrorism" activities, another $40 billion to bail out the airlines, and a twenty-year contract with Lockheed to produce military aircraft for $200 billion— enough to eliminate contagious diseases from the face of the earth. Yet our foreign assistance appropriations (except for military aid) have shrunk; we, the world's richest country, contribute only one-seventh of 1 percent of our GNP to foreign aid—the least of any industrialized country. A recent WHO report tells us that the total cost of providing safe water and sanitation to all of sub-Saharan Africa would be only $11 billion, only no one can figure out where the money will come from; and the U.N. is still a long way from raising a similar amount for its proclaimed Global Fund to combat AIDS, malaria, and TB. What kind of meanness is this? And what does it say about forms of racism, or "global apartheid," that value some lives—those in the U.S. and Europe—far more than others in other parts of the globe?

And the list goes on, with McDonald's, Coca-Cola, CNN, and MTV and all the uninvited commercial detritus that proliferates everywhere on the face of the earth and offends the cultural and spiritual sensibilities of so many— including transnational feminist travelers like me, when we find pieces of our local shopping mall transplanted to central Manila, Kampala, or Bangalore. But worse than the triviality and bad taste of these cultural and commercial barrages is the arrogant presumption that our "way of life" is the best on earth and ought to be welcome everywhere; or that our power and supposed advancement entitle us to dictate policies and strategies to the rest of the world. This is the face of imperialism in the twenty-first century.

None of this reckoning can comfort those who lost loved ones on

September 11, or the thousands of attack victims who lost their jobs, homes, and livelihoods; nor can it excuse the hideous crimes. As the Palestinian poet Mahmoud Darwish writes, "nothing, nothing justifies terrorism."[17] Still, in attempting to understand what has happened and think how to prevent it from happening again (which is probably a vain wish), we Americans have to take all these painful facts into account. The United States as the command center of global capitalism will remain ill equipped to "stop terrorism" until it begins to recognize its own past and present responsibility for many of the conditions I've listed and to address them in a responsible way.

But this would mean the United States becoming something different from itself, transforming itself, including abandoning the presumption that it should unilaterally police the world. This problem of transformation is at the heart of the vexing question of finding solutions different from all-out war. So let me turn to how we might think differently about power. Here is what I propose, tentatively, for now.

The slogan "War Is Not the Answer" is a practical as well as an ontological truth. Bombing or other military attacks on Afghanistan will not root out networks of terrorists, who could be hiding deep in the mountains or in Pakistan or Germany or Florida or New Jersey. It will only succeed in destroying an already decimated country, killing untold numbers of civilians as well as combatants, and creating hundreds of thousands more refugees. And it is likely to arouse so much anger among Islamist sympathizers as to destabilize the entire region and perpetuate the cycle of retaliation and terrorist attacks. All the horror of the twentieth century surely should teach us that war feeds on itself and that armed violence reflects, not an extension of politics by other means, but the failure of politics; not the defense of civilization, but the breakdown of civilization.

Tracking down and bringing the perpetrators of terrorism to justice, in some kind of international police action, is a reasonable aim but one fraught with dangers. Because the U.S. is the world's only "superpower," its declaration of war against terrorism and its supporters everywhere says to other countries that we are once again taking over as global policeman, or, as Fidel Castro put it, a "world military dictatorship under the exclusive rule of force, irrespective of any international laws or institutions."[18] Here at home a "national emergency" or "state of war"—*especially* when defined as different from any other war—means the curtailment of civil liberties, harassment of immigrants, racial profiling, and withholding of information (censorship) or feeding of disinformation to the media, all without any time limits or accountability under the dubious Office of Homeland Security and the "U.S.A. Patriot Act." We should oppose both U.S. unilateralism and the permanent security state. We should urge our representatives in Congress to diligently defend the civil liberties of all.

I agree with the Afro-Asian Peoples Solidarity Organization (AAPSO) in Cairo that "this punishment should be inflicted according to the law and only upon those who were responsible for these events,"[19] and that it should be organized within the framework of the United Nations and international law, not unilaterally by the United States. This is not the same as the U.S. getting unanimous approval from the Security Council to commandeer global security, which is a first step at best. Numerous treaties against terrorism and money-laundering already exist in international law. The International Criminal Court, whose establishment the U.S. government has so stubbornly opposed, would be the logical body to try terrorist cases, with the cooperation of national police and surveillance systems. *We should demand that the U.S. ratify the ICC statute.* In the meantime, a special tribunal under international auspices, like the ones for the former Yugoslavia and Rwanda, could be set up, as well as an international agency to coordinate national police and intelligence efforts, with the U.S. as one participating member. This is the power of international engagement and cooperation.

No amount of police action, however cooperative, can stop terrorism without addressing the conditions of misery and injustice that nourish and aggravate terrorism. The U.S. has to undertake a serious reexamination of its values and its policies with regard not only to the Middle East but also to the larger world. It has to take responsibility for being in the world, including ways of sharing its wealth, resources, and technology; democratizing decisions about global trade, finance, and security; and assuring that access to "global public goods" like health care, housing, food, education, sanitation, water, and freedom from racial and gender discrimination is given priority in international relations. What we even mean by "security" has to encompass all these aspects of well-being, of "human security," and has to be universal in its reach.

Let me again quote from the poet Mahmoud Darwish's statement, which was published in the Palestinian daily *Al Ayyam* on September 17, 2001, and signed by many Palestinian writers and intellectuals.

> We know that the American wound is deep and we know that this tragic moment is a time for solidarity and the sharing of pain. But we also know that the horizons of the intellect can traverse landscapes of devastation. Terrorism has no location or boundaries, it does not reside in a geography of its own; its homeland is disillusionment and despair.

> The best weapon to eradicate terrorism from the soul lies in the solidarity of the international world, in respecting the rights of all peoples of this globe to live in harmony and by reducing the ever increasing gap between north and south. And the most effective way to defend freedom is through fully realizing the meaning of justice.[20]

What gives me hope is that this statement's sentiments are being voiced by growing numbers of groups here in the U.S., including the National Council of Churches, the Green Party, a coalition of a hundred entertainers and civil rights leaders, huge coalitions of peace groups and student organizations, New Yorkers Say No to War, black and white women celebrities featured on Oprah Winfrey's show, and parents and spouses of attack victims, as well as some five hundred petitioners from women's peace groups here and across the globe calling on the U.N. Security Council to "Stop the War, Rebuild a Just Society in Afghanistan, and Support Women's Human Rights."

Maybe out of the ashes we will recover a new kind of solidarity; maybe the terrorists will force us, not to mirror them, but to see the world and humanity as a whole.

This essay first appeared in *Ms. Magazine* (December 2001).
© 2001 by Rosalind Petchesky.

NOTES

[1] Katha Pollitt, "Put Out No Flags." *The Nation,* October 8, 2001.

[2] Interview with bin-Laden, May 1998, "Frontline," (http://www.pbs.org/wgbh/pages/frontline/shows/binladen/who/interview.html).

[3] Paul Amar, Talk at Teach-In, Hunter College, New York, Sept. 24, 2001.

[4] Dozens of news reports noted the division within the Bush White House between the State Department on the one hand and Vice President Cheney/Secretary of Defense Rumsfeld/ Deputy Secretary of Defense Wolfowitz on the other.

[5] Interview with bin-Laden.

[6] Ibid.

[7] Eduardo Galeano, "The Theatre of Good and Evil." *La Jornada,* Sept. 21, 2001.

[8] Jack A. Blum, "Engagement Equals Survival." *The Sacramento Bee,* Sept. 16, 2001.

[9] Barbara Kingsolver, "And Our Flag Was Still There." *San Francisco Chronicle,* Sept. 25, 2001.

[10] Malise Ruthven, *Islam In the World.* New York: Oxford University Press, 1984: 27.

[11] Cynthia Enloe, *The Morning After: Sexual Politics at the End of the Cold War.* Berkeley: University of California Press, 1993: 173.

[12] John F. Burns, "Afghans: Now They Blame America." *The New York Times Magazine,* Feb. 4, 1990.

[13] Interview with bin-Laden.

[14] Ibid.

[15] Sumitha Reddy, Talk at Teach-In, City University of New York Graduate Center, New York, Sept. 21, 2001.

[16] United Nations Development Programme, Human Development Report 1998. Oxford: Oxford University Press, 1998, reported by Barbara Crossette, "Most Consuming More, and the Rich Much More." *The New York Times,* Sept. 13, 1998.

[17] Mahmood Darwish, Statement in *Al-Ayyam,* Sept. 17, 2001.

[18] "Fidel Castro Speaks about 'Infinite Justice.' Speech by Commander in Chief Fidel Castro, Sept. 22, 2001, Havana, Cuba. *NY Transfer News,* http://www.blythe.org.

[19] "Terrorism Invades America." Press Release Issued by Dr. Mourad Ghaleb, President, AAPSO, on behalf of the Permanent Secretariat, n.d. aapso@idsc.net.eg.

[20] Darwish.

The Color of Violence Against Women

ANGELA Y. DAVIS

This keynote address was delivered at the Color of Violence Conference in Santa Cruz, California on April 28, 2000.

I feel extremely honored to have been invited to deliver this keynote address. This conference deserves to be called "historic" on many accounts. It is the first of its kind, and this is precisely the right intellectual season for such a gathering. The breadth and complexity of its concerns show the contradictions and possibilities of this historical moment. And just such a gathering can help us to imagine ways of attending to the ubiquitous violence in the lives of women of color that also radically subvert the institutions and discourses within which we are compelled by necessity to think and work.

I predict that this conference will be remembered as a milestone for feminist scholars and activists, marking a new moment in the history of antiviolence scholarship and organizing.

Many years ago when I was a student in San Diego, I was driving down the freeway with a friend when we encountered a black woman wandering along the shoulder. Her story was extremely disturbing. Despite her uncontrollable weeping, we were able to surmise that she had been raped and dumped along the side of the road. After a while, she was able to wave down a police car, thinking that they would help her. However, when the white policeman picked her up, he did not comfort her, but rather seized upon the opportunity to rape her once more.

I relate this story not for its sensational value, but for its metaphorical power.

Given the racist and patriarchal patterns of the state, it is difficult to envision the state as the holder of solutions to the problem of violence against women of color. However, as the antiviolence movement has been institutionalized and professionalized, the state plays an increasingly dominant role in how we conceptualize and create strategies to minimize violence against women.

One of the major tasks of this conference, and of the antiviolence movement as a whole, is to address this contradiction, especially as it presents itself to poor communities of color.

The Advent of "Domestic Violence"

Violence is one of those words that is a powerful ideological conductor, one whose meaning constantly mutates. Before we do anything else, we need to pay tribute to the activists and scholars whose ideological critiques made it possible to apply the category of "domestic violence" to those concealed layers of aggression systematically directed at women. These acts were for so long relegated to secrecy or, worse, considered normal.

Many of us now take for granted that misogynist violence is a legitimate political issue, but let us remember that a little more than two decades ago, most people considered "domestic violence" to be a private concern and thus not a proper subject of public discourse or political intervention. Only one generation separates us from that era of silence. The first speak-out against rape occurred in the early 1970s, and the first national organization against domestic violence was founded toward the end of that decade.

We have since come to recognize the epidemic proportions of violence within intimate relationships and the pervasiveness of date and acquaintance rape, as well as violence within and against same-sex intimacy. But we must also learn how to oppose the racist fixation on people of color as the primary perpetrators of violence, including domestic and sexual violence, and at the same time to fiercely challenge the real violence that men of color inflict on women. These are precisely the men who are already reviled as the major purveyors of violence in our society: the gang members, the drug dealers, the drive-by shooters, the burglars, and assailants. In short, the criminal is figured as a black or Latino man who must be locked into prison.

One of the major questions facing this conference is how to develop an analysis that furthers neither the conservative project of sequestering millions of men of color in accordance with the contemporary dictates of globalized capital and its prison industrial complex, nor the equally conservative project of abandoning poor women of color to a continuum of violence that extends from the sweatshops through the prisons, to shelters, and into bedrooms at home.

How do we develop analyses and organizing strategies against violence against women that acknowledge the race of gender and the gender of race?

Women of Color on the Frontlines

Women of color have been active in the antiviolence movement since its beginnings. The first national organization addressing domestic violence was founded in 1978 when the United States Civil Rights Commission Consultation on Battered Women led to the founding of the National Coalition Against Domestic Violence. In 1980, the Washington, DC Rape Crisis Center sponsored the First National Conference on Third World Women and Violence. The following year a Women of Color Task Force was created within the National Coalition Against Domestic Violence. To make some historical connections, it is significant that the U.S. Third World

Women's Caucus formed that same year within the National Women Studies Association, and the groundbreaking book *This Bridge Called My Back* was first published.[1]

Many of these activists have helped to develop a more complex understanding about the overlapping, cross-cutting, and often contradictory relationships among race, class, gender, and sexuality that militate against a simplistic theory of privatized violence in women's lives. Clearly, the powerful slogan first initiated by the feminist movement—"the personal is political"—is far more complicated than it initially appeared to be.

The early feminist argument that violence against women is not inherently a private matter, but has been privatized by the sexist structures of the state, the economy, and the family, has had a powerful impact on public consciousness.

Yet, the effort to incorporate an analysis that does not reify gender has not been so successful. The argument that sexual and domestic violence is the structural foundation of male dominance sometimes leads to a hierarchical notion that genital mutilation in Africa and *sati,* or wife-burning, in India are the most dreadful and extreme forms of the same violence against women that can be discovered in less appalling manifestations in Western cultures.

Other analyses emphasize a greater incidence of misogynist violence in poor communities and communities of color, without necessarily acknowledging the greater extent of police surveillance in these communities—directly and through social service agencies. In other words, precisely because the primary strategies for addressing violence against women rely on the state and on constructing gendered assaults on women as "crimes," the criminalization process further bolsters the racism of the courts and prisons. Those institutions, in turn, further contribute to violence against women.

On the one hand, we should applaud the courageous efforts of the many activists who are responsible for a new popular consciousness of violence against women for a range of legal remedies, and for a network of shelters, crisis centers, and other sites where survivors are able to find support. But on the other hand, uncritical reliance on the government has resulted in serious problems. I suggest that we focus our thinking on this contradiction: Can a state that is thoroughly infused with racism, male dominance, class bias, and homophobia and that constructs itself in and through violence act to minimize violence in the lives of women? Should we rely on the state as the answer to the problem of violence against women?

The documentary, "Concrete and Sunshine,"[2] by Nicole Cousino (assisted by Ruth Gilmore) on California prison expansion and its economic impact on rural and urban communities includes a poignant scene in which Vanessa Gomez describes how the deployment of police and court antiviolence strategies put her husband away under the Three Strikes law.[3] She describes a verbal altercation between herself and her husband, who was angry with her for not cutting up liver for their dog's meal, since, she said, it was her turn to cut the liver.

According to her account, she insisted that she would prepare the dog's food, but he said no, he was already doing it. She says that she grabbed him and, in trying to take the knife away from him, seriously cut her fingers. In the hospital, the incident was reported to the police. Despite the fact that Ms. Gomez contested the prosecutor's version of the events, her husband was convicted of assault. Because of two previous convictions as a juvenile, he received a sentence under California's Three Strikes law of twenty-five years to life, which he is currently serving.

I relate this incident because it so plainly shows the facility with which the state can assimilate our opposition to gender domination into projects of racial—which also means gender—domination.

Militarized Violence

Gina Dent has observed that one of the most important accomplishments of this conference is to foreground Native American women within the category "women of color." As Kimberlé Crenshaw's germinal study on violence against women suggests, the situation of Native American women shows that we must also include within our analytical framework the persisting colonial domination of indigenous nations and national formations within and outside the presumed territorial boundaries of the U.S. The U.S. colonial state's racist, sexist, and homophobic brutality in dealing with Native Americans once again shows the futility of relying upon the juridical or legislative processes of the state to resolve these problems.

How then can one expect the state to solve the problem of violence against women, when it constantly recapitulates its own history of colonialism, racism, and war? How can we ask the state to intervene when, in fact, its armed forces have always practiced rape and battery against "enemy" women? In fact, sexual and intimate violence against women has been a central military tactic of war and domination.

Yet the approach of the neoliberal state is to incorporate women into these agencies of violence—to integrate the armed forces and the police.

How do we deal with the police killing of Amadou Diallo,[4] whose wallet was putatively misapprehended as a gun—or Tanya Haggerty in Chicago, whose cell phone was the potential weapon that allowed police to justify her killing?[5] By hiring more women as police officers? Does the argument that women are victimized by violence render them inefficient agents of violence? Does giving women greater access to official violence help to minimize informal violence? Even if this were the case, would we want to embrace this as a solution? Are women essentially immune from the forms of adaptation to violence that are so foundational to police and military culture?

Carol Burke, a civilian teaching in the U.S. Naval Academy, argues that "sadomasochistic cadence calls have increased since women entered the brigade of midshipmen in 1976." She quotes military songs that are so cruelly pornographic that I would feel uncomfortable quoting them in public, but let me give one comparatively less offensive example:

> The ugliest girl I ever did see
> Was beatin' her face against a tree
> I picked her up; I punched her twice.
> She said, "Oh Middy, you're much too nice."

If we concede that something about the training structures and the operations they are expected to carry out makes the men (and perhaps also women) in these institutions more likely to engage in violence within their intimate relationships, why then is it so difficult to develop an analysis of violence against women that takes the violence of the state into account?

The major strategy relied on by the women's antiviolence movement of criminalizing violence against women will not put an end to violence against women—just as imprisonment has not put an end to "crime" in general.

I should say that this is one of the most vexing issues confronting feminists today. On the one hand, it is necessary to create legal remedies for women who are survivors of violence. But on the other hand, when the remedies rely on punishment within institutions that further promote violence—against women and men—how do we work with this contradiction?

How do we avoid the assumption that previously "private" modes of violence can only be rendered public within the context of the state's apparatus of violence?

The Crime Bill

It is significant that the 1994 Violence Against Women Act was passed by Congress as Title IV of the Violent Crime Control and Law Enforcement Act of 1994—the Crime Bill. This bill attempted to address violence against women within domestic contexts, but at the same time it facilitated the incarceration of more women—through Three Strikes and other provisions. The growth of police forces provided for by the Crime Bill will certainly increase the numbers of people subject to the brutality of police violence.

Prisons are violent institutions. Like the military, they render women vulnerable in an even more systematic way to the forms of violence they may have experienced in their homes and in their communities. Women's prison experiences point to a continuum of violence at the intersection of racism, patriarchy, and state power.

A Human Rights Watch report entitled *All Too Familiar: Sexual Abuse of Women in U.S. Prisons* says:

> Our findings indicate that being a woman prisoner in U.S. state prisons can be a terrifying experience. If you are sexually abused, you cannot escape from your abuser. Grievance or investigatory procedures, where they exist, are often ineffectual, and correctional employees continue to engage in abuse because they believe they will rarely be held accountable, administratively or criminally. Few people outside the prison walls know what is going on or care if they do know. Fewer still do anything to address the problem.[6]

Recently, thirty-one women filed a class action law suit against the Michigan Department of Corrections, charging that the department failed to prevent sexual violence and abuse by guards and civilian staff. These women have been subjected to serious retaliations, including being raped again!

At Valley State Prison in California, the chief medical officer told Ted Koppel on national television[7] that he and his staff routinely subjected women to pelvic examinations, even if they just had colds. He explained that these women have been imprisoned for a long time and have no male contact, and so they actually enjoy these pelvic examinations. Koppel sent the tape of this interview to the prison and the medical officer was eventually dismissed. According to the Department of Corrections, he will never be allowed to have contact with patients again. But this is just the tip of the iceberg. The fact that he felt able to say this on national television gives you a sense of the horrendous conditions in women's prisons.

There are no easy solutions to all the issues I have raised and that so many of you are working on. But what is clear is that we need to come together to work towards a far more nuanced framework and strategy than the antiviolence movement has ever yet been able to elaborate.

We want to continue to contest the neglect of domestic violence against women, the tendency to dismiss it as a private matter. We need to develop an approach that relies on political mobilization rather than legal remedies or social service delivery. We need to fight for temporary and long-term solutions to violence and simultaneously think about and link global capitalism, global colonialism, racism, and patriarchy—all the forces that shape violence against women of color. Can we, for example, link a strong demand for remedies for women of color who are targets of rape and domestic violence with a strategy that calls for the abolition of the prison system?

I conclude by asking you to support the new organization[8] initiated by Andrea Smith, the organizer of this conference. Such an organization contesting violence against women of color is especially needed to connect, advance, and organize our analytic and organizing efforts. Hopefully this organization will act as a catalyst to keep us thinking and moving together in the future.

This essay originally appeared in *ColorLines* and *Sojourner: The Women's Forum.*

© 2001 by Angela Davis. The version used here is reprinted by permission of *Sojourner: The Women's Forum.*

NOTES

[1] Cherríe L. Moraga and Gloria Anzaldúa, eds., in *This Bridge Called My Back: Writings by Radical Women of Color,* ed., Cherríe Moraga and Gloria Anzaldúa (New York: Kitchen Table/Women of Color Press, 1983).

[2] Released in 2002. The scene described here did not make it to the final cut; however, the video is recommended for its overall presentation of the topics presented.

[3] California Codes, Penal Code Section 654–678.

[4] For details of this case, see http://www.amadoudiallofoundation.org/.

[5] Haggerty was a passenger in a car that was pulled over by police after a short chase. Police say she was shot dead when officers mistook the cell phone in her hand for a gun. Haggerty was nineteen at the time of her death.

[6] Dorothy Q. Thomas, ed., *All Too Familiar: Sexual Abuse of Women in U.S. State Prisons.* New York: Human Rights Watch, 1997.

[7] For details, see http://abcnews.go.com/onair/Nightline/nl991102.html.

[8] Incite! Women of Color Against Violence is based in Minneapolis and can be contacted through its Web site at http://www.incite-national.org.

Mother vs. Murder

DEBBIE NATHAN

It is hard to stay calm after seeing the baby's autopsy photograph. Entered into evidence in a Texas courtroom, it shows the infant Ramiro Pérez looking like a victim of African famine or the atrocities at Buchenwald. His tiny ribs are starkly outlined through his skin—every one of them. His belly sinks into his spinal column. His buttocks are no thicker than his thighs, and the skin hangs on them like the wrinkled sleeves of an old sweatshirt. On his face, the cheeks cave like a very old man's. His shrunken corpse weighed barely five and one-half pounds when this picture was taken. That is eight ounces less than at birth, seventy-five days before he was put on the coroner's scales in early 1998.

The person deemed most responsible for this horror is Ramiro Pérez's mother, Tina Rodríguez. She is a lifelong resident of the Hill Country—the lovely area just south and west of Austin that boasts gorgeous geography, countless bed-and-breakfasts, and a steady stream of tourists from throughout the country. In spring, 1999, media all the way to San Antonio buzzed about Rodríguez's trial for the capital murder of two-and-a-half-month-old Ramiro. "Starvation," boomed the headlines, for that was what the state of Texas was saying: that Rodríguez had deliberately deprived her infant son of food in order to kill him. The plan was carried out, prosecutors noted, in a rickety tin shack with no running water. Pictures of the miserable dwelling popped up repeatedly in the region's newspapers and on nightly TV news. In February 1999, Rodríguez had a trial in the charming Hill Country town of Boerne. The verdict was guilty, and she was sentenced to automatic life imprisonment.

It was one of the harshest punishments ever meted out in a child starvation case. Rodríguez will not be eligible for parole until 2039. Her husband, Noel Pérez, was also originally charged with capital murder. But after Rodríguez's trial he accepted a plea bargain to the less serious charge of child endangerment, which carries a maximum twenty-five years' imprisonment and possible parole in half that time. His bargain and sentencing got little publicity; by then the Hill Country had moved on to other things. The case, it seemed, was closed.

But disturbing questions remain. People who knew and worked with Rodríguez before she was arrested believe she was a troubled woman, but they do not think she deliberately murdered her infant. People who got acquainted with her at the trial—including members of the jury who convicted her—question why her lawyers didn't effectively suggest other possibilities for little Ramiro's death besides the prosecutor's monstrous scenario of maternal sadism. Nutrition experts speculate that the culprit was health problems: in Ramiro, in Rodríguez, or in both. A sociologist notes that women accused of killing their children are being judged and punished far more harshly now than they used to be. She worries that the new vengeance, with its images of mothers as wicked threats to their children, is the flip side of the equally pernicious myth of mothers as perfect nurturers. And the Rodríguez case was but one in a worrisome statewide trend: a 71 percent increase in deaths was attributed to child abuse homicide in Texas in 1998. There were 176 such cases during fiscal 1998, compared with about one hundred per year through most of the nineties. The early 1999 numbers are also high, and officials are at a loss to explain the increase.

✂   ✂   ✂

The details of Ramiro Pérez's death, and of his mother's life up to that death, are complex, unruly, and mostly unknown to the public or to Rodríguez's jury. The story takes place within the economic and social backwaters of Hill Country towns like Kerrville and Bandera, where the cheery antique stores and dude ranches hide an astonishing amount of poverty and trouble—perhaps especially for young mothers. Tina Rodríguez's life exemplifies a darker side of the Hill Country, one that never appears in chamber of commerce ads or travel magazines. Entering this bleak territory, we may be able to see more deeply, even past the terrible last picture of her child.

"We called her Gordy," Tina's mother, Lionor Rodríguez, testified on the second day of her daughter's trial, and she went on to explain that the nickname stuck because Tina is "big, like me, a little on the chubby side." Although mother and daughter both are barely five feet tall, each weighs at least 165 pounds. In Tina the bulk shows up in her round face, thick neck, and in her belly, which strains her dresses and pants even when she's not pregnant. But "Gordy" didn't always fit her. At birth in 1973, Tina and her twin sister, Cristina, were two months premature and weighed little more than two pounds apiece. Back then, doctors were just managing to save such small, undeveloped babies. With her twinhood, prematurity, and tiny size, Tina's infancy was remarkable. It was probably the last thing in childhood to make her feel special.

After their discharge from the hospital, Tina and Cristina joined five other siblings in a home where it was hard for any of the seven kids to get much parental attention. One problem was poverty. Lionor's husband, Mike Rodríguez, always supported the family as a construction worker. The work is hard and low-paying. But Rodríguez's education and earnings were constrained by the prejudice and segregation that reigned during his youth in the Kerrville area in the fifties. Lionor also grew up in the Hill Country, on a ranch where her parents worked as day laborers. For young Mexican Americans like them, the civil rights era still lay in the future. They were still relegated to segregated neighborhoods. In school they were punished for speaking Spanish, and their Anglo teachers told them not to bother with academic subjects or college.

Amid the ensuing cultural isolation, traditional customs continued, including the old-country, Catholic practice of marrying early and having many babies. Lionor was fifteen when she had her first child. Six more followed over the next fifteen years. The family lived in a run-down, ghettoized part of Kerrville known variously as The Barrio and Nigger Town. They are still there today, in an old clapboard house with peeling paint, moldy floorboards, and cracks snaking down the walls. The Rodríguez's insularity, large family size, and poverty were and still are common among Hill Country Hispanics.

In addition, Tina's family had its own problems when she was young. Due to marital difficulties—Lionor was jealous and convinced that Mike was running around on her—the couple split up for nine years, beginning when Tina was only a few months old. As Tina's kindergarten teacher, Jean Tally, remembers, Lionor had a rough time managing the household alone. Tina was a willful, mischievous child, recalls Tally. She and sister Cristina often came to school infested with lice. Lionor didn't seem neglectful, says Tally—just "overwhelmed." (When told of Tally's recollections recently, Lionor said she didn't remember anything about lice.) Despite the problems she perceived, Tally thought Tina "had what it takes" to make something of herself. She ran into her former pupil a couple of years ago in Kerrville. "She looked like she was doing so well; she said everything was great. I was so pleased."

But Tally was mistaken. Long before her meeting with Tina, things had started to go wrong. It's not that she was a bad student. By the early nineties, Tina was at Kerrville's Tivy High School, where she earned Cs, Bs, and an occasional A. Outwardly, she was a cheerful girl with full cheeks, a quick smile, and friends. She was also a devoted aunt to her big brother and sisters' babies, who were being born one after another in quick succession, just as their parents' had been. Tina changed her nieces' and nephews' diapers, prepared bottles, and babysat. But she also told her mother she didn't want her own children until she finished school and got married. She talked of attending college, and as an upperclassman, applied to the navy, thinking the government could help fund her higher education.

Yet Tina was also involved in a world her family was only dimly aware of. By high school, she was leaving home for days at a time, with no word on where she was going. Her mother figured she was at friends' houses, and the assumption had a precedent. Earlier, Tina had begun hanging out at the Lopez

Club, a tavern and dance hall just outside of Kerrville on the winding road to Bandera. Since the late eighties, the area has seen an influx of newcomers, mostly young men, from Mexico. They've come to work in ranching and in the construction industry, which has burgeoned during the last two decades as the Hill Country has attracted retirees and affluent refugees from cities such as San Antonio. Many of the immigrants who build infrastructure for these people are undocumented. But Lopez's is known as a place that the border patrol leaves alone. The father of one of Tina's girlfriends owned the club, and Tina started spending a lot of time with that family and away from hers. Saturday nights, she would go to the club and party. That is where she met Noel Pérez, a Mexican who spoke little English and had no papers.

With his football-player shoulders, longish black hair, high cheekbones, and cowboy shirts, Noel was as hard-looking as Tina is soft. The two started dancing together regularly. He was nineteen. She was twelve. By the time she was fifteen, Noel and Tina were "dating," she says, but they weren't having sex. Then, sometime in her junior year, according to her mother, Tina got pregnant by someone other than Noel—someone who apparently abandoned her soon afterward. "She wouldn't tell us who the father was," Lionor Rodríguez remembers. Today Tina still won't talk about him. She will say only that she had a Hispanic boyfriend who was native-born and cruel to her. Lionor remembers the miscarriage in Tina's third or fourth month of pregnancy. The dead babies were twins. Tina was devastated. She still mourns eight years later, Lionor says, and sometimes muses about what the babies would be doing now had they lived.

These are very private thoughts, though. To reporters, Tina will say only that a boy treated her very badly, and she vowed never again to get involved with someone raised in the United States. Noel Pérez was there for the rebound. "He was nicer to me than the one from here," Tina says. "He used to tell me endearments, to invite me to Mexico and tell me he would show me his land. He made me happy." But Tina says her mother rejected Noel because he was Mexican. Lionor denies this: "Whether they're from there or here doesn't matter," she insists. Tina, however, says her mother thinks Mexican men are invariably violent: "Once we were at my mom's house and there was a Mexican movie showing. A woman was with some guy and her husband came home and killed the woman and the man. And Mom said, 'See? That's why I don't like Mexican men.'"

Accurate or not, Tina's perception of her mother's xenophobia echoes observations from other Kerrville-area Hispanics about relations between local Mexican Americans and Mexican nationals. Martha Toles, a Mexican American who works at the Kerr County Mental Health Center, notes that foreign-born men often are looked down on by the area's Mexican Americans. Yet native-born Hispanic young men are moving out of the Hill Country. Thus, young women who want to "stay in the culture" increasingly are gravitating to Mexican-born partners, Toles says. That can provoke conflict between girls and their friends and families.

In Tina's case, the conflict seems less about foreigners versus natives than mother versus daughter. By the time she hooked up with Noel, Tina was already doing "rebellious" things to worry Lionor, says her sister, Connie. Hanging out with Noel was just one more disturbing act. But as Lionor explains it, her antipathy towards Noel was justified: she thought her daughter's partner was abusing her. Lionor says she noticed something wrong shortly after Tina graduated from high school in May, 1993. She could have joined the navy then; she'd been accepted. But she passed on the offer and instead married Noel in September, without telling anyone in her family about the wedding. Lionor knew only that Tina was pregnant, and that she and Noel were living in a trailer in Center Point.

She was shocked when she visited and discovered the dwelling had no electricity or water. "Tina's hair was filthy!" Lionor recalls. "I had to wash it for her." Connie remembers Tina telling her during this time about what happened when she broached the idea of a separation with Noel. "She said he threatened her with a gun. He said if she left he would kill her, the child she was expecting, and whoever she was living with." (Noel Pérez's lawyer would not allow interviews with his client.) At the end of May, 1994, eight months after her secret wedding, Tina gave birth to her first child, a son she and Noel named Paublo. Daughter Kassandra followed twelve months later. Barely eighteen months afterwards, Noel, Jr. was born.

It was now January, 1997, and Tina had three children in diapers—three children born in two and a half years. Ask her today why she had so many kids so quickly, and she seems not to relate to the question. "I've always wanted children," she said recently. "Noel and I planned to have six before we stopped." But her family remembers that after Kassandra's birth, Tina seemed overwhelmed. During her next pregnancy, with Noel, Jr., she denied for six months that she was expecting, even though people started noticing and asking her about it. By then, "she was quiet most of the time," Connie Rodríguez remembers. "She looked sad and sleepy. She seemed depressed. She had too many kids and too much work." The work was not just motherhood.

A few months after the birth of her oldest, Paublo, in 1994, Tina had taken a full-time job at Kerrville's Hilltop nursing home. Her supervisor, Tom Ventro, says she was a "terrific, hard worker" who made lots of friends. At first, she poured and served juice for the home's elderly residents. Her pay was minimum wage—at the time, $4.75 an hour. Full-time, that works out to less than $10,000 a year. Ventro later promoted Tina to a more responsible position, preparing desserts and serving meals. Yet she was still making only $6.50 an hour. Such poverty wages are common for women in and around Kerrville. Newcomer retirees, vacationers, and getaway homeowners need fast food outlets like Long John Silver's and Little Caesar's, where Tina's sisters, Connie and Mary Anne, work to support Connie's five children and Mary Anne's three. They need Wal-Marts, where another sister, Eva—who has eight children—is employed. They need old age homes, and someone to empty the bedpans. Or feed the patients, as Tina did.

Huge numbers of Hill Country women work hard at these low-paying jobs while their children are with babysitters or in day care. They do this in a region that—as Tina's former teacher Jean Tally puts it—"has always been rich and poor and nothing in between." Yet in the Hill Country's carefully groomed tourist image, only the affluent have a public face. "Poverty seems invisible," notes Sister Marge Novak. Novak, a Franciscan nun and nurse practitioner, teamed up with a doctor two years ago to open a free clinic in Kerrville for under- and uninsured women. When the two went out to drum up support from local socialites, Sister Marge remembers being told there was "absolutely no need for a clinic because there are no poor people around here." They opened the facility anyway. They are still shocked at their numbers: in less than twenty-four months, they've served five thousand woman patients—about evenly distributed between Anglos and Hispanics.

So, in addition to having too many children and too much work, Tina had too little money. But the problem wasn't just her low-paid job, or the need to pay for a baby sitter for the three kids while she worked. After all, she had a husband who did construction work—which, in the Hill Country, can pay upwards of ten dollars an hour. That adds up to $20,000 a year. Put that with Tina's $10,000 to $13,000, and the family might have been scrabbling. But it shouldn't have been destitute. Yet Tina was keeping another secret: in addition to her and the three children in Kerrville, Noel had a wife and children in Mexico, and he was sending them his and Tina's money.

Tina says she knew about the bigamy and the Mexican family when she married Noel. For years, he had been making visits to his hometown, and in the early nineties he already had four small children there by the same woman. She later announced that she was expecting a fifth child by Noel. One would think this would be a last straw for Tina. Yet today, she seems strangely impassive about the whole affair. "He was honest with me," she says. "He never beat around the bush. It might have made us short of cash. But I accepted the other family and loved those children like they were my own."

Tina's parents and siblings knew nothing about this second family. Norma Medina did. A middle-aged Honduran immigrant who works in housekeeping at Hilltop, she was good friends with Tina there. "Once she told me her husband was married," Medina recalls. "Once she said they were sending money to the kids."

Medina couldn't understand why Tina would go along with this. She was working full time, and sometimes double shifts so she could earn time-and-a-half wages. Yet on pay days, she would ask Medina for small loans—five, ten, or fifteen dollars—to buy milk for her babies. Medina started wondering if her friend was a victim of spousal battering. "Tina had Noel on a pedestal; she said he was a good man." But she also told Medina he was very jealous. When he picked her up from work, he never talked to her coworkers, and he acted as though Tina shouldn't, either. "I think he didn't want her to have friends," Medina says. And there was evidence of violence. "Once, she told me she hit him with a frying pan after he started hitting her. I think she was scared of him."

Tina's family was also noticing mistreatment. Connie Rodríguez regularly heard Noel ordering Tina around in a raised voice. Lionor remembers a hot summer day when Tina showed up for a visit in long sleeves. She had no explanation for the clothing, but when Lionor tried to touch her, Tina pulled back her arm and said it was "sore." Around the same time, Connie saw Noel hit his children. Connie urged Tina to break off with Noel, and suggested that she hide with relatives in Austin, or in the Mexican border city Juárez, where the Rodríguezes have family. "I don't know," Tina replied. "What if he finds me and goes through with his threats?" She made no move to leave. Connie became especially angry after Noel approached her one night and asked her to sleep with him. She told her parents, who told Tina. She said she didn't believe them.

During the time Tina's friends and family were becoming aware of her troubles, she and Noel and their three children were living in Kerrville, in a rented mobile home in a trailer park. In the tight Hill Country housing market, such places go for $500 a month, often excluding utilities. They are crowded with nearby neighbors, and in Tina and Noel's case, the neighbors apparently were watching them. In 1997, someone called Child Protective Services and anonymously reported suspicions that daughter Kassandra, about two at the time, had been sexually abused. An inquiry ensued, but the accusation was declared unfounded. Meanwhile, Tina was expecting again. As with her other pregnancies, she did not see a doctor. So she did her own math, which set her due date for late December or early January.

Life went on: she went to work, sometimes volunteered for extra shifts, and occasionally brought the children to work after picking them up from the baby sitter. Given her hard circumstances, things seemed as normal as could be expected. Then things took a turn for the worse. Late in 1997, the family moved—to Bandera Pass, a rural slum on the outskirts of Bandera. There, they rented the shack that would later become notorious in the media.

Actually, "shack" may be too generous: According to people who live near the ten-by-fourteen-foot tin structure, it was really intended to house goats. It had one room, one bed, and no running water. It was surrounded by mud, burnt trash, old toilet paper, and the smell of urine. Its location, in a *colonia* rivaling the worst such neighborhoods on the Texas-Mexico border, was a shocking world away from even the poorest homes in Kerrville. And it was yet another secret—both a public secret in the Hill Country, and one that Tina kept from her friends and family. "She told us she and Noel had found land and a trailer they were making payments on. She told us it was white and had a fence around it," remembers Tina's mother, Lionor. "She was so excited telling me about this new piece of land," adds Tom Ventro. "She said it had a trailer."

Tina says she and Noel ended up in the shack after they heard about a very cheap piece of land and a trailer in Bandera Pass, owned by relatives of a friend of Noel's. She says that by the time they arrived, someone else had taken the property. But she and Noel opted to stay in the area while they waited for another plot and trailer to open up. While waiting, they rented the shack for $200 a month. As miserable as it was, Tina says she preferred it to being "smothered" in Kerrville by her family's criticism of her husband. She didn't tell her parents her exact address. Once, they went to see her. Lionor recalls, "We looked and looked and never could find the trailer or the white fence. We were about to go to the police when we saw Tina and Noel's station wagon. My husband went up and knocked and knocked. Noel wouldn't let Tina open the door." Lionor now thinks Noel tricked Tina into moving to the shack.

Tina now was living in virtual isolation. Her only respite was her job, and not long after the move, her coworkers noticed she was going downhill. "The last few months of her pregnancy, she was coming into work dressed really ragged," recalls supervisor Ventro. "Like her shoes didn't match what she was wearing. She said it was because they were still unpacking." Norma Medina remembers that Tina seemed tired and depressed, and her skin looked yellow, as though she were anemic or sick. And Connie Rodríguez recalls a disturbing incident when Tina and the children visited her mother's house in Kerrville. "We had bought a whole box of chicken from Church's. Tina ate a lot, and her oldest kids"—who were only two and three years old—"ate two or three pieces each, and lots of rolls, and mashed potatoes. My kids said, 'Mom, look!' It was weird. We had to go buy more food."

That was in October of 1997. A few weeks later, just after Thanksgiving, Tina went into labor, even though she hadn't expected to for at least another month. While giving birth at Kerrville's Sid Peterson Hospital, she says she heard a nurse comment that the baby was premature. He emerged weighing five pounds thirteen ounces—small for a newborn, but not dangerously so. A doctor who later reviewed the infant's medical records said he seemed to have a gestational age of thirty-seven weeks instead of the average forty. That is early, but still considered normal, and the records say nothing about prematurity. The records also indicate that at first the infant's glucose levels were a bit low. But a later test was normal, so the baby was promptly discharged with his mother. She took him to the shack, and she and Noel named him Ramiro.

Tina was on maternity leave from work, but about two weeks after the birth, she visited Hilltop to show Ramiro off. "She had a baby carrier, filled with diapers and bottles," Ventro remembers. "She looked really happy— happier than a pig in fresh mud. But she still looked really ragged. And she wasn't her usual cheery self. It took us a little while to get her going." As for Ramiro, he "just looked tiny" to Ventro. Tina's explanation was that "he was premature." A few weeks later, she brought Ramiro to work again. Norma Medina remembers that the baby looked weak and skinny. But she didn't say anything to Tina. She didn't want to offend her.

Tina never came to Hilltop again. Almost daily, though, Noel drove her to her mother's house in Kerrville so she and the kids could take baths. Lionor had twenty-eight grandchildren at the time; she was caring for seven or eight of them every day while their mothers worked, and was also shopping and running errands. She was like the Old Woman in the Shoe, overwhelmed, as usual, and she and Tina didn't get along anyway. She noticed Tina breastfeeding Ramiro or giving him bottles. But the newborn was just one more child among many in the house. Lionor seldom took a good look at him.

Just before New Year's, Noel, Jr., who was by then eleven months old, came down with pneumonia. Tina took him to the hospital, and records show that besides treating him for his illness, medical workers also instructed his mother to stop feeding him watered-down milk. That was a practice the women in Tina's family had handed down for generations: making "formula" by mixing canned, evaporated milk with water and a little Karo syrup. The custom used to be universal and respectable in the United States: recipes appeared in baby-care books at the turn of the century, and were still showing up as late as 1994 in best-selling texts. Today, the mixture is considered risky, since cow's milk has been found to be hard for small babies to digest. More affluent, educated, literate parents have known this for a generation. Others haven't gotten the message. When they are short of funds for commercial baby formula, they frequently resort to cheaper cow's milk and the old recipe. And when they are really hard up for milk money, poor mothers are tempted to compensate by adding more water than usual.

Tina was definitely hard up. Often, when she visited her family in Kerrville, sister Connie would give her formula for Ramiro that Connie had bought for her own baby. Tina also sometimes breast-fed Ramiro—an unusual practice among working-class and poor women. Dedicated breast-feeding demands that a mother be with her baby almost constantly, which is impossible for women who have to work. Even to breast-feed part time, working women need several long breaks during the day to pump and save their milk. That perk is not available to most blue-collar and service workers. Today, breast-feeding in the United States is mostly confined to affluent women. Tina was exceptional: she says she tried it with all her children. She wanted to bond with them, and thought "breast milk is the best thing for babies." Yet there were no models among her friends or family to guide her. Her mother had bottle-fed all her children. So had her sisters. Tina got some instruction from the hospital after one of her children was born. After that, she was on her own.

Apparently, Tina did not understand that for a lactating woman to produce enough milk, breast-feeding needed to be done regularly, if not exclusively. Instead, she seems to have randomly fed Ramiro commercial formula, cow's milk, and breast milk, with no fixed schedule for these different foods. It's thus impossible to know whether Ramiro was getting enough nutrition, or—when his mother nursed him—if he got any nutrition at all. It was also impossible for a medical specialist to evaluate Ramiro's health. Tina never took him in for checkups.

Everything crashed on Wednesday, February 11, 1998. That evening, Bandera's Emergency Medical Services and Sheriff's Department got a call from Bandera Pass. An infant there was reported in serious distress after his mother discovered he was not breathing. When the ambulance and sheriffs arrived, they found Ramiro dead. According to affidavits produced later by emergency medical technicians Cindy Martin and Lynda Cook, Tina was at the scene, crying and distraught. When she remembered that Ramiro had not been baptized, she got so beside herself that Cook tried to calm her by faking the rite. Tina's grief over her son's death seemed wrenching and genuine.

Next day, however, Ramiro's body was sent to Austin for an autopsy. There, Travis County Coroner Roberto Bayardo took the gruesome photograph of the baby's wizened corpse. He cut it open, drained an eyeball, and sent the fluid for testing to measure biochemicals such as glucose, whose levels are used to diagnose many diseases. Even before the tests came back, Bayardo pronounced the cause of Ramiro's death as starvation. Bandera-area child protective services investigators entered the case. They noted disturbing details, such as that baby bottles found in the shack the night Ramiro died contained sour milk. By the end of February, Tina and Noel had been arrested.

⇾⇽   ⇾⇽   ⇾⇽

From that point, the story might have taken the usual turn. As horrific as it is to find a dead, emaciated infant in its parents' care, law enforcement authorities traditionally have blamed such tragedies on ignorance or carelessness. According to University of Texas–El Paso sociologist Martha Smithey, an expert on infant homicide, women such as Tina used to be put on probation or referred to parenting or nutrition classes. Since the late eighties, however, a national move to protect children has led to dramatically increased punishments for abusive and neglectful mothers. Even so, punishment for the accused in starvation cases has been relatively lenient. In Washington, DC in 1993, in the Chicago area in 1997, and in Kansas City in 1998, mothers of babies who died after wasting to skin and bones were charged with involuntary or other types of manslaughter. Such charges usually carry penalties ranging from probation to a handful of years in prison.

But Bruce Curry, district attorney for the Hill Country judicial region that includes Bandera County, yanked out all the stops as he charged Tina and Noel under a draconian Texas Penal Code statute. Enacted in the early nineties, it upgraded to a capital crime the first-degree murder of a child under the age of six. When the statute was being debated in the legislature, proponents painted culprits as homicidal male sex offenders and divorcing dads who kill their ex-wives and children. In fact, simply because children's caretakers are much more often female than male, most killers of small children are mothers and other women.

The capital charges leveled against Tina implied that she had cold-bloodedly planned her baby's death. Or if she hadn't planned it, she had at least known that what she did to Ramiro would cause him to die. Noel Pérez was charged under the same statute. Tina's family and coworkers didn't know what to make of Noel. But they were shocked that Tina was labeled a murderer. Her mother and sisters were angry with her for not noticing that something was wrong with Ramiro and taking him to a doctor. Yet they did not think she deliberately killed her son. They wondered whether he had succumbed to some undiagnosed illness. Or perhaps Tina herself had been sick in a way that interfered with her milk supply. Or maybe she had been so worn out by the demands of four very small children in a claustrophobic, rural shack with no running water or telephone—and so demoralized by an abusive husband—that, as Lionor Rodríguez puts it now, "Something went off and she wasn't there, like she was in outer space."

Because he was indigent, Noel was assigned two court-appointed attorneys. Tina's family wanted better for her than charity. They scraped together their savings and came up with $10,000—a huge sum for them, but laughable compared to the hundreds of thousands of dollars private lawyers typically charge to represent a capital murder defendant. The Rodríguezes took their money to Bruce Perkins, a Corpus Christi lawyer the family had used once before when one of Tina's brothers-in-law was in legal trouble. Perkins recruited Michael Collins, of San Antonio, as cocounsel. The family got what it paid for.

By early 1999, Tina's case had been downgraded: the district attorney had decided a jury might balk at the idea of executing her, and besides, Bandera County couldn't afford the money it would take to prosecute a death penalty case. But the state was still asking for a capital murder conviction, which would carry a heavier penalty than first-degree murder. Despite the gravity of the charge, the trial, which took place in February, was a bargain-basement fiasco. Perkins and Collins failed to present any testimony about their client's confusion over how to feed babies. They offered virtually no evidence of possible abuse by her husband. They made only the most cursory attempt to suggest that Ramiro might have had a disease that caused him to waste away.

Perhaps worst of all, the lawyers never interviewed Tina's coworkers to hear their recollections of her joy over Ramiro's birth. Nor did they talk to the emergency medical technicians, who could have testified about a mother's grief the night of her baby's death. Absent these witnesses, Tina came across as a person with no friends or coworkers, and no feelings for her child. The jurors—all middle-class Anglo men—saw only a few poorly dressed, intimidated family members: the kind of people for whom it's easy to confuse nervousness with sullenness. Tina seemed the same. When she answered questions, she came across as reserved, even sour. She showed strong feeling only twice on the stand. When she described the day she went into labor with Ramiro, she became downright animated, reciting attending nurses' names, using long, almost breathlessly involved sentences, and employing medical terms such as "consistent with" and "dilation." Her excitement during this testimony was eerie and sad: it seems that ever since she miscarried her twins, at the age of fifteen, Tina's role as bearer of children has been the sole basis of her identity. The jurors knew nothing about the twins, or anything of Tina's life. All they saw was the state of Texas insisting that this compulsive bearer of children, this veritable baby-making machine, would cruelly shut down as soon as its biological labor was done.

On the second occasion, Tina's dullness disappeared when she was asked to look at her son's autopsy picture. She began wailing so inconsolably that the judge had to call a recess. But jurors later said they wondered why she had been calm earlier in the trial, when her lawyers first showed her the picture. Even so, the panel wanted to give Tina a break. "Maybe she emoted on the stand because her lawyers told her to," juror Greg Deiley speculated during an interview months after the trial. Another juror, Donald Downer, said he and the others were looking for something—anything—to consider in Tina's favor. The jurors had been suspicious that Noel had done something terrible to Tina that affected her ability to care for her children. They speculated that Noel was pushing his wife around when they heard about the family moving from their decent mobile home in Kerrville to the Bandera Pass shack. "I really believe that, at the least, she was a controlled spouse," Downer says. He and the rest of the panel wanted to hear about possible health problems in Ramiro. "Her lawyers," Downer says, "could have brought somebody in to refute the prosecution's starvation theory. All it would have taken is one expert opinion. The defense attorneys were obviously not doing their jobs. But as a jury we were required to weigh only the evidence presented. And based on what we were given, there was really no option. We did what we had to do."

The trial lasted three days. In as many hours, the jury convicted Tina. Next day she was sentenced to prison, ostensibly for the rest of her life. Four months later, the district attorney offered Noel Pérez a bargain allowing him to plead to a more lenient charge than capital murder. Having accepted the deal, for a maximum of twenty-five years in prison but only half that much for good behavior, he is now doing far less time than his wife is.

Following the guilty verdict, Tina was assigned a court-appointed attorney for her appeal and habeas corpus (a presentation of new evidence to overturn the verdict and hold a new trial). Her new counsel is Adrienne Urrutia, a young criminal defense lawyer in San Antonio. Urrutia started making calls and dropping in on people. Immediately she discovered the emergency medical technicians from the night of Ramiro's death. She also found Dr. Steven Clarke, a University of Texas-Austin professor of nutrition. He examined Ramiro Pérez's medical and autopsy records and discovered several suspicious findings in the latter, including drastically low blood glucose levels. Low glucose, Clarke says, signals a rare metabolic disorder, pyruvic hydrogenase deficiency. Babies born with the illness lack an enzyme that helps convert food into the sugar—glucose—needed for growth and for life. The disease can cause newborns to lose weight, then suddenly go into a coma and die. Coroner Bayardo should have ordered tests to check for the disorder, says Clarke.

Urrutia also plans to present experts to testify about Tina's confusion over how and what to feed her child. Urrutia may put on testimony about how easy it is to watch a child lose weight without seeing a problem. And she may call specialists in battered-wife syndrome. They likely would testify that terror and low self-esteem often cause victims to deny abuse—even for years after being separated from their abusers. All this may happen if Tina Rodríguez gets a new trial. But it make take years to get a higher court decision. And there is no assurance that it will be in her favor. She could spend decades, if not the rest of her life, behind bars.

In March 2002, Urrutia argued a motion for a new trial before Judge Stephen Ables, who had presided over Tina's original proceeding in 1999. Ables denied the motion and Urrutia has since asked a Texas court of appeals to order a new trial anyway. The appeals court could have simply upheld Ables' decision; instead, it has ordered both Urrutia and the prosecution to restate their arguments in new briefs. As of this writing, the court still has not ruled on whether Tina Rodríguez's conviction will stand or whether she is entitled to a new trial. Her husand, Noel Pérez, remains in prison. The couple's three children, who were put into foster care immediately after their baby brother's death, were all adopted in 2001.

❅   ❅   ❅

Sociologist Martha Smithey has studied mothers from throughout Texas who were charged with killing their babies. She found that they have several characteristics in common. Virtually all are poor. Most have suffered sexual abuse. Typically, they were in abusive or conflict-ridden relationships with male partners when their children died. All seemed overwhelmed by the dilemma of mothering without adequate emotional or material resources. Yet they did not seek help. Their reticence does not come as a surprise. In our culture, Smithey says, femininity is still equated with the ideal of perfect motherhood, and not mothering perfectly means not being a good woman. The fiction is even more entrenched among Latinas.

Smithey fears that growing law-and-order responses to "bad" mothers will rigidify the "perfect mother" myth and make it even harder for women like Tina to seek the help they and their children need. Social services and social movements that realistically confront poverty, partner abuse, emotional trauma, and shame, Smithey says, are the real solution. Replacing these with harsh punishment simply pushes troubled mothers deeper into a closet of destructive behavior. And in Texas—where the number of child homicides is increasing—they are now being pushed towards Death Row.

"I do have to be thankful to the Lord that they decided not to execute me," Tina said in a jailhouse interview a few months after her trial. She had just been moved from prison, near Dallas, back to the Bandera County Jail so she could attend a hearing to terminate her parental rights to her surviving three children. During a two-hour conversation, she sat stonily, hardly moving, and continued her bleak defenses of her husband ("He's a jealous guy. It might have seemed to others that he was controlling, but no. We had our own relationship.") Her tone grew vaguely flat when speaking of her parents and sisters. She stiffened when asked about her childhood, her job, her youthful ambitions, and old hurts. It seemed she answered more from obligation than interest.

Then it came time to talk about her latest miscarriages. Shortly after her arrest for Ramiro's death, Tina discovered she was pregnant again. She talked about a sonogram that revealed twins. She talked about how her due date was supposed to be mid-fall. She was in jail, and jail was the first place she had ever received a medical diagnosis of pregnancy. Her lawyers asked the court to please release her until trial so she could get regular prenatal care. The court did not respond. She talked about the June day at the Bandera County Jail when she bent over while taking a shower and couldn't straighten up. She talked about sharp pains, about bloating, about being shackled, about being taken to the hospital in a squad car, about tests and doctors and nurses and amniotic fluid and dilation, and amid this torrent of pregnancy-and-labor talk, Tina stood up from her jailhouse chair, waved her hands, and raised her voice in excitement. For a moment she was alive again. She was a woman. A human being. A maker of babies.

The fetuses—two males—were so premature that they died minutes after birth. Afterwards, she named them Roman and Fabian. As things stand today, they are the last children Tina Rodríguez will ever bear.

Today Roman, Fabian, and Ramiro lie side by side in Guadalupe Cemetery, a small Hispanic burial ground in a wooded area near Kerrville's old Barrio. The twins' shared plot is a tiny, egg-shaped mound of dirt, bordered by white pebbles and decorated inside with stones arranged like a crucifix. Ramiro's grave is a little bigger. Someone has laid plastic flowers on it, and a cheap ceramic angel. There is also a potty seat: the little bedpan part that catches a toddler's pee and is pulled out to be dumped into a real, flush toilet. The potty seat is plastic and nursery yellow. It looks as light and buoyant as air. Perhaps to keep it from floating away in a good wind or rain, someone has filled it with dirt. The dirt makes it heavy and solid, as though it will stay by Ramiro Pérez's grave forever. But there is nothing growing in the potty seat. It doesn't look like anything ever will.

This essay was originally published in *San Antonio Current* (July 8–14, 1999).

Masked Racism: Reflections on the Prison Industrial Complex

ANGELA Y. DAVIS

Imprisonment has become the response of first resort to far too many of the social problems that burden people who are ensconced in poverty. These problems often are veiled by being conveniently grouped together under the category "crime" and by the automatic attribution of criminal behavior to people of color. Homelessness, unemployment, drug addiction, mental illness, and illiteracy are only a few of the problems that disappear from public view when the human beings contending with them are relegated to cages.

Prisons thus perform a feat of magic. Or rather the people who continually vote in new prison bonds and tacitly assent to a proliferating network of prisons and jails have been tricked into believing in the magic of imprisonment. But prisons do not disappear problems, they disappear human beings. And the practice of disappearing vast numbers of people from poor, immigrant, and racially marginalized communities has literally become big business.

The seeming effortlessness of magic always conceals an enormous amount of behind-the-scenes work. When prisons disappear human beings in order to convey the illusion of solving social problems, penal infrastructures must be created to accommodate a rapidly swelling population of caged people. Goods and services must be provided to keep imprisoned populations alive. Sometimes these populations must be kept busy and at other times—particularly in repressive supermaximum prisons and in INS detention centers—they must be deprived of virtually all meaningful activity. Vast numbers of handcuffed and shackled people are moved across state borders as they are transferred from one state or federal prison to another.

All this work, which used to be the primary province of government, is now also performed by private corporations, whose links to government in the field of what is euphemistically called "corrections" resonate dangerously with the military industrial complex. The dividends that accrue from investment in the punishment industry, like those that accrue from investment in weapons production, only amount to social destruction. Taking into account the structural similarities and profitability of business-government linkages in the realms of military production and public punishment, the expanding penal system can now be characterized as a "prison industrial complex."

The Color of Imprisonment

Almost two million people are currently locked up in the immense network of U.S. prisons and jails. More than 70 percent of the imprisoned population are people of color. It is rarely acknowledged that the fastest-growing group of prisoners are black women and that Native American prisoners are the largest group per capita. Approximately five million people—including those on probation and parole—are directly under the surveillance of the criminal justice system.

Three decades ago, the imprisoned population was approximately one-eighth its current size. While women still constitute a relatively small percentage of people behind bars, today the number of incarcerated women in California alone is almost twice what the nationwide women's prison population was in 1970. According to Elliott Currie, "The prison has become a looming presence in our society to an extent unparalleled in our history—or that of any other industrial democracy. Short of major wars, mass incarceration has been the most thoroughly implemented government social program of our time."[1]

To deliver up bodies destined for profitable punishment, the political economy of prisons relies on racialized assumptions of criminality—such as images of black welfare mothers reproducing criminal children—and on racist practices in arrest, conviction, and sentencing patterns. Colored bodies constitute the main human raw material in this vast experiment to disappear the major social problems of our time. Once the aura of magic is stripped away from the imprisonment solution, what is revealed is racism, class bias, and the parasitic seduction of capitalist profit. The prison industrial system materially and morally impoverishes its inhabitants and devours the social wealth needed to address the very problems that have led to spiraling numbers of prisoners.

As prisons take up more and more space on the social landscape, other government programs that have previously sought to respond to social needs—such as Temporary Assistance to Needy Families—are being squeezed out of existence. The deterioration of public education, including prioritizing discipline and security over learning in public schools located in poor communities, is directly related to the prison "solution."

Profiting from Prisoners

As prisons proliferate in U.S. society, private capital has become enmeshed in the punishment industry. And precisely because of their profit potential, prisons are becoming increasingly important to the U.S. economy. If the notion of punishment as a source of potentially stupendous profits is disturbing by itself, then the strategic dependence on racist structures and ideologies to render mass punishment palatable and profitable is even more troubling.

Prison privatization is the most obvious instance of capital's current movement towards the prison industry. While government-run prisons are often in gross violation of international human rights standards, private prisons are even less accountable. In March 1998, the Corrections Corporation of America (CCA), the largest U.S. private prison company, claimed 54,944 beds in sixty-eight facilities under contract or development in the U.S., Puerto Rico, the United Kingdom, and Australia. Following the global trend of subjecting more women to public punishment, CCA recently opened a women's prison outside Melbourne. The company recently identified California as its "new frontier."

Wackenhut Corrections Corporation (WCC), the second-largest U.S. prison company, claimed contracts and awards to manage forty-six facilities in North America, the U.K., and Australia. It boasts a total of 30,424 beds as well as contracts for prisoner health care services, transportation, and security.

Currently, the stocks of both CCA and WCC are doing extremely well. Between 1996 and 1997, CCA's revenues increased by 58 percent, from $293 million to $462 million. Its net profit grew from $30.9 million to $53.9 million. WCC raised its revenues from $138 million in 1996 to $210 million in 1997. Unlike those of public correctional facilities, the vast profits of these private facilities rely on the employment of nonunion labor.

The Prison Industrial Complex

But private prison companies are only the most visible component of the increasing corporatization of punishment. Government contracts to build prisons have bolstered the construction industry. The architectural community has identified prison design as a major new niche. Technology developed for the military by companies like Westinghouse is being marketed for use in law enforcement and punishment.

Moreover, corporations that appear to be far removed from the business of punishment are intimately involved in the expansion of the prison industrial complex. Prison construction bonds are one of the many sources of profitable investment for leading financiers such as Merrill Lynch. MCI charges prisoners and their families outrageous prices for the precious telephone calls that are often the only contact prisoners have with the free world.

Many corporations whose products we consume on a daily basis have learned that prison labor power can be as profitable as Third World labor power exploited by U.S.-based global corporations. Both relegate formerly unionized workers to joblessness and many even wind up in prison. Some of the companies that use prison labor are IBM, Motorola, Compaq, Texas Instruments, Honeywell, Microsoft, and Boeing. But it is not only the high-tech industries that reap the profits of prison labor. Nordstrom department stores sell jeans that are marketed as "Prison Blues," as well as T-shirts and jackets made in Oregon prisons. The advertising slogan for these clothes is "made on the inside to be worn on the outside." Maryland prisoners inspect glass bottles and jars used by Revlon and Pierre Cardin, and schools throughout the world buy graduation caps and gowns made by South Carolina prisoners.

"For private business," write Eve Goldberg and Linda Evans (a political prisoner inside the Federal Correctional Institution at Dublin, California) "prison labor is like a pot of gold. No strikes. No union organizing. No unemployment insurance or workers compensation to pay. No language problem, as in a foreign country. New leviathan prisons are being built with thousands of eerie acres of factories inside the walls. Prisoners do data entry for Chevron, make telephone reservations for TWA, raise hogs, shovel manure, make circuit boards, limousines, waterbeds, and lingerie for Victoria's Secret all at a fraction of the cost of 'free labor.'"[2]

Devouring the Social Wealth

Although prison labor—which ultimately is compensated at a rate far below the minimum wage—is hugely profitable for the private companies that use it, the penal system as a whole does not produce wealth. It devours the social wealth that could be used to subsidize housing for the homeless, to ameliorate public education for poor and racially marginalized communities, to open free drug rehabilitation programs for people who wish to kick their habits, to create a national health care system, to expand programs to combat HIV, to eradicate domestic abuse—and, in the process, to create well-paying jobs for the unemployed.

Since 1984 more than twenty new prisons have opened in California, while only one new campus was added to the California State University system and none to the University of California system. In 1996–97, higher education received only 8.7 percent of the state's General Fund, while corrections received 9.6 percent. Now that affirmative action has been declared illegal in California, it is obvious that education is increasingly reserved for certain people, while prisons are reserved for others. Five times as many black men are presently in prison as in four-year colleges and universities. This new segregation has dangerous implications for the entire country.

By segregating people labeled as criminals, prison simultaneously fortifies and conceals the structural racism of the U.S. economy. Claims of low unemployment rates—even in black communities—make sense only if one assumes that the vast numbers of people in prison have really disappeared and thus have no legitimate claims to jobs. The numbers of black and Latino men currently incarcerated amount to two percent of the male labor force. According to criminologist David Downes, "Treating incarceration as a type of hidden unemployment may raise the jobless rate for men by about one-third, to 8 percent. The effect on the black labor force is greater still, raising the [black] male unemployment rate from 11 percent to 19 percent."

Hidden Agenda

Mass incarceration is not a solution to unemployment, nor is it a solution to the vast array of social problems that are hidden away in a rapidly growing network of prisons and jails. However, the great majority of people have been tricked into believing in the efficacy of imprisonment, even though the historical record clearly demonstrates that prisons do not work. Racism has undermined our ability to create a popular critical discourse to contest the ideological trickery that posits imprisonment as key to public safety. The focus of state policy is rapidly shifting from social welfare to social control.

Black, Latino, Native American, and many Asian youth are portrayed as the purveyors of violence, traffickers of drugs, and as envious of commodities that they have no right to possess. Young black and Latina women are represented as sexually promiscuous and as indiscriminately propagating babies and poverty. Criminality and deviance are racialized. Surveillance is thus focused on communities of color, immigrants, the unemployed, the undereducated, the homeless, and in general on those who have a diminishing claim to social resources. Their claim to social resources continues to diminish in large part because law enforcement and penal measures increasingly devour these resources. The prison industrial complex has thus created a vicious cycle of punishment, which only further impoverishes those whose impoverishment is supposedly "solved" by imprisonment.

Therefore, as the emphasis of government policy shifts from social welfare to crime control, racism sinks more deeply into the economic and ideological structures of U.S. society. Meanwhile, conservative crusaders against affirmative action and bilingual education proclaim the end of racism, while their opponents suggest that racism's remnants can be dispelled through dialogue and conversation. But conversations about "race relations" will hardly dismantle a prison industrial complex that thrives on and nourishes the racism hidden within the deep structures of our society.

The emergence of a U.S. prison industrial complex within a context of cascading conservatism marks a new historical moment, whose dangers are unprecedented. But so are its opportunities. Considering the impressive number of grassroots projects that continue to resist the expansion of the punishment industry, it ought to be possible to bring these efforts together to create radical and nationally visible movements that can legitimize anticapitalist critiques of the prison industrial complex. It ought to be possible to build movements in defense of prisoners' human rights and movements that persuasively argue that what we need is not new prisons, but new health care, housing, education, drug programs, jobs, and education. To safeguard a democratic future, it is possible and necessary to weave together the many and increasing strands of resistance to the prison industrial complex into a powerful movement for social transformation.

This essay first appeared in *ColorLines* (Fall 1998).

NOTES

[1] Elliott Currie, *Crime and Punishment in America*. New York: Henry Holt & Co., 1998.

[2] Eve Goldberg and Linda Evans, *The Prison Industrial Complex and the Global Economy*. Berkeley: Prison Activist Resource Center, 1999.

Racism in U.S. Welfare Policy:
A Human Rights Issue

LINDA BURNHAM

*The Personal Responsibility and Work Opportunity Reconciliation Act,
commonly known as "welfare reform," was passed by the United States Congress
in the summer of 1996 and signed into law by then-President Clinton on
August 22nd. The legislation carried out the promise to "end welfare as we know
it," ending the entitlement of poor families to government assistance. Temporary
Assistance to Needy Families (TANF), the welfare program established as a result
of the legislation, includes many provisions that create hardships for current and
former welfare recipients, the majority of whom are women of color. Among
other things, welfare reform:*

- *coerces women into the labor force through Workfare and Work First programs*
- *gives substantial authority to the states to*
- *determine eligibility rules and benefit levels*
- *sets a two-year limit for receiving welfare benefits*
- *imposes a five-year lifetime limit for receiving welfare*
- *bars legal immigrants from receiving welfare for five years after arriving
  in the country*

The complex entanglement of race and socioeconomic stratification in the
United States ensures that certain areas of domestic policy are suffused and
tainted with racial bias, bear the imprint of a more frankly racist past, are particularly prone to political manipulation on behalf of the preservation of racial
privilege, and serve as touchstones for galvanizing key elements of a racist
consensus. U.S. social welfare policy is one such area.

The United Nations World Conference Against Racism is a fitting occasion
to examine the racist foundations and effects of welfare policy. The 1996
passage of the Personal Responsibility and Work Opportunity Reconciliation
Act (PRWORA),[1] commonly know as "welfare reform," underscored how
deeply embedded are racial bias and xenophobia in U.S. domestic policy. But,
of course, it is not racism alone that characterizes welfare reform. Researchers
and advocates have carefully explored the profound gender bias of the welfare
system.[2] The majority of women on welfare are poor women of color who face
the "triple jeopardy" of belonging to a disempowered class, marginalized racial
and ethnic groups, and a subordinated gender. Their experiences as welfare
recipients and as women who are being pushed off welfare into low-wage work

are framed by the integral nature of their identities and, consequently, the "simultaneity of their oppression." Welfare reform does not affect all women or all racial groups equally; women of marginalized racial groups are disproportionately represented among those receiving welfare. These women—and their families and communities—bear a disproportionate share of the burden of welfare reform's negative effects simply by virtue of their overrepresentation on the rolls. And, among women receiving welfare, some will bear the brunt of the racially discriminatory implementation of regulations and sanctions, while others will not.

Thus, welfare reform is a classic case study in the operation of what feminists of color have long identified as the "intersection of the structures of racial subordination, capitalist exploitation, and the hierarchical relations between the sexes"—structures that are "mutually reinforcing and interdependent."[3] Concepts of multiple structures or axes of oppression and compounded forms of discrimination, developed by activists and scholars over the course of thirty years, have more recently been brought into the framework of human rights discourse under the rubric of "intersectionality."[4] To more fully understand the particular vulnerabilities of women of color and communities of color to the negative effects of welfare reform requires an exploration of the structures and operations of racism within welfare policy.

Regulating Race

The strength of U.S. racism resides in the capacity of the state to sustain and justify, in different historical periods, the economic, social, political, and cultural privilege of the white majority, while simultaneously burnishing its image as the world's most advanced democracy. The moments when the legitimacy of the racial status quo has been most seriously threatened—during the antislavery and civil rights movements, for example—have been those moments when the contradictory character of these two impulses has been most successfully revealed. Central to the reproduction of relations of racial subordination are the economic and political mechanisms that recreate racially coded economic disadvantage. Welfare policy is one of those mechanisms. White advantage in access to land, capital, natural resources, the enslaved or profoundly exploited labor of others, and, for the white working class, favorable positioning in the labor market, has been a matter of state policy since the state's inception. And, though there is no denying the substantive democratic advances achieved by and for people of color, the preservation of white economic advantage remains a matter of state policy today.

The consequence of such policies is the concentration of the negative impacts inherent in capitalist production and accumulation within communities of color.

Today's remarkable racial differentials in income, wealth, educational attainment, and health status—multifactoral and multidimensional though they may be—are grounded fundamentally in the state-sanctioned subordination of people of color. Contemporary welfare policy reaffirms and strengthens the dynamic polarization of racial privilege and disadvantage.

Of course racial privilege is not fully compatible with the notion of a race-neutral state or multiracial democracy. But, in the long run of history, this is a relatively recent problem. For most of the nation's past, the savagery, immorality, inferiority, and ineducability of the darker races was a given. It is only in the past few generations that genetic inferiority has been delegitimized as the mainstream framework for understanding and explaining racial differences in socioeconomic status. The marginalization of this framework has left behind the conceptual conundrum of how to explain racial inequities without direct reference to either structured racial privilege or inherent racial superiority. It has also left behind the political puzzle of how to further the cause of racial subordination while clutching close the cloth of race neutrality.

Welfare policy is critical in this regard. It bears obvious and disturbing traces of primitive, atavistic racism, which is more powerful because it is unacknowledged and unspoken, and that is, consequently, most difficult to target and dislodge. The official stance of those who promulgated welfare reform is that the legislation is neither motivated by racial considerations nor discriminatory in substance. But welfare policy has long been a prime site for the reproduction, adjustment, and transformation of both racist social relations and ideologies of race. It is a crucial site for contesting the structures and dynamics of racism, as well.

Preparing the Ground

The decline in support for welfare coincides with a darkening of the welfare rolls. As the historically higher proportion of white recipients fell and the proportion of African Americans and Latinas rose, the program became increasingly vulnerable to cutbacks; to being used as a political cudgel by antitax, anti-big government conservatives; and to being wielded on behalf of white "backlash" and racial polarization.[5] Generations of right-wing ideologues evoked the image of the lazy, sexually irresponsible, African American welfare cheat, until that classic, iconic image contained within it sufficient emotive force to shift public policy. The explicit racial content of the conversation has shifted, from the "unmarried Negro women who make a business of producing children…for the purpose of securing this easy welfare money,"[6] to the "welfare queen" of the Reagan era, whose race was unspecified but universally understood. This "queen," playing a class-specific gender role, served as a "signifier of racial difference,"[7] reinforcing crucial social distinctions.

The highly charged debates among social analysts and politicians during the 1980s about the character and social impact of the "underclass" prepared the way for welfare reform. The term "underclass" masquerades as a locator of class position but, from the beginning, concerns about the "underclass" were concerns about "ghetto poverty" or "inner-city poverty"—that is, black poverty. "Underclass" discourse continued a long-standing U.S. tradition of using class to talk about race, using race to talk about class, and thoroughly confusing the two.

It also prefigured welfare discourse in three important ways. First, poverty was conflated with racial identity, which in turn was conflated with deviance and distance from the social values and sexual norms that purportedly govern mainstream America. "Underclass" served as a summarizing term for black deviance encompassing, at the least, criminality, promiscuity, irresponsibility, sloth, and dependence.

Second, the "underclass" debate was highly gendered; men and women played distinct roles, each contributive in its own way to regenerating poverty conditions. The men of concern to "underclass" analysts were generally young with low levels of educational attainment, weak commitment to the labor force, neglectful approaches to the responsibilities of fatherhood, and propensities towards criminal behavior. The women of "underclass" theory were also young and poorly educated. But their most salient characteristics were their low marriage rates, high out-of-wedlock birth rates, and high levels of dependence on welfare. "Underclass" discourse tended to reduce women to their biological capacities because perceived behavioral deviance, i.e., early childbearing and nonmarriage, were targeted as the main causative factors in persistent poverty.

This directly relates to the third way in which "underclass" theory anticipated the conceptual framework for welfare reform: poverty is regarded as a result of individual choices, behaviors, and failings—"personal responsibility"—not as a structural social dynamic.

A more recent trend in the scapegoating of women of color for social ills is the resurgence of anti-immigrant rhetoric featuring fears of inundation by the brown hoards intent on crossing the southern border and the overloading of U.S. social services by hyperfertile Latinas.

The public conversation immediately preceding passage of PRWORA was fundamentally anchored in and dependent upon the long, ignoble history of the racialization of poverty and poverty policy. It was a conversation whose deep historical roots created the basis for subtle forms of ideological dissembling, making possible the simultaneous evocation and denial of racist content, and rendering a profoundly regressive policy palatable to a distressingly broad swath of the political spectrum. But, whether frankly evoked or not, PRWORA is steeped in racist intent, is racially biased in its implementation, and, not surprisingly, has had a racially differentiated impact.

Intent

Neubeck and Cazenave argue persuasively that the "racial state" is far from neutral on the issue of the nation's demographic profile, and that a critical function of welfare policy is to deploy a range of disincentives meant to discourage poor black and brown women from having children. With the twin goals of limiting the birth rate of U.S.-born women of color and limiting entry to the U.S.—and the potential reproduction—of poor people from Mexico, Central America, the Caribbean, and Asia, welfare reform instituted such policies as the "family cap," the denial of benefits to teen mothers, the denial of benefits to legal immigrants, and the "illegitimacy bonus." The PRWORA was framed by the desire to insitute procreation-focused race population control and immigration-focused race population control . . . [addressing] the sentiment of many white political elites and other European Americans that the federal racial state must respond decisively to reproductive and immigration threats to the United States' white racial demographic status quo.[8]

The intense interest in, and interference with, the childbearing patterns of women of color is rooted in the fact that they reproduce not only individuals and families, but also subordinated ethnic and racial groups that are viewed as highly problematic components of the social whole. Women of color on welfare are targeted for particular forms of social control as a consequence of their role as "biological reproducers of ethnic collectivity"[9]—collectivities that are disproportionately impoverished.

The "family cap," a state option that disallows the provision of additional grant money to women who have children while on welfare, is an element of welfare policy that rests squarely on the mythology that women have additional children in order to collect additional state monies, and that the fertility of poor women of color is rapidly outpacing that of the white middle class. Though these fears may be grounded in race, class, and gender bias, they are not grounded in fact. The additional grant money provided for additional children under Aid to Families with Dependent Children (AFDC), predecessor of the current program, was so paltry as to serve, in strictly economic terms, as a disincentive to childbearing. Though the uninformed may have believed that substantial additional income was provided for each additional child, in actuality, under AFDC the average additional grant amount per child was a miserly $79 per month. And, belying fears of unrestrained fertility on the part of women receiving welfare, the majority of such families consist of a mother and one or two children (43 percent of families on welfare have only one child as compared with 41 percent of families not on welfare), and the birth rate of women receiving aid is actually lower than that of other women.[10] Nonetheless, anxieties that whites are being "outbred" are barely beneath the surface of the "family cap" provision.

Similarly, the "illegitimacy bonus," which rewards states monetarily for reducing the rate of births outside of marriage, and the denial of assistance to single teen mothers who are not under parental control, are attempts to modify poor women's sexual behavior and limit their fertility. These provisions reflect well-worn but still powerful notions about the deficient morality, hypersexuality, and heightened fecundity of women of color. They also revive the retrograde social stigma attached to "illegitimacy" by denying social support to children born to mothers who have chosen not to marry or who have been abandoned.

The idea that women of color on welfare are responsible for shifting the racial balance in the U.S. is unfounded, but it is undeniable that the population is undergoing a substantial, probably irreversible demographic shift—more apparent in some regions of the country than in others. The immigration legislation passed in 1965 removed racially biased quotas. This, in combination with complex global economic change, spurred migration to the U.S. from Asia, the Caribbean, Latin America, and, to a lesser extent, Africa. The consequent racially inflected xenophobia has impacted on many areas of public policy, at both the state and federal levels.

Several major immigrant-related themes became a significant part of the public conversation leading up to passage of PRWORA. These racially motivated claims asserted that "illegal aliens" were consuming an enormous share of public resources while contributing little or nothing to the U.S. economy; that immigrant women were bearing children in order to qualify for welfare; and that liberal welfare policies served as a migration incentive to poor people of color from all over the world. In these scenarios, the reproductive capacity of immigrant women is central insofar as they and their children are perceived to overburden the education, health, and public welfare systems.

Though "illegal aliens," i.e., immigrants without legal documentation to reside or work in the U.S., have never been eligible for welfare benefits, misinformation and confusion over their eligibility status served to stoke the racialized xenophobia that facilitated the passage of the anti-immigrant provisions in welfare reform legislation. Fujiwara has observed that PRWORA "codifies the popular racial politics that scapegoats immigrants and demands their exclusion and disenfranchisement from our increasingly multicultural society."[11]

The provisions of PRWORA that exclude documented immigrants who are not citizens from receiving welfare, Social Security Insurance, or food stamps for five years after their entry into the U.S. are clearly motivated by the desire to stem the tide of new immigrants. They will most likely have their greatest impact on women and children of color.

Implementation

The intentions behind welfare "reform" were not race neutral. Neither is its implementation. Although this is a grievously understudied area, there is increasing evidence to show that racial bias plays a significant role in how PRWORA is administered at the state and county levels.

One form of racial bias in implementation is the disproportionate application of punitive measures to people of color. The "family cap" discussed above punishes women for having more children while on welfare. But the "family cap" is a state option and one study has shown that (1) the states most likely to deny increases in grant size with increased family size are the states with high proportions of African Americans on the rolls, and (2) "restrictive TANF policies are most likely to be adopted in states where *both* Hispanics and African Americans receive aid in large numbers."[12]

There is troubling evidence as well of racial differentials in the imposition of sanctions for perceived violations of welfare rules and requirements. One study found that Native Americans and African Americans were the most likely of all racial and ethnic groups to be sanctioned. Of welfare recipients who were sanctioned, Native Americans were most likely to suffer the severe penalty of permanent loss of benefits. In fact, 47 percent were sanctioned in this way, compared with 34 percent of African Americans, 35 percent of whites, 30 percent of Latinos and no Asians.[13] Other studies show that blacks had their welfare cases closed due to "noncompliance" with program rules at significantly higher rates than whites.[14]

In addition to racial differentials in the application of welfare reform's punitive measures, there is also evidence of racial bias in the provision of information and services meant to support recipients in their transition to work and presumed self-sufficiency. Again, Native Americans fared particularly poorly, being the least likely of all groups to receive transportation assistance and, after Asians, the least likely to receive child care benefits.[15] A Virginia study that compared the experiences of black and white women on welfare found noteworthy differences in caseworkers' provision of information and assistance. Forty-one percent of white recipients were encouraged to raise their educational status as a way to better their chances in the work force. No black recipients were similarly encouraged. And, in a rural area of the country where reliable transportation is critical to getting and keeping a job, nearly half of whites were offered transportation assistance, while no blacks were. Gooden concluded that "white welfare recipients benefit considerably from the discretionary actions of their caseworkers."[16]

Language access is an additional area of discrimination in the implementation of welfare policy. Adequate translation services are rarely available in welfare offices and written notices are often in English only. Consequently, those welfare recipients with limited English skills face major barriers in gaining access to information about welfare-to-work requirements or services to which they are entitled. A study of Hmong women receiving welfare in Wisconsin found 90 percent with little or no English proficiency; 70 percent with no literacy in the Hmong language; and 62 percent with no formal education.[17] In California, Hmong, Cambodians, and Laotians all have very high rates of limited English proficiency[18] and a study of immigrant welfare recipients in one California county found that a substantial majority of the Vietnamese women and nearly half of the Mexican American women had limited or no proficiency in English.[19]

Other research reveals that substantial proportions of limited English speakers were provided with neither translators nor aid applications in their own languages.[20] The welfare bureaucracy is a formidable challenge to native speakers; for those without English language skills it can be impossible. Lack of translation is an especially serious problem in communities with both high levels of dependence on welfare and high rates of limited English proficiency—the case in Southeast Asian communities that rely on public assistance at three times the rate of African Americans and twice the rate of Latina/os.[21] Welfare reform is not being implemented fairly if large numbers of applicants and recipients cannot understand the notices that are sent to them and cannot communicate effectively with their caseworkers. To the extent that those affected are from communities of color, welfare policy is being implemented in ways that compound discrimination based on both immigrant status and race/ethnicity.

Impact

If welfare reform was motivated by racial bias, is intended to modify the behavior of women of color, and is being implemented in racially discriminatory ways, it should come as no surprise that women of color and their communities disproportionately bear the burden of the policy's negative consequences. Data on welfare reform's impact is seldom disaggregated by race, so it is currently not possible to conclusively demonstrate statistically that PRWORA is deepening racial inequality on a national scale. However, a number of trends point towards such a conclusion.

Welfare reform is exacerbating vulnerabilities that were already racially marked. Even before the passage of PRWORA, women of color and their families were disproportionately represented among the homeless, among those who experience food insecurity and hunger, and among those receiving low wages and working in substandard conditions. Welfare reform has heightened women's exposure to each of these situations.

Homelessness—Widespread family homelessness rose steeply beginning in the 1980s as the value of the welfare grant and the minimum wage dropped, low-wage work expanded, and housing costs ballooned. Negligible in the 1970s, family homelessness climbed to 27 percent of the total homeless population in 1985 and on to an estimated 37 percent in 1999.[22] The vast majority of homeless families comprises a single mother and her children.

Some communities of color experience homelessness at exceptionally high rates. African American women, for example, are massively overrepresented in the urban homeless population, constituting over 80 percent of homeless women with children in some cities; Puerto Rican women are also homeless in highly disproportionate numbers.[23] The particular vulnerability of women of color to homelessness is a consequence, in part, of high rates of reliance on welfare during a period in which the value of the welfare grant plummeted, putting shelter beyond the reach of many welfare recipients.

Immigrant women recipients are likely to experience severe overcrowding and to devote a huge portion of their income to housing. Many share housing with relatives or with unrelated adults; live in garages or other makeshift, substandard dwellings; and worry constantly about paying the rent.

There is increasing evidence, both anecdotal and empirical, that welfare reform has further jeopardized poor women's access to housing, contributing to rising levels of housing insecurity and homelessness. The author of one recent study noted, "Young children are without homes in the largest numbers since the Great Depression. Welfare reform has made things much worse. Shelters are overflowing and gridlocked."[24] A social service worker in a Salvation Army shelter in New Orleans, Louisiana, observed, "When I started here three years ago, we had plenty of family space. Since welfare reform, I don't have a bed."[25]

A few studies are beginning to confirm the anecdotal evidence of what happens when families hit the two-year time limit, or are removed from the rolls for noncompliance with work requirements. A survey conducted by social service agencies in six states found that 8 percent of the single parents who had stopped getting welfare in the previous six months had to turn to homeless shelters to house their families.[26] Seven percent of former recipients in Illinois who were not working became homeless. Prospects were not much better for former recipients who *were* working, of whom 5 percent became homeless.[27]

Homelessness widens the chasm between those who prosper and those who fall ever further behind. There are far more people of color on one side of that chasm than on the other. Welfare policy has narrowed poor women's access to safe and affordable housing, and, in doing so, has intensified the already disproportionate vulnerability of women of color to housing instability and homelessness.

Food Insecurity and Hunger—As is the case with homelessness, food insecurity and hunger are racially weighted conditions. One study by a national food bank network revealed that African Americans were represented among those using soup kitchens and food pantries at three times the rate of their representation in the population overall, while Native Americans were also substantially overrepresented.[28] Insofar as welfare reform exaggerates the vulnerability to hunger of poor women and their families, it may also be expected to deepen this racially inflected divide.

And the evidence is accumulating that, indeed, PRWORA has made women's struggles to obtain food for themselves and their families more difficult. Many former recipients can't pay for sufficient food; they and their families skip meals, go hungry, and/or use food pantries or other emergency food assistance.

The figures are astoundingly high. In New Jersey, half of former recipients surveyed reported an inability to feed themselves or their children sufficiently.[29] In an Illinois study, the population reporting the most difficulty with food insecurity was former recipients who were participating in the labor force, of whom 63 percent said that there was a time when they could not buy the food they needed.[30] The higher costs associated with participating in the labor force, combined with reduction or elimination of the food stamp allotment, meant that women's access to adequate food became more precarious rather than less so as they moved from welfare to work.

Welfare reform has also contributed to the underutilization of the food stamp program. Many families that leave the welfare system do not know that as long as their income remains below a certain level, they can continue receiving food stamps. Mistakenly believing that the termination of their TANF benefits disqualifies them for food stamps as well, they fail to apply or to reconfirm their eligibility. According to one study, among families that left welfare, only 42 percent of those who were eligible for food stamps were receiving them.[31]

Immigrant families have been hit particularly hard. A study of Los Angeles and San Francisco immigrant households whose food stamps had been cut found that 33 percent of the children in the San Francisco households were experiencing moderate to severe hunger.[32] Half of the Mexican American immigrant recipients in a Santa Clara County, California study had experienced food shortages, as had one-quarter of the Vietnamese women.[33] One out of three Hmong women recipients in Wisconsin reported running out of food in the six months prior to the survey and half said they had less food on the state's W-2 program than they had had on AFDC.[34] Food insecurity and hunger, conditions that are borne unevenly across the color line, have been exacerbated by welfare reform, further entrenching the racial divide.

From Welfare to Low-Wage Work—As others have cogently argued, welfare policy is also labor policy.[35] And indeed, within months of the passage of PRWORA, evidence was already emerging that workfare and Work First programs were depressing wages and displacing low-wage workers. In the boom economy of the mid- to late 1990s, employers recognized that "everyone has been raising wages to get people . . . and this [the influx of welfare recipients] will make it possible to hold pay steady."[36]

The work requirements and time limits that coerce women into the paid labor force are not implemented in a gender neutral or race neutral environment, and cannot be expected to be neutral in their impact. Thus, while the surge of former welfare recipients into the low-wage sector of the economy will worsen wages and working conditions for the poorest strata of the working class as a whole, some communities will be hit harder than others. Communities of color, with traditionally higher unemployment and underemployment rates, higher proportions of very low-wage workers, and lower median incomes, will be further disadvantaged by PRWORA policies that force women into a labor market in which they have virtually no bargaining power.

There are substantial racial differences among working women. Full-time, year-round Latina women workers earned a median annual income of $19,817 in 1998, considerably less than the $23,864 earned by African American women or the $27,304 white women earned.[37] All women are far more likely than white men to earn poverty level wages. But again, racial differentials are substantial. More than half of Latina workers, 51.8 percent, earn poverty level wages, compared with 40.7 percent of black women and 29.7 percent of white women.[38] Despite relatively low unemployment rates during the mid- to late 1990s, young women of color who had not attended college were at a distinct disadvantage. African American women with less than a high school education faced 1996 unemployment rates nearly twice as high as those of white women—20.9 percent vs. 10.8 percent—while 15.9 percent of Hispanic women at this educational level were unemployed. Underemployment rates were even higher. Analyzing the labor market conditions facing women on welfare, one researcher concluded: "Such high rates of un- and underemployment, which persist in a labor market that has experienced overall unemployment rates below 6 percent for over two years, suggest that it may be difficult for welfare recipients to meet the work requirements of the new welfare law."[39]

Former welfare recipients generally end up holding low paid, entry level jobs in the gender ghettos of service, sales, and clerical work. A study of the first two years of welfare reform in New Jersey found that the average hourly wage of those former welfare recipients who were working was only $7.31. More than a third were holding jobs that paid less than $6 per hour.[40] A 1997 national survey found that adults who left the welfare system and were employed had a median hourly wage of $6.61.[41] This would bring a family just above the official poverty level, but falls far short of a "living wage." Most former recipients who enter the labor force work at jobs that do not provide them with benefits. Less than one-quarter of these workers were covered by health benefits in one national survey.[42]

Far too many families end up in worse economic circumstances than they endured while on welfare. For example, a study that tracked families who left Wisconsin's welfare system found that during the first year off welfare, only half of the families had higher incomes than they had had while on welfare, even if they had been working while receiving welfare.[43] An examination of seven state studies of former welfare recipients found that in only two of the states were families' average annual earnings above the poverty line.[44]

Many women have been pushed off welfare but have not found employment. Several studies show that from 20–40 percent of former recipients find no work.[45] As more and more women reach their two-year and five-year limits—in an economy that is far less robust than it was when welfare reform was passed—they will face an even less welcoming labor market.

There is some evidence that racial disadvantage in the labor market is also being played out in terms of the rates at which different racial groups are leaving the rolls. Welfare use is declining rapidly among all races, but white recipients are leaving the welfare rolls at a much more rapid rate than are blacks or Latinos. In New York City, for example, the number of whites on welfare declined by 57 percent between 1995 and 1998, while the rate of decline for blacks was 30 percent and that of Latinos, 7 percent. White recipients have been leaving the rolls at faster rates than have minorities in states such as Illinois, Pennsylvania, Michigan, and Ohio, and have led the decline nationally as well.[46]

While there are no definitive explanations for this phenomenon, some of the factors may include: higher average educational levels among white recipients; greater concentrations of recipients of color in job-poor inner cities; racial discrimination in employment and housing; and higher child care costs for women of color due to the larger family size of some racial/ethnic groups. Gooden's findings regarding racial discrimination in the provision of information and assistance, as well as her findings of racial differentials in employment outcomes among black and white participants in a state welfare reform program, are clearly relevant here.[47] Though the combination of contributing factors is undoubtedly complex, the more rapid transition of white recipients into the labor force is an indicator of the racially disparate impact of welfare reform.

The passage from welfare to work is beset with difficulties. Women are forced into jobs earning poverty level wages that leave them worse off than they were while receiving welfare. With no benefits, transportation problems, and high child care costs, they struggle with the complex logistics of caring for their families while clinging to the bottom rungs of the economic ladder. Other women are sanctioned off the rolls or reach their time limits, but find no place in the paid labor force.

Women of color leaving welfare for work at poverty level wages will add to the black women and Latinas, as well as the women of some Asian communities, who are already substantially overrepresented within this stratum of workers. Women of color who are pushed off welfare but who find no work will join the disproportionately brown and black ranks of the unemployed.

The political impulse behind welfare reform, apart from being mean and socially regressive, was racist and xenophobic. Welfare reform is being implemented in ways that follow well-worn patterns of racial and anti-immigrant discrimination. And the negative impacts of welfare reform are unequally shared. Left unchallenged, this policy can only be expected to bolster white privilege and more deeply inscribe racial subordination.

Human Rights

Targeting U.S. welfare policy as a violation of human rights is one way in which welfare reform is being challenged. Scholars and activists alike are, increasingly, considering welfare policy within the framework of international human rights. Many have concluded that PRWORA is a violation of U.N. human rights conventions. For example, the imposition of the "family cap" and the denial of assistance to teen mothers who are not living with their parents are identified as violations of the Universal Declaration of Human Rights (UDHR) in that these provisions run contrary to the state's obligation to support families, regardless of their structure or the "legitimacy" of children. "Under the UDHR-based scheme...the family, in general, and motherhood and childhood, in particular, are entitled to special care and assistance from the state regardless of the marital status of the parents…"[48]

Time limits and sanctions, which may deepen family poverty, are condemned as undermining the rights of children to equal treatment, without distinction due to birth or other status.[49] And those excluded from assistance, including those convicted of drug felonies, children born after the "family cap," and immigrants without documents, "are guaranteed no economic and social rights at all."[50] The coercion of women into jobs paying poverty level wages, or off of welfare and into joblessness, is also a clear violation of the right to "free choice of employment, to just and favourable conditions of work and to protection against unemployment."[51] PRWORA runs directly contrary to the UDHR, the International Convention on Economic, Social and Cultural Rights, and the Convention on the Elimination of All Forms of Discrimination Against Women. Welfare reform is also incompatible with the objectives of the 1995 Beijing Platform for Action, a document that provides substance to the claim that "women's rights are human rights," and directs U.N. member states to take action to relieve "the persistent and increasing burden of poverty on women."[52]

The International Convention on the Elimination of All Forms of Racial Discrimination (CERD), ratified by the United States in 1994, and premised on the rights articulated in the UDHR, specifically condemns racial discrimination and enjoins states to eliminate "any distinction, exclusion, restriction or preference based on race, colour, descent or national or ethnic origin."[53] The convention condemns incitement to racial discrimination and, in Article 5(e), identifies the range of economic, social, and cultural rights to be guaranteed on a nondiscriminatory basis, including the rights to free choice of employment, just and favorable remuneration, housing, public health, medical care, social security, and social services.

Far from condemning and working to eradicate incitements to racial discrimination, U.S. government officials built upon a long tradition of such incitements to turn public opinion against social assistance for poor women and their families. By targeting women of color in intent, implementation, and impact, welfare reform substantially violates CERD, actively undermining racial equality in the enjoyment and exercise of human rights.

It is not so difficult to demonstrate that U.S. welfare policies deny women of color access to their full range of human rights. More difficult is to develop strategies, using the human rights framework, that effectively mobilize the social forces necessary to reconfigure those policies. But local, statewide, and national welfare rights organizations and networks are, increasingly, engaging in human rights education, documenting violations, and exploring ways to hold the government accountable for abandoning its treaty obligations. For example, the Kensington Welfare Rights Union (KWRU), in an intentional shift from a civil rights to an economic human rights framework, launched a 1997 national campaign to document violations of the Universal Declaration of Human Rights. After visiting with, and accumulating testimony from, poor peoples' organizations nationwide, KWRU published the *Poor People's Human Rights Report*,[54] which addresses violations of the human rights to employment, an adequate standard of living, and education articulated in UDHR Articles 23, 25, and 26. The Poor People's Economic Human Rights Campaign, a network of organizations initiated by KWRU, is united in its commitment to placing U.S. poverty in a global context, to basing its work on the leadership and organization of the poor, and to a "long-term struggle to translate the concepts of economic human rights into real programs for real people."[55]

The international human rights framework has great moral force and has been skillfully used by activists worldwide to bring violators to justice. What has yet to be incontrovertibly demonstrated is its efficacy in relation to U.S. domestic policy, particularly those policies that undermine economic rights. Many challenges remain. The grassroots human rights movement is relatively young. Mechanisms of accountability are highly complex and time consuming, requiring technical and financial resources well beyond the reach of most grassroots organizations. Hard issues must be confronted, notably the balance and relationship between strategies aimed at winning tangible victories and those that expose the U.S. government's moral and political hypocrisies; between local organizing and international advocacy; and between reforming domestic legislation and enforcing accountability to international human rights norms. The challenge for U.S. human rights activists is not only to arrive at a balance, where education, organizing, documentation, advocacy, and litigation at all levels can reinforce rather than eclipse one another, but also to convince others of the value of this integrated advocacy approach.[56]

There is, too, the far more basic issue of the traction of internationally recognized economic human rights in the context of economic systems fundamentally premised on the perpetuation of poverty and economic inequality.

Welfare rights organizations have begun to tackle these challenges. In doing so, they open a new chapter in the struggle for economic, racial, and gender justice.

Recommendations

PRWORA comes before the U.S. Congress for reauthorization in 2002. Organizations that advocate and mobilize for welfare rights, economic and racial justice, and women's rights have formulated a wide range of demands and recommendations for government action. Among the most important recommendations are:

- End the two-year and five-year time limits
- Count college education as a work activity
- Increase funding for child care subsidies
- Raise the minimum wage
- Support job development for living-wage jobs with benefits
- Increase funding for housing assistance
- Increase the food stamp allotment
- Ensure that all welfare recipients are informed of their rights and of the full range of services to which they are entitled

These measures would significantly improve economic circumstances for all women on welfare. However, given the racially discriminatory intent, implementation, and impact of welfare reform, it is crucial that the government "take effective measures to review governmental, national and local policies, and to amend, rescind or nullify any laws and regulations which have the effect of creating or perpetuating racial discrimination wherever it exists."[57] Among these measures must be the following:

- abolish the family cap
- eliminate the "illegitimacy bonus"
- restore benefits to teen mothers, whether living with their parents or not
- disaggregate data on the impact and outcomes of welfare reform by race and ethnicity—at the county, state, and federal levels
- restore benefits to immigrants
- monitor the provision of welfare services and the implementation of sanctions for racially discriminatory practices, and institute measures to eliminate such practices
- provide translation services at welfare offices and translate all forms and notices
- fund educational programs, including adult basic education and English as a Second Language, that address the particular needs of immigrant women

These recommendations are made within the context of the existing legislation. Nothing short of a complete overhaul of the U.S. social welfare system, a true reformation that places human needs as central, can eradicate the

racially discriminatory, gender biased, anti-immigrant, and antipoor foundations of a policy that so powerfully shapes the lives of U.S. women of color.

This essay first appeared in *Time to Rise: U.S. Women of Color–Issues and Strategies* (Berkeley:
Women of Color Resource Center, 2001).
© 2001 by Linda Burnham.

NOTES

[1] Public Law 104–193, 104th Cong., 2nd Sess. (22 August 1996).

[2] See Gwendolyn Mink, *Welfare's End.* Ithaca, NY: Cornell University Press, 2002; Mimi
Abramowitz, *Regulating the Lives of Women: Social Welfare Policy from Colonial Times to the
Present.* Boston, MA: South End Press, 1988.

[3] *Chicana Voices* (1986): 24.

[4] Kimberlé Williams Crenshaw, "The Intersectionality of Race and Gender Discrimination,"
background paper. Zagreb, Croatia: Expert Group Meeting on Gender and Race
Discrimination, November 21–24, 2000.

[5] Lucy Williams, *Decades of Distortion: The Right's 30-Year Assault on Welfare.* Somerville, MA:
Political Research Associates, 1997.

[6] Marilyn R. Allen, *Beacon Light-Herald* (March–April, 1961). Cited in Williams.

[7] Floya Anthias and Nira Yuval-Davis. *Racialized Boundaries.* New York: Routledge, 1992.

[8] Kenneth Neubeck and Noel Cazanave, *Welfare Racism: Playing the Race Card Against the
American Poor.* New York: Routledge, 2001.

[9] Ibid.

[10] Seavey, Dorothy, *Back to Basics: Women's Poverty and Welfare Reform.* Wellesley, MA:
Wellesley Center for Research on Women, 1996; and Welfare Law Center, *Welfare Myths:
Fact or Fiction? Exploring the Truth About Welfare.* New York: Welfare Law Center, 1996
(http://www.welfarelaw.org/publist.html).

[11] Lynn H. Fujiwara, "Impact of Welfare Reform on Asian Immigrant Communities," *Social
Justice,* 82, 1998.

[12] Joe Soss et al., "Predicting Welfare Reform Retrenchment: Race, Ideology and Economy in
the Devolution Revolution." Unpublished paper, 1999. Cited in Neubeck and Cazanave.

[13] Rebecca Gordon, *Cruel and Usual: How Welfare "Reform" Punishes Poor People.* Oakland,
CA: Applied Research Center, 2001.

[14] Steve Savner, "Welfare Reform and Racial/Ethnic Minorities: The Questions to Ask."
Poverty and Race 9, no. 4 (July/August 2000): 3–5.

[15] Gordon.

[16] Susan T. Gooden, "Race and Welfare: Examining Employment Outcomes of White and
Black Welfare Recipients." *Journal of Poverty* 4, no. 3 (2000): 21–41.

[17] Thomas Moore and Vicky Selkowe, *The Impact of Welfare Reform on Wisconsin's Hmong Aid
Recipients.* Milwaukee, WI: Institute for Wisconsin's Future, 1999.

[18] Deeana Jang and Luella J. Pensenga, *Beyond the Safety Net: The Effect of Welfare Reform on
the Self-Sufficiency of Asian and Pacific Islander Women in California.* San Francisco: Asian and
Pacific Islander American Health Forum, 1999.

[19] Equal Rights Advocates, *From War on Poverty to War on Welfare: The Impact of Welfare Reform on the Lives of Immigrant Women.* San Francisco: Equal Rights Advocates, 1999.

[20] Gordon; also Lissa Bell and Carson Strege-Flora, *Access Denied: Federal Neglect Gives Rise to State Lawlessness; Families Denied Access to Medicaid, Food Stamps, CHIP, and Child Care.* Seattle: Northwest Federation of Community Organizations and National Campaign for Jobs and Income Support, 2000.

[21] Fujiwara.

[22] United States Conference of Mayors, *A Status Report on Hunger and Homelessness in America's Cities.* Washington, DC: U.S. Conference of Mayors, 1999.

[23] Martha R. Burt and Barbara E. Cohen, "A Sociodemographic Profile of the Service-Using Homeless: Findings from a National Survey," *Homelessness in the United States,* vol.2: *Data and Issues,* Jamshid A. Momeni, ed., New York: Greenwood, 1990; and Ellen Bassuk et al., "The Characteristics and Needs of Sheltered Homeless and Low-Income Housed Mothers." *Journal of the American Medical Association* 276, no. 8 (1996): 640–646.

[24] Laura Griffin, "Welfare Cuts Leaving More families Homeless, Study Finds," *Dallas Morning News* (July 1, 1999).

[25] Kim Cobb, "Homeless Kids Problem Worst in Louisiana; Welfare Reform, Housing Crunch Are Among Reasons," *Houston Chronicle* (August 15, 1999).

[26] Arloc Sherman et al., *Welfare to What: Early Findings on Family Hardship and Well-Being.* Washington, DC: Children's Defense Fund and National Coalition for the Homeless, 1998.

[27] Work, Welfare and Families, *Living With Welfare Reform: A Survey of Low Income Families in Illinois.* Chicago: Chicago Urban League and UIC Center for Urban Economic Development, 2000.

[28] VanAmburg Group, *Second Harvest National Research Study.* Erie, PA: Van Amburg Group, 1994. Cited in Janet Poppendieck, "Hunger in the Land of Plenty," in *America Needs Human Rights,* Anuradha Mittal and Peter Rosset, eds. Oakland, CA: Food First Books, 1999.

[29] Work, Poverty and Welfare Evaluation Project, *Assessing Work First: What Happens After Welfare?* Edison, NJ: Study Group on Work, Poverty and Welfare, 1999.

[30] Work, Welfare and Families.

[31] Sheila R. Zedlewski and Sarah Brauner, *Are the Steep Declines in Food Stamp Participation Linked to Falling Welfare Caseloads?* Washington, DC: Urban Institute, 1999.

[32] Sandra H. Venner et al., *Paradox of Our Times: Hunger in a Strong Economy.* Medford, MA: Center on Hunger and Poverty, Tufts University, 2000.

[33] Equal Rights Advocates, *From War on Poverty to War on Welfare: The Impact of Welfare Reform on the Lives of Immigrant Women.* San Francisco: Equal Rights Advocates, 1999.

[34] Moore and Selkowe.

[35] Frances Fox Piven, "Welfare Policy and American Politics," in *From Poverty to Punishment: How Welfare Policy Punishes the Poor.* Gary Delgado, ed., Oakland: Applied Research Center, 2002.

[36] Louis Uchitelle, "Welfare Recipients Taking Jobs Often Held by the Working Poor." *New York Times,* sec. A10 (April 1, 1997).

[37] United States Department of Labor Women's Bureau, "Women of Hispanic Origin in the Labor Force," *Facts on Working Women,* no. 00–04, April 2000.

[38] Jared Bernstein, "The Challenge of Moving from Welfare to Work: Depressed Labor Market Awaits Those Leaving the Rolls." *EPI Issue Brief* no.116 (March 1997).

[39] Ibid.

[40] Anu Rangarajan and Robert G. Wood, *How WFNJ Clients are Faring Under Welfare Reform: An Early Look.* Princeton, NJ: Mathematica Policy Research, Inc., 1999.

[41] Pamela Loprest, *How Families That Left Welfare Are Doing: A National Picture.* Washington, DC: Urban Institute, 1999.

[42] Ibid.

[43] United States General Accounting Office, *Welfare Reform: Information on Former Recipients' Status.* Washington, DC: USGAO, 1999b.

[44] Ibid.

[45] Ibid.; Rangarajan and Wood; Loprest.

[46] Gooden.

[47] Ibid.

[48] Lisa Crooms, "The Temporary Assistance for Needy families Program and the Human Rights of Poor Single Women of Color and their Children," in *Women's Progress: Perspectives on the Past, Blueprint for the Future.* Conference proceedings. Washington, DC: Institute for Women's Policy Research, 1998.

[49] United Nations, *Universal Declaration of Human Rights.* General Assembly resolution 217 A (III)) Article 2 (10 December 1948); and Unitarian Universalist Service Committee, *America's Forgotten Families, Voices of Welfare Reform.* Cambridge, MA: Welfare and Human Rights Monitoring Project, 2001.

[50] Anuradha Mittal et al., "Welfare Reform Violates Human Rights," in *America Needs Human Rights.* Anuradha Mittal and Peter Rosset, eds. Oakland, CA: Food First, 1999.

[51] *Universal Declaration of Human Rights,* article 23(1).

[52] Fourth World Conference on Women, *Beijing Declaration,* paragraph 44. Beijing: FWCW, 1995.

[53] United Nations Office of the High Commissioner for Human Rights, *International Convention on the Elimination of All Forms of Racial Discrimination (CERD),* U.N. General Assembly resolution 2106 (XX, article 1(1). Geneva: United Nations, 1965.

[54] Kensington Welfare Rights Union, *Poor People's Human Rights Report on the United States.* Philadelphia: Kensington Welfare Rights Union, 1999.

[55] Willie Baptist and Mary Bricker-Jenkins, "A View from the Bottom: Poor People and Their Allies Respond to Welfare Reform," in *Lost Ground: Welfare Reform, Poverty, and Beyond,* Randy Albelda and Ann Withorn, eds., Boston, MA: South End Press, 2002.

[56] Ibid.

[57] *CERD,* article 2(1)(c).

Whose "Choice"? "Flexible" Women Workers in the Tomato Food Chain

DEBORAH BARNDT

My whole family [works] at McDonald's: my mother, my sisters, my boyfriend, often at different times. And my dad, a police officer, works from eleven in the night 'til six in the morning. So there's no time we can eat together. We just grab something and put it in the microwave.[1]

This narrative, by Tania, a York University student working at McDonald's, may resonate with many young women in the North. At the Southern end of the NAFTA food chain, Tomasa, a Mexican fieldworker for "Santa Anita Packers", one of the biggest domestic producers of tomatoes, describes her daily food preparations during the harvest season: "I get up at 3:00 A.M. to make tortillas for our lunch, then the truck comes at six to take us to the fields to start working by 7:00 A.M."[2]

An hour away at a Santa Anita greenhouse, Sara, a young tomato packer, tells us that the foreign management of Eco-Cultivos has just eliminated the two-hour lunch break, so workers no longer go home for the traditional noontime meal.[3]

These changes in the eating practices of women workers in the continental food system reflect several dimensions of the global economic restructuring that has reshaped the nature of their labor. Shifts in family eating practices have not been the "choice" of the women whose stories are told here, nor have they "chosen" the work shifts that involve them around the clock in growing and preparing food for other people.

"McDonaldization," initiated in the North and spreading to the South, and "maquilization," initiated in the South and now appearing in the North, are interrelated processes in the new global economy. McDonaldization, as George Ritzer describes it, is the model that the fast food restaurant has offered as a way to reorganize work in all other sectors. This model is based on efficiency, predictability, calculability or quantifiability, substitution of nonhuman technology, control, and the irrationality of rationality.[4] Central to this model is "flexible" part-time labor.

Originating in the maquila free trade zones of northern Mexico, *maquilization* now refers to a more generalized work process characterized by the feminization of the labor force, extreme segmentation of skill categories, the lowering of real wages, and a nonunion orientation.[5] In the traditional maquila sectors, such as the garment and electronic industries, there is full-time (though not necessarily stable) employment. However, the trade liberalization epitomized by NAFTA has opened the door for the development of maquilas throughout Mexico. "Agromaquilas," in particular, depend on more temporary, part-time, and primarily female labor.

Central to both the McDonaldization of the retail and service sectors and the maquilization of the agro-industrial and manufacturing sectors in the continental food chain are the interrelated processes of the "feminization of poverty"[6] and the "flexibilization of labor."[7] Since the 1960s, when export processing zones such as the Mexican maquilas began to employ primarily young women in low-skilled and low-wage jobs,[8] women have been key players in this new global formula.[9]

In the reorganization of work by global capital, women workers have also become key players in new flexible labor strategies, building on an already established sexual division of labor and institutionalized sexism and racism in the societies where transnational corporations set up shop. In these sectors of the global food system, women bring their own meaning to flexible labor as they juggle their lives as both producers and consumers of food, as both part-time salaried workers and full-time domestic workers in managing households.

Tomasita Comes North While Big Mac Goes South

In the Tomasita Project (a three-year cross-border research project conducted by the Department of Environmental Studies, York University–Toronto), the journey of the tomato from the Mexican field through the United States to the Canadian fast-food restaurant reveals the dynamics of globalization. While food production and consumption take place in all three countries, deep inequities, upon which nafta was based, remain among them.

The basic North–South contradiction of this continental (and increasingly hemispheric) system is that Mexico produces fresh fruit and vegetables (in this case, the tomato) for North American consumers, while Northern retail supermarkets[10] and fast food restaurants, such as McDonald's, are moving South at record speed[11] to market new foods, and new work and food practices, particularly as a result of NAFTA's trade liberalization. This contradiction is revealed in retail advertising, such as a Loblaws billboard promoting President's Choice products with an image of a Muslim woman in the desert with a shopping cart. The billboard proclaims "Food Means the World to Us." We are seduced by such images into consuming an increasing "diversity" and seemingly endless array of fresh, "exotic"[12] and nontraditional foods. Meanwhile, there are hidden costs under which these foods were produced— the appropriation of indigenous lands; the degradation of the environment and the health and dignity of workers; increasing poverty; deepening sexist and racist employment practices[13]—which are kept (carefully and consciously) from our view.

The Tomasita Project aims to uncover these costs, particularly by exposing the living and working conditions of the women workers whose labor (not by choice) brings the "world of food" to us. A deconstruction of the Loblaws' ad would reveal these women workers as the producers behind the food product, and show that they, too, are part of a global system that links agro-export economies (such as Mexico) with the increasing consumer demand in the North for fresh produce all year round.

Tomasita is a both a material and symbolic "ecofeminist"[14] tomato within globalized food production—from biogenetic engineering to intensive use of agrochemicals, from long journeys in refrigerated trucks to shorter journeys across supermarket counters where its internationally standardized "product look-up" numbers are punched in. Its fate is paralleled by the intertwining fates of women workers in the different stages of its production, preparation, and consumption. If the tomato is shaped by "just-in-time" production practices, women workers make this supply-on-demand possible through their flexible labor.

The tracing of the tomato chain builds on the tradition of "commodity chain analysis,"[15] which examines three interlocking processes: 1) raw material production, 2) combined processing, packaging, and exporting activities, and 3) marketing and consumptive activities.[16] The women workers who make the tomato chain come alive represent four different sectors of the food system—two in Mexico and two in Canada. In Mexico, they are the pickers and packers in Santa Anita Packers, a large export-oriented agribusiness; and the assembly-line workers producing ketchup at Del Monte, a well-established, multinational food processor. In Canada, the workers are cashiers in Loblaws supermarkets and service workers in McDonald's restaurants.

How do these women workers (both as producers and consumers) reflect, respond to, and resist the "flexible labor strategy" so central to corporate restructuring? There are, of course, obvious differences between the Mexican indigenous workers moving from harvest to harvest to pick tomatoes and the Canadian women slicing these tomatoes and stacking them into hamburgers. Yet, since NAFTA, there are increasing similarities in the feminization and flexibilization of the labor force in all four sectors and in all three countries. One of the similarities is the increasing participation of young female workers, who, from the perspective of the companies, are seen as both cheaper and more productive than comparable male labor.[17] Gender ideologies, culturally entrenched and reinforced by managerial practices, strongly shape this socially constructed reality.

Flexibilization: From Above and From Below

Key to global economic restructuring is the notion of flexibility. The term, however, changes meaning depending on whose perspective it represents. The perspective from above, from the vantage point of corporate managers, is different from the perspective from below, from the new global workforce. To some, flexibility implies "choice," but "whose choice" rules in a food system built on structural inequalities, which are based on differences of national identity, race, class, gender, and age?

For large transnational corporations, flexibility has meant greater freedom (provided by NAFTA and increasing support from the Mexican government) to set up businesses in Mexico, where businesses are offered lower trade barriers, property laws that allow greater foreign investment, decreasing subsidies, decentralization of production through subcontracting, and so forth. For large Mexican domestic producers such as Santa Anita Packers, trade liberalization has meant entering a globally competitive market with comparative advantages of land, climate, and cheap labor. Once producing primarily for national consumption, Santa Anita has become ever more export-driven—it now produces 85 percent of crops for export and, in the case of greenhouse production, 100 percent for export. The fruit and vegetable sector is one of the few winners under nafta in Mexico.

The meaning of flexibility changes when set in the context of the new global marketplace, where borders and nation-states are less and less relevant, and where production is increasingly decentralized while decision-making is increasingly centralized. In this context, "flexibility" also refers to the shift from Fordist to post-Fordist production practices. Fordism was based on scientific management principles and organization of tasks in assembly lines for mass production, with the production of large volumes being the objective. Post-Fordist or "just-in-time" production responds to more diversified and specific demands in terms of quality and quantity.[18] It is ultimately very rationalized, of course, as demonstrated by the processes of workplace McDonaldization in which new technologies allow greater control of inventory and labor, while decentralization of production allows companies to shift many of the risks to subcontractors. In talking about the globalized corporate world, or "globalization from above,"[19] then, flexibility is ultimately about maximizing profits and minimizing obstacles (such as trade tariffs, government regulations, underused labor, and trade union organization).

Women Workers' Experiences of Flexibility

What does flexibility mean, though, for the women moving the tomato through this continental food system, from Mexican field to Canadian table?

If we first look at the consumption end of the food chain, the fast food and supermarket workers in Canada, and then move to the source, where women plant, pick, pack, and process tomatoes in Mexico, we can learn how flexibilization has affected these women's daily lives. McDonald's "flexible labor strategies" have been key to the model of production of McDonald's and its competitors. McJobs, whether filled by students, seniors, or underemployed women, have always been primarily part-time (up to twenty-four hours a week). Part-time jobs do not require certain benefits and, because they are limited to short three- to four-hour shifts, do not require many breaks. Women student workers might be sent home after an hour or two if sales for the day are not reaching their predetermined quota. Karen, a university student, explains:

> They're supposed to make a certain amount of money an hour, say $1,300 between twelve noon and 1:00 P.M., and if they make less than that, for every $50 (under the quota), they cut half an hour of labor. Especially if you're newer, there's pressure to go home. It takes me an hour to get to work by bus, and I could be asked to go home after an hour of work.[20]

Flexibility of this temporary labor force is reinforced by the lack of trade union organization. Strong company-induced loyalty is fed by perks such as team outings, weekly treats, and training that inculcate a family orientation. It is meant to dissuade employees from seeking unionization or from complaining about their hours. Nonetheless, there are increasing efforts to organize McDonald's workers and there have been union successes in British Columbia and Quebec.

Loblaws

The experience of flexibility for women workers in the larger chains of the retail food sector, such as Loblaws in Canada, is just as precarious. Even though part-time workers are unionized, their working conditions have been eroded through recent labor negotiations. In the case of Loblaws, for example, a contract negotiated by the United Food and Commercial Workers Union eliminated almost all of the full-time cashier positions. Part-time cashiers are dependent on seniority for being able to choose their working hours. This particularly affects new cashiers, such as Wanda: "When you are low on the seniority list, you are lucky to get any hours. They might call you in once every two weeks for a four-hour shift."[21] This restriction on available hours also affects the cashiers' earning power. A cashier must complete five hundred hours before being eligible for a raise. At this pace, she could work at the starting wage for over two years. From the company's perspective, this shift to primarily part-time flexible labor is a conscious strategy; it is part of "lean production."

Del Monte

What does flexibility look like in the Del Monte food processing plant in Irapuato, Mexico? The production of ketchup in Del Monte takes place during a four-month period, from February through May. In part, this coincides with the peak period for harvesting tomatoes; thus flexibility in the agromaquilas depends, in part, on the seasonal nature of agricultural production (becoming less pronounced with the increasing phenomenon of year-round greenhouse production).

Another reason that production is limited to one period is to maximize the use of the food processing machinery and the skilled labor force. Del Monte's ketchup production employs a combination of Fordist and post-Fordist processes: it is an assembly line production from the dumping and cooking of tomatoes in big vats to the bottling, capping, and labeling on a mechanized line. Because other food processing (such as marmalade) uses the same machinery, the same full-time workers can easily shift from one product to another. Many are, in fact, multiskilled and are moved from one process to another, reflecting post-Fordist practices.

Such multitasking is another form of flexibility in the experience of the new global work force. Part-time women workers are brought on for the peak season only and for less skilled tasks. These women sometimes sit in the waiting room of the plant, hoping for a few hours of work, which are determined day by day. Flexibility reigns in a context where there is an oversupply of cheap labor, so companies can make such decisions on the spot, hiring and dismissing workers on a daily basis. This is another example of lean production, dependent on a disposable supply of female labor.

Santa Anita Packers

Finally we reach the source, Santa Anita Packers—the agribusiness that organizes production of tomatoes, from the importing of seeds to the exporting of waxed and packaged tomatoes in refrigerated trucks. Santa Anita, headquartered in Jalisco, central Mexico, uses a mixture of production practices and diverse applications of the notion of flexibility.

It is important to understand the historical development of the agro-export industry in Mexico[22] in the context of North–South political economic relations, which are based on ever-deepening inequalities, both between and within nations. Since the early part of the century, Mexican agriculture has been led by Northern demand for fresh fruit and vegetables, and by the use of cheap Mexican labor by U.S. agribusinesses on both sides of the border. While the Depression in the 1930s led to American workers taking over farm labor jobs from Mexican workers in the U.S. and also to a spurt of farm labor organizing, the availability of cheap Mexican indigenous migrant labor fed the postwar development of large agribusinesses in both countries from the 1950s onward. This transnationalization of the economy was built upon institutionalized racism and sexism within Mexico and the U.S., employing indigenous workers often as family units who were brought by the companies from the poorer states.

The sexual division of labor is seen most strongly in the packing plants, where a gendered ideology is used to justify the employment of women, as echoed by one of the company owners: "Women 'see' better than men, they can better distinguish the colors and they treat the product more gently. In selection, care, and handling, women are more delicate. They can put up with more than men in all aspects: the routine, the monotony. Men are more restless, and won't put up with it."[23]

The feminization of the global labor force, and thus the feminization of global poverty, has been based on the marginal social role that women play and on a social consensus that their domestic duties are primary. As Lourdes Beneria argues, "the private sphere of the household is at the root of continuing asymmetries between men and women."[24]

In the case of Mexican agro-industry, women are among the most marginalized workers, along with children, students, the elderly, and indigenous peoples. Sara Lara notes that agribusinesses exploit their common situation of "mixedness," referring to the fact that these workers already play socially marginal roles based on their gender, race, or age: "Women as housewives, indigenous peoples as 'poor peasants,' children as sons and daughters, young people as students, all as the ad hoc subjects of flexible processes."[25] It is important to integrate national identity, gender, race, class, age, and marital status[26] into any analysis of the new global labor force.

Deepening Inequalities: Flexibility for Whom?

In their restructuring, corporations have adopted a dual employment strategy that deepens the inequalities within the workforce and divides it into two groups: a "nucleus" of skilled workers who are trained in new technologies and post-Fordist production processes (quality circles, multiskilling, and multitasking) and who have stable employment; and a "periphery" of unskilled workers whose jobs are very precarious. McDonald's and Loblaws each has a small full-time work force, mainly male, while women make up the majority of the more predominant part-time work force.[27]

Tomato production in Mexico mirrors this dualism. Small numbers of permanent workers prepare the seedlings and the land for production, and later pack and process the tomatoes; a large number of temporary part-time workers pick tomatoes during the harvest seasons. Santa Anita, for example, employs *mestizos* (people of mixed race) from the local area for the jobs of cultivating the tomato plants, while hundreds of poor indigenous workers, brought in by trucks and housed in conditions of squalor in makeshift camps, do much of the picking during the three-to-five-month harvest season.[28] In this dual employment strategy, indigenous workers are again required to be the most flexible, which is yet another form of discrimination and exploitation.

Such flexibility has been integral to labor intensive and seasonal agricultural production for decades, though the composition of the migrant labor force has shifted over time. It is not uncommon for entire families to work together in the field, when the demand for labor is up. Children of local mestizo peasant workers join their families on weekends during peak season, while children of indigenous migrant workers, with neither school nor extended family to care for them, often work alongside their parents.[29] With increasing unemployment in Mexico, however, men are taking on agricultural jobs done previously by women, such as picking, and because the current economic crisis has increased the surplus of labor, companies choose the youngest and heartiest workers above the older ones (the ideal age seems to be fifteen to twenty-four, so workers in their thirties can already be considered less desirable). The flexible labor strategies of Mexican agribusinesses are predicated on race, gender, and age. And once again, flexibility is determined by the companies and not the workers.

Technological changes within the production process are integral to the application of flexibilization. Differences among workers (of gender, race, and skill) are accentuated with the increasingly sophisticated modes of greenhouse production and packing. Tomatoes in those plants, for example, are now weighed and sorted by color in a computerized process, which at the same time records the inventory and monitors the productivity of the workers. Through these changes, foreign managers and technicians are reorganizing production relations and the workday in ways that are also shifting social relations, both in the workplace and at home.

In a Santa Anita greenhouse, unproductive workers are dismissed daily, as there is always a plentiful pool of surplus labor to choose from. There are echoes here of the McDonald's worker being sent home when quotas are down and the Loblaws cashier not being called for weeks when she's not needed, as well as Mexican women waiting for a few hours of work on Del Monte's ketchup production line. Flexibility serves the companies' need to maximize production and profits; it does not always serve the needs of Mexican or Canadian women in this food chain to survive, to complement their family income, or to organize their lives and their double-day responsibilities. And as

Sara Lara concludes, "flexibility is not a choice for women," and "labor force management by companies is at the same time family management, that is, it reinforces particular family power relations."[30]

With NAFTA, the Mexican fruit and vegetable industry has been one of the only sectors to benefit from trade liberalization and has maintained an international competitiveness. Mexico has the advantage over its Northern partners in terms of land, climate, and cheap labor. The expansion of the agro-export industry, however, reflects a basic North–South contradiction between a "negotiated flexibility" and a "primitive flexibility."[31]

Large domestic companies in Mexico, such as Santa Anita, are becoming increasingly multinational, yet are still in the periphery of production decisions (controlled outside Mexico) and often lag behind in technological development. In the agro-export economy of Mexico, there is a growth of unstable and temporary employment in the still labor-intensive processes of production, sorting, packing, and processing. In these jobs, women, children, and indigenous peoples (the most flexible workers in a rural labor market) are managed by "primitive flexibility." Transnational companies, however, are located primarily in the more industrialized North and control production through ownership, subcontracting, and advanced technology (biogenetic engineering, sophisticated food processing, production of most of the inputs and machinery of production, and design of the commercialization and distribution systems). These transnationals employ the "nucleus" of skilled workers, with relatively stable employment, and manage this workforce through "negotiated flexibility."

Comparisons Across Borders: Women Workers as Producers and Consumers

Yet there are also increasing similarities between women workers in Mexican agribusinesses and food processing plants and women working as supermarket cashiers and fast food service workers in Canada. They play key roles in the implementation of corporate flexible labor strategies. As a result, they experience similar contradictions in their efforts to fulfill their dual roles as salaried workers in the food system and as consumers or providers of food for their families. Wanda, a Canadian cashier, feels some common bonds with Tomasa, a Mexican tomato fieldworker:

> Tomasa used to make her own tortillas but now she has to go and work, so she buys ready-made tortillas. And she's feeling that pull just like the North American women are: Should I stay at home with the kids? Should I go to work? She's feeling the economic thing, because everybody has to survive, everybody has to eat. She's taking care of the

family, that's a priority in her life; I'd like to think that in my life that's a priority.[32]

Wanda has reached a point in her career, after twenty-three years as a part-time cashier, where she now has seniority and so may choose her hours. She "chooses" to work three eight-hour days instead of six four-hour shifts, for example, because she moved out of town a few years ago and must now commute one hour to work, adding two hours to her workday. That "choice" is framed by the fact that if she transferred to a Loblaws that was closer to her home, she would lose her seniority. She also "chooses" to work on weekends, because, as a single mother, it is the only time her former husband can take care of her children, saving her child-care expenses. Her "choice" of hours allows her to be at home during most weekdays:

> As a single parent, I'm taking my kids to school, doing the piano lessons, the Brownies, that kind of thing. So I know which days I don't want to come down to Toronto to work, because it's quite a ways for me. Or if they have a pd day [professional development day for teachers], I don't go into work that day.[33]

Here is where the flexibility of women's labor comes head to head with other social contradictions of an institutionalized sexist culture. Corporate managers, in fact, often point out that their flexible labor strategy suits women who "choose" to have more time with their families, and therefore don't want to work full-time. And there is certainly some truth to this. Even some feminists argue that flexibilization can be reappropriated by women and men, if it challenges the sexual division of labor in the home and promotes more shared responsibility, while also shortening the work week. But it usually has little to do with "choice" and is often based on the assumption that women, not men or public child care, will take care of children and feed their families.

In the Mexican context, there is even less of an illusion of "choice" for indigenous women who are at the bottom of the hierarchy of workers, both locally and globally. While Santa Anita Packers brings indigenous families to work during the harvest season, they provide neither adequate housing nor child care, and it has been a struggle to get the children into the local school. It has been reported that company foremen became angry with indigenous women workers who brought their children tied to their backs to the fields and who stopped work, periodically, to breastfeed them. Here, in the most basic sense, the primary role that women fulfill in feeding their children is regulated by the company's rules. And though they have little choice but to bring their children to the fields, they also take tremendous risks in doing so. When we visited their camp, one baby was reportedly dying because, as the indigenous workers explained, pesticide residue on the mother's hand had entered the child's mouth during breastfeeding.

Since NAFTA, and with the deepening impoverishment of the rural population in Mexico, these indigenous families are forced to migrate from one harvest to another for even longer periods of the year. Whereas previously they may have been able to remain home for a few months and raise some of their own food, they are now permanently moving, by necessity, ready to go to wherever there is work.

The mestizo workers who live near the Santa Anita plant and only work seasonally experience the insecurity in another way. Due to erratic weather conditions, their work periods have been cut short, and the jobs available for them peter out. Describing the situation, Tomasa said:

> In the end, we were working one or two days a week, and then not at all. They don't even say thanks 'til the day that they return. Only when they begin to plant again in the next season, they come with their truck to take us back to the fields, no?[34]

This sense of never knowing when you are going to work, and often in the case of indigenous migrant workers, even where, is a permanent condition of agricultural fieldworkers. Canadian cashiers and fast food workers may know a week or two in advance what their shifts are to be, but the constantly changing hours often affect family routines, interactions and, especially, eating practices. It is not uncommon for a family to have no time when they can all sit down to a meal together.

Whose interests are served by this flexible labor strategy? Flexibilization as it plays out in the continental food system, and particularly in the lives of women workers in this food chain from Mexico to Canada, must be seen as "an ideology propagated by firm owners as a desirable future end state, and supported by conservative probusiness forces and governments in order to assist the private sector in achieving this goal."[35] It is part and parcel of lean production, maximizing efficiency and profits and leaving the most vulnerable and marginalized workers bound to the shifting winds of just-in-time production. In the end, they become just-in-time workers with no time of their own.

And what are the real choices for women in this system? Wanda, the Loblaws cashier, has taken a keen interest in this study and has read the stories of the Mexican workers. She concludes:

> I feel an overwhelming sadness and connection to all the women in the "tomato food chain." We all play a seemingly small part, but the ramifications of our work are enormous.... We are all entrapped in the corporate workings of flexibilization. However, the dilemma still exists for all of us in the food chain: we're trying to survive.[36]

I gratefully acknowledge the tremendous efforts of the graduate research assistants who worked from 1995 to 1999 on the Tomasita Project, helping to shape it and carrying out the interviews referred to in this article. Special thanks to Emily Levitt, Deborah Moffet, Lauren Baker (Mexican interviews), Ann Eyerman (McDonald's interviews), Stephanie Conway (Loblaws interviews), Egla Martinez-Salazar (review of Mexican interviews), Karen Serwonka (McDonald's interviews), Anuja Mendiratta, and Melissa Tkachyk (glossary).

Excerpted from *Women Working the NAFTA Food Chain: Women, Food and Globalization,* Deborah Barndt, ed. (Toronto: Sumach Press, 1999). Reprinted by permission of Sumach Press.

NOTES

[1] Tania (pseudonym), interview with author, Toronto, Ontario, February 1998.

[2] Tomasa (pseudonym), interview with author, Gómez Farías, Mexico, April 1997.

[3] Sara (pseudonym), interview with author, San Isidro Mazatepec, Mexico, April 1997.

[4] See George Ritzer, *The McDonaldization of Society* (Thousand Oaks, CA: Pine Forge Press, 1993). Ritzer notes that the new model of rationalization in our culture is no longer the bureaucracy, as Max Weber suggested, but the fast-food restaurant. He outlines the characteristics of this work organization based on 1) efficiency (from the factory-farm production of the ingredients to the computer scanners at the counter), 2) predictability (from the ambience and the personnel to the limited menu), 3) calculability or quantity, 4) substitution of nonhuman technology (the techniques, procedures, routines, and machines make it almost impossible for workers to act autonomously), 5) control (the rationalization of food preparation and serving gives control over the employees), and 6) the irrationality of rationality (for example, we see McDonald's as rational despite the reality that the chemicals in the food are harmful and that we can gain weight from the high calories and cholesterol levels).

[5] The four dimensions of maquilization, developed by J. Carillo as he observed restructuring in the auto industry, are elaborated by Kathryn Kopinak in *Desert Capitalism: What Are the Maquiladoras?* (Montreal: Black Rose Books, 1997): 13.

[6] Gita Sen and Caren Grown, *Development, Crises, and Alternative Visions: Third World Women's Perspectives.* New York: Monthly Review Press, 1987: 25.

[7] Kirsten Appendini, "Revisiting Women Wage-Workers in Mexico's Agro-Industry: Changes in Rural Labor Markets," *Working Paper 95, no. 2.* Copenhagen: Centre for Development Research, 1995: 11–12.

[8] The categorizing of so-called "low-skilled" work needs to be problematized, particularly when describing the kinds of tasks allotted to women in food production. Job tasks that correlate with women's domestic labor have almost universally been devalued and their counterparts in paid work have suffered a similar fate. While reigning gender ideologies purport that women are "naturally" more suited to certain tasks, Elson and Pearson argue that the famous nimble fingers are not "an inheritance from their mothers," but rather "the result of training they have received from their mothers and other female kin since early infancy in the tasks socially appropriate to woman's role." See Diane Elson and Ruth Roach Pearson, "The Subordination of Women and the Internationalization of Factory Production," in Nalini

Visvanathan et al., eds., *The Women, Gender, and Development Reader* (Halifax: Fernwood Publishing, 1997): 191–203.

[9] For a classic analysis of this development in the 1980s, see Swasti Mitter, *Common Fate, Common Bond: Women in the Global Economy* (London: Pluto Press, 1986).

[10] For a further elaboration of this North–South contradiction, see Deborah Barndt, "Bio/cultural Diversity and Equity in Post-nafta Mexico (or: Tomasita Comes North while Big Mac Goes South)," in Jan Drydyk and Peter Penz, eds., *Global Justice, Global Democracy* (Halifax: Fernwood Publishing, 1997): 55–69.

[11] While the presence of North American fast-food restaurants in Mexico is more visible, there has also been an incursion of the retail giants. Few are aware, for example, that the big Mexican supermarket chain, Aurera, is now owned by Wal-Mart, the Arkansas-based company that has become synonymous with corporate takeover, spelling death for smaller retail chains.

[12] The "appropriation" of the "exotic other" is the subject of the postcolonial theory and cultural studies examination of how difference is constructed within the politics of consumption to entice us into buying the mythical (and essentialist) look, the purity, the passion, the natural freshness of Southern peoples and lands. For an analysis of how Loblaws, and particularly President's Choice, has led the retail market in packaging difference, see C. Sachetti and T. Dufresne, "President's Choice through the Looking Glass," *Fuse Magazine,* (May-June 1994): 23.

[13] Analyses by ecological economists have helped to unveil the "hidden costs" in the production of the food we eat. William Rees, for example, advocates that we measure the "ecological footprint" of the goods we consume, and feminist ecological economist Ellie Perkins reminds us of the unpaid labor of women in managing the household. A more popular version of this analysis can be found in the cartoon story, "Tomasita Tells All: True Confessions of Tomasita, the Abused Tomato," an ecofeminist tale told from the perspective of the tomato forced onto this continental conveyor belt. Parts of this story appear in Deborah Barndt, *Tangled Routes: Women, Work and Globalization on the Tomato Trail* (Boulder, CO: Rowman and Littlefield, 2002).

[14] Ecofeminism offers an analysis that links the historical domination of women with the human domination of nonhuman nature. Although there are many different schools of ecofeminist thought, I support an analysis that proposes an integrative, historically and culturally contingent analysis of structural oppressions based on gender, race, and class, as intertwined with the exploitation of nature as a "resource." I don't ascribe to the stream of ecofeminism that suggests women (as an essentialist category) are inherently (biologically) closer to nature. See Noel Sturgeon, *Ecofeminist Natures: Race, Gender, Feminist Theory and Political Action* (New York: Routledge, 1997).

[15] See Gary Gereffi and Miguel Korzeniewicz, eds., *Commodity Chains and Global Capitalism* (Westport, CT: Praeger Publishers, 1994).

[16] See Laura Reynolds, "Institutionalizing Flexibility: A Comparative Analysis of Fordist and Post-Fordist Models of Third World Agro-Export Production," in Gereffi and Korzeniewicz, eds., *Commodity Chains and Global Capitalism.* Westport, CT: Greenwood, 1993): 143–160.

[17] Elson and Pearson, "The Subordination of Women and the Internationalization of Factory Production": 192.

[18] For a useful discussion of Fordist and post-Fordist production practices, particularly in terms of the model of fast food-restaurants, see Ritzer, *The McDonaldization of Society*: 150–153.

[19] Jeremy Brecher, John Childs, and J. Cutler, eds., *Global Visions: Beyond the New World Order* (Montreal: Black Rose Books, 1993).

[20] Karen (pseudonym), interview with author, Toronto, Ontario, February 1998.

[21] Wanda (pseudonym), interview with author, Toronto, Ontario, May 1997.

[22] See Sara Lara, "La Flexibilidad del Mercado de Trabajo Rural": *Revista Mexicana de Sociología* 54, no.1 (January-February 1994): 29–48.

[23] Conrado Lomeli, interview with author, Guadalajara, Mexico, December 1996.

[24] Lourdes Beneria, "Capitalism and Socialism: Some Feminist Questions," in Visvanathan et al., eds., *The Women, Gender, and Development Reader*: 330.

[25] Lara, "La Flexibilidad del Mercado de Trabajo Rural": 41. Translated from the Spanish by the author.

[26] Single women are preferred as packers, for example, because they are moved from one production site to another and housed in company homes in women-centered families. In the case of Mexican farm laborers hired by the farms program in Ontario to pick and pack our vegetables during the Canadian growing season, however, widows are preferred, reflecting a *machista* attitude that they're safer than married or single women in a foreign job (Irena [pseudonym], interview with author, Miacatlán, Mexico, December 1998).

[27] According to Statistics Canada, women are more likely to work part-time, by a ratio of 3 to 1, compared with men. *The Globe and Mail*, reporting on the study, states that "part-time employment was most prevalent among sales and service occupations, particularly in the food-service industry and among grocery clerks." *The Globe* quotes Gordon Betcherman of Canadian Policy Research Networks: "Many employers want to hire staff to work less than 30 hours a week because they can be more flexible in scheduling around peak demand and because they have to provide fewer benefits" ("Part-time Work Stats Questioned," *The Globe and Mail*, 18 March 1998: 6). A related article notes that the most predominant female occupation is "retail sales clerk," with "waitress" as number seven on the list ("He's a Trucker, She Types," *The Globe and Mail*, 18 March 1998: 1).

[28] The harvest season has varied tremendously lately, due to erratic weather conditions that are often blamed on El Niño. Unseasonal freezes have cut short the tomato season, causing companies financial losses and sending workers either on to other harvests or home to their villages where they seek casual labor to carry them through until the next harvest. In Gómez Farías, the workers lost three months of expected fieldwork and were eking out a living making and selling straw mats (Tomasa, interview).

[29] With the economic crisis in Mexico and deepening gaps between the rich and the poor, agricultural workers are part of a "family wage economy," requiring all members to work for the survival of the family. In *Desert Capitalism: What Are the Maquiladoras?* Kathryn Kopinak shows that while in 1981, 1.8 family members had to work to feed a family of five, by 1996, the number was 5.4. Though Northern economies are described as "family consumer economies" rather than "family wage economies," it is increasingly the case that working-class families also depend on multiple salaries, which are often from combinations of part-time jobs.

[30] Lara, "La Flexibilidad del Mercado de Trabajo Rural": 42. Translated from the Spanish by the author.

[31] Ibid.: 41.

[32] Wanda (pseudonym), interview with author, Toronto, Ontario, October 1997.

[33] Ibid.

[34] Tomasa interview.

[35] Kopinak, *Desert Capitalism*: 116.

[36] Wanda (pseudonym), interview with author, Toronto, Ontario, August 1998.

A Xicanadyke Codex of Changing Consciousness

CHERRÍE L. MORAGA

This essay was originally presented as the Kessler Award Lecture, sponsored by the Center for Lesbian and Gay Studies of The City University of New York, on December 8, 2000.

I. The Color of a Nation

They thought of the desert as colorless,
blind from its high noon bright.

They saw no hue,
its original inhabitants equally invisible,
their footprints camouflaged by the dusty imprint of wagon wheels
and hoof tracks.

Her name was written there in the dust.
Did you see her, she who wrote without letters,
the picture of a disappearing planet?

She knew in advance what it would mean, their arrival.
She saw us, her pueblo, a cactus tuna bleeding in the heat.

In 1996, I wrote a memoir entitled *Waiting in the Wings: Portrait of a Queer Motherhood.*[1] The book, which was initiated by my now-seven-year-old son's premature and threatened birth in 1993, was completed three years later, marked by the death of my son's paternal grandfather and the death of a beloved uncle. And in this manner pass the generations, and our lives.

Wings was an extended narrative describing my growing relationship with my child through conception, his birth in Los Angeles, his many months in the hospital, through the first three years of his life, and his final emergence into a thriving boyhood. I learned to write fiction in that narrative, drawing from whatever skills about dramatic tension and character development I had garnered as a playwright. Through the act of writing that so-called autobiography, I learned that a story well told is a story embellished and re-visioned, just like the stories that rose from my mother's mouth in our family kitchen some forty years earlier. The fiction of our lives—how we conceive our histories by heart—can sometimes provide a truth far greater than any telling of a tale frozen to the facts.

Through writing *Waiting in the Wings*, I learned to reconfigure and rearrange dates, names, chronologies in the effort to create a narrative generated by a relentless faith in dreams, memory, and desire. Since the completion of that memoir, I have witnessed my journal entries moving away from an "I" fixed on the exact record of my experience to something, I hope, much deeper: I have encountered the "I" of character who is and who is not me, but one that allows me the freedom of incorrect politics and a bravery not realized in my own life. So, what I present to you today is as much an autobiographical narrative as it is a dream waiting to happen, based on some irrefutable facts. Here are several.

Fact. I am a middle-aged dyke living in Oakland with my beloved and her sometimes-grown son and her growing preteen granddaughter and my blood-son, Rafael Angel. Fact. I got it all. A $40,000 debt, not counting a mortgage, but a woman and a sunset I can witness every clear night la creadora provides right from my front porch, above it all. I sit *above it all,* above the bay's horizon and the Airport Hyatt and Alameda's military base (turned-back Indian territory) and the Fruitvale barrio. I live with the barrio in my horizon, just south of my Berkeley whitedyke days and eight miles east of my early woman-of-colorhood in San Francisco. I got history in this territory and a woman my age that's as old as the hills which is why I took her on new cuz she remembered the hills of her own girlhood in Sacramento and southward all the way to Sandias, Tephuanes. And that matters to both of us. She taught me how to smoke a stick of tobacco like you're praying to some god; although I knew it before. Somehow. When she taught me, I remembered like most things she taught me that it was a matter of remembering. She taught me how to burn fire, even in the city. She taught me the importance of fire on a daily basis. Something you had to keep watch over, tend, nurture, coax along, and control. Like a boy. Who'da thought we'd live this long, raising babies and our babies' babies into our middle age? Like I said, I got it all.

Fact. My literary and theater career has been "marred" as much by my cultural essentialism as by my sexualized undomesticized lesbianism, to say nothing of my habitual disregard for the requirements of genre and other literary conventions. I don't know that I am a good writer. I believe I have, at times, well-articulated moments of insight, but I am not always convinced, no matter how many letters I get from those lonely queer and colored ones telling me that my words save lives that, in fact, words can.

Fact. We are a colonized people, we mechicanos, my woman reminds me when I find my stomach tied in knots each time I sit down to write. I experience myself writing beneath the suffocation of a blanket of isolation and censorship. The most virulent is self-imposed and lacks the high drama of senator-sanctioned obscenity charges. The censorship I have experienced has come in the not-so-idle threats of gun-toting maddog envidiosa coloreddykes and in just plain ole commercial disregard, where the money you need to do the work you do ain't there for the kind of work you do. This has especially been the case with my work in theater. I don't know, really, who my friends are as a writer, those with whom I share common cause. I wonder why so many of us, Chicana/o writers, remain so enamored of white people, their privileges, their goodies: the seduction of success. Why do we remain confused about who we are? Not Black. Not Indian. Not white. Then what? I believe that our confusion causes our writing to fall miserably short of the truly revolutionary literature it could be. I tend to read American Indian writers these days because they aren't afraid to betray America and always Toni Morrison because she's stayed Black looking back.

Fact. I have always lusted for women and am grateful that there was a lesbian feminist movement in 1974, which at the age of twenty-one allowed me to recognize and act on this loving without shame, justified it without apology, and propelled me into oppositional consciousness with Patriarchy. Mostly, I am grateful to that movement for saving me from many years of heartbreaking repression, I'm sure.

I'm also grateful, plain and simple, for her, my beloved, that there was a Chicano movement that invited her entrance, politicized and betrayed her, right around the same time that the white entitlement of lesbianfeminism betrayed me. I am grateful for those first moments of consciousness, always born from a living experience of injustice turned to righteous rage, that first experience of genuine collectivism, that blessed epiphany of art-inspired action. And I am equally grateful for those early betrayals that forced both of us to keep on looking elsewhere for a radical revisioning of our lives. Those betrayals have shaped my political consciousness more profoundly than any easy solidarity. There is no home, I learned, except what we build with a handful of others through a tenacious resistance to compromise.

In the small world that is my family we live as if our values shape the world at large or more accurately as if our values chisel away at some monolithic monoculture we attempt to subvert with our art, our blood, our daily prayer. This may be the truest fiction we inhabit, but it sustains us. For now.

Another maker of fiction, Spokane/Coeur d'Alene Indian Sherman Alexie, writes: "I made a very conscious decision to marry an Indian woman, who made a very conscious decision to marry me. Our hope: to give birth to and raise Indian children who love themselves. That is the most revolutionary act." When I stumbled upon these lines in Alexie's collection of poems and essays, *One Stick Song*,[2] my heart opened at the pure courage and simplicity of the statement. I felt him my relative in the naming of what I, as a xicanalesbian, have kept secret for so long. For as taboo as it is to admit within the context of the firmly inscribed multiracial social democracy progressives paint of their imagined America, I had a child to make nation, one regenerated from the blood nations Mexicans in this country are forced to abandon. I had an Indian child to counter the loss of my family's working-class mexicanindianism with each succeeding generation. I had a Xicano child cuz Raza's turning white all over the states.

Sometimes I think it is the "social advantage" of looking white enough to travel unnoticed amongst them that has put me in the position to recognize on a visceral level how spiritually unrewarding the white nation is. It may feed your belly but not your soul, I tell my Chicano students. And beneath this writing, I hear my son ask of his beloved gringo grandpa, my father, "What about Papa Joe?" How do you teach a seven-year-old the difference between institutionalized ignorance, racism, bigotry, class arrogance, and the individual white people, breeds, and mixed-bloods that make up our family? How do you teach a child the word "genocide" and still give him reason to love beyond his front door?

The evolution of my own changing lesbianchicana consciousness led me to make the same basic decision Alexie made: "to marry an Indian woman and to give birth to, and raise Indian children who love themselves." Not necessarily in that order, but, I believe, prompted by the same moral imperative. I can't write those lines, however, without acknowledging that from the perspective of most North American Indians, Chicanos are perceived as second-class Indians at best or no Indian at all, i.e. "Hispanic." I also can't write those lines without conceding that when most heterosexuals of color discuss "breeding" as a revolutionary act, they aren't necessarily thinking of their lesbian sisters and gay brothers as comrades in those reproductive acts of sexual resistance (especially given the white-washing queer identity has had in the national consciousness). Historically, we may have been invited to bed by those cultural nationalists, but not to the tribal councils.

But for Indian children to love themselves, they must love their sex organs and their sexual desire. They must love their lesbian mothers and aunties and queer fathers and cousins. They must develop a living critical consciousness about their land-based history, (outside of the whiteman's fiction), a history that remains undocumented by mainstream culture and is ignored by the queer, feminist, and "Hispanic" communities. They must remember they were here first and always, whether they call themselves, Chicano, Diné, Apache, Yaqui, or Choctaw; for that memory can alter consciousness and consciousness can alter institutionalized self-loathing in the service of genocide. Our children must become rigorous abolitionists of the slavery of the mind. They must think the taboo thought and cultivate in their own lives a profound knowledge about who they are, outside the framework of the U.S. Nation-state. I don't know exactly how to teach a counter culture of courage to my children, but I am working on it. And in this, I am not alone.

For these reasons, I believe my conversation about strategies for revolution as a xicanadykemama resides more solidly within the cultural-political framework of American Indigenism (North and South) than in any U.S. gay and lesbian or feminist movement, which remain, at their cultural core, Euro-American, in spite of a twenty-five-year history of people-of-color activism in those movements. I have for the most part removed myself from conversation with the gay and lesbian feminist movement because most of its activists do not share my fears and as such do not share my hopes.

Genocide is what I'm afraid of, as well as the complete cultural obliteration of those I call my pueblo and the planet that sustains us. Gay men and lesbians (regardless of race) have, in the last two decades, become intimately connected to the question of survival because of the AIDS pandemic. But, as AIDS activists have already learned, sometimes the hard way, AIDS and the threat of death impact people-of-color communities differently, gay *and* heterosexual. AIDS is just one more murderous face in the long history of the systematic annihilation of poor and colored folk across the globe.

So, I fear AIDS as I fear gang violence as I fear the prison-industrial complex as I fear breast cancer. But I also fear the loss of Nuevo México to New York artists; the loss of MexicanIndian curanderismo to new age healers; the loss of Día de los Muertos to San Francisco-style Halloween; the loss of Native tribal and familia social structures to the nuclear family (gay and straight); the cultural loss of kids of color to mixed-race adoptions (gay and straight); the loss of art to commerce.

I think of Adrienne Rich's words from a generation ago, "Every woman's death diminishes me." Twenty years later, I would amend Rich's statement and assert with equal lesbian feminist passion, "Every barrio boy's death diminishes me." I never knew I would experience it this way, this intimate sense de un pueblo in the body of a boy. Maybe motherhood has changed me. And then, I think not, except for a growing compassion for those I have loved the most intimately in my life: Mexican women, madres, unspoken and unspoken for. This love is what fundamentally propelled me to be a lesbian in the first place and remains so. And so, I suffer their sons, their fathers, our men. But I continue, a resistant combatant.

Journal Entry

The police delivered Linda's son to our door just before dawn this morning. He returned home a broken boy, crying as his mother patched him up from a yanked IV. Twenty-six years old, but in our bathroom, he is a boy of sixteen, wondering what had gone wrong, everything was going all right— the job, the car, the room, the "stuff"—I was doing so good, he cried. I watch the back of his neck as his head falls onto his chest wet with tequila tears, the sun-darkened brown of his skin against the white shirt collar, still crisp with starch. I see in him my own son's elegantly sculpted neck, the same silk of brown-boy color. I want to look away from this meeting of genera-tions, this juxtaposition of contradictions. My son of seven sleeping safely between the sheets, my woman of forty-seven, hours later, on the street with her grown son in search of the car he had abandoned the night before after a tequila-and-testosterone-driven fist fight after macho bravado and father failure and mother abandonment. Oh, so he sees it.

A week later the white Latin American therapist asks Linda, "What are you afraid of?" "That he'll be killed," she answers. I watch the therapist's face. He thinks she's being exagerada. Metaphoric. My woman, a veterana of a war the therapist does not witness. How is it we feel that our son's ability to flourish, to achieve some kind of real ánimo in their lives, is on our backs to carry? Their failure, our failure. How do we separate mother-guilt, collective and individual, from a righteous resistance to genocide? I am reminded of my comadre, Marsha. How she acknowledged in her mid-forties that she would never be free of the burden of her boy, that her son's "condition," she called it, meant he would never be a fully functioning adult. I felt an unbearable sadness for her. He was diagnosed schizophrenic. Still, I sometimes wondered, was her son's condition anything more than colored and queer in América: mixed-blood, mad, and male? A year later, he has murdered her. Marsha, like me, like my woman: a xicanadykemama.

He was one of the lost tribe. No romance about it. One of the lost ones who are so many of our sons now. I gotta boy following him. Somehow think if I do good by Linda's boy, twenty-six going on sixteen, my little boy got a chance. But it's hard to live up to. Big boy ain't my blood. I tell his mother, "I didn't break it." But I know in that resides the lie. We all "broke it," him, them. And I'm only as good as the chance I give him, even if we fail. "His blood is on my hands." I write these words like the beginning of a fiction about the end of a fact, but the question of his survival remains for both of us—for me and his mother. Somehow, this notion of us as a people, un pueblo, makes us mutually collectively responsible for one another's survival. The privatization of the American household makes no sense to us. He is family because he is Raza, although he and his kind hold my own life and my lesbianism in contempt. A living contradiction: the mutuality of our responsibility to one another in an individualistic culture that divides and most surely continues to conquer us through those divisions. This son of ours, my antagonist and this country's volatile victim at once. This threatened and threatening machito, who is my gente, child, brother. I want to write "brethren," for it is biblical, this grand story of nations and dislocations, exile and homecomings.

II. Homecoming

On Día de los Muertos, my Linda gathers all the orphans together—Mexican Indians and a few dispossessed white folk—and we pray. It is a vigil of sorts. By 9:00 P.M. my son is already a bundle of bones and cobija on the hardwood floor. Linda's granddaughter, Camerina, on the threshold of her bloods, stays up. Is it the pending menstruation, the hormonal eruption of her organism, that keeps her up? She has something to strive for.

I strive only for my son some days. Some days the pure joy I experience watching him jump off the play structure in the school playground at the sight of my car pulling up to the curb, his running toward it at full speed, back pack falling off one shoulder, an earnestness in his face is enough. What is enough for me is this pure recognition of the moment: these monkey bars, this asphalt playground with painted-on kickball fields and tetherball circles, *this momma arriving to pick me up as promised, knowing the afternoon snack will be waiting, the two hours of homework sitting at the kitchen table with sorta sister across from me, we both working word-problems onto a sheet of xeroxed preguntas. Momma working all the time with her hands, as we with our minds, cleaning the kitchen, banging around pots and pans, chop chop chop ajo, cebolla, celery into our evening dinner. My mother is not a housewife. She is queer and writes books, and wants something more for herself and her children — something more than careers and portfolios and mortgages. And what she wants is enough for all of us for now.*

I am wondering what is happening in my middle age. I have changed. I have less hope, it seems, but deeper dreams in my writing. I reference my son as I do because I know this is a fleeting moment of well-being, extended in his blessed childhood, where he is awake and full of hope that propels him forward into his life like the gestating hormones of his almost-sister. My lover's hormones and mine are not gestating so much any more. They are, I imagine, taking leave of their previous missions, four babies en total between us. Is this why I am sad? This death of the illusion that we are not dying?

Days later, I am on a plane returning from Los Angeles and my mother's eighty-sixth birthday celebration. I measure the ages of the passengers around me. There are those striving upward, ignorant of death. They are making money, careers, plans. There are those whose careers are what they have been. Their bodies worry them so. They try not to think about it, its enormous weight (the daily discomfort of those extra thirty pounds), its aching left hip, frozen knee, the sudden palpitations of the heart.

My mother is eighty-six years old today and continues to change into a woman I've never met, but must quickly learn to know. She repeats descriptions of events from yesterday and last week over and over again because they still interest her as she remembers them brand new with each telling. She asks the same question two and three times within a ten-minute span of a conversation. She brings out the same cup of coffee to serve someone, forgetting in the trip from kitchen to dining room who the someone was, although she's already asked and been told twice. The coffee she offered to serve me goes cold.

My mother is eighty-six years old today. My mother and Linda's son teach me daily not to expect anything. She is a deep bruise in my heart, he the constant ache of uncertainty. As I return home to Oakland, the sun sets pink and purple outside my window as I read Chicano poet Alfred Arteaga's new collection of verse.[3] He writes, "Gato and Xeritzín and all other souls alive, live only in the inks, in the red and the black, for only in codices do bodies truly animate." Then, I think, can't we just make art? There is a prayer in the writing. How is it I stray so far away? How is it I do not daily drag my woman into this prayer of art that sustains in the face of grave disappointment, all the small dyings of heart?

III. Some of My Best Friends Are

Nearly thirty years out of the closet and I really don't know what I have left to say to the white gay and lesbian community, except that I continue to be one, a lesbian, that just last night, on the eve of my woman's forty-eighth birthday, I made love to her like I remember wanting it as an adolescent. Thirty years ago, desire was a sad dream, thinking how queer (in the pre-eighties sense of the word) it was to want as I did.

Lesbian. Dyke. Queer. I'll go to the grave queer, I announce, fully knowing that no one can shake me from that rock bottom place of conviction about my desire. My racial identity has always been more ambiguous. The ground it stands on is built upon a memory for which I can make no clear accounting. I never met one of my Yaqui ancestors; never a relative who named us anything but Mexican so Mexican it is, but since my earliest childhood I knew Mexican meant Indian. And it was that naming of "Chicano" in the seventies that reminded me of that fact and that sent most of my relatives into political hiding. So, I knew "Indian" was dangerous, like lesbianism. Knew it could not be domesticated, tamed, colonized. Like "dyke." People (white, Black, and Brown alike) have tried to dislocate me from Chicanisma, half-breed that I am; but it is getting harder and harder to do so. I'm getting older. I've been standing on this ground for too long now. There are enemies from within and without. I've slept under the same roof and in the same bed with people for whom I remain unknown and unknowable. The bitter irony is that they never knew that they didn't know me. And *that's* a fact.

Several years ago, my compadre, Chicano playwright Ricardo Bracho, asked me how I identified myself politically, as a "Chicana lesbian" or a "lesbian Chicana"? As wordsmiths, of course, these distinctions mattered to us. I remember there was some discussion about how Spanish forces one to choose because Lesbiana and Lésbica occupy distinct locations as parts of speech, the first a noun, the second an adjective. English, on the other hand, allows for a bit more ambivalence, where the same *lesbian* is used for both the noun and the adjective and its signification relies exclusively on syntax. At the time, nearly a decade ago, we both agreed that I was surely a Chicana lesbian, in that order, where *Chicana* is the cultural *modifier* of the indisputable fact of my les-bianism. In a call for just such cultural specification, critiquing white middle-class women's cultural hegemony of lesbian sexuality, I wrote in 1982: "What I need to explore will not be found in the lesbian feminist bedroom, but more likely in the mostly heterosexual bedrooms of South Texas, L.A., or even Sonora, México."[4]

What I didn't know was how a thorough exploration of that sexuality on the sheets of my bed and the sheets of my writing would eventually separate me from the lesbian and gay movement. In contrast to what Ricardo and I had concluded in that kitchen conversation in the early 1990s, today I feel that my lesbianism modifies a growing Chicanisma, where the revolutionary consequence of my *cultural* identification generates my activism, my art, *and* my sexuality.

I still got white friends. Some of them are here tonight. Queer girls who sleep with each other and some who sleep with men, and who remain my friends because they are not safe women. They are not secure at night. They do not believe middle-class security will secure them. They are not fooled by professions and insurance policies and retirement funds. They are not fooled into believing that post-modern theory is the same as radical action or that tenure is a tent against the elements of oppression. And so, they remain my allies, these white women. Still, I don't see them that much any more.

There was a time, here in New York in the early 1980s, where I ran with a buncha white and Black literary girls and we had shared purpose cuz I was still thinking kind of black and white back then, never naming, except with great pains in my own private writings, what really wracked my soul at night: A desire for return more primordial than any simple cross-country relocation to Califas could fulfill. A longing for that Mexican Indian mother waiting for me at home in the body of my relatives here and gone, in the body of a woman my age and wanting.

For me, New York in the early 1980s was *Conditions* magazine, Kitchen Table: Women of Color Press, and New York Women Against Rape. It was a growing feminism of color that grew in its autonomous conversation just amongst us coloredgirls. And as that conversation evolved, so grew an activism, which separated many of us from white women, drawing us closer and closer not only to one another, but also to our specific cultural experience as Chicanas, cubanas, Lakota, English- and Spanish-speaking Afro-Caribbean women; as Chinese American and immigrant South East Asian.

In that specificity, I learned that for the most part, when white women spoke of women of color and racism, they were usually thinking black/white relations and, too often, African Americans were equally politically engaged in the same bipolared version of the history of U.S. race relations. Four years after the publication of *This Bridge Called My Back*,[5] it seemed that, in spite of my *theoretical* faith in an international feminism of color proposed by *Bridge* (which I still believe in), in *practice* my feminism of color was taking on a decidedly mechicana formation.

In the meantime, at night me and the Puerto Rican girls, and the Black girls that could dance salsa, went out and made out in bathrooms and somehow in that there was a place to be me. And I thank Sandra and Alma y las dos Mirthas for that. I thank Leota for an "Indianness" I couldn't even put a name to then, but knew my heart was working to live out in another decade. I thank even all "the women who hate me," to quote Dorothy Allison's book of poems.[6] Maybe cuz inspiring hatred gotta mean something was given and got up and gone when you left and that's somehow a tribute to what once was.

IV. What Once Was

Reading Amber Hollibaugh's *My Dangerous Desires*,[7] the history of a poor-whitegypsytrashfemcommiedyke rendered in the manner of a beautiful adventure book. It is my friend Amber's history and fantasy at once. The facts that make up her fiction. Closing the book, I think, *A damn worthy life. And she ain't even dead yet.* And through the history told of this complex and compelling woman and activist, the history of a movement is documented. I must confess I was a bit jealous of Amber's story; that for all its class betrayals, the gay and lesbian movement—that one movement—is where Amber finally found home. I was jealous because no movement has ever sustained me like that. My history, a solo journey it seems, traversing many movements of diverse, seemingly contradictory identities.

A few weeks ago, my Linda returned home with the news of Dolores Huerta's critical condition. She is mostly recovered now, but early that day I had a premonition of sorts, for some reason, about Dolores. I remembered Cesar Chavez' funeral, how I was unable to attend. How the "circumstances" of my life had prevented it. Today those "circumstances" have changed. Thinking of Dolores, I told myself that when she passed, I wanted to be present con mi familia, that this time I had a familia to be present with. Selfish thoughts about the markers of meaning in our own lives. These leaders: Both persons (our friends) and at the same time symbols. Audre Lorde was a symbol and a person and a friend. Artist-activist Marsha Gómez' intimate death continues to symbolize something great and powerfully humbling in my life. Maybe I, too, am a symbol to others, to young ones, as I age. I don't write this to aggrandize myself, only knowing that we are all just moments in a small and devastating history of a planet and its people.

I watch my mother aging daily and I live inside her body, watch the markings of my own body like the prediction of the future she already lives. I can't wait for her to die to write of that history. I can't wait to be a centenarian to remember. I remember now a future I fear I will witness and I quiet my justified paranoia by writing counter-tales of courage I may never live up to. It is autobiography in the truest sense: a record of my imaginings, as much as that of my experience. So that when I write in the voice of some one-hundred-year-old xicanadyke, armed and barricaded in her desert adobe, her lover of sixty years by her side, it is as much "me" as I can conjure in the best and worst of scenarios.

> *We are in a war against the U.S. government. We knew (hoped) it would finally come to pass, this meaningful way to end our lives here. Too horrible to think of dying without a fight, without reason for fighting. When I turned fifty, I began to mourn my ancestors, the recent ones known in my lifetime, who left with little resistance, except an entrenched bitterness. Flor and I shared this, this commitment to not die as one of them, to leave for our ungrateful children a legacy of self-defense, por lo menos.*[8]

The old women of this story, as much as the personal and political portraits painted in an essay, are my Xicanadyke codices of changing consciousness. As a child clandestinely dreaming of women in the early 1960s, I could never have imagined how "legitimate" in some select circles queerness would become. I also never knew how the color of that queerness (and its political conse-quences) would once again render my desire not only unlawful, but thoroughly revolutionary in its political promise.

A codex is a history told and foretold. I know a little bit about where I've been in the almost-fifty-years that is my life. I don't know where we're going. I can only guess, which is why I write, to guess at a future for which we must prepare. To that end, may we strive always for illegitimacy and unlawfulness, in this criminal culture. May our thoughts and actions remain illicit. May we continue to make art that incites censorship and threatens to bring the army beating down our desert door.

© 2001 by Cherríe L. Moraga.

<hr>

NOTES

[1] Cherríe Moraga, *Waiting in the Wings: Portrait of a Queer Motherhood.* Ithaca, NY: Firebrand Books, 1998.

[2] Sherman Alexie, *One Stick Song.* New York: Hanging Loose Press, 2000.

[3] Alfred Arteaga, *Frozen Accident: Philosophy of Spatial Act.* Unpublished.

[4] Cherríe Moraga, *Loving in the War Years: Lo Que Nunca Pasó por Sus Labios,* 2nd ed. Boston: South End Press, 2001: 117.

[5] Cherríe Moraga and Gloria Anzaldúa, eds., *This Bridge Called My Back: Writings by Radical Women of Color,* New York: Kitchen Table/Women of Color Press, 1983.

[6] Dorothy Allison, *The Women Who Hate Me: Poetry 1980–1990.* Ithaca, NY: Firebrand Books, 1991.

[7] Amber Hollibough, *My Dangerous Desires: A Queer Girl Dreaming Her Way Home.* Durham, NC: Duke University Press, 2000.

[8] From *A Cactus Tuna Bleeding in the Heat,* a work in progress.

From the First Intifada to the Second Intifada: Notes from an American Jew

LISA ALBRECHT

Forgetfulness leads to exile, while remembrance is the secret of redemption.

—Baal Shem Tov—plaque on the wall leaving
Yad Vashem, the Holocaust Memorial
Museum in Jerusalem[1]

This revised essay combines several pieces I've written over the past decade about the Israeli-Palestinian conflict. Together, I hope these words give readers a sense of the work of progressive Jews worldwide who are working for peace in the Middle East.

September 18, 2001—A Week After 9/11

I heard from Suha Hindeyeh, my old friend in Palestine, today. What a surprise! I had given up on getting a cyber-response, since I had e-mailed her several months ago. We met when I went on the women's peace brigade to Israel/Palestine in 1990. We hadn't talked in several years. The reason I wrote was to ask her for a new piece of writing about how Palestinian women activists are responding to the second *Intifada.* The editors of *Sing, Whisper, Shout, Pray!* were hungry to include current news about how the Palestinian women's committees were organizing. In the early 1990s, Suha had been the director of the Palestinian Women's Resource Center in East Jerusalem; it was a hub of feminist activism against the occupation. This is her e-mail to me:

> I have not written anything new. I am teaching at Birzeit University since last year. Things here are very worse. We have never witnessed such brutality. I am very sorry for what happened in Washington and NYC. It is really a human tragedy.

> Since the opening of the University, we cannot commute between Jerusalem, Ramallah and Birzeit, even on foot. Israeli soldiers are shooting, bombing and shelling. The University is practically closed by the occupation without announcing it because the road to Birzeit is closed. I send you an appeal by the University if something can be done.

> Birzeit University – Urgent Appeal – Lift the siege on education. Open the road to Peace through concrete action to protect the civilian population and civil life in Palestine. On 15 September

2001, more than 5000 students and over 700 faculty and staff commence a new academic year at Birzeit University—and will face a hard, humiliating and often dangerous journey by foot through two Israeli checkpoints as they attempt to reach their campus, classes, offices and laboratories.

Since March, 2001, students and teachers alike have borne the hardship of the closure of the main Ramallah-Birzeit road, and in these times, the only vital access to the University. Over the summer, the situation worsened and harassment and hardship have been institutionalized both for the Birzeit University community and for the residents of the 35 rural villages that use this road as their lifeline into Ramallah's services, jobs and supplies....

The Birzeit community has acted in peace, unity and dignity against the closure and for the right to education, freedom of movement and respect for persons. Over the past months, peaceful demonstrations, organized by the University and its friends, resulted in the filling in of the trenches that Israeli military bulldozers had gouged out of the road.... However, subsequent peaceful protests against the ongoing check point closure—including delivering notice to the soldiers on guard that their actions contravene international law—have not had long-term results....

We call on the international community to defend human rights by taking immediate action against this closure, which clearly violates the Fourth Geneva Conventions, to which Israel is a signatory, as well as the Universal Declaration of Human Rights.... (see www.birzeit.edu for updates.)

Spring, 1992—One Year After the Gulf War

These words are from an unpublished essay, and from a speech I delivered to the Minnesota River Peace Coalition on the first anniversary of the Gulf War.

My trip to Israel and Palestine in December, 1990 was a turning point in my life. In many ways, it also marked a turning point in my work. *Sing, Whisper, Shout, Pray!* was a process that began in December, 1987, the same month that the Intifada started in occupied Palestine. Since then, as part of this editorial collective, and as a white American Jew, I have sought ways to understand the relationship between anti-Semitism and racism in the U.S., and how it is connected to the Israeli-Palestinian conflict. I believe that they are intricately linked; American Jews cannot call ourselves antiracist and expect to find allies in people of color and non-Jews if we do not address the Israeli government's repression of the Palestinian people and the U.S. government's support of that repression.

What happened on my trip? Sixteen days before the Gulf War officially began with the bombing of Iraq, I was a member of a women's peace brigade, sponsored by the Middle East Children's Alliance, that went to Israel and Palestine. I walked through the Old City in Jerusalem. I touched the Western Wall, said a prayer for peace, and felt the presence of Jewish soldiers with guns all around me. My feet echoed off the marble floors of Yad Vashem, the Holocaust Memorial Museum, where images of Jewish resistance in the Warsaw Ghetto moved me to tears. At Yad Vashem, I searched the computer files for information about my father's family; he had met his half-sister, my Aunt Freida, for the first time when he was sixty-five years old. I wanted to know if there were other Albrechts from Gassi, Romania, and if there was a trail that led to any concentration camps, or beyond. I was unable to locate any new information. And so, my family history remains a mystery.

I stood vigil with Israeli Jewish Women in Black, feminist leaders of the Israeli peace movement, who protest the occupation and have been harassed and threatened by right-wing Israelis. These women stand vigil silently in many locations throughout Israel every Friday, before *Shabbat*. They are an intergenerational group—I talked with eight-year-old children, as well as eighty-year-old women, all carrying signs that said, "End the Occupation."

I met with Palestinian leaders of the Intifada and the peace movement, generous and kind people who knew I was a Jew, and respected and understood that there *are* U.S. and Israeli Jews who oppose the Israeli government's occupation of Palestine. They said again and again, "It is my duty…to tell you these stories." I walked through the Dheishah, Jelazone, and Jabalya refugee camps in the West Bank and Gaza; I saw children with rocks in one hand, waving the other hand with a "V" for peace, their eyes angry, yet filled with such a longing for an end to their pain.

What I found most startling about the Palestinian resistance was how much it looked and felt like the pictures I saw in Yad Vashem of Jewish resistance in the Warsaw ghetto. The hollow, dark brown eyes staring out. Hungry. Angry. Suffering. Jews in Poland fighting extermination, sealed in ghettos, with no escape. Palestinians fighting for statehood, barricaded in refugee camps, with no escape. The contradictions felt enormous. Palestinians today and Polish Jews yesterday, both struggling with dignity for their very existence. Except today, the oppressors are Jews.

I met with Palestinian leaders of the women's committees. Some were mothers whose sons had died, martyrs of the Intifada. These women served us

Turkish coffee in their one-room hovels in refugee camps, and apologized for not having more to feed us. They are often placed under twenty-four-hour curfew for days on end; during the Gulf War, the Israeli military quarantined them for over three weeks—no work and wages, no food, no doctors' visits. Few Palestinians work for living wages today, since many jobs have been lost to new Jewish settlers. Schools have been closed by the Israeli government during the Intifada, for fear that they are places where terrorist activities occur. Even the kindergartens.

The women leaders answered our questions with great dignity and passion, and urged us to go back to the U.S. and speak out, while their children played outside in the gutter, open sewage running between their legs. The mothers told us they do not urge their children to throw rocks and become martyrs; they fear for their sons' and daughters' lives, and understand their rage.

Since the Gulf War, I have spent many hours speaking before diverse audiences about these issues. I have attempted to honor the Palestinian people and their Israeli Jewish supporters by speaking out. During the war and for several months after it officially ended, I carted out my slide show for antiwar groups, feminist organizations, churches, and academics. I also spoke to a few Jewish groups, though not very many. They were not eager to invite me to talk, and many never returned my phone calls; they did not want to face the stories I wanted to tell them. They did not want to believe how the Israeli government is treating the Palestinian people.

I'd go to each of my talks feeling anxious, but eager to tell my story and show images of what we often do not see in the American media. I worried that I'd be verbally attacked by a Jew or an Arab person in the crowd. I feared that Arabs would challenge me because I always acknowledged anti-Semitism towards Jews while I addressed the violence directed at Palestinians. Would Arab people get angry because I focused on Jewish as well as Arab oppression? It never happened. The Arab people who heard me speak genuinely supported me. They did not ignore my references to anti-Semitism, nor did they deny that anti-Semitism exists.

However, the Jewish response to my talks was significantly different. I was often challenged, told that my history was incorrect and that I was lying about how Israeli Jews treat Palestinians. I'd come home after each "show" and get sick to my stomach. I naively thought that after showing the slides so many times, I would become immune to the images. I thought more Jews would support my work. Neither has happened.

When the first Scud missiles hit Tel Aviv, on January 23, 1991, the front page of the *Minneapolis Star Tribune*, like newspapers across the U.S., showed a sobbing, blood-covered Israeli Jewish woman holding an injured child in her arms. There was also a featured article about me in the same day's paper, "Making Peace with the Arabs: American Jew Wants Israel to Give Up Occupied Lands," with my picture covering a quarter of a page. After having read a story printed earlier in the week that implied that all Minnesota Jews totally supported the Israeli government and its persecution of Arab "terrorists," I had contacted the paper and urged them to report on the "other" Jewish perspective. After having been interviewed at my university office, I felt positive that the state's largest daily was willing to cover the story of a Jew who supports a two-state solution.

Now, several days after the interview, I walked across campus to my car and started listening for the latest war news. When I heard that a suburb of Tel Aviv had been bombed and that Jews had died, I started to throw up. I did not sleep that night; I watched CNN war news for hours, and inside my head, wrote and rewrote the reporter's story about me. By 5:00 A.M., I was driving around the neighborhood looking for an open corner store so I could find the newspaper.

It's hard to convey how scared I was that night. Yet, I also know my fear is nothing compared to the fear that Palestinians face each day in the West Bank, Gaza, and the Golan Heights.

Few American Jews speak out against the Israeli government. Those of us who do speak out rarely get mainstream media coverage. We are often labeled by other Jews as self-hating, anti-Semitic Jews, and as traitors to Israel. How dare I speak about Israeli violence towards Palestinians? How dare I speak, after only fifteen days there? How dare I speak out when Jews have been bombed in Israel?

Today, too many U.S. Jews and mainstream Jewish institutions have remained silent about the injustices of the Israeli government, a government that purports to speak on behalf of Jews across the globe. We are often afraid of anti-Semitism, the backlash against Jews. It is real, not merely a paranoid figment of Jewish imaginations, and it is on the rise globally. The Anti-Defamation League continually reports rises in anti-Semitic hate crimes in the U.S.[6]

We often react to any criticism of the Israeli government by saying that it is anti-Semitic. Our collective memory as a people is stamped with two thousand years of Jew-hating. Our twentieth-century consciousness is indelibly marked by the Holocaust and the fears that we might again become victims. U.S. Jews are taught by Jewish institutions to identify with Israel, "our" Jewish state, our safety net. We react to the idea of Palestinian statehood as if we are still victims. We fear that if we lose any Israeli land, we might lose all Jewish freedom. We often act like Israel is militarily weak, and on the brink of being swallowed up by its surrounding Arab neighbors. We emphasize Arab anti-Semitism, and rarely acknowledge that anti-Arab racism in Israel and the U.S. is part of the tinder that ignites the continuous violence.

This victim mentality pervades Jewish life. By acting as if Jews are victims, we justify Israeli violence against Palestinians. What I saw in Israel confirmed my worst fears. It is a military state, one of the most militarized on earth. By institutional design, Jews are not victims in Israel. Jews control land, water, the army, and all aspects of the political system. Yet, many Israeli Jews still see themselves as weak and powerless. And many U.S. Jews see ourselves as extensions of the Israeli people.

Fear of anti-Semitism is an excuse for not acting in the name of justice for Palestinians. Freedom for Palestinian people will also mean freedom for Jews. We are inextricably bound. The Palestinian people and their leadership acknowledge the existence of Israel. They want Jews to recognize their right to a state also. I believe that the only way we can stop the violence is if we agree to exist as two states, side by side. Yes, that means we must make a leap of faith. *Tikkun olum,* repair of the world, is a belief system that many Jews identify with. It is our ethical and moral responsibility as Jews to work for justice for all peoples globally.

For non-Jews engaged in the struggle for Palestinian statehood, I urge you to understand how Jewish history has shaped the different Jewish responses to the Israeli-Palestinian struggle. Challenge anyone, Jew or non-Jew, who uses anti-Semitism as an excuse for unequivocal support of Israeli policy. But you need to understand that to be my ally, you need to fight anti-Semitism also. Do not be silent.

Silence is as deadly as a gunshot to the heart. Silence kills—both Arabs and Jews. Silence is complicity. Each day many Palestinian families have lost their homelands of many generations in Gaza, the Golan Heights, and on the West Bank. Every day, Palestinian villages are surrounded by new Jewish settlements. Silence allows hatred to grow. Silence allows the chasms that separate Jews and Arabs to widen and solidify.

On this one-year anniversary of the terrible destruction of Iraq, and since the war and the unwarranted deaths of at least a hundred thousand Iraqi children, I urge each of you to never be silent. My friend Suha Hindeyeh, director of the Palestinian Women's Resource Center in East Jerusalem, taught me the Arabic word for teacher—*mu'alima*. It is my duty as a teacher/mu'alima, and our collective duty, to never be silent.

November 9, 2000—The Beginning of the Second Intifada

Remarks made at a University of Minnesota teach-in.

I am an American Jew who wants a just peace between Israel and Palestine. I have spoken out in this community for a two-state solution to the Israeli-Palestinian conflict since the first Intifada, which began in the fall of 1987. I am one of thousands of Jews all over the world who do not support Israeli government policy. We do not take the position of the mainstream U.S. Jewish community, which unequivocally supports Israel. We do *not* support the Israeli government's inhumane repression of the Palestinian people. We do *not* support the U.S. government's use of billions of dollars, our tax dollars, to fund Israel's violent military and economic domination of the Palestinian people. We challenge the U.S. media's incredibly one-sided coverage of this conflict. We work hard every day to get more information that accurately reflects what is really going on in Israel and Palestine.

In December, 1990, I was a member of a feminist peace brigade that visited and worked with Israeli and Palestinian women peace activists. This was my first trip to the Middle East; it occurred fifteen days before the Gulf War. I went on this two-week trip because I needed to be a witness, to see first-hand, if I was to continue to speak out for two states. We met with feminist members of the *Knesset*, the Israeli Parliament. We met with grassroots Jewish and Palestinian women activists in Jerusalem, the West Bank, and Gaza.

I consider myself a spiritual Jew, and a lover of peace, and a critic of Israel. I think you can be all of these things at once, though it is difficult. I have often been criticized by mainstream Jewish leaders, called pro-Palestinian, and accused of being anti-Semitic towards my own people.

On December 17, 1990, as part of the peace brigade, I went to Yad Vashem, the Holocaust Museum in Jerusalem. This day changed my life. I am going to read briefly from my journal from ten years ago:

"Forgetfulness leads to exile, while remembrance is the secret of redemption." This quote, by Baal Shem Tov, was on the wall as I left Yad Vashem today. Such contradictions. Earlier today, my first full day here, I saw Israeli soldiers with guns. I am already growing numb to it. So many soldiers with guns. It is a war zone. And the Palestinians are the victims today, like we Jews were yesterday.

I do not yet understand how and why the Jews of Israel (and the U.S.) do not see the connections. They say that remembering leads to redemption, but this historical moment tells me that the Jews in power have forgotten, and are becoming spiritually exiled.

I dreamt last night that when I awoke today I saw a beautiful bird. The Palestinians who are our guides in the Occupied Territories have been gracious, kind and open. The Old City was closed today. There was a general strike to protest the deportation of a number of Palestinians by the Israeli government. The Old City is walled, and "protected" further by soldiers everywhere. They search all Arabs at the gates. We went through without being checked. All the Palestinian storefronts were closed in solidarity with the strike. Old men wandered about, smoking cigarettes and talking among themselves. Children, mostly boys, ran around us, disappearing into narrow corridors; they beg for candy, then spit at the ground and say, "President Bush, President Bush." When pro-Palestinian graffiti appears on the walls, soldiers order Palestinians to paint over the signs in black immediately. The Muslim quarter is poor and rundown; it looks so much like the Jewish ghettos of Warsaw that I saw today at Yad Vashem.

In Lod, one hour from Jerusalem in Israel (not the Occupied Territories, but in Israel), we bussed to the Palestinian side of town. Shanties. Not much electricity. No running water in many homes. Nadja invited us into her home. She tells us that her kids always ask her why the Jewish kids across town have big schools and parks. Why do they have clinics and we don't? Why are their homes spacious? It felt like the deep South during the Civil Rights Movement in this country. Total segregation and apartheid. I don't understand; Why can't the Jews in power see?

It is now ten years later; the images are similar, except now the Israeli army uses live ammunition, Apache helicopters, and tanks made in the U.S.A. and purchased by our aid. The poverty and despair are worse for Palestinians, especially since the 1993 Peace Accord. Many of us believed there would really be a Palestinian state in our lifetimes. Now, there is *more* rage. I still think about the terrible, stark contrasts: pictures of Jewish freedom fighters in the Warsaw ghetto, and pictures of Palestinians fighting for their freedom in the refugee camps. They look the same.

I believe in my heart that many U.S. Jews live in total terror because of the memories we carry from the Holocaust. We have created a collective psychology that says, "Always look over your shoulder; someone is going to get you again. Just like the Nazis did." My mother told me this as a child. I believe that we have turned our fears inward and recreated ourselves as the "victim." Poor Israel, surrounded by all the Arabs. Poor Israel, being attacked by stone-throwing children. Poor Israel, being driven to the sea by millions of Palestinian terrorists. We have survived by doing unto others what was done to us. However, the reality is quite different. Israel is the most militarized country in the Middle East, bolstered by millions of U.S. dollars to arm itself.

The U.S. media tells us stories constantly of Israel, the victim. The media supports the U.S. government's support of Israel. We buy the images.

We must face the real truths. Since the second Intifada started, more than seven thousand Palestinians have been wounded, with an alarming number injured in the head and knees with live ammunition. Physicians for Human Rights "finds that the Israeli Defense Force has used live ammunition and rubber bullets excessively and inappropriately to control demonstrators, and that based on the high number of documented injuries to the head and thighs, Israeli soldiers appear to be shooting to inflict harm, rather than solely in self-defense."[2]

Media around the world tell these stories, but not U.S. media. We must challenge this. There are Jews in the U.S. and in Israel whose voices we have not heard. Progressive U.S. Jews draw our organizing strategies by listening to what Israeli and Palestinian activists are doing in Israel and Palestine. For example, the Israeli Committee Against House Demolitions, coordinated by American Jew Jeff Halper, says:

What must we do?

- International NGOs, faith-based organizations and political groups must join their extensive but scattered and poorly-focused networks into a coherent, adamant Campaign Against the Occupation. Each country must form a campaign team and those teams must develop a working framework of cooperation and joint action. The international and country-based teams should then establish contacts with Palestinian and Israeli organizations for purposes of

  - articulating our immediate concerns and demanding an end to the occupation now;

  - coordination;

  - the development of informational and campaign materials;

  - the dispatching of local delegations (Palestinian, Israeli and joint) for the purposes of lobbying, media work and appearing in public forums abroad. Effective lobbying in the American Congress, the European Parliament and in European capitals is essential. I would urge that joint Palestinian-Israeli delegations be sent with a simple, compelling message: we are on the same side, the side that aspires to a just peace that addresses the right of self-determination of the Palestinian people while bringing security, stability and economic development to the entire region;

  - the dispatching of international delegations to Palestine to engage in resistance actions, and to develop with them effective follow-up actions back home.

We also need more effective means of raising funds for our work, and of focusing our funding on campaigns and actions that bear directly upon the urgent task of ending the Occupation.

• Palestinian organizations must focus their efforts on a Campaign to End the Occupation Now, pulling together the agendas of their many organizations into a coordinated and effective effort. In my opinion, a close working relationship between Palestinian NGOs and those Israeli organizations that share in their agenda of ending the Occupation is essential for effective advocacy.

• Israeli peace and human rights organizations must also develop a more effective framework of action. Besides our scattered protest activities, we must find ways to effectively communicate with the Israeli public, and we must be much more involved in international networking and campaigns, including production of better informational materials. We must also seek ways to support Palestinian organizations.[3]

Since the Oslo Peace Accords, two hundred thousand new Jewish settlers have moved into the West Bank, where an extraordinary configuration of highways has been created by the Israeli government to cut off Palestinian communities from each other. This road system has military monitored checkpoints, not unlike the system that was dismantled in South Africa when apartheid ended. This system is also responsible for cutting off Palestinian access to water, another control by Israel to escalate Palestinian outrage.

All these actions are in direct opposition to the declaration of principles signed by the state of Israel and the Palestinian delegation on September 13, 1993: "The aim of the Israeli-Palestinian negotiations...is...to establish a Palestinian Interim Government...for a transitional period not exceeding five years, leading to a permanent settlement based on U.N. Security Council Resolutions 242 and 338...."

Resolution 242, passed on November 22, 1967, "emphasized the inadmissibility of the acquisition of territory by force" and "affirmed the Principle of Withdrawal of Israeli forces from territories occupied in the 1967 conflict."[4]

In the U.S., American Jews have formed a new national organization, *Brit Tzekek v'Shalom* (Jewish Alliance for Peace and Justice). Its founding principles are articulated as follows:

• Brit Tzedek v'Shalom supports the work of Israeli and Palestinian organizations that share our principles. We believe that the following principles and action are required in order to resolve the Israeli-Palestinian conflict in an equitable and nonviolent way:

- A complete end to the Israeli military occupation of the territories occupied since 1967 in the West Bank, the Gaza Strip and East Jerusalem with border adjustments agreeable to both parties.

- The establishment of a viable Palestinian state based on the pre-1967 borders alongside Israel with both states guaranteed the ability to maintain secure and recognized boundaries free from threats or acts of force.

- The establishment and recognition of Jerusalem as the capital of both states. Such recognition must also insure unfettered access to all religious sites in Israel and in the future Palestinian state to all Jews, Muslims and Christians, regardless of the nationality or sovereignty of the sites.

- A just resolution of the Palestinian refugee problem that takes into account the needs and aspirations of both peoples. Such a resolution is crucial to achieving a just peace, and therefore must acknowledge Israel's share of responsibility for the plight of Palestinian refugees while also respecting the special relationship between the State of Israel and the Jewish people.

- The termination of terrorism and state-initiated violence against all individuals with special care being taken to avoid harming civilians. We seek to build a future in which both peoples use non-violent means to resolve social and political inequities.

- The evacuation of Israeli settlements in the Occupied Territories. These settlements are a major obstacle to peace, a tremendous financial burden to Israel and do little, if anything, to enhance Israel's security. The settlements constantly expose to danger the settlers themselves and the Israeli soldiers sent to defend them, and they bring grave harm to the Palestinians living under Occupation. We call for bringing safely home to Israel the settlers from all settlements except those included as part of a negotiated and mutually agreed upon exchange of territories between Israel and Palestine in determining the final borders of both states.

- The recognition that as Jews and U.S. citizens, we have a special responsibility to urge our government to pursue policies consistent with the requirements of a just peace for Israel and the Palestinian people.[5]

Both the U.S. and Israel refuse to allow for U.N. leadership or peace-keeping forces to help resolve this conflict. We, alone, continue to veto any attempts by the U.N. to provide nonpartisan help; we keep saying that there can be no "fair" international peace-keeping force in this conflict, even though we have supported international peace-keeping forces all over the world in other conflicts. I ask you not to be silent. Listen to each other, both Palestinian and Jew. Do not give up; there is so much at stake. Too many have died. I will never forget what I saw in Jerusalem, in Lod, in Gaza, in Ramallah. I always carry the faces of the people of conscience and peace who work every day in Israel and Palestine. It is our duty as human beings, as citizens of the world, and as Jews and non-Jews to work for justice.

Peace...*Shalom...salaam.* To my Arab sisters and brothers, especially the Palestinian people—*shukran*/thank you for your courage. You have given me the courage to speak, and never be silent again. Shalom/salaam.

✺ ✺ ✺

See the following Web sites for further information:

Bat Shalom (Israeli/Palestinian feminist peace organization):
http://www.batshalom.org

B'Tselem (Israeli Center for Human Rights in the Occupied Territories):
http://www.btselem.org

Independent Media, Israel: http://www.indymedia.org.il/imc/israel

Physicians for Human Rights: http:www.phrusa.org

Birzeit University: http://www.birzeit.edu

Middle East Children's Alliance: http://www.mecaforpeace.org

Jewish Unity for a Just Peace: http://www.junity.org

✺ ✺ ✺

Thanks to many of my friends for their encouragement and support over the past decade. Our conversations have helped me do this work. Special thanks to Sharon Jaffe, Joanna Kadi, Irena Klepfisz, Barbara Lubin, Penny Rosenwasser, Matthew Lyons, Amy Beth, Noha Ismail, Fadia Abul-Hajj, Liz Kennedy, Bev Sorensen, and Pat Rouse. I take full responsibility for the ideas expressed in this essay.

NOTES

1 Baal Shem Tov was the founder of the orthodox, mystical Chasidic Jewish movement. He lived from 1698–1790. For further information, see Aryeh Kaplan, *Chasidic Masters: History, Biography, Thought.* Jerusalem: Moznaim, 1991. or http://members.aol.com/lazera/baalshem-tov.html.

2 To read the full report by Physicians for Human Rights, see http://www.phrusa.org/research/forensics/israel/Israel_force.html.

3 See http://www.icahd.org/eng/campaigns.asp?menu=4&submenu=3.

4 Institute for Palestine Studies, *The Palestinian-Israeli Peace Agreement: A Documentary Record.* Washington, DC: Institute for Palestine Studies, 1994: 117–18.

5 See http://www.brittzedek.org.

6 The Anti-Defamation League is a Jewish organization that fights anti-Semitism, bigotry, and extremism. It also takes a fairly strong position in support of the Israeli government. See http://www.adl.org.

Lurching Through These Frightening Days

ANONYMOUS

Fear grips my body to the point where I can't leave the house. I'm positive FBI agents wait for me outside the door. They're going to take me away. If I ask questions, if I mention civil rights, if I tell them I want to call someone, they'll say I'm non-cooperative, and punish me accordingly. How many agents will there be? How long will they keep me at their office? Will they make me wait for hours before they talk to me? I'm reasonably certain the experience will be so reminiscent of other times men had me locked in rooms that I will simply crumble. They'll take that as evidence I'm hiding something.

I can't believe I'm in south Florida where the hunt is on for any and all Arabs. Of all the places to be. Of all the places for some of the supposed hijackers to choose to live. Of all the places for them to rent cars. I wonder if the car I rented two weeks ago is now leading FBI agents here. I'm thankful most people here read me as Cuban. Is that a cowardly response?

This particular Friday, 14 September, crawls by. The morning has passed and the dog continues to wait patiently for her walk, which should have happened hours ago. Now it's 2:00. I alternate between TV news, which is having a profoundly negative effect on my whole being, and e-mail. The dog's big brown eyes follow me everywhere. She's the reason I finally force myself out the door. First I drink water and eat a sandwich; I haven't eaten before this because my stomach is tied in knots, but I know that experiencing low blood sugar while being interrogated will make it worse. I wear comfortable clothes, and tie a sweater around my waist because the FBI building is probably overly air conditioned and very cold.

The walk passes uneventfully, at least externally. Days pass. Still no knock at the door. Some of the fear lifts—emphasis on some—but I'm still checked out of my body and not present. The back of my neck and my head ache constantly. I can only cry when my lover puts her hands on me. I need to cry more, but I can't. My body's gone back into the mode it's taken years to break out of—locked up, shut down, tense, fearful. It's a reaction to trauma that makes sense, that I understand. And my understanding can't get me through to the other side.

Horror and fear and sadness have gripped me since Tuesday. I'm still trying to catch up with the reality of the disaster on American soil. Still trying to take in that hijacked planes blew up the World Trade Center and severely damaged the Pentagon, that thousands of lives are lost, that workers at the Pentagon never knew what hit their supposedly impenetrable fortress, that NYC's downtown core may never recover, that the war the U.S. has been waging around the world has come home with a vengeance. I'm still trying to take in 110 stories crumpling like a house of cards, to bodies flying out of windows as some people decided to jump rather than burn in an eerie and haunting reenactment of New York's 1911 Triangle Shirtwaist Factory fire, an important piece of history that no one references. I'm still trying to catch up with all those pieces of reality. Over the years I've come to believe humans are a slow, dense (in both good and problematic ways) species, with bodies that need time to fully absorb and then heal from cataclysmic and painful events.

I admit it. I'm slow. That took me years to understand, as I dealt with the aftermath of decades of torture, abuse, and neglect. I don't absorb huge, important pieces of information quickly and easily. Whether it's thousands of people dead in what used to be the World Trade Center, or whether it's the fact that many good people care about me and love me, I need time to take it in.

As that painful week crept by, as my physical and spiritual self attempted to keep up with too much information and too much terror, I listened as one white man after another, some representing the American government, some representing the American military, spoke in response to the hijackings and devastation. These men expressed outrage, a desire for vengeance, and plans for war. They reminded me of the early days in the rape crisis movement, when survivors talked about the rage their husband or father expressed upon learning the woman had been raped by another man. We came to understand that response as emotionally unhealthy and emotionally immature; as indicative of the fact that the man was unable to first, focus on the victim and support her, and second, feel the sadness and grief appropriate to the situation. I saw that response expressed over and over again in the aftermath of this tragedy, and it did not reassure me. The people who reassured me—some of whom I know, some of whom I heard on TV—are the people who grieve, who express confusion, who cry, who anguish.

I want the firefighters to finish their rescue work, move into the White House, and lead the country. New York's firefighters are familiar to me— working-class men who speak little and work with their hands. And that is what they did. Thinking not of themselves, thinking not of military strikes, simply doing the job that needs to be done—digging through the rubble to find survivors. This is a working-class response, I thought again and again, watching these guys turn their heads away from TV cameras, sip water, and return to Ground Zero. I trust this. They aren't speeding up international events to a pace no one except the truly evil and/or the truly numb can follow. They are focusing where the focus needs to be at the present time. What a different experience this would be if the men in the White House had kept the national focus where it needs to be—in New York and Washington, with the victims, the survivors, and their families/friends. What a different experience this would be if the government had dealt with the tragedy by staying with the tragedy. Instead, these men focused away from the tragedy and on the Arab/Asian world, with the same militaristic, imperialistic, racist attention they've given that part of the world for decades.

I managed to wean myself from the TV the day my fury erupted beyond its regular level as Dan Rather—my lover calls him Dan Lather and we both laugh—states that World War II began in 1941. The ignorance shown by American reporters and government/military officials of basic historical facts appalls and frightens me. I turned off the TV. I jotted down a list of questions that any semi-intelligent journalist would now be asking and attempting to answer: Why did this happen? Who hates America this much, and why? Are this hate and anger justified? What kind of foreign policy does the U.S. pursue, particularly in the Arab world? Which leaders, and which groups, has the CIA funded in the past twenty years? What does it mean that Osama bin-Laden is now vilified by U.S. intelligence when twenty years ago the CIA was funding him and other Afghanistan soldiers as they fought the Soviet Union? How do we define terrorism? Has the U.S. government/military committed acts of terrorism? Where does the Palestinian-Israeli conflict, and the U.S. support of Israel, fit into all of this? And finally, what about the claim, repeated over and over with no backing, that the destruction of the World Trade Center is the worst atrocity to take place on American soil? First, is it important and appropriate to rank atrocities? Second, how disrespectful is this claim for Native Americans? For Africans previously enslaved on American soil?

I wrote down these questions and then had to stop, because the back of my neck hurt unbearably, and I needed to pay attention. This pain isn't new to my body. It's come from direct experiences of torture and oppression, and from learning about the horrifying events of the past decades carried out against innocent people in Palestine, Lebanon, Iraq. El Salvador, Guatemala, Nicaragua. East Timor. The list goes on. The finger points back to the white men in the White House. On 11 September the inevitable happened, and the war came home. As wars tend to do, no matter how long it takes. And the American "leaders" didn't seem to understand this. Instead they talked of fresh new assaults on innocent people, on poor dark people, on ancient land, they talked in a way that indicated no lessons have been learned, they talked in a way that indicates American foreign policy will continue to thwart justice, liberation, and human rights for millions of people.

Their response disrupts me profoundly. I'm lurching through a triangle with one side made up of grief over the tragedy, one side made up of terror over American military retaliation, the third side consisting of fear for my personal safety. I've had no time to absorb any part of the triangle. I'm attempting to move on a timetable imposed by American "leaders," attempting to follow events that are happening way too fast, and, as I've learned over the years, healing can't happen this way.

We all need to heal. I say this to whoever reads this, the first anonymous article I have ever written, standing as a testament to the terror I feel as an Arab in the U.S. We all need to heal. We were traumatized by a horrific set of violent incidents on 11 September. I support each of you in your attempts to heal body/spirit/psyche from the trauma. I support you moving at your own pace. I urge all of us to cultivate our skill to do two things at once—to heal, *and* to be alert and active. "You can cry and fight at the same time," my karate teacher told me years ago as I begged her to let me stop sparring after an opponent's powerful kick between my legs left me reeling and weeping. (It also left me thinking: If it hurts me this much, imagine what it would do to a guy. Remember this.) I didn't know then that this teacher would become, had already become, one of my most important life mentors, that the two years I studied with her would prove important to my healing and my sense of self in ways I could neither imagine nor articulate. At the time, I was furious with her. I stomped back to the mats to resume sparring with my opponent who, in spite of her years of training beyond my own beginner status, suddenly couldn't get close to me because my defensive skills took a huge leap in only a few seconds. I cried, I fought, and I kept my opponent away from me.

My teacher's words hold true for me, possibly for many of us, today. To heal ourselves, to cry at the same time as we join together; to protest, to pray, to stand vigil, to fight. Not to put aside our need for healing as we contend with the larger political situation, but to do both.

At the same time, I call on non-Arabs and non-Muslims to stand up for those of us who are Arab and Muslim. I know you've heard this, but it bears repeating; we're under siege. We're being harassed, and beaten on the street. We're getting death threats, and at least three people have been murdered. No one is safe, least of all those with visible Arab features and Arab-accented English who wear Muslim dress. Allies—we need you. Stand up for us. Interrupt the comments you hear at work. Talk to the Arab Americans you know and ask them what you can do, on a physical daily level, to help. Call in to those damn radio shows and say something compassionate and intelligent. Write letters to the editor. Don't leave us alone. We're freaking out. Our terror is well grounded.

➤➤ ➤➤ ➤➤

I deplore the people who carried out the horrific acts of Tuesday 11 September. I grieve for the victims and survivors and families and friends devastated by the attacks. I honor the rescue workers for their beautiful and focused response to the tragedy, and I honor the citizens who committed acts of selfless heroism in the midst of fire, panic, and death. I support diplomatic and legal action to find who is responsible for Tuesday's actions, and I support a fair, legal, international trial if those responsible are found. I oppose military actions by the U.S. government. I oppose terrorist actions by the U.S. government—that is, actions designed to harm innocent women and men and children. I support the U.S. government in focusing its attention here at home, not only on the ravaged city of New York, but on the poverty, malnutrition, and inadequate education many Americans receive, and I support the U.S. government in making a decision to do better by these people. I support a shift in U.S. government foreign policy that will support justice and human rights for my sisters and brothers around the world.

⁔⁔⁔ ⁔⁔⁔ ⁔⁔⁔

As I stumble through these frightening days and nights, I try with each passing day to survive not only the external crisis but also my internal crisis of faith. My daily prayers have gone from a beautiful, simple, grounding ritual each morning to a difficult, excruciating, out-of-body experience that I put off later and later each day. When I do sit down and light my candles and begin to pray, I have trouble remembering what I'm doing and why. How can a spiritual response possibly be adequate to this situation? Can prayer help stop military retaliation?

It's been a healing experience for me to discover my own eclectic, earth-centered spirituality and incorporate it into my daily life. It's become part of the way I deal with and understand the world; it's moved me from a mostly political/social understanding into a more holistic understanding that integrates politics, spirituality, culture, and love. And while it is true that a spiritual response in and of itself is not adequate, I remind myself that a solely political response is not enough either. I continue to pray, even though my prayers feel grace-less and wooden.

Today I sought out the two "friends" I have made here in south Florida. I put the word *friends* in quotation marks because in some ways I barely know these retail workers whom I chat with several times a week. They are friendly, low-key men in their mid-forties; working-class, Catholic Latinos. I wanted to talk to them because I needed desperately to connect with a human who would not shove an American flag down my throat, and these are in short supply in south Florida at the moment. Only one was at his post; Emilio and

I chatted over hundreds of tomatoes that were on sale. He expressed horror over the devastation in New York, and horror over Washington's reaction. Emilio described Arabs and Muslims as beautiful people with a beautiful religion. "We cannot go to war with them," he said passionately, adding that he had been praying like the dickens and he hoped I was too. His heartfelt words and our authentic connection did not end my crisis of faith; however, they led to a tiny beginning of an inner shift.

And I end this essay here, having struggled a long time over how to end before concluding there is no clean stopping place, no obvious finishing line. This essay can't end neatly because not one piece of the triangle I referred to earlier has ended, neatly or otherwise. My grief about the tragedy remains, my terror about the American response remains, my fear about personal safety remains. We are in the midst of an unfolding set of experiences and the present moment is wavering, unstable, and unsettling. I close this essay with an acknowledgement of all of that.

In the Belly of the Beast:
Puertorriqueñas Challenging Colonialism

EL COMITÉ DE MUJERES PUERTORRIQUEÑAS–MIRIAM
LÓPEZ-PÉREZ-AIXA BORRERO, MARIGNA CAMACHO,
ELBA CRESPO, ANNETTE DIAZ, DOROTEA MANUELA,
AND MILAGROS PADILLA

The *Comité de Mujeres Puertorriqueñas–Miriam López Pérez* is a collective of
Puerto Rican women committed to the empowerment of all women. We are
a diverse group of women. We range in ages from midtwenties to forties and
represent the spectrum of racial characteristics that define our people as Puerto
Ricans. Among us there are heterosexual women and lesbians, middle- and
low-income women, women raised in Puerto Rico and women raised in the
United States, women whose predominant language is Spanish, and women
whose predominant language is English. We have come together to work
towards ending the injustices we experience in all aspects of our lives as Puerto
Ricans and as women.

The overall mission of the comité is to empower Puerto Rican women,
through collective action, to take control of our lives and to struggle in close
collaboration with other community organizations that strive for social change.
In our work, we prioritize raising consciousness regarding the social, political,
and economic reality of Puerto Rican women, with particular focus on the
effects of colonialism on the women in our community. We strive to develop
strong ties and solidarity with other oppressed women in the United States, as
well as with women in Third World countries. All of our work addresses the
particular effects of racism on the Puerto Rican community.

Our work has at its roots the conviction that to address issues affecting
Puerto Rican women, we must seriously and systematically challenge the
colonial relationship of the United States with Puerto Rico. Our understanding of the exploitation and racism that result from this colonial relationship
shapes our political development and our consciousness as oppressed women.
The oppression faced by women both in Puerto Rico and in the United States
is a direct consequence of the political, economic, and military interests of the
U.S. government. There is an urgent political need for other women living in
the United States to grasp this understanding and to join us in our struggle.

Colonialism: Its Effect on Our People

Although most official documents describe Puerto Rico as a "commonwealth
associated to the United States," with a governor, an advisory council, and a
bicameral congress, it is in fact the oldest colony in the world. Since 1898,

Puerto Rico has been an island territory operating within the limits of U.S. power and control. Before 1898, Puerto Rico was under the rule of Spain. As a result of the Spanish-American War, under the Treaty of Paris of 1898, Puerto Rico was ceded to the United States. U.S. military troops invaded Puerto Rico in that year and, against the will of the people, established a military regime that lasted two long years. Between 1898 and 1900, Puerto Rican patriots went to Washington to demand the establishment of a Puerto Rican military civil government on the island. The U.S. Congress ignored these demands and in 1900 the U.S. Congress unilaterally approved the Foraker Act, which has been described as the basis of U.S. colonial policies in Puerto Rico.

Since then, the United States has governed the island through a specific set of political structures affecting all social, economic, and political aspects of life in Puerto Rico and restricting external relations between Puerto Rico and other countries. Space limitations and the focus of this article do not permit a detailed discussion of all these political structures. What should be noted is that the U.S. military control of our nation is most clearly expressed through the presence of its armed forces, while U.S. economic control is evident by the presence of its corporate and financial institutions.

In 1917, the U.S. Congress replaced the Foraker Act with the Jones Act, and imposed U.S. citizenship on Puerto Ricans. This was done despite numerous petitions from the Puerto Rican people against citizenship and in favor of substantial reforms to the existing regime and consultation with the Puerto Rican people as the basis for establishing citizenship. Citizenship made Puerto Ricans available for compulsory service in the U.S. armed forces just as the United States was about to enter World War I. The imposition of citizenship therefore has allowed the United States to carry out more easily its imperialist and racist foreign policies. Moreover, Puerto Rico's location in the Caribbean makes the island a strategic territory from which the United States can carry out its political and military interventions in Central America, other Caribbean nations, and throughout Latin America. The U.S. National Guard of Puerto Rico has its own airport, air force, radar station, and training installations. In proportion to the population, it is the largest National Guard of the United States. In 1983, two hundred members of the Puerto Rican National Guard were sent to the borders of Honduras and Nicaragua. In 1988, the presence of the National Guard in Honduras was again confirmed; that year, thirteen hundred members of the Puerto Rican National Guard were sent to Panama when the U.S. government feared there might be a threat to its interests in the Panama Canal.

Puerto Rico has served as a contingency location for the warehousing of nuclear arms. U.S. military bases occupy 13 percent of all cultivatable land on the island. The U.S. Navy controls two-thirds of Vieques, an island to the east of the main island of Puerto Rico, which, together with Roosevelt Roads Base in Ceiba, Puerto Rico, constitutes one of the largest naval complexes in the world. Such a large military presence is significant; it ensures that Puerto Rico will be a target of attack in case of nuclear war. Given the geographic size of Puerto Rico, this would mean the elimination of our entire nation.

The United States' occupation of Puerto Rico has brought about dramatic changes in the island's economy. U.S. control resulted in the transformation of an agricultural economy into an industrial one dependent upon U.S. capital. The profits of economic production line the pockets of U.S. investors, giving little back to the Puerto Rican people. Lately, as U.S. manufacturing has abandoned Puerto Rico for even lower-wage markets, the unemployment rate has skyrocketed. At time of writing, that rate is 40 percent, and approximately 70 percent of the population is eligible for food stamps. The majority of the nation depends on subsidies from the U.S. government.

The colonial economic model imposed on Puerto Rico clearly does not meet the needs of our people. The result of this failed dependent economy has been the mass exodus of Puerto Ricans to the United States in search of economic stability. This migration keeps our nation geographically divided; there are more than three million Puerto Ricans living in the United States. However, the fulfillment of the promise of greater economic opportunities has eluded our people. Our U.S.-based community suffers disproportionately high rates of poverty, unemployment, housing shortages, infant mortality, AIDS, and other health problems resulting from lack of access to affordable care. These social and economic difficulties have taken their toll on our community, which has also seen marked increases in substance abuse and emotional illness. Racial violence and attacks on our language, on affirmative action, and on other civil rights are constant threats to our survival as a people here in the United States.

Despite our long history of oppression, the Puerto Rican people, both in our island nation and here in the United States, actively resist and struggle against colonialism and racism, working to end the oppression in our lives. Puerto Rican women take an active role as leaders in this resistance in our communities, at our work sites, and in our homes. Wherever there is an organized effort to combat colonialism, sexism, and racism, Puerto Rican women have been there, and we will continue to be there. (For more information on the history of the independence movement in Puerto Rico, see the suggested reading listed at the end of this essay.)

Effect of Colonialism on Women

U.S. political and economic interests in Puerto Rico have had a devastating impact on women. The control of reproduction is perhaps one of the most dramatic examples of the oppression of women as a means of maintaining political and economic interests in Puerto Rico. In order to control population growth, the United States manipulated not only women's social and economic realities but also those of the entire nation. In the 1930s an extensive campaign was launched to promote *la operación*—sterilization. Under the guise of promoting the economic development of the nation and women's participation in the labor force, the government encouraged women to seek sterilization. Hundreds of family planning clinics were established where women could get sterilized free of charge, and extensive "educational" campaigns were launched informing women that they would be free to work without the worry of families and would be freer to migrate to the United States if they had smaller families. Later, in the 1950s, once again to boost economic interests and women's participation in the labor force, Puerto Rican women were encouraged to use contraceptive foam and birth control pills, thereby becoming unknowing guinea pigs for pharmaceutical companies that were trying to promote their newly developed products. The strength of the pills used at that time was twenty times greater than what is now considered safe.

These abuses are not limited to the past; the effects of colonialism continue to shape the present and have an impact on women's lives here in the United States as well as in Puerto Rico. Limitations on women's reproductive health and freedom continue. Currently, more than one-third of women of child-bearing age living in Puerto Rico have been sterilized. Various studies in the United States among Puerto Rican women have found alarmingly high rates of sterilization—for example, 50 percent in Hartford, Connecticut, and 66.7 percent in Brooklyn, New York. Puerto Rican women have high rates of births by Cesarean section both here and in Puerto Rico. The contamination of food supplies with estrogen has resulted in unusually high rates of pubarche and thelarche, or precocious pseudopuberty—premature sexual and breast development in young girls—in Puerto Rico. Mortality resulting from breast cancer and cervical cancer is disproportionately high for Puerto Rican women. Lack of access to health care prevents early screening for disease and results in premature death for many of our women. This lack of access has a direct link to the economic situation in which our community finds itself. Unable to afford private medical care, our community must rely on public facilities, which are often overburdened and do not provide lin-guistically and culturally appropriate services. This is of particular concern as we face an organized English-only movement in the United States that would impose English as the nation's official language. Such a movement is a direct threat to bilingual education programs and other services that have been instituted to help ensure fuller participation of groups and communities whose first language is not English.

The message of colonialism is clear: not only is our land the property of the United States, but so are our people. Our physical health and our economic health are directly affected by the colonial policies in Puerto Rico. The forced migration that has resulted from colonialism affects us here in the United States as well, since we must confront and fight against racism daily. Women most often bear the brunt of these policies. Puerto Rican women experience racism and discrimination, which seriously affect their earning potential and limit their ability to gain economic independence. Participation in the labor force for Puerto Rican women is lower than that of other Latino populations. In addition, although Puerto Rican women have been integrated into the work force, they are concentrated in the lowest-paid occupations. More than 60 percent of Puerto Rican women work in service, clerical, or technical support jobs or in garment production—closer and close to the poverty line. This reduced earning power seriously affects the lives and the economic health of the women and children of our community; this is of particular concern for a community in which 40 percent of households are headed by women.

In Puerto Rico, workers in Mayagüez, the majority of whom are women, have been exposed to toxic gases in their workplaces. This exposure has resulted in a number of serious physical and emotional disorders for the workers. Government response (both U.S. federal and colonial Puerto Rican) has been to minimize the effects of this exposure or to attribute the symptoms exhibited by the workers to psychogenic stress disorder. This lack of response, or rather this inappropriate response, makes it clear where the priorities are: profits before people.

By now it should be clear that the colonial relationship of the United States with Puerto Rico affects women's lives on multiple levels both in Puerto Rico and in the United States. The economic and political structure in Puerto Rico, set in place by the U.S. government, attempts to limit and control women's lives. The migration that has resulted from a dependent economy has led many women to the United States, where they face additional burdens of discrimination in housing, employment, health care, and most other facets of their lives. It is crucial that all of this be taken into consideration when we develop strategies for empowerment of Puerto Rican women.

As Puertorriqueñas living and struggling against colonialism in the United States, we experience an urgent need for feminists in the United States to appreciate how our struggles against colonialism and racism are interconnected. We cannot emphasize enough the link between our struggle for national liberation and our struggle for emancipation as women. Though we currently live in the United States, we follow the model of our Latin American sisters—a model that recognizes that without women's participation there is no revolution, and that women's struggles are not separate from national liberation struggles. For us, as Puertorriqueñas, this model is of the utmost relevance and importance since we find ourselves here in the United States, in the belly of the beast. As such, our work is twofold: (1) empowering the women in our community so that women can be full participants in all stages of resistance to oppression; and (2) representing the needs of our community in other feminist organizations so that white feminists, in particular, can address how they contribute to the perpetuation of colonialism. The latter concern merits some special consideration.

As an example of how feminists can contribute to and perpetuate colonialism, consider the following advertisement for New Dawn Adventure: "Run by and for women; women's retreat on the small island of Vieques, Puerto Rico. Available for individual or group camping, workshops, *or a place to begin your exploration of the Caribbean*" [emphasis added]. If we recall that two-thirds of this same island is occupied by the U.S. Navy, little more explanation is necessary. A women-only retreat, run by non-Puertorriqueñas and designed for profit, further reinforces the message of exploitation that the U.S. military has already made clear. The U.S. Navy has displaced fishers and their families, and the presence of an outside business designed for profit—with the added reference to using the island as a starting ground for "exploration"—resonates of displacement and exploitation. Just as feminists have boycotted other causes that exploit people or nations in Central America, Latin America, and South Africa, they should boycott profit-making endeavors in Vieques.

Yet not all displays of colonizer ideology are this extreme or so clearly motivated by profit. Our experience over the years has taught us much. We often find ourselves in situations where our participation is solicited not because there is an understanding of how a particular issue might affect us as Puertorriqueñas, but rather to fulfill and complete the picture of colorful faces on a stage. In some cases it is our multilingual capacity that is being solicited. We are excluded from decision-making and agenda-setting but are later recruited to discuss "how to broaden our [read "their"] constituency." This attitude—which determines who sets an agenda and who prioritizes issues and then reaches out to get us to work on an issue that someone else has deemed important—is no different from the colonizer mentality that drastically undermined our nation's economy and then blamed us for not making a deficient system work. Therefore, U.S. feminists not only must become educated about the history of the United States with Puerto Rico, but also must also examine how they play out of these same histories.

Ending colonization benefits both the colonized and the colonizer. In *The Colonizer and the Colonized,* A. Memmi states that colonization distorts relationships, destroys or petrifies institutions, and corrupts individuals, both colonizers and colonized. If feminists are to achieve the goals of empowerment and liberation, then all feminists must take up the struggle against colonialism.

Puertorrequiñas as Organized Against Colonialism and Racism

Women organizing against repression and oppression is not new in Puerto Rico. Puerto Rican women have always been active and outspoken. As early as the 1500s, women like the *Cacica* (chieftain) Yuisa were actively resisting Spanish imperialism. In the late 1860s, Mariana Bracetti played a key role in a massive uprising against Spanish rule, *El Grito de lares* (the shout of the guardian of the house). Women such as Luisa Capetillo assumed leadership positions in labor movements and other struggles for civil rights and equality. Others, such as Julia de Burgos and Lolita Lebrón, were active voices in the national struggle against U.S. presence and control in Puerto Rico. Isabel Rasado was arrested in 1979, at age seventy-seven, along with twenty other *compañeros,* for protesting the military occupation on the island. At time of writing there are seven Puerto Rican women in U.S. prisons: Alicia Rodríguez, Aida Luz Rodríguez, Dilcia Pagan, Hayde Torres, Carmen Valentin, Alejandrina Torres, and Lucy Berrios. These women are political prisoners and prisoners of war, many of whom have been victims of harassment, physical and sexual assault, and other forms of repression. They are in prison because of their involvement in direct action to gain independence for Puerto Rico. In addition, Yvonne Meléndez spent a year and a half in prison and still awaits trial almost five years after her arrest; she must live under repressive restrictions imposed by U.S. courts that limit her freedom, even though one of the tenets of U.S. "justice" is that one is presumed innocent until proven guilty.[10]

These are but a few examples of the strength, dignity, and commitment to justice that characterize the spirit of Puerto Rican women. There are thousands of anonymous women who, in their daily lives and struggles, have been and continue to be the main sources of strength and the stabilizing forces within their families, their communities, the Puerto Rican culture, and the sociopolitical life of the nation. This strength and spirit of survival should be recognized and celebrated, for it serves as a context for understanding Puerto Rican women's response to difficult, painful, and life-threatening circumstances.

Such was the case with Miriam López Pérez of Boston. Miriam was a thirty-two-year-old mother of three at the time of her unexpected death in April

1987, a victim of the too-frequently tragic ending of domestic violence. Miriam had played a key role in her family. As is often the case with immigrant families, she carried out the tasks of the "cultural broker," the one to bridge two systems, two cultures, negotiating between Puerto Rican cultural expectations and the U.S. system of delivering services. Her parents and her sibling came to depend on her. Her children depended on her too.

Miriam confronted what is unfortunately the usual situation for poor women of color: discrimination, unemployment, lack of access to services. Yet she fought on, doing her best to protect herself, her children, and the rest of her family. In April 1987, after having appealed to the police for protection on numerous occasions, she was murdered by her ex-boyfriend. By some standards, Miriam would not be considered a political person. She was not an "activist" and she was not organizing the community. She was concentrating on defending her rights and those of her family. Yet her life and her death speak to the level of commitment and to the *espíritu de lucha* (spirit of struggle and survival) of Puerto Rican women as clear examples of what feminists mean when they say that the personal is political.

It was Miriam's death and the public response following it that helped to consolidate and formalize the Comité de Mujeres Puertorriqueñas–Miriam López Pérez. Many of us were active in other community struggles and had been working in efforts to support and defend the fifteen Puerto Rican nationalists who had been arrested and were being tried in Hartford, Connecticut. For years we had linked issues of national liberation with the struggle of Puerto Rican women. Miriam's death served as a catalyst to formalize this link. We took her name to honor her and to keep her struggle alive.

Miriam's death would have gone unnoticed had it not been for what was initially described in the media as "a group of angry Hispanic women." There was no public outcry, even though early newspaper reports clearly pointed to discrepancies between the police accounts and the family's reports of the events leading to her death. There was no response from "our" community agencies and male leaders. After all, this kind of thing happens in our community all the time. There was no response from the organized battered women's movement, although six months before Miriam's death there was much rallying after the beating death of a white woman in another section of the greater Boston area. Even after we brought attention to Miriam's death, advocates in the women's community referred to her death as the "South End case." Such depersonalization fosters anonymity and belittles our struggle as Puertorriqueñas. It relegates us to being simply residents of a section of the city without recognizing how such categorization might contribute to the very racism and classism that keep us oppressed.

The lack of response from Latino organizations and from women's organizations following Miriam's death reinforced what we, as Puerto Rican women, had always known. No one was going to take up our struggle. It was time to come together in our own organization to address our needs as Puerto Rican women—not as either Puerto Ricans or women, but as both. The comité was formed to create a forum where we could address all aspects of our lives and our political work.

The comité initially organized around the issue of domestic violence. Our early efforts focused on organizing the community to denounce the lack of protection for women of color and drew the connections between violence against women and the racism of city officials that contributed to the deaths of the women in our community. Our organizing strategy was clear: we had to make our concerns known publicly. We organized press conferences, visited homes door to door, and organized a candlelight march through the neighborhood streets, ending in a rally in front of police headquarters.

As our group developed, the need to broaden our strategies and educational efforts became obvious. We recognized that the eradication of domestic violence was a complex effort and that we had to address other sources of oppression that keep the women in our community disenfranchised and disempowered. Once again following the model of our sisters in Latin America, we organized an *encuentro* (dialogue) of Latina women in Massachusetts. The encuentro allowed us to share our experiences of oppression with one another and to develop a shared commitment and shared strategies for continuing our struggles. Some of the issues discussed at this event included violence as a tool of control, unemployment and homelessness as barriers to survival, the need to create a safe and enriching community for both lesbian and heterosexual Latinas, and the challenge of bilingualism that we and our children face.

The comité is a multi-issue organization in the sense that we do not limit ourselves to organizing around a single issue. At the same time we are a single-issue organization in that we see our work as consistently challenging racism and the manifestations of colonialism wherever these may present themselves. Therefore we might be involved in press conferences denouncing police brutality, in rallies and marches to the United Nations denouncing colonialism and calling for independence for Puerto Rico, in campaigns to assist in health care for Central American women, and in organizing activities to remember those in our community who are living with AIDS and those who have died of AIDS. We actively work to define our own agenda. For example, as the issue of reproductive rights has taken on a renewed sense of urgency within the feminist movement, the comité has taken a twofold approach. The first is to join with other women of color to define what reproductive freedom means to us as oppressed women, ensuring that the definition of reproductive rights is not limited to abortion; the second is to work with other women's organizations to ensure that our perspective as Puertorriqueñas is an integral part of the political agenda.

Over the years we have evolved into a strong political entity. We hold the following principles as guidelines for our work:

> We come together to work towards social change. We see the need to organize ourselves as women as a means to achieve these goals. Creating an organization is not, in and of itself, our final goal. We are a collective because we understand that individuals acting alone and individual actions by themselves do not bring about social change; social and political change require a collective, organized response to all forms of oppression.

> We actively support independence for Puerto Rico. We believe in and defend the right of all nations to self-determination and denounce all military, economic, and political interventions by one nation in another. Our struggle for liberation as women includes the struggles of women in other nations. Our work is not limited to our situation here; it includes solidarity with other women who struggle for their self-determination.

> We recognize that the foreign policies of the United States have a direct impact on the lives of all members of our communities. For example, funding needed for the development of affordable housing, quality child care, accessible and affordable health care, employment opportunities, and other programs critical to our survival is diverted to pay for military spending here and abroad. The U.S. government's defense of its political and economic interests is conducted at the expense of our communities in the United States and in Puerto Rico.

> We see empowerment as the active support and defense of Latinas' full participation in activities that will lead to social, economic, and political freedom. We view the defense of our rights as women as intrinsically connected to the defense of our human and civil rights as a Latino community. Women play a key role and must therefore be full participants in the struggle. To achieve this, there must be democracy in the home, and all barriers to full participation for women must be addressed and alternatives must be created.

We oppose and denounce racism and the use of violence as a tool of oppression and control. This violence takes many forms, including violence against women (domestic violence and sexual assault), racially motivated violence, and violence against the lesbian and gay community. Violence used as a tool of repression not only violates the human and civil rights of the individual affected but also reflects lack of respect and lack of value for all members of a community, including women, people of color, and the lesbian and gay community.

We believe in and defend the right to freedom of choice. This right to choose includes control over our own bodies, the right to decide if and when to have children, and the right to practice our sexuality in an atmosphere free of repression, including the choice of leading a bisexual or lesbian lifestyle. We denounce attacks on a woman's reproductive freedom, such as sterilization abuse, and denounce repression against lesbians.

We defend our cultural heritage, our Spanish language, and our bilingual status. We oppose all efforts to impose a monolingual status on our communities, such as that proposed by the English-only movement in the United States.

We value and respect the differences among us. We are committed to struggle to overcome artificial barriers created to divide us. We are committed to ending racism, classism, ageism, homophobia, and discrimination based on an individual's physical or mental abilities.

We understand that the same colonizer attitudes that keep Puertorriqueñas oppressed keep African American, Asian, Chicana, American Indian, and other women of color oppressed. We must join forces to define how we want to wage our struggle. In the same way as we make the connections between our national liberation struggles and our struggle as women, we see the need to work in coalition with other women. We believe the future of the women's movement in the United States lies in coalition-building and unity. We call upon other women to join us in denouncing U.S. colonialism, in particular in Puerto Rico.

Additional Sources

Edna Acosta Belena, ed. *The Puerto Rican Woman.* New York: Praeger, 1986.

A. Memmi, *The Colonizer and the Colonized.* Boston: Beacon Press, 1965.

"Puerto Rico: Women, Culture and Colonialism in Latin America," in *Slave of Slaves: The Challenge of Latin American Women.* Caribbean Women's Collective, eds. London: ZED Press, 1980: 132–146.

C. Rodriguez et al., *The Puerto Rican Struggle: Essays on Survival in the U.S.* New Jersey: Waterfront Press, 1984.

Hawai'i

HAUNANI–KAY TRASK

We are an island
and a history
and a myth.

We have a palace
and a flag
and an anthem.

We are crippled
and orphaned
and sentenced

to life imprisonment.
We are a country
chained to the map

of America.

Self-Determination for Pacific Island Women: The Case of Hawai'i

HAUNANI–KAY TRASK

Aloha mai. Aloha mai.

I am Haunaniokawekiu o Haleakala, descendant of Kiha a Pi'ilani of Maui. My mother is from Hana, my father from Kane'ohe, and my *kupuna* (elders) from Kaua'i and Maui. I am a Hawaiian woman. My people are the indigenous people of Hawai'i. Despite the control of Hawai'i by the United States of America, Hawaiians are not Americans. Nor are we Europeans or Asians. We are not from the Pacific Rim, nor are we immigrants to the Pacific. We are the children of the sacred land of Hawai'i Nei.

We believe that the first-born people of the land should govern their own land. The Tahitians should govern Tahiti, the Maori should govern Aotearoa (now called New Zealand), the Samoans should govern Samoa, the Kanaks should govern Kanaky (now called New Caledonia), the Chamorros should govern Guam, the Hawaiians should govern Hawai'i, and so on throughout the Pacific.

We believe this because without self-government, people of the land can no longer be who they are. They can no longer practice their ways of life, their caring for the land. Instead, they become mere servants of those who control their land, or they die.

At this moment, the peoples of the Pacific Islands are caught in many different struggles for self-government. Some have achieved a first stage of control and are now dealing with neocolonialism. Others, like the Kanaks, are engaged in decolonizing wars, and yet others, like my own people, the Hawaiians, are just beginning to think and act in conscious resistance to American control of their islands.

Whether Melanesian, Micronesian, or Polynesian, all Pacific Islanders are in some stage of struggle because we have all been colonized by the white world. Some of us have been given political independence because we had the historical luck to be conquered by a declining imperialist power—i.e., Britain—hence the nominal sovereignty of British possessions in the Pacific: Tonga, Western Samoa, New Zealand, Australia, and Fiji. (I say "nominal" because world powers continue to impinge upon Native sovereignty in many areas, ranging from resource exploitation to cultural degradation.)

Others of us were less fortunate and are now ensnared by France and the United States. France continues to hold major possessions in French—occupied Polynesia and New Caledonia, testing nuclear weapons in the former and waging a bloody battle against the Native Kanaks in the latter. The United States holds the Federated States of Micronesia, Belau, the Marshalls, Guam, and American Samoa as territorial pawns, refusing to accept responsibility for radiation poisoning, dispossession of lands, and military saturation. Hawai'i continues to be the American nuclear command center for the entire Pacific, while also being the most impacted-upon tourist destination per square mile in the world.[1] To this day, the United States, unlike France, denies that it has colonies, rendering independence struggles against America much more difficult.

Finally, all Pacific Islands, whether independent or not, suffer the predations of multinational corporations and the onslaught of the Japanese, who are, to many Native people, the new imperialists in the Pacific.

Colonialism in the Pacific

The impact of colonialism in the Pacific occurs in three stages. In the first stage, it has meant depopulation, followed by a long struggle for integrity and independence in the second stage. The failure to achieve independence often leads to a kind of living death, where the Native people are marginalized and increasingly exploited in a third stage.

Hawai'i is the worst example of the third stage. Euro-American penetration in the eighteenth and nineteenth centuries did more than kill 95 percent of our people. It depleted our strength through missionary conversion, cash-cropping of sugar and pineapple production, military encampment, and, in the twentieth century, commercialization of dynamic culture by honky-tonk tourism. Today, while our land continues to be leached away by rapacious development, our people suffer the worst health in the islands. Compared with other major ethnic groups in Hawai'i, our infant mortality rate is five times higher, and our life expectancy is ten years shorter. More Native Hawaiian children die in their first year of life than all the rest of the state's population up to the age of thirty-four. Our women have the highest rate of breast cancer in the United States. And our people as a whole suffer more chronic conditions, like respiratory ailments, than other ethnic groups. In fact, if you are a Native Hawaiian woman living in your ancestral homeland today, you are more likely to see your child die in infancy, to be unemployed throughout your life, to enter a drug treatment facility or be imprisoned at some point, to waste away from diabetes, or to end it all by suicide.[2]

Despite these realities, many of us who have not been killed or driven from the land or fatally assimilated still retain some connection to a past that once cared for the land and the people of old. For Pacific Islanders, this connection is cultural retention. In the Hawaiian view, the past is what stands before us (*ka wa mamua*), the future is behind us (*ka wa mahope*). We face our past, not our future, and we look to our past for lessons of survival in the present.

Therefore, it is in the context of our past and our culture that the issue of women's self-determination occurs. It does not occur in the context of the American women's movement, or of the French or the Japanese women's movements, or in the context of any other social, political, or environmental movement.

So the first question is, what does Pacific Island women's self-determination mean in the context of Pacific Island culture? Put another way, is political sovereignty for our people the first path to liberation for indigenous women?

For those of us in struggle against colonialism, the only answer is *yes*. And not a timid yes, but a firm, resounding yes. A yes that carries the knowledge of our ancestors. A yes that realizes and honors women's place as transmitters of culture. A yes that has chosen not to put individual rights above collective survival.

And what is the basis of this survival? Land. Unequivocally, in the first instance, land. Land—the Earth Mother, Papa. Land—*aina,* source of food and shelter. Land—keeper of our ancestor's bones.

In our culture, as in most Polynesian cultures, our islands are the elder sibling, first-born of the mating between Sky Father, Wakea, and Earth Mother, Papa. We, the Hawaiian people, are the younger sibling—second-born and thus born to care for and respect the elder sibling. As in the Polynesian family, so with our islands. Younger respects elder, who in turn protects and nourishes younger. The cycle is not only reciprocal, it is wise. Land that is tended and loved will flourish. A flourishing land will feed and clothe and perpetuate the people who care for her.

The land has many gods, many sacred places. She is first in the origin of our world, and when she is dead, we will all be dead. This is the root of indigenous knowledge. The land is all.

Pacific Islanders say this over and over to colonial powers, but to no avail. The French keep testing nuclear weapons, the Americans keep militarizing our lands and waters, and the Japanese keep pushing themselves into every corner of our islands as tourists and businessmen. They are all in search of something—a physical place or a cultural experience or just a diversion—that is different, more beautiful, and more friendly than what they call home.

These are the twin realities between which our struggle for self-determination is strung. Culture, ancient and wise, at one end. Imperialism, poisonous and seemingly all-powerful, at the other end. Between them are modern class formations: a growing urban proletariat, and a collaborating Native elite that is too willing to sell out for profit.

Definitions of Self-Determination: Collective and Indigenous

This is our present world: not wholly traditional but not completely industrial; not self-sufficient but not fully integrated into and dependent upon the West or upon Japan. Given this world, what would self-determination mean for Pacific Island women in the larger context of the historical moment?

First, I think Pacific Island women, like Hawaiian women, seek a collective self-determination. That is to say, they want to achieve freedom through and with their own people, not separated from them as individuals or as splintered groups. Such individualism and separation promise only more confusion and more alienation, the very maladies that so afflict industrial peoples.

To be Hawaiian, for example, is more important and truer to ourselves than to be Western-educated, nuclear-familied, rich, or propertied. This is why many Hawaiians continue to spend rather than save their meager earnings, to have so-called "illegitimate" children, and to be poor consumers. This is also why so many Hawaiians don't rise into the white middle class like Asians do in Hawai'i. Hawaiians hold other cultural values more dear: affection, generosity, traditional dance, and perhaps most telling of all, gathering together to share work, play, grief, and love. Tragically, we are imprisoned in a dominant culture that values and rewards unceasing work, accumulation of things, and calculation of every dollar, every child, even of every smile.

Therefore, self-determination for us means self-determination within our own cultural definitions and through our own cultural ways. It does not mean struggle as a class moving up and into the mainstream. Being Hawaiian-hyphen-Americans is not our intention. We are not immigrants seeking a better life. The best life Hawaiians ever enjoyed existed long ago, before the coming of white people to our land. Given this, why should we want to be like white people or like Americans? For Native people, forced assimilation and acculturation are nothing less than racism and, in extreme cases, genocide. Sovereignty, for us, promises the institutional and psychological opposite of racism. Sovereignty is the assertion that "what we are"—culturally, emotionally, and physically—is "what we prefer to be."

Second, our efforts at collective self-determination mean that we find solidarity with our own people, including our own men, more likely, indeed preferable, to solidarity with white people, including white feminists. Struggle with our men occurs laterally, across and within our movement. It does not occur vertically with the white women's movement and indigenous women on one side and white men and Hawaiian men on the other side.

The reasons for this should be obvious. We have more in common, politically and culturally, with our men and with each other as indigenous women than we do with white people, who are called *haole* in Hawaiian. This is only to make the point that culture is a larger reality than women's rights.

Then there is the historical hegemony of the haole and haole culture in Hawai'i, so that when Hawaiian women are with haole feminists, we see and hear the haole rather than the woman or the feminist. Haole feminists, for the most part, embody white privileges. They exude white culture, white power, white assumptions. Even their speaking habits, often so aggressive and formal in style, are an affront to Native Hawaiians.

It is imperative to understand that for us, the haole are the interlopers in Hawai'i, whether they happen to be feminists or Marxists or capitalists or California new- agers. Before they say a single word, they are already communicating that they are haole. In their presence, we feel vast differences in heritage and in values. Between Hawaiians and the haole, the cultural lines are drawn deep and fast across two hundred years of history.

At this point in our struggle, race and culture are stronger forces than sex and gender. We will make common cause with our own people, and other Native peoples, before we make common cause with non-Natives in our lands.

This does not mean, however, that white people, including white feminists, have no role to play in our larger struggle for self-determination. Their role is to support our efforts publicly, to form antiracist groups that address our people's oppression through institutional channels, and to speak out when we are attacked by other white people.

This last role is crucial. It is not the responsibility of Native people to answer white people who charge us with racism. We have more than enough to handle with our own struggles. It is, however, the duty of sympathetic whites to deal with their guilt by acknowledging that they live on stolen land. Then they should begin addressing hostile whites who oppose us. For Native nationalists there is a simple solution to the oft-voiced complaint, "I didn't steal your land, what can I do?" In Hawai'i, any haole who benefits by living on our land owes us support. And I don't mean liberal hand-wringing but *public, organized support.*

Haole feminists in Hawai'i suffer from an ignorance that seems to afflict Americans and white people in general: they are willfully ignorant of the geographic and cultural place they inhabit. Hawai'i, to most Americans, is just an extension of California and, like California, is without a history of conquest, of dispossession of Native peoples, of ongoing suffering and disenfranchisement of Native peoples. Unlike Hawaiians who are always made to be aware of their lack of control and "minority" difference (despite the numerical minority of white people in Hawai'i), Americans in Hawai'i assert their presence and their power through total ignorance of where they are, where

Hawai'i is (e.g., in Polynesia and not in California), and how they, themselves, are part of the dominant culture in Hawai'i.

Finally, self-determination for Pacific Island women means an indigenous, not a Western, definition of women's power. This power had often been more far-reaching and more respected in indigenous societies than haole feminist ideology, and strategy, imply. For example, women-selected male chiefs and men's and women's houses have been criticized by haole feminists as patriarchal customs. But a deeper, culturally aware perspective often reveals a different source and functioning of women's power—one not so obvious to haole eyes accustomed to atomized Western culture and the notion of "individual rights."

A major issue here is women leaders. Such women now form a visible front in Native movements throughout the Pacific. Maori women, Tahitian women, Hawaiian women, Chamorro women, Kanak women, Vanuatu women, women of the Solomons and of New Guinea have been active and outspoken in the struggles of their people. These women are not only young, they are middle-aged and elderly as well. They have come to be identified by white feminists as feminist leaders, that is to say, as women who have come into leadership in their movements as a result of a global women's movement and with Western-style women's rights in mind.

But my cultural perspective is that Native women leaders are only taking their older cultural roles—protecting the family, for example—and acting them out in a wider forum. It isn't feminism that has pushed women to the forefront of leadership. It is the traditional role of Native women in a changed political context, a context that has undermined their entire way of life, thrusting them out into a colonial world to do battle with the colonizers.

This analysis entails a Native angle of vision on women's leadership. It also entails a larger understanding of the primacy of colonialism in the lives of the colonized.

Actually, the whole question of women's leadership is secondary to the enormous problem of imperialism. If Pacific Island women, and particularly Hawaiian women, live in a white- and Japanese-dominated Pacific, why should we care about whether women are running for president of the occupying country responsible for our degradation? Indeed, why should we make common cause with white feminist issues when our cultural base, the land, is slowly being annihilated by the bulldozer or the warship or the nuclear cloud?

Issues of Self-Determination: Land Base, Cultural Identity, and Regional Security

As our understanding of self-determination is both collective and indigenous, so too are our specific issues.

Some form of territorial autonomy is a common goal of all Pacific Islanders. In the immediate future, this means independence for the Kanaks from the French. They have been supported by the South Pacific Forum (composed of independent nations in the South Pacific) and now by the United Nations, which has relisted New Caledonia as a non-self-governing territory, eligible for decolonization.

Following the Kanaks are the Tahitians, who have very active independence parties and a strong antinuclear movement. The territorial claims of the Maori, the West Papuans, the Marshall Islanders, the Chamorros, Australian aborigines, and the Hawaiians are close behind the Tahitians. All of these claims involve ancestral lands, self-governance, and the universal recognition of all people to determine their own economic and political future.

Intimately tied to the independence issue is the Nuclear-Free Pacific Movement. For more than two decades this movement has sought to end the presence of nuclear fuel and weapons, nuclear testing, and the mining of uranium in the Pacific.

Beyond this, the People's Charter for a Nuclear-Free and Independent Pacific unanimously supports "political independence" for all peoples of the Pacific, *and* a Pacific Nuclear-Free Zone to include all the areas of the Pacific bounded by Latin America, the Antarctic, the Indian Ocean, and the Association of Southeast Asian Nations (ASEAN) zones. This would include all of Micronesia, Australia, the Philippines, Japan, and Hawai'i. Although the South Pacific Forum's antinuclear Treaty of Rarotonga[3] is not as strong as the Melanesian spear group of Vanuatu, New Guinea, and the Solomons would like, it is still a clear statement to the world that the nations of the South Pacific wish to decide for themselves where the nuclear horizon will be. After suffering the poisoning of nuclear tests by the colonial powers, South Pacific nations are moving to restrict nuclearization as much as they can. It is instructive that Britain, France, and America have refused to sign the Treaty of Rarotonga, especially in light of Soviet and Chinese willingness to sign. Of course the Treaty does not include Hawai'i, which is flooded with American nuclear submarines, stored nuclear weapons, and American troops, which can be deployed to the South Pacific or Asia at a moment's notice.

The issue of nuclear militarization of the Pacific underscores the issue of protection of our lands and waters from environmental poisoning and exploitation. Apart from land-based resources—like gold in Melanesian nations and nickel in New Caledonia—this area of concern includes protection of (and fair rates for) fish, seabed minerals, and other ocean/land privileges held by foreign countries. Protection of the oceans is of paramount importance here, because all of the people of the Pacific Islands are dependent upon the seas as much as, if not more than, on their islands.

Protection and transmission of our island cultures goes hand in hand with protection of the ocean and land. At issue is the rapid and severe impact of foreign cultures and economies on peoples dependent upon subsistence lifeways, with little or no advanced technology. When coupled with the effects of tourism, rapid introduction of mass communication and transport can destroy cultures in less than a generation. This is what has happened in Hawai'i. And we, like other Pacific Islanders, realize how much Hawai'i exemplifies the power of colonialism to crush indigenous people.

The issue of foreign policy means a self-determination that asserts the right of Pacific Island peoples to venture out from under the Euro-American umbrella. The antinuclear stand of New Zealand that so angers the United States, the overtures of small island nations to the Russians for fishing agreements, and the skillful use of the United Nations and the Third World to bring global support to the cause of independence for the Kanaks are excellent cases of what Pacific Islanders must continue to do: assert their birthright to deal with whomever they choose on whatever terms they choose as sovereign peoples.

Finally, the need for Pacific regional security is demonstrated by the 1987 bombing of the Greenpeace ship Rainbow Warrior in Auckland harbor, and the subsequent admission by the French that their espionage agents were responsible. Events like this underscore the importance of unified positions on major issues affecting the region, like nuclearization, resource exploitation (particularly seabed mining), mass-based corporate tourism, and the role of multinational corporations generally. Without unity, colonial predators will feast on small island nations, while regional powers, like Australia, will join in the celebration.

These are the crucial struggles for all Pacific Island people: sovereign territorial control, a nuclear-free Pacific, protected environments and cultures, and regional security.

The Hawaiian Example

When applied to Hawai'i, these struggles are enormously magnified.

Imagine our lives.

We are 20 percent of a population overwhelmingly Asian and white. This means we are strangers in our own land. The economic, social, and political institutions, language, land tenure, transport, and communication systems in Hawai'i are all of American origin. Indeed, Hawai'i's ownership by the United States has been taken for granted for so long that Americans are shocked to learn how much they and their country are hated by Native nationalists. This hatred is the same hatred all Native peoples feel for occupying armies. Few

Americans know or care that Hawai'i was invaded by the American military in 1893, that our legally formed government was overthrown, and that our islands were forcibly annexed to the United States in 1898, against the wishes of the Hawaiian people. Since then, our ancestral lands have been continuously occupied by a foreign country and its military.

Now, we are desperately trying to preserve and transmit what is left of our language, our dance, and our religion. We are fighting on every island to stop resort development, missile-launching facilities, and the paving over of entire valleys with extravagant homes for the world's rich. We are protesting the biggest presence of American military anywhere on earth.[4] In the meantime, our people fill up the prison, unemployment, and homeless lists, or tragically give up Hawai'i altogether for life as the wandering dispossessed.

There is a fearful, crazy quality to our lives. At one and the same time, we teach traditional dance to our children, only to watch it degraded into tourist exotica; we stop one hotel only to learn that the land in dispute is zoned for another hotel a few years down the road; we assert our religion, asking the American courts to protect our volcano god, Pele, from development, only to learn that the government has plans to drill massive geothermal wells deep into her breast. We practice our religion by opening the Makahiki season—a period of four months in honor of the fertility god, Lono—on an island continuously bombed by the American military since 1941.

And while all this goes on, we are surrounded everywhere by millions of tourists, six million by this year's count. That works out to thirty tourists for every Hawaiian. What does this mean for us? It means that when we go to a *heiau* (temple) to worship, there are tourists making noise, leaving rubbish on the sacred stones, clicking cameras. It means that our beaches, once open and free to everyone, are now shoulder to shoulder with tourists demanding the shoreline for themselves. It means a huge increase in crime, the scarring of our lands with hotels, fast food outlets, gas stations, and freeways. It means, in a personally humiliating way, that I am now a tourist artifact, constantly bombarded by crude tourists asking me if I am a Native, if I can say something in Native, if I will let them take my picture.

This is the horror of the third stage of colonialism, where culture has been so thoroughly penetrated by commercialism: Native people become exotic ornaments for the First World.

Beyond the problems of tourism and cultural degradation, the whole question of territorial control in Hawai'i is further evidence of the complexity and depth of our colonization. The myths of democracy and Americanization as beneficial to Native Hawaiians have meant a Native population in the thrall of America. Decolonization must then shift from a primary focus on the mind of the colonized to a dual focus on reinvigoration of the Native culture, its superior land ethic and accompanying spiritual ethic, *and* an emphasis on political analysis of the colonial situation.

Since the modern Hawaiian movement began in 1970, land struggles have seemed, to many Hawaiians, a separate issue from cultural revival. Part of the reason for this is simply that those being evicted from our lands, or occupying military lands in protest of their use by non-Hawaiians, were not the same people striving to teach our ancient dance, create language-immersion schools for children, or save historic sites from demolition. This division actually reflects another problem, namely, the necessity for an evolution from cultural pride as Native Hawaiians to political resistance as Native nationalists. The first state is a precursor to the second. But the current problem for us Native nationalists is how to move our people from pride to resistance.

It is not simply that resistance increases the emotional and economic risks of an already burdened group but that the layers of colonization are so deep, the number of Hawaiians so small, and the opposing forces so overwhelming. We also have to contend with a public image that is far from sympathetic. Still, after more than fifteen years of struggle, the lessons are clear. Cultural revitalization without national consciousness sidetracks decolonization and maintains a large distance between cultural people and political people. Rather than one nationalist front, then, there is fragmentation and in-fighting that Americans profit from and enjoy.

The dangers of such disorder among our ranks are many. Tourism, like capitalism in general, thrives on anything that can increase profits. More authentic cultural rituals are easy prey to commodification, especially when so many of the Native people are already under the thumb of tourism as workers.

Second, the American myth of pluralism approves of ethnic diversity as long as it remains apolitical. In other words, traditional hula, Hawaiian language schools, and Hawaiian religion do not threaten American ideological hegemony unless they are attached to Hawaiian national consciousness rather than an American national consciousness.

Third, land struggles without a governing base are not national struggles and are, therefore, played out within the parameters of civil rights actions. The issue of indigenous claims is stillborn. Meanwhile, Marxists, white feminists, and liberals agitate against Native national consciousness by arguing that it is exclusionary, it is unfair (in the sense of antidemocratic), it is racist, and it is strategically unwise since, as the haole tell me daily, "you need all the help you can get."

In reality, the attitude of most Marxists and socialists is the same as that of white feminists and liberals on many issues. Few members of these groups are willing to question their presence on our lands, or to learn our history, especially the periods that involve the illegal and immoral actions of the American government. They all deal from ideological positions that are ignorant of what I would call a sense of peoplehood. And they all assume a similarity between the cultures of Native peoples everywhere, a similarity that conveniently excuses these foreigners from educating themselves about the particular place where they are living, including the Native people who have been dispossessed by foreigners to make way for foreigners. Armed with their ignorance, Marxists see class, not culture; white feminists see women, not people; and liberals see only individuals and individualism. None of these groups understands Native nations, despite the presence of over three thousand such in the United States. And all of these groups unthinkingly assume white culture as the unquestioned context within which political change will occur.

When we Native nationalists bring up Hawaiian culture and its inseparability from our people and our place, we are criticized for being romantic by the Marxists, for being racist by the liberals, and for being trapped in the patriotism of Western-style patriarchal nationalism by white bourgeois feminists.

To my mind, what all these positions have in common is the belief that culture is irrelevant, but not all culture, just Native culture. Such disregard for our culture in our own land recalls missionary imperialism in Hawai'i in the nineteenth century. Then, Hawaiians were bombarded by white people who fervently believed that Hawaiian culture was an impediment to the salvation of the soul. Today, Marxists believe it is an impediment to evolution and revolution, liberals believe it is an impediment to full civil rights, and white feminists believe it is an impediment to women's liberation. The similarities with missionaries are striking.

Regardless of what Marxists, liberals, and white feminists think about our alleged backwardness on the issue of culture, the main problem for our movement now is the lack of connection between cultural and political actions. I see this as a strategy question more than a theoretical problem, and I don't think it is insurmountable, given that in the last few years cultural leaders have begun saying publicly that they are nationalists. At the same time, political people have begun to see cultural revival as more central to psychological decolonization than they once believed. Apparently, the simple passage of time has allowed all of us in the movement to understand how culture and politics work together in strengthening our people's identification *as a people*. The depth of this identification is often a measure of the level of decolonization. Put bluntly, the more Hawaiians identify as Hawaiians, the less they are able to live with their identity as Americans and thus, with American ownership of their birthright: Hawai'i.

Indeed, the whole area of decolonizing the mind is very delicate. Language, for example, is a great decolonizer. Thinking in Hawaiian means, at the very least, thinking in the language of the land, of the culture, of alternative values and visions. Even without political analysis, Hawaiians who are familiar with their Native tongue are already thinking about things Hawaiian. They are more receptive to a Native nationalist argument because the language explains our commonalities as a people, that is, as a nation.

The same thing can be said for Hawaiians who know their history. Understanding the wisdom of the Hawaiian way on the land, and the rapid destruction of this way by the West, also makes for more receptivity to the choice of Native control and Native governance, that is, to the choice of Native nationalism.

Still, decolonization works in stages. And every place is unique in this respect. In my opinion, Hawai'i is the most colonized place in the Pacific. We have the most to fight against—for example, military saturation—and we are a minority in our own land. Unlike the Maoris', our islands are not territorially independent from the original colonial power. Unlike the Samoans, we do not control our islands, the bulk of which are held by the state of Hawai'i, the federal government, and a dozen or so major multinational corporations. Unlike the Tahitians, the vast majority of our people do not speak their native language. And our trust lands (like American Indian reservations, but without recognition of our nationhood) are controlled by the state and federal governments, which lease our lands to non-Natives.

On an ideological level, we are more integrated into popular culture, especially television and film, than are other Pacific Islanders. Popular culture alone is a tremendously powerful agent of colonization. Decolonizing young minds addicted to soap operas and MTV seems impossible without an alternative. Political analysis, unfortunately, is boring by comparison. This is where Hawaiian culture plays a significant role. It instills pride, it takes young minds away from colonial situations by providing physical and intellectual alternatives, and it opens up mental space for political analysis to slip in. But cultural activity must occur along with political analysis; otherwise they develop separately, and culture becomes an apolitical refuge from the colonial world. The potential for resistance is thus lost at the point of divergence, something Marxists fail to see because they are blind to the significance of culture in decolonization.

In the end, of course, decolonization is a long, generational process that can terminate at any plateau without bearing the fruit of Native national consciousness. Our only recourse is eternal vigilance, and the recruitment of young Hawaiians into the nationalist movement.

Conclusion

Colonialism in the Pacific has given rise to a movement among Native peoples for self-determination. Cultural identity, a land base, self-government, and regional security are major issues in these movements. Pacific Island women's self-determination is expressed within these parameters, as part of the broader economic and political context of their unique island group. Thus, what Pacific Island women contribute to their particular struggle for independence depends primarily on their cultural heritage and their colonial histories, rather than on feminist movements in the colonial nations. In the end, what Pacific Island women do will be different from what First World women have done, simply because the Pacific Islands are not the First World, nor are Pacific Island women First World women.

© 1992 by Haunani-Kay Trask.

NOTES

[1] For military information regarding Hawai'i, see U.S. Pacific Command, "Hawai'i Military Installations and Training Areas." U.S. Department of Defense, 1998. For tourist information regarding Hawai'i visitors, both east- and west- bound, see *Bank of Hawai'i Annual Economic Report,* 1999.

[2] For statistics on Hawaiian health see the following: David E. Stannard, "Disease and Infertility: A New Look at the Demographic Collapse of Native Populations in the Wake of Western Contact." *Journal of American Studies,* 24, 1990: 325–350; Mark Eshima, comp., *Native Hawaiian Data Book.* Honolulu: Office of Hawaiian Affairs, 1998: 414, Table 6.67; Merle A. Look and Kathryn L. Brown, *A Mortality Study of the Hawaiian People, 1910-1990.* Honolulu: The Queen's Health Systems, 1995. For a brief summary of contemporary health profiles of Native Hawaiians, see David E. Stannard, "The Hawaiians: Health, Justice, and Sovereignty." *Cultural Survival Quarterly,* 24, spring 2000: 15–20.

[3] For a discussion of the Pacific Theater as a nuclearized region, including the importance of the Treaty of Rarotonga, see the following: Stephen Henningham, "Keeping the Tricolor Flying: The French Pacific into the 1990s," *Contemporary Pacific* 1 (1 and 2) 1989; David Robie, *Blood on Their Banner: Nationalist Struggles in the Pacific.* London: Zed Books, 1989. For an analysis of the treaty, including the complete text, see Michael Hamel-Green, *South Pacific Nuclear Free Zone Treaty, A Critical Assessment, 1990.* Pacific Research Center, Australian National University. [The full text of the treaty can also be found at www.opanal.org/NWFZ/Rarotonga/rarotonga.htm. –Ed.]

[4] See "Hawai'i Military Installations and Training Areas."

Cincinnati, 1943

MITSUYE YAMADA

Freedom at last
in this town aimless
I walked against the rush
hour traffic
My first day
in a real city
where

no one knew me.

No one except one
hissing voice that said
dirty jap
warm spittle on my right cheek.
I turned and faced
the shop window
and my spittled face
spilled onto a hill
of books.
Words on display.

In Government Square
people criss-crossed
the street
like the spokes of
a giant wheel.

I lifted my right hand
but it would not obey me.
My other hand fumbled
for a hankie.

My tears would not
wash it. They stopped
and parted.
My hankie brushed
the forked

tears and spittle
together.
I edged toward the curb
loosened my fisthold
and the bleached laced
mother-ironed hankie blossomed in
the gutter atop teeth marked
gum wads and heeled candy wrappers.

Everyone knew me.

This piece first appeared in *Camp Notes and Other Poems,* originally published by Shameless Hussy Press in 1976 and by Kitchen Table/Women of Color Press in 1992. Currently published by Rutgers University Press, (New Brunswick, NJ, 1998) as *Camp Notes and Other Writings.*

The Real Southern Rebels

DENISE GIARDINA

I always considered myself a Southerner. People who heard my accent, especially Yankees who think everyone from the South talks the same, would agree. My eating habits tend to confirm my Southernness—I am partial to anything fried—though I try to stay away from grease these days, and I like greens and anything made from corn. I grew up with kudzu, the Grand Ole Opry, and people who put up preserves and who stop for funeral processions. I believe a house should have a front porch.

I always considered myself a Southerner. Then I moved to North Carolina.

I've lived in Durham the past two and a half years. This summer I'll be packing my bags and heading back to the Appalachian coal fields where I grew up. The coal fields are a tough place to live. Unemployment runs around 40 percent in places and money is scarce for schools and services because coal companies own most of the land and pay little tax. These same companies are stripping the hell out of the mountains and are destroying water tables. For anyone who cares about the place, living in Appalachia can be like watching your sister get beat up by her husband day in and day out, trying to stop the beating, and failing. Sometimes a person needs to look away.

I came to the Triangle for a change of scenery. I found much to enjoy here—great bookstores, a variety of restaurants, good friends—but I never felt at home. I've been wondering why. It has partly to do with landscape. Mountains imprint themselves on the souls of those who know them as children. The twists and hums of a prisoning hollow, the puffs of white steam rising from the hills in early morning or on a summer evening when the breeze turns cool, the awe-ful sight of an untidy range of peaks spilling one behind another—these things I crave. The pine-covered rises of the Piedmont have their own kind of beauty, but they aren't, somehow, enough.

And I miss much more than physical geography. Appalachia is culturally Southern in many ways, and the mountains and Deep South are also connected economically. But after putting in my time here, I've decided the two regions are like cousins with a strong family resemblance but different personalities.

My first sense of the connections and contradictions between the mountains and the rest of the South came back in the 1970s while watching the Academy Award-winning documentary *Harlan County, USA*. The movie followed events during the attempt by Harlan County, Kentucky miners to join the United Mine Workers of America, and the efforts of their company and the government to stop them. That company was Charlotte's Duke Power.

The bitter strike lasted for more than a year and ended only after a company guard shot a picket to death. The film included scenes of Duke Power press conferences, where one spokesman, asked about inadequate company housing provided for the workers, said, "[We plan to] upgrade our people—and they are our people—upgrade our people into trailers."

This plantation mentality that views workers as items on the inventory is not an attitude unique to Southern corporations. What is unique is the acceptance of the situation by Southerners, particularly white Southerners, not only as inevitable but as normal and even desirable. North Carolina business and political leaders even oppose a United Airlines facility that would bring hundreds of jobs to the state because they would be union jobs. North Carolinians seem to think that is just fine.

White Southerners like to think of themselves as rebels, to bask in their ancestors' defiance of the North. In fact, secession was one of the most anti-democratic rebellions in the history of the world, led by reactionaries looking to preserve their privilege and fed by other white men with no better sense than to go along, just so they could continue to claim they were better than Negroes. The South is a region that is used to being ruled by a big white man in a big white house, a region whose only significant act of rebellion by its white majority has been on behalf of the enslavement of its African American minority. And it still shows.

When coal field people look back and try to recover something of a democratic heritage with which to measure the present American mess, they find parents who went on strike and grandparents who lay down in front of strippers' bulldozers and great-grandparents who took up rifles against the coal companies, who even faced up to government troops on occasion, white and Black standing together despite individual bigotry. When white North Carolinians look back, they see a gaping hole, like a person born with some vital organ missing.

During the first year and a half I lived in Durham, a bitter coal strike ran its course in West Virginia, Virginia, and Kentucky. Most people here didn't notice, and many who did were probably unsympathetic to the miners on strike, even though it was the company that turned down a union contract it had previously honored and that cut off medical benefits to the elderly and disabled. Most North Carolinians saw another case of "union bosses" (a pet Jesse Helms epithet) causing trouble for fine upstanding American corporations and their employees who just want to make a hassle-free living.

Nothing could have been further from the truth of the situation, but to explain that to the average North Carolinian would take more time and space than I have here. A six-year-old in the coal fields knows more about unions than does a Tarheel[1] adult. Why are North Carolinians so blatantly ignorant about and opposed to unions? Race has to be a factor. The workers currently most likely to be organized in this state are poultry plant workers and migrant farm laborers, nearly all of them people of color. Only they have proud access to the rebellious history that democracy thrives on.

Working-class white North Carolinians, it seems, would rather be bossed around, abused physically, and underpaid than join an organization that puts them in solidarity with African Americans. In the mountains we call that cutting off your nose to spite your face.

North Carolina workers have rebelled on occasion. During the 1930s, Gastonia saw a bitter strike of mill workers. The powers that be played whites against Blacks, and cracked down hard. In other places—Detroit and Flint, Michigan, West Virginia, Kentucky—workers of that time also faced hunger and guns. They pulled together and endured. In North Carolina, people, especially white people, apparently decided unions weren't worth the trouble and gave up.

For forty years unions have been in decline thanks to the Taft-Hartley Act[2] and recent judicial decisions that make it almost impossible to win a strike. As a result, many unions have lost their militant edge. But in North Carolina, unions barely exist. While Carolinians and other Southerners continue their perverse attachment to so-called right-to-work laws (really right-to-have-your-life-run-by-your-employer laws), the South lags behind the rest of the nation in worker safety, workers' compensation, and wages.

Recently, in what one newspaper called "a graphic illustration of the power of business and industry," the North Carolina legislature voted overwhelmingly against expanding workers' compensation coverage to people with arm and leg injuries. The business lobby had a clear field as it stiff-armed legislators, because labor is practically invisible in this state. That absence makes itself felt in more than just workplace issues.

Take a state like Vermont, where socialist Bernie Sanders was elected from a blue-collar base while middle-class progressives mostly went for his Democratic opponent. Take West Virginia, a state of working-class people with blessedly few yuppies. West Virginia has a reputation for being backward, and yet all of its congressional representatives have liberal voting records and the state has a history of supporting measures like the Equal Rights Amendment. You will find old-fashioned crooks among West Virginia politicians, but few ideologues of the Helms variety.

West Virginia is not backward, but it is poor. It is poor in part because it has a work force with a reputation for standing up for itself. During the most recent strike, a West Virginia newspaper reported the state was being talked down on Wall Street because its government was reportedly too pro-worker. Meanwhile, Wall Street loves the South because Southern workers will take anything that is done to them. Great, say North Carolinians, as long as we get the jobs.

Yes, but what kinds of jobs?

A.O. Smith Company recently announced it would close an electric motor plant in eastern Kentucky that employed union workers and relocate it to Mebane. The Kentucky workers made $9.80 an hour. Nothing to get rich on, but still a living. The lucky people of Mebane will be getting the same jobs for less than $6 an hour—an opportunity to keep themselves in the ranks of the working poor with no workplace freedom. Aside from the questionable morality of happily taking food from two hundred Kentucky tables, Tarheels should consider that what goes around comes around. The North American Free Trade Agreement is here, thanks to the Clinton administration, and south of the border they work for $1 an hour, folks. North Carolina's faltering economy indicates Tarheels are already being hoisted on their own nonunion petard.

Time in the Piedmont has taught me there are Souths other than my own. Here I see lots of liberals who feel no connection to the working class, and I see a compliant white working class with no cohesive heritage except racism. No progressive movement will ever come of such a mix.

Then I think of the coal fields. Here miners took over a Virginia mine and talked about class war while even local government officials sat in front of scab coal trucks and were carted off to jail for supporting the strike.

And I recall an African American I met at a march who was president of his predominantly white union local and was jailed by the Feds in the 1970s for refusing to call his men off a strike. I recall visiting a remote West Virginia hollow and being lectured by an elderly white man about the evil of South African apartheid. He'd read about it in the *United Mine Workers Journal*. His counterpart in North Carolina would be reading Jesse Helms's newsletters and calling Nelson Mandela a communist.

Mountain people come in all kinds, and those hills hold their share of racists, sexists, and crooks. I've met conservative mountain people, but precious few outside of the larger towns who entertain illusions about our economic system. We've been contending for a hundred years with the same companies who own the oil of the Middle East. Mostly we've been losing, and lots of us have been forced into exile, but we're still holding on. If the union folded tomorrow, miners would still stand up for themselves, would still raise hell like their counterparts in the Soviet Union and Poland and Africa.

I can do without the BMWs, the Jesse Helms bumper stickers. I reckon I'll go back up home and set on that porch for a spell.

This essay first appeared in the *North Carolina Independent Weekly* (July 3, 1991, volume 9, number 27).

NOTES

[1] "A brigade of North Carolinians . . . failed to hold a certain hill [in a Civil War battle] and were laughed at by Mississippians for having forgotten to tar their heels that morning. Hence originated their cant name, 'Tar heels.'" *Overland Monthly,* Vol.3, 1869; quoted in Robert Hendrickson, *Word and Phrase Origins.* New York: Checkmark Books, 2000.

[2] The Labor Management Relations Act of 1947, known as the Taft-Hartley Act, weakened unions by placing limitations on the right to strike and permitting exemptions from union membership. It was passed over President Truman's veto.

Akwesasne: Mohawk Mother's Milk and PCBs

WINONA LADUKE

In the heart of the Mohawk nation is Akwesasne, or "Land Where the Partridge Drums." A twenty-five-square-mile reservation that spans the St. Lawrence River and the international border between northern New York and Canada, Akwesasne is home to about eight thousand Mohawks.

I'm riding the Akwesasne reservation roads with Katsi Cook, Mohawk midwife turned environmental justice activist. It is two o'clock in the morning, and Katsi is singing traditional Mohawk songs. Loud, so strong, is her voice. We are driving between Katsi's meetings, planes, and birth practice. The birthing chair she uses is wedged in her trunk between our suitcases. Her stamina is almost daunting. That may be the gift of a life-bringer, a midwife: all that power of birth and rebirth, which stays in your presence month after month. (Or, perhaps, it is just that she is a Mohawk. And, as Katsi jokes, *if you want something done, get a Mohawk to do it.*) My head droops to the side as we careen down the country roads of upstate New York, and my attention rivets back to her words, her company. Katsi is alternating between singing and explaining to me the process of bioaccumulation of polychlorinated biphenyls (PCBs) in breast milk. A combination of Mother Teresa and Carl Sagan.

She comes from a family whose tradition feeds her political work, and from a community with a long history of political resistance. "My father, mother, and grandparents of past generations distinguished themselves as political and cultural activists, who upheld community service as one of their highest standards," she explains. "My grandmother Elizabeth Kanatines [She Leads the Village] Cook, a traditional midwife, delivered me and many of the babies in my generation in the Mohawk territory at Akwesasne. My father, William Rasenne Cook, organized a cooperative at Akwesasne among the farmers and consumers. He also organized the peaceful ousting of New York state enforcement jurisdiction on our lands in 1948."[1]

Well, some things change, and some things do not. The Mohawks and Katsi Cook can tell you that. She is cut of the same cloth.

So it is that a culture and identity that are traditionally matrilineal will come into conflict with institutions that are historically focused upon their eradication. Katsi Cook, Wolf Clan mother and an individual who strives to uphold those traditions, finds that she must confront some large adversaries. Besides "catching babies," as she calls it, and raising her family of four children (the oldest of whom, Howie, bore her first grandchild in the winter of 1998),

Katsi finds herself in a standoff against her adversary, one of the largest corporations in the world: General Motors (GM). At its Massena, New York power train plant, General Motors has left a Superfund site—one with approximately 823,000 cubic yards of PCB-contaminated materials. GM has tainted the land, water, and ultimately the bodies of the Mohawk people, their babies included. Katsi's work is precedent-setting environmental justice work that links the intricate culture of the Mohawk people to the water, the turtles, the animal relatives, and ultimately the destruction of the industrialized General Motors Superfund site. "Why is it we must change our lives, our way of life, to accommodate the corporations, and they are allowed to continue without changing any of their behavior?" she asks.

The Mohawk Legacy

Mohawk legend says that at one time the earth was one, never-ending ocean. One day, a pregnant woman fell from the sky. A flock of swans carried her down to earth, gently placing her on the back of a large sea turtle. Some beavers then swam to the bottom of the ocean and picked up some soil and brought it back to this woman so she could have some dry ground on which to walk. She then walked in an ever-widening circle on the top of the turtle's back, spreading the soil around. On this giant turtle's back the earth became whole. As a result, North America is known today by the name Turtle Island.

As in the creation legend, the turtle remains the bedrock of many ecosystems. But snapping turtles found at so-called Contaminant Cove on the Akwesasne reservation contained some 3,067 parts per million (ppm) of PCB contamination; others were found with two thousand ppm PCB contamination. (According to EPA guidelines, fifty ppm PCBs in soil is considered to be "contaminated.") The story of how that turtle became contaminated in many ways mirrors the story of the Mohawk people of Akwesasne.[2]

> The Haudenosaunee, or Six Nations Iroquois Confederacy, is among the most ancient continuously operating governments in the world. Long before the arrival of the European peoples in North America, our people met in council to enact the principles of peaceful coexistence among nations and in recognition of the right of peoples to a continued and uninterrupted existence. European people left our council fires and journeyed forth in the world to spread principles of justice and democracy which they learned from us and have had profound effects upon the evolution of the Modern World.
>
> —Haudenosaunee Statement to the World,
> April 17, 1979[3]

The Mohawk people, like other Haudenosaunee, or Six Nations peoples, have lived in the eastern region of the continent for many generations. The Mohawks themselves are referred to as the Keepers of the Eastern Door of the Haudenosaunee Confederacy—the People of the Flint. It is said that the Six Nations peoples were once virtual slaves to the neighboring Algonkin peoples. Amidst their agricultural economy, they'd labored long and hard to pay the heavy tolls imposed upon them by the Algonkin.

But as the story goes, between miracles and sheer determination, the Six Nations peoples came to prosper in the region. As the generations passed, the differences grew between the peoples, and they divided into the Mohawk, Oneida, Onondaga, Cayuga, Seneca, and Tuscarora—the Six Nations. Early in their history, the great prophet Aiionwatha created the Haudenosaunee Confederacy, one of the most prominent and far-reaching forms of government ever created on the face of the earth. From this form of government came the concepts of constitutional government and representative democracy, the very foundation of the principles of the new American state. This form of government remains today in the Haudenosaunee Confederacy.

The Mohawk Nation expanded under the principles of the Great Law, established by Aiionwatha's teacher, the Great Huron Peacemaker. That law, *Kaienarakowa* (the Great Law of Peace and the Good Mind), upholds principles of kinship, women's leadership, and the value of the widest possible community consensus. Through these teachings and many others, the Mohawks eventually established communities scattered over fourteen million acres of land that straddle what would become the U.S.–Canada border. These lands would come to be home for seven major communities—Kahnawake, Kanehsatake, Akwesasne, Ganienkeh, Tyeninaga, Ohsweken, and Wahta.

While new American leaders such as George Washington, Patrick Henry, and Benjamin Franklin studied the Haudenosaunee government, they also engaged in land speculation over territory held by these peoples, and Mohawk lands were ceded through force, coercion, and deceit until fewer than 14,600 acres remained in New York State. By 1889, 80 percent of all Haudenosaunee land in New York State was under lease to non-Indian interests and individuals.[4]

For the Mohawks, words were not enough to defend their land. During the 1900s, additional land and jurisdiction grabs continued in Mohawk communities, along with Mohawk resistance to them. Whether through Katsi's father or the armed takeovers and struggles in the Mohawk communities of Ganienkeh (1974), Kahnawake (1988), or Kanehsatake (1990), the Mohawks have been vigilant in their commitment to their land, way of life, and economy.

Faced with heavy impacts on their traditional economy, the Mohawks adapted economically. First, as legendary high-steel workers, they built much of the infrastructure for eastern cities. Then, in more recent years, they have creatively used their strategic position on the national border to tap into the controversial "export-import" business, traversing colonial borders that separate the various Mohawk communities.

The Mohawks are also adept at both maintaining and recovering their culture and way of life. The Akwesasne Freedom School is foundational to that process. An independent elementary school run by the Mohawk Nation, the school was founded in 1979 by Mohawk parents concerned that their language and culture would slowly die out. In 1985, Mohawk-language immersion began. The Mohawk "Thanksgiving Address,"[4] which teaches gratitude to the earth and everything upon it, is used as the base of the curriculum. The students study the Mohawk ceremonial cycle, as well as reading, writing, math, science, and history, combining solid academics with Mohawk culture. "The prophecies say that the time will come when the grandchildren will speak to the whole world. The reason for the Akwesasne Freedom School is so that the grandchildren will have something significant to say," explains Sakokwenionkwas, or Tom Porter, a Mohawk chief.[5] (Porter is known for his recovery of traditional land. Leading some Mohawks into a different part of their traditional territory, Porter has successfully purchased some land and, with a number of traditional families, is in the process of restoring their village, on their own terms, and in their own way.)

Environmental struggles have also been a part of Mohawk history. In the 1950s, while Indian people nationally were mired in efforts to oppose termination, 130 acres of Akwesasne were flooded by the St. Lawrence Seaway project, and in 1967, nine thousand acres were flooded by the notorious Kinzua Dam project in upstate New York, which affected Seneca communities. In 1958, the New York State Power Authority attempted to seize half of the Tuscarora reservation; when the Tuscaroras physically blocked access to the site, "a 'compromise' was then implemented in which the state flooded 'only' 560 acres, or about one-eighth of the remaining Tuscarora land."[6]

Industry Takes Over

There is, through all of this, very little land left for the Mohawks and the Haudenosaunee. The St. Lawrence River, called *Kaniatarowaneneh,* which means "Majestic River" in Mohawk, has been the wellspring for much of Mohawk life. It has also been the target of much of the industrialism in the region. In 1903, the Aluminum Company of America (ALCOA) established a factory a few miles west of Akwesasne. Less than thirty years later, a biological survey noted serious local pollution problems. That was just the beginning.

In 1949, the St. Lawrence Seaway and Moses-Sanders Power Dam were built and hailed as the eighth wonder of the world. Dams and locks allowed huge ships to enter the Great Lakes from the Atlantic Ocean and produced cheap hydroelectric power that lured giant corporations to the St. Lawrence. In the late 1950s, General Motors, Reynolds, and Domtar (in Canada) became the Mohawks' neighbors, and the majestic river became a toxic cesspool.

In 1959, Reynolds established an aluminum plant one mile southwest of Akwesasne, and within a decade the facility was emitting fluorides into the atmosphere at a rate of four hundred pounds per hour. In 1973, pollution control devices reduced this level of emissions to seventy-five pounds per hour, but the cost of the pollution was high.[7]

According to Dr. Lennart Krook and Dr. George Maylin, two veterinarians from Cornell University, Mohawk farmers suffered severe stock losses of their dairy herds in the mid-1970s due to poor reproductive functions and fluorosis, a brittling and breakage of teeth and bones, which they found were linked to the fluoride emissions.[8] Additional studies have shown that area vegetation suffered as well. The impact on area wildlife is still unknown.[9]

Today, an estimated 25 percent of all North American industry is located on or near the Great Lakes, all of which are drained by the St. Lawrence River.[10] That puts the Akwesasne reservation downstream from some of the most lethal and extensive pollution on the continent.

Canada has singled out the Akwesasne Mohawk reservation from sixty-three Native communities in the Great Lakes basin as the most contaminated—a dubious honor. On the American side of the border, things aren't much better. Until the mid-1980s, five saturated lagoons and a number of PCB-filled sludge pits dotted GM's 258-acre property, adjacent to the reservation.[11]

Until 1978, when PCBs were banned, all of these companies used PCBs. Virtually all of those PCBs ended up in the surrounding water, soil, or air. Many of them have ended up in the fish, plants, and people of the Mohawk territory. An insidious chemical known to cause liver, brain, nerve, and skin disorders in humans, shrinking testicles in alligators, and cancer and reproductive disorders in laboratory animals, PCBs are among the most lethal poisons of industrialized society.

Studies of PCB contamination of alligators in the Everglades indicate a problem called emasculization—shrinking testicles in subsequent generations. A study of boys in Taiwan born to mothers exposed to PCBs found that they also had smaller penises. Studies of polar bears in the Arctic indicate dropping reproduction rates associated with PCB contamination, a concern in animals that are already threatened with extinction.[12] It will take a while for most Americans to consume levels of PCBs capable of causing such damage. But what happens if a segment of the population does become affected? Most of the information regarding the effects of PCBs and dibenzofurans (toxic chemicals formed by thermal degradation of PCBs) on human health is based on accidental poisonings.

In Japan in 1968 and in Taiwan in 1979, thousands of people accidentally ingested PCB-contaminated rice oil, which contained PCB concentrations as high as three thousand ppm. In Taiwan, twelve of the twenty-four people exposed died from liver diseases and cancers. Following both incidents, many people suffered from a severely disfiguring skin acne. Other problems included suppression of the immune system, making individuals more susceptible to many diseases. Thirty-seven babies born to PCB-poisoned Taiwanese women suffered from hyperpigmentation, facial swelling, abnormal calcification of the skull, low birth weight, and overall growth retardation. Eight of the infants died from pneumonia, bronchitis, or general weakness.[13]

Similarly, recent studies of malignant breast tumors indicate that PCBs may be linked to breast cancer. Researchers in Hartford, Connecticut, found that malignant breast tumors contained more than 50 percent as many PCBs as were found in the breast fat of women the same age and weight who did not have cancer.[14] Wayne State University's Joseph and Sandra Jacobson's study of 212 children reported worrisome data showing learning deficits in children who had the highest, although still modest, exposures to PCBs in the womb. Those children were reported to have scored about six points lower on IQ tests and also lagged behind on achievement tests that rely on short-term memory, planning ability, and sustained attention. Their word comprehension fell six months behind that of their less exposed eleven-year-old peers. Of the 212 children that were studied, 167 had been born to women who had eaten a modest amount of fish—at least 11.8 kilograms of Lake Michigan salmon or lake trout during the six years preceding their children's births.[15]

PCB Contamination at Akwesasne

In 1979, the Haudenosaunee called for thoughtful ways of living and issued the following statement to the world:

> Brothers and Sisters: Our ancient homeland is spotted today with an array of chemical dumps. Along the Niagara River, dioxin, a particularly deadly substance, threatens the remaining life there and in the waters which flow from there. Forestry departments spray the surviving forests with powerful insecticides to encourage tourism by people seeking a few days or weeks away from the cities where the air hangs heavy with sulphur and carbon oxides. The insecticides kill the black flies, but also destroy much of the food chain for the bird, fish, and

animal life which also inhabit those regions.

The fish of the Great Lakes are laced with mercury from industrial plants, and fluoride from aluminum plants poisons the land and the people. Sewage from the population centers is mixed with PCBs and PBS in the watershed of the great lakes and the Finger Lakes, and the water is virtually nowhere safe for any living creature.[16]

In 1981, the New York State Department of Environmental Conservation blew the whistle on General Motors' dumping of PCB-contaminated materials, reporting that there was "widespread contamination of local groundwater" by PCBs and heavy metals such as lead, chromium, mercury, cadmium, and antimony. Several Mohawks lived less than one hundred yards from the General Motors facility. At least forty-five Mohawk families drew their water from area wells, while over two syndrome families relied on water from an intake on the St. Lawrence River, which was only a half-mile from the GM plant.[17]

In October of 1983, after twenty-five years of dumping toxins, General Motors was fined $507,000 by the EPA for unlawful disposal of PCBs—in total, twenty-one violations of the Toxic Substances Control Act, or TSCA. Among the charges, General Motors was cited for ten counts of unlawful disposal of PCBs and eleven counts of unlawfully using PCB-laden oil in a pump house with no warning sign. At that time, GM received what was the highest EPA fine levied against a U.S. company for violations of the TSCA. The EPA placed the GM site on the National Priority List of Superfund sites that urgently need cleanup.[18]

But the EPA's early resolve quickly eroded. The latest battle with General Motors has been over regulatory gymnastics and some interesting redesignations of what the EPA admits is a very dangerous site. The EPA estimated that it could cost $138 million to clean up the GM site,[17] but during the mid-1990s has balked and backed down, redesignated and allowed for new proposals, proposals that would save General Motors a considerable amount of money. In August of 1990, the EPA suggested that "containment" rather than "treatment" can be appropriate for industrial sites contaminated with PCBs between ten and five hundred ppm. The redesignation by EPA meant that GM would have to dredge and/or treat only 54,000 cubic yards of contaminated soils, in contrast to the 171,000 cubic yards it currently has onsite or in nearby rivers and creeks. This redesignation of the numbers has saved General Motors over $15 million dollars in cleanup costs.[19]

"In one core sample of the river bottom at the GM site we tested, we found over six thousand ppm of PCBs," says Dave Arquette, an environmental specialist with the tribe. "GM put sand and gravel over those areas and considers that to be a permanent cap," he adds.[20] Today, the GM dump site is landscaped and covered with grass. But absent a liner under the waste, the GM contaminants still leach into the majestic river. The GM landfill "frustrates Tribal environmental standards applicable within the same ecosystem only a few feet away," according to the Akwesasne Task Force on the Environment.[21] "Capping is to cover up, not a cleanup," says an exasperated Jim Ransom of the task force.[22] The tribe's position is that the Mohawk PCB standard of 0.1 parts per million be applied to the entire cleanup, not just Mohawk land.

"This is a classic environmental justice site," says Ken Jock, a director of the Akwesasne Environment Program. A slight man with soft eyes and a quiet manner, he spends much of his time arguing with agencies about implementation of the law. His huge office is full of reports and photos documenting the extent of the contamination. The reports, photos, and sheer size of the Akwesasne Environment Program dwarf the infrastructure of most Indian nations in the country. Yet it seems that even with reams of paper, the action taken by federal agencies is minimal. "This all used to be a fishing village. That's all gone now. There's only one family that still fishes," Jock says. "We can't farm here because of all of those air emissions. Industry has pretty much taken the entire traditional lifestyle away from the community here."[23]

Today, 65 percent of the Mohawks on Akwesasne reservation have diabetes, says Jock. Henry Lickers, director of the environmental health branch of the Mohawk Council of Akwesasne, echoes Jock: "Our traditional lifestyle has been completely disrupted, and we have been forced to make choices to protect our future generations," says Lickers. "Many of the families used to eat twenty to twenty-five fish meals a month. It's now said that the traditional Mohawk diet is spaghetti."[24]

The Mothers' Milk Project

"The fact is that women are the first environment," says Katsi. "We accumulate toxic chemicals like PCBs, DDT, Mirex, HCBs, etc., dumped into the waters by various industries. They are stored in our body fat and are excreted primarily through breast milk. What that means is that through our own breast milk, our sacred natural link to our babies, they stand the chance of getting concentrated dosages." When the Mohawks found this out in the early 1980s, Katsi explains, "We were flabbergasted."[25]

Katsi Cook and other Mohawk women wanted to know the extent of their risk. In the fall of 1984, Katsi went to the office of Ward Stone, a wildlife pathologist. Stone's work documented toxicity in animals in the St. Lawrence/Mohawk/GM ecosystem and has been very influential internationally in the study and cleanup of the Great Lakes region. Stone showed that beluga whales of the St. Lawrence River carry some of the highest body burdens of toxic chemicals in the world and suffer from a host of problems, including rare cancers and pronounced disease and mortality among young whales. These whales have a reproductive success rate one-third that of belugas in the Arctic Ocean.[26] Katsi also went to the office of Brian Bush, a chemist at the Wadsworth Center for Laboratories and Research at the New York State Department of Health in Albany. She explained the concerns of the Mohawk women.

In 1985, Katsi helped create the Akwesasne Mothers' Milk Project in an effort to "understand and characterize how toxic contaminants have moved through the local food chain, including mothers' milk," as Katsi wrote. "You're not going to find a lot of women that went away to the universities and then came back to the community with degrees in environmental engineering," Katsi says. "It's hard to get the women involved although they are so impacted by all of this. Now [with the Mothers' Milk Project] the women are learning to apply science in their everyday lives."

Katsi's persistence, along with the work of Henry Lickers and Jim Ransom, former director of the St. Regis Mohawk Tribes Environmental Office, generated a bioaccumulative analysis of the entire food chain at Akwesasne, from fish to wildlife to breast milk. The collaborative epidemiological research project that ultimately resulted from Katsi's work was one of a scant eleven Superfund studies funded by the U.S. Congress, and the only one focused on human health.

Under Katsi's supervision, the research project studied fifty new mothers over several years and documented a 200 percent greater concentration of PCBs in the breast milk of those mothers who ate fish from the St. Lawrence River as opposed to the general population. "But their PCB levels came down after they stopped eating fish," Katsi explained. "I've got myself 0.108 parts per billion of mirex [a flame retardant], twenty-two parts per billion PCBs, 0.013 parts per billion HCBs, and 13.947 parts per billion DDC [a pesticide related to DDT] in my breast milk," Katsi said in an early 1990s interview, acknowledging the personal nature of the concern.[27] Related studies of fetal umbilical cord samples showed similar results. Subsequent studies indicated a decline generally, a result of the mothers reducing the consumption of natural foods.[28]

The Mohawk officials reassured the community that they could continue breast feeding their infants in spite of high levels of toxic contamination in the local fish and wildlife. But this advice was only viable because of the drastic reduction in the amount of fish consumed in the community.

Mohawk mothers voiced their anger at the contamination and the impact on their way of life. "Our traditional lifestyle has been completely disrupted, and we have been forced to protect our future generations. We feel anger at not being able to eat the fish. Although we are relieved that our responsible choices at the present protect our babies, this does not preclude the corporate responsibility of General Motors and other local industries to clean up the site," Katsi charges.

"The beauty of the response of the mothers," Katsi says, "is that they saw everything in a bigger picture. Many of us bless the seeds, pray to corn, and continue a one-on-one relationship with the earth." That process of remembering and restoring the relationship between people and the earth is a crucial part of healing the community from the violations of the industry in their way of life.

But "GM has been fighting us every step of the way," she says. In 1997, General Motors sat at the top of the U.S. Fortune 500 list.[27] It also sat on top of the world's Fortune 500 list. Not bad. So it's not like they couldn't spring some money for cleanup. But instead, they have degraded the Mohawks' water, air, and soil quality, and pushed for more lenient cleanup.

Part of the Mohawks' challenge is navigating the many jurisdictions and global corporations that have a stake in the region, as a bizarre result of colonialism. Akwesasne contends with two federal governments: Canada and the United States. Then there are two other governments—the province of Quebec and New York State. There are also several separate Mohawk jurisdictions, those recognized by the U.S. and Canadian federal governments, and the traditional Mohawk government. It seems that between them, no one can really make any progress. "New York State doesn't care, because as far as they're concerned, we're not part of New York State, we might as well be in Canada," says Ken Jock.[29] Canada views the problem as originating on the other side of the border, and among all of them, there seems to be limited application of the law. Except, that is, the law according to GM.

GM Goes Global

The Mohawk relations with GM, however, are not unique. In 1994, GM was hailed by *Multinational Monitor* as one of the ten worst corporations in the world and profiled in the illustrious Corporate Hall of Shame. GM was called on the carpet for the infamous exploding gas tanks, this time not on a Ford Pinto, but on a GM pickup. Two years before, the Council on Economic Priorities listed General Motors as a bad boy as well, mostly because of toxic releases. In its annual rankings in the Campaign for Cleaner Corporations, the council and a jury of investors, academics, religious institutions, and activists determine the largest culprits in relation to the environment. GM came in number two, after Cargill.[30] In 1988 and 1989, for instance, GM released nearly three times as much toxic material into the environment as Ford Motor Company, its principal competitor. The company is also potentially responsible for about two hundred Superfund sites.[31]

And the Mohawks' problems with GM are no longer just local problems for Mohawks; they are of urgent international concern. The national movement to stem the impact of PCBs and other toxic contamination, now often called "POPs," or persistent organic pollutants, is increasingly turning to international forums. POPs are airborne, ranging from the Arctic to the Antarctic, and are present in every segment of our environment. Theo Colburn, chief scientist to the World Wildlife Fund and author of *Our Stolen Future*, illuminates the scope of the problem in some remarks given at the State of the World Forum in 1996.

> Every one of you sitting here today is carrying at least five hundred measurable chemicals in your body that were never in anyone's body before the 1920s....We have dusted the globe with man-made chemicals that can undermine the development of the brain and behavior, and the endocrine, immune and reproductive systems, vital systems that assure perpetuity.... Everyone is exposed. You are not exposed to one chemical at a time, but a complex mixture of chemicals that changes day by day, hour by hour, depending on where you are and the environment you are in.... In the United States alone it is estimated that over seventy-two thousand different chemicals are used regularly. Two thousand five hundred new chemicals are introduced annually— and of these, only fifteen are partially tested for their safety. Not one of the chemicals in use today has been adequately tested for these intergenerational effects that are initiated in the womb.[32]

International discussions on POPs are now part of the United Nations, which in 1995 directed several international agencies to begin evaluating POPs, starting with the twelve most hazardous known substances (dubbed the "dirty dozen") and under a cooperative effort with more than one hundred countries.[33] It is hoped that an international protocol will stem their production and distribution. It will require much, particularly when one considers that the cleanup of a single site has met with so much red tape and foot dragging.

The Great Law of Peace and Good Mind

When you are out there on that river, you can think, you're at peace with yourself. You can talk to your Maker.

— Francis Jock, Mohawk fisherman[34]

Meanwhile, back at Akwesasne, Ken Jock and others are working on ecologically and culturally appropriate solutions. A new aquaculture project is underway. The fish farm consists of cages suspended off the bottom of the river, away from contaminated sediments. The fish are raised in the cages and fed on a diet of nutrient-rich, contaminant-free food. So far, the project shows promise and is expanding.

"The real question," Katsi says about all of this environmental justice work, is "how are we going to recreate a society where the women are going to be healthy?" That first environment, from Katsi's perspective, is the starting place for it all, and the best indicator. The first environment is about a baby, a woman, and family. Katsi's approach, not unlike that of her grandmother, the noted midwife from half a century ago, is that everything the mother feels, eats, and sees affects the baby. That is a part of the Mohawk belief system. That is why, whether it is GM contamination or the mental health of the mother, all must be cared for if the baby is to be healthy. And that is Katsi's work, holistic midwifery. "One home birth will impact thirty people," she tells me, and acknowledges it as a form of strengthening the social bonds of the community. She has deliveries coming up almost every month, but keeps her midwifery practice small so that she can attend to the holistic nature of bringing life into the world.

"The midwifery work is what keeps it all from being so damn depressing," she explains. "It's one thing to look at a statistic, it's another to look at and feel a baby," she continues. Katsi hopes one day to see a midwifery center and an exemption for aboriginal midwives to support their practices. "That is small remediation for the loss of self-esteem as a result of the breast milk contamination," she says.

In mid-September of 1997, Katsi Cook had her first face-to-face meeting with Carol Browner, then director of the Environmental Protection Agency. A decade after her first interactions with the federal agency, this would be the first time Cook would speak with Browner. She spoke mother to mother, explaining that the Mohawk mothers needed the EPA mother to help them. The Mohawks are hoping that the Great White Mother, the Environmental Protection Agency, will do her job. That she will protect the water, the air, the soil, and the unborn Mohawks. As of this writing, the Great White Mother has done little, but GM has budged slightly, because of all the community pressure. In 1998–99, some cleanup began. GM dredged some of the contaminants out of the bottom of the St. Lawrence and shipped them off to some unlucky community in Utah. According to Ransom, GM plans to "identify…hot spots inside the dump. Then, based on what they find, they may consider more remediation, or go back to…capping."[35]

According to the Mohawks, industry, along with government officials and policy makers worldwide, must heed the warnings that contaminated wildlife are sending before it is too late. The creation is unraveling, and the welfare of the entire planet is at stake. As the Mohawks would say, when the turtle dies, the world unravels. Instead of letting that happen, the Mohawks are determining their history. They are facing down General Motors, the Environmental Protection Agency, and the big industries. They are demanding a change and making their community stronger. Rebirthing their nation, from the first environment of the womb to the community and future generations, they are carrying on the principles of *Kaienarakowa,* the Great Law of Peace and the Good Mind.

Winona LaDuke, "Akwesasne: Mohawk Mother's Milk and PCBs" first appeared in *All Our Relations: Native Struggles for Land and Life* (Consortium Book Sales, 1999), now published by South End Press (Cambridge, MA, 2000).

NOTES

[1] This and other quotes from Katsi Cook are from an interview conducted on August 9, 1997, unless otherwise noted.

[2] Tim Bristol, "First Environment." *Turtle Quarterly,* fall 1992: 29.

[3] "Haudenosaunee Statement to the World." *Akwesasne Notes,* spring 1979.

[4] Ward Churchill, *Struggle for the Land.* Monroe, ME: Common Courage Press, 1993: 93.

[5] Akwesasne Freedom School literature, 1995.

[6] Churchill: 98.

[7] Janci Whitney Annunziata, "An Indigenous Strategy for Human Sustainability," Haudenosaunee Environmental Taskforce for the U.N. Environmental Program, 1992: 21.

[8] Annunziata: 21.

[9] Mary Francis Hoover, "Mohawk Land Under Attack: Akwesasne's Environment." *Turtle Quarterly:* 43.

[10] Akwesasne Task Force on the Environment, "Superfund Clean Up of Akwesasne: Case Study in Environmental Injustice." *International Journal of Contemporary Sociology,* October 1997.

[11] Hoover: 20.

[12] Theo Colburn, *Our Stolen Future: Are We Threatening Our Fertility, Intelligence, and Survival? A Scientific Detective Story.* New York: Penguin, 1997: 88–89, 151, 189.

[13] Hoover: 45.

[14] Laurie Garrett, "PCBs Linked to Human Breast Cancer: New Study Addresses Environmental Factors." *The Sun,* June 8, 1992: 3A.

[15] Janet Raloff, "Because We Eat PCBs…" *Science News Online,* September 14, 1996.

[16] "Haudenosaunee Statement to the World."

[17] Akwesasne Task Force on the Environment.

[18] Kallen Martin, "Akwesasne Industrial Contamination—Environmental Recovery." *Winds of Change,* summer 1996.

[19] Akwesasne Task Force on the Environment: 8, 9.

[20] Martin: 21.

[21] Akwesasne Task Force on the Environment: 9.

[22] Martin: 19–20.

[23] Interview with Ken Jock, August 10, 1997.

[24] Martin: 19–20.

[25] Winona LaDuke, "Katsi Cook, Mohawk Mothers' Milk, and PCBs." *Indigenous Woman,* 1993.

[26] See Donald A. Grinde and Bruce E. Johansen, *Ecocide of Native America: Environmental Destruction of Indigenous Lands and People.* Santa Fe: Clear Light, 1995: 171–203.

[27] LaDuke.

[28] Syuni-An Hwang, Edward F. Fitzgerald, Brian Bush, and Katsi Cook, "Exposure to PCBs from Hazardous Waste Among Mohawk Women and Infants at Akwesasne." *Technology: Journal of the Franklin Institute,* vol. 333A, 1996: 17–23.

[29] Interview with Ken Jock, August 9, 1997.

[30] Council on Economic Priorities, *Campaign for Cleaner Corporations.* Research Report, New York: December 1992.

[31] Council on Economic Priorities: 3, 4.

[32] Theo Colburn, Speech at State of the World Forum, San Francisco, CA, October 3, 1996.

[33] Colburn, speech.

[34] Mary Esch, "Local Reservation is Making News on the National Level." *Massena Observer,* December 17, 1987: 65.

[35] Interview with Jim Ransom, August 2, 1999.

Taking the River Back

MARY MORAN

Though we moved onto a mink farm, I don't remember the mink or the long rows of pens and kennels that they were raised in. Our house on that farm is just out of reach. I can almost hold the living room. But it pulls away.

The barn stands solid. Huge. And filled with hiding places. Our father punished my younger brother and me whenever he found us hiding in the barn. It was his, not our, place.

And the pigs. I remember the pigs. Round animals. Pink and black like the licorice candies we sometimes got at the grocery store in back of the tavern in Lily.

My brother and I hung over the tin fence watching the pigs hunt for corn and grain in the mud outside their shed. Mama didn't share our fondness and curiosity for the pigs. She told us to stay away from them because they were dirty.

She warned us to stay away from the Indians because they were dirty, too. She never told us that she was Indian and how my brothers and I were part of a tribal family in Canada.

There would be no Indians in our house. We had our father's skin. We would be Irish. And we would be clean. Our bodies scrubbed and white-towel rubbed. Our clothes laundered and pressed. And changed over and over again.

Before the snows came, we left Lily and drove up north to visit our relatives who lived in iron-ore country where we were born. That was the first time Uncle Will tried to tell my brothers and me what we weren't supposed to hear.

He started with his stories about working for the railroad before the accident that left him with a hand that looked like a bear's paw.

His voice changed when he started to talk about hunting. He said he was called *courier de bois,* half-breed trapper, in Canada.

He ran those stories through the woods of Ontario and then gathered us back on the riverbank to fish with him. Our unspeakable heritage began to skim the surface of the water in whispers.

Uncle told us about water spiders and how they went against the current, jumping over the ripples that pushed them downstream. He said they took the river back, all the way to its beginning place.

Traveling Through Big Mountain

JUDITH MCDANIEL

I sat on the dirt floor of Katherine Smith's hogan as she prepared fry bread over an open fire. Outside, only a few hundred yards away, run the high-power electrical wires that carry electricity down to Phoenix and Los Angeles, but in this hogan there is no electricity, no phone, no running water.

I had come to the Navajo/Hopi reservation to meet this woman and to see for myself the landscape of Big Mountain. I had been told this area is sacred to the Hopi and Navajo peoples, and when I left Katherine Smith later that night and drove the many miles of dirt road leading to a highway, I understood that belief in a new way. The moon was full; it highlighted the mesa rising, first on one side of the road, then on the other. At one bend in the road the mesa became rock sculptures, rising like proud elder spirits shimmering in the moonlight.

I had come to this hogan to say thank you to Katherine Smith for her endurance and her vision. I only meant to stay a few minutes, for I did not want to intrude, but her youngest daughter, Mary, told me that I could not leave a Navajo home without eating or it would be a great shame to them. "If we have sixty visitors a day," she said, "we eat sixty times." So I settled back on the dirt floor and watched as she mixed the flour and a little of the precious water, opened a can of beans, and placed it on the fire to warm.

I told Katherine Smith that I was a writer, and she said that she had written something once on a flag. What she wrote in the white stripes on the flag was that it had become the flag of cheaters and liars and greedy people who only wanted money. She wondered if U.S. citizens ever remembered what their flag had originally meant.

When the fry bread and coffee were ready, we all ate: first the company, then some of the family, finally Katherine herself. Her oldest son, Julian Begay, who was visiting, told me I should try a piece of the corn bread that was with the fry bread in the pan we were eating from. He said it was baked in an in-ground oven for a puberty celebration; when a young girl becomes a woman, Navajos bake this special kind of bread. I tasted it. At first it had a kind of fragrance, but by the second or third bite it was like corn bread, only a little grainy and very dry. He said they also used to have a ceremony with this kind of bread on the day when a baby in the family laughed for the first time, and I thought that was wonderful, to have a celebration when a baby laughs and becomes part of the family.

After we had eaten, Katherine began to talk a little bit about the day she had first seen the men building the fence across her land. She was out with the sheep. She said, "I was alone and I saw them and went over to them and told them to stop, that they weren't to build a fence there. They went away that day and the second day they came back and were building the fence again and I went in and got that old rifle," she gestured towards the corner where an old single-shot rifle stood, "and went out. There was a Hopi man dropping fence poles into the holes from a tank. They were using an old tank with a white star on its side to build this fence, a tank like they had used in Vietnam. And I thought that if they were going to make war in their own country, then I would respond. So I fired a shot over the head of the Hopi man who was dropping those fence poles into the holes and he just flew to the ground. He absolutely fell off the tank. Then I walked over to the policeman by myself and three policemen arrested me and took the gun and took me to Chinle to prison."

At that point Julian began to tell the rest of the story. Chinle is on the other side of the reservation, about sixty miles from Big Mountain. They put her in jail for the night and the next day she was called up before the judge along with a bunch of drunks. When she got in front of the judge he asked what she was here for. And she said she had no idea, because she wasn't going to give him any help. The men didn't show up to charge her because this judge didn't have any jurisdiction within the Navajo boundary where she had been arrested. So the judge released her. There she was, this sixty-seven-year-old woman released sixty miles from her home, and she started to walk home. Then the policemen came along and picked her up again and took her to the right jail, but still she was never convicted or sentenced. Julian thinks that people in Washington don't know what's going on in Big Mountain, how the elders are being harassed, that this is coming from the local authorities in Flagstaff. But I doubt that: I am sure it is orchestrated in Washington.

Just then a jet flew overhead. It flew incredibly low and the whole hogan shook. We couldn't talk. I couldn't imagine any other place where a jet would be allowed to fly so low over an inhabited area. As it flew by, the coyotes screamed in terror. Katherine's sister, Pauline Whitesinger, has said that half of her sheep are dead from this kind of flyover. Swan Eagle, one of the white women in the support camp, reminded me, when I asked about the flyover, that the U.S. government is waging "technowar" on these people, that it doesn't take a machine gun to wage war. Genocide in slow motion is more palatable.

The day before, I had interviewed Elmer Clark, a member of the Navajo-Hopi Land Commission, in his office in Flagstaff. He is a Navajo professional in his midthirties, obviously very concerned about the relocation problems being faced by those who have gone and those who have stayed. The commission has been hearing testimony from the people affected by the relocation. I read the testimony of Bert Toney, a sixty-three-year-old Navajo. Bert is an army veteran of World War II, and his four sons are vets now, too. In his testimony, Bert says he was born and raised at Echo Canyon, the homelands from which he was relocated fourteen years ago:

> I went to World War II. I was out front at the time the war was at its peak…and I know it's very fearful. Today it seems all my sacrifice and efforts have gone unrecognized. I was told to defend my land and took the oath in Phoenix. That's where I enlisted when I was drafted…. That land (Echo Canyon) over there was our grandfather's and it's been so for three generations. It's not something that's only recent. Our grand-fathers and grandmothers were exiled to Fort Sumner. Many of them at that time were massacred also. And the same thing continues today. It's no wonder you shed tears.
>
> So its real hard when something like this happens to you. When the Mother Earth you're born on and where your umbilical cord is buried; when the livelihood was strong, when the cornfields flourished, where there was no such thing as hunger; we never knew hunger when we had livestock; sheep, horses, and cattle were there to be cared for; where water is plentiful and strong, where our grandmother's house still stands.

Elmer Clark told me he had gone back to Echo Canyon with Bert Toney, gone back as an archivist with his camera and tape recorder, listening to Bert's stories about the land all the way down the winding obscure path to the canyon floor. He showed me some of the slides he'd taken that day, and the vistas from the canyon rim were breathtaking. Down in the canyon were several family hogans that had been partially bulldozed so Bert wouldn't move back in. In one corner of the canyon, by an old corral, was a shack that a Hopi family had built the year Bert moved out. They lived there for two years but the place has been deserted ever since, which is why Elmer and Bert were able to go back down the canyon. Bert takes his canteen with him on these trips to get water from the spring. He told Elmer that it was special water. He doesn't drink it up in one day. Bert says it is a way to maintain his sanity. He is in love with this area and his home, and he believes he will go crazy if he can't have this contact with it.

The Struggle

The struggle being enacted at Big Mountain and in Central America and South Africa and with the homeless people in Times Square and other urban centers is the same. It is a struggle over how we define the sacred. For if we are willing to disbelieve the fiction that the problem at Big Mountain is between the Navajo and Hopi peoples, or that the problem in Nicaragua is between the

Sandinistas and the Contras, then it is possible to see that there are two opposing "sacred" forces in these and so many other places around the world. Those two forces are the "sacred" profit motive of capitalism, which is in fact profane, and the sacred right of individuals to life and human dignity. But instead, just as the Reagan administration wanted us to believe it is really a conflict between communism and democracy in Central America, so we are being asked to believe that these native peoples who have lived together for (perhaps) thousands of years can no longer do so without the intervention of the United States government.

Those of us who have been to Central America know the struggle there is for something more concrete than the ideology of communism, real or imagined: it is a struggle for food, for the land reform that allows people to grow their own food, for the education that encourages free choices, and for the right to dissent without being murdered. That struggle is opposed by the corporate forces that want access to the land and other resources, access to a near-slave labor population. In the most extreme cases, achieving a profit requires genocide; there are simply too many people to feed and their labor is no longer necessary. Genocide is the result, if not the intention, of the high intensity bombing in El Salvador's rural areas, and in Guatemala with the forced relocation of the Indian people. Genocide is the result, if not the intention, of Congress's Public Law 93-531, which would relocate the Hopi and Navajo people in the Big Mountain area.

It seems almost irrelevant to catalog the corporate interests in Big Mountain. Driving to the north, through the Black Mesa area, I could not help but be aware of the richness under the earth, for the coal mining companies have torn the topsoil up and spilled the huge veins of coal out. Just above Tuba City I drove past an abandoned uranium processing plant with radioactive tailings open to the air. A barbed wire fence keeps the cattle and sheep out. Last year some children broke through the fence and played on the huge slag piles, unaware, of course, that they could be harmed by the radiation. Boeing owns 10 percent of Peabody Coal and Peabody owns the mineral rights to Big Mountain. As soon as the people can be forced off the land, Peabody will stripmine it; the Environmental Protection Agency has declared this desert "unreclaimable" and told Peabody Coal they don't even have to try and restore it. So this fragile ecological balance will be destroyed.

Boeing has sold enough jet airliners to South Africa to make South African Airways the aviator giant of the continent. It sells rotary blades for Huey helicopters to Central America. It provides AWAC surveillance crews and plans to advise the El Salvadoran military's bombing raids. Exxon, Bechtel, Citicorp, Chevron, Anaconda Copper all have similar patterns, involving them in the exploitation of native people and denying those people the right to live on and possess their own lands in Africa, Central America, and the U.S. Southwest. A young Navajo woman I spoke with, who was selling jewelry at Four Corners, said she wanted to own a piece of land some day that no one could take away from her. She wanted it not to belong to the tribal council and not to belong to the U.S. government, but to belong to her. "I don't think this is going to last," she said, waving her hand in the general direction of the reservation. "I think that they're starting to sell it off. They've already sold pieces of it and I just don't think this is going to be here much longer." And certainly in terms of the coal mining interests and the uranium mining interests, she is probably right.

And yet the illusion of relocation on reservation land continues. Part of Elmer Clark's job, as a Navajo-Hopi land commissioner, is to take families out to the New Land to which they would be relocated if they agree to move. From October to December of 1985, the year before the relocation became mandatory, he made six trips, each time showing ten to fifteen families the potential for creating a new life and new settlement. Everyone in the Southwest knows about the uranium spill into a river about forty miles north of the New Lands. Residents of the nearest community have reported contamination of wells. Elmer Clark said it was the issue every family on every trip asked him about, and it is the one about which he has no information. No effort has been made to clean up the spill and no agency—none—can guarantee that the water supply to the New Lands has not been contaminated. For herders and farmers, that news means the area is essentially unusable.

In addition, the Relocation Commission has refused to recognize, or certify as eligible for relocation funds, the extended family so central to the Navajo way of life. Generally only 50 percent of any family is certified; the other half is disqualified by stringent regulations. They are younger adults who may have chosen to live away from the family hogan for a year or so, men who have had to go to neighboring towns to work, and others. The elders, who usually do qualify, have responded by saying, "If relocation is going to happen, move my grandkids first, then my children. I want them to be accommodated, then I'll go." But the children are frequently ineligible for relocation funds, and so, says Clark, there is another impasse.

But the ultimate impasse may be the U.S. Congress, which has ordered the families to relocate while refusing to vote adequate funds to develop the areas into which they are to move. Clark suggested the Relocation Commission may have been responsible for drawing too grand a picture, trying to entice the families to agree to relocation at the beginning of the process. Commissioners went out to the reservation to find out what type of development—economic development, community development—they would like to see on the New Lands. Families said they wanted fire stations, police stations, senior citizens centers, preschools. And now, after all of that information gathering, families are being told that there will be no development, no community infrastructure, not even basic health care facilities. The money available for relocation is just for housing, water, and sewers. There are no jobs to earn the money needed to pay for utilities, to build new herds, to create a life comparable to what the families are told they must abandon. It is hardly surprising the struggle for Big Mountain is bitter.

Earth as Sanctuary: The Future

Katherine Smith's youngest daughter, Mary, wants to herd sheep like her mother. She has been away from home and decided to come back. Two years studying biology at UCLA convinced her that it wasn't "relevant," so she came home. I looked around the hogan as Mary told me this, looked at the wood stove in the center of the round room where Katherine cooked, looked at the loom on one wall, the narrow beds on the other walls. I wondered what it would be like to come home to this hogan to live with no running water or electricity. What did it mean that she could make such a choice? And I had no doubt it was a choice; Mary is an intelligent, attractive, articulate young woman who could have had, I would guess, almost any career she wanted in white society. She wanted nothing it had to offer. Her mother's way of life, she was telling me, offered her everything that mattered.

Katherine Smith is one of the four keepers of the Navajo sacred earth bundles. As a white person, I have almost no idea what that means. But as a person who cares about the earth's survival, I approach Katherine Smith, keeper of the earth, with awe and reverence. And despair.

Because here is one elder woman—joined with other men and women, it is true, but they are so few—who is in opposition to all of the forces of a modern technological capitalistic society that says she is anachronistic. Life isn't that way any more, those forces say, she has to change. And Katherine Smith says no. Katherine Smith says that it is we who live in this other society who are anachronistic, that is, out of time. The earth is time, all time. She says that if we destroy the earth, we will cease to exist.

Some of the people working on Big Mountain survival issues believe that Big Mountain today is the frontline, that all of the issues we have theorized about and worked for—those of us who stand for the earth—are being played out at Big Mountain: issues of how women are treated, how children are treated, how men and women can work together with mutual respect, issues of race and racism and cultural difference, and the suffering of land-based people all over the globe. I think they are right. I am sure that Big Mountain is one of the frontlines, just as surely as Nicaragua and South Africa and Times Square are, each in its own way.

And as I drove down from Big Mountain that night in the full moonlight, the beauty of the earth and my own inability to imagine that it and its keepers could survive brought me to despair.

I wondered what it meant that as an activist I have been willing to defy the laws of my country to offer sanctuary to Central American refugees fleeing oppression in their own countries, when there is no sanctuary here in these United States for Katherine Smith and her children. What does it mean that environmentalists create sanctuaries for birds and flowers and wildlife, when there is no sanctuary in which the sacred remains of Katherine Smith's elders can be preserved and reverenced? For to walk out in any direction from her hogan on Big Mountain is to walk to a sacred place. Sometimes it is hard for a white person to recognize a sacred place, but here the earth is scattered with remnants of ancient pottery and other artifacts. Stripmining this land will destroy more than the ecology of nature; it will be a sacrilege, destroying the spiritual and material balance of Katherine Smith's world. I believe our survival in this world depends on recognizing her right to survive in a world we share.

From January, when I visited Big Mountain, until July, when I began this essay, to think about Big Mountain has been to experience over again the despair I felt that night driving down from Katherine Smith's hogan, for I am afraid the people fighting for survival at Big Mountain—their own survival and this world's survival—may not succeed. But when I went back to my notes I rediscovered a conversation I had recorded with the white woman named Swan Eagle. She had helped Pauline Whitesinger herd sheep for a number of weeks.

Once Pauline had come back from a meeting with a government official who had told the people that those resisting relocation could expect to lose their lives. "Instead of getting upset," Swan Eagle reported, "Pauline told me prayers that can be said, and she said, 'They work, I know. They will keep the evil away.'" For Swan Eagle, the knowledge of those prayers was a major insight into how important the ceremonies are to this struggle. "The elders," she said, "do not believe that violence on their part will win the struggle. They do believe that the unity of all the races and the shared spirituality will succeed in keeping the evil away."

It is the Navajo and Hopi elders, the traditional leaders, who are guiding the resistance at Big Mountain, and this gives me hope. White people have never before—to my knowledge—stood with Indian people when they have been facing massacre, nor have white people been willing to place themselves so completely under the direction and guidance of Indian people. It is absolutely essential, of course, that those who are being affected by the potential relocation should be allowed to set the terms of their resistance, but that has not always been the reality of solidarity work when white people have been willing to undertake it. This is, I imagine, one of the reasons the support movement for Big Mountain has been so slow to grow: that absolute insistence that anyone coming into the Navajo/Hopi cultures be willing to recognize and honor and take direction from the leaders of those cultures. What will be special for the white person who can enter into the space at Big Mountain in a supportive way will be the gift of directly sharing the danger and oppression of the Indian resisters.

As I drove away from the reservation, I saw a Navajo man in a wheelchair hitchhiking by the side of the road, going the opposite way from me. He sat in the wheelchair, his face impassive, his arm out to wave down any willing driver. He was close to my age and I imagine he was a Vietnam veteran. He had lost the use of his legs. Perhaps he was about to lose his home to the strip-miners. And I wondered how much more he would lose in the struggle to survive. Bert Toney's grandparents were massacred; other Indians were exiled to Fort Sumner. The same thing continues today, Bert said, and he is right.

It's no wonder you shed tears.

This essay, now revised, first appeared in *Sanctuary: A Journey* published by Firebrand Books (Ithaca, NY, 1987).

Still "A Difficult Journey Up the Mountain"? Palestinian Women's National Versus Gender Politics 1919–2002

ORAYB AREF NAJJAR

Introduction

Poet Fadwa Touquan, sister of the famous nationalist poet Ibrahim Touqan (1905-1941), has provided a most poignant description of the connection between personal and political freedom.

In her memoir, *A Difficult Journey up the Mountain,* she writes:

> While I was in this state of mental confinement and alienation, my father came and asked me to write political poems. He wanted me to fill the gap left by Ibrahim. On any new national or political occasion he would come to me and ask me to write about it. An inner voice protested silently: How, by what right or reason, is my father asking me to compose political poetry while I am locked up in the house, never attending the men's meetings, never hearing serious discussions, never participating in the turmoil of life? I didn't even know what my home country looked like, since I was not allowed to travel....My father...made me feel impotent....A poet must be familiar with life and with the surrounding world before dealing with them in verse. Where, then, was I to obtain the necessary primary material?...Since I was not socially free, how could I possibly fight with my pen for political, ideological, or national liberation?[1]

Although Touqan, who was born in 1917, was writing about a more conservative time in her city of Nablus, she raises an important issue: The connection between women's personal and national freedom. Touqan's question is still so relevant that the entire history of the Palestinian women's movement can be understood as women's search for a balance between the two freedoms.

In what follows, I describe how Palestinians, in the organizations they formed, have dealt with sexual versus nationalist issues over the years. I show that even though nationalism took precedence over gender issues after the 1948 dispersal of Palestinians, in the founding of the General Union of Palestinian Women (GUPW) in 1965, and even in the founding of four new women's committees between 1978 and 1981, leaders of those women's committees have only recently realized that unless they take part in drawing up a progressive social agenda for women *before* a Palestinian state is formed, their political achievements will be forgotten.

Palestinian Women in Palestine: 1900-1948

Articulating gender-specific goals, even in times of peace, has never been easy for women of any nationality. For women who are part of a community facing outside threats of dispossession, and later, exile, the task has been submerged under the weight of daily necessity and the struggle for survival.

The history of women's activism since the early 1900s in what used to be called Palestine shows that the first organized women's societies were philanthropic in nature and depended on the charity of middle- and upper-class women. Describing the various societies that existed mainly in Jaffa and Haifa, Palestinian lawyer Matiel Mogannam writes: "In all cases the income of these Arab women's organizations is limited. It is generally formed of personal contributions and of the proceeds of bazaars and flower days, which are especially arranged to augment their revenues."[2] Mogannam speaks with admiration about Arab women's organizations in Syria and Lebanon, where the movement was "more social than political," where women were more involved in public life and used the press to advocate their cause.[3] Although a number of small philanthropic societies were formed earlier, the first large women's organization, The Arab Women's Union, was founded in 1919. Mogannam writes that the union had aims like those spelled out in a resolution of the first Arab Women's Congress in 1930: "To assist the Arab woman in her endeavors to improve her standing, to help the poor and distressed, and to encourage and promote Arab national enterprises."[4]

Jewish immigration into Palestine increased. In 1922, Jews made up 11 percent of the total population of Palestine. That increased to 30 percent in 1936. Most of the growth took place between 1933 and 1936, in response to the rise of Hitler and Nazi Germany,[5] but Palestinians felt threatened by the influx of Jews and resented having to pay for Nazi sins.

Women, like their male nationalist counterparts, believed that the flood of Jewish immigrants into Palestine was endangering the country's Arab character and that the survival of Palestinians as a community was the most pressing problem they were confronting. So while women's unions in other countries of the Arab world asked for raising the marriage age for women, abolishing polygamy and summary divorce, and improving women's educational opportunities, Palestinian women's organizations adopted a set of nationalist demands and at the same time continued to do philanthropic work for the poor.[6] It was not that women were unaware of the need for change, but many felt that such change could not be implemented under a foreign power whose motives were suspect.[7]

Women joined the struggle to rid the country of British occupation. Of the one hundred and twenty Palestinians who were killed by the British as they put down a nationalist rebellion in August 1929, nine were women.[8] On October 26, 1929, two hundred women attended the first Arab Women's Congress in Jerusalem. Predictably, most of the resolutions that women developed dealt with nationalist questions. The first resolution called for the abrogation of the Balfour Declaration of 1917, which promised Jews a national home in Palestine; the second dealt with demands for a national government; and the third dealt with development of national industries and economics, according to Mogannam, who explains women's political involvement by noting: "The Arab women…found themselves unable to shirk the responsibility which was thrust upon their shoulders. Hundreds of men were sent to prison, hundreds of homes unmercifully destroyed, hundreds of children became orphans…. It was not strange, therefore, that such distressing circumstances as those in which Palestine was found in 1929 should have resulted in the greatest change in the life of the Arab women in Palestine and in the concentration of their forces."[9]

Although women continued to minister to the needy, such work increasingly took on a nationalist coloring. In 1930, for example, women bought two plots of land in Hebron and dedicated the land as a trust to benefit the families of three prisoners the British had sentenced to death.[10] Women stepped up their activities as Palestinians were preparing for what came to be called the 1936 Revolt, a popular rebellion that culminated in a six-month strike designed to force Britain to stop Jewish immigration to Palestine. Even women of the conservative but nationalist city of Nablus, Fadwa Touqan's city, took a leading role in public demonstrations against British immigration policies. Nationalist Akram Zuaytir , founder of the Independence Party, describes that involvement in his diary:

> April 30, 1936. I most admire what I heard today from female students of Nablus who came to the house to announce their readiness to sacrifice their souls for the sake of the homeland. The female students have formed a committee to represent them…and have decided to march in a demonstration tomorrow, and it is the first female demonstration in Nablus. They have agreed on a program, they have sewn Arab flags, they have prepared nationalist songs. [11]

The next day, Zuaytir writes:

> Today in Nablus was the great marvelous day for young female students, the demonstration was the largest ever in Nablus. By the time it got to be 3 P.M., thousands of people and delegations from villages met where the female students of Nablus were assembled…. And when the female students appeared carrying Arab flags and chanting for the homeland, we met them with thunderous applause…. Miss Yusra Said

Touqan was the first speaker, she saluted the martyrs, and announced the solidarity of the Arab woman with the nation in serious struggle, and she strongly attacked British policy. She was followed by Miss Ilham al-Masri who encouraged struggle and the continuation of the strike, and she called for the downfall of British imperialism. [12]

Seven female speakers followed, and the thrust of their speeches was nationalist. The women were not asking for anything for themselves, but for independence and freedom for the whole country. Their involvement had a strong symbolic component. It signaled to the British and Zionist forces that now all of Palestinian society had been recruited for the struggle. But it also signaled that the energy of the most educated of women was going to be spent on nationalist issues, rather than on improving the status of women. Newspaper articles written by women and published in the 1930s confirm women's preoccupation with politics.

Palestinian Women in the Diaspora: 1948-1965

Neither the women nor the men who went on strike for six months in 1936 in an attempt to change British immigration policy could stem the tide of Jewish immigration. In the 1948 Arab-Israeli war, Palestinian society itself was dismantled. Between 600 thousand and 760 thousand Palestinians fled or were expelled from Palestine to refugee camps in the countries surrounding Israel between December 1947 and September 1949.[13]

Palestinian women increased their philanthropic work because of the conditions they faced after the loss of Palestine: An opponent with superior resources (the newly formed state of Israel); lack of territory from which to launch a struggle or in which to develop autonomously; dispersion, which made the reproduction of the community difficult; and the repeated crushing and scattering of the national movement, preventing the accumulation of organizational experience, self-knowledge, and records.[14] All these conditions weighed down on women. Basic survival was at stake.

By the end of June 1953, there were 871,748 Palestinian refugees depending on relief from the United Nations for rations. The refugees formed a substantial addition to several countries ill-equipped to handle their needs.[15] World Bank reports show that unemployment of the refugee population stood at more than 50 percent until 1954. The influx of unskilled laborers—former farmers—depressed the wage scales by one half in some areas, and by one third in others.[16]

The collapse of the socioeconomic structure of Palestinian society after 1948, however, hastened the entry of women into the work force. The financial burden for supporting the family fell on the family as a whole rather than on the man, who had historically been defined as the head of the household. This shift decreased the rigidity of traditions that had circumscribed women's educational and work opportunities.[17] "Several hundred individuals from Palestine's intelligentsia moved to Kuwait between 1948 and the early 1950s.... The expertise and levels of education that this class possessed provided it with the keys to survival most needed in the Arab world at that time."[18] Among Kuwait's new immigrants were women who contributed to women's education in Kuwait and other oil-producing countries. These female pioneers have led Ann Dearden to describe Palestinian women as "torchbearers for women's emancipation" because they have gone to less advanced countries and "are providing a living example of how, in a Muslim society, women may lead useful outgoing lives without loss of dignity or principle."[19]

Not all women found good jobs abroad. Refugee women—former farmers—were at the bottom rung of the work scale. Such women held, and still hold, low-skilled labor-intensive jobs wherever they live. Because of the harsh economic conditions in refugee camps, dispossessed Palestinian women who had slowly reentered the middle class felt lucky compared to the families still in refugee camps. The services they provided were philanthropic in nature and provided basic necessities to refugee families.

Palestinian Women and Formal Political Parties in the Arab World: 1950s and 1960s

In the 1950s and the early 1960s, women's organizations based in East Jerusalem in the West Bank, in Amman, Jordan, in Lebanon, and in Syria continued to dispense services to the refugee population, the way they dispensed services to "the less fortunate" in Palestine. Host Arab governments stipulated that these groups concern themselves only with relief work and avoid politics, so women who were interested in politics joined the mostly underground existing Arab political parties. Political parties had progressive rhetoric on women's issues, but were unwilling to risk their other programs for women. But more important, the degree of poverty and hopelessness among the refugee population made it impossible for middle-class women to lobby for reform even when feminist consciousness was spreading among the middle classes in the 1960s. Explains Rosemary Sayigh: "So profound is the idea that women's political action should be gratuitous and unrewarded...that most Palestinian women find feminism, understood as women's *claims*, morally shocking." As one Jerusalem activist put it, "I would feel guilty if I asked for more rights as a woman at a time like this." Most of women's labor in political movements is voluntary, unpaid, and undemanding.[20]

But it was not the Arab-inspired political parties alone that had problems with effecting major changes in the status of women. The Palestine Liberation Organization (PLO) also saw women *only* in terms of their potential for serving the national struggle.

The Palestinian Liberation Organization and the "Woman Question": 1964-1978

The PLO involved women in the organization from the very start,[21] but, as Issam Abdel Hadi, later president of the General Union of Palestinian Women (GUPW) Executive Committee explains, "In 1964 when the PLO was established, we were chosen to be delegates to the Palestine National Council...*not as women but as national figures*. I was a member of the preparatory committee in Jerusalem, later twelve women were elected (there were over 450 men). I felt the establishment of the PLO was a glimmer of hope, a beginning of national mobilization. We had been deprived of our identity for twenty years.... We were all yearning for something, for anything, and *we wanted to turn all our activities into political activity*" [emphasis mine]. Even the establishment of the GUPW had little to do with liberating women. Says Abdel Hadi, "In August 1965, *at the suggestion of the PLO*, we held a conference and invited representatives from all over Palestine to create an organization to represent and mobilize Palestinian women, and to work *for the liberation of Palestine*. This was the beginning of the General Union of Palestinian Women (GUPW). *Our constitution was based on the PLO national charter*"[22] [emphasis mine].

The Palestinian case is not unusual. Revolutionary movements need all the support they can get and are eager to involve women because women bring with them skills that are useful to any revolution. But this type of inclusion has a price for women: It offers them a false sense of liberation, and pushes their own demands to the background. A few younger PLO female cadres attempted to make the PLO more responsive to women's issues, but there was resistance to any deviation from Palestinian nationalist goals. When the leadership of the GUPW chose a slogan as the theme for the Fourth General GUPW Congress in February 1980, "Towards a More Effective Participation in the Revolution," Yasser Arafat rejected it because he saw it as too critical of the status quo.[23]

Although PLO leaders encouraged women to join the organization, officials saw women mainly as sisters, wives, and mothers of revolutionaries, only occasionally as commandos themselves. But of all the roles assigned to women, their reproductive role was the most valued. In a speech to the Palestinian community in Abu Dhabi, Yasser Arafat told his audience that he expected twelve children from every family.[24] Women were seen (and many saw themselves) as helping the revolution when they had numerous children, raised them as revolutionaries, and bore their loss with dignity. A series of interviews conducted in 1968 by central information of the largest commando group, Fatah, illustrates the reproduction of a culture of sacrifice through women:

The Voice of Asifa (Storm) announcer: Here is the mother of a martyr from Palestine, the hero Mohammad Diab…expressing sincerely the stand of mothers of heroes…here is her touching nationalist reply:

Mother: The martyr, may God bless his soul…was a revolutionary from childhood, anything that had to do with the homeland, he was the first to give a speech or encourage youths his age…. But what hurts as a mother of the martyr Mohammad Diab is that his birth, his receiving his university degree, and his martyrdom were on the same day and time….What is the value of our lives when we are scattered (*musharradeen*)…without a country….I want to direct a word to the mothers of the strugglers (*Mujahiddeen*) and to every Palestinian mother because we are the ones who encourage our children and instill courage and a nationalist spirit in them. We have to raise them to regain our land with their blood….We must not be sorry for our children because our country has to be regained, and it will not be regained except with the blood of the martyrs…. Jerusalem is calling you and your children, get up and heed its call…. Don't be afraid of death…also girls, you must join in the battle.[25]

The sister of Lutfi Kilani, killed on November 28, 1968, ties his death to international liberation struggles around the world: "When they brought him to us as a martyr, it was not a surprise…. Everyone at home was expecting it …. Revolution is sacrifice…. All the revolutions of the world gave young men and blood until liberation…. I think that my role is to teach the girls at my school to sacrifice, and in any case, I find revolution in the breast of every student. I swear to my brother…to continue in the road he traveled until victory, or until I die and follow him in the procession of heroism and sacrifice."[26]

Elevating the status of women who sacrifice is useful both for the reproduction of Palestinian community and for the acceptance of the heavy toll that protracted conflict exacts from it. While it is true that the PLO provided women with jobs at its factories and helped the families of fighters financially, its assignment of heroic roles to women was not accompanied by a willingness to examine their status in Palestinian society. Members of the PLO mediated in individual disputes between women and their families, but the various institutions of the PLO, including the GUPW, were not willing to tackle such thorny issues as polygamy. In fact, Fatah, the largest constituent group of the

PLO, insisted on leaving room for more than one wife on the identity cards of its commandos, whereas other [leftist] organizations did not.

Because the GUPW was established "to liberate Palestine rather than to liberate women" the Palestinian leadership did not ask, What can the PLO do for and with women? It asked instead, What can women do for the PLO? And while GUPW cadres recruited families to help the "Revolution," important Fatah male intellectuals continued to insist that the "woman issue" was a "secondary struggle,"[27] and many women agreed with that assessment.

Several factors made the GUPW less effective than it could have been: The location of the main office, funding, and representation. The fate of the GUPW was closely tied to the fate of the PLO. The constitution of the union stipulates that its headquarters be located in the country that hosts the principal PLO office. Thus, when Jordan closed the PLO office in 1966, it closed the GUPW as well. When women continued to work in an unofficial capacity, Jordan still cracked down on all types of Palestinian political activity, especially after the 1970 Palestinian-Jordanian confrontation. Explains Laurie Brand, "The union once again found itself in a state of organizational limbo, a situation that lasted until the union was completely reorganized in Beirut in 1974.[28]

Women who were disbanded in Jordan reorganized and continued to offer the same services under the aegis of different charitable societies until they formed the Women's Union in Jordan (WUJ). Brand notes that "the WUJ leadership included women from a broad range of political affiliations—the Communist Party, the Democratic Front for the Liberation of Palestine (DFLP), the Popular Front for the Liberation of Palestine (PFLP), Fatah, and some independents—all of whom had nationalist inclinations and who sought to further Palestinian-Jordanian cooperation. The political bent of the union led it to take a real interest in women's concerns. Its efforts to study and improve women's economic, legal, and social status in the kingdom meant that WUJ simultaneously became involved in a variety of political issues, both domestic and foreign, primary among them the Palestine question."[29] But the lobbying efforts of this group led to its suppression in 1981. And even though the group won in court, the Jordanian Ministry of Interior continued to obstruct the union's work and replaced it with a women's organization closely tied to the regime.[30] When the PLO was chased out of Lebanon in 1982, the GUPW moved to Tunis.

An examination of brochures written by the PLO Information Services in Lebanon as well as in Tunis reveals an obsession with women's "revolutionary role" as fighters, who work "side by side" with men. But these brochures, by their very nature, are not designed to address the cost to women of Palestinian patriarchal society. As a result, nationalist literature constitutes the bulk of what is written about women.[31] Even in the 1980s and 1990s, when the PLO established Palestinian women's research centers, the object of those institutions was to recruit women for the Palestinian cause, rather than to research the problems and needs of women in Palestinian society. And because funders determine what women's organizations do, most of the research that has attempted to document women's living conditions has been done by academic women and, recently, by institutions and women's committees in the West Bank, rather than by the GUPW.[32] Funding of the GUPW has always been poor, even though the members bring in revenues from the various projects they sponsor, and the GUPW is not as structured as the new women's committees discussed below. Some leftist women's groups have also criticized the way women make it to the top in PLO-run institutions.[33]

While the leftist streams within the PLO outside the occupied territories have called for reform, they have not seriously attempted to give priority to women's rights on the agenda of the organization. The leftist philosophy of organizing women and the progressive attitude towards social work can be seen more clearly in women's organizations in the West Bank and Gaza. These organizations are allied with the PLO, but have flourished perhaps because of their distance from the official PLO "outside" male leadership and because the women who run these organizations determine their agendas.

Women's Committees in the West Bank: 1978-1994

Like all Palestinian institutions, women's organizations have been affected by developments in the PLO. Between 1965 and the early 1970s, the PLO stressed armed struggle for the liberation of Palestine (thus the recruitment of women commandos). But in the 1970s, the PLO, as well as West Bank institutions, started to stress nation-building, and women started organizing in groups that shared similar ideology. However, women were also active in agitation against the occupation. Women were so active in the organization of strikes and demonstrations in the occupied territories that in June 1980, the Israeli military government forbade all women's organizations and charitable societies to assemble, publish information, or make public declarations. The order came after women held a sit-in opposite the three houses sealed in Nablus the week before.[34] Israeli military authorities found it necessary to restrict women's nationalist activity because of their continuing involvement in demonstrating. Women called for, organized, and participated in 84 percent of the demonstrations that took place in 1968, and 71 percent of the demonstrations held in 1976. Women were responsible for 55 percent of the sit-ins in 1969 and 100 percent of the sit-ins of 1974. The 1980s order did not decrease women's involvement. Women were responsible for holding 100 percent of the sit-ins held in 1983.[35]

But there were important changes on the Palestinian scene that worked in women's favor. By the time the Tenth Palestinian National Congress met in Cairo in April 1972, the PLO had softened its line on armed struggle, and had started to encourage community organizing or "institutional resistance," which involved Palestinians in the building of institutions that would help them bear the onslaught of land confiscation, repression, and deportation.[36] Various forms of volunteer work flourished in the West Bank.[37] A number of young women activists, heavily involved in the budding volunteer movement, at first tried to work within traditional women's societies but were dissatisfied with them because they found the top-down approach to social work unsatisfactory.

Initially, the women's movement consisted of women from different political streams as well as independent women. On March 8, 1978, a group of women met with the intention of discussing women's affairs. The group did not remain united for long. Four groups, representing the ideological divisions within the Palestinian movement, eventually emerged. Women affiliated with the DFLP established the Palestinian Union of Women's Work Committees (PUWWC) under the slogan "Towards a Unified Popular Women's Movement."[38] The Communist Party established the Union of Palestinian Working Women's Committees in March 1980, and announced that its goal was to make up for insufficient attention paid to working women and to union affairs. Women sympathetic to the PFLP established the Palestinian Women's Committee in March 1981, a group that more explicitly addresses sexual politics in its writing than do other groups. Fatah women established the Union of Women's Committees for Social Work in June 1982. The fourth group is the most socially conservative in its organizational structure.

A seminar held by a women's committee provided some insight into the kind of thinking the activists involved in committees espouse. Architect Suad Amiri, a university professor who does volunteer work for the committees, said that some charitable societies understand the nature of their work from a capitalist perspective. That viewpoint suggests that the bourgeoisie alone are able to produce and be counted upon to donate to the poorer classes from a humanitarian perspective. She stressed the need to change such an approach [to one where women are productive and help themselves].[39] And while the new committees differ from the charitable societies in their approach to social work, both types of organizations agree that Palestinian women should not use the confrontational tactics used by women in the West to demand their rights. Leaders of these committees argue instead that disadvantaged women first need to be empowered through literacy classes and job training, through the creation of strong unions, the provision of health care that is responsive to the needs of the rural poor, and the creation of structures that involve women in decision-making about the projects set up in their communities. That is what the new committees try to do. What follows is a summary of the organizers' analyses of such issues as class, education, health, politics, and religion, as well as a description of what they have attempted to do in those areas.

Class—In the 1920s, most of the women who did social work, and who took part in demonstrations and letter-writing campaigns against the British, were upper-class women, mostly wives and relatives of the Palestinian elites in power.[40] Rosemary Sayigh writes that "class, sect and region appear to be critical factors influencing family attitudes towards its female members, with middle-class [Palestinian] Christians of the coastal cities among the first to adopt liberal practices, and with conservatism appearing more resistant in the rural hinterland, provincial towns, and among lower middle social strata."[41] Upper class women did volunteer work before 1948, but the poor bore the brunt of British practices. The PLO in Lebanon tried to involve "the masses" in its revolution, but the priorities of social work were determined by centralized planning and involved the masses mostly at the level of execution.[42]

The strategy of establishing women's committees in the West Bank after 1978 evolved as a reaction to earlier, failed attempts to attract women from refugee camps to various activities. Activists concluded that they could not recruit women for volunteer work (let alone nationalist activity) without paying attention to social constraints to which women are subjected. Before women could work within their communities, *they had to be allowed to leave their homes.* Women's sensitivity to rural and refugee needs resulted in the recruitment of an increasing number of women of rural or refugee origin into women's committees. An examination of the change in the photos in women's publications over time tells the whole story. The early photos of the women's movement in the 1920s and 1930s feature city women in Western dress. Today's newsletters feature rural and refugee women, mostly in traditional dress, not only as participants, but as part of the leadership.[43]

The building blocks of the committees of the Palestinian Federation of Women's Action Committees (PFWAC)—the new name of PUWWC, since June 1987—are the "basic units" deliberately kept to between fifteen and thirty members to encourage local democratic decision-making in refugee-camp neighborhoods and villages. Members of each base unit decide which projects to adopt in its community. Most women appear to want kindergartens in their villages, evidenced by the fact that in 1987, 1,504 children were registered in kindergartens that were started and run by the basic units of PFWAC. When we consider that all four committees run kindergartens, the number of children served is impressive."[44]

The needs of rural and refugee women are also great because high taxes exacerbate poverty. Israel extracts higher taxes from the Arab population than from its own, but spends less money on services than it does in Israel. Statistics issued by the Israeli authorities in March 1987 show that Israel collects $383 million in taxes from the occupied territories and allocates $240 million for expenditures in the territories.[45] The only way for women's committees to gain credibility with rural and refugee women is by responding to their physical needs. Committees have attempted to involve poor women in the process of determining which services are most needed, as well as in decisions about how they should be implemented. The organizational structure of PFWAC reveals how it is designed to involve village and refugee women in communal decision-making.[46]

The model for development advocated by these and other groups, "developmental from below," has resulted in a call for a shift in Palestinian developmental policies from one concentrated mainly in towns to one serving towns as well as villages. The village is now seen as a vital place for Palestinian activity. A kindergarten in the village of Hizma, for instance, was used as a model kindergarten. Trainees from *towns* were sent to the *village* for training.

Education—In the Palestinian experience, the education of women and their entry into the work force were extremely important for the changes that took place in the role of women. In 1930, Palestinian women represented only 20 percent of the total number of students in British government schools.[47] The number of Palestinian women at all levels of education has increased dramatically.[48] Since Palestinians became refugees in 1948, families have seen education as a ticket out of poverty. Women's groups share the general enthusiasm for education and occasionally procure scholarships for women to study abroad. Members of the committees encourage parents to allow their daughters to complete high school, but until recently such attempts were sporadic and reactive. Women's groups did not make demands on national institutions regarding the mass education of women, even though they themselves used creative ways to reach illiterate older women. For instance, women's committees are actively trying to decrease the high dropout rate of older learners by scheduling classes at appropriate times and by making child care available to learners.

For all the slogans about "national liberation," activists discovered that revolution in Palestinian society would be incomplete if women had no tools for self-improvement. Research in the Ramallah area revealed that the literacy rate for women over 50 is 0 percent and for those over 40 it is 30 percent.[49] As a result, some of the women's groups offer literacy classes in villages with the cooperation of the Higher Council of Literacy. The record of PFWAC on literacy is the best among the four groups because that committee has made literacy an issue in its policy statements and in its conventions. PFWAC, as well as other groups, also attracts women through the screening and discussion of various videotapes on topics ranging from medical information to women's liberation struggles in South Africa, Asia, Latin America, and the Arab world. In Beit Anan village, for example, thirty women attended a videotape showing of *The Peasant Revolt* (in Egypt).[50] For women isolated by the borders of occupation, the discussions help them to feel that they are part of an international liberation movement and provide them with inspiring examples of political action.

Health—Health professionals, many of whom are volunteers for the women's committees, note that females will benefit more from a women's movement that is aware of and addresses the health needs of rural and refugee women and their children than from a movement that generates slogans about gender inequality without knowledge of the health situation of its constituents. Furthermore, researchers note that often the health problems of the poor have more to do with distribution of health-care facilities than with gender issues. Villages suffer the most because most hospitals and health-care facilities are located in the towns. Research on village women, conducted by Dr. Rita Giacaman, has placed the mortality rate at between fifty and one hundred per thousand.[51] Dr. Mohammad al Faqih of the United Nations Relief and Works Agency's al-Am'ari Camp Health Center puts the overall neonatal mortality rate at 40 per 1,000 births in refugee camps. These figures do not even tell the whole story. Dr. Muhiyeh Khalifeh notes that in 1980, only 44.8 percent of all deliveries took place in hospitals, so it is difficult to get accurate mortality figures.[52]

Palestinians have recognized the importance of health in the empowerment of people and have started to change their planning strategies accordingly. Bir Zeit Women's Charitable Society, with the help of Bir Zeit University, started maternity clinics in twenty-six villages in the late 1970s. In 1979, the Union of Palestinian Medical Relief Committees was established by doctors and medical personnel who volunteer their services. UPMRC has taken a holistic approach to health care following its mandate to provide Quality Health for All. On the level of Primary Health Care, UPMRC operates 25 Community Health Centers in towns and villages throughout the West Bank and the Gaza Strip. These Health Care Centers focus on preventive, promotive as well as curative care. UPMRC mobile clinics bring services to villages and towns under difficult circumstances, such as closure and curfews, and to deprived and remote areas. Often, and particularly during times of conflict, Palestinians are unable to reach clinics, and thus UPMRC must bring its services to the people. The Well-Baby and Child Health Program: UPMRC strives to reach to most vulnerable members of Palestinian society, which includes infants and children. UPMRC conducts screenings, vaccinations and educational programs in order to ensure that infants and children are well prepared to live healthy lives. Women's Health Program: This comprehensive program focuses on addressing the major health issues that Palestinian women face throughout their lives. It combines health care service provision, education and awareness raising and staff training. Through this program, women in even the most remote villages in Palestine have access to vital services such as health education, pre-natal, post-natal and family planning care, as well as a host of other basic and specialized services that address their specific needs.

The union believes its greatest achievement lies in training female health workers—123 in its first eight years. Ninety of those graduates now work in the union on various projects. In 1993 alone, the health centers served 205 thousand people, made eleven thousand home visits, and provided educational prevention activities for thirty-four thousand people.[53]

Women and Politics—Early research about Middle Eastern women has structured our knowledge about them in ways that misrepresented women's contributions to building their countries. Most research in English was done by social scientists who "tend[ed] to draw exclusively upon other Western language sources, to rely upon each other as sources for their 'conclusions.' Thus a very narrow, ethnocentrically oriented base of opinion about Arab women constitutes the bulk of the literature currently available on the subject. Most of the early studies, really little more than impressionistic assertions about Arab women, were done by men with little or no access to the subjects of their study or by westernized Arabs alienated from their own mass societies."[54]

Carolyn Fluehr-Lobban notes that "Until recently the literature on Arab women has revealed more about the biases of Western writers than it has about the actual lives and activities of women….Increasingly the literature is beginning to answer some of the questions that have disturbed observers of life in the Arab world who have gone beyond the tourist view of oriental rugs, camels, and veiled women. How is it that these apparently weak and pitiable women, so constrained by Arab men and Islam, often stand out as some of the strongest figures in the society?" Fluehr-Lobban quotes a 1973 study by Davis when she concludes that "ethnographic evidence suggests a different picture of traditional Arab culture, a society segregated by sex to be sure, but a society where the world of women emerges with as much integrity and scope as the world of men."[55]

Some mainstream Western politicians and leaders of the United States' feminist movement who have come in contact with Palestinian women have not been thrilled at how involved the latter are in national politics. During the 1985 Nairobi women's conference, for instance, Maureen Reagan, as well as some other U.S. and Israeli women, attempted to prevent the "politicization" of the conference by the introduction of the subject of Israeli occupation. Palestinian women argued that one could not improve the overall condition of women without working for the end of occupation. Occupation affects every aspect of women's lives. According to then Israeli Defense Minister Yitzhak Rabin, eighteen thousand Palestinians had been arrested even before the end of the first year of the 1987 uprising. The figure translates into a larger number of women transformed into single parents. Leaving the agony of being separated from a loved one aside, the trip to prison on visiting days takes up most of the day. When children are traumatized because Israeli soldiers break into their homes at night, bed-wetting increases; when schools are closed as collective punishment for eighteen months, and universities for four years, women's time is stolen. When land is confiscated, when water use is restricted, and when Israel takes more in taxes than it provides in services, Palestinians—especially women without partners—suffer the consequences. Between December 9, 1987, and January 31, 1993, Israelis killed 1,137 Palestinians; injured 121,246 (injuries requiring hospitalization); deported 483; administratively detained (i.e., imprisoned without trial) 15,320; confiscated 87,741 acres; demolished or sealed 2,072 houses; and uprooted 130,411 trees. The Israeli army also placed Palestinians under curfew for 11,151 days in various areas with populations of over ten thousand, and placed the entire West Bank and Gaza under almost constant curfew from January 16 to February 18, 1991. Between September 28, 2000 and July 23, 2002, 1,788 Palestinians were killed and more than 20,000 were injured. [56] All the injured, imprisoned, and newly landless have mothers, grandmothers, wives, aunts, sisters, or daughters whose lives have been made harder by Israeli acts of repression. Activists like to point out that when 1.7 million Palestinians are placed under curfew, families of twelve are restricted to a two-room shack under conditions of fear and scarcity, women still give birth during curfew, and children still get sick in the middle of the night, when no one dares move to get help.

Women who used to live in homes that have been destroyed as collective punishment not only lose a husband or a son to prison, but have their homes literally demolished right under their noses *before* the male of the family is tried in a court of law for whatever offense he may have committed. Is the blowing up of a home a domestic or a political issue? Female activists argue that such an act puts politics right inside the home, where it belongs, and that to ask such women not to politicize the occupation constitutes gross insensitivity to the women's right not to be deprived of their homes as collective punishment.

Writings that ignore the effects of war and occupation tend to overempha-size gender-specific problems caused by the conservative interpretation of Islamic law. On the other hand, writings that stress the nationalist issue alone, to the exclusion of discrimination against women in Palestinian society, downplay the role of conservative interpretations of Islam in preventing women's issues from being tackled head-on. The relationship of women to Islam is more complex than either of the two positions admits.

Palestinian Women and Islam

No one can dismiss the influence of Islam on women's legal rights and on women's status in society. But Islam does not exist in a void, and it interacts with material and political conditions to affect women. Like all religions, Islam is interpreted, and it is up to women to see that they take part in that process. Palestinian writer Nadia Hijab observes that "blaming Islam" ignores the fact that cultural attitudes, including Islamically inspired ones, change remarkably quickly, and with the active support of the government, when the need and opportunity arise.[57] Jordan, faced with a labor shortage in 1976, aggressively recruited women for nontraditional jobs in the labor market, using all the information channels at its disposal. By 1986, however, when the need for labor lessened, "there was 'almost an official policy,' to encourage married women to stay at home."[58]

Hijab adds that a serious problem feminists face is that family law and women's personal rights are debated almost entirely within an Islamic framework by both conservatives and liberals. This type of debate is tricky for liberals. Fundamentalists know and do not mind the fact that Islamic concepts are not in accordance with European ones. Liberals, on the other hand, "have to go through mental contortions to prove that women and men are equal in Is-lam; the conservatives see men and women as having been created complementary rather than equal, and this is not, for them, a bad thing."[59] Agreeing to debate the issue from a conservative Islamic, rather than a secular developmental, perspective places liberal women at a disadvantage. Says Jane Smart in another context: "It is a dilemma that all radical political movements face, namely the problem of challenging the form of power without accepting its own terms of reference and hence losing the battle before it has begun. Put simply, in accepting law's terms in order to challenge law, feminism always concedes too much."[60] By adding other elements to the debate by stressing inno-vative programs in education, child care, and health care, Palestinian women's committees place women in a better position vis-a-vis the conservatives.

But when women leave the interpretation of women's role in society only to conservatives, their power is usurped the way it was in Gaza in the mid-1980s. According to anthropologist Rema Hammami, religious forces in Gaza waged a campaign to impose the *hijab* (head cover) on women. By a combination of intimidation and a redefinition of the *hijab* as a nationalist gesture against ostentatious dress in times of trouble, religious groups made it impossible for women of Gaza to go out without it. It took the United National Leadership of the uprising *a year and a half* to issue a leaflet against harassing women who choose not to cover their heads. And even when the condemnation came, it did not inspire unreserved confidence, "The leaflet's main priority is not to roll back the suppression of women but to arrest the potential for disunity caused by attacks on women."[61] But the reaction of women's groups, says Hammami, is even more disturbing. Women's committees reacted in writing even *after* the leadership of the Intifada did. Instead of placing the blame where it belonged, on conservative Palestinian society, they blamed Israeli forces and collaborators.

The reaction of the United National Leadership and the women's committees prompted Hammami to conclude that neither the unified leadership nor the Higher Women's Council (of the four women's groups) acknowledged the extent to which nationalist forces bought into the *hijab* campaign. The fact that religious groups promulgated it and that conservative elements in Palestinian culture oppose women's political independence was never adequately addressed. Leaflet No. 43 dealt a blow to undemocratic processes and validated at a critical moment, but in words only, women's right to choose. Its title, "A Call for Unity," reflects the absence of real self-criticism. Keeping the religious groups in the fray and the nationalist consensus going was deemed more important than confronting sexism and reactionary elements. In the end, not only will women be the victims, but so will the left and secular forces.[62]

Hammami's prediction came true sooner than expected. In April 1990, Hamas religious activists stormed a women's committee production project in Rafah and harassed its members. Hamas activists elsewhere later made pronouncements from a mosque that women should not be allowed to go out without a male member of the family.[63] Religious activists were fighting the Left's influence and its involvement in developmental work in two ways, by providing services of their own, including kindergratens, and by waging a campaign against liberal dress. Although the women's groups have finally formed a committee to confront the trend, it is too early to tell whether all of women's gains will be wiped out because they were too busy confronting Israelis to estimate the danger an extreme fundamentalist interpretation of Islam poses to women's freedom.

The Women's Movement Finally Confronts Gender Issues

This review of the history of the women's movement shows that women gained acceptance for their involvement in social life by defining their activities as political and nationalist in nature and by essentially avoiding questions of sexual discrimination. This strategy has served them well in the past. But as women's concerns have started to shift to include a call for gender equality and an examination of women's legal rights, resistance to women's organizations has increased.

Opponents of changing the status quo for women in the Arab world always gain an advantage when they redefine feminism as a bid for the practice of premarital sex, as in, "they're only interested in liberation from here [the waist] down."[64] Such a redefinition automatically delegitimizes *all* of women's demands. Nadia Hijab explains that those who fear the effect of the change of women's role in the family "find conclusive support for their position in what they see as the breakdown of society in the West. They hold the erosion of family ties responsible for a range of social ills…from the loneliness of the old to drug addiction among the young, from violence and crime to immorality."[65] But in the West Bank, changes in the philosophy of organizing women have been taking place at a speed that is breathtaking, given that it took women from 1919 to 1989 to begin to articulate a women-centered rather than a nationalist- centered agenda.

The West Bank organization al-Haq ("Right"; formerly "Law in the Service of Man" until women protested the sexist terminology) organized a series of workshops in preparation for the convention on "Women and Law" planned for September 16 to 20, 1994. The most encouraging fact about the convention was that the workshops were held in different locations in the West Bank and Gaza to ensure maximum participation. Workshops were held in Hebron on July 5, 1994 on "Women and Health Rights"; in Toulkarm on July 15, on "Personal Status Law"; in Ramallah on July 17 on "Vocational Training"; in Beit Sahur on July 19 on "Violence Against Women"; in Nablus on July 22 on "Women, Work, and Benefits"; and in Gaza on July 29 on "Women and Political Life." Several lecturers called for making substantial changes in the letter of personal status law (now based on Islamic law as well as on fragments of Napoleonic, Turkish, and Jordanian laws). More important, said some of the women, laws already on the books should be applied equally to both sexes. Speakers insisted that such changes be part of the constitution, that women be included in legislating for the new Palestinian state that will emerge if Israel pulls out of the West Bank, and that they be included in planning for economic development. The July 19 workshop, for example, defined relations of economic dependence on men as "economic violence." Speakers also suggested that women form strong lobby groups to ensure fairness to women in the new state for which they are preparing.[66]

A women's delegation met with Yasser Arafat in the city of Gaza and stressed the need for adding to the constitution legislation that ensures women's "full rights, total and unabridged," as the report of the meeting noted. The women reminded Arafat of women's political as well as social sacrifices.[67] With that meeting, women have declared that they are no longer content to serve the national cause only to be relegated to the background when independence is achieved as was the case with Algerian women.

Leaders of the women's movement now realize that the weakness of the Palestinian women's movement was not caused solely by Islamist dictates, but by women who work for the national movement on Arab-Israeli issues without demanding gender-specific rights that shield them from the redefinition of all their actions in sexual terms. But women's reluctance to lead the debate on gender issues until recently should not obscure the important shift that has been taking place in the organizational form of the groups, in the nature of their activities, and in their ideology since 1978. The changes can be detected in the attention active women are beginning to pay to the language of published material about women, in the coalitions they make with international as well as Israeli women, and in their serious discussions on gender issues.

Language—Even as women leaders insist that the nationalist struggle is more important than the personal struggle for individual rights, stronger feminist language is being written in women's publications or heard in forums dealing with women's issues. In a seminar entitled "The Struggle of Palestinian Women, Obstacles and Ambition," we hear that "women are the working class of men, and the division of labor between them is like the division between the worker and the capitalist; it is men who own the means of production and who run work and who take surplus production. These conditions are indicators of the present social economic system.... Making women conscious of their rights under the prevailing social system creates an internal struggle within women. An understanding of the political role women play and its connection to structural changes is one approach to solving the conflict and placing it within its proper path, the path of social liberation of women."[68] At present, pronouncements like these mean that the consciousness of oppression is beginning to creep into the women's literature.

The first conference to deal with women (rather than with women only as participants in the nationalist debate) was held in Jerusalem in July 1988, under the auspices of the Arab Thought Forum. Explains one working paper of the conference: "The Intifada (Uprising) has placed the issue of women in the circle of serious attention, this was no accident. It is the vital role of

Palestinian women during the Intifada that made it possible."[69] During this forum participants stressed the importance of ensuring women's full representation in any future Palestinian state in order to secure their full liberation.[70]

The loudest calls for change have come from independent academic women who do not belong to any of the committees but are critical of some of the writings about women. Some of the research on the status of women (like Abu-Ghazaleh's research below) is done by independent academic women, but there is no doubt that women's groups have been affected by it. During the Intifada, Ilham Abu-Ghazaleh, who teaches linguistics at Bir Zeit University in the West Bank, showed that while newspapers are aware of and glorify women's nationalist action in the street, Palestinian poetry was retaining its stereotypical images of Arab women. Poets, instead of celebrating women's action, stress their physical appearance (long hair, tiny waist) and their biological function (giving birth). On the street, in real life, women rescue men from Israeli troops, and sometimes die for it. In poetry, on the other hand, women tearfully wait inside their homes for the men to return and listen to descriptions of the outside world as men see it.[71] But women not only are seeing the outside world without help, but also are increasingly joining with other women in coalitions that will prove to be beneficial to them in the long run.

The Power of Coalitions—Palestinian women's committees and charitable organizations are divided along factional lines inside and outside the occupied territories. Despite these divisions, there are some encouraging signs on the horizon. Women have been trying to unite since 1986. The four women's committees held a single unified meeting in 1987 for the first time on International Women's Day. During the Intifada, women formed a higher council to coordinate their activities. Coordination seeks to improve national resistance rather than to discuss a women's agenda, but the joint meetings have resulted in a better women's agenda . None of the women's groups alone is strong enough to influence Palestinian politics; only unity among them will place the issue of gender discrimination on the national agenda. The best chance for creating a just society lies in their creating a strong movement with a women's platform before the establishment of a Palestinian state.

On November 15, 1988, Palestinians unilaterally declared their independence in a document that stressed the rights of women. If the committees translate the progressive 1988 declaration into law and insist that laws need to be supported by a progressive structure of education, health, and social equity, women's committees will become a permanent part of the Palestinian political scene. If each of the four groups continues to function alone, the groups can easily be swept aside by Hamas, the religious movement.

Contact with International Women's Groups—Women's groups have always sought international support for the national issue (that is, their struggle with Israel) but not for feminist issues. Palestinian women believe that the tactics of the Western feminist movement (the direct approach of charging men with sexism, chauvinism, and the militant tactics of the early feminist movement) are not appropriate in the Middle East because of the different family dynamics operating there. Women (and men) live with their families until they get married and physical independence is harder to achieve under those conditions.

Furthermore, Palestinian women fault the Western feminist movement for its overemphasis on individualism over community and for its demand for equal opportunity within existing social structures, rather than for working to change the oppressive effects of those structures on the disadvantaged in the society. Palestinian female leaders believe that the mainstream U.S. feminist movement has not come to grips with how gender, race, and class intersect within the social structure, making the experience of poor Black and white women totally different from the experiences of white middle class women. The Palestinian women's movement has been aware that, to free women to work outside the home, family-like services need to be provided—thus, the strong kindergarten movement led by women's groups.

Despite these differences in approach, dialogue with Western women's delegations has been beneficial to both sides. Palestinian women initially had defensive answers to the questions Western feminists asked about women's status, but the questions helped women's committees verbalize their views on the connection between the personal and the political-national as they see it. Western women who discussed feminist issues with the leaders of the Palestinian women's movement also benefited from observing a movement that is more aware of class issues than are some mainstream Western feminist organizations, and by seeing how people who organize around the concept of "community" (as opposed to individual freedom) approach the problem of empowering women through involvement in the national struggle.

Palestinian publications after the 1985 Nairobi conference stressed the value of knowing that Palestinians were not alone in their struggle. One observer listed other benefits: "There seemed to be a clearer understanding in the West that problems women faced because of their sex could not be isolated from the problems they faced as a result of military occupation, apartheid, or famine. At the same time, there was a stronger feeling in the Third World that women should not wait for a solution to political or economic problems to achieve their human rights."[72]

In addition to the exchange of experiences, international and women's organizations offer practical types of assistance, such as help in midwifery training or kindergarten teacher training. These contacts and services give women a certain degree of independence from funding restrictions faced by the GUPW, and at the same time legitimize their activities on the international level.

In 1991 the Women's Studies Center (WSC), established in 1989, started publishing in a pamphlet called *Spark* with selections from its women's magazine, *al-Mar'ah* (*Woman*). The first issues of *Spark,* published in December 1991, explained that "through this publication [women] hope to build bridges with overseas readers and sister organizations and enhance their awareness of developments in the Palestinian women's movement and of issues of particular concern to Palestinian women." In its first issue, the WSC translated articles about domestic violence, polygamy, and an examination of issues surrounding frequent pregnancy and childbirth. In its eighth and ninth issues (June 1993), *Spark* dealt with a feminist conference the director of WSC, Suha Hindeyeh, attended in Italy and reported on conversations with Arab women filmmakers.[73]

In the recent past, because women's political actions were "unrewarded and undemanding," female nationalist activists were their own worst enemies when they assumed that their activism on behalf of nationhood for Palestinians would automatically result in gains for women once their nationalist goals were achieved. But the success of Gaza fundamentalists in forcing women to wear the *Shari'a* dress made female political activists aware that what feminist academic and independent women were saying all along was true: Unless women change personal status law, equality will be impossible no matter how progressive the Palestinian constitution sounds.

The most encouraging development since Palestinian women first met in 1919 was the September 1994 conference in which women's issues that were identified in workshops that discussed the issue on a national level. These discussions will result in concrete demands on the Palestinian (mostly male) leadership for substantive changes and additions to the family status laws used in the occupied territories.

Contacts with Israeli Women—A new and still controversial development on the Palestinian scene is the increasing contact between Israeli women's peace groups and Palestinian women's groups. Such contacts would have been unthinkable a few years earlier, when all Israelis were indistinguishable from one another. But when Israeli women started questioning the Israeli military machine, and when "Women in Black" demonstrated weekly for the end of occupation, despite the abuse heaped on them by Israeli extremists, Palestinian women softened their stand on meetings with Israelis. Now members of the Palestinian women's committees regularly meet with Israeli women who believe that Israelis should negotiate with the

Palestinians and accept the concept of self-determination that is bound to lead to a two-state solution.

Despite the Uprising of September 2000, Palestinian and Israeli women have continued to work together for peace. On April 22, 2002 , they issued the "Israeli and Palestinian Women Joint Peace Statement" issued by Bat Shalom and the Jerusalem Center for Women (http://www.una-oc.org/ipjoint.htm). The statement included the following:

> It is our role, women on both sides, to speak out loudly against the humanitarian crimes committed in order to permanently subjugate an entire nation. Right now, in the face of uncontrolled military turmoil, we jointly ask the international community of states to accept its duty and mandate by international humanitarian law to prevent abuses of an occupying power, by officially intervening to protect the Palestinian people.
>
> Beyond the immediate crisis, we know that there is one future for us both. The deliberate harming of innocent civilians, Palestinian or Israeli, must not be condoned. By working together we improve our chances for a better future.... Women have already begun to give substance to the recognition that a just peace is a peace between equals. When we call for a Palestinian state (on the territories occupied on 4th of June 1967) alongside the state of Israel, we envision true sovereignty for each state, including control over land and natural resources. We envision a settlement based on international law, which would endorse sharing the whole city of Jerusalem, the dismantling of the settlements, and a just solution to the question of refugees according to relevant UN resolutions. In continuing our joint work together, we want not only to achieve an end to the occupation; we want to help create the conditions for a life of security and dignity for both peoples.

In the conclusion to my 1992 book, *Portraits of Palestinian Women*, I wrote that, "To date, not a single [women's] group has managed to present its vision of women's role in Palestinian society other than in broad generalities of wanting women to work 'side by side' with men. No group has yet come up with a blueprint for what Palestinian society needs to do to improve the education of women, their health, their work opportunities, and their legal status." I am pleased to note that change came almost as soon as the book was published. In 1992, the Women's Technical Affairs Committee (WATC) was formed during the preparations for Israeli-Palestinian negotiations. As a result, closer cooperation developed between three political women's committees and independent female professionals. Up to that point, there was little representation of women within the various technical committees. No official body addressed specific women's issues or catered to their needs.

During the years 1992-1996, the WATC succeeded in placing Palestinian women's issues on the national agenda. During the first two years of operation, WATC depended on the voluntary work of its members: Sixteen women activists representing three political groups and some women's study centers, in addition to independent professionals. In 1994, the WATC succeeded in attracting funds for the employment of a director and a secretary. In 1996 a fourth main political group of women joined the WATC, as did the Palestinian Health Coalition and al-Haq, a human rights organization. Together, they formed a strong lobby to consolidate their efforts to secure equal rights for women in Palestinian society by abolishing all forms of discrimination against women, and assisting in the creation of a civic democratic society characterized by equality and social justice. The fifth political group, the Palestinian Women's Committees, also joined WATC in the same year.

Today, WATC, a respected Palestinian non-governmental organization, is a coalition of women affiliated with six main political parties as well as independent professional women and representatives of various women's study centers and human rights organizations. WATC's headquarters is in Ramallah, with a branch in Gaza. Regional coordinators are located in all parts of Palestine.

Between 1995 and 1996, WATC implemented twelve projects that involved lobbying for more rights for Palestinian women, training women in various skills, networking with a large number of women's institutions and informing the public about the challenges facing women and advertising their achievements.

Achievements of WATC

As a result of committed and professional lobbying and campaigning efforts, WATC succeeded in achieving the following:
- a large number of modifications on draft legislation (civil status law, civil administration law, and election law) has been achieved
- women are no longer required to obtain the permission of their male guardian in order to apply for a travel document
- women may keep their maiden names after marrying
- women are no longer required to take along a chaperone while taking driving lessons
- women may open bank accounts in their children's names, which was a right given only to men by some local banks
- widows can have passports issued for their children without obtaining the permission of their in-laws
- women are now eligible to three months' maternity leave and one hour a day for nursing, according to the new Civil Administration Law

- a greater percentage of women are now holding decision-making posts within the government; the number of female general directors in ministries was raised to twenty-three in 1996
- at least twenty-nine women have been appointed to positions on local councils and municipalities as a result of WATC advocacy work

The strategic plans of WATC include: Promoting gender-sensitive policies and legislation; developing the self-assertiveness of women, using the latest methods of adult education and training; enhancing women's participation in political life at all levels, especially the decision-making level; lobbying decision-makers in Palestinian society to promote equal rights for women; and empowering and supporting existing women's committees and groups on the operational and organizational level to improve cooperation and networking between them.

Other WATC goals include:

- reaching more rural women in the West Bank and Gaza Strip by targeting more villages and increasing the number of female volunteers who work in their local communities on women's issues
- increasing young women's awareness of women's status
- training women in lobbying skills and providing them with opportunities to put those skills into practice
- lobbying to increase the number of females in local councils and municipalities
- empowering various women's committees (by working with women at the grassroots level), discovering their needs, and giving them suitable training to improve their performance and ability to reach more women

Areas that still need work include:

- continuing the work to enable women to have passports issued for their children without male consent
- continuing to promote a quota policy that will ensure women obtain 30 percent of the seats in the Legislative Council and municipal councils
- continuing the work on legal reform and lobbying for gender-sensitive laws in an attempt to protect women from all forms of discrimination and violence

WATC and Education

The Women's Affairs Technical Committee is providing more educational and work opportunities for women as alternatives to early marriage and powerlessness. Although the school enrollment rate of girls and boys is equal, the number of girls who leave school at the secondary level is larger than the number of boys. Poor families who cannot afford to pay the travel expenses of all their school-age children inevitably decide to pay for the boys rather than the girls. Reasons for leaving school vary for the sexes. Boys leave to help support their families, while girls leave to get married. Early marriage is a problem for many rural women with no educational and work opportunities. About 37 percent of rural women marry before the age of eighteen. Moreover, the fertility rate decreases with the increase in female education.

Many poor parents do not mind educating their daughters but cannot afford the cost of transportation to a nearby town or village. To solve the problem the Women's Affairs Technical Committee–Palestine, created a sponsorship program in 1997 to cover the travel costs for needy girls in order to give them the opportunity to continue their secondary education.

Conclusion

Because of the recent shift in focus of Palestinian women's activities from resisting Israeli occupation to the new emphasis on improved and more equitable gender relations, Palestinian women will not have to settle for political freedom at the expense of personal freedom. Instead, they hope to enjoy equal rights in a society that respects them as equals. If those new amendments now slated for debate pass, Palestinian women's journey up the mountain will be less arduous than it was when the young poet Fadwa Touqan was making her difficult journey up her mountain in Nablus in the 1930s.

Perhaps the most important thing that can be said about the Palestinian women's movement is that its leaders have benefited from what happened to Algerian women after the fight for independence from France was won. Algerian women sacrificed for the revolution, but did not enjoy its rewards in the form of more personal rights. Palestinian women who had insisted on working almost exclusively for national ends under Israeli occupation realized that with the coming of the national authority in 1994, their agenda needed to change. Women concluded that national ends are best served by giving women more personal and educational rights and opportunities. This realization made activist women change their goals and strategies and increase their lobbying of the Palestinian legislature. The legislature has been responsive to many of the women's demands. The opposition to some legislation on personal rights continues to come from Islamists. So more pressure needs to be applied to achieve real equality, but the pressure will be successful only when the Palestinian secular government feels strong enough to face Islamist pressure groups on several remaining issues.

Useful links on Palestinian Society:

http://www.pngo.net The Palestinian Non-Governmental Organizations Network (including women's groups)

http://www.wameed.org Women's Studies Center

http://www.pcbs.org Palestinian Central Bureau of Statistics (good statistics on women in all areas /in English)

http://www.passia.org Palestinian Academic Society for the Study of International Affairs- East Jerusalem (click on links)

http://www.planet.edu Palestinian Academic Network PLANET (click on Links

http://www.birzeit.edu/links/index.html Birzeit University's Guide to Palestinian Web Sites

http://www.palestinemonitor.org/links/links.html The Palestine Monitor: The Voice of Civil Society

http://www.pal-pwws.org Palestinian Working Woman Society

http://www.pal-watc.org Palestinian Women's Technical Affairs Committee

http://nonprofnet.ca/wao Women Against Occupation

http://www.amin.org Arabic Media Independent Network (some articles in English)

http://www.hdip.org Health Development Information and Policy Institute

http://www.upmrc.org The Union of Palestinian Medical Relief Committees UPMRC (strong on services to women)

http://www.electronicintifada.org The Electronic Intifada (information on the media and links to Arab sites)

NOTES

[1] Fadwa Touqan, "Constrained Adolesence," in *A Difficult Journey Up the Mountain,* Hannah Amit-Kochavi, trans., *New Outlook,* January-February, 1987. One of Touqan's poems is included in J. Bankier, et al., eds., *Twentieth Century Women's Poetry in Translation: The Other Voice.* New York: W. W. Norton, 1976:150.

[2] Matiel Mogannam, *The Arab Woman and the Palestine Problem.* London: Herbert Joseph, 1937: 63.

[3] Ibid.: 64

[4] Ibid.: 55.

[5] Simha Flapan, *The Birth of Israel: Myths and Realities*. New York: Pantheon Books, 1987: 8.

[6] Ghada Talhami, "Women in the Movement: Their Long, Uncelebrated History." *Al-Fajr* (English), May 30, 1986: 8.

[7] Mogannam: 63.

[8] Isiah Jad, "From Salons to Popular Committees: Palestinian Women 1919–89," in *Intifada: Palestine at the Crossroad*, Jamal Nassar and Roger Heacock, eds. New York: Praeger, 1990: 127.

[9] Mogannam: 69.

[10] Ibid.: 58.

[11] Akram Zuaiter, *The Palestinian National Movement 1935–1939*. Beirut: Al-Yasar Publications, 1980: 81.

[12] Ibid., 82.

[13] Benny Morris, *The Birth of the Palestinian Refugee Problem*. Cambridge: Cambridge University Press, 1989: 1.

[14] Rosemary Sayigh, "Palestine." *Third World Quarterly*, vol. 5, no. 4, October 1983.

[15] Refugees formed 53 percent of the population of Jordan, 12 percent of the population of Lebanon, 3 percent of the population of Syria, and 28 percent of the population of Gaza, then under Egyptian administration. See James Baster, "Economic Aspects of the Palestine Refugees." *Middle East Journal*, vol. 8, 1954: 55.

[16] G. Hazboun and B. Salihi, "The Workers and the Movement in the Occupied Territories 1967–1983," part 2, *Al-Kateb*, June 1984: 23–35.

[17] Ghazi Khalili, "The Palestinian Woman and the Revolution." *Journal of Palestine Studies* (winter 1977): 164–165 (translated from *Shu'un Filastiniyya*, October–November 1976).

[18] Shafeeq Ghabra, "Palestinians in Kuwait." *Journal of Palestine Studies*, vol. XVII, no. 1, winter 1988: 63.

[19] Ann Dearden, ed., *Arab Women*. Minority Rights Report No. 27. London: Minority Rights Group, December 1975: 15.

[20] Rosemary Sayigh, "The Mukhabarat State: Testimony of a Palestinian Woman Prisoner." *Race and Class*, vol. 26, no. 2 (autumn 1984): 24.

[21] See Cheryl Rubenberg, *The Palestinian Liberation Organization, Its Institutional Infrastructure*. IAS Monograph Series No. 1 (Belmont, MA: Institute of Arab Studies, 1983). Julie Peteet, in "No Going Back: Women and the Palestinian Movement" (*MERIP* no. 138, January–February 1986: 20–24, 44), writes that "from the late 1960s until 1982 when the PLO moved to Tunis after the Israeli invasion of Lebanon, the Palestinian national movement in Lebanon recruited women and instituted a variety of social services geared to their needs..... Though still a minority in political organizations, women joined all spheres of the resistance. Few attained leadership positions, and most were concentrated in the social services sector. Nevertheless, women were now more than wives and mothers; they were now fighters, leaders, workers, students, activists, cadres and martyrs. These roles and status informed a new sense of identity and aspirations."

[22] Soraya Antonios, "Fighting on Two Fronts: Conversations with Palestinian Women." *Journal of Palestinian Studies*, vol. 7, no. 3, 1979; reprinted in *Third World, Second Sex*, M. Davies, ed.. London: Zed Press, 1983: 34.

[23] Sayigh, "Palestine": 884.

[24] For example, in a collection of Arafat interviews with a number of Arab publications reprinted in a book published by Arafah Publishers, Jerusalem, 1988.

[25] "Shihadat Min Ard el Maaraka" ("Testimonies from the Battlefield"), transcripts of PLO broadcasts. *Lebanon War* (March 15–23, 1978): 67.

[26] Ibid.: 68.

[27] Sayigh, "Palestine": 83.

[28] Laurie Brand, *Palestinians in the Arab World*. New York: Columbia University Press, 1988.

[29] Ibid.

[30] Ibid.: 198, 200–202.

[31] For example, critiques by Ilham Abu-Ghazeleh "Women in Poetry," *Al-Kateb* (The Writer), June 1989, and *Jad*, op. cit. Najah Manasrah, a West Bank writer, says that woman's status has not kept up with her role in the street. Manasrah ("Early Marriage: Temporary Retreat in the March of Palestinian Women," *[Al-Kateb]*, May 1989, 55) writes: "The important role of Palestinian women during the Intifada is responsible for the exaggerated optimism that is reflected in the writings of non-specialists, or in the optimism that can be detected in the declarations of the leaders of the women's movement in our country. If we see that great changes have taken place in the role of women, and even though we're optimistic about the improvement of that role, role changes are not automatically followed by change of status." An early critic of Palestinian gender relations is novelist Sahar Khalifah (see her *Wild Thorns,* London: Zed Press, 1976).

[32] For an example of the most typical type of research about women, see the GUPW pamphlet *From the Palestinian Women's Struggle* (Beirut, n.d.). Also see the PLO pamphlets, *The Woman's Role in the Palestine National Struggle* (Beirut: PLO Department of National Information and Guidance, n.d.). available in English and French; and *The Role of Women in the Intifada*. Tunis: Carthage Press, 1989 (Arabic).

[33] For a critique of how some female leaders got their positions, see Fawzia Fawzia, "Palestine: Women and the Revolution," in *Sisterhood is Global,* Robin Morgan, ed. Harmondsworth, Middlesex: Penguin Books, 1985: 539–548.

[34] Al-Hamishmar, June 2, 1980.

[35] Palestinian Union of Women's Work Committees, Statistics (1987): 9

[36] Salim Tamari, "What the Uprising Means." *Middle East Report* (May–June 1988).

[37] For example, in 1985, the Voluntary Work Committee established in 1979 said it cultivated nineteen thousand dunams of land as part of a program to assist Palestinian farmers (*Al-Fajr,* March 8, 1985: 3). Bir Zeit University requires students to put in 120 hours of voluntary work as a prerequisite for graduation.

[38] PUWWC was renamed the Palestinian Federation of Women's Action Committees (PFWAC) in June 1987. I use PFWAC throughout this article.

[39] PFWAC, Tarik el Mara'a. *Seminar on the Development of the Women's Movement and Its Problems in the Occupied Territories* (March 1982): 38.

[40] Rosemary Sayigh, "Introduction," in *Portraits of Palestinian Women,* Orayb Najjar, with Kitty Warnock. Salt Lake City: University of Utah Press, 1992: 19.

[41] Rosemary Sayigh, "Encounters with Palestinian Women Under Occupation." *Journal of Palestine Studies,* vol. 10, no. 4, summer 1981: 13.

[42] Peteet, "No Going Back."

[43] See the photograph of a delegation of Palestinian women outside the British High Commissioner's Office residence in Jerusalem in Walid Khalidi, *Before Their Diaspora: A Photographic History the Palestinians 1976–1948* (Washington DC: Institute for Palestine

Studies, 1984: 101). For the portrayal of women in general, see Sarah Graham-Brown, *Images of Women: The Portrayal of Women in Photographs of the Middle East 1860–1950* (London: Quartet, 1988). Also see photos in newsletters of all four women's committees.

[44] The involvement of mothers' committees in the planning process to improve kindergartens (rather than having to accept centralized planning) has made kindergartens more responsive to the special needs of working women. In some cases, women themselves decide whether a facility stays open in summer or during the weekend.

[45] Azmi Bishara, "The Third Factor: Impact of the Intifada on Israel," in *Intifada: Palestine at the Crossroad,* Jamal Nassar and Roger Heacock, eds. New York: Praeger, 1990: 271–286.

[46] See the chart of the structure of PFWAC in Najjar, *Portraits of Palestinian Women:* 136–137. The shift in recruitment strategy was essential because of the composition of the Palestinian population. At present, there are more than six million Palestinians living all over the world (2001). Whereas 70 percent of Gaza's inhabitants live in refugee camps, 15 percent of the inhabitants of the West Bank are refugees from former Palestine (L. Hajjar, M. Rabbani, and J. Beinin, "Palestine and the Arab-Israeli Conflict for Beginners," in *Intifada: The Palestinian Uprising Against Israeli Occupation,* Zachary Lockman and Joel Beinin, eds. Boston: South End Press, 1989: 105).

[47] Ylana Miller, *Government and Society in Rural Palestine: 1920–1948.* Austin: University of Texas Press, 1985: 130.

[48] Statistics between 1948 and 1967 show an increase in the ratios of females to males in all stages of education. United Nations schools where Palestinian refugees study had 13,079 boys and 15,489 girls in elementary schools, and 5,558 boys and 6,185 girls at the preparatory level (ninth-grade) (United Nations Relief and Work Agency Staff, 1986: 8).

[49] For more information about women and literacy, see Najjar, *Portraits of Palestinian Women.*

[50] PFWAC *Newsletter* (January 1986): 6.

[51] Interview with Dr. Giacaman, Ramallah, July 19, 1986.

[52] Nanar Sa'id, "Maternity: High Risk in the West Bank." *Al Fajr,* March 8, 1985: 7.

[53] "Fifteen Years of Service and Creative Development." *al-Talia,* July 14–20, 1994: 170.

[54] Nancy Adams Schilling, "The Social and Political Research of Arab Women: A Study in Conflict," in *Women in Contemporary Muslim Societies,* Jane Smith, ed. London: Associated University Presses, 1980: 118.

[55] Carolyn Fluehr-Lobban, "The Political Mobilization of Women in the Arab World," in *Women in Contemporary Muslim Societies:* 235, 236. The S.S. Davis quote is from "A Separate Reality: Moroccan Village Women," Paper read at the Middle East Studies Association, Milwaukee, Wisconsin: 12.

[56] *The Washington Report on Middle East Affairs.* July/August 1993: 65. Also see http://www.upmrc.organization.

[57] Nadia Hijab, *Womanpower: The Arab Debate on Women and Work.* Cambridge: Cambridge University Press, 1988: 11.

[58] Ibid.: 114.

[59] Ibid.: 35.

[60] Carol Smart, *Feminism and the Power of Law.* New York: Routledge, 1989: 5.

[61] Rema Hammami, "Women, the Hijab and the Intifada." *Middle East Report,* May–August 1990: 28.

[62] Ibid.

[63] Ibid.

[64] Sayigh, "Encounters with Palestinian Women": 16.

[65] Hijab: 13.

[66] "Women's Workshops to Strengthen Palestinian Women Under the Supervision of al-Haq Institution." *al-Talia,* July 14–20, 1994: 15. Also see "Under the Supervision of al-Haq, Two Workshops in Beit Sahur and Nablus." *al-Talia,* July 23–August 3, 1994: 15.

[67] "Women's Workshops to Strengthen Palestinian Women."

[68] *Development Affairs,* 1988: 11.

[69] Ibid.: 12.

[70] Ibid.

[71] Abu-Ghazaleh, "Women in Poetry." *Al-Kateb (The Writer),* June 1989: 65–76.

[72] Sayigh, "The Mukhabarat State": 26.

[73] See *Spark,* December 1991 and June 1993.

Impasse

MARY TALLMOUNTAIN

*Excerpted from the novel Doyon, set in Nulato village. Nulato is a dot at the
edge of the Yukon River on the subarctic map of the vast interior of Alaska.
During World War I, Lidwynne, three-year-old daughter of terminally tubercu-
lar Indian/Russian Mary Joe, is adopted by the white American doctor and his
wife, and lives with them in the U.S. Government Hospital.*

Under the bed, Lidwynne was singing the words of one of Mamma's Indian
songs softly, for the ears of her pretend friend, LO-SE EVNS.

Nellie came out of the kitchen. "That's a pretty song," she said, "but what does
it mean?"

Lidwynne peeked out. "It means there's the seagull and there's the
porcupine." She slid out and gazed up, up, to see Nellie's soft brown eyes and
the hand held out to her.

Nellie reached down and squeezed the hand Lidwynne stretched up. "Did
you ever see a porcupine?"

"No. But one time, Mamma and Michael did."

"Where did they see him?"

"Up Four Mile, Nellie. At fish camp."

Nellie's forehead seemed to squeeze itself together, and her voice rose a little.
"Don't be careless, dear. You meant to say *up at* Four Mile, didn't you?"

Lidwynne shook her head vigorously. "*Up* Four Mile is the way Mamma
and everybody says it. When I say it I mean *up,* too. It's *up the river!*"

Nellie patted Lidwynne's hair and straightened it neatly. "*Up at* sounds
better, though."

Lidwynne stared at the floor. Inside herself she muttered to LO-SE, "She
doesn't know how we talk. But we can talk *our way,* can't we?"

Nellie asked, "Where were you when your Mamma and brother Michael
saw the porcupine?"

"Don't you remember? I was gone away with you. It was when we went on
the Teddy T, upriver to Ruby."

"Yes, that was the time." Nellie sat down close to where Lidwynne was
sitting hunched up beside the bed. Lidwynne wanted to make up some more
words for Mamma's song. Already, some of it was hiding in her mind, and she
started singing the words, real low.

Nellie's forehead grew those funny ridges across it again.

"Please don't frown to me," Lidwynne said.

But Nellie kept her face that way and sat on the bed. Looking down at Lidwynne, she said, "I want to tell you something important. I know you love to talk Indian. But you're getting to be a big girl. You're five, almost six. Only you don't speak English yet. You ought to be speaking it all the time. Then, when we go Outside, people can understand you."

Lidwynne was surprised. She thought Nellie liked Indian words. "Mamma and I and Michael talk Indian all the time." She smiled at Nellie and hummed a little more of the song. "Say 'Oh my!' to me, Nellie," she said. She loved the way Nellie said "Oh my!" to her when she'd done something specially nice. This time Nellie wouldn't, even when Lidwynne put her hand on Nellie's knee and asked quickly, "Aren't you glad I've got a new song?" because Nellie was looking as if she were getting ready to say no. "Well then, can't I just sing the song inside my self?"

"That's what I mean, dear. Please promise to try very hard to *think* English words. When we go Outside, you won't speak Indian words, because people won't understand you. So don't you see you must begin now to speak English."

"I like English," Lidwynne said slowly. "I learned to read it from my books, when you showed me how."

"But now you need to use it. Using Indian words interferes with your good English."

Lidwynne thought Nellie was different today. These mornings she would always be singing to herself. This morning she had been very quiet in the kitchen. "Why can't I talk both ways?" she asked.

"Because you will be living Outside."

Lidwynne put her fists on her hips. "Oh, I hate Outside! Why do we have to go there?"

"Are you sure you really hate Outside?"

"Why do you talk about it all the time?"

"Because you said you liked Outside when I talked about it, and you wanted to go there."

"I'm very busy. Here in Nulato is where I'm busy. I don't want to go Outside any more."

"You don't want to go to Oregon where it's warm? Where it won't be cold like it was last winter?"

"You told me it rains a lot Outside. I don't like rain."

"Nice warm rain, Lidwynne. There's no snow where we're going. You'll like that."

"No, I love snow. Here in the village we like snow."

"Don't you want to see the animals in the zoo? And the elephant?" Nellie said "elephant" in her high voice.

"Are there elephants Outside?" But she already knew.

"Don't be stubborn. You know there are. I've told you so."

Real bad, Lidwynne wanted to see the elephant. There were lots of things she wanted to see, but they were far away. She brightened. "I can look at elephants in my books."

"It's much better to look at real live elephants."

"Why can't Mamma and Michael and Daddy Clem go Outside with us?"

Nellie seemed not to have heard her. "You'll have good new things to eat. You won't have to live in two places any more."

"I like what I eat right here."

Nellie's lips looked as straight as a ruler, and she gave Lidwynne a kind of long stare. "I'm not going to argue with you. We are going Outside."

"Will we come back here?"

"It won't be possible."

Lidwynne's stomach felt as though she were alone in an empty room. It wasn't any use talking. "Why do we have to go Outside?" she asked anyway.

"Because Doctor Daddy and I are tired. He's been working in the Yukon a long time. We both need to rest. Besides, you'll get to see Aunties, and Grandma, and Uncle Kay, and all your cousins."

"My aunties and uncles and my cousins live here, and Grandpa. Grandmother's here too, up there in the graveyard." She couldn't get Nellie to understand. "Nobody ever goes away from here," she said.

"Don't you remember that you're our little girl now?"

"I'm Mamma's girl too, and I'm Daddy Clem's girl."

Nellie looked out the window. "You remember when we were in Ruby that day?"

Lidwynne nodded. "A little bit, maybe."

"It was two years ago, and you were almost four. We went to see the Judge, and he gave you an apple. He wrote out a paper that said Uncle Sam decided you'd be Doctor Daddy's and my little girl. That means we adopted you."

She remembered the apple. When she tried to see the judge in her mind, she couldn't see his face, just his thin gray whiskers. But she could see the new red sweater and cap Nellie got her in the store, there at Ruby. She remembered, too, a little cub bear on a chain, going around and around a stake stuck into the muddy street, and how she cried because he couldn't get away.

"Adopted, adopted," she said, in a high voice. Nellie had talked to her about that when it first happened, but her words had all gone into the back of Lidwynne's head where things went that made her feel funny. She felt funny now. Nobody else ever got adopted. She wanted to find out what it meant, even though she'd heard about it before, and really ought to remember.

"Adopted," she repeated. "I heard Grandpa say we don't have that word in Nulato. He was mad when he said it."

"We have that word in Nulato now, Lidwynne. You're adopted."

Lidwynne asked, 'What does adopted mean?" She kept forgetting. Nellie's thumbnail dug into her knuckle, and Lidwynne thought it must be hurting. Nellie leaned forward and looked straight into Lidwynne's eyes. "It means your Mamma said she would let us have you, and you could live with us and be our little girl. So she wrote her name on that paper the Judge gave us."

"Why did she? Didn't she want me?" Lidwynne stared up under her bangs at Nellie.

"Oh, darling, your Mamma is sick. She can't dress you and cook for you. She wants you to be warm and eat well, and live with us in the hospital. Now come here, and stop hiding your face." She reached out her arms.

"I like Mamma's *yah*," Lidwynne said, crawling into Nellie's lap.

"Don't say '*yah*.' Say 'house.' You can't always have two houses, dear."

Lidwynne thought, No, Mamma's cabin isn't a house, it's a *yah*. "I like to have Mamma's house and your hospital, both." She patted Nellie's face. "I like having two houses."

"This is your house now. You live here with Doctor Daddy and me, even though you go and see your Mamma in her house sometimes."

Lidwynne thought that over. She didn't understand how Mamma could be sick, unless—"Oh, I see. Mamma got that germ you had last winter when everybody was right here in the hospital, and you were taking care of them, and you got that germ!"

"No, your Mamma has something a little harder to get rid of. It's called tuberculosis and she has to rest a lot."

"Oh." Lidwynne grew very quiet. It was nice and warm in Nellie's lap, and for a minute everything was wonderful. Even if something was wrong with Mamma, she was sure to get better. And if she had to go Outside away from everybody, she could take LO-SE along. She would always have LO-SE. When they were alone, she talked out loud to LO-SE. She was Lidwynne's best secret. "You mean I'm Doctor and Nellie Merrick's little girl," she said.

Nellie's brown eyes smiled. "That's the stuff!"

Lidwynne sang some more. "*Mats hodee*," the words went. She loved that song about the seagull.

"I'm going to keep after you till you stop using those words." Nellie bounced her up and down, rocking at the same time.

"Those Indian words? I forgot, Nellie. Mamma is an Indian. Is Mamma bad?"

"No, dear, of course she isn't. Indian is not bad. But when you go Outside, you will still be a little girl that's part Indian. It isn't bad being part Indian. But it will be easier for you if you talk English and act white."

Lidwynne shook her head. "I look like Indian."

Nellie said, real close, "But it will be easier for you to talk English. Let's say it like this: You need to forget some of the old Nulato ways, and start being the kind of little girl who lives Outside."

This reminded Lidwynne of LO-SE, and she hummed the song again, this time careful not to sing the words. She said them to LO-SE in her mind. Next, she thought about the beautiful red sweater. There were lots of things like that Outside. It would be nice to go Outside for a little while, maybe. And if she needed to sing Indian or talk Indian she would just have to go under the bed with LO-SE. Nobody else seemed to know LO-SE was there, even, so she finally realized LO-SE was made of some stuff they couldn't see.

Nellie put her face against Lidwynne's. The comfortable feeling crept back. "Some day you'll start to call me Mother," Nellie said. She put Lidwynne down and went back into the kitchen. After a while Lidwynne heard her singing.

≫€   ≫€   ≫€

Late in the fall Lidwynne's whole family went to their camp at Four Mile for the last salmon run, but Lidwynne couldn't go. Nellie got her up early, and they went down to the bank to watch Mamma and Michael and Grandpa leave with Uncle and Auntie and all the cousins.

Mamma carried Michael over and picked Lidwynne up too. Her cheek felt real cold against Lidwynne's. "*Snaa,* my child, already it's dog salmon time. Soon now, your birthday is coming." Mamma's cheek felt wet.

Lidwynne said, "I must have forgotten my birthday!"

"Are you still sleepy?" Mamma held her so tight it hurt.

"Yes, I'm sleepy." Lidwynne didn't move.

"You be a good girl," Mamma whispered. "Maybe the Doctor and Nellie will bring you back to see us."

Over Mamma's shoulder Lidwynne saw Nellie's thin, crying look.

She squeezed Michael, and his little voice said her name. His eyes were round like the moon. Mamma took him to the family canoe and sat down with him in her arms. Her long black hair covered their faces.

Just the way it was, Lidwynne remembered his eyes. She remembered his eyes better than any others. The canoes and her family's faces went away upriver, till she couldn't see the people waving. Michael got smaller and smaller. He was so small, her brother.

Walking back to the hospital, she held Nellie's hand. "He'll cry, and I won't be there," she told Nellie.

Nellie tried to cheer her up and wiped her face with one of her white hankies with crocheted edges. "You'll have a birthday next month. Won't that be fun?"

"Mamma said I forgot it. Did I forget?"

"Seems to me you haven't talked much about your birthday."

"How could I have forgot that?"

"You've been very busy."

"Will I be six?"

"Yes, you'll be six."

"I'm an old little girl," Lidwynne said.

Korea

MERLE WOO

My grandmother named her Korea. The oldest girl in the family.
The exact year of her birth is still in question. Maybe 1896.
You see, it was an obsession with her to keep her age from
everyone;
she even changed her birth certificate.

Since she was the only one of her eight children who was
born in their home country, grandmother named her Korea.

Korea Chang.

Although, thought my mother, her little sister Helen,
ugly, she loved her in a sometimes cruel way, and
they were always close all their lives,
all over the world.

My mother Helen—
Wanted a more glorious, beautiful, and romantic life.
Didn't want to be just a plain old "Helen."
So my mother changed her name to Helene.

But, Korea Chang:

She grew up in Shanghai. My mother was there too.
The park outside the International Zone had a sign that said:
"No Dogs. No Chinamen."

Korea Chang changed her name to Cora Chandler to live better
in the world.

And she was so beautiful:

    Had the strong high cheekbones of Korea—
    and eyes—big, round, and full,
    but with a hint of Korea.
    She dyed her hair to a flaming red,
    until the roots turned grey, then dyed it silver.
    Wore sea-green, silver-flecked mascara—
    Cora Chandler with her false eyelashes,
    White face makeup and rouge over the high cheekbones.

Came to the U.S. single and with a baby girl—

> Named Gloria—after Swanson
> (Later had Wally—after Beery).

Popular with men, with sailors—
In her sunglasses worn all the time,
shading the beautiful dark eyes.

How she took care of her face:
Cold cream every night, told my mother—

> "Now, Helene—cream and lotion every night on the
> places age hits the most: the hands, neck, elbows.
> Cover the forehead! Keep the deadly wrinkles away."

> The wrinkles will keep the men away. Success away.

My mother followed in her footsteps, naming two of her children
in the same fashion—

> Ronald—after Colman
> Merle—after Oberon.

But mother wouldn't, couldn't hide her heritage.
Married Chinese, had Korean Chinese children.

You know, we couldn't visit my Auntie Cora in San Mateo
while we were growing up.

She feared the neighbors finding out—
Might be suspicious if they saw a bunch of Asians
climbing out of an old Buick and going into her house.

I would sit under the table while Helene and Cora talked
at our flat in San Francisco.

Of men, work, family.
Reminiscing about their lives as young women:

> How Helene with her retarded daughter, Christina,
> stayed with Cora. And while Cora worked in a factory,
> Helene kept the tiny apartment, taking care of their
> two girl-children.

Two single mothers—
Korean women in Chicago during the 20s.

I loved their stories,
My aunt's biting humor and sharp tongue—
Made me laugh.

Stories about her kind of people at the horse races,
Reno: gamblers, prostitutes, lesbians.

Even as a teenager, I would still drift in to hear their talk.

Oh, she did become bitter over the years.
Sarcastic tones in all her phrases—
Words like "fat," "ugly," "pig," "poor," and "stupid"—
referring to her family.

Her succession of houses, a descent into poverty.
Dying of stomach cancer, fragile and broken,
in Nairobi, East Palo Alto.

How I admired this woman:

She loved me and treated me good,
always giving me talcum powder in pink satin boxes,
and pungent perfumes in exotic glass bottles,
racy negligees in sizes too big.

She taught me that life is harsh—
Taught me to fight with whatever tools I had.

She used her looks and the values she had no choice but to accept.

One tool I have is the message of her life—
And that tool is really a weapon.

This poem first appeared in *Yellow Woman Speaks* (Seattle: Radical Women Publications 1987). Copyright © 1982 by Merle Woo.

Josephine and Me: Teaching About Racism in Women Studies

MERLE WOO

Today I'd like to take teacher's prerogative and change the subject for class. I'm going to talk, I hope, for about twenty minutes or so, and then Josephine will say a few words, and then I want to open it up for discussion. I've been somewhat angry (mostly at myself) about what happened in class last week. Been thinking about it and having discussions with Josephine. And now that we've come up with an analysis I want to address the issues of that day, and I am confident we can all learn from the experience.

Women studies is one segment of the women's movement. More and more it is becoming the *academic* arm of feminism rather than an extension of the communities that put women studies on college campuses. And racism is still a central issue. Well, even worse, in general society racism is on the rise! We have to be part of the solution of ending racism, if we want true liberation for all women.

But fighting racism is still not seen as integral to feminism. One reason there is a reluctance (or refusal) to address race is that women would then have to address class as well.

Remember how we read in Assata:

> As far as i was concerned, it didn't take too much brains to figure out that Black people are oppressed because of class as well as race, because we are poor and because we are Black. It would burn me up every time somebody talked about Black people climbing the ladder of success. Anytime you're talking about a ladder, you're talking about a top and a bottom, an upper class and a lower class, a rich class and a poor class. As long as you've got a system with a top and a bottom, Black people are always going to wind up at the bottom, because we're the easiest to discriminate against. That's why i couldn't see fighting within the system. Both the democratic party and the republican party are controlled by millionaires.[1]

Could it be that radical feminists[2] in particular, have a problem with this concept? That the history of people of color in this country is a history of super-class exploitation? Native American peoples were either forcibly removed from their land or massacred. For four hundred years, Africans were brutally enslaved. Latinos/Chicanos (if not already in the U.S.) and Asian/Pacific Islanders were brought here deliberately—in chains, by coercion, or with false promises of a life free from starvation and poverty—to fill those lower rungs of the ladder. Our history is the history of the proletarianization of nonwhite peoples.

Earlier in the semester, we had read Oliver C. Cox, a Black Marxist sociologist, who wrote:

> In the case of race relations the tendency of the bourgeoisie is to proletarianize a whole people—that is to say, the whole people is looked upon as a class—whereas white proletarianization involves only a section of the white people. The concept "bourgeois" and "white people" sometimes seems to mean the same thing for, with respect to the colored peoples of the world, it is almost always through a white bourgeoisie that capitalism has been introduced .... It is this need to proletarianize whole peoples which introduces into the class struggle the complicating factors known as race problems.[3]

Could it be that when radical feminists focus only on sexism as being the central and key oppression, the result is a lack of genuine solidarity with other groups? That the oppression of men of color and white working-class men is completely ignored? For radical feminists, the origin of women's oppression is the patriarchy, and so addressing the need to abolish capitalism and imperialism is not a priority. They believe that when capitalism is abolished, sexism will still remain. But, what is the praxis for radical feminism?

In the San Francisco Bay Area, radical feminism remains entrenched in the women's community—where the central tenet is the oppression of women by men. Where women are still seen as a separate class, with men, all men, being part of the ruling class. A biologically deterministic view! Now this contradicts any theory around race, a Marxist class analysis, and the potential for people to change.

Connected to this concept is also a trendy narcissism, a hold-over from the sixties, and evolving into new-age Me-ism, crystal-gazing, identity and lifestyle politics. Radical feminists tend to be inward-looking versus outward-looking, and so if all they see are themselves—primarily white, college-educated, privileged women, who have never worked a permanent forty-plus-hour week, and who do not identify with women who must work at "women's jobs," they turn up their noses at the majority of working-class women in society.

I'm really tired of hearing radical feminists say they never learned to type because they would never be caught doing clerical work. Or they say that they would never work for big corporations, like the phone company, and prefer to work in the women's community. This kind of elitism prevents acknowledging those women who have no choice, or who have made a *different* choice than they!

Today some academic women arrogantly brag about having studied all the "big" feminist of color writers like Audre Lorde, bell hooks, Barbara Smith,

Mitsuye Yamada, Nellie Wong, Louise Erdrich, and Paula Gunn Allen; Cherríe Moraga and Gloria Anzaldúa. To put these women of color on a pedestal without absorbing their life's lessons, or without being critical of their diverse theories of social change, is simply racist love. It's racist to dehumanize people of color in any way. As an Asian Pacific American, I have had to fight against *positive* stereotypes that are supposed to make us "better than" all other communities of color: We're the "model minority." This is dehumanizing and divisive.

There is a segment of the San Francisco lesbian, gay, bisexual and transgender community that is becoming more conservative, more insulated; and there is a tendency, in the face of AIDS, not to turn outward, but to turn inward. They've bought into the moralism of right-wing reaction, and in their desperate dash for "respectability" and acceptance *under capitalism,* mimic the monogamous nuclear family.

Recently, I was one of the judges in a lesbian/gay "family fiction" contest. In nearly all of the stories there was absolutely no social consciousness whatever. The stories depicted a very separatist, very privatized environment. All were very white. "Castro Family Fiction" is what I call it. It's very interesting to note, of course, that a lesbian/gay fiction contest would be modified by making it a *family* fiction contest in the age of AIDS. For heaven's sakes, us queers are supposed to challenge the heterosexist and sexist family structure, not *join* it!

Pat Parker said that when AIDS first hit the gay community, white gay men kept insisting it was not a gay disease.[4] But now that it has been proven that people of color communities are being hit, with women of color and children hit disproportionately, many white gay men are silent on that subject. When talking about AIDS and people of color communities, we have to address not only safer sex practices, but poverty, drugs, lack of educational opportunities, and the need for free quality healthcare.

Me first is the name of the identity-politics game. But in the end, it isn't our individual identity that matters, but whose needs we all have to address to liberate everyone. It's the political program that matters—theory and practice. A white woman can be a multi-issue revolutionary feminist. I know many of these. An Asian Pacific American lesbian can be a conservative. This is a theory class, and all semester long we've been looking at the connections between race, sex, sexuality, and class. I recall one of you during the semester saying that socialist feminist theory seemed the most multi-issued, but that socialist feminists focus on class too much. Well, I'm sorry about that. We didn't make up the objective reality that racism, sexism, and heterosexism are integral to, part and parcel of keeping the working class divided—they are the main tools of class exploitation.

The Issue

OK. So now given all of that, let's get to what happened in class last week. Because lo and behold, this was a classic example of some dynamics of racism in women studies. And of how practice is the direct result of the theory you hold.

We were talking about the Hedda Nussbaum case where her partner, Joel Steinberg, beat their little girl to death. Joel had battered Hedda for years, and both she and Joel were cocaine addicts.

You will remember that Josephine, who is our one Chinese American students and one of four women of color in a class of twenty-six, had a question about whether or not Hedda had any responsibility to save that child who was lying on the bathroom floor for hours before she died, while Hedda performed her routine tasks.

Immediately, at least four white women jumped in, stopped Jo short, and went on about the cycle of violence and battery, the *total powerlessness* of women caught in that kind of domestic situation. They said that Hedda had no responsibility for that child, and couldn't be faulted for not picking up the phone and dialing 911.

I got back to Jo and asked her if she wanted to add to what she had begun to say. She said no. She was done. She was fed up and done.

Now, two things are at issue here regarding racism and women of color. First, there's the obvious. The white women who interrupted her did not even let her finish. They weren't even listening to what she had to say *as though she had nothing worthwhile to say at all!* Is it because these white women, having taken all these women studies courses and knowing all this radical feminist theory, had the answers? And that a Chinese American woman had nothing to say about battery at all? To interrupt her like that is downright racist.

The second issue is that Jo may have had an opposing theory to the radical feminists', based on the fact that she is an Asian woman. To ignore the contributions of women students of color who are bringing to this class a history and personal knowledge of race, sex, and class oppression is racist and self-destructive.

None of you, all semester long, has openly disagreed with me when I've talked about the leadership of women and lesbians of color. No one has questioned the rationale that the most oppressed shall lead in the movements for radical social change because being at the bottom, their perspective is the most clear and, out of necessity, their conscious vision is a militant and collective one. And yet you don't even listen to a woman of color who might have a different perspective. You effectively denied her leadership.

Radical feminism, with its roots in the New Left, in narcissism and identity politics, has dispensed with the concept of leadership. Of the New Left, Clara Fraser, Jewish socialist feminist theoretician and cofounder of the Freedom Socialist Party, wrote:

> Born of ideological anarchism, the current network of collectives, "alternative institutions"...deplore and detest organization and leadership, which they label as anti-human, Leninist-machine, imperialistic constructs.

> The New Left still supplants program and leadership with the cult of "human relations," "relating to people," and following after the spontaneity and given level of consciousness of the masses. The functions of leadership—to guide, coordinate, supervise, initiate, advise, teach, organize—is anathema to them....The New Left pontificates that "lifestyle IS our politics" and "lifestyle humanism means no leaders."[5]

The feminist slogan, "The personal is political," has come to mean that lifestyle IS our politics, e.g., any lesbian having a lesbian relationship is being a political person. And denying any need for leadership in the movements for social change means you have no responsibility yourself, either to lead or respect other women's leadership, to be accountable. Do what you want, where you want, how you want.

Jo might have taught you something she's known all along—something about collective responsibility.

I want to read you an excerpt from Barbara Omolade's "It's a Family Affair: The Real Lives of Black Single Mothers":

> All my close women friends and I are Black single mothers .... We share similar past experiences of poverty, mental torment and physical abuse, self-doubt and confusion. But now we are heading our households and raising our children in well-functioning families.

> If any of us were frozen in those past crises brought on by unemployment, lack of decent, affordable housing, or trouble with our spouses or mates, we would have seemed destined to live out the stereotype of perpetual poverty and despair.

> In fact, after surviving the trauma of losing a loved one through separation, divorce, or death, most Black single mothers slowly stabilize their families.[6]

There is within our people of color communities a sense of responsibility to each other, our families—for good or ill—and to our communities. I'm not saying that we all escape that cycle of despair that comes from poverty and a constant violent war going on against us in our Chinatowns, ghettoes, barrios. But the point is that many women of color and working-class white women hold Hedda Nussbaum accountable. Of course, to a lesser degree than Steinberg. But we do not see ourselves as totally powerless in the clutches of the patriarchy. This could lead us to a horrible and suicidal cynicism and to separatism. We know that our children have the least power, and we take responsibility for them, and attempt to protect them against the enemy, any enemy, if it's a man or The Man.

Omolade also says,

> Most Black single mothers are the working poor.... We commute daily to city, state, and federal government agencies. As paras, aides, and clerks, we are the backbone of the hospital, child care, and nursing home systems. Although the wages are low and the work tedious, Black women stay with their city jobs for years because they offer stability and benefits.[7]

If women of color have a loyalty to their communities, they also embody a solidarity with their class. My own mother, a Korean American, is a testament to the tedious work, rotten working conditions and low pay women of color are forced into. But, at the same time, she talked about the self-respect that came from a job well done and her integrated workplace where people are faced with racism, sexism, and class oppression every day, and where it is very clear who the enemy is: management. Working-class people, without much choice in where they work, learn a respect for collective leadership, responsibility, and organization; if they're unionists, they learn about solidarity and strength on the picket lines.

You didn't learn from Jo or what she had to say. And you lost out.

Every semester I see women of color sign up for classes and then drop out. They are very, very precious to me, to the other faculty of color, and to progressive white faculty and students in women studies. And I want to see our classes addressing their needs, and nourishing their voices, leadership, and theoretical skills.

I'm also not letting racist faculty off the hook. Students are getting racist theory somewhere, or they're not being called on it, or they're seeing faculty being racist themselves. There exists some misleadership in women studies.

Last semester a white woman kept going on about how she—pacifist that she was—condemned the "physical cruelty" of Audre Lorde's mother in *Zami* and Maxine Hong Kingston's mother in *Woman Warrior*.[8] I told her, and other women students of color told her, that was a racist statement. Our mothers may seem "cruel and violent" (and objectively, hitting children isn't right—we're not talking about condoning, but *understanding*), but they have the monumental task of warning our children of the much more intense violence out there in society.

There's police brutality. Militarism. The neo-Nazis are out there, Operation Rescue, and Roe v. Wade going down the tubes. And a capitalist economy in chaos with the concomitant rise of violence against women, people of color, immigrants, lesbians, gays, bisexuals, and transgenders—the entire working class! There isn't going to be any coalition-building if the basic respect isn't there for women of color and their potential for leadership. What I want to see being built is an anticapitalist mass movement that would really change everything at its root, and achieving—finally—a socialist feminist revolution that has integral to its program antiracism and the abolishment of every single other form of discrimination that exists in this rotten society today.

Race, sex, sexuality, and class are not just words. There are whole histories behind those words. And when they all connect up in women/lesbians of color, that history is embodied in their lives. And their lives form theory, which catapults us into a certain direction for action.

Until white feminists acknowledge the need to address race, sex, and class issues in all their specificity, i.e., having an understanding of the particular conditions and histories of Asian women in America, the feminist movement will remain peripheral and irrelevant to the majority of these women.

Some of you want women of color to be just like you. No challenge, no threat. We're all the same under the skin.

That's not the objective reality. And there is no instant solution, but a lot of hard work that is complicated and complex, where you have to look at every situation with a dialectical materialist eye. You point out similarities and analyze those differences, in all their objective particularities, and respect them. You fight for women whose histories, language, and culture are totally different from yours and love how your own world has become so much richer. If you really want liberation, you must create a solid political relationship with women of color. Yes, you can say we all suffer from sexism and most of us from class exploitation, but you have to acknowledge that because of racism, the oppression of women of color is so much more intense. You need to make the fight against race and class oppression your fight.

And when you talk about female genital mutilation in Africa, or bound feet and female infanticide in China, make sure you also add that the U.S. government has a program of genocide through sterilization of women of color, and that's pretty inhuman, too. Or compare what American women are brainwashed to do to themselves in terms of breast implants, plastic surgery, and diets! My point is that women of color are not the exotic "other." We have a common cause because we have a common enemy: patriarchal capitalism and imperialism.

> We need a lot of collective drive and commitment for the long haul. Josephine, would you talk about what you've been thinking?

Josephine said something like this:

> Some of my friends told me not to take a women studies class because there is racism. But I did anyway because I wanted to see if I would learn anything about being a Chinese American woman.
>
> Usually, I don't speak out very much in any of my classes, not because I don't want to, but because I'm slow to pull my thoughts together and by that time everyone else has said what I was going to say. Everyone seems to know much more than I do.
>
> Merle's been trying to get me to speak out all semester. She says, just say what you know and it will always be relevant. My auntie gets beat up by my uncle when he gets drunk. And she doesn't say anything because everyone she knows is all wound up tight together by family, church, and our community—yeah, Chinatown West, the Richmond District.
>
> But still she's the best mother to my cousins and my sisters and brothers too. And she works. So that's why I asked that question.
>
> This whole thing has been really hard but at the same time empowering. Others in the class have supported me because I spoke out and had a different opinion. And now I'm also part of solving a problem. I learned from Mitsuye Yamada that we APA women can no longer contribute to our own stereotype of the quiet, studious, ready-to-please Asian woman. I have a new awareness now and that is going to make me more visible than ever. I'm going to continue to speak out and demand that others be responsible for any disrespectful actions towards me.

Discussion

There was silence in the classroom for several minutes. Then a white woman, who hadn't been one of those who interrupted Jo, said that theory and action *were* connected, and that if women didn't formulate their theories with great care, racism would continue. She added that a theory that finds the origins of women's oppression in private property and the nuclear monogamous family *will* have a different practice for liberation than a theory that says that the patriarchy/men are the enemy.

A Black woman spoke about the similarities in the racist way she was treated in the psychology department. She said it was intolerable that this should happen in women studies.

A white woman, who *had* interrupted Jo, said that only today did she really understand that what may be merely an intellectual exercise to her, could be painful and real to women of color. She said that because she was committed to antiracist activism, in the future she would see any racist attack as a personal attack on her.

A Chicana said she was so relieved that what had happened last week was discussed in class. As a young feminist, she has felt alienated from ethnic studies because of sexism and homophobia and from women studies because of racism. She thought we were moving forward.

For the sake of feminism, we must move forward.

Conclusion

As faculty, we have to be extremely conscious and respond immediately when racism rears its ugly head. We can be living examples on how to deal with racism, spontaneously and collectively, and when we do so, successfully, students also learn and are encouraged to speak out: They will gain a discerning eye and ear and be ready.

As an Asian Pacific American lesbian and socialist feminist activist, I know I was more angry on that day in class than I should have been. I think the main reason is that I was angry with myself, because I didn't stop the racism *as it was happening!*

I learned once again that my job as a lecturer is not just to teach subjects isolated from the students themselves. The dynamic in a classroom where students are encouraged to speak out will create situations that can turn into vital lessons about life. Our faculty and students must together fight racism. Women studies, like ethnic studies, was born out of the need for liberation. We must take advantage of every opportunity to provide the tools for communication, education, and united fronts to attain democracy and freedom.

NOTES

[1] Assata Shakur, *Assata: An Autobiography,* Westport, CT: Lawrence Hill & Co., 1987: 190.

[2] The subject of this class came up in the context of having studied radical feminist and socialist feminist theories on the roots of women's oppression.

For radical feminists, the oppression of women by men/patriarchy is the primary oppression. Sexism cannot be eradicated by massive economic, political, and social change, such as in a socialist revolution. Sex, not class, is the determining factor in radically altering society. Using an inherently biologically determinist view, radical feminists see women's oppression as the result of the male tendency towards violence and aggression. Women are naturally gentle and nurturing. Solutions for women's liberation vary: separatism, the creation of a women-only society or a women's culture, drastically decreasing the numbers of men in the world; and/or becoming a lesbian.

Socialist feminists trace the roots of women's oppression to the beginning of the monogamous nuclear family and the concomitant rise of private property, which today has evolved into a class society of capitalists, who own the means of production, and workers who sell their labor: the haves and have-nots. Socialist feminists connect women's oppression, heterosexism, and racism to class exploitation, and all must be struggled against simultaneously in order to liberate the most oppressed workers: women/lesbians of color. Socialism is a way of collectivizing production and wealth, with all workers gaining hegemony. A socialist revolution is the prerequisite for women's emancipation, and feminism is essential to socialism. Where male supremacy functions, real socialism does not, because socialism connotes a higher form of human relations than can possibly exist under capitalism.

[3] Oliver C. Cox, *Caste, Class & Race.* New York: Doubleday, 1948: 344.

[4] At the Empowering Women of Color Conference, University of California, Berkeley, April 15, 1989. Pat Parker, a Black revolutionary feminist poet, died of metastasized breast cancer later that year.

[5] In "Woman as Leader: Double Jeopardy on Account of Sex," Seattle: Radical Women Publications, 1972: 6.

[6] Barbara Omolade, "It's a Family Affair: The Real Lives of Black Single Mothers," Freedom Organizing Series #4, New York: Kitchen Table/Women of Color Press, 1986.

[7] Ibid.: 4.

[8] Audre Lorde, *Zami.* New York: Crossing Press, 1982. Maxine Hong Kingston, *Woman Warrior.* New York: Knopf, 1976.

Ah Chenk

NELLIE WONG

Ah Chenk was what we kids called him
Ma Ma's brother-in-law
but whose wife died
in the village in Toishan

Ah Chenk came once a month
from *Ai Fow* to visit us in Oakland
Oh, how my mouth watered
at the thought of his visit

In his three-piece suit, his gold watch
fob hanging from his vest,
Ah Chenk brought pink boxes filled
with *cha sieu bow, hah gow,*
bock tong go and *gin duey*

And we kids would devour them,
happy that we had a rich uncle
or so we thought, who made sure
our rumbling bellies got filled
with what *we thlee yip* folks
called *cha ngow*

At least once a month
Bah Bah would drive us
in his '39 green Chevy
to visit *Ah Chenk* in *Ah Fow*

Yeah, the Big City's lights
thrilled us as we crossed the Bay Bridge
as Leslie, Flo and I squirmed
in the back seat, talking and laughing

Our bellies growled until
Ah Chenk took us above
the Stockton Street tunnel
to the corner coffee shop on Bush Street

and ordered us prime rib of beef
mashed potatoes and custard pie
How American we felt
as we savored the tender beef in our mouths

Back down on Stockton Street
we walked into the laundry
where Chinese men ironed, where the irons
hissed and hissed as crisp white shirts
came out fresher than new

Who would have known *Ah Chenk*
dressed in his three-piece suit
on his visits to Oakland
but in his shop, with his shirtsleeves rolled up,
was a laundryman

Ah Chenk was handsome,
slender and dapper, his eyes sparkled
as if he were truly wealthy,
not the image that Westerners imagined
of a Chinese laundryman

who sent a picture of himself
as a young man to China
and procured himself a young bride
When Auntie arrived in San Francisco
she was shocked that her groom was silver-haired

Ah Chenk fathered four children
with his bride whom we called *Ah Thlaw*
who had to work to provide
for their growing family

Ah Chenk, I can't forget him
How urbane and sophisticated his air
but whose heart flowed with love,
his hands carrying pink boxes,
with his jade and gold ring glistening

Quicker than he could wink his eye
Ah Chenk would thrust a crisp $5 bill
into each of our hands,
even though it wasn't Chinese New Year.

GLOSSARY

Ai Fow – Big city, San Francisco

Thlee yip – The fourth dialect, Toisanese

Cha ngow – Tea pastry or dim sum ("a little bit of heart"). *Cha sieu bow, hah gow, bock tong go,* and *gin duey* are all types of *cha ngow*

Ah Thlaw – Auntie

© 2001 by Nellie Wong.

History Lesson

JANICE GOULD

A terrible pestilence, an intermittent fever, was reported as having almost depopulated the whole valley of Sacramento and San Joaquin.... The country was strewn with the remains of the dead wherever a village had stood, and from the headwaters of the Sacramento to the King's River only five Indians were seen.

—H. H. Bancroft, *The Native Races,* vol. 1,
Wild Tribes (1883)

1832

All this fall we have watched our families sicken
with astonishing rapidity. In a fever they chill to the bone,
then break into a profuse sweat. The shuddering heat and cold alternate
till they are too weak
to rise from where they lie
and they simply die. In our village no adults are left,
just one woman so heartbroken she can do nothing
but wail and smear her shorn head with pitch.
The children not stricken with fever neither sleep nor eat.
They shrink with fear and grief, for the dead
clamor about us, even in this silence,
and poison the air with their stench.
There are too many to bury. We must wander away.
We cannot stay here.

Wandering, I thought I would feel no more.
Then I came to a place that filled me with disgust and shame
though at first only confusion and fear.
The skinned carcasses of hundreds of elk
lay swelling in the rain
at the foot of Sutter's Buttes.
Two white men lived there in a canvas tent.
Up they panted when they saw me
and pointed their guns at my chest.
If I escaped, it was only with a prayer,
for it seems they kill everything that goes about on legs,
and upon doing this, cut away and take the skin
and leave the meat to rot for black-winged birds of prey.

1849

General Bidwell has hired us on to work at his gold diggings
on the Feather River. If we work well, we'll be paid
two red handkerchiefs a day.
Otherwise we'll be paid but one.

1851

Several headmen among us Maidu have signed a treaty
with the white government.
We are to stay on the land between Chico and Oroville,
clear up to Nimshew, and we are not to stray.
For this the men will receive a pair of jeans,
a red flannel shirt, and a plow.
Women will get a linsey gown,
a few yards of calico, scissors, and thread.

1852

At first we could not understand how the whites could settle
on the land granted us by the Treaty. They came in droves.
Then we learned the U.S. Senate had secretly rejected all treaties
with Maidu and other Indian tribes, and we were to be removed
to Nome Lackie reservation, several miles away.

1863

They told us, *Because of conflict between Indians and whites
you will be moved for your own safety to Round Valley reservation.
It is in Mendocino county, some three days' march away.*

It has taken two weeks, and of the 461 Indians who began this
miserable trek,
only 277 have come to Round Valley.
Many died as follows: Men were shot who were seen trying to escape.
The sick, or old, or women with children
were speared if they could not keep up,
bayonets being used to conserve ammunition.
Babies were also killed, taken by the feet
and swung against trees to crack their skulls.

1984

There are some things I don't want to think about.
That chapter, for example, on California Indians that read:
California Indians were a naturally shiftless and lazy people.
The Mission padres had no trouble bringing them into the Mission
for these Indians were more submissive than the Plains warriors.
California Indians were easily conquered.
When Mama was brought to the city,
she heard a neighbor remark,
"Why did they ever adopt an Indian? Don't they know
Indians are too dumb to learn anything?"
Mama thought, "I'll show her!" and went off to Juilliard and Columbia.
But later, when she came to marry my dad,
Her future mother-in-law turned to him and said,
"Why, she speaks English as well as we do!"

Mama used to say, "Why can't you kids learn anything?
What's wrong with you? Are you too dumb?
Perhaps you're just lazy and stupid.
Why don't you do as well as your friends?
Why do you give up? Why do you want to fail?
Why don't you make the effort?"
But how could we answer?

Sometimes I wake up in the night clenching my fists, crying.
This morning it was because when I tried to report about Christopher
Columbus, the whole
class turned away, bored,
and began to talk amongst themselves.
"Christopher Columbus," I began, "had two motives
behind his voyage. He was intrigued by the discovery
of hitherto unknown languages,
and by the discovery of skull shapes and sizes
unlike the European."
Here I held up a small, round, discolored skull, then continued,
"Christopher Columbus meant
to sail around the world
till he found a language
with a shape which matched its sounds."
I held up an alphabet in beautiful calligraphy.

I knew the class did not care
and I raged into a frenzy, beating desktops,
throwing chairs aside.
The professor got up to leave the room,
her eyes sad and frightened.
I glared at her.
"You can finish your talk," she said,
"when you pull yourself together."

I stood in a corner of the room
and cried in humiliation and grief.

This poem first appeared in *Beneath My Heart* (Ithaca, NY: Firebrand Books 1990).
© 1990 by Janice Gould.

III: THE MYTHOLOGY OF RACE, THE REALITY OF RACISM

Shame On!

CHRYSTOS

(There are many forms of genocide and this is one)

fake shaman give me some money
I'll make you a catholic priest in a week
couple thousand I'll name you pope
of our crystal breakfast cereal circle of healers

Give me some money   you'll be free
Give me some money   you'll be whole
Give me some money   you'll be right

with past lives zooming by your door
Steal from anybody to make a paste-up tacked-on
holy cat box of nothing
I tell you I'm sincere & that excuses everything
I'm a sincere thief   a sincere rapist   a sincere killer

My heart is pure my head is fuzzy give me some money
& you'll be clear
Your pockets will be anyhow
Give me a dime   I'll erase your crime
Give me a dollar give me a ten give me a thousand
fastest growing business in america

is shame men shame women
You could have a sweat same as you took manhattan
you could initiate people same as into the elks
with a bit of light around your head
& some "Indian" jewelry from hong kong why you're all set
Come on now take something more that doesn't belong to you
Come on & take that's what you know best
White takes   Red turns away
Listen I've got a whole bunch of holey underpants
you could use in a ceremony you can make up yourself
Be a born again Indian it's easy

You want to buy spiritual enlightenment we got plenty
& if you act today we'll throw in four free 100-watt lightbulbs
so you can have your own private halo
What did you say? You met lynn andrews in person?
That woman ought to be in a bitter herb stew
I'll sell you lies half-price better than hers
america is starving to death for spiritual meaning
It's the price you pay for taking everything
It's the price you pay for buying everything
It's the price you pay for loving your stuff more than life
Everything goes on without you
You can't hear the grass breathe
because you're too busy talking
about being an Indian holy woman two hundred years ago
You sure must stink if you didn't let go
The wind doesn't want to talk to you
because you're always right
even when you don't know what you're talking about
We've been polite for five hundred years
& you still don't get it
Take nothing you cannot return
Give to others   give more
Walk quietly   Do what needs to be done
Give thanks for your life
Respect all beings
    simple
      & it doesn't cost a penny

In honor of Muriel Miguel & Spiderwoman Theatre

This piece first appeared in *Dream On* (Vancouver: Press Gang Publishers, 1991).

On Being White and Other Lies

MAB SEGREST

Four years of full-time anti-Klan organizing and I began to get sick. First it hit my stomach, and I was up all night puking. That was the week after Eddie and Tim, Tuscarora Indians, walked into the local newspaper office in Robeson County with sawed-off shotguns and held twenty people hostage for most of the day. While I and a host of others waited outside, they finally released everyone after the governor promised to investigate racist violence, drug trafficking, and law enforcement complicity in both. I got home and got well, then it hit my throat and came and went for another three months. The first time, I was back in Robeson County, after Lumbee Indian leader Julian Pierce was killed the month before he would have beat the white power structure in a fair election for district attorney by consolidating Black, Indian, and poor white votes. Later it hit me in a motel in Shelby, where we were trying to build up local support for a case against neo-Nazis who murdered three young men in an adult bookstore, "to avenge Yahweh on homosexuals."

I slowed down then and started tracking another way; my road map was not the spidery back roads of North Carolina, but history. I knew I needed to understand the genesis of the violence that was sickening me.

A year or so into the process, I found James Baldwin's piece "On Being White and Other Lies" on microfiche in the Duke University library. Baldwin's face watched from the opposite page, light off his features showing as whiteness on the duotone, his intelligent eye emerging from the blackness like a galaxy, Andromeda perhaps. But in his universe it was definitely I who was under observation:

> America became white—the people who, as they claim, "settled" the country became white—because of the necessity of denying the Black presence and justifying the Black subjugation. No community can be based on such a principle—in other words, no community can be established on so genocidal a lie. White men—from Norway, for example, where they were Norwegians—became white by slaughtering the cattle, poisoning the wells, torching the houses, massacring Native Americans, raping Black women. This moral erosion has made it impossible for those who think of themselves as white to have any moral authority .... It is the Black condition, and only that, which informs the consciousness of white people. It is a terrible paradox, but those who believed that they could control and define Black people divested themselves of the power to control and define themselves.[1]

Baldwin's words resonated with my own sense of whiteness. I could see the country was going backwards, and I understood instinctively from my childhood in the Jim Crow South what that meant. This knowledge had brought me to anti-Klan organizing, and it also fed my deepening sense of crisis. But I also came to suspect that these changes, the bloody effects of which I had experienced so intimately working for North Carolinians Against Racist and Religious Violence, might involve more than just the rollbacks of the civil rights movement I had lived through in my adolescence. What was the larger historical framework, and what did it mean?

I was convinced that most white progressives hugely underestimate the power of race in U.S. history as well as the degree to which racial struggles have shaped other political struggles in this country. I suspected that both feminism and the gay and lesbian organizing I had done for over a decade had been as profoundly shaped by race as by gender, but with far less acknowledgement. I had spent many of my years in these movements trying to ensure that my new women's community would not replicate the segregation of my Alabama childhood, but I often felt my head bloody from beating it up against a familiar wall of what felt like willed ignorance, or disoriented from wandering in fogs of personalization and guilt. If "racism equals power plus prejudice," as the antiracist formula states, how do we really go about explaining this "power" to people in ways that help them to understand what a huge force it is we are up against, how inevitably we all have been shaped by it, and how much we need to do beyond "fixing" ourselves?

As I worked on these questions, the globe shifted: the Soviet bloc collapsed, the Sandinistas lost the Nicaraguan election, Nelson Mandela walked out of a South African jail, Bush Sr. went to war against Iraq, and a hard-line coup against Soviet Premier Mikhail Gorbachev brought the end of state-sanctioned communism in the Soviet Union and that union's collapse by the year's end. How did these volatile and massive international shifts relate to my sense of growing crisis at home, as Los Angeles burned in the wake of Rodney King's judicial beating and the economy unraveled to the extent that Bill Clinton could defeat George Bush in the 1992 race for the presidency?

In an attempt to answer, or at least more fully frame, some of these questions, I set out to write a history of racism as it emerged in what is now the United States. The immediate context for the project was my participation in the editorial collective of *The Third Wave: Feminist Essays on Racism,* which publisher Barbara Smith of Kitchen Table/Women of Color Press had approached me and several other women to edit in 1988.[2] Barbara assembled a multiracial group of women: Jacqui Alexander, an African Caribbean woman living in Boston (then later in New York); Sharon Day, an Ojibwe from Minnesota; Norma Alarcon, a Chicana at Berkeley; Lisa Albrecht, a Jew relocated from New York to Minnesota; and me, a white Southerner.

Early in the process, we came up against the question of how anti-Semitism would be incorporated into the anthology. Was anti-Semitism a form of racism within the U.S. context, or not? To answer that question with any integrity, I realized that I needed a clearer sense of what racism is in the United States, how it has evolved. I soon learned that I would have to understand more about capitalism as well.

Putting together the anthology became a major learning experience for me. As we met in each of our home communities to discuss manuscripts and the emerging vision of the book, we also shared our lives and cultures. In the context of our continuing discussions I would hear what to me was new information and say, "You should write that up for the book." The response I often got was, "I already know that. I want to do something that is fresher for me." It occurred to me that I could take on as my part of the project some of these understandings that seemed so basic to particular cultures yet were so foreign to people outside. The bibliography for this essay emerged from those *Third Wave* discussions, as my coeditors recommended books and I read them. I began to synthesize what I was learning into very rough drafts, which I brought back to the collective for comment. Whatever strengths this essay has, they have arisen from this collective process.

I have attempted this overly ambitious project, not with a scholar's time and degree of specialization, but with an organizer's urgency. It is the result of a rich collective process I underwent with women who became my friends. They helped me to struggle with and against a knowledge that was coming to me through the pages of books, their usually remote and objective tone reinforcing the very white emotional denial that created the devastation in the first place.[3] This "book learning" was balanced by the passionate oral histories of communities in struggle that we shared.

My coeditors also urged me to find a way to close the distance between myself as a white person (a lesbian, a woman) and the material. Near the end of my reading, I remembered part of my mother's legacy. Before she died, she passed on to me the genealogical work done by her cousin to establish her father's lineage back to emigration to the British colonies from England in 1613. She thought that someday I or my siblings might want to belong to the United Daughters of the Confederacy, the Daughters of the American Revolution, or the Colonial Dames—all women's organizations whose membership is predicated on proving European pedigree. As my mother explained it, the genealogies were designed to help me "know who I am." I got out those family papers and decided to put them to use, as a way to locate myself within this history and to frame it in more personal and immediate terms.

My goal, then, is to provide an overview of the history of racism in the U.S. that can be read in one (long) sitting: a place for beginning students and activists to understand the extensive and cruel history of institutional racism, as well as for others more veteran to review this history in light of the present emergency; to understand how capitalism has worked with racism to write various of us into it differently according to gender, class, sexual orientation, religion, nationality, geography, and skin color; and, most importantly, to talk about strategies and goals as we work to move into a very different history. The essay has had an additional value for me in getting a historical perspective on my own family's emotional dynamics.

Commerce Capitalism

"So great a supply exhausted in so short a time...."

My great-great-great-great-great-great-great-great grandfather Ambrose Cobbs landed at Yorktown, Virginia on the "Treasure" in 1613 with his brother Joseph. The Cobbses were among the earliest emigrants to America from Devonshire, Lancaster, London, and northern England. Ambrose had been born in 1590, two years after the English navy defeated the Spanish Armada and opened up North America to British conquest. Ambrose arrived six years after the first settlement at Jamestown, only three years after the "starving time," when colonists living in cave-like holes dug up and devoured newly buried corpses, one man killing his wife, salting and eating all parts of her except her head. European settlers in such new worlds probably often found themselves in such desperate situations, acting similarly savage and animal-like, responses that intensified their need to project such characteristics on the peoples they encountered.[4]

Ambrose and Joseph came to what we now call North America as settlers. Joseph's wife and two sons came over to join him in 1624; Ambrose married Anne and settled in York County, Virginia, where they were granted three hundred and fifty acres of land. These Cobbses were part of the worldwide, massive burst of discovery, colonization, and conquest that catapulted Europe out of feudalism and into commerce capitalism, the first stage of capitalist expansion that would amass the huge amounts of resources needed to make the industrialization of Europe and the United States possible. Its cost I can only describe as a maniacal decimation of other peoples and resources across the globe.

Western Europe, of course, did not invent empire building: the conquest of other peoples and appropriation of their resources justified by a sense of the conqueror's superiority.[5] But capitalism and modern technology allowed these behaviors much more global and totalizing effects than they had ever had before in what we know of human history. By 1914, Europe would control 80 percent of the globe: 283 million Europeans would rule nine hundred million non-European peoples.[6] Racism in the United States today cannot be understood outside of this context: that is, the emergence of capitalism in its commercial, industrial, and financial stages, and the global imperial agenda that it required.

In Africa and Asia, Europeans initially conducted their business from fortifications and limited their emphasis to trade, given the geographical, political, and climatic considerations in those vast continents. But the Americas, New Zealand, Australia, and South Africa became settler colonies, to which people like Ambrose Cobbs brought their families, intending to stay and take advantage of economic and political opportunities. Of all these settler colonies, only in the Americas would European colonials import Africans for slave labor, and it is from this fusion of settler colonization and chattel slavery that the particularly vicious character of U.S. racism emerges. "There is not a country in world history," concludes historian Howard Zinn, "in which racism has been more important, for so long, as in the United States."[7]

Ambrose and Joseph landed in Virginia six years before the first shipment of "negars" to the British colonies would debark in Virginia in 1619, recent starvation having sharpened British appetites for a source of added labor. By the Cobbs's arrival, however, European enslavement of Africans was almost two centuries old and had become "a fixture of the New World" in Latin America and the Caribbean. The English got the idea of enslaving Africans from Spain and Portugal. Explorers had brought Africans to Portugal to serve as slaves in the fifteenth century.[8] Slavery did exist in the African states to which Europe turned for slaves, but with nothing like the severity or inhumanity that European slavery derived from a relentless pursuit of profits and from racial hatreds.[9]

The Spanish and Portuguese also led the way in exploration and colonization, establishing the first basic and deadly practice of racism in the Americas: the genocide of native peoples necessary to control the new lands, and the enslavement of Africans for the labor needed to tap their wealth. Spanish *conquistadores* rapidly destroyed the centralized states of the Aztecs and Incas in a short period of time, partly because of the hierarchical nature of those cultures, partly because the Spanish had the advantage of gunpowder, horses, iron, and bacteria that spread European diseases with fatal results among the indigenous population.[10] By the end of the sixteenth century, Spain had a colonial empire twenty times its own size. So vast a territory would require massive amounts of human labor to yield its riches.

The Spanish first tried indigenous labor, but the Indian population was soon decimated by the brutal nature of that labor and by disease. As one Jesuit remarked casually in 1583, "No one could believe that so great a supply [of labor] could ever be exhausted, much less in so short a time."[11] Practically the entire Indian population of the Caribbean was wiped out by the end of the seventeenth century. In 1492, indigenous people in the Americas totaled at least seventy million; by 1650, they had been reduced to 3.5 million.[12]

For anyone trying to understand racism, this terrible history brings us to a crucial question: What could allow for the deaths of 66.5 million people? Or for the deaths of an estimated fifty million Africans in the beginning centuries of the slave trade? [13] The Spanish and Portuguese, like the British after them, seemed driven by a psychosis of domination. It affected kings as well as soldiers, workers as well as priests. When Columbus wrote home about his first encounter with Indians, he described their amiability and their love towards all others in preference to themselves, and his own confusions as to whether they had any private property.[14] When Cortez's forces slaughtered the Aztecs at the fiesta of Toxcatl, it came (according to an Aztec who was present) "at this moment in the fiesta, when the dance was loveliest and when song was linked to song, [when] the Spaniards were seized with an urge to kill the celebrants."[15]

When the exploring party of Cabeza de Vaca lost three of its men in an accident, the survivors were amazed when the Indians who discovered them sat down among them and expressed a loud and earnest grief, feelings that the Spanish had not been able to muster for their own people.[16] It is this failure to feel the communal bonds between humans, I think, and the punishment that undoubtedly came to those Europeans who did, that allowed the "community of the lie" to grow so genocidally in the soil of the "New World." Historian Howard Zinn has pointed to a possible source of this European malady: Tribal life in Europe, with its more communal spirit and kinder rules and punishments, had been destroyed by the slave societies of Greece and Rome.[17] What took its place was an individualism that was only sharpened by the drive for private ownership as Europe emerged from feudalism. The massive denial that results from the destruction of communal bonds is the undergirding of the epistemology or the "way of knowing" of genocide: We do not feel, and thus we cannot "know."

The silver that indigenous people were forced to mine during this period of genocide fueled Europe's economy while it killed the native people and sapped the natural resources of the colonies. By 1650 silver was 99 percent of the mineral export of Spanish America, exceeding by at least three times the total European reserve. It passed to Dutch, French, Genoese, English, and German bankers. This enormous capital in northern Europe fueled the spirit of enterprise and financed manufacturing, which propelled the advent of the Industrial Revolution. The concentration of global wealth in Europe prevented the accumulation of industrial capital in the lands that produced the wealth. Conquest had shattered the foundations of native civilizations, and forced labor in mines or plantations destroyed the collective farming system, further punishing the people and land from which European wealth flowed. These historically created patterns of poverty are the source of what we now call "underdevelopment."[18]

Having exhausted the native supply of labor, the Spanish needed an alternative. However, the kidnapping and importing of Africans to use as slave labor did not become a profitable alternative until European consumption of chocolate and coffee imported from the colonies made the demand for sugar skyrocket. By the end of the 1500s, sugar was the most valuable agricultural product in international trade. The profits from sugar production offset the costs of the slave trade and opened Africa up as a new supply of labor.[19] It seems no accident that two of the cash crops that would make slavery profitable—sugar and tobacco—were highly addictive substances; and the physiological responses to these substances further incorporated racism into the European body, demarcating European and "Other" as consumer and consumed. No wonder that in the late twentieth century, people all across the United States flock to a host of "Twelve Step" programs that offer a solution (whatever their political strengths and limits) to a proliferating sense of addiction.

England did not realize the potential in overseas exploration until the reign of Queen Elizabeth. The English did not get to Africa until 1550, and their encounter there with Africans would reverberate in the American colonies. The English, hailing from a small northern island, had more limited cultural experience than the Spanish or the Portuguese, who had both been conquered by a darker-skinned, more advanced Moslem civilization during the Middle Ages. When these Englishmen met Africans for the first time, one of the most fair-skinned peoples on the globe came into contact with one of the darkest, a difference reinforced by the existing dichotomy between dark and light in British culture. It led the English to see the Africans as both "black" and "heathen" and to link them immediately with barbarity, animalistic behavior, and the devil (not a healthy combination).[20]

The English were coming from a culture in which the Protestant Reformation required of its pious aspirants self-scrutiny and internalized control at an expansive time when medieval moral restraints seemed to be disintegrating. British (and other European) explorers projected their disquieting sexual feelings on the darker, seemingly less inhibited peoples with whom they came in contact. For example, Europeans found both apes and Africans similarly lustful ("sexuality was what one expected of savages"). They concocted stories of cross-species copulation and of apes attacking African women.[21] It was with a shock of recognition that I read of these accounts in Winthrop Jordan's *White over Black*.[22] I had just cowritten *Quarantines and Death: The Far Right's Homophobic Agenda,* which discussed the contemporary neo-Nazi "explanation" for the origins of AIDS as cross-species copulation between Africans and monkeys.[23]

That such racist mythology could find resonance across four centuries (I don't think the Nazis had been reading Jordan or the writings of early explorers) is cause for alarm. I hardly believe in "racial memory," but in the absence of such biological theories we have to account for the ways in which such cultural residues are kept alive and passed on from century to century. I think in the twentieth century the presence of overtly fascist movements is one medium of transmission, which is one reason why such movements are allowed by capitalists, the state, and regular white folks to operate.

This tendency of Christian European men to project sexual desire on an Other, then to exterminate the "polluted," was already in practice in the witch-burnings in Europe in the late Middle Ages and early modern periods. Estimates of the number of women executed range from thirty thousand to nine million[24]—in a time period that coincides with the beginnings of imperial conquest. Excessive female sexuality, as church documents explained, made women susceptible to witchcraft. "From 1480 to 1700, more women were killed for witchcraft than for other crimes put together," explains historian E. William Monter.[25] The emerging nation-state also needed to assert control over its male subjects' bodies at home and overseas. In 1533 Henry VIII's parliament made the act of sodomy a crime, the first in a series of statutes that recodified as felonies crimes that were previously under the jurisdiction of church courts.[26]

Sixteenth-century biblical justifications for slavery based on the story of Noah and Ham also show how the European mind linked sexuality with racism. In fact, the Genesis story has no mention of race or color. After the Flood, Noah's son Ham looked on his father's nakedness while he lay drunk in his tent, the violation of a patriarchal injunction. For this, Noah cursed Canaan, son of Ham, saying he would be a "servant of servants" to his brothers.[27] According to Elizabethan commentators, Ham's posterity was cursed also with becoming "so blacke and lothsome, that it might remain a spectacle of disobedience to all the worlde. And of this blacke and cursed Chus came all these blacke Moores which are in Africa."[28] At a particular historical moment, emerging racism adopted patriarchy for its own ends.

Jews, the primary Other in Europe for much of the Middle Ages, were also receptacles of European Christian men's projections, and also received punishment. The Christian Crusades of the eleventh century intensified religious anti-Semitism in Europe, as did the role that Jews were forced to play in the money economy that emerged in part from the Crusades. Usury, like sexuality, was considered a sin, so Jews were forced as money-lenders into the marginal economy until that cash economy became profitable. Then they were forced out in country after country, until capitalism replaced feudalism in Europe, with Christians in firm control of financial resources and with Jews as a convenient buffer class to obscure the real source of class oppression and to hedge Christians against their own guilt over a burgeoning materialism.

When the British turned to the West in search of profits for the private London Company, the history of European anti-Semitism, racism, and sexual repression shaped the laws and attitudes of their first permanent settlement at Jamestown, the entry point of the Cobbses into the history of North America.

Ambrose Cobbs died in 1656. His son Robert Cobbs had been born in 1620, the year the pilgrims landed at Plymouth Rock. Robert Cobbs lived his sixty-two years in York County, Virginia, eventually holding the authority of justice of the peace and high sheriff. His life spanned the period when the practice of African chattel slavery developed in Virginia, a shift that also brought the emergence of white identity.[28]

The British in America followed Spanish and Portuguese patterns of genocide of indigenous people and enslavement of Africans. Some historians feel, however, that British racism was even harsher than the Spanish variety, partly because the British did not have to reckon with the competing interests of the Catholic Church and partly because British capitalism was more ruthless as Britain gained control of the slave trade.[29] The British policy regarding the racial identity of the offspring of interracial unions was also much more rigid than the Spanish version. British colonies used what Marvin Harris calls the "rule of hypo-descent," which categorized anyone with any African parentage as belonging to the subordinate race. This practice allowed plantation masters to have sexual access to Black women without jeopardizing the inheritance of white children; it also ensured that "whites" would remain relatively "pure," while "Blacks" became increasingly hybrid.[30]

The British employed slavery first on their sugar plantations in the Caribbean. As with Spanish silver, profits from the slave trade fueled European industrial development. The Royal Africa Company had been chartered in the 1670s, and between 1680 and 1688 it paid 300 percent in dividends, although 35 percent of its African (human) cargo did not survive the Middle Passage. Slave traffic made Bristol, its shipping center, Britain's second-largest city and Liverpool the world's largest port. Liverpool slave merchants made more than 1.1 million pounds a year from the Caribbean trade (at a time when an Englishman could live on six pounds a year). Banks grew, and Lloyds made money by insuring each step of the process. These slave profits financed Britain's Great Western Railway and its industries, and subsidized the invention of the steam engine.[31]

The slave trade profited New England as well. In the mid-1700s, northern slave ships left Boston for Africa with rum to trade for slaves, then sailed to the Caribbean and traded slaves for molasses, bringing that back to Massachusetts to distill into rum, with big profits made from each transaction. This slave trade helped develop the northern naval industry and distilleries and created a market for agricultural and manufacturing exports.[32]

This history of European–U.S. economic development provides the context we need to understand programs such as affirmative action, which seem a puny enough redress for centuries of rape of resources and labor and women. According to 1990 U.S. census figures, African Americans still make only half the wages of whites, but have one-tenth the wealth, because many whites are still inheriting the cumulative effect of centuries of appropriation.[33]

Sugar made slavery profitable in the Caribbean. Tobacco was the cash crop on the Atlantic seaboard, and in the tobacco colonies of Virginia and Maryland, African slavery developed in three phases. Between 1619, the year before Robert Cobbs was born, and 1640, the year after his family received a land grant, the British imported Africans gradually, with no set policies. But by 1640 evidence mounts that Africans were being subjected to the twin characteristics of slavery: lifetime servitude and inherited slave status. Both of these were very different from the indentured servitude of Europeans and the "tendency toward liberty" of English common law. Along with this emerging practice came the debasement of Africans through discriminatory laws and practices, such as the barring of interracial sexual unions and not allowing Africans to purchase arms.[34] British jurisprudence—the American version of which various Cobbses would help to implant—codified an emerging American racism. Little wonder that when I sat in North Carolina courts monitoring trials of racist attackers, I despaired of justice from a legal system that itself helped to invent the racist distinctions between "slave" and "free."

The Cobbses probably used their three hundred and fifty acres to grow tobacco, the main cash crop of Virginia. That acreage hardly made them part of the planter aristocracy; but it was probably a large enough tract to "require" a small number of slaves. The Cobbses were probably also affected in the 1660s when the price of tobacco dropped in Virginia, and with this economic pressure "unmitigated capitalism" (in Stanley Elkins' terms) became "unmitigated slavery," as colonists realized the extra dividend of inherited slave labor.[35] As justice of the peace, Robert Cobbs doubtless reacted fearfully and forcefully to Bacon's Rebellion in 1676, an uprising of African slaves and white indentured and unemployed workers against the planter aristocracy.

To forestall such revolutionary alliances across race lines, colonial rulers had already begun extending to all European settlers the rights initially given to Englishmen. By 1671, the British began encouraging the naturalization of Scots, Welsh, and Irish to enjoy "all such liberties, priviledges, immunities whatsoever, as a naturall borne Englishman." In the same decade, the Virginia assembly passed a law that "the conferring of baptism doth not alter the condition of the person as to his bondage or freedome":[36] that Africans could be converted to Christianity but still remain slaves. (I wonder whether Robert Cobbs in his role as first vestryman of Bruton Parish Church in Williamsburg agonized at all over the contradiction between "saved" soul and enslaved soul.) Historian Winthrop Jordan comments, "From the initially most common term *Christian,* at mid-century there was a marked drift toward *English* and *free.* After about 1680, taking the colonies as a whole, a new term appeared—*white*"[37] [emphasis added].

Robert Cobbs's life spanned the period in U.S. history when white people were "invented" to give Europeans a common identity against Africans. His son Robert Cobbs, Jr. was born in 1660 and lived until 1725, serving as constable and vestryman. It was during Robert Jr.'s lifetime that slavery was finally consolidated into a police state in the mid-Atlantic colonies. By 1705 Virginia consolidated a generation of random statues into a "slave code." With police power and the legal equation between Africans and slavery in place, African slaves were brought to the colonies in unprecedented numbers in a period that Jordan calls the "unthinking acquiescence" to slavery and its presuppositions.[38]

This creation of white identity in late seventeenth-century Virginia is what James Baldwin recognized. The implications are profound: If we white folks were constructed by history, we can, over time and as a people, uncon-struct ourselves. The Klan knows this possibility and recognizes those whites who disavow this history as white niggers, race traitors, and nigger lovers. How then, to move masses of white people to become traitors to the concept of race?[39]

Industrial Capitalism

"Slavery is nothing compared to it...."

My great-great-great-great-grandfather James Cobbs, born in 1735, was a captain of the militia in the American Revolution—he is my claim to membership in the D.A.R. After the war, he was granted large tracts of land in Kentucky and South Carolina, which he willed to his sons at his death on or before 1800.

During James Cobbs's lifetime, Europe entered a new phase of capitalism, its industrial phase, made possible by technology that adopted new energy sources and machines for manufacturing and by the development of the factory system. Profit-making from manufacturing was at the heart of industrial capitalism, as money became concentrated in the hands of the middle class. Both the American Revolution and the Civil War would be fought over who would reap the profits of industrialism on the vast continent. In the British colonies, commerce capitalism had demarcated whiteness against and above both Africans and Indians; in the new nation, industrial capitalism would add Mexicans and Asians to a racially demarcated underclass.

As the market revolution expanded, African, Indian, Mexican, and Asian peoples were written into sectors of the economy differently. African Americans were tied to the Southern agrarian/slave economy, Mexicans to the "free" and soon-to-be freed territory of the Southwest appropriated after an official war, and Asians to the "free" agricultural and industrial labor system of California and Hawaii. Indians resisted incorporation into any labor system and thus were the objects of open warfare, land appropriation, and the reservation system.

The American Revolution was fought on the cusp of the Industrial Revolution in America. It was precipitated by England's victory over France in a struggle for control of increasingly profitable colonies in North America, the West Indies, and India. After four global wars fought in the first half of the 1700s, England emerged in 1763 as the leading colonial power in the world, a position the British would hold until the mid-twentieth century, when the United States assumed hegemony.

England's victory over France, however, led to the loss of her richest claim, the thirteen colonies in North America, because England began to tighten the bonds of empire that previously had been laxly enforced in America, in order to pass on the costs of the war. British taxation, passed through such acts as the Stamp Act and the Tea Act, led to the colonists' cry of "no taxation without representation" and to the Continental Congresses and the Declaration of Independence.

The "self-evident truths" that Jefferson used to explain the colonists' revolt were not merely the more cold-blooded "right" to profit, but the "inalienable rights" of "life, liberty and the pursuit of happiness"—hardly consistent with the practices of genocide or chattel slavery that had helped create the profits the colonists were so loathe to have taxed. In fact, the new Constitution, passed in 1787, wrote racial inequity into the nation's founding document in the "three-fifths compromise," in which slaves were counted as three-fifths human for the purpose of determining the population base for propertied white male representation. Abolition of the slave trade ("the Migration or Importation of such Persons as any of the States now existing shall think proper to admit") was forbidden for twenty years.[40]

If the white framers of the Constitution did not apply natural rights to Blacks and Indians, the people of Haiti did, as Haiti became the next country in the Americas to follow the revolutionary example, overthrowing French domination in a bloody revolt. The aftershocks of Haiti's uprising persuaded Napoleon to sell off the Louisiana Territory to the United States in 1803, ironically opening up more territory for slavery and for relocation of Indians. The Haitian Revolution also terrified the white authors of American liberty, inspired North American slaves, and sent tremors through Southern households, including, perhaps, the Cobbs's.

One of the first concerns of the new nation was economic independence from Britain. The large-scale agriculture of the plantation system in the South was the Southern face of the Industrial Revolution. Textile manufacturing in the North using the new technology ushered in the beginning of the factory system in the United States, which was based in New England but that used Southern cotton. Thus when the Industrial Revolution reached American shores, it set up interdependent but competing economic systems, one dependent on "free" white labor, the other on the slave labor of Africans.

James Cobbs's son Thomas Cobb (born in 1764, the year after the Treaty of Paris, and part of the first generation to drop the "s" from "Cobbs") sold off part of the land he inherited from James and moved to Georgia. He was a lawyer and became a judge. He died in 1816, willing his farm to his son. Perhaps he moved south in the years after the revolution because of depleted soil and a glutted tobacco market, which brought a severe depression in the tobacco colonies. The price of slaves declined, and there was reason to believe that slavery as a practice might pass.

But here the momentum of racism overrode short-term economic motives, and the planters sustained their losses. The invention of the cotton gin in 1792 broke the bottleneck in textile production and ushered in "a period of economic change...that, in degree, compared favorably with any changes in the history of agriculture."[41] Cotton became the new cash crop on which slavery could thrive. The United States produced six thousand bales of cotton in 1792; by 1810 it was producing 178 thousand bales, and by 1860, more than five million.[42]

About the time Thomas Cobb left Virginia and headed with his family to Georgia, the economic center of the slave colonies shifted from the mid-Atlantic to the "Cotton Kingdom" of the deep South, where soil had not been depleted by tobacco production. The new states of Louisiana (1812), Mississippi (1817), and Alabama (1819) were swelled by slaves and by immigrants like Thomas Cobb. The population of the Cotton Kingdom rose from forty thousand in 1810 to one million thirty years later.[43] The abolition movement won the end of the international slave trade in 1808, but a white supremacist economy adjusted, as the Atlantic states substituted breeding slaves as the "cash crop" to replace tobacco—what historian John Hope Franklin calls "one of the most fantastic manipulations of human development in the history of mankind."[44]

In 1790 there were fewer than seven hundred thousand slaves in the United States. By 1830 there were two million. By 1860 there were almost four million slaves.[45] At the turn of the eighteenth century Boston Judge Samuel Sewall had declared, "[Africans can] never embody with us and grow up into orderly Families, to the Peopling of the land."[46] Clearly, the American "family" was being ideologically constructed as white. The bonds of biological and emotional families outside of whiteness had no protection, an inhumanity that, I suspect, has considerably eroded emotional bonds within white families as well.

Southern and westward expansion created the need for a new Indian policy. From the first colonial settlements in the early 1600s, North American Indians (in less hierarchical, more egalitarian tribal arrangements than those of the Aztecs or Incas)[47] had resisted assimilation into the labor system. At first, settlers in clearly vulnerable positions on the edge of the continent were friendly to the Indians who helped them survive. Then, when the English settlements became permanent and stockpiled arms, their attitudes had shifted. The Massachusetts colonists had massacred the Pequots only sixteen years after the first settlements in New England, at about the same time slavery was consolidating in Virginia. As one colonist described the attack: "[Many Indians] were burnt in the fort, both men, women, and children; others [who were] forced out...our soldiers received and entertained with the point of the sword. Down fell men, women, and children."[48] The Pequots were the first New England tribe to feel the genocidal impact of the English and the implications of their style of battle, intended, in the words of one officer, to "conquer and subdue."[49] By the French and Indian War (1754–63), every colony but Georgia and Pennsylvania had engaged in a bloody war with the tribes in its region, as native resistance to the colonial presence intensified.

After the revolution, the "white lie" of the new nation showed in an Indian policy that developed in the highest councils of state into a cold-blooded rationale for "extinction." In 1783, Congress forbade white settlement on Indian lands, the first of many such statements to be ignored by settlers and land speculators. In 1786, Secretary of State Henry Knox shifted Indian policy from "right of conquest" to "right of purchase" unless in a "just war"[50]—a shift that led mainly to manipulative purchases and an increase in legalistic explanations for war.

President Thomas Jefferson, "author of American liberty," began a two-faced Indian policy of urging assimilation but planning for Indian removal. He viewed the hunting, nomadic life of most tribes as lazy because it did not fit into the mostly agrarian U.S. economy. He urged "his children" to give up hunting and learn to farm—to "persuade our red brethren then to be sober, and to cultivate their lands; and their women to spin and weave for their families."[51] On the other hand, he waged a secret campaign for Indian land, regarding the territories newly acquired by the Louisiana Purchase as a good place to relocate Indian tribes.

One deliberate intent of encouraging Indians to abandon hunting was to turn them into debt-ridden consumers at government trading posts: "To promote this disposition to exchange lands, which they have to spare and we want, for necessaries, which we have to spare and they want, we shall push our trading uses, and be glad to see the good and influential individuals among them run in debt," Jefferson wrote to Governor William Henry Harrison, who was legally responsible for keeping white settlers away from Indians in his territory. If any tribe were to fight back, they would "[seize] the whole country of that tribe and [drive] them across the Mississippi."[52]

By the 1820s, the western territories opened by the War of 1812 were viewed by settlers as good places to relocate native peoples, since the West with its treeless plains was considered unsuitable for white people.[53] Between 1816 and 1848, twelve new states joined the union, carved out of Indian country. John Adams wrote to a friend in 1818, "Shall we say that a few handfuls of scattering tribes of savages have a right of dominion and property over a quarter of this globe capable of nourishing hundreds of millions of happy human beings?"[54] According to President John Quincy Adams' memoirs, Secretary of State Henry Clay explained in a 1825 cabinet meeting how it was "impossible to civilize Indians," so they were "destined to extinction" and although he would never use or countenance inhumanity towards them, he did not think them, as a race, worth preserving. He considered them as essentially inferior to the Anglo-Saxon race, which was now taking its place on this continent. They were an improbable breed, and their disappearance from the human family would be no great loss to the world.[55]

In 1828, Georgians such as Thomas Cobb's son William, itching for land of the "Five Civilized Tribes," passed laws extending the state's control over Indian lands, in clear violation of the Constitution. When the Cherokees refused to emigrate after the Indian Relocation Act of 1830, Supreme Court Chief Justice John Marshall upheld their position but President Jackson refused to enforce it, forcing relocation instead, explaining that contact with whites would "degrade and destroy Indians." In 1812, Jackson had led forces that killed eight hundred and fifty Creeks at the Battle of Horseshoe Bend, "those deluded victims doomed to destruction by their own restless and savage conduct."[56] On the Cherokees' "Trail of Tears," a forced march to Oklahoma begun in 1836, one-quarter to one-third of the sixteen thousand Cherokees died. President Jackson's blatantly unconstitutional action was a disregard for the facade of "justice" that Jefferson could not have mustered.

Several thousand Seminoles in Florida, many of them escapees from Georgia and South Carolina, refused to relocate. They were joined by several hundred African Americans, escaped slaves or the descendants of slaves, who could slip on and off plantations, bringing information gathered by slaves. Under the leadership of Chief Osceola, they waged a guerilla campaign (the Seminole War) against the U.S. troops Jackson sent with instructions to find their villages and to capture or destroy the village women.[57] "If strong measures are not taken to restrain our slaves, there is but little doubt that we should soon be assailed with a servile as well as Indian war," reported Major Benjamin Putnam to the Secretary of War.[58] [William Cobb of Columbia County, Georgia served under Jackson against the Seminoles and escaped slaves.]

The Seminole War was only one of many acts of resistance by people of color to the racist practices of Europeans. From the beginning of the slave trade, as Vincent Harding chronicles, Africans had seized control of slave ships or jumped overboard, preferring drowning to slavery; once in the Americas, many Africans ran off to join bands of Maroons in the Caribbean or the Seminoles in Florida, or to initiate slave rebellions on plantations. In 1831, several years before the Seminole War, Nat Turner led a slave uprising in Virginia that killed sixty whites in twenty-four hours, explaining to his followers that theirs was not a war "for robbery, nor to satisfy our passions;...[but a] struggle for freedom."[59] From the beginning, Indian tribes had engaged in prolonged warfare against white encroachment.

While William Cobb was soldiering for Jackson, the movement to abolish slavery became the first strong interracial antiracist movement in the United States. The egalitarian strain in Christianity, combined with a rise in humanitarianism, produced the white abolition movement, which for the first time among whites challenged slavery in an organized way. Of the fifteen known white condemnations of slavery before 1750, all were by Quakers, who themselves had undergone years of persecution for doctrinal heresy.[60] White abolitionism coincided with a growing number of free Blacks in northern states. The doctrine of natural rights that justified the American Revolution, if it did not in fact protect African Americans or Indians, did give ideological impetus to both white and Black abolitionists. In 1794, delegates from nine antislavery societies met in Philadelphia. Northern states abolished slavery in the two decades after the revolution, and many southern states allowed manumission, or voluntary freeing of slaves. By 1808, the first year after the constitutional protection of the slave trade expired, abolition sentiment and fear of Black uprisings was enough to induce the abolishment of the international slave trade—the high-water mark of early abolitionist struggle.

The 1830s brought a new upsurge in abolitionist organizing, as sharpening economic differences between the slave states of the Cotton Kingdom and the wage labor of the Northeast caused increasing sectional conflict. White abolitionists led by William Lloyd Garrison took on a more militant stance, abandoning gradualism to argue for immediate abolition. In 1831 the New England Anti-Slavery Society and in 1833 the American Anti-Slavery Society were founded.

It was from this interracial abolition movement that the first feminist or "woman rights" organizing emerged. Black women such as Maria Steward, Harriet Tubman, Sojourner Truth, and Sarah Redmond and the white Grimke sisters (who had been run out of South Carolina for their opposition to slavery) joined the question of racial slavery with that of women's rights. They had the cooperation of male supporters of women's rights such as Frederick Douglass. This radical analysis emerged as a contradiction to the moment when growing industrialism encouraged the "cult of true womanhood," confining pious, domestic, submissive, and pure—therefore middle-class— "true" women to the home at a time when more and more poor women were entering the factory work force.[61] Disagreements over the role of women in the abolition movement eventually helped to split the American Anti-Slavery Society. White racism also split the abolition movement.

Martin Delany observed that African Americans within the abolition movement occupied a similar "underling position" to whites as in the general culture, fueling racist practices that contributed to increasing autonomy in

Black organizing. By 1830, there were 319 thousand free Blacks in the United States, many of whom were subject to the Northern racism of white mob violence and denial of education and jobs and land that would become the model for Jim Crow. A radical Black analysis began to emerge from such people as David Walker and Martin Delany, who began to target not just slavery but the federal government for its anti-Black policies, combining an analysis of racism for the first time with an analysis of economic exploitation. Delany began to advocate for more separatist and nationalist Black strategy, while Frederick Douglass continued to argue for integration into the U.S. political system.[62] Historian Vincent Harding points to a similar emergence of Black nationalist strategies from a disillusionment with interracial activism in the 1960s.

Indian-fighter William Cobb's life spanned the advent of the market economy in the United States. In the early years of the nineteenth century the "market revolution" marked the takeoff of the U.S. economy in a period of entrepreneurial ferment. In 1800, the cost of transporting a ton of goods thirty miles overland was as much as shipping it three thousand miles to Europe. Advances in transportation and increasing urbanization (the U.S. urban population increased from 5 percent to 20 percent from 1800 to 1860) broke down barriers and created the space in which a sectored market emerged as a central force in U.S. society, with the East providing manufactured goods and commerce, the West foodstuffs, and the South cotton both for eastern textile mills and for Europe. Because cotton was the commodity that sold on an international market and thus brought in extra capital, the entire economy depended for its growth on the cotton trade, which depended on stolen Indian land and unpaid African labor.[63]

The Jackson administration (1828–1836) had been a period of increased democratization for white U.S. citizens as frontiersmen challenged the patrician rule of the previous forty years. Constitutional changes in a number of states widened suffrage, in some cases giving the vote to all adult white males. These votes brought Jackson to the White House. In the late 1600s, white rights had expanded at a period of intense contraction of rights for Africans (the consolidation of chattel slavery). In the 1820s, expanding white political freedom across class lines came at the same historical moment as Indian removal, Sam Houston's appropriation of Mexican land, and a viewing of African Americans as "anti-citizens."[64] White democracy, it seems, gets built on the backs of people of color, a fact that gives white people a very different subjective experience of U.S. democracy than many people of color have. Congressman Alexander Duncan observed without conscious irony in 1845: "There seems to be something in our laws and institutions peculiarly adapted to the Anglo-Saxon American race, under which they will thrive and prosper but under which all others wilt and die…. There is something mysterious about it."[65]

The market revolution reshaped U.S. citizens not only as consumers, but also as workers subject to the labor discipline required by industrial capitalism. A white working class emerged, defining itself in republican terms as "free laborers" in contradistinction to the despised and forced labor roles of African slaves. Labor historians George Rawick and David Roediger have suggested that Blacks came to symbolize their preindustrial way of life for whites: "Increasingly adopting an ethos that attacked holidays, spurned contact with nature, saved time, bridled sexuality, separated work from the rest of life and postponed gratification, profit-minded Englishmen and Americans cast Blacks as their former selves."[66]

William Cobb's son James was born in 1835, the year before his father went off to fight in the Seminole Wars. James would himself fight in the Civil War to defend the agrarian slave economy against the wage labor system of the North as the culmination of the competition over which form of economy would prevail in the expanding U.S. territories. If Robert was the first "white" Cobbs, James was the first "Southern" one, since defense of the increasingly profitable slave system rose to fever pitch and consolidated the identity of the slave states as "Southern" in the three decades before the Civil War broke out. James joined the Fifth Texas Regiment of the Confederate cavalry. Like Thomas Cobb's migration to Georgia, his grandson James' migration to Texas in 1857, where he went to practice law, was made possible by appropriation of land—this time, the land of Mexico. After the Louisiana Purchase, the next major block of territory to the west belonged to Spain. Jefferson had commented in 1809, "[The Spanish borderlands] are ours the first moment war is forced upon us."[67] It was the kind of "just war" that the U.S. government had become expert in rationalizing against Indians.

"New Spain" reached from what is now Utah to Central America in 1810 when the native or *mestizo* (mixed race) inhabitants of Mexico began their revolution against Spanish colonial control. The country of Mexico that they won in 1821 was already sapped of many of its resources because of three hundred years of colonial rule. Mexico was bankrupt and needed time to build a unifying infrastructure. The United States, on the other hand, was an expanding white settler state, its Southern economy underwritten by slave labor and its profits firmly in the hands of its industrial class. The U.S. population encompassed seventeen million people of European descent, three million slaves, and fewer than a million Indians; Mexico's population was four million Indians and three million mestizos and Europeans.[68] Anglo-Americans began to covet Mexican territory more aggressively after Mexican independence. Sam Houston and Stephen Austin's men took more than a million square miles and established the Republic of Texas by defeating the army of Santa Anna in 1836. Then in 1845, the United States annexed Texas and provoked a war with Mexico by claiming territory extending to the Rio Grande. U.S. victory resulted in Mexico's ceding what is now California, New Mexico, Nevada, parts of Colorado, Arizona, and Utah for only $15 million. The statement of rights for former Mexican citizens that Mexican negotiators fought to include in the Treaty of Guadalupe Hidalgo was uniformly violated, and Mexican Americans quickly became an underclass in the rapidly expanding Anglo-American political and economic system.[69]

With California part of U. S. territory, the country had reached the Pacific Ocean; the invention of steam transportation, both trains and boats, opened up Asia as a source of markets and labor. European imperialism in Asia was likewise creating conditions that propelled its work force towards the United States. Most of the Chinese immigrants came from Guangdong, driven to the United States by peasant rebellions and the British Opium Wars of 1839–42 and 1856–60. Many Chinese immigrated to avoid starvation.[70]

Asians were the only non-European peoples during the nineteenth century who immigrated to the United States for economic opportunity. (Mexicans were incorporated by land appropriation, as were Indians. Africans were imported for slave labor.) They were treated very differently from European immigrants, however. Immigration policy, repression, and racist violence were used to keep Asians as a "reserve labor force." As with Africans in the Caribbean, the pattern of Asian labor was established on island sugar-cane plantations in Hawaii. William Hooper, a Boston visitor to a sugar mill on the island of Kauai in 1835, noticed a small group of Chinese workers and wrote home to the New England businessmen who had sent him there: "They have to work all the time—and no regard is paid to their complaints for food, etc., etc. Slavery is nothing compared to it."[71]

At about the same time the Royal Hawaiian Agricultural Society was importing Chinese to Hawaii, Chinese also began immigrating to the West Coast of the United States. The year after the Treaty of Guadelupe Hidalgo ceded California to the United States, gold was discovered there, bringing a wave of new settlers to the great "Gold Rush of '49." There were 325 Chinese among the prospectors in 1849. Three years later, twenty thousand Chinese had immigrated, and by 1870 there were sixty-three thousand Chinese in the United States, 77 percent in California, where they constituted one-quarter of the entire work force. In the first year or two, they were welcomed, but the nativism of white miners rapidly contracted the space in which they were allowed to operate.[72]

James Cobb lost his law library in a fire in 1860. Penniless, he taught school in Liberty, Texas, until Texas seceded from the union. James joined Company F of the Fifth Texas Regiment as a private, and he was soon promoted to second, then first, lieutenant. He was captured at the battle of Gettysburg and spent the rest of the war in a series of Northern prisons. Soon after the war, he settled in Alabama. According to family records, there he "made a name and fame as a jurist and statesman of which Alabama may well be proud…succeeding in every thing that he undertook and with energy and foresight made his impress in politics, in the church, and in his daily intercourse with his fellow man." Other records show that he was one of many white men instrumental in reasserting white supremacy, both regionally and nationally, in the decades following the South's defeat in the Civil War.

Finance Capitalism

"Nothing we could do but take them all…."

James Cobb returned to Alabama part of an army whose defeat had settled the issue over whether slave or wage labor would prevail and opened up all the mainland territory to the expanding industrial economy. In Europe and the United States the years between 1870 and 1914 brought a new surge of industrial and technological progress. The invention of electricity, wireless telegraphy, refrigeration, the dynamo, and the gas engine helped create the "New Industrial Revolution." It was fueled by industrial research that systematized inventions, mass production techniques, and the assembly line, and breakthroughs in chemistry that created new synthetic materials, such as early plastics. Business consolidated into huge new structures, such as trusts and cartels, to control markets and sources of raw material necessary for the new products. Increasingly, the chief source of profits would come from the process of finance itself. The northern United States, Germany, and Japan emerged to rival Britain as industrial powers.

Within the United States, burgeoning industry brought suddenly skewed distribution of wealth.[73] In 1889, total manufacturing capital in the United States was $5,697 trillion; in 1900 it was $8,663 trillion. In 1890, the wealthiest 1 percent of families owned 51 percent of real and personal property, while 44 percent of families at the bottom owned only 1.2 percent. The 88 percent of families in the poor and middle classes owned only 14 percent of the wealth. These inequities, periodic depressions, and the expanding power of business brought intense labor agitation in the late nineteenth century, as new waves of immigrants from Eastern Europe entered the industrial work force. These Eastern European workers were often viewed as different "races" from Northern Europeans;[74] however, much as in the 1600s, when other Northern Europeans were given the privileges of Englishmen, after Reconstruction the category of "whiteness" was expanded to take in all Europeans (even Jews). Eastern Europeans battled their way into the white working class, while non-Europeans were often excluded from the unions and the economic progress that resulted from labor struggles.[75] Like the "cult of true womanhood" that worked to draw the line around who was a "real woman," race ideology created a highly elastic "cult of true whiteness"; both of these seemingly biological categories drawing their power in part from their volatility and their power to exclude.

This expanding economy, whose benefits within the United States flowed differentially according to race, led the United States for the first time to carry out imperial conquests beyond the limits of North America and eventually to overtake Britain as the world's foremost imperialist power. The imperialism that accompanied finance capitalism linked people of color in the United States even more closely to their continents and nations of origin. As in industrial capitalism, in finance capitalism the roles of various nationalities and communities of color within the United States depended in part on the respective group's role in a sectored economy.

When James Cobb returned from Yankee prison camps, emancipated slaves in the South were experiencing a brief period of increased freedom and economic promise during Reconstruction. The Thirteenth, Fourteenth, and Fifteenth Amendments helped to rectify the injustice built into the original Constitution, not only for African Americans but for other people of color as well. But after four decades of intense sectional conflict, Northern and Southern whites closed ranks, to the detriment of all people of color both in the United States and globally.

In 1874, James Cobb was elected judge in Macon County on the Democratic ticket, and he did his part to restore white rule to his county, sentencing two Black legislators to the chain gang for larceny and adultery and persuading a white Republican to leave town by indicting him for perjury. Judge Cobb opposed the white businessmen in Tuskegee who supported Booker T. Washington's plans to build a school for African Americans. Cobb was elected to Congress in 1884.[76]

James Cobb's training as a lawyer and his role as a judge were in keeping with those of his Cobb forebears, who were consistently part of the judiciary and police in the emerging racist disciplinary structures. He was not, nor were they, part of the capitalist class who owned the plantations or, after the war, profited hugely from the development of an industrial economy. During his lifetime, New South industrialists would link up for the first time with

Northern capitalists. Sharecropping and debt peonage replaced slavery for Black workers, who were shut out of most union organizing during this period as white workers joined the mill villages in the textile industry of the newly industrializing South.

As the South shifted back towards white control, marking James Cobb's passage from defeated soldier to Democratic judge, Northern opinion also began to shift. Former abolitionists, like "neoconservatives" a century later, moved to the right, speaking for the prosperous, educated classes. In publications such as *The Nation* and *Atlantic Monthly,* these men "mouth[ed] the shibboleths of white supremacy regarding the Negro's innate inferiority, shiftlessness, and hopeless unfitness for full participation in the white man's civilization."[77] A succession of Supreme Court decisions between 1873 and 1898 closed the political space opened by the post-Civil War amendments, leading to "separate but equal" segregation in *Plessy v. Ferguson* in 1898.[78]

As racist propaganda and state-instituted repression surged, racist violence escalated, fueled by a racist mythology. Philip Bruce explained in *The Plantation Negro as a Freeman* (1889) that Black males, cut off from the civilizing influence of whites, had regressed to African type and were raping white women.[79] Whites rioted and murdered all over the South, lynching 2,060 Blacks between 1882 and 1930, some of the victims children and pregnant women. It was not so much the African who had regressed: some of the Black victims were castrated, burned at the stake, decapitated, or blinded with hot pokers.[80]

In the 1880s and 1890s, a severe economic depression fueled an insurgent interracial populism that offered a radical challenge to the Southern elite. Tom Watson, foremost leader of Southern populism, declared the Populist Party would settle the race question "by presenting a platform immensely beneficial to both races and injurious to neither." Watson explained that race hatred rested on "the keystone arch of financial despotism which enslaves you both…[and] a money system which beggars you both." In Georgia in 1892, two thousand armed white farmers came to the defense of a Black populist threatened with lynching, and in 1896 Georgia populists denounced the lynch law. Blacks were admitted to the inner circles of the party, serving with whites as party delegates and officials and speaking from the same platform to interracial audiences.[81]

This class alliance alarmed Southern conservatives, who had made their alliances with Northeastern financial interests, and they mounted a campaign of repression, using fraud, terror, and race-baiting. Conservatives stole Black votes, and Populist Party candidates were defeated by these forged ballots. The resulting frustration and bitterness dissolved the Black-white coalition, leading the way for intensified racial repression and violence. Tom Watson turned racist and campaigned in 1906 on what Woodward calls a platform of "Negrophobia and progressivism."[82]

In the 1890s, James Cobb seems to have stolen at least one, if not two, elections from Populist candidates. Voter fraud was so obvious in 1894 that Congress threw out his election and seated his Populist opponent. By the turn of the century, the South was in the throes of a resurgent white supremacy. All over the South, legislatures enacted segregation laws and disenfranchised Black as well as poor white voters, inaugurating the rule of "Jim Crow." One of James Cobb's last official acts in 1901, before he went to New Mexico for his final years at the age of sixty-six, was to participate in the Alabama Constitutional Convention that brought segregation and disenfranchisement to Alabama.

African Americans, numbering about eight million, were the largest nonwhite population in the United States at the turn of the century. But the rising racism fueled by expanding capitalism devastated other communities of color as well. The Chinese had migrated to the West Coast in large numbers in the 1840s, 1850s, and 1860s. Capitalists in California looked to the Chinese to do the hard labor that white workers refused to do, in building the western section of the transcontinental railroads, providing service work in mining camps, performing back-breaking agricultural production, and carrying out manufacturing in western cities. "The introduction of machinery was rendering Black labor obsolete, it was claimed, for what was required in an industrial mode of production was a 'much higher standard of intelligence.'" Chinese became both servants and factory proletariat.[83]

In 1882, organized labor turned against "coolie" workers, and Congress passed the Chinese Exclusion Act, barring the entry of Chinese laborers into the country and denying them the vote and citizenship. Chinese were also the targets of white mobs, with eighteen Chinese lynched in Los Angeles in a single incident in 1871, and twenty-eight Chinese murdered in Rock Springs, Wyoming, in 1885.[84] Like the African presence during slavery, the Chinese presence on the West Coast helped to consolidate the white working class. Many white workers got a start towards economic self-sufficiency, as one railroad builder explained, "by controlling Chinese labor on our railroad."[85] The Chinese functioned as a kind of internal colony of "nonwhites allowed to enter as 'cheap' migratory laborers and members of a racially subordinated group, not future citizens of American society."[86]

Indians, who were not willing to be assimilated into the U.S. work force, fought a new set of wars for western territory. The federal government's genocidal policy towards Indians, established in the early years of the century, played itself out. After the Civil War western expansion into "treeless" territory, once thought unfit for white habitation, led to demands for a new wave of military conquest of Indian tribes. There were bloody battles in the 1870s and 1880s, with surviving members of tribes put in reservations, land that government policy then set out to steal. The Dawes Severalty Act of 1887 intended to break up communally owned reservation land and allow for purchase of "surplus" by white settlers, leading to a decline in reservation land from 138 million acres in 1887 to seventy-eight million in 1900. In 1890 at Wounded Knee, the U.S. Army attacked warriors of the Ghost Dance, the last burst of Indian resistance in the nineteenth century, killing 146 men, women and children. By 1910, the policies of Jefferson and Jackson had borne their deadly fruit: there were only 222 thousand Indians in the United States, a population reduced by two-thirds in only a hundred years.[87]

In the Southwest, the years of rapid industrialization after the Civil War brought the appropriation of Mexican American land and the forcing of Mexicans into a dual-wage labor system in mining and agriculture. New Mexico and Arizona remained territories until the twentieth century because their populations were not white majorities. In New Mexico, where land was the major resource, the Anglo-American colonizers destroyed communal land holdings through the use of private land grants. Anglos also took control of the open range, where cattle raisers established monopolies on grazing and pushed out Mexican subsistence farmers, who began to accumulate in urban *barrios,* or neighborhoods.[88]

The completion of the railroad opened the Southwest to an intensified exploitation of its mineral and agricultural resources, in which Mexican American workers became the lowest level of labor in the mines, on the railroads, and on communal farms. Often Anglo workers insisted on twice the wages of Mexican workers.[89] Throughout the Southwest, Mexican Americans fought back against white violence, and armed rebellion was common. When even the most radical unions excluded Mexican American workers, they organized in *mutualistas* (unions). In the Clifton-Morenci strike of 1903, upwards of fifteen hundred miners—80 percent to 90 percent Mexican or Mexican American—armed themselves and occupied the mines. Strikes in 1906, 1915, and 1917 convinced mine owners that Mexicans were hardly "docile" laborers, and farmers began to import Filipino workers to replace them.[90]

The treatment of the four major non-European populations by whites in the United States over the course of the nineteenth century shows the way in which an expanding white supremacy scripted people of color into specific economic and psychological roles. "Next to the case of the black race within our bosom, that of the red on our borders is the problem baffling to the policy of the country," former President James Madison explained in 1826.[91] Slavery in the nation's "bosom" made anti-Black racism inescapably intimate and domestic; the relative independence of indigenous people on the "frontiers" caused open warfare that led to the decimation of Indian peoples and the reservation policy. These racist practices and ideas were then extended to other non-European people. Sam Houston explained glibly when he took over Texas that the United States had always cheated Indians, and Mexicans were no better than Indians.[92]

Planters in Hawaii expected to find "coolie" labor "far more certain, systematic, and economic than that of the native," as one explained.[93] There, planters systematically diversified immigrant populations, paying Portuguese, Japanese, Chinese, and Koreans different wages for the same work to prevent class solidarity. "By employing different nationalities, there is less danger of collusion among laborers and the employers [are able to] secure better discipline," a planter explained.[94] On the U.S. mainland, the Chinese were identified with the already developed stereotypes used on African Americans and were called "nagurs."[95] The Chinese were also viewed as quieter and more intelligent and generally more fitting for an industrial labor force. By playing off national and racial groups, capitalism created not one but a series of racisms that buttressed each other and a series of working classes that allowed people of color to be played off against one another. It was a potent strategy.

It was not just white men who shifted sharply to the right in the last half of the nineteenth century. White women leaders of the woman rights movement accompanied them, breaking with the interracial, antiracist origins of U.S. women's organizing in the abolition movement. The split came with the debate on the Fifteenth Amendment. By 1867, it became clear that Republicans would allow female suffrage or Black suffrage, but not both (and excluding, in both cases, Black women). White feminist leaders Susan B. Anthony and Elizabeth Cady Stanton teamed up with millionaire Democrat George Train, who financed *The Revolution,* their woman rights newspaper, and implemented an increasingly racist suffrage strategy. "While the dominant party have with one hand lifted up TWO MILLION BLACK MEN and crowned them with the honor and dignity of citizenship," it read, "with the other they have dethroned FIFTEEN MILLION WHITE WOMEN—their own mothers and sisters, their own wives and daughters—and cast them under the heel of the lowest orders of manhood."

Stanton, writing of a lynching in Tennessee, said, "The Republican cry of 'Manhood Suffrage' creates an antagonism between black men and all women that will culminate in fearful outrages on womanhood, especially in the southern states."[96]

The American Equal Rights Association, founded by Susan B. Anthony, Elizabeth Cady Stanton, and Frederick Douglass, split into two suffrage organizations after its 1869 meeting because of increasing racism within the movement.[97] After 1870, when the Fifteenth Amendment was passed, both Black men and women agitated for the female vote, including Black elected officials in Reconstruction governments. Black woman rights activists again came in conflict with white women leaders during the antilynching campaign spearheaded by Ida B. Wells-Barnett. "The colored race multiplies like the locusts of Egypt," Frances Willard of the Women's Christian Temperance Union had written, "and the grogshop is its center of power."[98]

In white feminist circles, there were no antiracist leaders in the tradition of the Grimke sisters. The complicity of white women in the mythology of rape doubtless contributed to the escalation of racist violence, as right-wing feminism emerged. By the 1910s, Black women had organized independently in the club movement and were fighting not only for women's votes, but for the votes of Black men lost to post-Reconstruction disenfranchisement in the Southern states. In 1918, after the Nineteenth Amendment passed the House, white feminist organizers again capitulated to racism to get the support of Southern senators. "Negro men cannot vote in South Carolina and therefore negro women could not if women were to vote in the nation," Alice Paul of the Women's Party reassured the *New York World*.[99]

After the eventual passage of the Nineteenth Amendment, Black women continued to press white feminist organizations to work against their disenfranchisement in the Jim Crow South, with little success. In the South, however, Jesse Daniel Ames and the Society of Southern Women for the Prevention of Lynching took on the white power structure in the name of "white womanhood," and an interracial YWCA movement brought women together to work against racism.

Like the suffrage movement, the birth control movement took a decidedly racist and elitist turn, as leaders like Margaret Sanger capitulated to the eugenics movement. "More children from the fit, less from the unfit—that is the chief issue of birth control," she explained in 1919, and by the 1930s, her rhetoric was virulently racist and she began to advocate sterilization of the "whole dysgenic population."[100]

One major factor in the national move to the Right was a new wave of U.S. imperialism towards peoples of color globally. In 1898 the United States went to war with Spain over Cuba and the Philippines, and U.S. victory brought eight million people of color under U.S. control. To many whites, the new colonial possessions symbolized national greatness, a coming of age on the world stage, and expanded access to new markets, especially in Asia.[101] The "English virtue" of empire sparked a new sense of brotherhood among English-speaking peoples and a sense of Anglo-Saxon superiority.

In the United States, these concepts echoed the race theories being propagated in Europe in the late nineteenth century, where "scientific racism" gave ideological justification for European imperialism. From the beginnings of colonialism, the intellectual machinery of Europe had been busy explaining what "race" meant in a context that justified European dominance, shifting from a religious to a scientific explanation as Europe emerged from the Middle Ages. Early race theories that supplanted the interpretation of the story of Ham in Genesis were concerned with whether humans developed from a single stock in a short period of time or whether many races evolved differently in different places.

Opposition to the slave trade at the end of the seventeenth century prompted European scientists to consolidate the theory of race, drawing on both anthropology and evolution to justify racist practices. In 1843, the English Ethnological Society grew out of the activities of the Aborigines Protection Society. British scientists felt a need to understand "the whole mental condition of the savage...so different from ours"; subjects of the Empire that represented "almost every known modification of the human species whose varied and often conflicting interests have to be regulated and provided for."[102] Although Charles Darwin did not himself assign superiority to particular traits or place races in position on the evolutionary scale, his followers did. They used the doctrine of natural selection, or "survival of the fittest," to explain the superiority of conquering European culture: "As the Indian is killed by the approach of civilization, to which he resists in vain, so the black man perishes by that culture to which he serves as a humble instrument."[103] Cultural traits such as language and physical traits such as facial features were dangerously confused into a biological determinism designed to show European superiority.

Within this biased framework, various tests were used to classify humanity into diverse racial groupings. The test of language arrived at groupings of three or seven main races. Physical characteristics such as skull size were used to clarify the Frontal (European), Parietal (Mongol), and Occipital (Negro). Facial angle was used to conclude that the "receding forehead and projecting jaws of the Negro" represented "ignorance and brutality" in contrast with the "harmonious" Saxon/Celt/Scandinavian "broad forehead...a special fullness in the intellectual and moral regions." Often the reason scientists would challenge a particular system would be that it lumped in Europeans with less "evolved" races. While all non-European "races" were inferior, in British thought the Negro came in for special fear and hatred: "His energy is considerable: Aided by the sun, he repels the white invader."[104]

Darwin himself underlined the subjectivity—thus the irrationality—of racial classifications:

> Man has been studied more thoroughly than any other organic being, and yet there is the greatest possible diversity amongst capable judges whether he should be classed as a single species or race, or as two (Virey), as three (Jacquinot), as four (Kant), five (Blumenbach), six (Buffon), seven (Hunter), eight (Agassiz), eleven (Pickering), fifteen (Bory St. Vincent), sixteen (Desmoulins), twenty-two (Morton), sixty (Crawfurd), or sixty-three (Burke).[105]

Anti-Semitism evolved within this race-conscious European climate from eighteen hundred years of persecution aimed at Jews as a religious group ("Christ killers" or "poisoners of wells") to persecution aimed at Jews as a race. Not unlike his British counterparts, German philosopher Arthur de Gobineau was convinced that "the racial question overshadows all other problems of history, that it holds the key to them all, and that the inequality of the races from whose fusion a people is formed is enough to explain the whole course of its destiny."[106] In Germany, nationalism fed by Germany's defeats fueled a sense of Teutonic destiny. Race was seen to determine the fate of civilizations. German philosophers fused the ideas of the German people, or *volk,* with the idea of the state as a transcendental essence to which the Jew was the primary outsider. The term "anti-Semitism" itself was coined during this period by a German racist, Wilhelm Marr, to promote Jew hatred.

Hitler and his party of National Socialists would take these racist, anti-Semitic ideas to their genocidal conclusions. In *Mein Kampf,* he wrote, "The racial question gives the key not only to world history, but to all human culture," for "in the blood alone resides the strength as well as the weakness of man." The Aryan race is the "bearer of human cultural development" and was therefore chosen to rule the world. The state must "set race in the center of all life…not only of assembling and preserving the most valuable stocks of basic racial elements in this people, but slowly and surely of raising them to a dominant position."[107]

"The mightiest counterpart of the Aryan is represented by the Jew," Hitler explained. "Jewry is without question a race and not a religious fellowship" because "if worst came to the worst, a splash of baptismal water could always save the business and the Jew at the same time."[108] At the end of the nineteenth century, Jews were being allowed into the white working class in the United States, at the same time that they were being cast as the most reviled racial Other in Europe (an indication, among other things, of the extreme malleability of the concept of race).

The climate that fostered scientific racism also began to evolve medical distinctions between homosexuals and heterosexuals. Doctors such as England's Havelock Ellis, who were investigating questions of sexuality in the late 1800s, reported an outpouring of stories from the newly labeled homosexual population. Many indigenous cultures in North America had allowed community members, such as the *berdache,* cross-gender identification, practices severely discouraged by Christian missionaries. With urbanization, white medical writers came to see homosexuality not as sodomy, a punishable but discrete offense, but as a kind of gender identity, a personality type with specific behaviors that they usually assumed to be pathological. Between the 1880s and World War I, homosexuals emerged as a "sexual minority of sorts."[109] Scientific racism, as well as psychiatry, contributed to early homophobic discourse. In an atmosphere where the propagation of the white race was the key to a nation's destiny and the fittest were assumed to be white, the newly discovered white homosexual's alleged inability to have children was seen as "degenerate."[110]

In the United States by the beginning of the twentieth century, Anglo-Saxons, not "Aryans," were the superior racial group. The virtues of these Anglo-Saxons, according to *Our Country,* an influential report on missions published in 1887 and paraphrased by historian Nell Painter, were "a sense of fair play, the ability to gain wealth honestly, the enjoyment of broad civil liberties in democracies in which every man had an equal vote, the genius for self-government and for governing others fairly and the evolution of the highest civilization the world had ever known."[111] Theodore Roosevelt, imbued with a sense of Anglo-Saxon manhood, declared in 1895 that "this country needs a war."[112]

President McKinley explained his decision, three years after Roosevelt's declaration, to keep the Philippines after the Spanish-American War: "We could not leave them to themselves—they were unfit for self-government— and they would soon have anarchy and misrule over there worse than Spain's was…there was nothing left for us to do but to take them all."[113] The white lie refined its concept of democracy as an exclusively Anglo-Saxon preserve at a time when the United States was extending increasingly antidemocratic control over huge numbers of people of color.

My grandfather Ben Cobb, one of Judge James Cobb's seven children, lied about his age and, perhaps harking to Roosevelt's call to Anglo-Saxon manhood, went off at sixteen to enlist in the Spanish-American War. He didn't get to fight in 1898, but spent his time camped in Florida, where he did get malaria. He later became an engineer and spent a good bit of time in Central America working on the Panama Canal. But his health had been weakened by disease, and he died in the influenza epidemic of 1918, when my mother was three.

It is with James and Ben Cobb that I begin to pick up the trail, the emotional scent, of family history. "Men and wars! Men and wars!" Mama would sometimes exclaim bitterly; but she too was an Anglophile, reading my brother and me to sleep at night with tales of English adventure, from *Robin Hood* and *King Arthur* to *When Knighthood Was in Flower* and *Under Drake's Flag.* She loved her daddy the way women love men they never knew except through other people's stories. Mother said that my grandmother hated Judge Cobb because he beat his children. Ben was a wanderer, an adventurer, maybe trying to escape his power-hungry father; and I don't think it was coincidental that many of the places to which my mother liked to travel—often needing to get sick to get to do it—were places he had been. In my forties I have begun to deal with the effects of my sense of abandonment from her absences, my panic from her sickness: issues usually privatized in therapeutic discussions of "dysfunctional families," but in fact with historical causes and dimensions, racism not the least of them.

The Spanish American War that eventually killed Ben Cobb marked the beginning of the United States' rise to global economic supremacy in a century when intense rivalries among industrial powers would contribute to two world wars. World War I brought the beginning of the watershed shift from Britain to the United States as premier imperial power. The Allies turned to New York to borrow money to finance the war. The dollar joined the pound as a major reserve currency, or that national currency (and/or gold) that is used to pay off the balance of payments of nations that import more than they export. These reserve dollars act as IOUs that can only be used to purchase U.S. goods at U.S. prices, making the role of the dollar an instrument of massive economic control.[114] The increased trade that resulted helped the U.S. to shift to the status of creditor nation and begin international lending on a large scale, bringing profits from the interest. In 1913, the Federal Reserve Act made international branch banks legal, marking the beginning of a web of U.S. financial networks that would increasingly span the globe. When World War II devastated Europe for a second time, the dollar finally beat out the pound as primary reserve currency, requiring that the leading trading nations keep their reserves in U.S. banks.

As the U.S. gained its status as the premier capitalist country, for the first time in four centuries serious challenges emerged to the capitalist/imperialist system. The threat of international socialism manifest in the 1917 Bolshevik Revolution presented an alternative to the imperialist system.[115] Within the United States, the Great Depression, brought on by excesses of capitalism such as stock speculation, high tariffs, and skewed distribution of income, brought riots and strikes from both white workers and people of color. Armed white farmers in Arkansas seized food supplies, five hundred unemployed people rioted in Detroit, Boston children raided a luncheon for Spanish War vets, three hundred thousand Southern textile workers went on strike, and Black Alabama sharecroppers fought off sheriff's deputies when they came to confiscate their land.[116]

This uprising occurred near my home county. The fact that Black sharecroppers fired on white law enforcement officers to defend their property brought immediate reprisal. Vigilante violence by white groups followed the incident, and two of the Black farmers died in jail of untended wounds. Survivors received prison sentences of up to twelve years.[117] My paternal grandfather, Fletcher Segrest, was sent by local law enforcement out to the hospital to question one of the surviving members of the Sharecropper's Union shootout about possible communist influence. These and other insurgencies necessitated a "New Deal" between workers, owners, and government, a reorganization of U.S. capitalism through increased federal regulation, deficit spending, and a coopting of socialist policies in a range of welfare state reforms. Both world wars also weakened Europe's hold on its colonial empires, which became too expensive to maintain. After World War I, strong national movements across the globe won political independence from former European colonizers, a process accelerated by World War II and extending into the 1960s.

Fascist movements emerged in the 1920s in Germany, Italy, and Japan and were propelled into power by the Great Depression. They offered a challenge both to communism and to the leading industrial countries, but not to capitalism itself. As Hitler explained, "Let these 'well-bred' gentry [capitalist leaders] learn that we do with a clear conscience what they secretly do with a guilty one."[118]

Bertram Gross explains that the fascists were "heretics seeking to revive the old [capitalist] faith by concentrating on the fundamentals of imperial expansion, militarism, repression, and racism." They mobilized the discontented and alienated in order to "channel the violence-prone" and they manipulated and tolerated anticapitalist currents to ultimately build a firmer base for capitalism. "Above all," Gross explains, "the fascists wanted 'in.'"[119]

Albert Speer explained Nazism as "the first dictatorship of an industrial state in this age of technology, a dictatorship which employed to perfection the instruments of technology to dominate its own people."[120] The Germans employed unprecedented repression on their own people, focusing, as Hitler explained, on "the annihilation of the Jewish race throughout Europe."[121] Concentration camps built and supplied by German firms became the focus of wholesale gassing and cremating of twelve million people (six million Jews, as well as communists, gypsies, homosexuals, and the sick or insane), slave labor (7.5 million civilian foreigners working for the Reich), medical experiments, and "recycling" of human remains. Beyond the concentration camps, fascists in Germany, Italy, and Japan (the so-called "Axis powers") "destroyed the very liberties which industrialization had brought."[122] The needs of the master race justified imperialism and the militarism required for it and for domestic repression. These racist theories were used against not only Jews. but also Africans (by Italians), Slavs (by Germans), and Chinese and other Asians (by the Japanese).[123]

My two uncles, Ben Cobb's sons, fought in World War II, as did my own father, who was in the air force. He was shot down over Germany, and he spent two years in a German POW camp before being liberated by Allied armies in 1945. The defeat of fascism made World War II a "good war," although the internment of Japanese Americans, the decision to drop the atomic bomb on Hiroshima and Nagasake, and the experience of Black soldiers on their return home showed that there was a need to defend democracy beyond its white preserves at home as well as abroad. Like many men and women of their generation, my parents turned from the defeat of German Nazism to a fervent Cold War confrontation with communism. They also began to anticipate the postwar uprising of African American Southerners that announced itself most publicly with *Brown v. Board of Education* in 1954.[124]

As bankers and industrialists in the U.S. had anticipated, the victory of the Allies over the Axis brought the United States to a uniquely new global leadership role in what *Time/Life* magnate Henry Luce dubbed "the American century." World War II had brought unprecedented cooperation among political and military leaders, businessmen, and scientists. At the close of the war they worked to consolidate a world capitalist bloc under the leadership of the United States with myriad channels of influence, "a loose network of constitutional democracies, authoritarian regimes, and military dictatorships described as the 'Free World,'" Gross explains. The net result was "a remarkably flexible control system in which competing views on strategy and tactics make themselves felt and are resolved through mutual adjustment," allowing business to operate both through and beyond the state.[125] As colony after colony won independence, they were brought into the burgeoning capitalist financial networks as the price of their independence, a process known as neocolonialism.

Within these networks, the poorer, "underdeveloped" countries were at a permanent disadvantage. When they ran up deficits that their reserve currency could not cover and were refused credit by banks, they were forced to undertake severe internal adjustments: austerity measures that raised prices, lowered wages, and shifted spending from social services towards the military. The United States, on the other hand, could maintain yearly deficits without having to induce the kind of austerity measures that would have had severe political repercussions, both in terms of encouraging domestic revolutionary movements and increasing governmental repression. The United States used the money from its deficit to finance its military machine, to lend military and economic aid to its allies (including forgiving debts for its client states who behaved, and for foreign investments that brought countries more tightly into its economic sphere).

The United States maintains a deficit because of its flexibility of resources, because it generates much of its income from its financial services, and because it can extend itself credit due to other countries wanting dollars in a way that they do not want Third World national currencies. "If we had not been world banker...we would have been in the same situation as other countries face," explained Secretary of the Treasury C. Douglas Dillon in 1963, "as soon as we got into deficit we would have had to balance our accounts one way or another."[126] Once again, political openness in the United States was built on the backs of people of color.

World War II also brought a shift within the United States away from self-sufficiency in raw materials, one of the "striking economic changes of our time," according to a commission on foreign economic policy;[127] and the intensified need for overseas raw materials coincided with the growth of the "Second World" of the communist empire. Three-fourths of the imported materials in a Department of Defense list of necessary stockpiles came from underdeveloped areas,[128] a "Third World" beyond Europe, North America, Japan, and the Soviet Union. Explained W. W. Rostow, President Johnson's advisor on national security affairs, to a joint congressional committee: "The location, natural resources, and populations of the underdeveloped areas are such that, should they become effectively attached to the Communist bloc, the United States would become the second power in the world.... In short, our military security and our way of life as well as the fate of Western Europe and Japan are at stake in the evolution of the underdeveloped areas."[129]

These far-reaching shifts in world finances helped to shape racial policies and practices within the United States. Intensified racism at the end of the nineteenth century had brought an upsurge in Black antiracist organizing, marked by the beginning of the NAACP (National Association for the Advancement of Colored People) and the Urban League. World War I brought increased economic opportunities to as many as one million African Americans who left the South looking for industrial employment formerly denied by industries and by white unions, but now available because of war-induced labor shortages. Black soldiers came home from fighting a war to make the world "safe for democracy" to race riots, lynchings, and a resurgence in the Klan. With a powerful and growing urban base in the North, Black militancy increased in the 1920s, with an international focus: W. E. B. Du Bois called a Pan-African Congress to meet in Paris during the Versailles conference; Marcus Garvey promoted Pan-Africanism with his Universal Negro Improvement Association; and the Harlem Renaissance brought an unprecedented cultural resurgence.

Immigration policy shifted under the new global pressures of the American century, affecting especially Asian immigration, which had been severely limited since the Chinese Exclusion Act in 1882. World War II had also brought the internment of 110 thousand Japanese Americans here while German Americans went on with their daily lives. But after the War, the quotas limiting non-European immigration, in place from the beginning of the century, finally gave way under pressure from Cold War competition for Third World resources. In 1952, the Immigration and Nationality Act (also called the McCarran-Walter Act) finally made legal the naturalization of any person regardless of race, for the first time making immigrants from Japan, Korea, and other parts of Asia eligible for citizenship.[130] In 1956, the Republican Party came out in favor of easing immigration restrictions—the same year its platform called for "the establishment of American naval and air bases all around the world."[131] Political refugees from Cuba and Indochina were admitted in large numbers after the U.S. failed to dislodge communist governments. In 1965, the McCarran-Walter Act was amended to abolish the national origins system and substitute seven preferential categories, including refugees "fleeing a Communist or Communist-dominated country." Asians began to immigrate to the U.S. in record numbers—one and a half million people between 1966 and 1983,[132] creating a brain drain and siphoning off wealth from the Asian continent. Capitalism's economic competition with communism helped to shift immigration policy and thus the racial demographics of U.S. society.

The deficit in U.S. mineral resources contributed to a shift in policy towards American Indians as well, as mineral resources on reservation lands became more coveted. Indian policy after the Dawes Severalty Act had followed a colonial pattern, destroying collective structures and fostering dependence on an emerging welfare apparatus. From 1880 to 1930, fifty thousand Indian children were sent, by force or otherwise, to Indian boarding schools to encourage assimilation. Between 1881 and 1934, Indian land declined from 155 million acres to seventy million acres.[133] In 1924, Congress granted full citizenship, finally, to Indians. In 1928, the Meriam Survey described unrelieved poverty on reservations as a result of land policies. Because corporations wanted access to mineral leasing, the Indian Reorganization Act of 1934 gave power for economic planning to a "tribal council" system, settling up Indian leadership that would collaborate with corporate pillaging and further usurp traditional structures.

Roosevelt's "New Deal" and World War II helped to dislodge the biological approach of "scientific" racism, whose genocidal ends Hitler made clear. From the 1930s to 1965, the "ethnicity theory" of race operated as the progressive/liberal consensus. First articulated by sociologists at the University of Chicago in the 1920s, it theorized a "race cycle" of contact, conflict, accommodation, and assimilation based largely on the experience of European immigrants, an approach that has been increasingly challenged by class (mostly Marxist) and nation-based (anticolonial) theories of race.[134] Jim Crow still gripped the South, but the integrationists won the confrontation within the Democratic Party in 1948.

As the U.S. competed with the Soviet Union for Third World resources, domestic racism became an international issue. "We cannot escape the fact that our civil rights record has been an issue in world politics," Truman admitted in 1946. "Those with competing philosophies have stressed—and are shamelessly distorting—our shortcomings."[135] Third World revolutionary movements were growing in Indochina, the Philippines, Indonesia, and Africa. Truman appointed a committee on civil rights in 1946, and in 1948 issued an order barring racial segregation in the armed forces.

In 1954, after decades of work by the NAACP to shift court findings, the Supreme Court in *Brown v. Board of Education* reversed the 1898 *Plessy v. Ferguson* ruling that had made "separate but equal" school facilities legal at the end of Reconstruction. Challenging the Southern apartheid put in place as Jim Crow, the Black freedom movement erupted in the South, targeting school desegregation and voting rights.

In early January 1965, Sammy Younge, one of the young Black men and women across the South who responded to this movement, was shot and killed by a man named Marvin Segrest, a cousin of my father's, after Younge insisted on using the "white" bathroom in the gas station where Marvin

Segrest worked. Segrest claimed he had shot in self defense and was acquitted by an all-white jury. Activist James Forman called Younge "the first Black college student in the movement to have been killed," a murder that "marked the end of tactical nonviolence."[136] That year I was sixteen, and deeply disturbed by the eruptions of racist violence around me.

School desegregation and voting rights came in the South with federal enforcement, much reviled by white Southerners. The need for the United States to consolidate its relationships with newly independent Third World countries probably helped motivate the Kennedy administration to overturn the Jim Crow structures put in place in the South after Reconstruction. As Black freedom struggles moved north and became less assimilationist and more militantly nationalist, the federal "support" of the civil rights movement turned to opposition, as George Wallace had predicted. Martin Luther King, Jr. was assassinated after he linked Black civil rights struggles in the United States with the issue of domestic poverty and with anti-imperialist struggles in Vietnam. Numerous Black Panthers and other Black leaders were murdered by federal and state law enforcement officers.

This militant Black organizing triggered renewed militancy in other Third World communities within the United States, as well as student rebellions and the anti-imperialist opposition to the war in Vietnam. Vietnam became the first U.S. military defeat in history, and the militant antiwar movement at home helped to put some brakes on U.S. military power. This revolutionary upsurge also triggered a "Second Wave" of feminism, in a way similar to the emergence of early woman rights out of the abolition struggles. Gay and lesbian liberation movements also erupted from the homosexual subcultures that had been developing since the late 1800s, inspired by and using political models of both feminism (itself highly influenced by antiracist struggles) and Black freedom struggles. It was this lesbian-feminist politics into which the great-great-great-great-great-great-great-great-granddaughter of Ambrose Cobbs of Jamestown came out in the mid-1970s.

In this essay, I have tracked ten Cobbs, from the sweating pews of Virginia churches; to Florida swamps, dodging 'gators and searching human prey; to the Alabama bench, gaveling Reconstruction officials off to the chain gang. I have traced my white history through a particular set of white men because they are the ones who constructed white history and because my mother's papers did not include the genealogy of daughters and mothers. I suspect from my knowledge of own mother's and grandmother's experiences that this matrilineal history is fraught with much more ambivalence and opposition. My father's side of the family would bring a more working-class world view. Likewise, if I have tracked ten of these ancestors back to English origins, I find it hopeful that I am left 1,014 more possibilities of something other than "pure" European blood.

"It is the Black condition, and only that, which informs the consciousness of white people," wrote James Baldwin. And on another occasion: "As long as you think you're white, there's no hope for you."[137] I have worked in this essay to both think myself, and unthink myself, white (the related project, which I have engaged in other places, to *feel* myself both white and not-white); to regain the power, in Baldwin's terms, to "control and define" myself by excavating the Black (and "red" and "brown" and "yellow") condition within my own white history. For it is only through acquiring an awareness of racist consciousness (a necessary corollary to antiracist practice) that we as white people will ever have any other community than the community of the lie.

This essay first appeared in *Memory of a Race Traitor* (Cambridge, MA: South End Press, 1994).

NOTES

[1] James Baldwin, "On Being White and Other Lies." *Essence* (April 1984): 90–92.

[2] *Sing, Whisper, Shout, Pray!* is the eventual outcome of our work on *The Third Wave.*

[3] Thanks especially to Jacqui Alexander for many careful readings of drafts and for her confidence that I would indeed, someday, finish the essay in a useable form. Thanks also to Barbara Smith for close editing and encouragement and to Tobi Lippin and Peter Barnes for feedback and support.

[4] Howard Zinn, *A People's History of the United States* (New York: Harper & Row, 1980): 24. The most recurrent explanations for the psychology of white racism (as distinct from its material base) draw heavily on Freudian theories of repression and projection, as do Rawick, Roediger, Takaki, and Jordan.

[5] For more on the precapitalist "tendency to seize upon physical differences as the badge of innate mental and temporal differences," see Thomas Gossett, *Race: The History of an Idea in America* (Dallas: Southern Methodist University Press, 1975): 3–16. "Prior to 1500 differential valorization of human races is hardly noticeable," historian Magnus Morner comments of "the hierarchic classification of human races dictated by European ethnocentricity," in *Race Mixture in the History of Latin America* (Boston: Little Brown, 1967: 6). Michael Omi and Howard Winant agree: "Race consciousness, and its articulation in theories of race, is largely a modern phenomenon" dating to European explorers' "discoveries." *Racial Formation in the United States.* (New York: Routledge, 1989): 58.

[6] T. Walter Wallbank, et al., eds., *Civilization Past and Present,* vol. 2, 5th ed. (Chicago: Scott, Foresman & Company, 1965): 280.

[7] Zinn: 23.

[8] Winthrop Jordan, *The White Man's Burden: Historical Origins of Racism in the United States.* (London: Oxford University Press, 1974): 33. *White Over Black: American Attitudes Toward the Negro 1550–1812* (Baltimore: Penguin, 1969) is a longer version of this excellent book, which was abbreviated in *The White Man's Burden* to make it more accessible to students. References are to *The White Man's Burden* unless otherwise specified.

[9] Zinn: 26–28. "African slavery is hardly to be praised. But it was far different from plantation or mining slavery in the Americas, which was lifelong, morally crippling, destructive of family ties, without hope of any future" (27).

[10] Marvin Harris, *Patterns of Race in the Americas* (New York: W.W. Norton, 1974): 12.

[11] Quoted in Gilberto Freyre, *The Masters and the Slaves* (New York: Knopf, 1956): 178.

[12] Eduardo Galeano, *Open Veins of Latin America: Five Centuries of the Pillage of a Continent.* Cedric Belfrage, trans. (New York: Monthly Review Press, 1973): 50.

[13] Zinn: 29.

[14] "The Columbus Letter of March 14, 1493," quoted in Virgil J. Vogel, *This Country Was Ours: A Documentary History of the American Indian* (New York: Harper & Row, 1972): 34.

[15] Aztec's account of the incident as given later to the priest-historian Bernadino Sahagún, quoted in Vogel: 35–36.

[16] "The Narrative of Alvar Nuñez Cabeça de Vaca," quoted in Vogel: 37.

[17] Zinn: 26–27.

[18] Galeano: 33–34.

[19] Harris: 12–14.

[20] Jordan: 4–7.

[21] Jordan: 17, 18, 22.

[22] Jordan: n.8.

[23] Mab Segrest and Leonard Zeskind, *Quarantines and Death: The Far Right's Homophobic Agenda* (Atlanta: Center for Democratic Renewal, 1989): 29.

[24] See Mary Daly, *Gyn/Ecology: The Metaethics of Radical Feminism* (Boston: Beacon Press, 1978): n.183.

[25] E. William Monter, "Pedestal and Stake: Courtly Love and Witchcraft," *Becoming Visible: Women in European History,* Renate Bridenthal and Claudia Koonz, eds. (Boston: Houghton Mifflin, 1977): 133. Perhaps in the witch craze the trajectory of European misogyny (a much longer story than that of the racism traced here) intersects with the trajectory of European racism in a way that we have not fully understood, as Harriet Desmoines suggested to me in response to this section of the essay—for example, in the breaking of the European peasant movement leading towards land enclosure (a technique used also against people of color to break up communal ownership and economic and spiritual connections to the land).

[26] Ed Cohen, "Legislating the Norm," *Displacing Homophobia,* special issue of *South Atlantic Quarterly,* vol. 88, no. 1 (Winter 1989): 185–186.

[27] Jordan, *White Over Black:* 18

[28] Quoted in Jordan, *White Over Black:* 41.

[29] See, for example, Stanley Elkins, *Slavery: A Problem in American Institutional and Intellectual Life,* 2nd ed. (Chicago: University of Chicago Press, 1971): 38–44.

[30] Harris: 37. See Patricia Williams, *The Alchemy of Race and Rights* (Cambridge, MA: Harvard University Press, 1991) for a brilliant examination of the history and implications of her own "hybrid" origins.

[31] Galeano: 91–93.

[32] Galeano: 95.

[33] "Rich Got Richer in '80s, Census Report Says," *Raleigh News and Observer* (January 11, 1991).

[34] Jordan: 40, 4.

[35] Elkins: 44–49.

[36] Quoted in Vincent Harding, *There Is a River: The Black Struggle for Freedom in America* (New York: Random House, 1983): 27.

[37] Jordan, *Black Over White:* 93–95.

[38] Jordan: 46, 57.

[39] See Margo Adair, "The Subjective Side of Politics," unpublished essay. The People's Institute for Survival and Beyond (1444 N. Johnson St., New Orleans, LA 70116) shapes much of its work with white people against racism on this historical knowledge of the ideological construction of whiteness.

[40] Article II, Section 2 of the U.S. Constitution tied representation and taxes to "the whole Number of free persons, including those bound to Service for a Term of Years, and excluding Indians not taxed, three-fifths of all other persons." The prohibition against abolishing the slave trade was in Article II, Section 9.

[41] John Hope Franklin, *From Slavery to Freedom: A History of Negro Americans,* 3rd ed. (New York: Random House, 1969): 147–149.

[42] Franklin: 171.

[43] Ibid.

[44] Franklin: 178.

[45] Franklin: 186.

[46] Quoted in Jordan: 73.

[47] Harris: 3–4.

[48] Quoted in Richard Drinnon, *Facing West: The Metaphysics of Indian Hating and Empire Building* (Minneapolis: University of Minnesota Press, 1980): 42.

[49] Quoted in Drinnon: 43–44,

[50] Quoted in S. Lyman Taylor, *A History of Indian Policy* (Washington, DC: Bureau of Indian Affairs, 1973): 35.

[51] Quoted in Drinnon: 86.

[52] Quoted in Drinnon: 89.

[53] Gossett: 231.

[54] Quoted in Drinnon: 76–77.

[55] Quoted in Drinnon: 179.

[56] Quoted in Ronald T. Takaki, *Iron Cages: Race and Culture in Nineteenth Century America* (Seattle: University of Washington Press, 1979): 96.

[57] Takaki, *Cages:* 101–102.

[58] Quoted in Harding: 109–111.

[59] Quoted in Harding: 95.

[60] Jordan, *White Over Black:* 194–195.

[61] Paula Giddings, *When and Where I Enter: The Impact of Black Women on Race and Sex in America* (Toronto: Bantam, 1984): 48–50.

[62] See Harding, Chapter 9, where he quotes Delany: "We are politically not of them, but aliens to the laws and political privileges of the country" (174). Delany's emerging Black nationalism was influenced by the nationalism sweeping Europe. Delany prefigures Du Bois in his observation: "It would be duplicity longer to disguise the fact that the great issue, sooner or later, upon which must be disputed the world's destiny, will be the question of black and white, and every individual will be called upon for his identity with the one or the other" (186).

[63] Takaki, *Cages:* 75–79.

[64] Dave Roediger, *The Wages of Whiteness: Race and the Making of the American Working Class* (London: Verso, 1991): 57.

[65] Quoted in Gossett: 235.

[66] Roediger: 95. See also George Rawick, *From Sundown to Sunup: The Making of the Black Community* (Westport, CT: Greenwood Publishers, 1972).

[67] Quoted in Rudolfo Acuña, *Occupied America: A History of Chicanos,* 3rd ed. (New York: Harper & Row, 1988): 6.

[68] Acuña: 1–2, 12.

[69] See Acuña's chapter, "Legacy of Hate: the Conquest of Mexico's Northeast."

[70] Ronald T. Takaki, *Strangers from a Different Shore: A History of Asian Americans* (Boston: Little, Brown & Company, 1989): 32–33.

[71] Quoted in Takaki, *Strangers:* 22.

[72] Takaki, *Strangers:* 79–81.

[73] Nell Irvin Painter, *Standing at Armageddon: The United States, 1877–1919* (New York: W.W. Norton, 1987): xvii, xx.

[74] Painter: 21–22.

[75] Omi and Winant: 64–65.

[76] Robert J. Norrell, *Reaping the Whirlwind: The Civil Rights Movement in Tuskegee* (New York: Vintage, 1986): 10, 19–20.

[77] C. Vann Woodward, *The Strange Career of Jim Crow,* 2nd rev. ed. (London: Oxford, 1966): 70.

[78] In the Slaughterhouse Cases of 1873, in *U.S. v. Reese,* and in *U.S. v. Cruikshank* in 1876, the Court cut back sharply on privileges and immunities seen as under federal protection, limiting the scope of the Fourteenth and Fifteenth Amendments. Civil rights cases of 1883 nullified portions of the Civil Rights Act, the legislative enactment of the Fourteenth Amendment, saying that Congress could restrain states but not individuals from acts of racial discrimination and segregation. In *Hall v. De Cuir* (1877) and *Louisville, New Orleans and Texas Railroads v. Mississippi* (1890), the court ruled that states first could not prohibit, then could require, segregation, leading towards the 1896 *Plessy v. Ferguson* decision that "legislation is powerless to eradicate racial instincts" and that "separate but equal" facilities were constitutional. *Williams v. Mississippi* (1898) "completed the opening of the legal road to proscription, segregation, and disfranchisement by approving the Mississippi plan for depriving Negroes of the franchise" (Woodward: 71). "Just as the Negro gained his emancipation and new rights through a falling out between white men, he now stood to lose his rights through the reconciliation of white men" (Woodward: 70).

[79] Giddings: 27.

[80] Manning Marable, *Race, Reform and Rebellion: The Second Reconstruction in Black America, 1945–1982* (Jackson: University of Mississippi Press, 1984): 8.

[81] Woodward: 60–65.

[82] Woodward: 79–80, 90.

[83] Takaki, *Cages:* 219.

[84] Painter: 162.

[85] Takaki, *Strangers:* 28.

[86] Takaki, *Strangers:* 31.

[87] Painter: 163.

[88] Acuña, Chapter 3, "Freedom in a Cage: The Colonization of New Mexico": 54–81.

[89] Acuña: 90–91.

[90] Acuña: 98, 103.

[91] Quoted in Drinnon: 182.

[92] Quoted in Gossett: 233.

[93] Quoted in Takaki, *Strangers:* 24

[94] Takaki, *Strangers:* 25.

[95] Takaki, *Cages:* 217–219.

[96] Quoted in Giddings: 66.

[97] Commented Frances Ellen Harper, "The white women all go for sex, letting race occupy a minor position. Being black means that every white, including every white working-class woman, can discriminate against you" (Giddings: 68).

[98] Quoted in Giddings: 91.

[99] Giddings: 160.

[100] Linda Gordon, *Woman's Body, Woman's Right* (New York: Grossman, 1976). See the section on "Eugenists," 274–290, especially 281–282.

[101] Painter: 147.

[102] Quoted in Christine Bolt, *Victorian Attitudes to Race* (London: Routledge & Kegan Paul, 1976): 1–2.

[103] *Journal of the Anthropological Society of London* (1864): lxvii. Quoted in Bolt: 20.

[104] Robert Knox, *Anthropological Review,* vol. 8 (1870): 51, 243–246, 456. Quoted in Bolt: 22.

[105] Charles Darwin, *The Descent of Man,* vol. 2 (London: J. Murray, 1871): 225–226.

[106] Quoted in Lucy S. Dawidowicz, *The War Against the Jews 1933–1945* (Toronto: Bantam, 1976): 41.

[107] Quoted in Dawidowicz: 23–24.

[108] Quoted in Dawidowicz: 14.

[109] John D'Emilio and Estelle B. Freedman, *Intimate Matters: A History of Sexuality in America* (New York: Harper & Row, 1988): 227.

[110] Havelock Ellis and John Addington Symonds, *Sexual Inversion* (New York: Arno Press, 1975): 137. Ellis, according to Gordon (283), favorably reviewed eugenicist Lothrop Stoddard's *The Rising Tide of Color Against White World-Supremacy in 1920* (New York: Scribner, 1922).

[111] Painter: 149–150.

[112] Quoted in Painter: 150.

[113] Quoted in Painter: 147.

[114] Harry Magdoff, *The Age of Imperialism: The Economics of U.S. Foreign Policy* (New York: Monthly Review Press, 1969): 85–88.

[115] Magdoff: 40.

[116] Zinn: 380–381, 386.

[117] For one version of this story, see Robin D.G. Kelley, *Hammer and Hoe: Alabama Communists During the Great Depression* (Chapel Hill: University of North Carolina Press, 1990): 50–53. For another, see Theodore Rosengarten's *All God's Dangers: The Life of Nate Shaw* (New York: Knopf, 1974).

[118] Quoted in Bertram Gross, *Friendly Fascism: The New Face of Power in America* (Boston: South End Press, 1982): 21.

[119] Gross: 17.

[120] Quoted in Gross: 25.

[121] Quoted in Gross: 24.

[122] Gross: 22.

[123] Gross: 23.

[124] *Brown v. Board of Education of Topeka*, 1954.

[125] Gross: 34–36.

[126] See Magdoff: 91–99 on the dynamics of devaluation. The quote is from testimony before the Joint Economic Committee of the Congress of the United States, Hearings on the United States Balance of Payments, Washington, DC, 1963, Part I, 83–84 (Magdoff: 104–105).

[127] Quoted in Magdoff: 49.

[128] Magdoff: 51.

[129] Quoted in Magdoff: 54.

[130] *Recent Activities Against Citizens and Residents of Asian Descent, A Report of the U.S. Commission on Civil Rights,* Publication No. 88, 1988: 11–12.

[131] Quoted in John Lukacs, *Immigration and Migration: A Historical Perspective* (Monterey, VA: American Immigration Control Foundation, 1986): 14–15.

[132] U.S. Civil Rights Commission: 13.

[133] Edward H. Spicer, *A Short History of the Indians of the United States* (New York: D. Van Nostrand, 1969): 113, 116.

[134] Omi and Winant: 14–24.

[135] Quoted in Zinn: 440.

[136] Forman: 23–24, 25.

[137] See Roediger: 6.

Who Is an Indian? The Minnesota Chippewa Tribe Struggles for Land and Sovereignty

MARCIE MCINTIRE

In 1988, the Minnesota Chippewa Tribe began working to revise their consti-tution. One of the issues to contend with is the issue of enrollment. Tribal enrollment was a policy instituted by the U.S. government to limit access to tribal rights, particularly rights to land, by establishing strict standards of who belongs to the tribe. The Indian Reorganization Act of 1934 imposes a set of severe restrictions on who can identify themselves as Minnesota Chippewa. The restrictions are based on the abstract concept of "blood quantum."

American Indian people currently comprise the only group within this country who are required by the government to furnish proof of their ancestry. No one would dream of demanding a white or a Black person prove their race. Yet the United States secretary of the interior requires all Indian people to be enrolled in a federally recognized tribe in order to be considered American Indian. During the monthly meeting of the Grand Portage Reservation Business Committee held on November 30, 1988, the question of changing the enrollment provisions of the tribal constitution was discussed. The discussion centered on the issues of blood quantum and the diminishing number of enrollees.

Basically, new members are enrolled in the tribe if they have a least one-quarter Minnesota Chippewa Indian blood. According to the constitution, you must be a descendant of a person enrolled in 1890 at the White Earth, Leech Lake, Fond du Lac, Bois Forte, Grand Portage, or Mille Lacs reserva-tions in order to have "Minnesota Chippewa Indian blood." The number of enrollees is diminishing because many of the babies being born to current enrollees do not meet the one-quarter Minnesota Chippewa Indian blood requirement. One of the reasons for this is that tribal members marry and have children with non-Indian people. A second reason is that tribal members marry and have children with Indian people who come from reser-vations other than the six Minnesota Chippewa Tribe reservations. So we have the phenomenon of children being born with less than one-quarter Minnesota Chippewa Indian blood who consequently cannot be enrolled and will therefore not be considered American *Indian.*

But there is no such thing as racial purity except as a figment of a bigoted imagination. Prior to the European conquest of the Americas, Indian people traveled great distances to trade, to form political alliances, and to marry persons outside of their tribes or locales. The concept of an Indian person being a descendant of only one particular tribe, reservation, or group of reservations is absurd.

Revisions to the Minnesota Chippewa Tribe constitution will have to consider the question of degree of Indian blood, if the tribe wants to have sufficient members to govern the reservations adequately. The realities of blood quantum will have to be examined.

For instance, if a person's parent or grandparents were enrolled with Red Lake or one of the Canadian (Ojibwe) reserves, they may be a full-blood Chippewa Indian but can only be enrolled as one-half or one-quarter with the Minnesota Chippewa Tribe. This is true even if all the other ancestors were Minnesota Chippewa. The descendants of these people will not enjoy the rights and privileges of the Minnesota Chippewa Tribe if they do not marry someone from one of the six reservations who is also enrolled with sufficient blood quantum to produce children having one-quarter Minnesota Chippewa Indian blood or more. But if a person is Indian, shouldn't they be enrolled regardless of which tribes or reservations their ancestors came from?

Placing the burden of blood quantum on people is not congruent with the ideals and emotions surrounding love and marriage. The decision to marry another person and to have children is not going to be based upon whether or not they are enrolled with one of the six Minnesota Chippewa Tribe reservations. Such concerns surround the breeding of animals; they should not be imposed on human beings.

This essay first appeared in *The Circle*.
© 1993 by Marcie McIntire.

What Do You Want to Be Called?

SUZAN SHOWN HARJO

What do you want to be called, *American Indian* or *Native American*?

This is the most common question other people ask us. This is not a question we ask each other and there is no pressing need for us to answer it right now. It is a good question to mull over, if only to let others know what we'd rather not be called. For decades, my stock answer has been that they're both wrong, so use them interchangeably.

"Indians," of course, comes from the lost European sailors who washed up on our shores in 1492 and thought they were in India. The misnomer made it into the legal and historical literature and the U.S. Constitution—in the part about who counts for representation and tax apportionment, "excluding Indians not taxed." It is used for the body of law called (what else?) federal Indian law.

It could have been worse. "Savages" was the term used in the Declaration of Independence—"merciless Indian Savages," to be exact. Rather than judges, policymakers, law students, and attorneys poring over federal Indian law, their jurisprudential focus could have been "federal Savage law." (Or, the worst, "redskins" or "squaws," the most popular American pejoratives.)

"American Indians" has the added complication of invoking the Italian navigator, Amerigo Vespucci, who brought us the renaming of the entire hemisphere. So, what's the problem? It furthers the impression that we didn't exist or had no words for "us" or "we" or "her" or "continent" or "hemisphere" before 1492.

"Amerindians" was devised later as a term for all Indians throughout the Americas and to distinguish Indians here from the ones in India. The choice of some Indianists, mostly in governmental and anthropological businesses, it never gained wide usage, happily.

"Native Americans" was a well-meant effort from the 1960s to put aside "American Indians" and to introduce the concept of originating in this place. It carries the same problem as the latter term, implying that we just barely predate the coming of the Europeans. The other problem with "Native Americans" is that many non-Natives in the United States consider themselves Native Americans. In response to a 1980s questionnaire, a high number of delegates to the Republican and Democratic conventions checked the box marked "Native American." Nearly all were non-Natives who said in follow-up calls that they thought the term meant "born in the United States." Since they weren't immigrants, they said they were Native Americans.

A similar term, "First Americans," may have been well intended, but always sounds condescending. "First Americans" conveys the misimpression that we arrived ten minutes before the first boat from Europe. This is what manifest-destiny archeologists and anthropologists have been trying to prove for more than a century and are arguing today in the Kennewick Man case— that this hemisphere was totally empty until people started migrating across the Siberian land bridge and by sea from Europe and Polynesia. These scientists never make the case for migrations from Africa or for early travel by Indians in any direction. Their points are political, not scientific, and intended to prove that we were not native to this place and that "other immigrants" had the right to take the land because it wasn't really ours.

"First Nations" is the preferred term in Canada and enjoys some small support in the United States. First Nations people never warmed to "Native Canadians" or "Native Americans," which are commonly heard in Ottawa. "L'Indian Rouge," the term of choice in France, was iced by First Nations people, even those on the French side of the English-only campaign in Canada.

The positive aspect of "First Nations" is that it puts nations and sovereignty right out front. Its main negative is that it lacks the dimension of individual people.

"First" has the general problem identified earlier, and the broad connotation that what's ours is theirs. But, there is another way to look at "first," particularly when it's linked with "nations." There is a legal concept of first in time, first in right. In U.S. water law, Indian water rights are considered prior and paramount because we saw it, drank it, and splashed in it first.

In Central and South America, the despised word is "Indios." There are some who say that the lost Spaniards and Italians were not calling Native Peoples "Indios" as in people of India. Rather, this thinking goes, they were saying "in Dios," as in "of God," and admiring the children of God. This explains, no doubt, why priests and sailors killed and hacked off hands and feet of Indios who would not forsake their "Godless ways."

I don't buy the *in Dios* story and am not a fan of any version of "Indian." What set me against "Indian" was a conversation with the first Englishman I ever met, when I was twelve. "Indian," he asked, "are you a red Indian or one of our Indians?" It was like a trick question with no right answer.

The word "Indios" almost derailed the 1976 formation meeting of the World Council of Indigenous Peoples at Port Alberni, Canada. Delegates from Bolivia wanted to use "Indios" in the organization's title because, in this hemisphere's countries where Spanish and Portuguese are the main languages, the word may as well mean "dirty dog" or "peasant." They favored "Indios" because it identified and united us by our mutual oppression.

Delegates from outside this hemisphere—including the Sami who herd reindeer in Scandinavia and the Maori who ranch cattle in New Zealand—rejected the notion of being part of a group calling itself "Indios" or "Indians." The delegates from Australia told us that they preferred the term "Aboriginals" for themselves and the new group. They also were emphatic that it was never proper for anyone to call them "Aborigines."

"Indigenous Peoples" stands for tribal peoples worldwide. The United Nations declared the Year (1992) and then the Decade of Indigenous People. This set off a struggle among U.N. members about whether the latter word should be "people" or "peoples." Some countries wanted the word to be singular, so that it carried no recognition of sovereign or group rights. Others wanted it pluralized so as to include individuals and human rights, along with nations, tribes, and groups.

Although it sometimes sounded like a half-s argument, it was an important debate, one that the U.S. government is still having with itself. Proponents of the word *indigenous* like that its root is "gene," implying family and relatedness. This cuts the other way, too, suggesting race-based relationships, rather than political status and nationhood. In English, where the word is strongly connected to flora and fauna, *indigenous* connotes something closer to plants than to people.

It sounds somehow more dignified in Spanish—*Indigena*. I am told that the word in Latin America is used interchangeably with "Indio," but is more acceptable to Pueblos Indigena because, unlike "Indios," it is not synonymous with "primitive."

"Native Peoples" is the term I favor these days. "Native" places us here, with origins in our lands, and it has the pluralized "peoples" for both human beings and sovereignties. Its next-best attribute is that it's not any of the other terms.

So, what do we want to be called? The answer is, we are busy with cultural reclamation. We want to be called by our proper personal and tribal names. We do not want to be called "redskins," "squaws," or "savages," or to have any references to us in sports.

We have not gotten around to deciding what we want to call ourselves collectively, but that could change at any time.

Until then, thank you for thinking of us, especially in positive terms, and we'll get back to you on this.

Letter to Hassan

JOANNA KADI

Now is not a good time. You crept down the mountain in the too-large suit of your dead brother. The Israelis shot him precisely at noon. You clung to a cheap suitcase in your left hand, dreams in the right. Immigration is chess with a deadly twist. *Faceless key players orchestrate pawns.*

You kissed your mama you kissed your niece there being no one else left because the earth had swallowed them you picked up one foot then the other. In this fashion you arrived and found out how much you did not know. *All pawns sit in terror, mouths gaping. Although our dulled eyes decipher empty spaces on the other side of the board(er)(land), we cannot interpret this game. Sometimes we move at dizzying speeds, other times we sit and sit. Trying to outwait hunger and bombs.* You and I collided in dream land. Our only possible meeting place. You can't come here and I can't go there. You remind me of a second cousin. Always a tiny country, Lebanon shrinks again as pieces fall away. A greedy entity devours her. Israel cuts through and leaves a wake. I remember. My second cousin Hafed visited twenty years ago, proposed marriage to my sister. No, she said. He returned to south Lebanon the day of yet another Israeli bombardment. A quick demise, or lingering under the rubble? *This chess game with a deadly twist speeds up and slows down. Sometimes pawns move with dizzying speeds. More often than not we wait. Waiting destroys people.* I peered unblinkingly as you trudged steadily along the mountain path. I knew what you did not. Namely, traffic in pawns moves at a snail's pace. You clenched your fist around your flimsy valise and a wad of bills that to you seemed large. Always a tiny country, Lebanon contracts as another expands. You clutched a hopeful dream in your right hand. Hope is perilous when accompanied by ignorance. *When the faceless key player said This wad of bills is woefully small, when the faceless key player said You cannot slide across to the empty space on the other side, you did not know what to do and neither did I.* Once again you folded back the too-long sleeves of your brother's one suit. The Israelis gunned him down as he pruned olive trees. Threats to security lie everywhere and no pawn must be left unturned. You walked and I followed. We slip through in our dreams, more so than in waking life. Our hands could not mark each other although the same spot of brown earth absorbed our tears. Arab tears have become cheap like Arab lives. *The chess game has slowed to a halt even though many openings call from the other side of the board. Those in charge don't care. They never will.* I walked and you followed. The possibilities for dream connections surprise me. Memories of dead brothers marked our trail. As a pawn on the other side of the board I could do no more than slide through to you and Lebanon in the night. *Now is not a good time.*

This piece first appeared in *Mizna: A Journal of Arab-American Literature.*

Parasites and Pioneers: Antisemitism in White Supremacist America

MATTHEW NEMIROFF LYONS

Preface

I wrote "Parasites and Pioneers" between 1989 and 1993, almost ten years before the publication of *Sing, Whisper, Shout Pray!*[*] It reflects my thinking—as well as the political events and intellectual discussions—of that time. I still hold to its core approach and arguments: The U.S. system of racial oppression has sometimes defined Jews as White and sometimes as non-White, and these shifts have alternately dampened, fueled, and again dampened anti-Jewish discrimination and violence. But becoming White has involved losing Jewish culture and internalizing anti-Jewish stereotypes, processes that have especially targeted Jewish women. Also, White privilege does not necessarily protect Jews against antisemitic scapegoating and in some ways may reinforce it, because stereotypes of the privileged, powerful Jew are central to such scapegoating.

Untangling these issues remains vitally important not just for the sake of historical clarity, but to strengthen our work against oppression, and to explore and honor the complexity of who we are as individuals, as communities, and as a society.

Yet there are many things I would change if I were writing "Parasites" today. A number of points strike me now as oversimplified or outdated, and of course the essay could not take account of scholarship since it was written. Without going into exhaustive detail, this preface will touch on some of the essay's major gaps and limitations as I see them now.

An important theme in "Parasites" is the immediate danger the neonazi

---

[*] In preparing "Parasites and Pioneers" for this book, I made a few factual corrections, improvements in phrasing, and stylistic changes to the text, and consolidated the notes slightly. Otherwise the essay that follows the preface remains unchanged from the form previously intended for publication.

A few of the stylistic changes deserve explanation because they are more or less nonstandard. I capitalize *White* where it refers to an ethnoracial group, in the same way that I capitalize *Black* or *Native American*. I spell *antisemitism* without a hyphen or capital "S" because the term means the targeting of Jews, not of "Semites." This contrasts, for example, with *anti-Catholicism,* which targets Catholics, an actual group of people. I spell *neonazi* as distinct from *neo-Nazi* because to me *nazism* refers to a general political category, while *Nazism* refers specifically to Hitler's National Socialist Party and the ideology and system associated with it. This parallels the standard distinction between *fascism,* referring to a general category, and *Fascism,* referring to Mussolini's organization and regime in Italy.

Right posed for Jews in the early 1990s. The situation looks a bit different ten years later. Aryan Nations, the leading neonazi group of the nineties, has virtually collapsed, and other groups have declined or been placed on the defensive. Yet the factors that helped the neonazi movement grow remain widespread, and it is likely that far Right groups of one sort or another will see a resurgence in the foreseeable future.

"Parasites" did not anticipate the brief but explosive growth of the Patriot/armed militia movement in the mid-1990s. The militias and the Patriot movement were never a mere front for neonazis, as some critics claimed, but neonazis were a significant part of the movement's hodge-podge of survivalists, libertarians, Christian theocrats, and far rightists of various kinds. Antisemitic themes—explicit and veiled, intentional and unintentional—heavily influenced Patriot movement warnings about an elite plot to impose a tyrannical world government. These ideas circulated widely among the movement's millions of adherents. The armed militia wing of the Patriot movement shrank in the late 1990s, but this decline left a core of militia activists who were more zealous and more bigoted.

If I were writing "Parasites" now I would say more about the Christian Right, whose agenda centers on reinforcing heterosexual male dominance and traditional gender roles. Already a vast movement in the 1980s, the Christian Right in the nineties deepened and expanded its grassroots organizing through initiatives such as Pat Robertson's Christian Coalition. At the same time, tensions developed within the movement between pragmatists such as Robertson, committed to winning political power through the Republican Party, and hard-liners who demanded theocratic control over all areas of society. Hard-liners spearheaded a series of assassinations and other terrorist attacks against abortion providers. Yet all wings of the Christian Right were influenced by *dominionism,* a call for Christian men to take control of political and cultural institutions and exercise dominion over sinful secular society. Dominionism is inherently anti-Jewish and a direct threat to all non-Christians and all advocates of an open, pluralistic society.

Another problem in "Parasites" is that its broad-brush historical analysis oversimplifies some concepts and discussions. For example, the essay offers a one-sided treatment of the "cult of true womanhood." It's true, as "Parasites" notes, that this nineteenth-century doctrine tightened the social rules restricting middle-class women to the domestic sphere. The true womanhood doctrine arose just as the domestic sphere was shrinking, with the removal of productive tasks such as spinning and weaving to workplaces outside the home. However, there is another side to this that "Parasites" failed to address. As a number of women's historians have shown, many nineteenth-century women also used the cult of true womanhood to justify their social and political activism, arguing that their domestic role as nurturers and educators required them to take an active role in civic life. This approach to activism resonates in interesting ways with the work of twentieth-century Jewish women such as Clara Lemlich Shavelson, a labor activist who turned to organizing working-class wives and mothers after becoming a wife and mother herself.[1]

"Parasites" also oversimplifies when it suggests that antisemitism may intensify "in the event of a major economic crisis." Economic distress is only one of several factors that can fuel antisemitism. Other factors include a backlash against social, cultural, or political change; fear of losing traditional status and privileges; a sense of disempowerment in the face of massive public and private bureaucracies; and the existence of anti-Jewish organizing and propaganda networks. All of these contributed, for example, to the rise of the Patriot movement in the 1990s. Economic crisis and hardship have played little or no role in the growth of the Christian Right, whose core support has been among prosperous, middle-class suburbanites.

However, economic grievances sometimes do feed antisemitism, and Jews' concentration in positions of relative privilege outside the centers of power increases our vulnerability to scapegoating, as "Parasites" argues. A similar kind of scapegoating is at work when Korean or Arab shopkeepers in poor communities are targeted as major representatives of the oppressive power structure. Unfortunately, "Parasites" relies on twenty-five-year-old statistics about Jews' roles in the economy, and so this part of the argument needs to be updated.

Since writing "Parasites," I have become more cautious about using leftist jargon words such as "imperialism," "ruling class," and "labor aristocracy," which express valid and important concepts but may distract many readers from the intended meaning unless they are explained carefully. I've also learned to question the term "cheap labor," which "Parasites" presents as a simple, straightforward concept. No person's labor is inherently cheap. Rather, oppression compels some workers to accept less money for their labor. Unless this is addressed directly, the term "cheap labor" runs the risk of victim-blaming.

"Parasites" describes U.S. society as an example of *settlerism*. The concept of settlerism is helpful because it explains the combination of rigid racial caste divisions and weak or nonexistent remnants of precapitalist society. Most theories of racial oppression ignore this combination, but it is vital for understanding why antisemitism developed differently in the United States than it did in Europe. However, the concept of settlerism carries a lot of baggage. It was largely developed by revolutionary nationalists such as J. Sakai, who claimed that all people of color in the United States constitute separate oppressed nations or national minorities.[2] I disagree with this claim but did not address it in "Parasites."

Sakai rightly emphasized that White privilege brings not just an illusion of superiority, but also concrete benefits that people of color generally do not enjoy. But Sakai tended to present this as a simple matter of White workers enjoying higher wages, better working conditions, and more opportunities to acquire property than do workers of color. That has often been true, but I question whether it has always been true. White privilege has involved a shifting mix of political, legal, social, cultural, educational, and economic benefits, and implying that this mix can be reduced to economics only weakens the argument "Parasites" tries to present.

Sakai criticized efforts to romanticize White labor activism in the United States, detailing the long history of White working-class complicity in oppressing people of color. But he interpreted this history in a one-sided way, claiming that settler privilege has eliminated any genuine White working class. Far more descriptive and useful is the argument that White workers hold an essentially *contradictory* status in the United States, being both relatively privileged to various degrees and also exploited. The Sojourner Truth Organization, a Midwest-based Marxist group, advanced this position in the 1970s.

Although the settlerism model remains valuable for contrasting the U.S. and European contexts, today I would combine it with other models of racial oppression. Historical scholarship on Whiteness broadened dramatically in the 1990s. Works by Theodore W. Allen, Noel Ignatiev, Ian F. Haney López, and others showed how U.S. society has created and periodically reshaped Whiteness as the dominant racial category. Each of these writers treats racial oppression as a core feature of the United States that offers European Americans concrete social privileges, but they don't reduce this to economics or trivialize the major divisions that also exist within White society, such as class. These historical studies are part of a larger emerging field of scholarship on Whiteness, encompassing work in sociology, women's studies, cultural studies, and other disciplines. This discussion (like much good scholarship generally) has been stimulated by interchange between academia and people active in a range of social movements.[3]

The most relevant historical work of this kind is Karen Brodkin's book, *How Jews Became White Folks and What That Says about Race in America*. Like Allen, Ignatiev, and Haney López, Brodkin explores the nature of Whiteness and of race in general by looking at a moment when race categories originated or changed. Unlike these other authors, Brodkin pays special attention to women's experiences and how gender, race, and class affect each other, and she focuses, of course, on Jews. Ranging from memories of her own childhood to "the metaorganization of American capitalism," *How Jews Became White Folks* offers a rich and engaging historical analysis.

Brodkin describes Jewish ethnic identity in the early twentieth century—when Jews in the United States were predominantly working class and defined as "not quite white"—with special focus on Jewish socialism's defining role for the community and on the gap between Jewish womanhood and dominant White ideals. In showing how Jews and other Southern and Eastern European ethnics became White after World War II, Brodkin concentrates on the GI Bill of Rights and related federal programs. She describes the GI Bill as "the most massive affirmative action program in American history," and one that mainly helped men of European origin. During the 1950s and 1960s, Brodkin argues, Jewish intellectuals fashioned "a new, hegemonic version of Jewishness" that was male-centered and that portrayed Jews as a model minority of hard work and family values. She also traces many ways that Jews in this period expressed ambivalence about Jewishness, Whiteness, and the costs of mainstream acceptance.[4]

My own work over the past decade has focused less on Jews' changing racial status and more on the issue of scapegoating. I spent most of the 1990s working with Chip Berlet on the book *Right-Wing Populism in America: Too Close for Comfort.*[5] The book looks at movements that have combined phony or distorted anti-elitism with campaigns to intensify oppression. For example, the Jacksonians of the early nineteenth century loudly denounced "the money power" and helped propertyless White men win the vote, but they also sharpened racism against Black people and American Indians and glorified laissez faire capitalism. Such movements partly exploit legitimate grievances but channel them in ways that reinforce social hierarchies. Some, but not all, of these movements have promoted antisemitic scapegoating—particularly the myth of an evil, superpowerful Jewish conspiracy.

Right-Wing Populism in America includes detailed discussions of several antisemitic movements and organizations, including the 1920s Ku Klux Klan, Henry Ford's propaganda campaign and industrial empire, the fascist and ultraconservative movements of the 1930s, and the neonazi, Christian Right, and Patriot/militia movements of recent years. In some cases, these discussions correct distortions or oversimplifications in "Parasites." (For example, the 1920s Ku Klux Klan was stridently Protestant but not particularly tied to Protestant fundamentalism, and only some of the antisemitic right-wing movements of the 1930s can properly be described as fascist.)

This is a painful, scary time. I wrote most of "Parasites" in 1990–1991, and the essay closes with reflections on the U.S.-led war against Iraq—a war that has not ended, as U.S.-imposed sanctions still kill thousands of Iraqi children every month. But I write now in the aftermath of September 11, 2001, when four teams of hijackers brought sudden mass murder to New York; Washington, DC; and Pennsylvania. Since September 11, the U.S. government has embarked on a new round of war, this time centered on Afghanistan. Parallels with the campaign against Iraq are numerous and vivid: the demonization of brutal ultrarightists previously supported by the United States; the lies that proclaim America's love for freedom and hide the United States' own terrorist crimes; the thinly veiled drive to control oil supplies; the bombing campaigns and "accidental" civilian deaths; the increased attacks on civil liberties in the United States; and the surge of violence and harassment against Muslim, Middle Eastern, and South Asian people, including friends of mine.

Antisemitism is a secondary but real issue in this mix, as it was in the Gulf War. After September 11, articles circulated widely on the Internet suggesting that Jews (specifically, the Israeli secret service) secretly orchestrated the hijacking attacks. Many far rightists blamed Jews indirectly, treating the September 11 crimes as retribution for the U.S. alliance with Israel and supposed Jewish dominance over U.S. foreign policy. At the same time, some portrayals of the conflict exploited fears of antisemitism to help justify U.S. militarism or attacks on Muslim and Arab people.[6]

Antisemitism, both real and fictitious, also figures in the deepening catastrophe of the Israeli-Palestinian conflict. Anti-Jewish bigotry is a reality among some Palestinians and their supporters, yet the charge of antisemitism is too often pinned on legitimate criticisms of Israeli rule. Random violence against Israeli Jewish civilians has no justification, yet U.S. accounts often portray such violence in ways that mask or justify the Israeli state's greater and far more systematic violence against Palestinians.

In organizing against war and bigotry, questions of antisemitism present complex challenges for both Jews and non-Jews. For example, when and how do we name ourselves as Jews? Where do Jews "fit" in discussions of diversity, coalition-building, or social justice, or discussions of U.S. Mideast policy? When do claims of antisemitism enable Jews to avoid dealing with our White privilege? When do Jews become convenient targets of blame, onto which non-Jewish Whites can shift their own responsibility for racism?

Seventeen days after the September 11 mass killings, my grandfather died. Leo Nemiroff deeply embodied the radical humanism—salted by pain, leavened with humor—that is central to my family's heritage of Jewish culture. Leo was one of my most important teachers. As a teenager first exploring radical politics, I treasured the long talks with Leo about history and theory and the sometimes bitter lessons of past struggles. Leo encouraged me to hope and work for a better world, but he taught me also to keep questioning, and to beware any movement or organization that claims to have all the answers. For that and everything else, Leo, *spasibo*, thank you. This preface and the essay that follows are dedicated to your memory.

M.N.L.
October 2001

>€   >€   >€

Introduction

Once again, hatred of Jews has become a major force on the far Right in the United States—more so than at any time since World War II. For decades, Ku Klux Klansmen and neonazis had talked about merging their two movements, and in the 1980s it finally started to happen. Old style, segregationist Klan factions stagnated or went under, while new organizations like the Aryan Nations, the Order, and White Aryan Resistance (WAR) drew fresh strength by fusing White supremacy with fascist ideology and goals. Estimates place the movement's core membership in the tens of thousands, with perhaps ten times as many supporters.[7] "The new strategy is not to put people in their place; it is not to make a sub-class out of them and to exploit, or super-exploit, their labor. It is genocidal. It is exterminationist."[8] To groups that embrace this doctrine, people of color are "subhumans" corrupting White society through race mixing, while gays and lesbians undermine supposedly natural sex roles and the reproduction of the White race. And behind them stand the Jews, who secretly wield vast power in a plot to control the world.

The LaRouchian fascist movement, which has avoided an open White supremacist focus, also grew during the 1980s and early nineties, building a major fundraising, espionage, and electoral network. Masked by populist rhetoric and obscure code words, scapegoating of Jews form the core of Lyndon LaRouche's doctrine.[9]

To all antifascists who take the far Right seriously, these developments mean that analyzing and fighting antisemitism are important not only morally, but also strategically. Jew-hatred is not, as some have argued, just an archaic prejudice slowly on its way out; it is once again a useful organizing tool for the most vicious political organizations in the country. And in a

period when millions of people have shown support for Christian fundamentalism, it is difficult to dismiss this as a lunatic fringe phenomenon that
cannot spread.

Both the limits and the extent of antisemitism deserve careful attention.
Jews in this country do not face institutionalized discrimination, exclusion,
or exploitation, except in extremely limited spheres. Most of us do not, as
Jews, face the systematized, everyday violence meted out to women, people
of color, or gays and lesbians. Open hostility to Jews is taboo in many
sections of our society. But stereotyping and prejudice remain common, even
among progressive-minded people. Anti-Jewish threats, harassment, and
physical attacks are reported regularly in all regions of the country. Jewish
culture is widely invalidated or rendered invisible. And some forms of open
antisemitism—notably JAP-baiting, which targets Jewish women—have
won disturbingly wide acceptance.

Why has antisemitism been stronger or more organized in some periods
and locations than in others? Is Jews' oppression a form of racism or is it
something different? How can Jews hold White privilege and be targets of
antisemitism at the same time?

These questions cannot be answered in the abstract, or within the limits of
one's personal experience. We need to look at the historical context and
processes involved. One obstacle to understanding antisemitism in the
United States, I believe, is that we have too often relied on a European
yardstick to measure the problem here. Judging North American Jews' experience against the thousand-year horror of Europe, some people have
declared the United States a benign exception where Jew-hatred need not be
taken seriously. Others have collapsed the United States and Europe into one
entity, implying that it is simply luck that has shielded Jews here from
pogroms and mass murder.[10]

I will look at Jews' oppression in the context of three factors: class, gender,
and race. The politics of class and gender have been intimately linked to anti-
semitism since its beginnings. The politics of race set Jews' experiences in the
United States apart from those in Europe. Within the U.S. framework of
White supremacy, Jews have sometimes been positioned above, and
sometimes below the color line, and this shifting status has dramatically
affected the degree and nature of The United States inherited antisemitic traditions from Europe, where Jews had long been marginalized within the
Christian feudal order. But here antisemitism entered a different context: *settlerism,* the new society created as millions of Europeans overran the
continent. Through the late nineteenth century, settlerism in the United
States mitigated the traditional dynamics of anti-Jewish persecution in two

ways: (1) by building capitalist society "on fresh ground," so that institutional vestiges of feudalism and Christian theocracy could not survive as they did in much of Europe; and (2) by defining Jews from the beginning as "White"— i.e., as members of the privileged settler population.

Between about 1880 and 1940 the racial hierarchy was in flux, as millions of culturally alien immigrants from Europe—including Jews—formed an intermediate group above people of color but below people of northwest European origin. Anti-Jewish hostility rose sharply but temporarily during this period, declining as most Jews were integrated into White society. (A small number of Jews in the United States today are people of color, many of them "Oriental" Jews.) Loss of traditional culture has been the lasting price of White privilege for Jews and many other European immigrant groups. But antisemitism persists and has the potential to get worse again. Following the traditional European pattern, Jews have tended to fill roles as visible agents of the power structure, which makes us particularly vulnerable to scapegoating in times of crisis.

My analysis draws on several currents of political thought, each of which has its own strengths and weaknesses. The work of Jewish feminists over the past two decades has been invaluable in exposing both blatant and subtle forms of antisemitism today—including anti-Jewish attitudes among some feminists and leftists—and has provided important insights into relationships between antisemitism and other forms of oppression, notably homophobia, sexism, and racism.[11]

On the class dynamics of Jews' oppression, I have been influenced by several Marxist studies of antisemitism, beginning with Abram Leon's book, *The Jewish Question: A Marxist Interpretation*. As other Marxist historians have pointed out, Leon tends towards economic reductionism. But his theory of a Jewish *people-class* offers a healthy counterweight to the ideological and psychological determinism common in liberal discussions of Jews' oppression.[12]

My discussion of settlerism as a key feature of United States society draws on revolutionary nationalist thought, especially J. Sakai's *Settlers: The Mythology of the White Proletariat*. In critiquing the view that racism can be reduced to a "bad idea," Sakai elucidates the material reality of White privilege, the differences between settler society and colonialist Europe, and the transition process that many European immigrants have faced in order to become White.[13]

Background: Antisemitism in Europe

Religious antisemitism developed in Europe under the Christian theocracy of the Middle Ages. The Church persecuted Jews as Christ-killers. Jews were portrayed as materialistic, scheming, deceitful, cowardly, bloodthirsty, smelly, and repulsive. They were defined as sexually threatening or deviant: Jewish women as aggressive whores, Jewish men as effeminate beings who menstruated as punishment for refusing to accept Christ. Medieval anti-semitism was closely intertwined with misogyny and the witch persecutions. (Christianity blamed witchcraft on women's supposedly defective nature.) Both witches and Jews were labeled agents of the Devil who parodied Christian rituals, defiled sacraments, poisoned wells, and murdered children. Just as Jewish men were degraded by associating them with female-ness, the witches' gathering was called *Sabbat* and *synagogue* to link it with "demonic" Jewish ritual.[14]

Feudal law restricted Jews to so-called nonproductive jobs such as merchant and moneylender. Thus they became a people-class—an ethnically distinct community identified with a specific economic niche. There were non-Jewish creditors as well, and many Jews who were not moneylenders or merchants, but money and commerce professions took on a central, defining role for Jewish communities as a whole. Some Jews prospered in these occu-pations, but their status was always shaky. Christian kings and nobles relied on Jews for commerce and credit, but if their debts got too big, religious zeal gave them an excuse to throw the Jews out and seize their wealth. During a social or political crisis, Jews became handy scapegoats to deflect the people's anger away from the Christian rulers. Many peasant revolts involved massacres of Jews. Thus Jews faced repeated cycles of tolerance, persecution, and expulsion.[15]

With the rise of capitalism and modern nation-states, Jews were forced out of their traditional commercial niche. Racial antisemitism began to emerge as early as the fifteenth century and took clear shape in the nineteenth century, as part of the "scientific" theories of race that Europeans were devel-oping to justify their intensified conquests in Africa and Asia. Before, Jews had been attacked as nonbelievers who could save their souls by converting to Christianity. Now Jewishness was declared a permanently imprinted evil essence. European racism defined Jews (unlike many of the colonized peoples) not as a useful, inferior group to be exploited, but as a parasitic threat with no productive role in society.

Through documents such as the phony *Protocols of the Elders of Zion,* racial antisemitism depicted a hidden, superpowerful, international Jewish conspir-acy bent on world conquest. Racial antisemitism identified the Jews with "parasitic" finance capital—as opposed to "productive" industrial capital. Thus it represented a vulgarized critique of capitalism: a "socialism of fools."[16]

The United States: Antisemitism and Settlerism

The United States has been a place of relative safety for Jews, where anti-semitism has loomed periodically, but has never approached the violence or intensity it reached in medieval and modern Europe. At the root of this difference, I believe, is the way that settlerism has shaped U.S. society: a European American empire built on conquered land, in large part with the labor of conquered peoples.

On many of the lands they colonized around the world, Europeans imposed only a small garrison force to rule over the native people. In North America, as in Australia, South Africa, and some other areas, they created a wholly new society, moving in by the millions and clearing the existing societies out of the way. Settlerist expansion in the continental United States region took place steadily from 1607 until the end of the nineteenth century, as the rapidly growing European American population displaced and massacred Native Americans, conquered the northern half of Mexico, and imported millions of Africans as slave laborers. Since then, many key features of settlerism have persisted, although transformed by industrialization and the rise of modern imperialism.[17]

Settlerism created a new, "pure" capitalist society. In Europe, antisemitism developed under feudalism, a system in which commerce was marginal and political authority was explicitly Christian. European capitalism grew out of the contradictions within feudal society. In many European countries, such as Germany, vestiges of feudalism persisted long into the modern capitalist era. Jews were often caught in the middle in the struggle between the feudal and capitalist orders. The United States, however, has been capitalist from the start, and has no feudal past or traditions. As one consequence of this, separation of church and state was quickly established as a principle of the U.S. political system. Although the U.S. government has in fact restricted religious freedoms for some groups (such as American Indians), religious Jews have been free to practice their faith.

Since at least the late seventeenth century, the line between people of European descent and people of color has always been more rigid and violent than any divisions between European American ethnic groups. The conquest of Native America and the enslavement of Africans led to an ideology of White superiority and a system of White privileges. At a time when European peasants were being pushed off the land into the cities, settler expansion made cheap land available in North America.[18] Long before the profits of imperialism created an economically privileged "labor aristocracy" in Europe, super-exploitation of Black, Mexican, and Chinese workers created a large White labor aristocracy in the United States. This material and cultural division within the working class has offered capitalists a safety valve for deflecting class struggle away from themselves. In this context Jews' traditional function as scapegoats for the rulers has been less important.

Settlerism has intensified gender oppression, while White fears of supposed sexual transgression have fueled efforts to strengthen the color line. For women of color, White supremacy has meant a long history of rape and sexual exploitation by White men, combined with stereotypes of lustfulness and promiscuity on the one hand, strength and sexlessness on the other. For White women, racism has often been the rationale for so-called protection in the form of constricted roles and intensified subordination.[19]

White supremacy has sometimes stereotyped men of color as sexually aggressive and dangerous—such as in the colonial-era stories of Indian warriors kidnapping settler women, as well as the Black rapist myth dating from the late nineteenth century. In other cases it has stereotyped them as sexless, or as effeminate—such as Chinese men in late nineteenth-century California, who were portrayed as Blacks in women's garments and forcibly restricted to restaurant and laundry work (cooking and washing).[20]

Jewish immigrants, both female and male, have faced strong pressures to conform to White gender roles and family structures. Sexual stereotypes of Jews inherited from Europe have been compounded by the clash between "Old World" and "New World" cultures. Based on traits adapted to life in Eastern Europe, Jewish women have been labeled as too masculine, Jewish men too feminine.

Settlerism has also set up a pattern of nativist hostility to foreigners. White privilege is a valuable item, and in the United States it has not been automatically available even to all Europeans. Employers have exploited many European immigrant groups as sources of cheap labor, while the native-born White working and middle classes have repeatedly attacked immigrants' cultures, assaulted them physically, and campaigned for their exclusion. Irish immigrants, for example, faced nativist racism in the mid-nineteenth century, combined with anti-Catholic scapegoating that strongly paralleled traditional Jew-hatred. Unlike the oppression of people of color, however, most discrimination against European national minority groups has been temporary. Through Americanization, the Irish and other Europeans could become White—the price of White privilege was giving up most of one's traditional culture.

Jews' oppression in the United States has involved a combination of European American nativism and traditional antisemitism. Thus anti-Jewish discrimination reached its peak during and shortly after the mass European immigration of the late nineteenth and early twentieth centuries. Americanization, a process most Jews had undergone by the mid-twentieth century, had contradictory effects: It reduced discrimination against Jews by attacking Jewish culture. It brought millions of Jews middle-class prosperity, but in the process drew many of them into highly visible positions as agents of the power structure. Thus Jews have remained vulnerable to the deeper current of anti-semitic prejudice and ideology that has persisted below the social surface and on the fringes of political life.

Colonial Period to Civil War

The first Jewish immigrants to North America were predominantly affluent Sephardic Jews from Spain, Portugal, and their American colonies, where Judaism was forbidden. Jews faced special restrictions in many of the British colonies, such as bans on voting or holding office, but—unlike Jews in most of Europe—they were usually allowed to practice their religion and run their communities without state interference. The Declaration of Independence and the Bill of Rights strengthened the principle of religious equality. Many states were slow to put the principle into effect. (New Hampshire, the last holdout, did not grant Jewish men the right to vote until 1877.) But local discriminatory policies found no endorsement at the federal level.

Between 1840 and 1870 the Jewish population in the United States rose from fifteen thousand to 170 thousand. Most of the newcomers were German-speaking Jews from Central Europe, who faced special restrictions, taxes, and economic hardships at home. They were part of a large mid-nineteenth-century influx of Germans to North America, and frequently lived among Christians in German communities across the United States. The German Jews were predominantly lower middle class upon arrival; many of them prospered here in skilled crafts and small businesses, especially retail trades. The newcomers included many single women who often worked as schoolteachers, domestic servants, or sales clerks. The German Jews moved with the frontier and established trading centers in small towns across the Northeast, Midwest, Far West, and South. Reform Judaism, which by the 1880s was the dominant sect among German Jews in the United States, was at that time an assimilationist movement to Westernize or "rationalize" Jewish worship. Reform leaders declared that Jewishness was strictly a religious matter, part of the private sphere. Partly because of pressure from Jewish women, they introduced some changes allowing women greater opportunities to participate, such as abolishing segregated worship.[21]

But German Jews entered U.S. society at a time when the sphere considered proper for White women was shrinking. Many productive tasks that women had traditionally performed in the home, such as making cloth and clothing, were being industrialized. Many occupations previously open to women were being closed off. The "cult of true womanhood," which began to take shape in the 1830s, imposed new, rigid standards of feminine respectability. The "true woman" must be delicate, submissive, pious; her sphere was the home and family. Since this ideology evolved as growing numbers of poor immigrant and, later, Black women were becoming wage workers, it sharpened class and race distinctions and represented the restrictive side of White privilege for women. The true womanhood cult placed special pressures for conformity on Jewish immigrant women, who were outsiders with a long history of isolation, seeking acceptance into White middle-class society.[22]

Traditional antisemitic prejudices, such as the Shylock stereotype of the rich, greedy, cruel Jew, were indeed widespread during this period. But most discriminatory laws had been removed by the 1830s and, until the 1870s, Jews encountered only sporadic hostility and discrimination. By and large they were accepted as a part of the United States' prosperous, rapidly expanding settler society. As the editors of one frontier newspaper wrote in 1851:

> In vain have nations and sects hurled anathemas against...the Jew....
> He belonged to a superior race....He was a WHITE man—he was of
> the God-appointed, ruling, progressive race of humanity, for such all
> nature, all experience, all the philosophy of facts, and the attestations
> of religion, prove the white race to be.[23]

But White privilege did not entirely protect Jews from antisemitism. Upwardly mobile Jews, ironically, "met a distrust that spread along with their increasing assimilation."[24] Traditional antisemitic fears revived and mingled with new stereotypes of the Jewish nouveau riche. During the Civil War, Jews were suspected of secretly trading with the enemy, which at one point caused General Grant of the U.S. Army to expel all Jews from the area under his command. (President Lincoln immediately rescinded the order.) In the 1870s, wealthy Jews began to be barred from hotels and summer resorts. Combined with nativism, this discrimination would soon spread to other spheres.

Mass Immigration and the Nativist Response

Like Western Europe, the United States received large numbers of Eastern European Jewish immigrants in the late nineteenth and early twentieth centuries. In both places, this was a time of profound social change, including imperialist conquests overseas, rapid industrialization, the growth of cities, the beginnings of commercialism, and shifts in roles for women and men. In both places, a sharp antisemitic reaction ensued, as Jews provided a convenient scapegoat for social and political grievances. But the United States, unlike Western Europe, was already internally divided along racial lines. White supremacist violence intensified during this period, including mass lynchings of African Americans and a campaign of terror to drive out Chinese workers. The logic of the United States' racial hierarchy both stimulated and restricted the anti-Jewish reaction.

The forms of White rule in late nineteenth-century America dictated capitalism's need for immigrant European labor. "Neither the family farms of the Midwest nor the plantations of the South—even after these shifted from slavery to sharecropping—had the capacity to generate the kind of massive labor surplus needed for rapid industrial growth."[25] Native-born White workers were concentrated in the skilled trades, from which most Blacks, American Indians, Mexicans, and Asians were forcibly excluded. In agriculture, service work, and in some cases mining, people of color provided much of the economic substratum on which an industrial society could be built, but not until World War I would they be admitted to factory work in substantial numbers.

Immigration from Southern and Eastern Europe—particularly including that of Italians, Slavs, Hungarians, and Finns as well as Jews—offered the necessary work force. This "new" immigration wave began in the 1880s and soon outstripped the "old" immigration of Germans, British, Irish, and Scandinavians. About fifteen million new immigrants arrived between the 1880s and the beginning of World War I in 1914, including two million Jews. Southern and Eastern Europeans provided cheap industrial labor in the factory towns of the Northeast and Midwest. By 1909, they constituted over one-third of the work force in the United States' main industries.[26]

Jewish immigrants differed from other newcomer groups in several ways. They came fleeing not only poverty, but also pogroms and government persecution. Unlike most of the other new immigrants, who came from backgrounds in farming or unskilled labor, few of the Eastern European Jews had worked the land, while many had experience in skilled crafts and business. These backgrounds would help Jews to advance economically in the United States. Many Jews also brought with them years of political experience in the radical movements of Eastern Europe.

The Jewish immigrants also included an unusually high percentage of women. During the period 1899–1909, for example, about 43 percent of Jewish arrivals were female, in contrast to only 24 percent of other Eastern and Southern European immigrant groups.[27] Jewish women brought a strong tradition of assertiveness, economic initiative, and business responsibility from Eastern Europe, where they often played the leading role in supporting and managing the household. This clashed directly with the United States' true womanhood ideal. In the United States, young Jewish women joined the wage work force in large numbers, and many were active in the labor movement and other political efforts. Immigrant Jewish men, meanwhile, often bore a gentle, dreamy, soft-spoken image based on a traditional male emphasis on spiritual reflection and scholarship, which did not fit with U.S. standards of masculinity. Thus Eastern European Jews threatened White American gender boundaries, perhaps more than did other European immigrant groups.

But upon arrival in the United States, most of the Jews shared with other new immigrants a harsh life shaped largely by working-class status. Wage work meant low pay, long hours, monotonous tasks, and difficult and often dangerous conditions. For women these problems were compounded by sex discrimination, often including sexual harassment on the job. Outside the workplace, conditions were often equally harsh.

Like the Irish in the mid-nineteenth century, Southern and Eastern Europeans were widely defined as racially inferior, and occupied a middle position economically and socially: below native-born Whites and immigrants from Northwestern Europe, but above Asians, Blacks, Mexicans, and American Indians. Supposedly, Finns were "Mongolians," Slavs and Hungarians were "Huns," and even Italians were descended from "Asiatic hordes."[28] Such claims, combining traditional nativism with new racial doctrines from Europe, enabled Whites to protect the color line upon which their own privilege depended. Unlike the racial categories imposed on Blacks, Indians, Mexicans, and Asians, however, the new immigrants' non-White status was ambiguous, controversial, and temporary.

Discrimination and attacks against the new immigrants were widespread. Italians were a prime target of nativist violence. Catholic, impoverished, more than half of them illiterate, sometimes relatively dark-skinned, Italian immigrants were stereotyped as bloodthirsty criminals, and lynched in town after town through the 1890s. Southern Whites particularly feared Italians as a threat to the racial order. In Louisiana, five Sicilians were murdered for associating with Blacks "nearly on terms of equality."[29]

Mass immigration and the nativist upsurge coincided with important changes in European American gender roles and family structure. The cult of true womanhood was in crisis as growing numbers of women moved into the world outside the home. The number of European American and European immigrant women in wage work doubled between 1890 and 1910. Although initially concentrated in fields defined as women's work, such as domestic service, increasingly these women went into factory and, a bit later, office work. Often technological changes in production coincided with a shift from male to female employees, as women were favored for many unskilled tasks—and paid less than men.[30]

But the shift out from the home included "not only single working-class women who held jobs, but also millions of middle-class women, single and married, who joined women's clubs, social reform groups, and suffragist chapters."[31] Social critics blamed women's movement into traditional male spheres for many social problems, both real and imagined, such as a rising divorce rate, decreasing family size, a decline in so-called traditional values, and the spread of prostitution.

Nativism and efforts to preserve female domesticity represented parallel defensive reactions to rapid social change. The two ideologies flowed together in several important political campaigns, such as the "race suicide" propaganda that peaked during the first decade of the twentieth century. Eugenicists warned of a high birthrate among Southern and Eastern Europeans and a declining birthrate among native-born Whites—usually blamed on women shirking their motherly duties. There were also close parallels between the campaigns to restrict immigration and to limit women's entry into the job market. "Protective" labor legislation excluded women from many occupations—based on claims that women were naturally weak and vulnerable—in order to protect men's jobs, wages, and economic control over wives and daughters. Similarly, immigration restrictionists accused the new immigrants of lacking racial fitness. Working- and middle-class Whites, who often feared the newcomers as competitors for jobs or fomenters of class conflict, increasingly supported immigration restriction. Industrialists tended to oppose it—because they benefited from cheap immigrant labor—while favoring efforts to Americanize the immigrants to undercut their political radicalism. The big capitalists softened their opposition after World War I, when large numbers of Black and Mexican farmers began to move northward and offer new sources of cheap labor, and in 1921 and 1924 Congress sharply reduced all immigration from Eastern and Southern Europe.[32]

While nativism and sexism were contributing factors, the antisemitic wave they helped to stimulate targeted all Jews—women and men, immigrant and native-born alike. From the 1880s on, there were periodic demonstrations, riots, and assaults against Jews and their property. In the early 1890s, mob attacks in New Jersey and Louisiana forced many Jews to flee.[33] Discrimination trickled downward from the wealthy social clubs and hotels, and was increasingly designed to block Jewish entry into the middle class. In the 1890s and 1900s, Jews were barred from private schools, university faculties, housing, and jobs. Later, as Jews flooded into colleges after World War I, many universities established quotas limiting the number of Jewish students.[34]

In the 1890s, for the first time, the Jewish banker became an important theme in U.S. politics. The agrarian People's Party (Populist Party) opposed the monetary gold standard as part of its radical-reform program. Since Jews were commonly identified with gold, some reformers, such as Ignatius Donnelly and William Jennings Bryan, vulgarized the Populist program by blaming rich Jews. Fears of a Jewish plot to wreck the economy peaked during the severe depression of 1893. Such fears recurred during the depression of 1914, the recessions of the early 1920s, and the Great Depression of the 1930s. As in Europe, anti-Jewish scapegoating tended to be strongest in times of socioeconomic crisis.[35]

Fear of Jews, of foreigners, and of women's movement out of the home all converged in the early twentieth-century campaigns against organized prostitution under the label White slavery. Ideas connecting Jews and prostitution in this period show how persistent were the old stereotypes of Jewish sexuality:

> Outside the Jewish community, the Jewish prostitute herself was sometimes idealized by non-Jews—she was the turned-on tart. And she commanded a higher price than others, especially if she happened to have red hair. In San Francisco, at the turn of the century at least, the redheaded Jewish whore was all the rage, perhaps because she was seen as exotic.[36]

For Jewish males, the corresponding stereotype was the procurer: an evil, secretive figure, who preyed on women sexually for money. Reformers portrayed White slavery as a huge international conspiracy run by foreigners—especially Russian Jews—destroying young innocent White women from the countryside.[37]

The Leo Frank case, culminating in the first antisemitic lynching in U.S. history, drew on images of the Jewish White slaver, as well as economic fear of Jews stimulated by the depression of 1914. Frank, a Jewish businessman from New York, owned a pencil factory in Atlanta. One of his employees, a fourteen-year-old White Christian girl named Mary Phagan, was found raped and murdered there in 1914. Frank was quickly charged, tried, convicted on flimsy evidence, and sentenced to death. When rich Northern Jews sent money for a legal fight to overturn the conviction, a statewide backlash developed against the imagined Jewish plot. Tom Watson, former Populist leader turned reactionary, spearheaded the campaign. In his newspaper he warned of plans to flood the country with "the very scum and dregs of the *Parasite Race.*" He called Frank the "lecherous Jew…, the lascivious pervert guilty of the crime that caused the almighty to blast the Cities of the Plain." Watson wrote that "the black man's lust after the white woman is not much fiercer than the lust of the licentious Jew for the Gentile."[38]

In 1915, after the governor had commuted the death sentence, vigilantes calling themselves the Knights of Mary Phagan dragged Frank from prison and murdered him. Two months later the lynchers burned an enormous cross on Stone Mountain overlooking Atlanta. In an era when Italian laborers were lynched by the dozens and Blacks and Mexicans by the hundreds or thousands, Frank's murder stands alone as a fatal anti-Jewish attack. But the lynching caused half of Georgia's three thousand Jews to flee the state, and it became a catalyst for something much bigger. In November 1915, fifteen men refounded the Ku Klux Klan in a ceremony on Stone Mountain, and adopted the flaming cross as their new symbol.[39]

Intensified racism and nativism during and after World War I offered favorable conditions for reviving the Klan, which had been dormant since the 1870s. Eighteen major anti-Black pogroms took place during the war, directed largely against African Americans who were moving north to find work and escape conditions in the South. The Red Scare of 1917–1920 targeted not only socialists and anarchists, but European immigrants in general. The Klan brought together all of these themes. It was anti-Black like the original Klan of Reconstruction years, but it was also antisemitic, anti-immigrant, anti-Catholic, and to some extent antilabor. By the early 1920s, the Klan had millions of members, including President Harding, and wielded wide-ranging political powers. However, lacking a coherent political strategy and discredited by scandals within its leadership, the Klan quickly collapsed in 1925.

Paralleling the rise of the Protestant fundamentalist movement at about the same time, the Klan focused much of its energies on supposed moral purification of White Protestant America. To the Klan, "the Jew stood for an international plot to control America and also for the whole spectrum of urban sin—for pollution of the Sabbath, bootlegging, gambling, and carnal indulgence."[40]

The Klan's focus on antisemitism tended to be stronger in the North than in the South, where Klan-sponsored boycotts of Jewish businesses repeatedly failed. This contrast points to the process by which Jews were being integrated into the White supremacist social framework. As historian John Higham has noted, the struggle "to uphold white supremacy in the face of a colored race," at that time fiercest in California and the South, tended to pull Jews more closely into the White privileged group. Hostility towards Jews tended to be greatest in places such as Minneapolis, whose population was overwhelmingly of European descent.[41]

Through the early 1900s, Jewish involvement in labor unions and the socialist movement helped engender a new stereotype, the Jewish radical. Following the Red Scare of 1917–1920, antisemitic propaganda portrayed Jews not only as financial parasites, but also as the masterminds behind Bolshevism.[42] A major piece of "evidence" for the international Jewish plot was the fraudulent *Protocols of the Elders of Zion,* which was brought to the United States in 1918 by Czarist army officers fleeing the Bolshevik Revolution. Henry Ford's newspaper, the *Dearborn Independent,* drew heavily on the *Protocols* in a tirade against "the International Jew" published on and off through the 1920s.

Ford's propaganda campaign prepared the way for a new upsurge of anti-Jewish sentiment during the depression years of the 1930s, and for the large fascist movement that developed with it. The fascists pulled antisemitism out of the nativist mosaic in which it had been embedded, and made it the central tenet of their ideology. Where the Klan and other nativists had a largely conservative vision of White supremacist America, fascists envisioned a new, totalitarian order. The fascists emphasized national chauvinism, but their movement went beyond the traditional parameters of native-born Whites. Father Charles Coughlin appealed largely to Catholics through the National Union for Social Justice and the Christian Front, while Italian fascist groups and the pro-Nazi German-American Bund recruited European immigrants predominantly. These organizations worked together with William Dudley Pelley's Silver Shirts, followers of Gerald L.K. Smith and Gerald Winrod, and many other native fascist groups. Fascism even recruited African Americans in small numbers, mainly on the basis of solidarity with the Japanese as fellow people of color.

The fascists were fiercely anticommunist and opposed to the liberal New Deal reforms, but they also condemned finance capital and advocated vague plans for halting economic exploitation. Fortunately, many different fascist groups and leaders competed for primacy within the movement without finding any solid unity. Often hatred of Jews provided the least common denominator for bringing together the different factions.[43]

The fascist movement was not the only political expression of antisemitism in the 1930s. More brutal in effect were the actions of the Roosevelt administration and the State Department (the latter dominated by antisemites in the old Yankee patrician mold). When masses of European Jews were trying to escape from German Nazism, the U.S. government refused to allow entry to more than small numbers of refugees. In this way, the immigration restriction movement's legacy helped Hitler to conduct his own race purification plan.

Assimilation: Gain or Loss?

While discrimination and organized antisemitism isolated Jews through the first decades of the twentieth century, economic and cultural forces were working to integrate the immigrant Jewish national minority into White society. In the space of one or two generations, the majority of Jewish families moved from the sweatshops and immigrant ghettos into the offices and suburbs of the middle class. This process brought a dramatic improvement in the material conditions of life, but it also reinforced a tendency for Jews to reject and deny their cultural traditions—i.e., to internalize antisemitism.

At the beginning of the twentieth century, the Yiddish-speaking national minority constituted a new type of Jewish people-class. In contrast to their traditional "middle men" roles of European Jewry, most of these Jews were workers, heavily concentrated in the garment industry. Geographically, Jewish immigrant life centered on New York's Lower East Side. Yiddish united the community linguistically and culturally. The combination of class exploitation and national oppression, together with the stream of Jewish radicals immigrating from Czarist Russia, produced a socialist political ferment that influenced the entire community. Yiddish became "for a short period of time a Left-oriented language and culture," a self-sustaining web of radical thought and action.[44]

Jewish women played a key role in developing Yiddish radical culture. Evelyn Torton Beck notes that Yiddish "belonged to the women; its literature was developed (by men) so that women, who were not trained in Hebrew, would be able to read."

> It is associated with warmth, emotion, home, nurturing, and rooted-ness—even in exile. Like women, Yiddish was elevated (often sentimentalized, especially after World War II), but also denigrated. It was seen as impure (a dialect of German, rather than a language of its own), unacademic, and overly emotional.[45]

In Russia, women were many of the organizers in the Jewish Labor Bund, a socialist organization that emphasized Yiddish and called for Jewish "national cultural autonomy" in Eastern Europe. In New York, many women supported and led a range of political efforts: socialist, feminist, anarchist, antiwar, and others. Some were active as writers, in the Yiddish theater, and in the political-literary networks of cafés, lectures, and discussion circles. Some rejected the dominant sexual morality—as lesbians, as opponents of marriage, or as promoters of sexual equality between women and men.[46]

Jewish women were the backbone of the labor movement in the garment industry, which employed more workers in New York City than any other industry. The New York City shirt-waist makers' strike of 1909–1910 included twenty thousand workers—most of them women, two-thirds of them Jewish. Such activism extended beyond workplace issues. In 1902, Jewish women organized a successful boycott of butcher shops to protest high meat prices. The boycotters picketed, seized, and burned meat in the streets. The *New York Times* commented, "They are very ignorant…. They do not understand the duties or the rights of Americans. They have no inbred or acquired respect for law and order as the basis of the life of the society in which [*sic*] they have come." In both of these actions, women had to contend not only with the hostility of businessmen and police, but also with the condescension of male leaders who sought to contain or bargain away the women's militancy.[47]

The high degree of radical ferment within the Jewish community proved temporary and transitional. Like the other European national minorities, Yiddish-speaking Jewry was a troublesome intrusion, which White society began to digest immediately. Jewish immigrants were isolated from their cultural roots in Europe, subject to capitalist and White supremacist rules governing economic opportunity in the United States and to the growing power of commercialized, mass culture. These impersonal forces ultimately played the biggest role in assimilation. But in the early years, at least, such forces found conscious voice and direction among some representatives of White society.

Industrialists, working through organizations such as the Inter-Racial Council, promoted Americanization heavily as a way to discipline their work forces and undercut the threat of revolutionary activism. Their efforts were backed up by state laws promoting Americanization and English-only rules, and by sections of the White labor aristocracy. The newspaper for the conservative United Garment Workers of America (whose Jewish members had split off to form the more leftist Amalgamated Clothing Workers) declared that:

> Much of the extreme radicalism in some of our unions today may be traced to the foreign membership who are unnaturalized and who have a hatred for our institutions, and are secretly or openly working for their overthrow.[48]

One of the first industrialists to put Americanization into practice was Henry Ford, who set up the Ford English School and required his foreign employees to attend.

> The first thing that foreign-speaking employees learned in the Ford School was how to say, "I am a good American." Later the students acted out a pantomime [in which] a great melting pot (labeled as such)

occupied the middle of the stage. A long column of immigrant students descended into the pot from backstage, clad in outlandish garb and flaunting signs proclaiming their fatherlands. Simultaneously from either side of the pot another stream of men emerged, each prosperously dressed in identical suits of clothes and each carrying a little American flag.[49]

German Jews were on the frontlines of this assault on immigrant national culture. As Americanized Jews they held an intermediary position between the Eastern European immigrants and White society, and their response to the Yiddish-speaking community blended class antagonism with internalized antisemitism. Most German Jews were prosperous; a few very wealthy. They owned many of the sweatshops in which early Yiddish-speaking immigrants worked. Yiddish culture offended their belief that Jewishness should be kept out of sight, and they feared that the newcomers were provoking antisemitism that would threaten their own newly acquired status. As one of their publications, the *Hebrew Standard*, anxiously declared: "The thoroughly acclimated American Jew…has no religious, social or intellectual sympathies with [Eastern European Jews]. He is closer to the Christian sentiment around him than to the Judaism of these miserable darkened Hebrews."[50]

German Jewish philanthropies provided the newcomers with charity, but generally in a condescending or even hostile manner. These agencies also helped to furnish employers with cheap labor and strike-breakers. The Educational Alliance, in New York City, was the most prominent of the Americanization agencies formed by German Jews. Most classes at the alliance initially banned Yiddish as a "jargon" not worthy to be called a language, and members were punished or even expelled for its use. Even after softening its policy, the alliance pressed immigrants to abandon Yiddish as quickly as possible.[51]

In the long run, such external propaganda and pressures on the Yiddish-speaking community were only able to transform it so profoundly because of tensions within the community itself. Although working-class radicalism was key in promoting and shaping Yiddish culture, Orthodox Judaism remained a stronghold of conservatism against the antireligious socialists and anarchists. Male supremacist leadership undercut the power of Jewish women's activism. Despite the temporary equality that mechanized labor imposed, many immigrants retained the skills and consciousness of artisans or small businesspeople. And despite their community's assertive vitality, many Jews carried a burden of hopelessness, insecurity, and self-contempt imposed by centuries of repression. Such factors pushed many Jews to accept the terms on which White America offered prosperity.

Even before World War I, Jews were beginning to move rapidly into small business and white-collar work. Jews' roles in Eastern Europe had equipped them with many administrative and artisan skills which, combined with their emphasis on formal education, enabled them to rise more quickly than any other immigrant group. By the end of World War II, Jews were concentrated in white-collar positions and moving increasingly into professional work. A sizeable minority remained in blue-collar positions, notably in New York's garment industry, but they tended to move into the more privileged ranks as Black and Puerto Rican workers filled the lower-status jobs.[52]

As they rose economically, Jews changed culturally. "This process involved moving out of the old neighborhood and changing names, dress, manners, and speech patterns in order to project the image of an American or perhaps a German-American. Often Orthodoxy would be abandoned in exchange for Reform or Conservative Judaism or, in some cases, no religion at all."[53] Jewish socialists tended to abandon or tone down their radicalism. Jewish socialist institutions designed to maintain Yiddish culture, such as the Workmen's Circle, began moving steadily to the right once a substantial number of their members moved up and out of the working class. So long as there was a steady stream of fresh immigrants to replace those who left, the Yiddish community could flourish despite this drain. Once immigration was cut off in the 1920s, cohesive forces within the community proved too weak to hold it together.

Cultural change affected attitudes towards male and female behavior. European- American norms dictated that in a successful family, the wife was strictly a homemaker while the husband was the breadwinner and controlled all major economic decisions. "Both the corruption of Jewish life and values and the absorption of American attitudes toward women often resulted in a feeling of contempt for the same survival qualities of women so admired in *shtetl* culture."[54] Women were pressured not to appear direct, articulate, competent, or strong, but rather to follow U.S. patterns of femininity. Instead it was men who were expected to assert these qualities, and to avoid the "feminine intellectual" image inherited from Eastern Europe.

But Americanization also brought Jews important benefits. For millions of Jews it facilitated release from harsh poverty, exhausting and dangerous labor, overcrowded housing, disease, prostitution, and crime. To some it brought broader opportunities for learning. To some it offered a chance to escape from the harsh authority of parents or rabbis, the God-sanctioned contempt for women, or the endless strictures that theocratic tradition imposed on daily life and thought. To free oneself from such restrictions was healthy and positive; to equate the restrictions with Jewishness itself, as many did on one level or another, was to internalize antisemitism.

Americanization coercively alienated Jews from their own traditions in a number of ways. Economic necessity forced many religious Jews to work on the Sabbath. Fear of discrimination made Jews change their names and men remove their yarmulkes and cut their beards. Gentile standards of beauty later pressed thousands of Jewish women to have their noses surgically altered. Americanization reinforced the psychology of oppression that Jews had long carried with them: many learned to be ashamed of their backgrounds, and to internalize anti-Jewish stereotypes and attitudes of self-hatred, fear, powerlessness, arrogance, and mistrust. The process left a legacy of cultural invisibility and loss with which many Jews continue to struggle today.

Privilege and Scapegoating

Jewish assimilation tended to reduce open antisemitism. The fascist movement, after reaching a high point in the late 1930s, collapsed with the United States' entry into World War II in December 1941. Yet the war temporarily strengthened unorganized hostility to Jews. Fears of a Jewish conspiracy also played a significant role in the Cold War hysteria of the late 1940s and early 1950s, which included the Rosenberg/Sobell spy case and the congressional investigation of communist influence in Hollywood.[55]

Nevertheless, overt anti-Jewish propaganda and discrimination declined sharply in the postwar years. Most of the systematic barriers that Jews had faced in jobs, housing, education, and other areas were removed. A long period of U.S. economic prosperity reduced the impulse to scapegoat Jews, and revelations about the Nazi genocide in Europe heavily discredited antisemitism. But the central factor was the change that had taken place in the country's racial hierarchy: by the 1950s most of the European immigrant national minorities—including Jews—had become integrated into the White working and middle classes.

Is this decline of Jew-hatred permanent, or is it the downward swing of a cycle that could turn upward again—as antisemitism has so often done in the past? Since the oppression of Jews in the United States has had two components historically—nativism plus traditional antisemitism—both answers are correct in part. The decline of nativist antisemitism is permanent, because that movement developed under the historically specific conditions of industrialization and mass European immigration—events that cannot recur here in the same way. But the fact that most North American Jews are now unequivocally White and economically privileged does not mean the end of antisemitism—just as White supremacy's elevation of European American workers does not mean that capital has ceased to exploit White labor. Anti-Jewish attacks have continued (on a smaller scale than before): slurs and graffiti; vandalism against synagogues, Jewish homes, and businesses; harassment and threats; and physical attacks. For several reasons, antisemitism has the potential to get significantly worse: (1) Jews' roles in the class structure make us vulnerable to renewed scapegoating, especially in the event of a major economic crisis; (2) despite a widespread taboo against open Jew-hatred, antisemitic attitudes persist across class, color, and political lines; and (3) antisemitism is a central part of today's far Right, which is stronger now than it has ever been in fifty years.

Although Jews no longer constitute a people-class, they are once again concentrated in "middle-man" roles—positions of relative privilege outside the centers of power. According to figures from the late 1970s, almost three-quarters of Jews in the paid work force are either professionals or administrators. Close to 50 percent are employed in trade and finance; those in manufacturing are concentrated in consumer goods and other light manufacturing. Almost half of Jews in the labor force are self-employed.[56] Although a tiny number of Jews have become wealthy, few of them have reached the top levels of the most powerful corporations. The ruling class remains WASP-dominated. Meanwhile, a sizeable minority of Jews remains poor—especially elderly Jews and Jewish women.

Holding occupations such as shopkeeper, landlord, teacher, social service worker, lawyer, and bureaucrat makes Jews prime targets for scapegoating. To poor and working-class people—most of whom never meet any rich capitalists—such jobs represent the most visible kind of status and power. Seeing Jews in these roles can reinforce the myth that Jews are the main oppressors. Jews' prominence (partly real, partly fictional) in journalism and the film industry does the same thing on a bigger scale.

As in the past, economic privilege plus a persistent sense of vulnerability has drawn the official Jewish leadership into closer alliance with the WASP power elite. Mainstream Jewish organizations have moved steadily to the right in recent decades. After being won over to political Zionism in the 1940s, most hardened by the late 1960s into rigid supporters of Israeli government policies. In the 1970s, such groups played a leading role in opposing affirmative action programs. Jewish organizations such as the Anti-Defamation League (ADL) and periodicals such as the *New Republic* have also repeatedly exploited the charge of antisemitism to attack political opponents (particularly Blacks and left-wing critics of Israel) and to intensify Jews' sense of isolation. Such manipulation discredits genuine concern about Jew-hatred.

True, antisemitism is a reality within segments of the African American community, and the government's repression of the Black liberation movement in the 1960s and early seventies left a wake of political frustration in which anti-Jewish scapegoating could gain ground. A 1977 "Blacks and Jews" issue of the *Black Books Bulletin,* for example, included such assertions as "the Jews' grand strategy has been to use Blacks as their major tool in their quest for world power and domination." In 1988, National Black United Front Chair Conrad Worrill said that Black people were upset about Jewish "domination": "The Jewish people have amassed a great deal of wealth in the Western World. I would say that Jews control insurance, the banks, merchandising, and trade."[57]

But charges of "Black antisemitism" must be weighed carefully and in context. Jews and other Whites have frequently criticized Blacks for antisemitism while ignoring or rationalizing anti-Black racist behavior. Even when presenting a seemingly more balanced view, they have often treated Black antisemitism and Jewish racism as equivalent phenomena. They are only equivalent if we consider attitudes while ignoring the social framework: nearly all Jews in the United States hold White privilege while Blacks do not; Blacks face pervasive, institutionalized racist violence, bigotry, and discrimination, while Jews do not.

Highlighting the complexity of this issue was the August 1991 explosion in the Crown Heights section of Brooklyn, when long-standing neighborhood conflict between Black people and Lubavitcher Hassidic Jews erupted in several days of street fighting. Here anti-Jewish scapegoating and violence was mingled with legitimate Black grievances against Lubavitchers' systematic racist behavior, institutionalized White privilege, and preferential treatment by the city government. Yet mainstream media accounts tended to ignore the systemic context and to focus one-sidedly on Jews and other Whites as victims and Blacks as victimizers.

Too often, legitimate African American demands and grievances have been portrayed as antisemitic, such as Black support for affirmative action programs or criticisms of Israel's close ties with apartheid South Africa. Too often, Jews have focused on Blacks as an easier target, while playing down White antisemitism.

Compare the treatment of Louis Farrakhan's Nation of Islam (NOI) and that of the Christian Right. Farrakhan has certainly made reprehensible statements, such as: "I am your last chance, Jews. You can't say 'never again' to God, 'cause when he puts you in an oven, you are in one indeed!" He has promoted bigots such as Steve Cokely, who charged that Jewish doctors have injected Blacks with AIDS. In the early 1990s, NOI cultivated an alliance with Lyndon LaRouche's neonazi movement, reprinting its articles, cooperating on electoral work, and praising LaRouche publicly.[58] Farrakhan's religious antisemitism is to be condemned along with his many other reactionary beliefs: he endorses homophobia and women's subordination, glorifies petty capitalism, and advocates a theocracy based on medieval Islamic law. But it should be noted that Farrakhan has never been accused of any role in any physical attack upon Jews.

Legitimate opposition to Farrakhan's ideas does not explain the full weight of invective that many Jews and other Whites have applied to him. Leonard Zakim of B'nai Brith reportedly described Farrakhan as "the most notorious anti-Semite of this century," a remark that he presumably regretted.[59] Chanting demonstrators have called for his death. Farrakhan is targeted this way because he is anti-Zionist, Muslim, and, above all, Black. Racism has led many Jews and other Whites to exaggerate and distort his message, and to demand—in the spirit of McCarthy-era loyalty oaths—that other Black leaders denounce him to prove their own legitimacy.

In contrast, the White-dominated Christian Right—a much larger, richer, and more powerful movement than the Nation of Islam—has received only light criticism for its hostility to Jews. The movement's campaign to Christianize every area of life is anti-Jewish by definition. But while they make no secret of their hatred for women's liberation and homosexuality, most Christian Right leaders adhere to what Andrea Dworkin has called "pedestal anti-Semitism." As one Moral Majority official explained: "I love Jewish people deeply. God has given them talents He has not given others. They are His chosen people. Jews have a God-given ability to make money...they control the media, they control this city...."

A brief furor did ensue after a 1980 political rally where the Reverend Bailey Smith, president of the Southern Baptist Convention, said, "With all due respect to these dear people, my friends, God Almighty does not hear the prayer of a Jew." Jerry Falwell "clarified" Smith's remark by explaining that God does hear the prayers of "redeemed" (i.e., Christianized) Gentiles and Jews.[60] But in general, establishment Jewish groups have been quick to forget such incidents.

The Christian Right's staunch pro-Zionism (combined with pedestal anti-semitism) has served it well as a political shield, enabling it to form coalitions with conservative Jewish groups. Ronald Sobel of the ADL urged, "we ought to accentuate the pluses we have in our relationships with evangelicals. One of these pluses is our common concern about Israel." To the ADL and many Jewish organizations, one's stand on Israel is the key factor in assessing anti-semitism. But fundamentalists favor Israel for their own reasons: to them, Israel's establishment is a sign that Christ's second coming is near. Many believe that Christ's return will be preceded by a world war centered on Israel, and that at the final Judgment all except true Christians will die.[61]

As Andrea Dworkin has suggested, alliance with the Christian Right also offers conservative Jewish men a way to reassert their masculinity, threatened not only by traditional stereotypes, but also by the memory of German Nazism, which castrated large numbers of Jewish men in the camps and "castrated" the people as a whole through mass murder:

> In associating with the Christian Right, there is a repudiation of homosexuality…a strong move against women (reestablishing male dominance), and in general making an alliance with the rulers—with the Christians who run a Christian country.

> Believing they can fit in—assimilate—these Jews are turning to the one group of people—the fundamentalists—who will never forget that "the Jews killed Christ." Anything not to be that castrate, that homosexual; there is more dignity in the killing of Christ than in the concentration camps where the measure is masculinity.[62]

The interplay that Dworkin notes between misogyny and internalized antisemitism has also been pivotal to the rise of the "JAP" (Jewish American Princess) stereotype, created by Jewish male novelists of the 1950s and 1960s such as Herman Wouk and Philip Roth. The term JAP evokes the racist "kill Japs" propaganda of World War II. Through the stereotype, Jewish men have projected on women their own self-contempt and fear of embodying the rich Jew stereotype. Another factor, argues Evelyn Torton Beck, is that "middle-class American Jewish men view the large numbers of Jewish women who have successfully entered the workforce as professionals as a serious economic and ego threat." The JAP is portrayed with "thick" lips and a supposedly funny accent, which are presented as negative traits. She is materialistic, greedy, vain, shallow, manipulative, lazy, and parasitic. She is "both sexually frigid (withholding) and a nymphomaniac"—combining Jewish greed and "the misogynist stereotype of the insatiable woman, the woman who is infinitely orgasmic, who will destroy men with her desire."[63]

In recent decades JAP-baiting has become one of the most common ways of attacking Jews, but has often been trivialized because it targets Jewish women. Particularly prominent on college campuses, JAP-baiting includes both the threat and practice of violence—for example, "Slap a JAP" contests, a cartoon suggesting ways to "exterminate" JAPs, and verbal rape in the form of the slogan, "Make her prove she's not a JAP, make her swallow." In the 1980s, a Jewish man in Arizona was acquitted of murdering his wife after his lawyer persuaded the jury that the killing was justified: the woman had provoked it by being a JAP.[64]

Many Jewish feminists such as Evelyn Torton Beck have focused attention not only on antisemitism in society at large, but also within the women's movement itself. This effort crystalized with the development of Jewish identity politics, as Jewish women have challenged invisibility and asserted Jewish culture in feminist and lesbian contexts. In many respects, the work of Jewish feminists has paralleled and overlapped with efforts by socialist Jews to confront antisemitism on the Left and to raise a distinct Jewish radical voice. Thus many of the anti-Jewish tendencies noted among feminists apply to socialists and other leftists as well.[65]

As Jewish feminists have shown with numerous examples, antisemitism in the women's movement takes many forms. Some feminists have perpetuated stereotypes of Jews as controlling, loud, demanding, or exotic. Some have referred to Jews only negatively—as oppressors, wealthy, or right-wing. Some have developed new versions of old myths–for example, blaming Jews for killing the Goddess or creating patriarchy. Some have belittled the seriousness of antisemitism, or suggested that the fight against Jew-hatred must be subsumed in other struggles. Some have responded with hostility to expressions of Jewish identity. Jewish feminists note that internalized oppression has often led Jewish women to collude with or even participate in such hurtful actions, or to keep silent about their Jewishness. "Jewish invisibility is a symptom of anti-Semitism as surely as lesbian invisibility is a symptom of homophobia."[66]

Addressing antisemitism in the women's movement has raised difficult issues. Many non-Jews (and some Jews) have responded with defensiveness or denial. At the same time, Jewish feminists have sometimes raised the issue of antisemitism in ways that deflect attention away from their own White privilege, or have unfairly singled out non-Jewish women of color for special criticism.[67] For many Jews in the women's movement, as in various sections of the Left, the question of Zionism in relation to both racism and anti-semitism has been a major point of conflict.

Zionism and Anti-Zionism: A Necessary Detour

"Any anti-Zionist position is...anti-Semitic," wrote Di Vilde Chayes, a Jewish lesbian feminist group, in 1982.[68] Many Jews across the political spectrum believe that Jews need a homeland to ensure survival, and that to call for the dissolution of the Jewish state of Israel is antisemitic. Many Jews who hold this position are critical of Israeli government policies, and many also support the creation of an independent Palestinian state. But even Jews who do not call themselves Zionists often believe firmly in the existence of the Jewish state, the bottom line of Zionist ideology today.

I am an anti-Zionist Jew: I believe that Israel should not exist as a Jewish state. Zionism is wrong because it is based on ethnic exclusivism and internalized antisemitism. Creation of an independent Palestinian state alongside Israel (as opposed to partial "autonomy" in a couple of tiny enclaves) could relieve some of the worst symptoms of Israeli rule, but it would not address these basic problems.

Left anti-Zionism cannot be equated with the neonazis, who hate Israel because they hate Jews. Still, some left anti-Zionists have acted and spoken in antisemitic ways or shown insensitivity to Jewish concerns. For example, some anti-Zionists have equated all Jews with Zionism or all Israelis with the Israeli government. Some have dismissed any talk about Jewish culture or antisemitism as racist or distracting. Some have trivialized the Nazi genocide, or equated Israeli rule with Nazism. Some have exaggerated the power of a supposed Jewish lobby or international Zionist conspiracy. Some have incorrectly labeled Zionism a form of White supremacy, ignoring the fact that roughly half the Israeli Jewish people are "Oriental" Jews (people of color).[69] Some have stated or implied that Israeli Jews should be driven out or killed. Some have dismissed any sympathy with Israeli Jewish victims of Palestinian violence as inherently reactionary. These actions can play into antisemitism and discredit legitimate criticisms of Zionism.[70]

Jewish feminists and leftists have encountered many cases of antisemitic behavior passing as anti-Zionism: a political rally in New York City where demonstrators chanted "Down with the Jews!"; or newspapers and journals that would only print Jewish-identified material by "balancing" it with pro-Palestinian articles. At the 1980 United Nations Women's Conference in Copenhagen, where the U.N. resolution declaring Zionism a form of racism set the terms of debate, women reported numerous calls for Jews to be killed, and a general climate of anti-Jewish intimidation.[71]

I do not want Israeli Jews to be expelled or killed, but rather to share the land under terms of justice and equality with Palestinians. Israeli Jews are not simply a collection of individuals, nor a religious group. The Zionist project brings together Jews from many different nations and ethnic communities and welds them into a new Israeli nation, with its own language, economy, and culture. Ironically, Zionist ideology, which declares that all Jews everywhere form one abstract nation, does not and cannot recognize either this concrete Hebrew-speaking national entity or the diverse and conflicting national traditions within it.[72]

Israeli fundamental law, equivalent to a constitution, defines Israel as "the sovereign state of the Jewish people" (an extraterritorial group), rather than a state of its own citizens (Arabs as well as Jews).[73] It declares that "gathering in the exiles is the central task of the State of Israel and the Zionist movement." Thus Israel exists primarily to serve Jews, to the exclusion of other citizens. By law, "all" Jews (with some exceptions) may claim Israeli citizenship "by return," while Palestinian Arabs may not, although hundreds of thousands of them have been forced to live in exile for decades. By law, 92 percent of Israeli land may not be sold or leased to non-Jews. By law, most Palestinian Arabs have no property rights and are defined as "absentees," even if they live in Israel. By law, national development is in the hands of agencies that serve only Jews. This is what the Jewish state means. Without this, Israel would not be a Jewish state. This is legal racism.[74]

Many liberal Jews avoid this issue. New Jewish Agenda, which went further than most U.S. Jewish groups in the 1980s in criticizing oppression of the Palestinians, called on Israel to adopt a constitution guaranteeing all residents equal rights, but also endorsed Israel's self-definition as the state of the Jewish people. They did not explain how Israel could grant special status and priority to one group and also guarantee equal rights for all.[75]

Like the United States, Israeli society is based on settlerism: the colonization of Palestinian land and labor. During the 1948 war, Israeli armed forces deliberately caused 750 thousand Palestinians to flee, by conducting a series of civilian massacres. During and after the war, Israel demolished four hundred of the five hundred Palestinian villages within its borders, and seized large tracts of land from Palestinians. From the early 1900s until midcentury, the pseudosocialist Labor Zionist movement pursued the "conquest of labor": forcibly excluding Palestinians from working in Jewish-run projects and businesses. In many cases the businesses replaced Palestinian workers with "Oriental" Jews brought in specifically for that purpose. Later the policy shifted and Israeli Jews began to exploit Palestinian workers as a cheap work force for menial jobs, increasingly relying on workers from the Occupied Territories. Many of the pseudosocialist *kibbutzim* (Jewish communal farms) have long barred Palestinians and "Oriental" Jews from becoming members, while using their low-paid labor.[76]

Israeli settlerism is a particularly virulent form of the Western intervention—political, military and economic—that bolsters oppressive societies throughout the Middle East. Palestinians fleeing Israeli rule have borne the full weight of this interlocking system. Seeking refuge and work in other Arab countries, they have often been exploited as a stateless labor force and subjected to harsh government persecution.

The 1993 accord between Israel and the Palestine Liberation Organization (PLO), which established limited Palestinian "autonomy" in Jericho and the Gaza Strip, did virtually nothing to transform genuine power relations—except to give the PLO shared responsibility for policing the Palestinian people. Creation of a genuine Palestinian state in the Occupied Territories would go somewhat further, offering Palestinians possible relief from the harsh burden of exile, military rule, and cultural and political repression. Even this, however, would not change the colonial relationship between Israeli settler society and Palestinian labor. It would not restore to Palestinians the land stolen from them within Israel's borders. It would not change the racism in Israeli fundamental law. Palestinian national liberation requires an end to Israel's discriminatory Jewish-state laws and policies, and to the class and cultural hierarchies that oppress Palestinians throughout the Middle East.

Political Zionism, the movement to build the Jewish state of Israel, has been called "the liberation movement of the Jewish people." Yet this movement has been a disaster not only for Palestinians, but also for Jews. Political Zionism was founded on the beliefs that Jews are a foreign presence in all countries outside of Palestine and that antisemitism is natural and inevitable whenever Jews live among other people—thus we should accept it rather than fight it. The Zionist movement repeatedly attacked Ashkenazi, Sephardi, and other Jewish cultures. Theodor Herzl, founder of political Zionism, denounced Yiddish-speaking Jews in antisemitic terms as cowardly, profit-hungry, treacherous, scheming, dirty, repellent. (Note that Yiddish was associated with women, whereas Hebrew, which the Zionists promoted, had for centuries been the nearly exclusive province of men.) In Israel, the Ashkenazi-dominated power structure has worked to stifle and marginalize African and Asian Jews' cultures and histories, while repackaging their music, crafts, and foods as exotic tourist items.[77]

The Nazi genocide is often cited as proof that Jews must have a homeland "to ensure our survival as a people." This argument carries great emotional power because it speaks to the grief and fear that millions of Jews feel in the wake of Nazi terror. But it overlooks one fact: A homeland does *not* ensure survival. The Polish state did not save the three million non-Jewish Poles murdered by the Nazis. The USSR, with one of the most powerful armies in the world, did not save the twenty million Soviet citizens killed during World War II. The Jews in Palestine were not saved by Zionism, but because they happened to be in a place that the Nazis did not conquer.[78]

The leadership of the Zionist movement during the Nazi period ranked the creation of a Jewish homeland a higher priority than protecting Jewish lives. Shortly after the Nazis' 1938 *Kristallnacht* pogrom, which killed one hundred Jews, the British government offered to provide immediate refuge to thousands of Jewish children from Germany. David Ben-Gurion, later Israel's first prime minister, opposed the plan:

> If I knew that it would be possible to save all the children in Germany
> by bringing them over to England, and only half by transporting them
> to Eretz Yisrael, then I would opt for the second alternative. For we
> must weigh not only the life of these children, but also the history of
> the People of Israel.[79]

The Israeli state has followed a similar policy of subordinating the needs of
Jews to its own ends. Through the 1960s and 1970s, the Israeli government
blocked independent Western Jewish groups trying to aid Soviet Jews. During
the 1980s, Israel pressed other governments—especially the United States—
to limit Soviet immigration, in order to force Soviet Jewish emigrés to settle
in Israel. The United States instituted such restrictions in 1989, resulting in a
mass influx to Israel. Israel has developed close ties with antisemitic governments in Ethiopia, South Africa, and most notoriously Argentina, where the
neonazi military junta conducted systematic terrorism against Jews.[80]

Far from freeing Jews from the dangers of antisemitism, Zionism has
expanded Jews' traditional role into the international sphere. Many Arab governments use Israel as a scapegoat to draw popular resentment away from
their own role in imperialism, capitalism, and repression. Far from giving
Jews a "normal" nation-state, Zionism has created a state that is heavily militarized, perpetually at war, and massively dependent on foreign subsidies.

Israel's semitheocracy gives Orthodox rabbis legal authority over all issues
of personal status for Jews—"the famous private sphere in which civilly subordinate women are traditionally imprisoned"—including marriage, divorce,
abortion, rape, and domestic violence. Jewish women may not testify in
religious courts; husbands alone may grant divorce, and their decisions are
final. In the most common form of pornography in Israel, published in
mainstream magazines, "Jewish women are sexualized as Holocaust victims
for Jewish men to masturbate over.... The themes are fire, gas, trains, emaci-
ation, death."[81] Like JAP-baiting in the United States, this enables Jewish
men to channel their own self-hatred into hatred of women.

Until the 1940s only a small minority of North American Jews endorsed
political Zionism. A broad spectrum of Jewish political tendencies has rejected
the concept of a Jewish state in Palestine, ranging from the Jewish Labor Bund
to pre-1930s Reform Judaism to the Orthodox Jews of Neturei Karta.[82]

It is important for us to acknowledge and confront anti-Jewish tendencies
when they appear under the guise of anti-Zionism. It is also important for us
to counter misinformation about supposed Israeli democracy and the Zionist
"liberation" movement, and to act in solidarity with Palestinians working for
a just peace free of colonial and ethnic oppression.

Antisemitism and Neonazi Organizing Today

False claims that anti-Zionism equals antisemitism, and that hostility to Jews is rampant on the Left, help obscure the vastly greater danger of antisemitism on the Right. Religious antisemitism finds broad appeal, espoused by reactionary Christian (and to a lesser extent Muslim) groups, while the neonazi movement's racial antisemitism offers the biggest immediate danger of organized anti-Jewish violence.[83]

The Nazi-Klan convergence has infused White supremacist politics with a new, antisemitic direction and focus. The imagined Jewish conspiracy gives the far Right a way to define the power structure it is fighting: a superhuman force that stands behind other, more direct threats. Neonazis counterpose the image of the Black rapist, who attacks White Christian women in person, with that of the Jewish pimp, who kidnaps and corrupts them through his organization. They blame supposedly promiscuous gay men and Blacks for spreading AIDS, but warn that rich Jews are encouraging the epidemic to weaken White Christian society.

The far Right capitalizes on the real fears and frustrations of White farmers, blue-collar workers, the lower middle class, and alienated youth. Thus Posse Comitatus, for example, gained a substantial following among Midwestern farmers in the 1980s by opposing bank foreclosures. Posse members consider all existing government above the county level to be illegitimate. They condemn corrupt politicians and judges, bankers, agribusiness, the Federal Reserve, the Internal Revenue Service, immigrants, and of course the rich Jews who supposedly control it all behind the scenes.

For most far-right groups, White supremacy remains an explicit, central article of faith. Nazi/Klan groups warn that self-assertive Blacks and a supposed flood of Asian and Latin American immigrants threaten to overwhelm the White race, as "race-mixing" erodes its genetic and moral purity. They have continued the Klan tradition of racist assault, harassment, and murder in all regions of the country. In recent years, fascists have also increasingly targeted lesbians and gay men, as in January, 1987, when "former" members of the White Patriot Party murdered three gay men in Shelby, North Carolina, and seriously wounded two others, in an execution-style attack. Neonazi propaganda and violence have helped to stimulate a much broader wave of hate violence against members of oppressed groups within U.S. society.

Most neonazis uphold a traditional form of sexism in keeping with that of the Christian Right: men are superior to women by nature and must protect them, the nuclear family must be defended, and sex is for reproduction not pleasure. But racism gives these themes an added intensity: *White* men must control *White* women in order to safeguard racial purity and ensure lots of White babies.

Homosexuality, in this framework, threatens the White race's ability to reproduce itself and undermines the gender roles needed for racial dominance. Yet "revolutionary" sections of the neonazi movement have also promoted a kind of fake feminism, analogous to vulgar anticapitalism: an ideal of White women and men as equal comrades-in-arms. The Aryan Women's League, affiliated with White Aryan Resistance (WAR), claims that the Jews invented male supremacy, and calls for "Women's Power as well as White Power."[84]

The "revolutionary" wing of the Nazi/Klan movement seeks to overthrow the United States government or at least secede from it. This tendency draws supporters from many local Klan chapters, Posse Comitatus groups, and the Christian Identity movement (which claims that Anglo-Saxons, not Jews, are the true children of Israel). Richard Butler's Aryan Nations, based in Idaho, has provided an umbrella formation for many groups of this tendency. In 1983 members of the Aryan Nations formed an underground organization known as the Order, which declared war on the "Zionist Occupation Government" (ZOG for short). They raised about $5 million through counterfeiting and robberies of banks and armored cars, some of which they passed on to other Nazi/Klan organizations. The Order's most notorious action took place in June, 1984, when members murdered Alan Berg, a Jewish radio talk-show host in Denver.

The U.S. government cracked down hard on the Order. The state can accept right-wing terrorism directed against the Left (such as the 1979 Greensboro massacre, which two federal agents helped to plan) but not against its own rule. Order founder Robert Mathews was killed and many other members imprisoned. But in 1988, fourteen fascist leaders, including Butler, were acquitted in Arkansas of seditious conspiracy charges, leaving most of the underlying political-military network intact.

Tom Metzger, a former California Klan leader, heads another branch of the Nazi movement's "revolutionary" tendency: White Aryan Resistance. Metzger, like many European fascists, advocates so-called Third Position politics: rejection of both capitalism and communism. This political philosophy has its roots in the extreme anticapitalist wing of Hitler's Nazi Party. Metzger expounded his philosophy at the 1987 Aryan Nations Congress:

> WAR is dedicated to the White working people, the farmers, the White poor....This is a working class movement....Our problem is with monopoly capitalism. The Jews first went with Capitalism and then created their Marxist game. You go for the throat of the Capitalist. You must go for the throat of the corporates. You take the game away from the left. It's our game! We're not going to fight your whore wars no more! We've got one war, that is right here, the same war the SA fought in Germany, right here; in the streets of America.[85]

Metzger supports "White working-class" militancy, stresses environmentalism, and has opposed U.S. military intervention in Central America and the Persian Gulf. Metzger's television program, *Race and Reason*, has been broadcast on cable television in dozens of cities. Through its Aryan Youth Movement wing, WAR was particularly successful in the 1980s in recruiting racist skinheads, who include thousands of young people clustered in scores of violent, pronazi formations. Metzger and WAR's position in the neonazi movement was partially weakened in October, 1990, when they were fined $12.5 million in a civil suit for inciting three Portland skinheads who murdered Ethiopian immigrant Mulugeta Seraw.[86]

In contrast to "revolutionary" neonazi groups, a "reformist" wing of the movement seeks to build alliances with established conservatives. This tendency includes Willis Carto's Liberty Lobby, which has a radio network of some 150 stations and a weekly paper, *The Spotlight*, with a circulation over one hundred thousand. Carto also founded the Institute for Historical Review, which claims that the Nazi genocide never happened, and the Populist Party, which in 1988 ran ex-Klan leader David Duke for president.[87]

Partly influenced by Willis Carto, Lyndon LaRouche has developed one of the strongest but least-recognized neonazi organizations in the United States. A former Trotskyist, LaRouche founded the National Caucus of Labor Committees (NCLC) in 1968 as an offshoot of the radical student movement. But in the early 1970s LaRouche used cult pressure tactics to consolidate his control over the NCLC and turn it into a right-wing fascist group.[88]

LaRouche has been guided by the insight that in order to win political power, fascists must make themselves useful to the ruling class. In Italy and Germany, capitalists backed fascism as a way to smash the large, militant labor movement and the Left. At first LaRouche experimented with a street-fighting strategy, including physical attacks on communists and Black nationalists. But the Left's decline in the 1970s meant this approach was unlikely to win major capitalist support. LaRouche therefore adopted other approaches to build his organization in a period of relative social stability.

First, his followers built an extensive network for spying, propaganda, and dirty tricks to make themselves useful to the upper levels of government, business, and organized crime. The LaRouchians have reported to intelligence agencies in the United States, South Africa, West Germany, and elsewhere. Their dirty tricks record includes helping Jesse Helms retain his U.S. Senate seat in 1984 by gay-baiting his opponent, and branding George Bush an agent of the Trilateral Commission in 1980 to help Ronald Reagan win the Republican presidential nomination.

Second, the LaRouchians began to develop a mass base through populist electioneering. Since 1980, the LaRouche network has fielded thousands of candidates and received millions of votes in Democratic Party primaries across every region of the country. The LaRouchians spearheaded the 1986 California ballot initiative to quarantine people with AIDS, which received two million votes. With this vote "LaRouche scored a major ideological breakthrough for neo-Nazism in America. He took a previously taboo idea— enforced isolation for the Scapegoat—and elevated it into a topic of legitimate discourse."[89]

During the 1980s the LaRouchians raised an estimated $200 million through legal and illegal fundraising efforts—a feat far beyond any other fascist organization in U.S. history. In 1988 LaRouche was imprisoned for several years for tax evasion and mail fraud conspiracy related to fundraising, yet his organization continued to run strong.

Although LaRouche's world view divides humanity into superior and inferior "species," his organization has often played down White supremacist themes. Since about 1990, the LaRouchians have made a push for African American support, recruiting a few right-wing Black spokespeople such as Rev. James Bevel and forming an alliance with Farrakhan's Nation of Islam.[90]

Similarly, LaRouche hides his antisemitism by pointing to a number of Jews among his supporters, and by using a variety of code words for Jews, from the commonplace ("Zionists") to the esoteric ("Babylonians"). LaRouchian propaganda constantly invokes sinister conspiracies linked to prominent Jews such as "[Henry] Kissinger's friends, the Rothschild family, and other representatives of Britain's financial power." (Like Hitler, LaRouche believes that Britain is controlled by the Jews). In classic antisemitic fashion, LaRouche draws a phony distinction between "productive" industrial capital and "parasitic" finance capital. This enables him to be procapitalist and seemingly anti-imperialist at the same time: "Imperialism was not the result of capitalist development; it was the result of the conquest of power over capitalist nations by a usury-oriented rentier-financier interest older than feudalism."[91]

LaRouche's reputation as a kook has helped to shield him from criticism and organized opposition. But other neonazis have begun to learn from his successes. David Duke, for example, long modeled his electoral strategy after LaRouche.[92] In 1988 he ran in a series of Democratic presidential primaries before turning to the Populist Party ticket, then adopted the Republican Party label the following year to win entry into the Louisiana state legislature. In 1990 he received 605 thousand votes and raised $2.2 million in the race for U.S. Senate. Emulating LaRouche, Duke sought token Black support in the form of civil-rights worker turned right-winger James Meredith. Like

LaRouche, Duke cultivated a public image of antielitist conservatism, while promoting hard-core fascist racial ideology behind the scenes. The combination helped to give neonazi politics a new chance at respectability and a broader constituency that may outlast David Duke himself.

Organizing against neonazis and hate crimes offers both special opportunities and special pitfalls. Knowing that we are all targeted can provide an immediate, concrete reason for political alliances between Jews, gays and lesbians, people of color, women, immigrants, workers, and leftists. In many communities, diverse coalitions against "hate" have formed, providing a valuable framework to learn about each others' histories and struggles, and important lessons in the challenges of coalition work. But in seeking a broad base of support, some antinazi campaigns face a temptation to misrepresent the struggle as a conflict between a supposedly democratic mainstream and an extremist fringe. There is nothing un-American about the far Right: it gives raw, open expression to violence deeply rooted in U.S. society. At their best, antinazi coalitions highlight this connection and offer a bridge to challenging mainstream systems of oppression as well.

Conclusion: Antisemitism in the New World Order

From racist skinhead gangs to JAP-baiting, from the Christian Right's pedestal antisemitism to the neonazis' racial ideology, Jew-hatred remains a serious force in the United States today. Antisemitism no longer involves widespread, institutionalized violence and discrimination, as it did in the early twentieth-century United States, when Jews were commonly categorized as non-White. But for many Jews, White privilege has come at the price of cultural invisibility and loss. Economic gains have also left us vulnerable to age-old forms of scapegoating. To fascists and demagogues who want to exploit people's real grievances against the government and economic system, "the Jewish conspiracy" still offers a valuable target.

The U.S.-led Gulf War against Iraq highlighted not only antisemitism's persistence here, but also how routinely the issue of antisemitism is distorted and manipulated. Saddam Hussein's scapegoating of Israel, threats of poison gas, and missile attacks against Israeli civilians played into George Bush's cynical effort to brand him an "Arab Hitler." Few noted the U.S. government's own antisemitism. Bush (whose "New World Order" rhetoric echoed Hitler) first set up Israelis to be bombed, then exploited Holocaust imagery to help justify his own mass murder of Iraqis. The mass media helped out: while systematically hiding the hundreds of thousands of Iraqis killed and wounded in the U.S.-led bombing, they paraded graphic photos of a prostrate, bloody Israeli woman injured by an Iraqi missile. The selective portrayal of victims was racist against Arabs, but also, more subtly, anti-Jewish: the equation Israel=woman=victim evoked the World War II stereotype of passive ("effeminate") Jews being led to the slaughter.[93]

Regarding the antiwar movement, liberal writers such as Todd Gitlin made vague, sweeping charges of "left antisemitism" (often with little or no documentation), while virtually ignoring the LaRouchian fascists' coordinated, nationwide effort to parasitize the movement.[94]

While pro-Zionist Christian fundamentalists praised the anti-Iraq war for bringing us closer to Armageddon, right-wing opponents of Israel condemned it. The war brought to the surface a split among mainstream conservatives between *New Republic*-style neoconservatives and so-called paleoconservatives, led by syndicated columnist Patrick Buchanan, who denounced Bush's war in antisemitic terms. According to one paleocon, "most neocons are Jewish." The Populist Party and other neonazi groups praised Buchanan and tried to draw him into an alliance.[95]

Antisemitism will not go away by itself, and it may get worse. The Soviet bloc's collapse has weakened the ideological power of anticommunist scapegoating, leaving a gap that antisemitism could help to fill. The United States' long-term economic difficulties offer potentially fertile ground for anti-Jewish sentiment. Opponents of antisemitism need to confront squarely the organized forces of Jew-hatred on the Right, and the systems of capitalism, male supremacy, and White supremacy that sustain them.

© 2001 by Matthew Lyons.

This essay was written with the support, criticism and bibliographic advice of more people than I can name individually. Among them are Lisa Albrecht, Evelyn Annuß, Sander Gilman, John Goetz, J.K. Langford, Robert Schmidt, Mab Segrest, Paul Seidman, Barbara Smith, the *Settlers* study group, my 1990 Ithaca study group, and members of the John Brown Anti-Klan Committee (New York City chapter). My thanks to those both named and unnamed.

For advice and comments that helped me in writing the preface, my thanks to Chip Berlet, David Lyons, Sandra Lyons, Claire McGuire, and laurie prendergast.

NOTES

[1] On the cult of true womanhood, see Paula Baker, "The Domestication of Politics: Women and American Political Society, 1780–1920," in *Unequal Sisters: A Multicultural Reader in U.S. Women's History,* Ellen Carol DuBois and Vicki L. Ruiz, eds. (New York: Routledge, 1990): 72, 87 n36. On Clara Lemlich Shavelson, see Karen Brodkin, *How Jews Became White Folks and What That Says about Race in America* (New Brunswick, NJ: Rutgers University Press, 1998): 131–132.

[2] See J. Sakai, *Settlers: The Mythology of the White Proletariat* (Chicago: Morningstar Press, 1983).

[3] See Theodore W. Allen, *The Invention of the White Race*, vol. 1, *Racial Oppression and Social Control* (New York: Verso, 1994), and vol. 2, *The Origin of Racial Oppression in Anglo-America* (New York: Verso, 1997); Noel Ignatiev, *How the Irish Became White* (New York: Routledge, 1995); and Ian F. Haney López, *White By Law: The Legal Construction of Race* (New York: New York University Press, 1996). For a small sampling of the many other recent works on Whiteness, see Michelle Fine, et al., eds., *Off White: Readings on Race, Power, and Society* (New York: Routledge, 1997); George Lipsitz, *The Possessive Investment in Whiteness: How White People Profit from Identity Politics* (Philadelphia: Temple University Press, 1998); and Birgit Brander Rasmussen, et al., eds., *The Making and Unmaking of Whiteness* (Durham, NC: Duke University Press, 2001).

[4] Brodkin, *How Jews Became White Folks*. The quotations are from pp. 38 and 139.

[5] See Chip Berlet and Matthew N. Lyons, *Right-Wing Populism in America: Too Close for Comfort* (New York: Guilford Press, 2000).

[6] See Esther Kaplan, "Antisemitism after September 11th," *The Public Eye 16,* no. 2 (Summer 2002): 26–32.

[7] See Elinor Langer, "The American Neo-Nazi Movement Today," The Nation 251, no. 3 (July 16–23, 1990): 85; *When Hate Groups Come to Town: A Handbook of Effective Community Responses, 2nd ed.* (Atlanta, GA: Center for Democratic Renewal, 1992): 183.

[8] Ken Lawrence, "Klansmen, Nazis, and Skinheads: Vigilante Repression," *CovertAction* 31 (Winter 1989): 32.

[9] See Dennis King, *Lyndon LaRouche and the New American Fascism* (New York: Doubleday, 1989).

[10] For a sampling of historical studies of U.S. antisemitism, see David A. Gerber, ed., *Anti-Semitism in American History* (Urbana: University of Illinois Press, 1986).

[11] For examples of Jewish feminist writings about antisemitism, see Evelyn Torton Beck, "From 'Kike' to 'JAP'," *Sojourner: The Women's Forum* (September 1988): 18–20; Beck, "The Politics of Jewish Invisibility," *NWSA Journal* vol. 1, no. 1 (1988): 93–102; Beck, ed., *Nice Jewish Girls: A Lesbian Anthology,* rev. ed. (Boston: Beacon Press, 1989); Elly Bulkin, "Hard Ground: Jewish Identity, Racism, and Anti-Semitism," in Elly Bulkin, et al., *Yours in Struggle: Three Feminist Perspectives on Anti-Semitism and Racism* (Brooklyn: Long Haul Press, 1984); Andrea Dworkin, "Israel: Whose Country Is It Anyway?," *Ms.* (September-October 1990): 69–79; Dworkin, *Right-Wing Women* (New York: Coward-McCann, 1983); Dworkin, "The Sexual Mythology of Anti-Semitism," in *A Mensch Among Men: Explorations in Jewish Masculinity,* Harry Brod, ed. (Freedom, CA: Crossing Press, 1988): 118–123; Melanie Kaye/Kantrowitz and Irena Klepfisz, eds., *The Tribe of Dina: A Jewish Women's Anthology* (Montpelier, VT: Sinister Wisdom Books, 1986); Elinor Lerner, "American Feminism and the Jewish Question, 1890-1940," in *Anti-Semitism in American History:* 305–328; Letty Cottin Pogrebin, "Anti-Semitism in the Women's Movement," *Ms.* (June 1982): 45–74. See also the periodicals *Lilith* and *Bridges*. For a polemical critique of Jewish identity politics, see Jenny Bourne, "Homelands of the Mind: Jewish Feminism and Identity Politics," *Race & Class,* vol. 29, no. 1 (1987): 1–23.

[12] See Abram Leon, *The Jewish Question: A Marxist Interpretation* (New York: Pathfinder Press, 1970). For sympathetic critiques, see Maxime Rodinson, "From Jewish Nation to Jewish Problem," in *Cult, Ghetto and State: The Persistence of the Jewish Question,* Jon Rothschild, trans. (London: Al Saqi Books, 1983): 68–117; and Ilan Halevi, *A History of the Jews: Ancient and Modern,* A.M. Berrett, trans. (London: Zed Books, 1987): especially pp. 107–111. For a Marxian discussion of Jews in the United States, see Arthur Liebman, *Jews and the Left* (New York: John Wiley & Sons, 1979).

[13] For examples of revolutionary nationalist discussions of the United States, see Sakai, *Settlers,* and its companion volume, E. Tani and Kaé Sera, *False Nationalism/False Internationalism:*

Class Contradictions in the Armed Struggle (Chicago: Seeds Beneath the Snow, 1985); James R. Forman, *Self-Determination & the African-American People* (Seattle: Open Hand Publishing, 1981); and Phillip Horne, *Beyond Racism: Colonization of U.S. Blacks from Slavery to Superexploitation* (Philadelphia: Institute of Black Studies, 1978).

[14] On the relationship between medieval antisemitism and the witch persecutions, see Rosemary Radford Ruether, *New Woman/New Earth: Sexist Ideologies and Human Liberation* (New York: Seabury Press, 1975): 89–114.

[15] See Leon, *The Jewish Question;* Rodinson, "From Jewish Nation to Jewish Problem"; and Halevi, *A History of the Jews,* especially pp. 107–111.

[16] See Moishe Postone, "Anti-Semitism and National Socialism: Notes on the German Reaction to 'Holocaust'," *New German Critique* 19 (Winter 1980): 97–115. The phrase "socialism of fools" is from August Bebel (1840–1913), a leader of the German Social Democratic Party. The Protocols of the Elders of Zion has been published in many editions, such as *Protocols of the Learned Elders of Zion,* Victor E. Marsden, trans. (New York: Gordon Press, 1978). On the origins of the *Protocols,* see George L. Mosse, *Toward the Final Solution: A History of European Racism* (Madison: University of Wisconsin Press, 1985): 116–120.

[17] My analysis of settlerism, White supremacy, and the material benefits they accord to White workers are based primarily on Sakai, *Settlers,* although I reject Sakai's claim that there is no genuine White working class. See also James Boggs, "Uprooting Racism and Racists in the U.S.A.," *Black Scholar* (October 1970).

[18] On the connections between land expropriation in Europe and settler expansion in North America, see Starhawk, *Dreaming the Dark: Magic, Sex & Politics* (Boston: Beacon Press, 1982): 192–199.

[19] See Angela Davis, *Women, Race and Class* (New York: Random House, 1983); Paula Giddings, *When and Where I Enter: The Impact of Black Women on Race and Sex in America* (New York: Bantam Books, 1984); Rayna Green, "The Pocahontas Perplex: The Image of Indian Women in American Culture," *Massachusetts Review* 16 (Autumn 1975): 698–714; and Asian Women United of California, eds., *Making Waves: An Anthology of Writings by and about Asian American Women* (Boston: Beacon Press, 1989): 2–4, 308–326.

[20] On the Indian captivity literature, see Richard Slotkin, *Regeneration through Violence: The Mythology of the American Frontier, 1600–1860* (Middletown, CT: Wesleyan University Press, 1973): 94–115; and Mark Thomas Connelly, *The Response to Prostitution in the Progressive Era* (Chapel Hill: University of North Carolina Press, 1980): 117–118. On the sexual stereotyping of Chinese men, see Sakai, *Settlers:* 35–36.

[21] See Charlotte Baum, Paula Hyman, and Sonya Michel, *The Jewish Woman in America* (New York: Dial Press, 1976): 24–28.

[22] See Gerda Lerner, "The Lady and the Mill Girl: Changes in the Status of Women in the Age of Jackson," in *The Majority Finds Its Past: Placing Women in History* (Oxford: Oxford University Press, 1979): 15–30; Giddings, *When and Where I Enter:* 47–48; and Baum, et al., *Jewish Woman in America:* 28–30.

[23] Quoted in John Higham, *Send These to Me: Immigrants in Urban America,* rev. ed. (Baltimore: Johns Hopkins University Press, 1984): 149–150.

[24] John Higham, *Strangers in the Land: Patterns of American Nativism 1860–1925* (New York: Atheneum, 1972): 26.

[25] George M. Fredrickson, *White Supremacy: A Comparative Study in American and South African History* (Oxford: Oxford University Press, 1982): 200–201.

[26] Sakai, *Settlers:* 61.

[27] See Joan Younger Dickenson, *The Role of Immigrant Women in the U.S. Labor Force, 1890–1910* (New York: Arno Press, 1980): 59, 65–66.

[28] Sakai, *Settlers:* 63; and Higham, *Strangers in the Land:* 51.

[29] Higham, *Strangers in the Land:* 169.

[30] See Dickenson, *Role of Immigrant Women:* 17–18, 75–86; and Alice Kessler-Harris, *Out to Work: A History of Wage-Earning Women in the United States* (Oxford: Oxford University Press, 1982): 108–141.

[31] Ruth Rosen, *The Lost Sisterhood: Prostitution in America 1900–1918* (Baltimore: Johns Hopkins University Press, 1982): 45.

[32] On race suicide propaganda, see Linda Gordon, *Woman's Body, Woman's Right: A Social History of Birth Control in America* (New York: Grossman Publishers, Viking Press, 1976), especially pp. 139–157. On protective labor legislation, see Kessler-Harris, *Out to Work:* 152–158, 180–214; and Baum, et al., *Jewish Woman in America:* 144–145. On immigration restriction, see Higham, *Strangers in the Land.*

[33] Higham, *Strangers in the Land:* 92–93.

[34] On anti-Jewish quotas in colleges, see Sabrina Gee and Deborah Tirschwell, "Aii Yaa/Oy Vey: The Misuse of Quotas against Jewish and Asian Americans in North America's Institutions of Higher Education," unpublished manuscript.

[35] Higham, *Strangers in the Land:* 92–94, 184–186, 277–286.

[36] Baum, et al., *Jewish Woman in America:* 175.

[37] On the White slavery controversy, see Rosen, *Lost Sisterhood:* 112–135; Connelly, *Response to Prostitution:* 114–135; and Baum, et al., *Jewish Woman in America:* 170–175.

[38] First Watson quote is in Higham, *Strangers in the Land:* 186. Other Watson quotes are in Paul E. Grosser and Edwin G. Halperin, *Anti-Semitism: The Causes and Effects of a Prejudice* (Secaucus, NJ: Citadel Press, 1979): 246–247. See also Wyn Craig Wade, *The Fiery Cross: The Ku Klux Klan in America* (New York: Simon & Schuster, 1987): 143.

[39] See Wade, *Fiery Cross:* 143–145; and Bulkin, "Hard Ground": 116–117.

[40] Higham, *Strangers in the Land:* 286.

[41] Higham, *Send These to Me:* 141–149.

[42] President Wilson took it for granted that "the Bolshevist movement had been led by Jews." Lenin himself was often referred to as a Jew. See Zosa Szajkowski, *Jews, Wars, and Communism,,* vol. 2, *The Impact of the 1919–20 Red Scare on American Jewish Life* (New York: Ktav Publishing House, 1974): 153, 159.

[43] See Morris Schonbach, *Native American Fascism During the 1930s and 1940s* (New York: Garland Publishing, 1985): 266.

[44] Liebman, *Jews and the Left:* 32–33.

[45] Evelyn Torton Beck, "Why Is This Book Different From All Other Books?" in *Nice Jewish Girls,* Beck, ed.: xixn. On the stigmatizing of Yiddish as a women's language, see also Sander Gilman, *Jewish Self-Hatred: Anti-Semitism and the Hidden Language of the Jews* (Baltimore: Johns Hopkins University Press, 1986): 75–76.

[46] See Baum, et al., *Jewish Woman in America:* 77–89, 159–161; and John D'Emilio and Estelle B. Freedman, *Intimate Matters: A History of Sexuality in America* (New York: Harper & Row, 1988): 229–230.

[47] Sara Schulman, "When We Were Very Young: A Walking Tour Through Radical Jewish Women's History on the Lower East Side 1879–1919," in *Tribe of Dina,* Kaye/Kantrowitz and Klepfisz, eds., 235–236, 249. In 1910, male union leaders bargained away the shirt-waist makers' demands for tougher health and safety regulations. These compromises "may very well have resulted in the death of 146 workers in the Triangle Waist Company fire a year later, on Saturday, March 25, 1911" (Baum, et al., *Jewish Woman in America:* 148).

[48] Szajkowski, *Jews, Wars, and Communism,* vol. 2: 117.

[49] Higham, *Strangers in the Land:* 247–248.

[50] Liebman, *Jews and the Left:* 150.

[51] Szajkowski, *Jews, Wars, and Communism,* vol. 2: 122; and Liebman, *Jews and the Left:* 153.

[52] See Liebman, *Jews and the Left:* 195, 359; and Baum, et al., *Jewish Woman in America:* 123–124.

[53] Liebman, *Jews and the Left:* 156.

[54] Baum, et al., *Jewish Woman in America:* 139. See also Elizabeth Ewen, *Immigrant Women in the Land of Dollars: Life and Culture on the Lower East Side, 1890–1925* (New York: Monthly Review Press, 1985).

[55] See Cedric Belfrage, *The American Inquisition: 1945–60* (New York: Bobbs-Merrill, 1973).

[56] The figures cited here on Jews' occupational distribution are from Liebman, *Jews and the Left* (603–604), published in 1979, and may have changed slightly in the interim. Probably the number of self-employed has declined and the number of professionals has increased.

[57] William H. Prichard, William H., "Blacks, Jews, and Negro Zionists: A Crisis In Negro Leadership," *Black Books Bulletin* 5, no. 4 (Winter 1977): 20. On Black-Jewish relations see also Melanie Kaye/Kantrowitz, "Class, Feminism and the Black-Jewish Question," unpublished manuscript; Adolph L. Reed, Jr., "Demystifying Black Jewish Relations," *Genesis II,* (February–March 1987): 13–19; Jonathan Kaufman, *Broken Alliance: The Turbulent Times Between Blacks and Jews in America* (New York: Charles Scribner's Sons, 1988); Amiri Baraka, "Confessions of a Former Anti-Semite," *Village Voice* 25, no. 51 (December 17, 1980): 1, 23; and James Baldwin, "Negroes are Anti-Semitic Because They're Anti-White," *The Price of the Ticket* (New York: St. Martin's Press, 1985): 425–433. Worrill quoted in Brian Klug, "The Philosophy of Cleaning Clothes," *Searchlight* 163 (January 1989): 19.

[58] Farrakhan quoted in Salim Muwakkil, "Louis Farrakhan and the Rhetoric of Racial Division," *In These Times* 9, no. 40 (October 23-29, 1985): 9. On Cokely see Klug, "The Philosophy of Cleaning Clothes": 19. On the NOI-LaRouche alliance see Chip Berlet, "LaRouche Quietly Invades Anti-War Movement," *In These Times* (January 30, 1991): 12; Dennis King, "David Duke and Lyndon LaRouche: The Rise of Neo-Nazism in the Electoral Arena," lecture at Cornell University, Ithaca, New York, May 2, 1991; and *New Federalist* (September 28, 1990).

[59] Quoted in Playthell Benjamin, "The Attitude Is the Message: Louis Farrakhan Pursues the Middle Class," *Village Voice* (August 15, 1989).

[60] See Steve Bruce, *The Rise and Fall of the New Christian Right: Conservative Protestant Politics in America 1978–1988* (Oxford: Oxford University Press, 1988): 127; Pogrebin, "Anti-Semitism in the Women's Movement": 62; and Matthew C. Moen, *The Christian Right and Congress* (Tuscaloosa: University of Alabama Press, 1989): 40. The phrase "pedestal anti-Semitism" is from Dworkin, *Right-Wing Women.*

[61] Ronald B. Sobel, "The Religious Right: Questions for Jews," *ADL Bulletin* 38, no. 1 (January 1981): 4; and Sara Diamond, *Spiritual Warfare: The Politics of the Christian Right* (Boston: South End Press, 1989): 131–134.

[62] Dworkin, *Right-Wing Women:* 139–141.

[63] Quotes in this paragraph are from Beck, "From 'Kike' to 'JAP',": 18–20.

[64] See Beck, "From 'Kike' to 'JAP'"; and Shirley Frondorf, *Death of a "Jewish American Princess": The True Story of a Victim on Trial* (New York: Villard Books, 1988).

[65] For discussions of antisemitism in the feminist movement and the Left, see Beck, "The Politics of Jewish Invisibility"; Beck, "Why Is This Book Different…?": xx–xxxi; Bulkin, "Hard Ground": 145–153; Annette Daum, "Blaming the Jews for the Death of the Goddess," in *Nice Jewish Girls,* Beck, ed.: 303–309; Irena Klepfisz, "Anti-Semitism in the Lesbian/Feminist

Movement," in *Nice Jewish Girls,* Beck, ed.: 51–57; Roger S. Gottlieb, "The Dialectics of National Identity: Left-Wing Anti-Semitism and the Arab-Israeli Conflict," *Socialist Review* 47 (September–October 1979): 19–52 (as well as Peter Johnson's reply to Gottlieb, and Gottlieb's reply to Johnson, in the same issue of *Socialist Review*); Arthur Liebman, "Anti-Semitism in the Left?" in *Anti-Semitism in American History,* Gerber, ed.: 329–359; Steven Lubet and Jeffry (Shaye) Mallow, "That's Funny, You Don't Look Anti-Semitic: Perspective on the American Left," in *Chutzpah: A Jewish Liberation Anthology,* Steven Lubet, et al., eds., (San Francisco: New Glide Publications, 1977): 52–56; and Miriam Socoloff and Henry Balser, "Jewish, Radical and Proud," in *Chutzpah,* Lubet, et al., eds.: 45–46.

66 Beck, "Why Is This Book Different…?": xvii.

67 See Barbara Smith, "Between a Rock and a Hard Place: Relationships Between Black and Jewish Women," in *Yours in Struggle:* 74–78; and Bulkin, "Hard Ground": 148–150.

68 Di Vilde Chayes, "An Open Letter to the Women's Movement," *off our backs* (July 1982): 21.

69 *"Oriental" Jews* is a term encompassing most non-Ashkenazi Jews, including Jews of Arab, Ethiopian, Indian, Iranian, Kurdish, and Sephardi descent. (Ashkenazi Jews are of central and eastern European descent.) I place the word "Oriental" in quotes because of the racist connotations often attached to it. The phrase *Sephardi Jews* is sometimes used as a generic term for non-Ashkenazi Jews, but I find this misleading. Sephardis are Jews of Spanish or Portuguese descent, whose culture blended European and Arab influences under Islámic rule in Spain, and many of whom found refuge in Turkey and North Africa after the Christians reconquered the Iberian peninsula and threw them out. To subsume all non-Ashkenazis under the label "Sephardi" obscures the existence of many other non-Ashkenazi Jewish cultures.

70 See Alisa Solomon, "Jewish Feminists Speak Out on Israel," *Bridges* 1, no. 1 (Spring 1990/5750): 41–56; Lubet and Mallow, "That's Funny, You Don't Look Anti-Semitic"; Bulkin, "Hard Ground": 154–186; and the discussion of Zionism, antisemitism, and racism in the July, August-September, and October, 1982 issues of *off our backs.*

71 On the 1980 U.N. Women's Conference in Copenhagen, see Pogrebin, "Anti-Semitism in the Women's Movement": 48–49, 62, 65; and Bulkin's critical comments about Pogrebin's article in "Hard Ground": 169–174.

72 On the Israeli-Jewish nationality, see Arie Bober, ed., *The Other Israel: The Radical Case Against Zionism* (Garden City, NY: Doubleday & Company, 1972): 176–181, 237–242; Alain Gresh, *The PLO: The Struggle Within: Towards an Independent Palestinian State,* A.M. Berrett, trans. (London: Zed Books, 1985): 40–42; and Moshe Machover and Said Hammammi, "To Live Together," in *Forbidden Agendas: Intolerance and Defiance in the Middle East,* Jon Rothschild, ed. (London: Al Saqi Books, 1984): 383–387.

73 On the racism inherent in the Zionist conception of a Jewish state, see Roselle Tekiner, *Jewish Nationality Status as the Basis for Institutionalized Racism in Israel* (London: EAFORD [International Organization for the Elimination of All Forms of Racial Discrimination], 1985); Nira Yuval-Davis, "The Jewish Collectivity and National Reproduction in Israel," in *Women in the Middle East* (London: Zed Books, 1987): 60–93; Dworkin, "Israel: Whose Country Is It Anyway?'; Uri Davis, "Israel's Zionist Society: Consequences for Internal Opposition and the Necessity for External Intervention," in *Judaism or Zionism?: What Difference for the Middle East?* EAFORD and AJAZ [American Jewish Alternatives to Zionism], eds. (London: Zed Books, 1986): 176–201; Elmer Berger, "The Unauthenticity of 'Jewish People' Zionism," in *Judaism or Zionism?* EAFORD and AJAZ, eds.: 133–147, especially pp. 140–142; and Walter Lehn, "The Jewish National Fund," in *Settler Regimes in Africa and the Arab World,* Ibrahim Abu-Lughod and Baha Abu-Laban, eds. (Wilmette, IL: Medina University Press International, 1974): 43–53. Certain groups of Jews have been denied the right to automatic Israeli citizenship "by return." For example, gay and lesbian Jews have been excluded at least until recently, and Ethiopian Jews were excluded until 1975.

[74] Israel's fundamental laws articulate its primary racial division—between Jews and non-Jews. White supremacy operates as a second-order division within this framework, creating a three-tiered structure: on top, Ashkenazi Jews (of central and eastern European descent); in the middle, "Oriental" Jews (Arab, Sephardic, Sephardi, African, and Asian); on the bottom, Palestinian Arabs. The claim that Israel is the state of the entire Jewish people helps to rationalize the dominance of Ashkenazis within Israeli society: Ashkenazis long formed a minority of Israeli Jews, but a large majority of Jews worldwide. This "imbalance" also presumably fed the Israeli government's eagerness to admit large numbers of Soviet (Ashkenazi) Jews.

[75] See the New Jewish Agenda National Platform (adopted November 28, 1982): 6.

[76] See Rosemary Sayigh, *Palestinians: From Peasants to Revolutionaries* (London: Zed Books 1979): 64–92; Uri Davis, "Israel's Zionist Society": 180, 196n–197n; *Settler Regimes in Africa and the Arab World*,196–197n; James J. Zogby, "The Palestinian Revolt of the 1930s," in *Settler Regimes in Africa and the Arab World*, Abu-Lughod, ed.: 103–105; Edward Said, *The Question of Palestine* (New York: Random House, 1979): 21; Moshe Machover and Mario Offenberg, "Zionism and Its Scarecrows," *Khamsin* 6 (1978): 46–59; Emmanuel Farjoun, "Palestinian Workers in Israel: A Reserve Army of Labor," in *Forbidden Agendas,* Rothschild, ed.: 77–122; and Moshe Semyonev and Noah Lewin-Epstein, *Hewers of Wood and Drawers of Water: Noncitizen Arabs in the Israeli Labor Market* (Ithaca, NY: ILR Press, 1987).

Labor Zionism's policy of racial exclusivism fits a pattern often followed by other settler working-class movements: In the United States, White socialists and other labor activists played a leading role in the bloody campaigns from the 1870s to early 1900s to force Chinese and Japanese workers out of the California labor market. In South Africa in 1922, the Communist Party supported a nationwide general strike by White workers under the slogan, "Workers of the World Fight and Unite for a White South Africa!" (See Sakai, *Settlers:* 35–36, 60.)

[77] See "Zionism and Anti-Semitism" in *The Other Israel,* Bober, ed.: 167–75; Gilman, *Jewish Self-Hatred:* 238–240; Machover and Offenberg, "Zionism and Its Scarecrows": 34–46; and Ella Shohat, "Rethinking Jews and Muslims: Quincentennial Reflections," *Middle East Report* (September-October, 1992): 28–30.

[78] See Boaz Evron, "Holocaust: The Uses of Disaster," *Radical America* 17, no. 4 (July-August 1983): 7–21.

[79] Quoted in Lenni Brenner, *Zionism in the Age of the Dictators: A Reappraisal* (Westport, CT: Lawrence Hill, 1983): 149.

[80] See William W. Ohrbach, "Israel vs. Soviet Jewry," *Response* 38: 7–19; *Soviet Jews: Whose Humanitarian Concern? The New York Times* (March 1, 1987): 3; (March 30, 1987): 8; (June 18, 1987): 31 (column by Pamela B. Cohen and Micah H. Naftalin); (July 16, 1987): 9; Noam Chomsky, *The Fateful Triangle: The United States, Israel and the Palestinians* (Boston: South End Press, 1983): 110, 169n; Bulkin, "Hard Ground": 155–156, 205n; and Bishara Bahbah, *Israel and Latin America: The Military Connection* (New York: St. Martin's Press, 1986): 130–131.

[81] Dworkin, "Israel: Whose Country Is It Anyway?": 74–77.

[82] On the Bund's anti-Zionism, see for example, *The Jewish Labor Bund, 1897–1957* (New York: International Jewish Labor Bund, 1958). The Reform Jewish anti-Zionist tradition is continued by American Jewish Alternatives to Zionism, Inc. (AJAZ), 501 5th Avenue, Suite 2015, New York, NY 10017. See for example, EAFORD and AJAZ, *Judaism or Zionism?* Neturei Karta, affiliated with the Satmar court of Hassidism, continues the Orthodox Jewish anti-Zionist tradition. See for example Moshe Shonfeld, *The Holocaust Victims Accuse* (Brooklyn, NY: Neturei Karta, 1977).

[83] See Elinor Langer, "The American Neo-Nazi Movement Today," *The Nation* 251, no. 3 (July 16-23, 1990): 82–107.

84 See Mab Segrest and Leonard Zeskind, *Quarantines and Death: The Far Right's Homophobic Agenda* (Atlanta, GA: Center for Democratic Renewal, 1989); Gene-Gabriel Moore, "North Carolina's War Against Gays," *Christopher Street* 121 (1988): 14–18; and Monique Wolfing, discussion with Tom Metzger on *Race and Reason,* aired on San Francisco public access television, May 1989. Wolfing was leader of the Aryan Women's League. See also Helen Zia, "Women in Hate Groups," *Ms.* (March-April 1991): 20–27.

85 "Metzger Begins Move to the Top," *The Monitor* (Center for Democratic Renewal), (January 1988): 5. See also Lawrence, "Klansmen, Nazis, Skinheads": 33.

86 "What Next for Metzger & WAR," *The Monitor* (March 1991): 9.

87 "Far Right Takes Anti-War Stance," *The Monitor* (March 1991): 11.

88 My discussion of Lyndon LaRouche is based on Dennis King, *Lyndon LaRouche and the New American Fascism* (New York: Doubleday, 1989), and on lectures by King at the Marxist School in New York City on May 11, 1989, and at Cornell University, Ithaca, NY on May 2, 1991.

89 King, *Lyndon LaRouche:* 143.

90 Farrakhan has been endorsed not only by the LaRouchians, but also by the New Alliance Party (NAP), an ostensibly leftist, feminist, progay organization widely denounced as a political cult. NAP leader Fred Newman once led his followers into an alliance with the LaRouchians in 1973–1974, including a few months as members of the National Caucus of Labor Committees (NCLC). Former Newmanites such as Dennis L. Serrette, NAP's 1984 presidential candidate, report that Newman's methods of organizational control closely resemble LaRouche's and that people of color hold prominent positions but no real power within the NAP. See Chip Berlet, *Clouds Blur the Rainbow: The Other Side of the New Alliance Party* (Cambridge, MA: Political Research Associates, 1992); Bruce Shapiro, "Dr. Fulani's Snake-Oil Show," The Nation (May 4, 1992): 585–594; and articles in *Radical America 21,* no. 5, by Berlet, Serrette, Ken Lawrence, Charles W. Tisdale, and Leigh Peake. *(Clouds Blur the Rainbow* is available from Political Research Associates at 678 Massachusetts Avenue, Suite 205, Cambridge, MA 02139-3355.)

91 "Imperialism…" is quoted from Lyndon H. LaRouche, Jr., *The Power of Reason, 1988: An Autobiography* (Washington, DC: Executive Intelligence Review, 1987): 191. "Kissinger's friends…" is quoted from Christopher White, "George Bush's Countdown to Middle East War," *New Federalist,* extra edition (January 1991).

92 Dennis King, lectures May 11, 1989, and May 2, 1991.

93 I am grateful to Patricia Zimmerman for pointing out the media's use of the missile victim photo, and its significance (personal communication, February 1991).

94 See Todd Gitlin, "Toward a Difficult Peace Movement," *Village Voice* (February 19, 1991): 34; and Alisa Solomon, "Between Iraq and a Hard Place," *Village Voice* (February 5, 1991): 29. For a critical discussion see Jean Tepperman, "Scud Shockwaves Hit Bay Area Jews," *San Francisco Bay Guardian* (February 13, 1991): 15–16.

95 See "Leaders Wrestle with Faith and War," *Christianity Today* (February 11, 1991): 50; and "Far Right Takes Anti-War Stance," and "Pat Buchanan and His 'Amen Corner,'" *The Monitor* (March 1991): 10–13.

Multiplicity

EDÉN TORRES

Teaching ethnicity
introducing multiplicity
Promethean confrontation
directed information.
Jueros like mad albino wasps
land and sting
recoil and foil the lesson plan
inside their heads
entitlement rings
and egos swell.
    I sacrifice in sweat divine
pop peyote
and swallow whine
Porque todos son muertos
passing in time,
whose investment in evil
cannot survive.
    But at night I am underground
with a nation of *lobos solos*
aztlanitos y mestizos
Fronting with the pack
Sublimating the lack
of *cultura pura*
con Puerto Rican Powwows
Native *carnival*
Black *conjunto*
Chicano New Year
(silk dragons and all)
    Bienvenido a la frontera
Ay te watcho guapo
What I really want, *chulito*
is to teach Spanglish 101
But my brutal university
does not recognize

the emotional adversity
and drain
of m o n o l i n g u a l i s m.
Cannot understand
having to represent
mi gente no decente
I learned long ago
there's no power in a brown Ph.D.
just a little money for the family.
     And when I die
my last known residence
will be
the corner of 4 sacred directions
and irony.

The Cult of the "Perfect" Language:
Censorship by Class, Gender, and Race

MITSUYE YAMADA

This article is an expanded version of a talk given at a plenary session at
"Parallels and Intersections: A Conference on Racism and Other Forms of
Oppression," sponsored and organized by the Women Against Racism
Committee, Women's Resource & Action Center, University of Iowa, on April 8,
1989. It was originally published in Sowing Ti Leaves: Writings by
Multicultural Women.[1]

Thanks to prodigious research by women scholars in the past two decades,
we are beginning to see a fuller picture of women's history through recovered
writings of that part of women's lives that has been left out of traditional literature and recorded documents. As the results of their research began to
reach the popular market in the early 1970s, I read, with a sense of exhila-
rating excitement, the letters, diaries, poems, and songs collected in works
such as *By a Woman Writt: Literature from Six Centuries By and About Women*[2]
and *The World Split Open: Four Centuries of Women Poets in England and*
America, 1552–1950.[3] I was especially struck by what these women dared to
"complain" about in their writings. The writers were not high-born ladies
writing letters and poems to while away their time; many were working
women, either trying to make a living as popular writers or working in textile
mills and mines. These collections of recovered works give women, as one of
the editors so aptly states, "their own voice in their own time."

Among these diggings, I looked in vain for small nuggets, maybe a few
specks, by my own immediate "mothers" in this country. Even in the more
recent, voluminous, and extraordinary collection, *The Norton Anthology of*
Literature by Women,[4] a work that makes us acutely aware of "women's
cultural situation" in a female context, early Asian women's voices are absent.

In the light of increasing interest in the experience of Asians in America, a
similar search is underway among Asian American scholars to recover our
historical past in this country. A few early polemical works in English have
surfaced about the exclusion movement directed against the Chinese and
Japanese immigrants in the late nineteenth century and early twentieth
century, but generally research in this area has resulted in historical and sociological assessments by recent scholars about what happened to Asian
immigrants. Very little has been written by the Asians themselves about how
they were personally affected by nativist attitudes that were translated into

anti-Asian immigration policies, except perhaps for those remarkable and poignant poems literally dug into the walls of the immigrant detention halls on Angel Island. The value of these poems has only been recently recognized, and the poems have been translated and published.[5]

Finally, only in the past decade or so have we begun to listen to the words of the old immigrants themselves as they reminisce in their native languages about their early experiences. A few oral history projects are underway to compile and translate these stories into English from their original languages. I have heard of a few personal diaries by first-generation Issei women, but they remain in the hands of their families, untranslated, and therefore inaccessible even to the diarists' own Nisei children.[6] An exciting prospect for some future researcher in Asian Pacific American history may be to look for "letters home," which surely must exist among personal papers, hidden away by families in boxes throughout Asia.

We now know that such writings, especially the intensely personal accounts, are building blocks to the dreams of future generations of writers. Had the writings by early immigrant Asian women been accessible in whatever form, they might have become grist for my own creative efforts when I was growing up. For myself, I yearn to read personal accounts by those Asian women who struggled beside their men. As I dipped into the new collections of women's writings, I felt a gnawing sense of regret that such primary materials by pioneering Asian women written "in their own voice in their own time" are almost nonexistent.

Meanwhile, what about the treasures that are being lost today as thousands of new Asian immigrants struggle to live, study, and work among us? We accept the loss as inevitable. Like those other Asians before them, we reason, they have no time to write, for they are too busy working, studying, and becoming "acculturated." But all immigrants from different parts of the world have been faced with the same problems. In the early 1900s a number of Jewish and Italian immigrant writers, most notable among them Anzia Yezierska, author of *The Bread Givers* (published in 1925),[7] wrote about the day-to-day struggle of the immigrant in the New World. Among the Asians, we do have a few autobiographical works, but on the whole, except for Carlos Bulosan's writings,[8] they are "East meets West" observations, primarily designed to charm the hearts of American readers.

Could there be other factors involved that make Asians, more than other immigrants, reluctant to express themselves openly? Can they be persuaded to tell us in any language they now speak, in any way they know, something about the foundation of culture and myth that shapes our lives? If our past history is any guide, the answer is "Probably not," except for those who are writing for the many foreign-language weekly newspapers in their own communities. As for the rest of the immigrants, they are caught in "the cult of the 'perfect' language." Their lives are in constant transition, as are their languages; a crucial part of their life experiences may never be recorded.

Through examining my own culture, my mother's experiences as an immigrant woman, and my own experience as a Japanese American, I will explore some of the cultural barriers that are peculiar to transplanted Asians, particularly the women. I belong to a still relatively small group, Asian Pacific American women writers, who are second-, third-, and fourth-generation writers primarily educated in the American public school system. Very little in the literature, by men or women, that was presented to us during our school years spoke to our specific experiences.

If we are now writing about our respective heritages from a vast array of Asian traditions, or about our identities within the American cultural landscape, or about our self-image in the American political context, we do so by forging our own way. A recently published anthology, *The Forbidden Stitch: An Asian American Women's Anthology,*[9] offers a nearly comprehensive bibliography but cites only a few works dated before 1970. Our Asian ancestors have been around for more than a hundred and fifty years, but most of their experiences have never been recorded *as they occurred,* even in their own languages.

Most of our writings are what we might call "retroflexive," bending back over territory trod by our parents or ourselves in a process of rebirth. Some of us, not aware at first of our "difference," had begun to write just as we began to perceive ourselves as "other" in a majority culture not our own, and of course by then we were writing in literate English. Even those of us who initially spoke another language didn't "come out" as writers until we became socially acceptable in English. Our main goal was to learn to write grammatical English and then to speak it without a trace of a foreign accent, if possible. Anything less, we assumed, would have been unacceptable. My ninety-year-old mother, for example, took English lessons seventy years ago for a short period and today speaks it only well enough to carry on a simple conversation with her grandchildren and great-grandchildren. She gave up trying to learn years ago because, she says, she could "never, never get it right."

After my father's death more than thirty years ago, my mother came to live with my husband and me and our growing family of small children in suburban New York, and she moved with us to California several years later. In both places, she felt isolated from old friends and from other Issei, the Japanese communities in Seattle where my father and she usually lived before World War II and later in Chicago, where they settled after the war. Helping us raise our children and watching the family dynamics among us had obviously triggered long-suppressed and anguished memories of "those early days" when she came to live with a man she hardly knew, five thousand miles away from family and friends in Japan.

It was then that I began to hear touching stories I had never heard before: stories about her fears as a lonely young mother with small children, trying to cope in a strange country, separated from her immediate neighbors by language and culture. As the self-appointed family historian, I first started to record those stories by translating them into English, "for the sake of your Sansei grandchildren," I told her, but she would always admonish, "Don't write these things down; they aren't worth anything. It's too embarrassing; I hardly learned to speak English properly after all these years." She persisted in discrediting the value of her own stories because they could not be written down in proper style. I thought about capturing what she herself referred to as her special brand of "broken English" (the expression reflects our attitude towards those who do not speak as we do, as if language were an immutable artifact, like a precious marble statue, rather than a dynamic, living force).

The process seemed to me simple enough at first. All I had to do, I thought, was let her see her own words in print between the covers of a published book, and she would come to know that her language, and hence her experience, had a valid place in this culture. I wrote the poem "Marriage Was a Foreign Country" and showed her the typed-up version. (The poem was later included in a book of my poems.)[10]

When we land the boat full
of new
brides
lean over railing
with wrinkled glossy pictures
they hold inside hand
like this
so excited.

"See, Mother, here it is, these are your words, your life." But she would insist that I translate her words into "correct" English. When I countered that people would be more interested in hearing her real voice, she fretted that I was trying to expose her ignorance. She was adamant about my not embarrassing her by making her sound "crude and uneducated." I have tried to respect her wishes by "cleaning up" some of her most glaring grammatical errors and malapropisms, but because the emotional impact of her devastating experiences needed to be retained, I asked her if she would permit me to retain the flavor of her speech pattern in some way in the poem. She responded, *"Soshitara, warawarenai yoni shite chōdai,"* then, "Don't make me into a laughing stock."

"Nobody will laugh at you," I would persist, but our conversation often ended with a variation of, "Yes they would because I sound like an illiterate lower-class person."

My mother is not the only person who associates language with class. Most Americans share the dictum that correct English is spoken by proper, well-educated Americans who use it to discuss serious matters; flawed English spoken with an accent (with the exception of the upper-class British accent) is spoken by the lower class and is usually the object of ridicule. The hierarchical language that existed in Japan when my mother was growing up, she found, was very much in force here as well.

My mother came to the United States at nineteen years of age in 1918 to join my father, who had earlier gone to Japan to "find a wife" and then returned to his job in Seattle. She was born and raised in Fukuoka Prefecture on the island of Kyushu and speaks two different Japanese dialects: the Tokyo dialect considered to be the standard speech, and the country dialect of her prefecture. She had very carefully cultivated her Tokyo dialect to teach it to my three brothers and me. It was the dialect she used exclusively when she spoke in the company of her new friends among the immigrant Japanese in Seattle. I suggested to her that she write down those stories about her early days of adjustment to American culture in Tokyo dialect, exactly as she told them to me, but was puzzled when she even resisted that. Gradually, I learned what the problem was: through the years she learned that to the contemporary Japanese in her native land, her Tokyo speech, like that of most Issei here, had become old-fashioned and quaint after several decades of isolation from a changing mother tongue. Increasingly, she became reluctant to even think of writing a letter to her educated relatives in Japan, she said, for fear of being judged unschooled by them.

I was undaunted. Well then, why not write her stories down in her own country dialect somewhat modified, so that I could understand it? I remembered that she spoke "another language" besides the Tokyo dialect I knew. I learned this for the first time on our visit to Japan when I was a child. On that occasion, much to my astonishment, the minute we got off the train in Fukuoka, she began rattling off in a strange tongue to the throng of relatives who had come to meet us. This must have been her language, the language of her thoughts, but she never permitted herself to reveal it in "full bloom" even to us, her children. When I brought up this possibility she said, Oh no, people would laugh. Didn't I know that country dialect, like street and peasant patois in print and on the stage, is often the language of light comedy in Japan (except, of course, to the native speakers)? I had no quick response to this. I was reminded of hillbilly speech, which is often the subject of ridicule and scorn here. She brought up other examples: the *kyogen,* those short farcical and stupid antics of the commoners between performances of deadly serious Noh dramas. Ah yes, I would note, just like the comic relief segments in Shakespearean tragedies. I was amazed by the logic of her arguments but was nevertheless increasingly irritated by what I thought was her stubbornness.

In some ways, I was trying to find another project for my widowed mother, who had become completely involved in her role as grandmother to my children since moving in with us. I tried different approaches. It's different in this country, I would tell her. People in America are charmed by country and other kinds of dialects because these are considered to be part of the folk culture, like the patchwork quilts that she was so skillful at making. In fact, there are many written materials in the language of Black people as well as in pidgin English spoken in Hawai'i, I would say, but she could not be persuaded. She knew that these were not languages used for educated discourse or in serious writing.

At one point when she became tearfully defensive, I had to admit I was pressing too hard and finally realized she was not simply making excuses for herself. Here was a woman with incredible stories to tell, who is capable of speaking and writing in three different languages, but whose stories would never be recorded in any of those voices because she herself had judged them flawed in some way. Separate social attitudes towards each of them, one reinforcing the other, have silenced her. In this country she faced the most common social attitudes towards her "broken English," almost on a daily basis. She remembers only too vividly the number of times salespersons shouted at her or spoke to her in a truncated, childlike way, as if she were hard of hearing or a person with limited mental faculties. *Hakujins* (white people), she complains, assume that people who speak less-than-perfect English or speak it with an accent (or both) are "flawed" in other ways. She became a victim of "the cult of the 'perfect' language," which exists even today in many other cultures as it does here. She is silenced multiply: by class attitudes towards language in both cultures; by herself in Japanese; and by us in English.

In addition to class attitudes that had the effect of self-censorship for my mother, strong gender-linked differences in Japanese speech must have compounded her difficulties in learning English as "perfectly" as she had hoped to. I had not realized until quite recently how much more complex learning a new language must have been for my mother than for some other immigrants. There are many sex-specific terms in spoken Japanese, not to mention the numerous socially determined ones, to complicate matters for someone as strictly bound to observing social decorum as she was. It must have required a kind of mental gymnastics to try to find the "right words" in translating her thoughts into American English. The much-quoted Virginia Woolf spoke of habits of the mind and the choice of subject matters that hampered the literary output of women writers of her time. Woolf told us that she had succeeded in killing "The Angel in the House" but that there are still "many ghosts to fight, many prejudices to overcome."[11]

My own struggles in learning Japanese as a small child may be a case in point. I learned quite early that certain forms were correct for my brothers to use but not for me. My three brothers used the first person singular pronoun *boku,* but when I did so, I was told I mustn't talk "like a boy." Girls must use the more polite form *watashi* in informal conversation, and *watakushi* in formal settings, I was told. In confusion I simply referred to myself by name—"Mitsuye would like a glass of milk." I did not know then that it is not necessary to use pronouns in most verbal constructions in Japanese.

As we grew older, I learned that certain forms of expression became even more complex, especially for girls. For example, my father simply said, *"Hitostu kure"* ("Give [me] one") to my mother at the dinner table. When my brothers and I were quite young, the informal *"Hitostu chodai"* was acceptable, but I soon learned (at about age twelve) that the informal language I had learned as a child is spoken only to one's peers, and since I never spoke Japanese to my brothers or to my friends, a whole new way of speaking to one's superiors, a "ladylike" polite way, had to be learned. And so, instead of *"Hitostu chodai,"* I was told to say, *"Hitostu kudasai masen ka?"* ("Won't [you] please give [me] one?")

An avid reader of novels in those days, I used to sit at the kitchen table recounting in Japanese the plot summary of the story I happened to be reading while my mother prepared the family dinner.[12] It was a special time for us because my older brothers were outdoors playing and dinner preparation for a full-course meal was very often an elaborate ritual for my mother. Suddenly, at around age eleven or twelve, the age a girl must become a "lady," I stopped doing this and spoke to her as little as possible in Japanese because of her constant unpleasant interruptions. She was not aware that in her effort to teach me the absolutely proper Japanese (so that I would not disgrace myself in public as an adult woman, she said) she not only succeeded in muzzling me, but effectively put a wedge in our relationship that would not be removed for many years.

During my early teens I learned in an interesting way that Japanese men's language is more open and free. As a teenager with literary aspirations, I often sat, enraptured, in our dining room watching a group of twenty to thirty poets spend long hours scribbling Japanese characters on strips of paper on their laps. I was not there as a participant at these monthly meetings of my father's poetry society, the Senryu Kai, but as part of the kitchen help, serving tea, *makizushi,* and assorted snacks prepared by my mother. I looked forward to these meetings because of the thrill of watching the calligrapher brush fluid black characters on a long roll of paper pinned to the whole length of our dining room wall. Listening to the poets intone their short lines as the calligrapher made his brush strokes was a special treat for me, though I understood only snatches of the words. After each reading, there would be audible murmurs of appreciation or bursts of laughter.

Senryu's short, fourteen-syllable verses about the daily cares and concerns of the poet were written in concrete language with wit and humor. The humor was often sardonic and, I gathered, frequently scatological and bawdy, but as long as I kept a straight face through the "punch line" as they laughed raucously, my father and his friends assumed that their jokes were slipping by this properly brought up teenage girl. My mother would call me back into the kitchen from time to time and tell me to do my job and not listen to any of the "male silliness" going on out there in the dining room.

There was one woman in the group, a Mrs. Kawaguchi, but she was so "different" from any Issei woman I knew that I did not consider her sitting there writing senryu among the men at all strange. She out-talked the men in her low raspy voice, laughed out loud with her mouth open, and smoked and drank, just like my father and the other men in the group. My mother and her friends had taught me by example that women should speak with discretion in high-pitched voices and in a childlike manner in the presence of men and must always laugh politely, covering their mouths with their hands. And as far as I knew, none of my mother's friends smoked or drank.

Furthermore, and more shocking, was that Mrs. Kawaguchi talked like the men, using the kind of language Mother would have considered coarse and definitely unladylike. Like my father, she would demand, *"Hitostu kure"* ("Give [me] one") as she held out her plate for another helping of sushi to the man at the other end of the table. Not only that, she and the men addressed each other as *kimi* ("you"), a pronoun form I was told I must never use. It is only for boys, I was told, when they talk to each other or for grown men in addressing other males. As they gossiped about an absent poet, Mrs.

Kawaguchi would say *"anno yatsu"* meaning "that person," an especially vulgar expression I was told was only for men. Obviously the men accepted her as one of them, a fellow poet. Mrs. Kawaguchi's presence in our dining room, "acting like a man," irritated my mother and fascinated me.

On one occasion when I returned to the kitchen with a pot of tea saying, "Mrs. Kawaguchi says this tea is cold," my mother hissed savagely and said under her breath, "That woman has two small children at home. What is she doing here in the company of men writing senryu?" To my mother, writing senryu, like drinking and other forms of debauchery, was all right for men, but women, especially mothers of small children, had more important things to do. I must have looked surprised, more by her tone than her words. Noticing my expression, she explained, "She could be writing haiku, at least. Senryu is not for women. Men are 'lousy'; it's their nature." She was speaking Japanese interspersed with English words. I knew she had meant to say "rowdy," and I could not resist breaking into a wide smile, as I must have done at her malapropisms on many other occasions. I was amused, I remember, by her inadvertent cleverness: senryu is indeed "lousy" because it is boisterous, coarse, repellent, and bad. She immediately directed her anger at me, "And you, a young girl like you shouldn't be standing there *pok'kan to shite*, like a dummy, listening to such stupidity!" The onomatopoeic Japanese word *pok'kan*, which imitates the hollow sound of an empty vessel, might have come right out of one of the senryu poems. Its harsh ring used to intimidate me when I was a small child, but I was, by this time, an arrogant high school teenager studying English.

By then I had been taught the difference between "good" poetry and "bad" poetry in my literature classes, and my mother's words must have reinforced my learning. In my English classes, I was reading sonnets by the likes of Shakespeare and John Donne and publishing some of my own in the school's creative writing magazine. I must have agreed with her that indulging in expressing one's angers and frustrations using unadorned language or body metaphors was frivolous and vulgar. This particular incident, among all the memories of Senryu Kai meetings my father had at our house, remains vivid in my mind. It may have been the time I had processed the information about "proper" and "improper" language for poetry, especially for women, and came out on the side of "proper" academic poetry. In fact, it would take me almost thirty-five years after writing my "camp poems" about my experiences in a concentration camp in Idaho during World War II before I took them to be "serious" poetry. Those poems were not crafted sonnets; neither were they "haiku-like." They were simply notes of everyday happenings I jotted down during my internment, more like my father's senryu.

The language of haiku is symbolic, encoded, implicit; therefore, presumably elegant and ladylike. The language of senryu, on the other hand, is concrete, direct, explicit; therefore "inelegant." Oddly enough, the mother I knew with only family members present was not ladylike—quiet and demure. She was commanding, strong, and frequently given to angry outbursts. Ironically, the haiku form that she admired so much would have been too subtle for her to express the intensity of her passions forcefully and directly. Still, she would not have permitted herself to join the men in her own dining room writing senryu alongside Mrs. Kawaguchi. During those Senryu Kai meetings, she demonstrated clearly that she resented the position of serving those who were indulging themselves writing poetry in her dining room, but she kept her anger in check and simmering beneath a swift, efficient surface as she worked. I remember trying to keep an emotional as well as a physical distance from her whenever possible during those times, for I knew I would become the target of her anger if I stood around.

Generally speaking, the Nisei, born and raised in a society less bound by class than the Issei and having learned English at a younger age, were not hobbled by old-country traditions. One might assume, then, that the Nisei would be freed from what Tillie Olsen calls the "unnatural silence"[13] imposed by varying social and psychological circumstances. Such an assumption would be only partially true, judging from the types of writings that the Nisei, as well as children of immigrants from other Asian countries, have traditionally done in the past decades. Personal narrative and imaginative writings would tell us what forced acculturation *feels like,* but we have many more historical and sociological studies by Nisei and other scholars *about* our history than personal accounts or fictional stories that would expose how we feel about our experiences.

Persons who are constantly on the watch about their language form, the way they speak or write, are more likely to guard their thoughts and feelings more carefully. Most Nisei who grew up before World War II will remember that the pressure to learn to speak American English "like a white person" was very great.[14] In fact, some Nisei have deliberately resisted learning Japanese in order to be "more American." Some of us tried to give up our original language because, we were told, hanging on to it would hamper our progress in learning "perfect" English and would make us seem "un-American." For us, cutting away the Japanese language from our consciousness seemed a simple way of casting our lot with the American majority. By disassociating ourselves from "alien languages" spoken by our parents and newly arrived Asian immigrants, we believed we were freed of the complex issues of identity that plagued our parents. We were embarrassed by our mothers who, it seemed, were either incapable of learning or refused to learn to speak English. (The fathers, because they were out in the work force, generally spoke communicable English.) Many of us had school friends with European immigrant parents who were adjusting remarkably well; why couldn't our mothers be like them?

Most Nisei could not understand the terror our mothers felt in being forced to reject everything familiar to them. For the most part, our mothers became adjusted to wearing shoes and Western dress, to eating American food, and even to seeing their children rapidly drifting away from them by adopting American ideas and manners. Most of us thought little about the racist nature of the laws aimed specifically at Asian nationals, such as the restrictions against their becoming naturalized U.S. citizens and buying land in this country. We were not sensitive to the notion that our mothers may have been unwilling to give up what seemed to them the only vestige of their heritage, their native language, that could not be invaded by the foreign culture that surrounded them every day. As products of the American educational system, we Nisei already believed in the Protestant work ethic: You can attain anything and get anywhere you want if you work hard enough at it. The corollary to that, of course, is obvious: It must be your own fault if you aren't getting anywhere.

An incident during World War II would illustrate to what extent some of us had been indoctrinated and had internalized this old saw. During the planning stage of the removal of the West Coast Japanese to concentration camps a few months following the outbreak of World War II, Milton Eisenhower, then director of the War Relocation Authority, apparently sought the opinion of one of the older Nisei leaders in the Japanese American community about the management of the Japanese in the camps. In his response to the director, our spokesman suggested that schools should be set up in these camps and include in their curriculum speech classes to eliminate all traces of the "Japanese American accent or mannerism" so that we would not encounter prejudice against us when we left camp. This nation was alive and well. More than three decades later, in the 1970s, an enterprising couple in California advertised in Vietnamese and Korean language newspapers: "Learn to speak American in six weeks! Erase your Asian accent and get higher paying jobs!" "Speak American" became the buzzword. Although quite a number of Vietnamese people I met during those days spoke functional English, they were led to believe that all their problems would be solved magically and simply if they took this six-week course. Needless to say, this couple did a brisk business.

The enormous success of the "U.S. English" movement, actively supported by the former U.S. Senator S.I. Hayakawa, can be attributed to support from both new and old immigrants as well as from the general public. The immigrants have been loathe to express opposition to the English-only movement for fear of appearing to be anti-American, while much of the nonforeign white population has rallied around this issue with a renewed sense of patriotism. It has given the latter an outlet for their resentment against the infusion of Asian immigrants and other refugees in our communities, with their various "foreign and alien" languages and cultures.

In 1987, the voters in California, in their seeming concern for national unity, overwhelmingly passed an "English-only" initiative. This initiative made English the official state language in California and has served to encourage the already percolating xenophobia among us. Since the passage of this initiative, there has been a series of troubling incidents, such as the reprimand issued to hospital workers at the University of California in San Francisco for speaking Spanish and Tagalog to fellow workers and attempts to prevent donations of Chinese-language books to the library in a community in southern California. Such incidents serve to divide us more than bilingualism or multilingualism ever could. The insidiousness of the movement becomes quite apparent. Facility in learning "perfect" English among the newly arrived immigrants has become a measuring stick to test their loyalty to their adopted country.

No one, the recent immigrants least of all, wants to be locked up in what are often referred to as "language ghettos." Most immigrants understand that becoming proficient in English is a way of finding a better way of living in this country. However, the English-only movement is primarily a negative campaign. Its tactics aim to limit the rights of the new immigrants, specifically Latinos and Asians. More damaging than disenfranchising the immigrant population by relegating them to second-class citizenship are attempts to convince them that they are second-class people in the eyes of the "world." When children are told in a disapproving way to "speak only in English," they perceive that English is "better." In first grade I was forced to sit crouched in the kneehole of the teacher's desk for hours in punishment for speaking to my brother in Japanese (only a year apart, we started first grade together). Did I know that this was being done "for my own good" so that I would learn English more quickly? Among other things, I learned that speaking Japanese in public leads to humiliation. The lines were clearly drawn. English is like Sunday clothes and is the superior language. By extension I learned that the whites who speak it must be the superior race, and I must learn to speak as the whites do. At that very young age, I was already on my way to what Elizabeth Dodson Gray labels "hierarchical thinking."[15]

Gray, a feminist theologian, believes that we must change the way we think about differences. She writes:

> When we are responding to differences (whether man and woman, or man and whale, or man and chimp, or man and God), our perceptions are dominated and distorted by the hierarchical paradigm. Almost in the same instant that we perceive difference, we are looking to ascertain rankings of power, moral or economic value, and aesthetic preference. We do this whether it is a different animal, a different culture, or a skin pigmentation that is different.
>
> The hierarchical paradigm...is a veritable contact lens. So intimately is it a part of how we perceive that we seem never to assess difference as just that—different. Instead we insist upon *imposing comparative rankings which are incomplete and often self-serving* [italics mine].[16]

In her sweeping book on how our religious and cultural attitudes are destroying the environment, Gray writes that diversity in nature is not only desirable but necessary for our survival. With the present interest in cultural diversity, we may be moving in the right direction, though to some of us, it seems to be at a creeping pace. Many Asian American writers who now speak and write well enough to not be an "embarrassment" to our races have taken on the task of being interpreters of our immigrant parents' experiences and of exploring our own relationships with them. A few of us are published by small presses.[17] Some short prose works have appeared in recent major multicultural anthologies.[18] An even smaller minority of Asian writers, most notably Maxine Hong Kingston and Amy Tan, have been published by major publishers.

Recognizing that powerful social forces have kept us unnaturally estranged from our parents' cultural heritages has been a crucial step for us, the second and third generation of children of immigrants who are writing today. We must find ways of letting the newer immigrants know that they do not have to wait to completely "master" American English before we will listen to them. We must let them know that there is a downside to being "perfect." Those of us who have been around long enough know about the "model minority" syndrome. We know that the more we strive for "perfection," the more isolated we become.

Nor can we wait for some major American writer to write for the new immigrants, as suggested by Bharati Mukherjee, an East Indian American writer. In an article that appeared in *The New York Times* on the occasion of her becoming "naturalized" (as some wag put it, the foreign-born are "unnatural" until they become U.S. citizens), this writer of acutely insightful stories about cross-cultural adjustment problems writes, "There is a blind spot in American writing, and even our best writers are guilty of passing over one of the biggest stories in recent American history: While American fiction is sunk in a decade of minimalism, an epic is washing up on its shores." Mukherjee laments the loss of those stories by new Americans who have "lived through centuries of history in a single lifetime" and who are "bursting with stories." She challenges current American authors to awaken to the rich source of materials among the immigrant population.[19]

The loss of those stories is real, but I do not agree with her. I hope that we do not have to wait until some accepted American writer with perfect English adopts the immigrants as interesting "subjects" before their experiences can be considered "universal" and therefore a bona fide part of American culture. The act of writing itself is a transforming process, as most of us who have taught writing know. Our own writings shape us. There are thousands of immigrant Asians out there who may not know until they are encouraged to write about it what it is that they have to offer us in the Western world. Many of these people come from countries that have been colonized and recolonized and have seen first-hand what several successive wars in their lifetime have done to their countries.

Many of these Asians, unlike the other immigrants before them throughout our history, did not come willingly to seek better economic conditions. Many of these new immigrants remain here somewhat reluctantly because of political conditions in their own countries and, like my mother, are resisting the traditional acculturation process. Their collective experiences could tell us much about the effects of destructive modern politics. They could tell us a great deal about the process of migration. They could tell us something about the psychological effects of inevitable transformation. We should be encouraging them to record their experiences "in their own voice in their own time."

On a global scale, the cult of the "perfect" English language is seen by many in other countries as a form of cultural imperialism. A few years ago when I visited Japan, I met with a group of Japanese feminists in Kyoto, most of whom were teaching at least one course in women's studies in the neighboring colleges. One of the women remarked that the only women among them who get invited to participate in conferences in the United States by women's or academic organizations are bilingual Japanese women. As if, she said ruefully, monolingual Japanese are not as politically aware of feminist issues or as well informed on scholarly topics. Contrary to popular belief, she felt expressing oneself freely in one's native language through a competent translator is preferable to speaking in one's second language. So again, it is perceived even in Japan that we use English proficiency as a measure of intelligence and judge people accordingly.

What will it take for us to create a climate of acceptance and tolerance for differences among us? For one thing, we need to release ourselves from this trap of linguistic purism in order to develop a healthy attitude towards the numerous patois around us and accept them as legitimate forms of expression in our culture. We would not be encouraging a "kind of illiteracy," as one of my colleagues said to me recently. (Besides, how many average Americans speak or write "perfect" English?) Instead, our language would be enriched by creative neologisms introduced into it by new immigrants. We should arrive at a level of sophistication where individualistic idioms in whatever form of mixed, communicable patois that are among us can be accepted into the language with ease. The human mind is capable of dealing with several levels of expressions, sometimes switching back and forth, at other times simultaneously, as those of us who have raised children know.

If we are all to be liberated from this tyranny of hierarchical language, we must fight those many ghosts, overcome those many prejudices. When that happens, we will be hearing more from our immigrant sisters as they write about their experiences in their own unique, individual voices in all the different stages of their development.

NOTES

[1] Mitsuye Yamada, *Sowing Ti Leaves: Writings by Multicultural Women* (New York: Kitchen Table/Women of Color Press, 1991).

[2] Joan Goulianos, ed., *By a Woman Writt. Literature from Six Centuries By and About Women* (Baltimore: Penguin Books, 1974).

[3] Louise Bernikow, ed., *The World Split Open: Four Centuries of Women Poets in England and America, 1552–1950* (New York: Random House, 1974).

[4] Sandra M. Gilbert and Susan Gubar, eds., *The Norton Anthology of Literature by Women* (New York: W.W. Norton & Company, 1985).

[5] Him Mark Lai, et al., eds., *Island: Poetry and History of Chinese Immigrants on Angel Island 1910–1940* (San Francisco: Hoc Doi Project, 1980). Distributed by San Francisco Study Center.

[6] The Japanese terms *Issei, Nisei,* and *Sansei* literally mean "first generation," "second generation," and "third generation," respectively. *Issei* generally refers to the immigrants who came to the United States to work, settle, and raise their families. *Nisei* refers to the American-born and -educated children of Issei, and *Sansei* to their children.

[7] Anzia Yazierska, *The Bread Givers* (New York: Persea Books, 1925).

8 A comprehensive bibliography of literature and literary criticism by Asian Americans now available for scholars is *Asian American Literature: An Annotated Bibliography,* by King-Kok Cheung and Stan Yogi (New York: Modern Language Association, 1989).

9 Shirley Geok-lin Lim and Mayumi Tsutakawa, eds., *The Forbidden Stitch: An Asian American Women's Anthology* (Corvallis, OR: Calyx Books, 1988).

10 Mitsuye Yamada, *Camp Notes and Other Writings* (Piscataway, NJ: Rutgers University Press: 1998).

11 Virginia Woolf, *The Pargiters* (New York: Harcourt Brace, 1978).

12 Years later, after World War II, when I returned home from college, my mother told me she saw the film version of *Les Misérables* and remembered she had heard the story from me during this period. The detail she remembered particularly was the story of the "poor little mother who sold her hair and teeth to keep her baby fed and clothed." She said laughing, "You were too young to understand what you were reading. How indignant you were over the cruelty toward the girl 'just because she had a baby.'"

13 Tillie Olsen, *Silences* (New York: Delacort Press/Seymour Lawrence, 1978): 6.

14 The following discussion reflects the general attitude of the American-born Nisei, although I am technically not a Nisei, having been born in Japan. As a child of Issei parents and someone who was primarily educated in the United States, however, I speak from the Nisei point of view. On the other hand, because I grew up as a Japanese national, like my parents, I was more aware of the Issei's sensitivities than the average Nisei. We were barred by law from becoming naturalized United States citizens until the passage of the Walter McCarran Immigration and Naturalization Act of 1953 when I was thirty years old.

15 Elizabeth Dodson Gray, *Green Paradise Lost* (Wellesley, MA: Roundtable Press, 1981): 20.

16 Gray: 11.

17 Among them *Seventeen Syllables and Other Stories* by Hisaye Yamamoto (Kitchen Table/Women of Color Press, 1988), and *Through Harsh Winters: The Life of a Japanese Immigrant Woman,* by Akemi Kikumura (San Francisco: Chandler & Sharp, 1981).

18 For example, Merle Woo's "Letter to Ma," reprinted in *New Worlds of Literature,* an anthology of multicultural writers (New York: W.W. Norton, 1989).

19 Bharati Mukherjee, "Give Us Your Maximalist," *New York Times Book Review* (August 28, 1988).

The Secret, 1893

HUANANI-KAY TRASK

White Americans and blackmail,
a Native Queen.

From the gunboats, swarms
of bluejackets.

In her palace, a conspiracy
of thieves.

At once, a fallen
government.

Hawai'i, this murdered
country, lying by the roadside
of history.

The Homeland, Aztlán

GLORIA ANZALDÚA

El otro México

El otro México que acá hemos construído
El espacio es lo que ha sido
territorio nacional.
Este el esfuerzo de todos nuestros hermanos
y latinoamericanos que han sabido
progressar.

—Los Tigres del Norte[1]

"The *Aztecas del norte*...compose the largest single tribe or nation of Anishinabeg (Indians) found in the United States today.... Some call themselves Chicanos and see themselves as people whose true homeland is Aztlán [the U.S. Southwest]."[2]

Wind tugging at my sleeve
feet sinking into the sand
I stand at the edge where earth touches ocean
where the two overlap
a gentle coming together
at other times and places a violent clash.

Across the border in Mexico
  stark silhouette of houses gutted by waves,
    cliffs crumbling into the sea,
      silver waves marbled with spume
        gashing a hole under the border fence.

          Miro el mar atacar
         la cerca en Border Field Park
      con sus buchones de agua,
an Easter Sunday resurrection
of the brown blood in my veins.

Oigo el llorido del mar, el respiro del aire,
  my heart surges to the beat of the sea.

In the gray haze of the sun
  the gulls' shrill cry of hunger,
    the tangy smell of the sea seeping into me.

      I walk   through the hole in the fence
          to the other side.
Under my fingers I feel the gritty wire
 rusted by 139 years
    of the salty breath of the sea.

Beneath the iron sky
Mexican children kick their soccer ball across,
run after it, entering the U.S.

          I press my hand to the steel curtain—
    chainlink fence crowned with rolled barbed wire—

rippling from the sea where Tijuana touches San Diego
unrolling over mountains
              and plains
                    and deserts,
this "Tortilla Curtain" turning into *el río Grande*
    flowing down to the flatlands
              of the Magic Valley of South Texas
      its mouth emptying into the Gulf.

1,950 mile-long open wound
              dividing a *pueblo,* a culture,
              running down the length of my body,
                    staking fence rods in my flesh,
                    splits me   splits me
                          me raja   me raja

          This is my home
          this thin edge of
          barbwire.

          But the skin of the earth is seamless.
              The sea cannot be fenced,
          el mar does not stop at borders.

To show the white man what she thought of his
arrogance,
Yemayá blew that wire fence down.

This land was Mexican once,
was Indian always
and is.
And   will be again.

Yo soy un puente tendido
del mundo gabacho al del mojado,
lo pasando me estira pa' 'trás
y lo presente pa' 'delante.
Que la Virgen de Guadalupe me cuide
Ay ay ay, soy mexicana de este lado.

The U.S.–Mexican border *es una herida abierta* where the Third World grates against the first and bleeds. And before a scab forms it hemorrhages again, the lifeblood of two worlds merging to form a third country—a border culture. Borders are set up to define the places that are safe and unsafe, to distinguish *us* from *them.* A border is a dividing line, a narrow strip along a steep edge. A borderland is a vague and undetermined place created by the emotional residue of an unnatural boundary. It is in a constant state of transition. The prohibited and forbidden are its inhabitants. *Los atravesados* live here: the squint-eyed, the perverse, the queer, the troublesome, the mongrel, the mulatto, the half-breed, the half dead; in short, those who cross over, pass over, or go through the confines of the "normal." Gringos in the U.S. Southwest consider the inhabitants of the borderlands transgressors, aliens—whether they possess documents or not, whether they're Chicanos, Indians, or Blacks. Do not enter, trespassers will be raped, maimed, strangled, gassed, shot. The only "legitimate" inhabitants are those in power, the whites and those who align themselves with whites. Tension grips the inhabitants of the borderlands like a virus. Ambivalence and unrest reside there and death is no stranger.

In the fields, *la migra.* My aunt saying, "No *corran,* don't run. They'll think you're *del otro lao.*" In the confusion, Pedro ran, terrified of being caught. He couldn't speak English, couldn't tell them he was fifth generation American. *Sin papeles*—he did not carry his birth certificate to work in the fields. *La migra* took him away while we watched. *Se lo llevaron.* He tried to smile when he looked back at us, to raise his fist. But I saw the shame pushing his head down, I saw the terrible weight of shame hunch his shoulders. They deported him to Guadalajara by plane. The furthest he'd ever been to Mexico was Reynosa, a small border town opposite Hidalgo, Texas, not far from McAllen. Pedro walked all the way to the Valley. *Se lo llevaron sin un centavo al pobre. Se vino andando desde Guadalajara.*

During the original peopling of the Americas, the first inhabitants migrated across the Bering Straits and walked south across the continent. The oldest evidence of humankind in the U.S.—the Chicanos' ancient Indian ancestors—was found in Texas and has been dated to 35,000 B.C.[3] In the southwest United States, archaeologists have found twenty-thousand-year-old campsites of the Indians who migrated through, or permanently occupied, the Southwest, Aztlán—land of the herons, land of whiteness, the Edenic place of origin of the Azteca.

In 1000 B.C., descendants of the original Cochise people migrated into what is now Mexico and Central America and became the direct ancestors of many of the Mexican people. (The Cochise culture of the Southwest is the parent culture of the Aztecs. The Uto-Aztecan languages stemmed from the language of the Cochise People.[4]) The Aztecs (the Nahuatl word for people of Aztlán) left the Southwest in 1168 A.D.

> Now let us go.
> >   *Tihueque, tihueque,*
> *Vámonos, vámonos.*
> >   *Un pájaro cantó.*
> *Con sus ocho tribus salieron*
> >   *de la "cueva del origen."*
> *los aztecas siguieron al dios*
> >   *Huitzilopochtli.*

Huitzilopochtli, the god of war, guided them to the place (that later became Mexico City) where an eagle with a writhing serpent in its beak perched on a cactus. The eagle symbolizes the spirit (as the sun, the father); the serpent symbolizes the soul (as the earth, the mother). Together, they symbolize the struggle between the spiritual/celestial/masculine and the underworld/earth/feminine. The symbolic sacrifice of the serpent to the "higher" masculine powers indicates that the patriarchal order had already vanquished the feminine and matriarchal order in pre-Columbian America.

At the beginning of the sixteenth century, the Spaniards and Hernán Cortés invaded Mexico and, with the help of tribes that the Aztecs had subjugated, conquered it. Before the conquest, there were twenty-five million Indian people in Mexico and the Yucatan. Immediately after the conquest, the Indian population had been reduced to less than seven million. By 1650, only one and a half million pure-blooded Indians remained. The *mestizos,* who were genetically equipped to survive smallpox, measles, and typhus (Old World diseases to which the natives had no immunity), founded a new hybrid race and inherited Central and South America.[5] *En 1521 nació una nueva raza, el mestizo, el mexicano* (people of mixed Indian and Spanish blood), a race that had never existed before. Chicanos, Mexican Americans, are the offspring of those first matings.

Our Spanish, Indian, and mestizo ancestors explored and settled parts of the U.S. Southwest as early as the sixteenth century. For every gold-hungry *conquistador* and soul-hungry missionary who came north from Mexico, ten to twenty Indians and mestizos went along as porters or in other capacities.[6] For the Indians, this constituted a return to the place of origin, Aztlán, thus making Chicanos originally and secondarily indigenous to the Southwest. Indians and mestizos from central Mexico intermarried with North American Indians. The continual intermarriage between Mexican and American Indians and Spaniards formed an even greater *mestizaje.*

El destierro/ The Lost Land

> *Entonces corre la sangre*
> *no sabe el indio que hacer,*
> *le van a quitar su tierra*
> *la tiene que defender,*
> *el indio se cae muerto,*
> *y el afuerino de pie.*
> *Levántate, Manquilef.*
>
> *Arauco tiene una pena*
> *más negra que su chamal,*
> *ya no son los españoles*
> *los que les hacen llorar,*
> *hoy son los propios chilenos*
> *los que le quitan su pan.*
> *Levántate, Pailahuan.*

—Violeta Parra, "Arauco tiene una pena"[7]

In the 1800s, Anglos migrated illegally into Texas, which was then part of Mexico, in greater and greater numbers and gradually drove the tejanos (native Texans of Mexican descent) from their lands, committing all manner of atrocities against them. Their illegal invasion forced Mexico to fight a war to keep its Texas territory. The Battle of the Alamo, in which the Mexican forces vanquished the whites, became, for the whites, the symbol for the cowardly and villainous character of the Mexicans. It became (and still is) a symbol that legitimized the white imperialist takeover. With the capture of Santa Anna later in 1836, Texas became a republic. Tejanos lost their land and, overnight, became the foreigners.

> *Ya la mitad del terreno*
> *les vendió el traidor Santa Anna,*
> *con lo que se ha hecho muy rica*
> *la nación americana.*
>
> *¿Qué acaso no se conforman*
> *con el oro de las minas?*
> *Ustedes muy elegantes*
> *y aquí nosotros en ruinas.*

—from the Mexican corrido,
"Del peligro de la Intervención" [8]

In 1846, the U.S. incited Mexico to war. U.S. troops invaded and occupied Mexico, forcing her to give up almost half of her nation: what is now Texas, New Mexico, Arizona, Colorado, and California.

With the victory of the U.S. forces over the Mexican in the U.S.–Mexican War, *los norteamericanos* pushed the Texas border down one hundred miles, from *el río Nueces* to *el río Grande*. South Texas ceased to be part of the Mexican state of Tamaulipas. Separated from Mexico, the Native Mexican–Texan no longer looked towards Mexico as home; the Southwest became our homeland once more. The border fence that divides the Mexican people was born on February 2, 1848 with the signing of the Treaty of Guadalupe-Hidalgo. It left one hundred thousand Mexican citizens on this side, annexed by conquest along with the land. The land established by the treaty as belonging to Mexicans was soon swindled away from its owners. The treaty was never honored and restitution, to this day, has never been made.

The justice and benevolence of God
Will forbid that...Texas should again
become a howling wilderness
trod only by savages, or...benighted
by the ignorance and superstition,
the anarchy and rapine of Mexican misrule.
The Anglo–American race are destined
to be forever the proprietors of
this land of promise and fulfillment.
Their laws will govern it,
their learning will enlighten it,
their enterprise will improve it.
Their flocks range its boundless pastures,
for them its fertile lands will yield...
luxuriant harvests....
The wilderness of Texas has been redeemed
by Anglo–American blood & enterprise.

—William H . Wharton[9]

The Gringo, locked into the fiction of white superiority, seized complete political power, stripping Indians and Mexicans of their land while their feet were still rooted in it. Con el destierro y el exilio fuimos desuñados, destroncados, destripados—we were jerked out by the roots, truncated, disemboweled, dispossessed, and separated from our identity and our history. Many, under the threat of Anglo terrorism, abandoned homes and ranches and went to Mexico. Some stayed and protested. But as the courts, law enforcement officials, and government officials not only ignored their pleas but penalized them for their efforts, tejanos had no other recourse but armed retaliation.

After Mexican American resisters robbed a train in Brownsville, Texas, on October 18, 1915, Anglo vigilante groups began lynching Chicanos. Texas Rangers would take them into the brush and shoot them. One hundred Chicanos were killed in a matter of months, whole families lynched. Seven thousand fled to Mexico, leaving their small ranches and farms. The Anglos, afraid that the *mexicanos*[10] would seek independence from the U.S., brought in twenty thousand army troops to put an end to the social protest movement in South Texas. Race hatred had finally fomented into an all-out war.[11]

My grandmother lost all her cattle,
they stole her land.

"Drought hit South Texas," my mother tells me. "*La tierra se puso bien seca y los animales comenzaron a morirse de se'. Me papá se murío de un heart attack dejando a mamá pregnant y con ocho huercos,* with eight kids and one on the way. *Yo fui la mayor, tenía diez anos.* The next year the drought continued *y el ganado* got hoof and mouth. *Se cayeron* in droves *en las pastas y el* brushland, *panzas blancas* ballooning to the skies. *El siguiente año* still no rain. *Mi pobre madre viuda perdió* two-thirds of her *ganado.* A smart *gabacho* lawyer took the land away mamá hadn't paid taxes. *No hablaba inglés,* she didn't know how to ask for time to raise the money." My father's mother, Mama Locha, also lost her *terreno.* For a while we got $12.50 a year for the "mineral rights" of six acres of cemetery, all that was left of the ancestral lands. Mama Locha had asked that we bury her there beside her husband. *El cementerio estaba cercado.* But there was a fence around the cemetery, chained and padlocked by the ranch owners of the surrounding land. We couldn't even get in to visit the graves, much less bury her there. Today, it is still padlocked. The sign reads: "Keep out. Trespassers will be shot."

In the 1930s, after Anglo agribusiness corporations cheated the small Chicano landowners out of their land, the corporations hired gangs of mexicanos to pull out the brush, chaparral, and cactus and to irrigate the desert. The land they toiled over had once belonged to many of them, or had been used communally by them. Later the Anglos brought in huge machines and root plows and had the Mexicans scrape the land clean of natural vegetation. In my childhood I saw the end of dryland farming. I witnessed the land cleared; saw the huge pipes connected to underwater sources sticking up in the air. As children, we'd go fishing in some of those canals when they were full and hunt for snakes in them when they were dry. In the 1950s I saw the land, cut up into thousands of neat rectangles and squares, constantly being irrigated. In the 340-day growth season, the seeds of any kind of fruit or vegetable had only to be stuck on the ground in order to grow. More big land corporations came in and bought up the remaining land.

To make a living my father became a sharecropper. Rio Farms Incorporated loaned him seed money and living expenses. At harvest time, my father repaid the loan and forked over 40 percent of the earnings. Sometimes we earned less than we owed, but always the corporations fared well. Some had major holdings in vegetable trucking, livestock auctions, and cotton gins. Altogether we lived on three successive Rio farms; the second was adjacent to the King Ranch and included a dairy farm; the third was a chicken farm. I remember the white feathers of three thousand Leghorn chickens blanketing the land for acres around. My sister, mother, and I cleaned, weighed and packaged eggs. (For years afterwards I couldn't stomach the sight of an egg.) I remember my mother attending some of the meetings sponsored by well-meaning whites from Rio Farms. They talked about good nutrition and health, and held huge barbecues. The only thing salvaged for my family from those years are modern techniques of food canning and a food-stained book they printed made up of recipes from Rio Farms's Mexican women. How proud my mother was to have her recipe for *enchiladas coloradas* in a book.

El cruzar del mojado/Illegal Crossing

> *"Ahora si ya tengo una tumba para llorar,"*
> *dice* Conchita, upon being reunited with
> her unknown mother just before the mother dies
>
> —from Ismael Rodriquez's film,
> *Nosotros los pobres*[12]

La crisis: Los gringos had not stopped at the border. By the end of the nineteenth century, powerful landowners in Mexico, in partnership with U.S. colonizing companies, had dispossessed millions of Indians of their lands. Currently, Mexico and her eighty million citizens are almost completely dependent on the U.S. market. The Mexican government and wealthy growers are in partnership with such American conglomerates as American Motors, IT&T, and Du Pont, which own factories called *maquiladoras*.[13] One-fourth of all Mexicans work at maquiladoras; most are young women. Next to oil, maquiladoras are Mexico's second-greatest source of U.S. dollars. Working eight to twelve hours a day to wire in backup lights of U.S. autos or solder minuscule wires in TV sets is not the Mexican way. While the women are in the maquiladoras, the children are left on their own. Many roam the street, become part of *cholo* gangs. The infusion of the values of the white culture, coupled with the exploitation of that culture, is changing the Mexican way of life.

The devaluation of the peso and Mexico's dependency on the U.S. have brought on what the Mexicans call *la crisis. No hay trabajo.* Half of the Mexican people are unemployed. In the U.S. a man or woman can make eight times what they can in Mexico. By March 1987, 1,088 pesos were worth one U.S. dollar. I remember when I was growing up in Texas how we'd cross the border at Reynosa or Progreso to buy sugar or medicines when the dollar was worth eight pesos and fifty centavos.

La travesia: For many *mexicanos del otro lado,* the choice is to stay in Mexico and starve or move north and live. *Dicen que cada mexicano siempre sueña de la conquista en los brazos de cuatro gringas rubias, la conquista del país poderoso del norte, los Estados Unidos. En cada Chicano y mexicano vive el mito del tesoro territorial perdido.* North Americans call this return to the homeland "the silent invasion."

> *"A la cueva volverán"*
>
> —El Puma *en la canción "Amalia"*

South of the border, called North America's rubbish dump by Chicanos, mexicanos congregate in the plazas to talk about the best way to cross. Smugglers, *coyotes, pasadores, enganchadores* approach these people or are sought out by them. *"¿Qué dicen muchachos a echársela de mojado?"*

> Now among the alien gods with
> weapons of magic am I.
>
> —Navajo protection song, sung when going into battle[14]

We have a tradition of migration, a tradition of long walks. Today we are witnessing *la migración de los pueblos mexicanos,* the return odyssey to the historical/mythological Aztlán. This time, the traffic is from south to north.

El retorno to the promised land first began with the Indians from the interior of Mexico and the mestizos that came with the conquistadores in the 1500s. Immigration continued in the next three centuries; in this century, it continued with the *braceros* who helped to build our railroads and who picked our fruit. Today thousands of Mexicans are crossing the border legally and illegally; ten million people without documents have returned to the Southwest.

Faceless, nameless, invisible, taunted with *"Hey cucaracho"* (cockroach). Trembling with fear, yet filled with courage, a courage born of desperation. Barefoot and uneducated, Mexicans with hands like boot soles gather at night by the river where two worlds merge, creating what Ronald Reagan called a frontline, a war zone. The convergence has created a shock culture, a border culture, a third country, a closed country.

Without benefit of bridges, the *"mojados"* (wetbacks) float on inflatable rafts across *el río Grande,* or wade or swim across naked, clutching their clothes over their heads. Holding on to the grass, they pull themselves along the banks with a prayer to *Virgen de Guadalupe* on their lips: *Ay virgencita morena, mi madrecita, dame tu bendición.*

The Border Patrol hides behind the local McDonald's on the outskirts of Brownsville, Texas, or some other border town. They set traps around the riverbeds beneath the bridge.[15] Hunters in army green uniforms stalk and track these economic refugees by the powerful night vision of electronic sensing devices planted in the ground or mounted on Border Patrol vans. Cornered by flashlights, frisked while their arms stretch over their heads, *los mojados* are handcuffed, locked in jeeps, and then kicked back across the border.

One of every three is caught. Some return to enact their rite of passage as many as three times a day. Some of those who make it across undetected fall prey to Mexican robbers such as those in Smugglers' Canyon on the American side of the border near Tijuana. As refugees in a homeland that does not want them, many find a welcome hand holding out only suffering, pain, and ignoble death.

Those who make it past the checkpoints of the Border Patrol find themselves in the midst of a hundred and fifty years of racism in Chicano *barrios* in the Southwest and in big northern cities. Living in a no-man's borderland, caught between being treated as criminals and being able to eat, between resistance and deportation, the illegal refugees are some of the poorest and the most exploited of any people in the U.S. It is illegal for Mexicans to work without green cards. But big farming combines, farm bosses, and smugglers who bring them in make money off the "wetbacks'" labor—they don't have to pay federal minimum wages, or ensure adequate housing or sanitary conditions.

The Mexican woman is especially at risk. Often the *coyote* (smuggler) doesn't feed her for days or let her go to the bathroom. Often he rapes her or sells her into prostitution. She cannot call on county or state health or economic resources because she doesn't know English and she fears deportation. American employers are quick to take advantage of her helplessness. She can't go home. She's sold her house, her furniture, borrowed from friends in order to pay the coyote who charges her four or five thousand dollars to smuggle her to Chicago. She may work as a live-in maid for white, Chicano, or Latino households for as little as $15 a week. Or work in the garment industry, do hotel work. Isolated and worried about her family back home, afraid of getting caught and deported, living with as many as fifteen people in one room, the *mexicana* suffers serious health problems. *Se enferma de los nervios, del alta presión.*[16]

La mojada, la mujer indocumentada, is doubly threatened in this country. Not only does she have to contend with sexual violence, but like all women, she is prey to a sense of physical helplessness. As a refugee, she leaves the familiar and safe home ground to venture into unknown and possibly dangerous terrain.

> This is her home
> this thin edge
> of barbwire.

This essay first appeared in *Borderlands/ La Frontera: The New Mestiza.* (Spinsters/Aunt Lute, 1987, 1999)

© 1987, 1999 by Gloria Anzaldúa. Reprinted by permission of Aunt Lute Books.

NOTES

1 Los Tigres del Norte is a *conjunto* band.

2 Jack D. Forbes, *Aztecas del Norte: The Chicanos of Aztlán.* Greenwich, CT: Fawcett Publications/Premier Books, 1973: 13, 183; Eric Wolf, *Sons of Shaking Earth.* Chicago: University of Chicago Press/Phoenix Books 1959: 32.

3 John R. Chávez, *The Lost Land: The Chicano Images of the Southwest.* Albuquerque: University of New Mexico Press, 1984: 9.

4 Ibid. Besides the Aztecs, the Ute, Gabrillino of California, Pima of Arizona, some Pueblo of New Mexico, Comanche of Texas, Opata of Sonora, Tarahumara of Sinaloa and Durango, and the Huichol of Jalisco speak Uto-Aztecan languages and are descended from the Cochise people.

5 Reay Tannahill, *Sex in History.* Briarcliff Manor, NY: Stein and Day/Scarborough House, 1980: 308.

6 Chávez: 21.

7 Isabel Parra, *El Libro Major de Violeta Parra.* Madrid: Ediciones Michay, 1985: 156–157.

8 From the Mexican *corrido,* *"Del peligro de la Intervención,"* Vicente T. Mendoza, *El Corrido Mexican.* México, D.F.: Fondo De Cultura Económica, 1954: 42.

9 Arnoldo De León, *They Called Them Greasers: Anglo Attitudes Toward Mexicans in Texas, 1821–1900.* Austin: University of Texas Press, 1983: 2–3.

10 Chávez: 79. The Plan of San Diego, Texas, drawn up on January 6, 1915, called for the independence and segregation of the states bordering Mexico: Texas, New Mexico, Arizona, Colorado, and California. Indians would get their land back, Blacks would get six states from the South and form their own independent republic.

11 Jesús Mena, "Violence in the Rio Grande Valley," *Nuestro* (January/February, 1983): 41–42.

12 *Nosotros los pobres* was the first Mexican film that was truly Mexican and not an imitation European film. It stressed the devotion and love that children should have for their mother

and how its lack would lead to the dissipation of their character. This film spawned a generation of mother–devotion/ungrateful–sons films.

[13] For a discussion of the maquiladora system, see Deborah Barndt, "Whose 'Choice'? 'Flexible' Women Workers in the Tomato Food Chain, in Section I of this volume.

[14] From the Navajo "Protection Song" (to be sung upon going into battle). George W. Gronyn, ed., *American Indian Poetry: The Standard Anthology of Songs and Chants.* New York: Liveright, 1934: 97.

[15] Grace Halsell, *Los ilegales.* Mayo Antonio Sánchez, trans. *Editorial Diana Mexica,* 1979.

[16] Margarita B. Melville, "Mexican Women Adapt to Migration," *International Migration Review* (1978).

Three Movements in A Minor

GRACE POORE

I wonder how many lesbians realize that closets are not identical, that different realities define our closets, and that the difference in our closets defines the ways in which we choose to Come Out. For instance, with non-immigrant lesbians—women who carry their homes with them, some in exile, some on the run, and others who are simply, yet not merely, travelers—nonimmigrant by virtue of our choice not to become citizens, not to immigrate but to temporarily reside, live, love, work in one country, pay taxes, join community struggles, contribute art and thought, women who reject the terms "illegal" and "alien," and like all other lesbians contend with the risk of hate violence and housing or job discrimination, but unlike other lesbians, also contend with immigration.

The U.S. immigration process is designed to disempower and intimidate. It is arbitrary in its use and abuse of power. Anyone who encounters it finds herself also encountering U.S. foreign policy. For the lesbian, the encounter includes homophobia. For the brown lesbian from the geographic Third World, the minefield is even more treacherous since she has to simultaneously negotiate racism, sexism, orientalism, classism, and lesbophobia while facing the possibility that her application for immigration may be denied for some or all of these reasons. It is this uncertainty about one's life that amplifies the powerlessness a lesbian feels in the face of so complete and arrogant an authority as the immigration department. Even more so, it is the lack of information about rights and options that erodes a lesbian's self-confidence, makes her "paranoid," and leads to her isolation—an isolation exacerbated by her reluctance to talk about a situation that most Americans are either ignorant or unconcerned about. This is the struggle that lesbians who are "citizens" do not see by virtue of their "legal" status in a country. This is the reality that gets left out of the gay rights agenda, the people of color agenda, the women's rights agenda, the lesbian agenda.

I. Eviction

Improperly filed. Rejected.

Three words that translate eviction. Ghost moving in fog, she wonders, pack first but store where? Leave for but go where? Goodbye but for how long? Lover is here, conference next month, film in progress, manuscript incomplete...should this all go in boxes?

No appeal necessary. Work authorization revoked.

Like she is not even here: the woman whose plants need watering, ceiling needs repair. The woman with ivy creeping over her kitchen window so the sun has stopped breaking in. She asks for voluntary departure.

Dictionary definition: *Voluntary*—*"Proceeding from the will or from one's own free choice; intentional; volitional. Done without compulsion. Performed without legal obligation."*

Eviction by some standards can also mean voluntary departure. Tonight, her sobs do not come, trapped inside tunnels of fear that lead her back to the same place...same place every time. Because her mind will not see beyond deportation. Yet.

II. Translation

When my status with the U.S. Immigration Department was pending, I used a pseudonym under which I did much of my writing and public speaking. At one of these presentations, I became acquainted with a South Asian lesbian who, later on, called me a hypocrite for using a pseudonym. "How can you claim to be out?" she asked. "You're hiding behind another name." When I explained that even with a pseudonym I was publicly out, visible and vocal, she did not understand. She felt betrayed. In her mind, there was only one state of closeting—one way of being out. She could not envision the multiple possibilities for creative resistance by being simultaneously out of and inside the closet. She could not see that by negotiating in and out spaces differently, one could participate in subverting homophobia and heterosexism.

"Passing" occurs in all communities struggling for liberation. In the gay community, there are lesbian women who opt for the illusive safety of the closet and distance themselves from gay politics. There are lesbians who usurp the lesbian community and resources while gaining the benefits of passing as heterosexual. There are also lesbians who not only do nothing to confront homophobia, but also actively sabotage other out lesbians for fear that by association, their own identities will become known. These women see out lesbians as a threat to their secret lives, a potential danger to their improvised sexual arrangements. They seek to destroy what "outness" can bring. Lesbians who live their lives this way and collude in their own oppression violate other women through a fear that overrides a sense of accountability. They put at risk women like themselves striving to live out their own sexual identity without censure or persecution. They are silent when the specter of homophobia, and in particular, lesbophobia, rears its evil head.

Perhaps it was knowing the potential for such betrayal that caused the woman I met to call me a hypocrite. Perhaps it was a past experience of being caught in the crossfire of someone else's internalized and externalized homo-phobia that polarized us. Perhaps she assumed that with a double name I could avoid naming my Self.

It is true that many nonimmigrants tell ourselves that the INS has better things to do than go after some lesbian from Bombay/Hong Kong/Chile living in Trenton/DC/LA—but we also know the risk. We understand why some of us never march on the outside of Gay Pride contingents in case of cameras. Why many of us fear going to bars in case of a raid. Why we only do radio interviews, never have our photographs taken, or get married. Why I—hard-line, separatist, feminist, lesbian—sought the protection of my closet without apology while standing in a public forum, talking about needing to fight homophobia while using another name.

For even with a pseudonym there was risk as there was resistance (if I couldn't sign petitions, I distributed them; if I couldn't lead meetings, I organized them; if I couldn't do civil disobedience, I wrote). The fear of exposure was always present, but the closet was a shield, not an obliteration of who I am. It was a way to be out without being caught by the INS.

Of course, there was also humor in all of this, when I could attend a gathering and be two persons at once, talking about "each other" as if we were old friends. Or confuse myself with the identity games I played—who was I supposed to be today when I went to this conference? Who did I say would speak on that panel? Was the airline reservation for so-and-so or so-and-so?

So the question remains: does the politics of coming out invalidate the politics of a double identity? Even with my green card today, I am suspended between borders, between definitions of legal and illegal, resident and non-resident. Even with my green card I am labeled an alien. The question of survival is not necessarily about being in or out. It is about remembering that going in and out of closets is a strategy for working to remove the conditions that make my closets necessary in the first place.

III. Transnation

In a heterosexist culture, lesbians will always be undocumented/evicted women, and in a country like the U.S. where immigration rules impose (unofficial?) restrictions on gays and lesbians seeking permanent residence, the terms "undocumented" and "illegal alien" are a double irony for the lesbian who gets married to escape the oppression of INS rules and to become "legitimate." On one hand, her legitimacy with the INS is possible only because she agrees to pass for a heterosexual by marrying, even if her charade is "only" for two years. On the other hand, she experiences the hypocrisy of having left her home country to avoid marriage, only to end up marrying in the U.S. for the right to stay.

As an alternative to a green card marriage, a lesbian can ask an employer to sponsor her. If her employer is a university or major corporation, she is fortunate, since these organizations often treat sponsorship as merely a formality. However, many more lesbians get sponsorships through businesses that often expose them to the indignities and exploitation of employers who use the power imbalance to their advantage. This kind of arrangement can and, often, does replicate the abuse of power that green card wives who are battered experience with their real or paper husbands. The potential for such abuse is not limited to women who work in sweatshops or on tomato farms. Neither is it limited to women receiving wages "under the table." Instead, women who are legally employed by progressive, social-change, and even feminist organizations are also vulnerable—to power shifts within the management, to the faltering of political correctness in favor of the bottom line. These lesbians, like those in sweatshop and agribusiness industries, are reminded of how expendable they are, how much of a liability (rather than an asset) they are to their organizations.

Imagine within such a scenario the emotional and psychological cost to a feminist lesbian activist who is nonimmigrant, undocumented, deportable. Who is not eligible for welfare benefits, and whose right to live in the U.S. is tied to the very organization she works for. Her nonprofit feminist sponsor becomes an anathema, like a corporate sponsor might be—with all of its power plays and incongruities; with all of its diversity doublespeak.

It is no wonder that many lesbians "prefer" to risk marrying for a green card because at least as "wives" they can leave jobs that treat them badly, travel a little more freely in and out of the U.S. and, at least for now, as someone's spouse, have access to emergency welfare benefits. Yet, in this scheme of survival strategies, where is there space for a lesbian, or for that matter any woman who finds marriage oppressive under any circumstances? When will there be a debate about making immigration possible without marriage, whether that marriage is heterosexual or gay? How does an underground that helps undocumented women negotiate a system as green card wives benefit lesbians who don't wish to be wives? Is the risk of rape or domestic violence any less for a lesbian married to a paper husband? Is the cost of paying for a green card sponsorship all that different from paying a dowry? Even if the sponsoring "husband" were a friend, where no payment exchanged hands, is a green card marriage not also an arranged marriage? Perhaps the greatest irony is that the danger of being caught as a pseudo-wife is greater than that of being caught with a pseudo-name.

It should not be difficult to imagine that for some women these contradictions are too great, where self deserts self, breaks down into shadows that offer no refuge from internal eviction—where collusion between immigration and marriage erodes personal and political integrity and exacts the gift of psychic death.

Marriage for anyone can always be an option. My question is, why does it have to be the "option of choice?" Why do U.S. lesbians who reject it for themselves offer marriage as an acceptable option for lesbians who are not citizens or immigrants—as if the personal and political choices for refusing to marry are somehow less valid for *Third World* lesbians simply because they are Third World—as if immigration to the United States needs to come at any cost, including compromising on the conscientious objections to marriage?

At the same time, why do non-U.S. lesbians who opposed marriage at home find themselves advocating it when they come here? Exclusion by immigration versus inclusion by marriage—we barter one oppression for another while leaving intact one of the most powerful and insidious institutions of heteropatriarchy. For even reconstituted as an egalitarian bond between two equals, and despite its revised renderings as a "union," a "commitment ceremony," a "joining of journeys," marriage is still a mechanism by which the state organizes society, by which citizens and noncitizens, immigrants and nonimmigrants are rewarded and penalized. By which men are still granted greater benefits over women.

It is time to stop privileging marriages—gay, green, or otherwise. We need to be creative in the use of our minds and resources to develop other alternatives—like a sanctuary, for instance, one that enables lesbians to live and work in the U.S without taking the marriage route. One that might involve the lesbian and gay community "setting up organizations" to sponsor lesbians via employment opportunities. One that might include individuals who officially "hire" lesbians for one job while in fact paying them to engage in political and creative work of their choice. One that could become a forum to advocate self-petitioning for green cards so that lesbians can apply on their own merit. One that could be a network of homes across the country that helps protect and keep hidden undocumented lesbians facing deportation or detention in any one of the immigration prisons that the U.S. operates around the country. One that could extend legal recognition to lesbians to become political asylees on the basis of their status as evicted endangered women, fleeing honor rape, forced marriage, coerced pregnancy, electroshock treatments, psychosurgery, institutionalization, torture, imprisonment, police abuse, community harassment, and perhaps, death by execution.

There will always be lesbians who are "illegal aliens" and there are many undocumented lesbians who are "illegally married." Unless we make immigration a gay rights issue, a women's rights issue, a people of color issue, many of us will be suspended between closets, with or without our pseudo–names.

In *Webster's Dictionary*, the definition for *sanctuary* is "a consecrated place …immunity from law." *Sanctuary* by our definition could be an option for nonimmigrant lesbians so they can have immunity from multiple evictions.

A version of this article appeared in *Trikone Magazine* (January 1997).
© 1997 by Grace Poore.

Crossing the Bridges of Pain: Racial Factors in the Colombian "Drug War"

BERTA I. PEREA

My telephone rang on Saturday night, January 22. It was my brother, Walter Dionne Perea, telling me that our great-aunt, Josephine "Pipia" Romana, 103 years old, had passed away. Both of us broke down and cried. We were very sad.

On Christmas, by tradition, everybody born and raised on the Pacific coast of Colombia plans a return home to our native land; but I had missed this year. People working in the cities and in other parts of Colombia save money all through the year to bring home in December. Christmas is the time for celebration, reconciliation, remembrance, and unity. In addition to the Catholic ceremonies, we practice many other rituals that keep us in touch with the past. We also introduce those newly born to our traditions. Among my immediate family members, only my six living brothers and one sister made that long trip. My other three sisters remained in Bogota taking care of my father, who was very ill. My mother and I were in New York.

Pipia was the oldest woman in our African Colombian family. She was the one who linked the past to the present, and the present to the future. She was like the family Bible that kept the oral traditions, memories, and stories of everyone born, raised, and dead in my hometown of Condoto Choco. She kept the record of events and of any new arrivals to our town. She knew all about our revolutionary movements and struggles that took place a century before her birth.

We had reason to cry. It was the last time I heard my brother express his strong feelings about life and death. "Lucky, Pipia lived so long!" he said. "The blessing that she gave us on New Year's Eve is still in my memory. I knelt in prayer before my departure from Contodo Choco, and she begged our ancestors for our protection, hoping that everybody would be together for next year's festivities. I did not want her to leave. She was not really sick. How could it be possible that two weeks later she is dead?" My brother was depressed, and could not stop crying.

I used the opportunity to talk about Walter's plans in case my father died soon. But he rejected the idea that we make such preparations for a person who was still alive: in his understanding, to do so was to invite that person's death.

"Let's deal with the problem when it happens," he urged. "My wish is that you, Berta, always remember that we are the children of the mining land. Our ancestors fought for these lands. Technically everything there belongs to us. We have the responsibility to return there, even after death.

"In the reality of Colombia," he continued, "with this ongoing internal armed conflict, no one feels safe, even in their own houses. I don't know if after this conversation, I will have the chance to talk to you again."

I cut my brother off. "You are too melancholy," I told him. "Please stop. We need to have a more positive frame of mind."

"No sister," he replied. "Yesterday (Friday January 21) was my first day back to work." Walter was a teacher at the San Luis Gonzaga high school in Copacabana, in the Medellin region. "Since September 2000, I've been threatened by various people at work, including some parents and students. Yesterday morning, for instance, I had a conversation with some of my students who failed my math class last November. They called themselves members of La Banda los Azulitos, a teenage gang known as the Blue Boys. They made it clear that they don't like me, and that this year they plan to clean the school of foreigners and black teachers like myself."

Before Walter moved to Medellin, he was the principal of Santa Rita Agricultural High School in Choco. In 1996, guerrillas showed up in this isolated village and killed people they called *soplones* (messengers) of the Colombian army. To protect his life, Walter moved away. He believed that by going to a big city, Medellin, he was exercising his human rights. The only school where he could find a job was the all-white high school of San Luis Gonzaga. But some students, born and bred in this industrial city, could not deal with having a black teacher from a marginal region, such as Choco.

"A girl who is part of this group even lives in my building,' Walter continued. "I personally saw her selling drugs to other students in the school. Her father is involved in the same business, too. I am desperately looking for a new apartment. These students promised that I would not wake up to see the sunrise again or to teach any other white, local, *paisa* kids."

I started crying. I spoke to my brother in vain about the seriousness of the threats. I could not encourage Walter to return to Choco because our home region was almost as violent. It would not be safe for him to travel there. I implored him to leave his apartment immediately, and to look for legal protection. I even suggested that he travel to Bogota and present his passport to the American embassy, even though appointments for visas to the U.S. require a wait of almost two years.

"The problem for me is more complicated," Walter told me. "It is a question of honor, honesty, and respect. I am a teacher of principles. I'm not going to run away because my students or anybody else wants me to. I'm not going to pass students if they don't deserve it or if they're not prepared to function at the next math level. I'm not going to leave Colombia like you and everyone else. At this point in history, the nation needs us. Our people need professionals and intellectual people to help the nation rise from the unspeakable, horrible conditions created by violent people, who are hungry for power and money. These people ignore the fact that those who are suffering and dying are their own people, Colombian families, and our culture."

After a moment of silence, I understood that Walter was not afraid; he was mentally prepared and motivated by a powerful sense of purpose. Still, I tried again to urge him to run away by reminding him of our last conversation with Sekai Holland, a Zimbabwean activist who was in Bogota in 1988. "Do you still remember what she told us after our Afro-Colombian Women's Center and its activists were threatened by secret police officers who accused us of being communists?" I asked. "Please repeat what she said to us."

"I know, I know," Walter responded. "She said, 'Did you see the sky? What is there? Too many clouds…the sky is full of our leaders that have been killed. They will never return to us.' Walter," I continued, "I don't believe that we need to continue sacrificing our lives for the sake of progress and for a more democratic society. In the end, new leaders will not care about those who have died defending ideologies. It has happened before; Colombians tend very easily to forget the past.

"Now Walter," I urged, "I heard in the news that every Colombian state has a committee created to protect displaced and threatened people."

"Yes," he confirmed, "that institution was created in 1992 by the Colombia Congress under Law 1645. In theory, it was established to protect people with problems like mine, but in practice it is a bureaucratic committee that only defends people with good political contacts or money. Think about it, Berta: who are the five people on this committee? One represents the Department of Procurement. Another represents Internal Research and Finances. One represents the governor, another workers' ministers, and the last one the teachers' union. Most of these people are on the side of the government and are not interested in solving our problems. To them, someone like me just represents statistical information that further disturbs the image of Colombia they're trying to project. You know that Colombia today is at war. Under these conditions, it is impossible for these five people to protect all Colombian citizens living in Antioquia State."

Then Walter spelled out for me just what all this meant for him, as an individual seeking personal safety. "Just yesterday morning,'" he told me, "I visited that office in Medellin. I soon discovered that getting legal protection is a complicated process that takes way too much time. Even though we are the ones whose lives are threatened, the burden of proof is on us to show the danger we're in.

"I asked the bureaucrats if I could take time off my job in order to dig up the necessary evidence. The answer was no. They demanded four letters: from my school principal, the Department of Finance, the Department of Procurement, and the mayor of Medellin. Each letter has to prove that I have a valid case. In addition, I would have to write another letter describing my situation.

"How long would this process take, Berta? It's not like you visit those offices and they write these letters immediately. Once your life has already been threatened, do you think you would live long enough to complete this complicated process? And then they told me that even collecting the proper evidence wouldn't guarantee protection or a safety transfer."

This was my last conversation with Walter Dionne.

The Afro-Colombian Heritage

Condoto Choco is a small mining community on the Pacific coast of Colombia. It was here that my siblings and I were born and raised. Most of the Pacific coast is a tropical rain forest, with a mostly warm and wet climate and lush vegetation. Rain falls year round, totaling over eighty-five inches annually.

Our African Colombian ancestors gravitated to this environment, so similar to their equatorial homeland. As a result, the Pacific coast is known as "the black region of Colombia." Our ancestors have populated this area since the beginning of colonization. Later, their numbers swelled with the separation of Portugal from Spain (1640), when a considerable mass of Africans was contracted as slave labor for the mines of Nueva Granada (known today as the Bogota Cundinamarca region). Until then, they had worked primarily in *haciendas* or farmlands.

During the seventeenth century, the British monopolized the mining industry and brought with them a massive number of Africans to work in the gold mines of the Pacific coast. Since their introduction to these lands, and after the era of slavery (1817–1851) ended, African descendants remained in the region, living in the *centros de cimarrones* (free territories), mining towns, and farmlands.

With the official end of slavery, the land passed from one generation to the next. Everyone living in the gold and platinum land belonged to the same two ethnic groups: Native Colombians or Indians, and African Colombian descendants. We called ourselves "the authentic people." We were close to nature. We never made a distinction between races or classes. Everybody was interrelated and cared for one another.

The only strangers in our lands were the *gringos* of the American consortium known as the Mining Gold and Platinum Corporation. The centralized

Colombian oligarchy negotiated the exploitation of our mineral resources with the American mining companies. For almost a century they have been there with high technology (*dragas*) extracting our precious metals.

For hundreds of years, our land was isolated from the rest of the nation. Even today we continue to live with minimal resources and infrastructure: that is, few roads, schools, and hospitals; no electricity; and no other means of communication. In our rain forest land, the riches of the subsoil and the rivers were our most important sources of survival. Our major rivers—the Atrato, San Juan, Baudo, Patia, Timbiqui, Isquande, Cauca, and their tributaries—were navigable for their entire lengths. Our centuries-old market towns grew up along the rivers, allowing transportation of goods and people to the rest of the country. Our memories, language, and traditional beliefs sprang up around the rivers and the rain forest. The spirits of dead ancestors and lesser gods are represented in every single aspect of this natural world.

The traditional religion, the climate, and the land remain very important to us. In many ways, the people of the Pacific coast bless our isolation from the rest of the country. The customs common to other parts of Colombia more strongly reflect colonial socioeconomics, which were designed primarily to serve Western needs. In isolation, my ancestors were able to live in harmony with our environment and traditions.

The Death of an Activist

After Walter and I completed our conversation, I asked my mother to remind me to visit the Immigration and Naturalization Office at the federal plaza on Monday. I was now even more determined to work on the application for her U.S. citizenship, and to submit legal petitions for my seven brothers and three sisters working in the combative cross-fire war lands of Colombia.

We started the process late. I returned home on Monday afternoon with the proper application papers. Switching on the TV, I heard chilling news on CNN's Spanish service: Teachers from Antioquia had gone on a four-day strike, demanding that the Colombian government raise their pay retroactive to the year 2000. My brother Walter was a teachers' union delegate from Antioquia, representing the municipality of Copacabana. That was why it was always hard for me to find him at home. The Supreme Court of Colombia had ruled that increases in workers' salaries had to be based on the national inflation rate, but the government had steadfastly refused to apply that court decision to teachers. As a union delegate, Walter had often told me that the Colombian government considered teachers its worst enemies.

Four days later, on January 26, the teachers' strike ended. I left a message on my brother's answering machine, asking him to call me back in New York.

That afternoon, as soon as he returned from school at his apartment in Copacabana, he called our sister Gloria in Bogota. He asked about the health of my father, who had been hospitalized with a critical heart problem. Walter told Gloria that he planned to take the first plane leaving Medellin for Bogota. Meanwhile, he said, he would remain in his apartment, grading students' papers and waiting for my call. Gloria heard the sound of his doorbell. Walter put her on hold and went to his second-floor window to check who was there. Then he told Gloria he had to hang up; some people from his school were at the building's front door. My sister hung up the phone, expecting that they would talk later, when Walter arrived in Bogota. That phone call never came.

Instead, it was my phone in Brooklyn, New York that rang that night. I leapt to answer it, so as not to wake up my two children: six-year-old Caramina and Tomin, aged four. They needed to sleep a bit longer before their Saturday morning dance classes. "*Diga* (hello)," I said into the mouthpiece. I heard my sister Gloria crying at the other end of the line. I clasped my chest. I was prepared for the worst: Was it my Dad? "Nooo," she sobbed. Had our sister Amparo's drug problems finally killed her? "Nooo," cried Gloria. "Who is it?" I demanded, my voice rising with anxiety.

"It's Walter. He was found dead," she said.

"Nooo!" Now it was my turn to cry. "It is not possible," I insisted. My overburdened heart fell even further when I realized it was up to me tell my mother that her favorite son was dead. I went from the phone to kneel on my bed and I prayed, asking Him to guide me to the best way to relay this terrible news. Then I went to the kitchen, drew a clear glass of water, lit a white candle, and prayed some more.

I called my husband, Craig, from the basement and told him what I had just learned. We could not believe the news. "You need to be strong," Craig urged. "Remember that your mother is here." Immediately, we started calling Walter's apartment in Medellin to verify the news. We left messages on his answering machine. I called some of his best friends. We were hoping that somebody would call us to deny the news. But half an hour later, someone returned our call and confirmed the truth. That's when the nightmare started.

We called all the airlines that travel to Colombia to get a ticket. Most of them were closed. We also called my relatives in Condoto to tell them that Walter's wish had been to return to them, to his homeland. I asked my cousin Elda to take charge of the funeral and ceremonies. She was also responsible for finding food and lodging for the visiting mourners.

Meanwhile, my brothers and sisters were in Bogota with my father in a hospital, waiting for my phone call. Nobody had money that night to buy a ticket, because they had all been displaced from their jobs and homes by force. Nobody even knew where my brother's body was in Medellin. When the news about his death spread, union leaders, black activists, some friends, and relatives were charged with moving Walter's body to a funeral home and from there to Choco.

Finally, I mustered the courage to go to my mother's bedroom. I gave her some sleeping pills, telling her that the doctor had prescribed them for the pain from a recent fall on New York's icy streets. After she took the pills, I gave her the bad news. My mother was more serene and calm than I. She lowered her eyes, cried silently, and questioned me about the decision to travel.

"You know that Colombia is in a state of war and that they are kidnapping people. Are you going?"

"Yes mother" I said. "Everything is ready."

"It is not a good idea to take the children—do you know why?"

"Yes, Mother" I replied. To take children on such a trip would be to expose them to kidnapping by armed thugs who believe that anyone traveling from the U.S. is rich.

Then I said to my mother, "I have to dress you, and in two hours we need to be at Kennedy Airport."

Over a series of phone calls, Walter's friends and associates in Medellin filled in the details of his last moments. According to his girlfriend, Maye, Walter had lived in a four-story attached house. There were several apartments, with little space for privacy. One apartment was occupied by the family of one of Walter's students: the woman who did his cleaning, laundry, and cooking. When the doorbell rang, everybody was at home. Tenants opened their windows, because the visitors had rung the wrong bell.

Witnesses later told the police that four youngsters from Walter's school (one of whom was female) and one adult had entered his apartment. From the street, people heard my brother yelling and screaming. The visitors turned up the music, forced Walter to leave his apartment, slashed him with knives all over his body, and then proceeded to shoot him four times. All this happened right in front of his building—but nobody in the neighborhood would admit that they had seen it. I have hired various private investigators, but since Colombian social order is maintained under a military state of siege, impunity for Walter's killers remains in place.

That Friday I was deeply grief-stricken. At work, we had ended the fall semester. The teachers' union was negotiating a new contract. The city mayor refused to negotiate; instead, he insulted educators and made impossible demands. In my school, some coworkers had made nasty comments about teachers' delegates and others teachers who had lost their jobs or been transferred to other schools. I was confused, recognizing that even in

America, people did not appreciate and respect the role teachers play in society and in their students' futures.

During the previous semester, some activist teachers who had sacrificed their free time tutoring students, writing new curricula, and implementing changes in the school system had been laid off. In the view of some administrators, they were endangering the good order and represented a threat to the administration. My mind truly was jumping back and forth between the high price that conscientious teachers paid for trying to introduce changes in New York's school system and the difficulties my family and my people were facing in Colombia.

Money Changes Everything

The harmonious and balanced lifestyle my people had always enjoyed on the Pacific coast of Colombia started changing in the 1980s, when foreign governments and private investors urged the government to build new roads and bridges over our most important rivers. Local authorities believed that the main objective of these investments was to connect the Pacific land with the rest of Colombia. The reality is that the roads and bridges were built to transport products to the overseas shipping ports for trade with Colombia's inland industrial cities. Our coastal plains were just an obstacle to be bridged so the money could flow more freely past us. The new development did nothing to help the black community improve their lives.

Roads and bridges turned also into the open door that brought private investors and white Colombians seeking easy profits. They confiscated people's properties and pillaged the region's natural resources: Gold, platinum, copper, oil, wood, palm products, *borojo,* coconut products, etc. The Pacific coast has much unused land and forests and one of the largest hardwood reserves in Colombia. It also has enough hydroelectric potential to provide electricity to the rest of the country. It has extensive mineral resources and the best isthmus between two major rivers (the Atrato and San Juan) that could be broached to connect the Pacific and Atlantic oceans.

People of the Pacific coast feel they live with the tragedy of occupying a land that has much importance to other people. The "progress" that was foisted on us marked the beginning of massive displacement. Very little of the profit reaped from our lands was shared with the African Colombians. The "interior people" or *colonos* (white men) arrived in our land with modern weapons and new technology, specifically intending to divide people and take over, destroying the ecosystem and killing the heads of many families.

My people were not prepared to respond to the modern world at this level. My own family has been deeply affected.

The Flight Home

My mother and I flew from New York to Bogota, where a local carrier took us to Quibdo. From there, we traveled to Condoto by bus. In the plane, I started remembering my last conversation with my brother. With tears in my eyes, I also mentally recited a fragment of Tupac Shakur's song "Changes": "That is the way it is...things will never be the same."

I thought about the assassination of my older brother Marcelino, who was killed in 1987 at the age of thirty-three, and my older nephew, Wilmer, assassinated in 1997 at the age of seventeen under similar circumstances. Marcelino died fifteen years ago, when the struggle between two Western ideas—communism and capitalism—was so strong in Colombia. Maybe if Marcelino had not defended one of those ideologies he would still be alive today. In both incidences, the bodies disappeared. When my family finally found them, their organs had been removed by traffickers. In addition, Marcelino was found with no fingernails or testicles. He had been a worker at the Colombian National University in Bogota. The ideas Marcelino and his union defended at that moment are not the same ones on the minds of many Colombians today. While in the past, people were able to identify a direct enemy—the government, controlled by the same oligarchies—the present political situation is very complex. Many Colombians do not have a clear picture of the many reasons contributing to the destruction of the social order. Today the Colombian power conflict, manipulated by both external and internal forces, limits the level of the people's resistance and mobilization.

I remembered that when Walter and I were college students in Bogota, Marcelino tried insistently to stop us from being on the frontlines of the students' march movement. Marcelino's long experience at the national university union had convinced him that Colombian violence has a long history of human rights violations. Civilians have been always the victims of the past four decades of brutal armed conflict between the national army, the guerrilla movement (which has lost its leftist character), and the right-wing paramilitary forces. Marcelino always said to us, "Please be clear that you are black. As African descendants, we have other priorities. Get educated, then go back to your homeland to organize our family and our own community."

Even though we carry revolutionary ideas in our blood, like many other Colombians, I was tired of having constant tragedies in my life.

Retro-Excavating Machine: The White Tactics to Take Over My Land

The armed conflict between guerrillas, the drug trade, paramilitary fighters, and the Colombian army forced many white miners and farmers from Uraba Antioquia and the coffee plantations of Risaralda to migrate to the Pacific coast region. They brought their heavy technology to Choco mining lands and from there, they extended their influence across the entire region. The colonos developed the same strategies used by the gringos to take over and expropriate our land. They changed the ways the small rivers ran, closed the branches, and destroyed the tributaries supplying waters to their gold mines.

The colonos knew that the basic sources of survival for people were the land and the rivers. They dirtied the rivers' water that people used to meet their most immediate, fundamental needs. With the river branches broken, people were no longer able to continue working in their mines. Then the colonos offered people a percentage (20–80 percent) of total gold and platinum production in exchange for their lands. The African Colombian miners were not allowed to supervise the exploitation of their lands; they were forced to accept the conditions imposed by the white men, who argued that they needed the rest of the money for their machinery and the guerrillas' protection fees. The African Colombian miners did not understand the game. They gave away their lands, in part to support Colombia's war. Black activists tried to stop landowners from giving in to the colonos; but most African Colombian miners had never seen so much money before. They reasoned that at their age, they would never have the chance to buy the heavy equipment needed to exploit the minerals under their feet. So they gave away their best investment and their only riches: the land.

Soon, a new group of Colombians followed the original Antioquenos colonos, accompanied by guerrillas and paramilitaries. These groups demanded a "quota," or portion, of the production. The makeup of our population changed rapidly. Pale faces occupied our streets and bars. Prostitution and weapons were in every corner of our towns. We started seeing people with various types of weapons and uniforms all over our land. In a few months, African Colombian miners had no money and no land, even for farming. They were victims of extortion. People were in a panic. The peace of the land disappeared.

Government armed forces showed up, too. African Colombians were in the middle of the cross-fire. The armed groups took control of our rich land, whose strategic location allowed them to bring in new weapons and take out coca. Innocent people started dying. Native and African descendants felt intimidated. As more of them became victims of selective assassination and massacres, many moved away. Since then, our forest land has become known for drug plantations, uncontrolled exploitation of mineral resources, and guerrilla and paramilitary conflict that threatens and kills thousands of innocent people.

People left their peaceful land for a marginal existence in slums in the worst parts of Colombia's cities. As professionals, teachers, peasants, students, and native people from the Pacific coast were forced to migrate to the biggest cities to escape the war, massive displacement of the population increased dramatically. Human rights violations have soared to unprecedented levels. As of winter, 2001, more than two million people had been displaced by the conflict, 60 percent of them Afro-Colombians.[1]

In Colombia, there are no statistics on how many African Colombians were forcibly displaced from their homes. According to the New York newspaper *Hechos Positivos,* approximately 392 thousand families—a total of 1,900,000 people—suffered forced displacement between 1985 and 1999. In 1999 alone, around three hundred thousand people were displaced from their homes.

Virlenice Diaz lost her son during this terrible time. After the funeral, she told me, "When we were on the land at least the mayor and governors of Choco were black. Now in the cities, we have no access to economic and political power. It is in these arenas that we suffer problems of discrimination. The Colombian government and many of its people are racist. Here in the cities we have no name. Our families are broken up. We are the black parents with no jobs, who watch helplessly as our teenagers join the armed forces of Colombia, the guerrillas, and the paramilitary groups. Our children are on the frontlines because they have no economic opportunities. They are the first ones shouting in defense of the interests of these groups."

Now I am here in this airplane crying over the death of my brother. I also cry for the past that will never return. I cry for my family and for many other Colombian families that are probably suffering the same pain. I feel deeply frustrated. I did not save my brother in time. Our leaders are dying, as are many Afro-Colombians in positions of power. They can't protect their own lives. They can never return home again, except perhaps in death.

Displacement: Resistance or Racism?

The people of the Pacific coast are victims of problems that they never created. They feel betrayed by their environment, because the region's strategic location and tropical weather conditions facilitate the easy growth of coca and the transportation of illegal weapons. My people clearly understand that they are the victims of a dirty game between gangs: the government army, the paramilitary/guerrilla groups, and the United States.

These groups are unexpectedly showing up in our communities looking for great profits and seeking out informers about their enemies' tactics. Some of my people, as a form of resistance, choose to remain in silence, and they get killed. Those who provide information are executed by rival military groups, and those who do not provide the correct answers are assassinated because their clients think they support rival groups. It is a dilemma. It happened last year in cities like Bagado and Ungia (Choco), and in Riosucio and Apartado (Antioquia).

It happened in June, 2001, in the lower reaches of the Baudo River and in May, 2002 in Bohaya village, Choco. In isolated Bohaya, the villagers who survived the massacre ran to their church, thinking that the paramilitaries and guerillas would respect its sanctity. Instead, the combatants shot deadly gas into the church. A hundred and nineteen African Colombians, including children, women, and elders, died. These people had deliberately avoided direct confrontation with the armed forces. They were simply trying to escape the cross-fire. Their reward was death.

Apart from its literal impact, displacement symbolizes institutionalized domination over the subordinate Afro-Colombian population. My people, terrorized by the powerful armed groups, have not had the opportunity to reciprocate: they can't trade beating for beating, death for death, slap for slap, or insult for insult. As a new form of survival and resistance, we have institutionalized displacement.

It is not a coincidence that the majority of the people being displaced happen to be black. This emphasizes the racist nature of the displacement, economic exploitation, and massive expulsion of people from their homes and lands on Colombia's Pacific coast. Violent intimidation, more deaths, destruction of lives, and environmental disaster are all part of the program. Displacement further tears apart extended family members, breaks down customs and traditions, and contributes to more poverty throughout Colombia.

I had a personal conversation with Relicario Machado, a former religious leader in the village of El Salado. He said:

> We live in peace in our towns, working in the mines, and growing the banana and tropical fruits. We use to hunt and fish in the rivers too. Right now, we are not able to do these activities. In defense of their lives, many of our relatives have run away from their homeland, with no clothes and no personal property. I took the risk of returning to El Salado, because I did not like the way people live in the city. Over there, I had lost authority over my surviving family. I was never able to work and life was difficult for an old man like me. People in the city need money all the time, you pay money for everything. There are no

job opportunities for anyone. People could not even sell anything on the streets because the police arrest them. I returned to my village when I heard that my brother was killed. At my age, I have nothing to lose.

"What was your impression when you arrived at the El Salado-Panamericana village?" I asked another elder, who wants to remain anonymous. He answered,

I was very sad when I returned there. I found too many new white faces. These people are the current owners of the best houses and best located lands around the Panamericana road. In addition, they are the owners of the machinery, weapons, and local businesses. When I noticed that, I became upset but I understood I could not complain.

Yesterday morning, one of these people said to me that I don't look happy working for him. He put a weapon in my face when I tried to retaliate after we found a dead man's body in the forest. I cried and I turned around looking for a machete, which no one had. To prevent any revolution these people had collected our tools and guns. Look around, all twenty-six of these men and women that you see walking around here, they are working for these people. Some of them are messengers (spies) or work in the coca plantations of the displacers. Every weekend when they get paid, all of their money gets spent in the white men's businesses on their personal needs.

I asked Relicario about other changes happening in our community. He said:

I don't want to traumatize you, since you are just trying to bury your brother's body, and you have a very long way to go. But it looks like our culture and traditions are dying. People don't walk on the streets late at night any more. We don't show up in *novenas, arruyos, gualis,* and *velorios* (ancestral rituals). We don't have weapons to fight these foreigners. I believe that the current situation is worse than any other in Colombia's history. At least in the past, our revolutionary leaders were able to identify their enemies and retaliate, and they were united. Right now I'm really confused.

Because there is not an open Afro-Colombian insurrection, many observers perhaps believe that African Colombians are taking a passive role in this racist war and economic expropriation. We might look like a disorganized community that just lets things happen. Some may speculate that people are still waiting for the government's army to show up and rescue them, or that they are using displacement as a way to run away from the problem.

The conditions I have described have changed the social status of the Afro-Colombian families living in the Pacific littoral. From being the powerful ones who controlled the riches and the environment, we are now the subordinate ones. As a subordinated class, my people could not afford the luxury of organizing armed confrontation. They do not have modern weapons. The consequences could be dangerous and suicidal. We have too many disadvantages. The circumstances can turn very complicated for us as activists.

The Need for Organization

How might my community organize and fight back? There is not any Afro-Colombian family, living in a rural or urban community, that has been not devastated by colonization, racism, and this horrendous war. Truly, people feel intimidated by the sound of weapons and shattered by the cries of women, who scream again, because their only surviving child has been murdered by violent people.

Is displacement a solution to our critical problems? Or is it adding new contradictions to our lives? Many Afro-Colombian miners and peasants predicted that leaving our homeland would provide them with some kind of protection from the government. That never happened. More and more intruders are arriving in our towns. Life in the white industrial cities is no better. We are strangers in our own country.

Moving away from our towns and villages is a way of giving more power to the intruders. It also exposes us to the devastating experience of being surrounded by people who identify us by skin color and socioeconomic status.

These impressions have not changed since I left Colombia after the funeral of my brother in February 2001. I returned four months later, when my father passed away in Bogota. In keeping with the tradition, hundreds of displaced people were at the velorio in the funeral home. Even through the pain of my personal loss, I was able to see that displaced people live in greater poverty and have no jobs. Boarders share rooms, or are even entirely homeless.

As with my brother, my fathers' body was moved to Condoto Choco. This time it was by land. The guerrillas and paramilitaries had total control over Choco's two main roads and rivers. Every piece of land on the stretch of road that separates towns is dominated by one of these groups. In each place, drivers and passengers are forced to present an I.D. or pass (like the pass system in South Africa), and to pay taxes and quotas. These roadblocks are also used to hijack trucks, cars, merchandise, food, and medicine, and to kidnap soldiers, teenagers, and any blacks known to hold positions of power. Many kidnapped people, unable to pay, are found floating in the rivers. The guerrillas and paramilitaries use the roads for extortion and to deny blacks freedom of movement.

In spite of all the violence and misery, people in Condoto Choco are starting to create change. They are beginning to realize that their lives are not completely in the hands of the violent. They are aware of suspicious visitors and activities. They are connected interdependently with other Colombian union movements. Also, large numbers of protesters—teachers, health providers, and transit workers—are beginning to challenge the state. These people oppose any governmental action that threatens employment. Some local Afro-Colombians have started investing in the mining industries and acquiring heavy technology. Other Afro-Colombians are making progress in breeding animals and creating farms for agriculture.

In addition to seeking out new economic opportunities, many activists are focusing on the need to restore traditions and introduce new methods into the old ones. They are trying to create new forms of resistance to domination.

During my father's funeral, I was very impressed to hear teenagers playing traditional instruments (reserved in the past to the elders) and singing songs (even during the velorios and novenas) appropriate to this occasion. After the funeral, the streets were full of people, and a children's parade began. Parents watched their children playing traditional music, marching, and dancing. It was a sign of revival and a move for restoration of their spirits. Despite the pain caused by my father's death, I was happy to see some changes. The culture and tradition are still there. People are learning to depend more and more on their own resources for survival. They are learning not to let the weight of this racist war break down their lives.

I remained in Condoto for four weeks. During this time, l was able to interview community leaders of various political persuasions. We held many meetings with the community to discuss new ways of organization. Everyone understood the need to reclaim our economic power and the necessity of empowering traditions, so that displaced people would be drawn back to their homelands. Many angry speeches were made, demanding peace. In unity, we were able to pray to the spirits of those innocent ones killed during this war. We prayed for more organizational and economic support in our communities.

The truth is that people in the towns have begun to understand that life is no better in the racist cities. People are coming out of the shadows. The spirits of our ancestors have begun to break down the fear of death. People now have courage. Their self-esteem is returning, and consequently they have created ways in this racist world to proudly address the task of creating a new revolution.

Could this rejuvenation undermine racism, guerrillas, and paramilitarism? It is hard to predict. The people's stand could be perceived as a threat to the imposed order, thus provoking harsh retaliation. Still, people continue challenging the system, protesting, and holding strikes. Living in Colombia, it is difficult not to get inflamed by the passion of the war. The movement I've describing here is just the beginning.

La lucha continúa—the struggle just continues.

NOTE

1 *The Colombian Media Project Bulletin* (Winter 2001-2002): 10.

Multiracial Feminism

BECKY THOMPSON

Whereas militant white women of the late 1960s and early 1970s found little workable space in the white feminist movement, the situation for the next cohort of white women—those who came to feminism in the mid-1970s and the 1980s—was quite different. By the late 1970s a decade of self-conscious organizing among lesbians and gay men meant that issues of sexuality could not be sidelined as they had often been in the civil rights movement, the Black Power movement, and the early second-wave liberal feminist movement. Black, Latina, Asian, and Native American women's efforts to create autonomous organizations led by women of color in the 1970s—organizations that did not include men or white women—created a foundation for coalition politics between women of color and white antiracist women in the 1980s. With these organizations and the concurrent explosion of writing by women of color as their base, women of color confronted what history-of-consciousness theorist Chela Sandoval identifies as "the ideological differences [that] divided and helped to dissipate the movement from within between the years 1972 and 1980."[1]

Organizations of women of color became bridges between the nationalism of the 1960s and the multiracial feminist activism of the 1980s. By the early 1980s, there were multiple venues for collaboration. It was in this context, and in response to the limitations of mainstream feminist organizing, that a small but growing group of white women began to articulate an explicitly antiracist feminist politics.

From the beginning, the story of the emergence of white antiracist activism has been intertwined with and dependent upon the development of feminism among women of color. For the most part, the story of antiracist white activism simply is not told in the recent histories of radical, liberal, or cultural feminism, since much of antiracist white feminist work has been in reaction to what Chela Sandoval refers to as "hegemonic feminism."[2] As is true of the story of white antiracist activism in the Civil Rights and Black Power movements, the story of white antiracism in feminism cannot be separated from the work of women of color at the level of culture, strategy, or ideology.

That there is no single source history of contemporary African American, Latina, Asian American, and Native American feminisms complicates a tracing of white antiracism, since it was through feminism developed by women of color that white antiracist feminism emerged. The tendency in much white feminist history to marginalize the activism of women of color is a key reason for this absence. Differences in the histories of these groups is another reason why the stories have largely been told separately. Although separate tellings do justice to the different histories of women of color, white antiracism did not form solely alongside Asian American and African American feminism, for example; rather, it developed through the interaction among and between feminists across race. I open this essay, then, with a brief sketch of the development of feminism among women of color, even though I am cognizant that an abbreviated rendering runs the risk of flattening significant differences among African American, Latina, Native American, and Asian American women.

Organizing by Women of Color in the United States

During the early period of the feminist movement (the late 1960s and early 1970s), women of color in the United States were working on three fronts: forming women's caucuses in existing mixed-gender organizations, developing autonomous feminist organizations, and working in white-dominated feminist groups.[3] This three-pronged approach contrasts sharply with the common notion that feminism among women of color emerged in reaction to (and therefore later than) white feminism.

Among the earliest women-of-color organizations were women's caucuses formed within existing Third World and nationalist organizations. These caucuses either remained within such organizations or became autonomous. The Third World Women's Alliance, for example, grew out of Student Nonviolent Coordinating Committee (SNCC) chapters on the East Coast and focused on racism, sexism, and imperialism.[4] One of the earliest feminist activist organizations of the second wave was a Chicana group, Hijas de Cuauhtemoc, founded in 1971 and named after a Mexican women's underground newspaper that was published during the 1910 Mexican Revolution. The feminist consciousness-raising group that led to the founding of Hijas de Cuauhtemoc was initially convened by women in the United Mexican American Student Organization, which was part of the Chicano student movement of the late 1960s.[5] Many of the founders of Hijas de Cuauhtemoc were later involved in launching the first national Chicana studies journal, *Encuentro Feminil.*

An early Asian American women's group, Asian Sisters, focused on drug-abuse intervention for young women in Los Angeles. It emerged out of the Asian American Political Alliance, a broad-based, grassroots organization largely fueled by the consciousness of first-generation Asian American college students.[6] Networking between Asian American and other women during this period included participation by a contingent of a hundred and fifty Third World and white women from North America at the historic Vancouver

Indochinese Women's Conference (1971) to work with Indochinese women against U.S. imperialism.[7] Asian American women also provided services for battered women, worked as advocates for refugees and recent immigrants, produced events spotlighting Asian women's cultural and political diversity, and organized with other women of color.[8]

In her history of the early Asian women's movement (1966–1974), Miya Iwataki writes that by the early 1970s Asian American women were building organizations directed to, for, and by women while "remaining integrated with the movement as a whole." About these dual commitments Iwataki writes, "The roots of the woman's question are centuries deep, and like the roots of centuries-old trees, cannot be suddenly ripped out of the soil without leaving huge gaps and fissures that would be destructive to the rest of the ecology (or the communities). A separatist woman's movement would fall right into the divide and conquer tactics of the government."[9]

The best-known Native American women's organization of the 1970s was Women of All Red Nations (WARN), initiated in 1974 by women, many of whom were also members of AIM, founded in 1968 by Dennis Banks, George Mitchell, and Mary Jane Wilson.[10] WARN's activism included fighting sterilization in public health service hospitals, suing the U.S. government for attempts to sell Pine Ridge water in South Dakota to corporations, and networking with indigenous people in Guatemala and Nicaragua.[11] WARN reflected a whole generation of Native American women activists who had been leaders in the takeover at Wounded Knee, South Dakota in 1973, on the Pine Ridge Reservation, and elsewhere. WARN, like Asian Sisters and Hijas de Cuauhtemoc, grew out of, and often worked with, mixed-gender nationalist organizations.

The autonomous feminist organizations that women of color were forming during the early 1970s drew on nationalist traditions through their recognition of the need for independent organizations led by people of color.[12] At the same time, unlike earlier nationalist organizations that included men and women, these were organizations specifically for women. Among Black women, the foremost autonomous feminist organization of the early 1970s was the National Black Feminist Organization (NBFO). Founded in 1973 by Florynce Kennedy, Margaret Sloan, and Doris Wright, it included many other well-known Black women, including Faith Ringgold, Michelle Wallace, Alice Walker, and Barbara Smith. According to Deborah Gray White, "more than any organization in the century [NBFO] launched a frontal assault on sexism and racism."[13] Its first conference in New York was attended by four hundred women from a range of class backgrounds.

Although NBFO was short-lived nationally (1973–1975), chapters in major cities remained together for years, including one in Chicago that survived until 1981. Although its members employed the tool of consciousness-raising also used in white feminist groups, the content of these sessions was decidedly Black women's issues: stereotypes of Black women in the media, discrimination in the workplace, myths about Black women as matriarchs, and Black women's beauty and self esteem.[14] NBFO also helped inspire the founding, in 1974, of the Combahee River Collective, an organization named after a river in South Carolina where Harriet Tubman led an insurgent action that freed seven hundred and fifty slaves. The Combahee River Collective not only led the way for crucial antiracist activism in Boston through the decade but also provided a blueprint for Black feminism that still stands a quarter of a century later.

A foundational principle of the Combahee River Collective statement was the concept of identity politics. In 1977, members of the collective wrote, "We believe that the most profound and potentially most radical politics come directly out of our own identity, as opposed to working to end somebody else's oppression. In the case of Black women this is a particularly repugnant, dangerous, threatening, and therefore revolutionary concept because it is obvious from looking at all the political movements that have preceded us that anyone is more worthy of liberation than ourselves. We reject pedestals, queenhood, and walking ten paces behind. To be recognized as human, levelly human is enough."[15] Identity politics did not mean there were any natural, inevitable, or necessarily long-lasting alliances among Black women simply on the basis of a shared identity. In fact, the Combahee River Collective knew better than that even in 1977; class and educational differences between women in the collective threatened to destroy it on more than one occasion, and eventually did.

Identity politics underscored the reason why separate caucus groups were a necessary component of coalition work. Just as Black women needed time to look each other in the eye, white women needed to confront the ways they failed to take racism seriously. Identity politics was the strategic basis for Combahee's protests against the Boston Police Department and the media in 1979, when those two institutions attempted to dismiss the murders of twelve black women (based on the notion that they were alleged to be prostitutes and therefore not worthy of protection or investigation).

For Combahee, taking identity politics seriously as a strategy meant recognizing it as a two-step process. Identity politics was more than naming an identity based on group affiliation: it was the naming of that identity for the purpose of subversive action. Because Black women had been murdered,

Black women needed to be the ones to name the strategies for organizing on behalf of Black women's safety.[16] In her journal entry about the organizing in 1979, Barbara Smith wrote, "That winter and spring were a time of great demoralization, anger, sadness and fear for many Black women in Boston, including myself. It was also for me a time of some of the most intensive and meaningful political organizing I have ever done. The Black feminist political analysis and practice the Combahee River Collective had developed since 1974 enabled us to grasp both the sexual-political and racial-political implications of the murders and positioned us to be the link between the various communities that were outraged: Black people, especially Black women; other women of color; and white feminists, many of whom were also Lesbians."[17]

Of the coalition between Black and white women that developed during that time, Smith wrote, "This is *new*. Black and white, feminists and non-feminists, women have never come together and worked on a woman's issue, an issue of racial-sexual politics, at least not in this era. I am thinking about the anti-lynching movement at the beginning of the century as the nearest parallel—and that of course was different. So this has never been tried before. It could work. I think about sitting up at Harriet Tubman House three or four years ago in CESA [the Committee to End Sterilization Abuse] trying to figure out how to involve Third World women in our work. And now it is the other way around. White women taking leadership from Black women around one of those 'universal' issues we as Black feminists have always said would pull in everyone."[18]

The Combahee River Collective saw race, class, and gender as interlocking and refused to rank one oppression over another. In recognizing a "simultaneity of oppressions," the members of Combahee were following in the footsteps of their foremothers who had argued for a multidimensional analysis in previous decades.[19] Combahee also offered an anticapitalist, anti-imperialist critique that drew on Black Marxism and nationalism of the 1960s and earlier.[20] A dramatic departure from the past, however, was Combahee's explicit attention to sexuality in addition to race, class, and gender.

Combahee was critical of a narrow Black nationalism that was male dominated. At the same time, Combahee rejected the separatism of some white lesbians as untenable, given Black women's commitment to working with Black men. In the space between Black male nationalists and white lesbian separatists were Black lesbians who, though representing one of the smallest subsets of people in liberation struggles, fashioned a stunningly inclusive definition of feminism. Barbara Smith writes, "Feminism is the political theory and practice that struggles to free all women: women of color, working-class women, poor women, disabled women, lesbians, old women—as well as white economically privileged, heterosexual women. Anything less than this vision of total freedom is not feminism but merely female self-aggrandizement."[21]

This definition of feminism went far beyond white feminist definitions in its refusal to sideline any woman—most particularly women of color—in the process. This expansiveness, along with Combahee's commitment to socialism and their international perspective, resulted in a Black feminist politics that, as sociologist Patricia Hill Collins has noted, was about "fairness, equality, and justice for all human beings, not just African American women. Black feminism's fundamental goal of creating a humanistic vision of community is more comprehensive than that of other social action movements."[22]

Alice Walker's 1983 term "womanism," like Smith's definition of feminism, also offered an understanding of women's liberation that went far beyond white feminist versions of the time.[23] The politics emerging among many Chicanas in the 1970s had similar breadth and scope. One term used, "Chicana womanism," bridged antiracist and antisexist struggle. Like Walker's "womanism," this term distinguished Chicana liberation from liberal or radical white feminism while holding Chicanos accountable for challenging patriarchy within Latino struggles.[24] According to Chela Sandoval, each of these terms—and others: Gloria Anzaldúa's "new *mestiza*," Audre Lorde's "sister outsider," Maxine Hong Kingston's "woman warrior"— and all the political and cultural work they represented made the emergence of U.S. Third World feminism impossible to ignore.[25]

A third location in which women of color worked in the 1970s was white-dominated, early second-wave feminist organizations. Just a few of many examples: Margaret Sloan and Pauli Murray helped found the National Organization for Women in 1966 and continued to try to push for a multidimensional feminist politics in that organization for many years. Doris Wright, who helped found NBFO, was also a founding member of *Ms. Magazine* in 1972. Elizabeth Martinez was one of the initial members of New York Radical Women, along with Chude Pam Allen, Kathie Amatniek Sarachild, Shulamith Firestone, and Anne Koedt.[26] Celestine Ware, author of *Woman Power,* one of the earliest radical feminist books, was a founder of the New York Radical Women.[27]

I note these examples (and many more are to be found) in part to counter the tendency in white feminist historiography to consider the feminism of women of color and white feminism as completely separate in the early years. This tendency not only renders invisible women of color's early contributions to and interventions in white-dominated feminism, but it also fails to account for the skills required to negotiate in multiple communities simultaneously. Chicana studies scholars Beatriz Pesquera and Denise Segura write, "It is theoretically possible and likely that Chicanas' multiple sources of group identification conflict at times with one another, rendering the development of a group consciousness based on the privileging of one social location over the others ahistorical and untenable."[28] This part of the story—the balancing acts—is especially relevant for white antiracist women who, since the 1970s, have often found themselves straddling multiple communities as well.

Each of these arenas of activism had its own struggles, a reality compounded for women of color, who had commitments in more than one location. Members of women's caucuses in mixed-gender nationalist groups faced the challenge of keeping the attention on women: as leaders, in the organization's priorities, and in networks with other groups. As Angela Davis writes, "Even though we may have considered the feminism of that period white, middle-class, and utterly irrelevant, we also found compulsory male leadership utterly unacceptable."[29] The struggles of members of autonomous groups led by women of color included finding common ground when class, color, and sexual differences came to the fore. Women of color involved in white-dominated organizations struggled to be heard when outnumbered and to be respected rather than tokenized. Not surprisingly, a great deal of the most successful and longest-lasting organizing took place in autonomous organizations—organizing that within a decade enabled a vibrant women-of-color movement to emerge.

Through the 1970s and 1980s, grassroots activism by women of color focused on multiple issues: organizing for reproductive rights, especially against sterilization abuse; building battered women's shelters and rape crisis centers; advocating for welfare rights; sponsoring Black, Latina, and Asian American women's conferences; developing Black and Latina women's studies in higher education; supporting workplace organizing; and opposing police brutality.[30]

This activism, in concert with an explosion of writing by women of color, made a much wider space for feminism among women of color. The literary, political, and artistic writing of the 1970—Toni Cade's *The Black Woman;* Ntozake Shange's *For Colored Girls Who Have Considered Suicide / When the Rainbow Is Enuf;* Maxine Hong Kingston's *The Woman Warrior; Conditions: Five, the Black Women's Issue;* Audre Lorde's *The Cancer Journals*—reflected an extraordinary range of artistic and political contributions.[31] The writing included a dizzying array of genres—theory, poetry, plays, songs, novels, essays, autobiography—all of which pushed beyond existing intellectual and cultural boundaries.

By the early 1980s "the development of women of color as a new political subject" had clearly taken place due to substantial work done in multiple arenas.[32] According to Angela Davis, "most people date this new political subject from 1981, when *This Bridge Called My Back: Writings by Radical Women of Color,* was first published."[33] Originally conceived of by Chicana lesbians Cherríe Moraga and Gloria Anzaldúa in 1979, *This Bridge Called My Back* reflected the tremendous cultural work and activism of women of color in the years before its publication.[34] It was published at a time when the editors and many contributors saw a real possibility for a unified Third World women's movement, a movement made possible by women of color putting themselves and each other at the top of the agenda.

In the foreword to the second edition of *This Bridge Called My Back,* Moraga writes, "In response to a proliferation of writing by women of color up until 1980 which in the name of feminism focused almost exclusively on heterosexual relations—either by apologizing for or condemning the sexism of Third World men—*Bridge* intended to make a clean break from that phenomenon. Instead, we created a book which concentrated on relationships *between women.*"[35] About the title of the book, Moraga explains, "[It] was a way to make physical our experience of having to bridge…. It acknowledges the fact that Third World women *do* lay their bodies down to make a connection. But at the same time, being able to say it in a way where it's not a submission, it's a self-declaration: I am a bridge. I lay myself down; I'm the one doing it, no one's pushing me down."[36] It is this paradoxical message, in part, that gave the book its power. In her review of *This Bridge Called My Back,* Paula Gunn Allen, a Laguna Pueblo/Sioux–Lebanese woman, writes that the book "provided me ways to view myself and my history/experiences that gave me order, coherence and meaning. I was by turns delighted, enraged, grieved and stunned. I was deeply conscious of how wounded I have been."[37]

The vision for the contributors to *Bridge* was to find ways for women of color to communicate and activate together—mother to daughter, sister to sister, lover to lover, friend to friend; in small and large groups; through artistic connection and activist organizations; locally, regionally, and internationally; across multiple divides. Merle Woo, the daughter of a Korean mother and Chinese father, writes "A Letter to Ma," about how her radicalism is informed by her heritage, what it took for her parents to send her to college, why her mother's stories and her grandmother's stories have been so hidden, and why she came to identify herself as an Asian American feminist.[38] Mitsuye Yamada's "Asian American Women and Feminism" sees women of color in the United States as a link to Third World women throughout the world.[39]

In her letter to Third World women writers, "Speaking in Tongues," Gloria Anzaldúa urges herself and other women writers to "forget the room of one's own—write in the kitchen, lock yourself up in the bathroom. Write on the bus or the welfare line, on the job or during meals, between sleeping or waking." For Anzaldúa, writing by women of color is a lifeline between them. She writes, "In the San Francisco area, where I now live, none can stir the audience with their craft and truth saying as do Cherríe Moraga (Chicana), Gennie Lim (Asian American), and Luisah Teish (Black). With women like these, the loneliness of writing and the sense of powerlessness can be dispelled. We can walk among each other talking of our writing, reading to each other. And more and more when I'm alone, though still in communion with each other, the writing possesses me and propels me to leap into a timeless spaceless no-place where I forget myself and feel I am the universe. *This* is power."[40]

Although *Bridge* was written by and for women of color, it and other writing of the period exposed growing numbers of white women to the politics articulated by women of color. Political scientist Jane Mansbridge writes, "Despite the efforts of individual Black and Latina and Asian women to influence their mostly White organizations and their standing up at conferences to present their points of view, it was not until a significant literature by women of color appeared that the larger feminist movement began to learn significantly from those differences and be transformed. It was too painful for each Black woman individually to have to teach the White feminists in her organizations about their experiences. But through the written word, which can teach many at once, and through the controversies and understanding generated when people talk about what they have read, the movement as a discursive entity is now beginning to absorb, confront and be transformed by these new insights."[41]

White readers of *This Bridge Called My Back* and other writing by women of color of that period had much to learn about racism. Sherna Berger Gluck writes, "By 1982, on the heels of difficult political struggles waged by activist scholars of color, ground breaking essays and anthologies by and about women of color opened a new chapter in U.S. feminism. The future of the women's movement in the U.S. was reshaped irrevocably by the introduction of the expansive notion of feminismS [*sic*]."[42]

This Bridge Called My Back; Home Girls: A Black Feminist Anthology; and Beth Brant's edited volume, *A Gathering of Spirit: Writing and Art by North*

American Indian Women, were all wake-up calls for white women, alerting them to the fact that dealing with racism was an absolute must.[43] In the preface to *This Bridge Called My Back,* Cherríe Moraga writes, "What drew me to politics was my love of women, the agony I felt in observing the straight-jackets of poverty and repression I saw people in my own family in. But the deepest political tragedy I have experienced is how with such grace, such blind faith, this commitment to women in the feminist movement grew to be exclusive and reactionary. *I call my white sisters on this.*"[44] In "—But I Know You, American Woman," Judith Moschkovich explains that as a Latina, Jewish, immigrant woman, she knows much more about white Anglo culture than white Anglos know about her culture. In response to the many women who have assumed that it is her responsibility to educate them, she says, "Anyone that was raised and educated in this country has a very good chance of being ignorant about other cultures.... It's a sort of cultural isolationism, a way of life enforced on the people in this country so as to let them have a free conscience with respect to how they deal with the rest of the world." To that ignorance Moschkovich replies, Educate yourself: "I say: *read and listen.* We may, then, have something to share."[45]

The works in *This Bridge Called My Back* and other writings of the time provided a sturdy and clear template for white antiracist activism for the 1980s and beyond. Among its directives were the following: Do not expect women of color to be your educators, to do all the bridge work. White women need to be the bridge a lot of the time. Do not lump African American, Latina, Asian American, and Native American into one category. History, culture, imperialism, language, class, region, and sexuality often make a monolithic concept of a "woman of color" indefensible. Listen to the anger of women of color. It is informed by centuries of struggle, erasure, and experience. White women, look to your own history for signs of heresy and rebellion. Do not take on the histories of Black, Latina, or American Indian women as your own. They are not and never were yours.

Many white women came to see antiracism as a centerpiece of feminism through the activism and writing of women of color. Equally important, the identity politics first articulated by the Combahee River Collective opened a way for white women to explore how their own multiple identities—class, religion, family, sexuality—might inform their strategies for opposing racism.

Turned Away, Stepped Back In

Along with this "new political subject" among women of color came the creation of a space, a testing ground, and the possibility for an increasing number of white women to develop antiracist feminist politics. Among them were white women activists of the 1960s who had steered clear of feminism in the early 1970s. The presence of prominent women of color who were embracing class- and race-conscious feminist politics forced them to reexamine their belief that feminism was by definition white and bourgeois.

Naomi Jaffe, who had turned away from white radical feminism in the early days (late 1960s and early 1970s), came back to it later, mainly through her work with Black and Latina women, particularly lesbians. When I interviewed her in 1997, she was working at Holding Our Own, a multiracial feminist funding organization in Albany, New York, where she has been on the staff since 1991. The Women's Building in which Holding Our Own has an office is sandwiched between Lawau's Braids and Beauty Salon; the Tattoo Shop; AAA Used Furniture; a leftist, independently owned bookstore; the Last Straw Cafe; and Alewaba African Braids. Unlike many women's centers, which are housed in white sections of town, this one is in a central location within a working- and middle-class Black community. Not that maintaining this location has not been a struggle, Naomi tells me: getting the Women's Building to value and nurture a thoroughgoing commitment to diversity has not been an easy task. But the struggle has been worth it.

One question, of course, is how and why a woman who initially left the women's movement—a former member of the radical feminist organization Women's International Terrorist Conspiracy from Hell (WITCH) in New York—came to consider feminist organizing key to her activism. As was the case for other women I interviewed, not until the early 1980s did Naomi begin to see that feminism and an anti-imperialist perspective need not contradict each other. After she came up from the underground (in 1978), Naomi moved to Minnesota with her partner, who was going to chiropractic school. Naomi tried to get involved with activism but had trouble "rejoining" the movement. Eventually she began doing antiapartheid work in the Twin Cities. Although there were some South Africans in the movement, Naomi had almost no contact with Black or Native American women in the area, an absence she had also experienced in the late 1960s. The antiapartheid movement was largely white women and Black men. She remembers, "I was working full time and I was pregnant and very tired when I read *This Bridge Called My Back,* just when I needed it most. I read *This Bridge* and I realized, oh, that is what has been missing all my life—women of color."

Although it was a number of years before Naomi began working primarily with women of color, her basic insight remained. Once she moved to Albany, she worked with the Central America solidarity organization there, which included some Latinos, most of whom were Central Americans. But it was a predominantly white organization, and there were very few Latinas. Naomi and a few others worked to change the racial consciousness of the organization by sponsoring multiracial events. But Naomi continued to feel isolated: "There was still this pull to be in organizations that were all white, and I decided that I wasn't going to do that any more. I couldn't do it as a white person in a predominantly white organization. I needed to be situated differently. I needed to be in rooms that were predominantly filled with people of color in order to figure out what work I had to do. I had never done that. I had been an activist for twenty-five years, and I had never worked in predominantly people-of-color organizations."

During this period Naomi was also asked by women in her community to account for the ways heterosexism had shaped her life, resources, and assumptions—to figure out how being a straight woman affected her activism. For Naomi, confronting issues of homophobia and sexuality finally guided her to work directly with women of color. In a Nicaraguan women's solidarity group the two lesbian members said it was not a comfortable place for them. Naomi remembers them saying, "This is a married women's club and that does not work for us." The married women said, "Oh God, we can't deal with this. We have so little time. We have our kids and our families and our jobs and we are trying to do this one thing. We can't do ten things. We can only do one thing." That, Naomi says, "is when I remembered where I came from in my feminist life." She said to the other straight women, all of whom were younger than she, "'You guys don't understand. You guys wouldn't be here if it weren't for lesbians. There were no women's organizations in solidarity with anything when I started doing political work. The way we got to a point where we can have feminist organizations is a struggle led by lesbians. We wouldn't be here. Homophobia is not just another issue. It is the work we are doing. If we can't do this right, we can't do anything. We won't have any women's organizations.' So I remembered where I came from, just in the nick of time. I had come from a feminist background, but I hadn't done feminist work for many years…. When it came to arguing issues around homophobia, I found myself arguing a position that I didn't know I understood."

Soon after taking that position, Naomi went to a gay and lesbian rights march in Washington in 1983. "At that point, I was trying to figure out ways to be an ally of lesbians. So I went to this march with a couple of lesbian women I had known from the Nicaraguan affinity group. It was really affirming. They were just so welcoming of me. They made this big beautiful banner that said, 'Commies, Dykes, and Friends for Liberation.' I saw it and felt like allies were welcome. I started making connections with lesbians in the community, including lesbians of color. The lesbian feminist community, with all its deep contradictions, was a little more multiracial than the other parts of our movement." Through these connections Naomi got involved with Feminist Action Network (FAN), a predominantly lesbian and woman-of-color activist organization. Naomi remembers, "I thought it was one of the most wonderful things that ever happened to me, when I got invited to join this group. I was so thrilled. It was just where I needed to be working, in a place where issues of race and gender and sexuality are predominant. A place led by women of color, led by lesbians."

Suzanne Ross's entry into feminist organizing was also a direct consequence of working and developing friendships with Black feminists. Her long-term political work with women across race has taught her much about her complex and sometimes contradictory position within multiracial feminism. She was raised in the late 1930s and early 1940s in a Jewish family that lived in Europe and Palestine to escape the Holocaust. In the 1960s and early 1970s Suzanne became an activist against the Vietnam War and U.S. imperialism. While earning her Ph.D. in psychology, she also became a lifelong advocate for young people through her work with African American adolescents. By the early 1970s, Suzanne was teaching at Lehman College and began working closely with Audre Lorde, J. D. Franklin, and other Black women scholars. Although she was aware of the feminist movement in the 1970s, "I didn't like it even though I always had an inclination and identified with the politics." Suzanne was asked to speak at the first feminist conference at Barnard College in 1970, but she turned the opportunity down: "I didn't like the fact that it wasn't as militant at that time, I lumped all of them as racists. I had a very undialectical understanding of it. I saw it as too white, too lacking in militancy, too elitist. The stereotype of the white women's movement is what I bought into and missed a lot of opportunities to either raise it to a different level or relate to it differently. I always posed it against the antiracist movement."

Suzanne saw the class makeup and whiteness of the movement as a tragedy but did not, at that point, try to intervene. Until the mid-1970s she kept her distance from feminist activism. Once she began teaching and organizing alongside Black women, she began to examine her initial reaction to feminism. Meeting and working with Black feminists is "what turned me around. A lot of them gave me a hard time for not taking the feminist movement seriously enough. With someone like Audre Lorde, her mere presence, you couldn't say that feminism was white. Barbara Smith and hattie gossett became friends of mine. I met hattie on a trip to Cuba along with Toni Cade Bambara. She is an amazing thinker and a wonderful human being who taught me a lot. These women taught me a lot." By the late 1970s

Suzanne had added the term "feminist" to the term "revolutionary" to describe her politics. Since the mid-1970s her feminist activism has primarily taken place in multiracial organizations composed largely of women of color, including her annual work with a multiracial collective for International Women's Day.

It was precisely the emergence of a multiracial movement that was attempting to come to terms with race, sexuality, and gender that made room for Suzanne, Naomi, and other militant women of the 1960s to apply the skills they had developed in the Civil Rights and Black Power movements. Because of their involvement with and commitment to women of color, they could no longer reject feminism as inherently racist. Moreover, identity politics first articulated by Black women gave them tools to understand how what Adrienne Rich termed the "politics of location" informed their perspectives.[46] For Naomi, that meant dealing with the ways heterosexism kept women of color and white women from connecting with each other. The lessons Suzanne learned working with African American adolescents and feminists of color required her to reconsider feminism as key to revolutionary politics. Multiracial feminism allowed Suzanne and Naomi to see that women of color had been invisible to them in the 1960s. For both women, multiracial feminism provided a community they had missed in the 1960s.

White Antiracist Feminism: Stumbling Blocks, Turning Points

Whereas some white women came to antiracist feminism after having been involved in the Civil Rights and Black Power movements, a younger cohort of white women—most of whom were in their twenties at the time—was first exposed to race consciousness through multiracial lesbian feminist contexts. Unlike white militant women of the 1960s, these women came to political consciousness through feminism at a time when women of color had made it clear that to call oneself a "feminist" and not deal with race is not to be a feminist. As one woman said at the National Women's Studies Association (NWSA) conference in 1981, "Shall we, as Third World women, decide to 'join' the 'movement'? We can't join the movement...because we are the movement."[47]

One woman I interviewed, Laurie Holmes, describes her entry into activism as having been filtered from the beginning through her work in a multiracial work force and multiracial feminism. Laurie was raised in a Protestant family in working- and middle-class bedroom communities in New England. As a child she was involved in a local United Church of Christ community, where lessons of race revolved around Martin Luther King Jr.'s "I Have a Dream" speech and the idea that all people are equal. As a teenager she began to believe that the world she was living in was not "the real world," so she set her sights on moving to a multiracial city. She moved to Boston at the age of seventeen, in 1976, and she soon came out as a lesbian. She began living with "other women who were discovering women's music, and got very psyched about feminism." In the gathering places she frequented—Saints, a women's bar; the Cambridge Women's Center; and women's concerts and conferences—she soon heard Black, Latina, and Asian American women saying that white women needed to do a serious examination of their racism. "The scene I have in my mind is of women of color standing up at concerts and conferences, talking about the work white women needed to do, immediately. I agreed with them and believed them. The message I heard was that white women had a lot of fucking work to do on ourselves. Go do it. Simple as that. I said, yeah. That is true for me. I have a lot of work to do. I had no idea where to start, but I am going to do it. I felt like I needed to start schooling myself."

Laurie's education about race began when she started driving a public school bus soon after Boston began school desegregation. In 1972 the National Association for the Advancement of Colored People (NAACP) and Black parents had sued the Boston School Committee to challenge school segregation.[48] The school bus drivers supported desegregation while, as an organization, modeling an integrated group that many hoped would exist in the school as well. The drivers drove children to and from school through angry crowds and barrages of rocks and other violence from whites opposed to integration. Laurie believes that the seven years she drove a bus "ended up being the best schooling I could have ever had. I joined what I think was one of the very few integrated work forces in Boston, along with the Gillette Company and maybe the post office. We were really mixed. Folks from all over the city. There was just so much in it for me. I got to know every single neighborhood in the city. I got to become friends with the kids on an ally level rather than from a position of authority." Had Laurie been a teacher, there would have been a formalized process for interacting with the parents. Because she was a bus driver, relationships could develop more naturally.

At the same time, Laurie began "hitting up against my own racism." She believed a lot of stereotypes about neighborhoods and city life. But "going into neighborhoods and listening to the way people talk, I noticed my own fears as I developed relationships with people of color.... The most classic stuff is thinking some place is a bad neighborhood, but then, going in and seeing how people live busts all of that." Laurie had big fears that people of color were going to reject her. "My racism told me that I want to be friends with everybody, but no people of color would want to know anything about me. So let me not push myself onto them." This too was a fear she began to confront. Laurie sought information everywhere. "I was trying to read. I didn't read. I am probably the least well-read antiracist activist in the world. You could probably name any number of theorists and I probably haven't read them. But I started reading novels written by women of color."

Laurie was also part of a bus drivers' union that was predominantly Black both in the rank and file and in the leadership, and 25–35 percent women.[49] The union, which was well known for its organization and cohesion, staged several successful strikes to secure a decent wage, benefits, and accountability in hiring. In the process, according to Laurie, the bus drivers "did the kind of struggling with each other that people do in developing relationships." For example, as one of the only out lesbians in the union, Laurie "was hanging out with a lot of Black men who I think hated the idea of lesbianism. And yet we were all developing relationships across lines of difference that I believe challenged all of us." One year Laurie tried to play on a softball team with a group of Black women bus drivers. "They didn't have any white players on the team and no lesbians. They let me play, but it didn't work out as a positive experience.... It didn't get comfortable enough. They had social gatherings after games, but I never knew where those were. I somehow didn't get myself there. I wanted to challenge myself to do that and I wanted to build relationships with those women, but it was really hard. And we didn't find a way to articulate together what was in the way."

Despite difficulties, people in the union kept working together. Laurie remembers Mel King (a progressive Black leader who ran for mayor of Boston under the Rainbow Coalition in 1983) coming to their union meetings. "He would rally us together. I remember this one meeting where he had us all hugging each other. It was wonderful. I remember those as really great times. Probably greater than they were, but I felt like we were walking the talk. We weren't talking that we were doing antiracism work, ever. That is true of my whole story. We were just doing it. We were trying to get the kids to school on buses. We were trying to get a better contract. We were aware that we were a diverse group of folks. We spoke of an appreciation of that which worked in our favor." At that time Laurie and many others across race believed that busing was the "only way that communities of color were going to get equal resources.... We would line up with police escorts and go into South Boston and have rocks thrown at us. That kind of stuff. It kind of felt that all of us were united—the drivers and the parents and the kids on the buses. Trying to keep the kids safe and get everybody where they needed to go."

Through a combination of lessons she learned as a bus driver and from multiracial lesbian feminism, Laurie was coming to believe that fighting racism centered on being part of people's real-life struggles. Of her work at that time, Laurie says, "I would have called it activism. I just wouldn't have called it antiracism. I am here because this is my job. Antiracism has always been a subtitle for other work I am doing." Laurie continued to develop organizing skills she associated with feminism: consensus-making, building activist organizations through individual relationships, and "giving everyone a voice that wants to be involved." There were times, however, in the early 1980s, where the life she was leading and her work with lesbian feminist organizing felt separate to her. She would drive a bus in multiracial communities as part of a multiracial union during the day and then go to the Cambridge Women's Center, which was mostly a white feminist center, at night. For example, the affinity group she was involved with in the early 1980s, Lesbians United in Nonnuclear Action (LUNA), did a great job of confronting the larger, male-dominated, antinuclear organization Clamshell Alliance, "pushing their way into the decision-making process if they had to." But the lesbian affinity group itself was mostly white. Laurie pushed to get the alliance to think beyond white women, working, for example, to make sure the story she wrote about Karen Silkwood was translated into Spanish.

Over time Laurie's community was becoming more and more mixed racially. In 1981 she fell in love with a Puerto Rican woman who had three children. That relationship and her parenting pulled her away from white feminists and towards daily life in a Puerto Rican family. "In those days," she explains, "it was not cool to be a lesbian and have boys…. My focus was really at home. Little boys were not accepted. I had four brothers and no sisters and always loved boys. I didn't move away from feminism. I moved away from feminists."

Not until the 1990s—when Laurie began working at the Elizabeth Stone House, a grassroots mental health alternative founded in 1974 by a group of radical social workers and women who had formerly been incarcerated on psychiatric wards—did Laurie find a place where her feminism and antiracism need not be separated. She recalls, "As soon as I walked through the doors at the Stone House, I felt like I had come home…. It was a place that consciously thought through its policies to reflect the experiences of the people it serves and to walk that politic and honor the experience of everyone walking through the door…. Through a process of plenty of struggle, the organization is explicit about reflecting the communities it serves—women of color, lesbians, bilingual, bicultural women—and operates based on a non-hierarchical model."

Laurie's story illustrates the tensions felt by a group of white women in the late 1970s and early 1980s who, in their attempts to understand race,

class, gender, and sexuality, ended up straddling several worlds simultaneously. She, like many lesbian feminists of her generation, first began dealing
with racism because of what she was learning from women of color. Laurie
was working in a multiracial, highly politicized setting at a time when many
white people were openly hostile towards school bus drivers and their young
charges. Laurie came out as a lesbian into an increasingly vocal and politicized gay and lesbian community at a time when, as she remembers it, "gay
and lesbian pride marches were political rather than a picnic." For Laurie,
the personal was political, and the political was personal in every aspect of
her life.

Ruth Frankenberg also links her consciousness about racism directly to
lessons learned from women of color during the rise of Third World
feminism. Ruth grew up in England and moved to northern California in
1979. As a child she saw the world as both an insider, being white and
English-speaking, and an outsider, being the daughter of a Jewish father and
Protestant mother, a child of leftist parents, and from a single-parent
household in a period when divorce was not yet common. As a young adult,
Ruth was involved in challenging the National Front, a neo-Nazi organization that was gaining political power in England in the mid-1960s. During
that period, she identified herself as a socialist feminist. When she moved to
Santa Cruz in 1979, she quickly learned that the feminist movement in
Britain lagged behind the movement in California, which meant she still
considered antiracism and feminism as completely separate. Like many white
women who came to see the two as intertwined, Ruth learned much from
women of color who considered themselves feminists or were intensely
involved in women's rights issues. A Puerto Rican woman who had come of
age in the National Welfare Rights Organization (NWRO) became Ruth's
particular mentor and friend.[50] Ruth began to recognize racism in the
feminist movement, in graduate classes and scholarship, and in American
culture and daily life.

Like many white women, Ruth initially responded to these lessons with
disbelief. In graduate school, where women of color and white women
students were openly confronting issues of race, Ruth remembers stages of
her own reactions. At first she thought the women of color were kidding or
wrong when they identified limits of socialist feminism. She went though a
"whole process of trying to prove them wrong on everything and thinking
that they must be thinking about liberal feminism, not Marxist feminism."
She then went through a lengthy period of feeling great "shame about being
part of this big category of people called white people, or this subcategory
called white women, or even smaller category called white feminists, who

were not on the right side but on the wrong side." Until then Ruth had felt like "one of the good guys.... So it was an about-face.... Being very conscious that everything I thought I knew I didn't know. Because everything I thought I knew was inadequate." During that period Ruth went from thinking everything she had learned and thought was right to thinking nothing was. She assumed everything a person of color said was correct, which became a real bind for her when two people of color disagreed.

A turning point came when she became close friends with an Indian woman who, like Ruth, was an immigrant. "She had experienced a lot of misrecognition and misunderstanding and nonrecognition as an Indian who had been a feminist activist and a leftist in India who then came here and encountered a lot of the same kinds of incomprehension from women of color that you might get from white people—the presumption of how could there be a feminist movement in India?" Ruth's relationship with her friend taught Ruth to "think for myself": to question her own limited knowledge as a white woman but not glorify women of color in the process.

As Ruth continued to engage with African American, Puerto Rican, Chicana, and South Asian women—through both friendships and activism—she began to uncover part of what makes confronting racism so scary. In an open letter to Gloria Watkins (bell hooks), who was also enrolled in a graduate course Ruth was taking, Ruth included an analysis of another white woman in the class who Ruth believed did not want to confront her own racism because the woman thought it would mean questioning her own self-worth, her Ph.D., and her credibility. Ruth's appraisal was accurate, but with time she began to see that her analysis of the other white woman applied to herself as well. She was projecting on another white woman her own fears. "Everything I knew to be true was really dubious, so in other words, for me, my political work, my academic work were very connected. I mean, you have your line, your act. So if Gloria was right, then everything I knew was wrong, therefore my entire epistemology was up shit creek. So in that sense, I feared for my Ph.D., my intellectual credibility, my competency, and therefore my self-worth. My self-worth was very tied to...my political consciousness."

Ruth was aware of the problems with white women's identities, but at that period in her life she had trouble claiming those problems as her own. Instead, she made it another white woman's problem, setting herself up as separate from other white women. "I ended up in a very polarized situation where my whole first-year cohort [in graduate school] hated me, because it was a very strong cohort of white feminists. I thought they hated me because of the line I was taking about racism, and in fact that was true. But the other thing that was true is that, had I been ten years down the road with my practice of antiracism, I could have addressed all of this in a different way. One thing that is changed about me is my improved ability to talk with other white people about racism in a way that doesn't freak them out. So I was going like a herd of elephants, blundering through with my new shock, horror, discoveries." Ten years down the line, Ruth might have "had the honesty to take it on myself, to take on my issues, and then say, 'I wonder if that issue is true for this other person as well.'"

About two years into the process of developing race consciousness, Ruth "hit the wall." She explains, "I got to this place where I had no place to sit or fit.... I was in this body that was entirely filled with white privilege; that was the totality of myself." Although Ruth had white friends, she had no white allies. A lot of her "white friends literally didn't want to deal with me because they felt I was too closely identified with my friends of color.... But, to be really frank, I don't think those white friends were interested in a thoroughgoing engagement with racism." During this same period, Ruth also could not figure out if she was a lesbian or not, which only added to her confusion and tentativeness.

Amid this cognitive dissonance Ruth became very sick. She returned to England to take care of her grandmother, who was recuperating from surgery. In the process she learned much about the health care system, the social welfare system, and her own mother's struggle to care for her mother. At the same time she was doing graduate work on the difference race makes in how feminists talk about female consciousness. "All of that helped me to remember that there is no binary path.... Women's lives are shaped not just by race but by a range of other issues as well."

In the ten years between Ruth's "going like a herd of elephants" and finding a way to walk with other white people, she did a lot of learning. She came out as a lesbian, continued to sustain long-term relationships with women of color, and began finding ways to develop close friendships with white antiracist women. She came to trust that her partner "would equally well call me on my racism and support me on my antiracism." From Ricky Marcuse and Terry Berman, both white antiracist consultants and teachers, Ruth learned that antiracist work for white people requires "doing the work from a place of self-love."

All these influences led her to see antiracist work as a political as well as a spiritual process. Coming from a left background, she had grown up with a narrow understanding of what constitutes "activism." She now has a larger understanding. She has also come to believe that her biggest challenge is "working with other white people around racism.... My work is really about waking white people up to who they are in terms of racial formation."

By the time Ruth and Laurie came to feminism (in the late 1970s and early 1980s), there were multiple arenas in which white women learned that dealing with race and women's multiple identities was essential. They did not come of age as feminists thinking feminism started and ended with white women. It was a time when race was an openly contested issue in multiple places: in conferences, speak-outs, and political forums; in neighborhood organizing; in women-founded organizations; and in intimate interracial relationships and friendship circles.

At the same time, there are important differences in their stories, differences that speak to the range of ways in which white women contended with race through feminism in the late 1970s and 1980s. Much of Ruth's early exposure to and many of her conversations with women of color took place in a university setting, in writing, and through multiracial feminist theory. Laurie, by contrast, went to college "for a quick minute" but dropped out after coming to believe that Hampshire College (a small alternative liberal arts school in a predominantly white community) was as unreal an environment as the bedroom communities in which she had grown up. Her early understanding about racism took shape in the working world, among and with working-class people. For her, antiracism was always work she did through other work—driving a bus, raising a family, resisting separatist politics—straddling many worlds simultaneously.

Alongside this key difference are important parallels in Ruth's and Laurie's stories that are indicative of the dilemmas many white women faced during this period. Their stories of coming to consciousness about antiracism cannot be told without attending to their private as well as their public lives. The lessons they learned in intimate relationships were as compelling as those they learned in the work world. Both women attributed early lessons about race to women of color—lessons they learned in conferences, conversations, organizing, and intimate relationships. Both went through a period of isolation from other white women. Ruth's isolation is captured in her story about projecting on another white woman her own fears and confusion; Laurie's is expressed in her skepticism about separatist politics and limits she experienced in white-dominated feminist circles. To me, it is telling that neither of them saw other white women as their potential allies in taking on issues of race in the late 1970s or early 1980s. In fact, both women's coming to consciousness as white antiracist women slightly predated what was, by the mid-1980s, the emergence of a more visible group of white antiracist feminists.

Conclusion

The striking differences in the views held by militant white women about early second-wave feminism, as compared to the experiences of women who came to feminism by the late 1970s and early 1980s, led me to ask two questions about feminist movement history: What pushed the Naomi Jaffes and Marilyn Bucks of the world (left, militant, and anti-imperialist women) away from feminism in the 1960s and early 1970s and then pulled them towards it in the 1980s? What opened a space for some white women to see antiracism—from the outset—as a quintessential feminist principle? In both cases, the emergence of feminism spearheaded by women of color created a context for making issues of race and racism central feminist priorities.

In *White Women, Race Matters,* Ruth Frankenberg raises a key question about why the women's movement came to be known as white: "Class- and nation-based movements [of the 1960s and early 1970s] were themselves the inspiration and in some ways provided the moment of origin for second-wave feminism or 'women's liberation.' Not only did they provide models for the women's movement, but many women activists either moved from antiracist movements into the feminist movement or participated simultaneously in both. The obvious question here is why, given these origins, by the mid-1970s, the most clearly audible feminist discourses were those that failed to address racism?"[51] The most obvious answer to this question involves the gaze of the mass media, which was directed almost entirely at radical white feminist actions. But the mass media is certainly not the sole culprit. White women who conceived of feminism as finally getting to "their issue," as if racism was not also a white feminist question, also played into the image of feminism as a white woman's issue. Nationalist politics of the time—which recognized the value of autonomous political organizations—also contributed to separate spheres for women of color and white women. These and other factors contributed to an image of feminism that excluded both Black, Latina, and Asian American feminist work and white women who refused to let go of an antiracist analysis.

Incorporating their experiences into the story of early second-wave feminism requires consideration of a number of key realities. First, the growth of organizations of feminists of color in the 1970s and 1980s contributed to the willingness of anti-imperialist women to treat feminism as central to their politics. Second, the stories of these antiracist white women also counter the notion that the "best days of the movement were over by the mid or even early 1970s."[52] What feminist Ellen Willis identifies as the height of the radical feminist movement (1968–1974) was a period in which many antiracist women absented themselves from white feminism.[53] Considering 1968 to 1974 the height of the radical feminist movement really only considers white women who saw sexism as the ultimate oppression.[54] In fact, from the perspective of white antiracism, the early 1970s were a low point of feminism, a time when many women who were committed to an antiracist analysis had to put their feminism on the back burner in order to work with men and women of color and against racism. For antiracist white women, the best days of feminism were yet to come. As Barbara Smith explains, the early 1980s was "the period when those issues that had divided many of the movement's constituencies—such as racism, anti-Semitism, ableism, ageism and classism—were put out on the table."[55]

From a multiracial perspective, a high in the feminist movement took place in the early to middle 1980s with the rise of feminism and coalition-building among women of color and with the emergence of a small but important white antiracist voice.[56] Barbara Smith writes that "the most progressive sectors of the movement responded to the challenge to transform their analysis and practice in order to build a stronger movement that encompassed a variety of feminisms."[57] What white feminist scholars typically consider the period of abeyance of the feminist movement in the 1980s was actually the height of multiracial feminism.[58]

Viewing feminist history from the point of view of multiracial feminism does not invalidate the import of dates often assigned to a timeline of second-wave feminism: the founding of the National Organization for Women (NOW) in 1966; the formation of the first radical feminist group, New York Radical Women, in 1967; the *Roe v. Wade* Supreme Court decision legalizing abortion in 1973; the founding of the Coalition of Labor Union Women (CLUW) in 1973; and the struggle to ratify the Equal Rights Amendment from 1970 to 1982. It does, however, add a whole new set of dates to that timeline, including the rebellion at Attica Prison in 1971; Angela Davis's acquittal on all charges in 1972; the founding of WARN in 1974; the work of the Combahee River Collective from 1974 to 1979; the conference on racism and sexism cosponsored by NBFO and the Sagaris Collective in 1976; the murders of antiracist activists in Greensboro, North Carolina, in 1979; and the publication of *This Bridge Called My Back* and *Home Girls* in the early 1980s. Adding these dates to the story of second-wave feminism provides a necessary introduction to understanding the development of antiracist consciousness within multiracial feminism of the late 1970s and beyond.

When the various political generations of white antiracist women are included in the telling of second-wave feminist history, commonly accepted ideas about the origins of feminism must be reconsidered. The most problematic is the notion that white women brought feminism to women of color. From the perspective of many white antiracist women, it was largely the other way around. White women, whose early political training was in the Civil Rights movement, saw modeled all around them Black women leaders who not only were the backbone of the movement but also provided much of its vision. White women involved in the antiwar movement who developed an international, anti-imperialist analysis considered militant women in Vietnam, Cuba, and Puerto Rico as their role models—women who, as Marilyn Buck says, not only fed the troops but "were the troops." White women who avoided early second-wave feminism because of its white biases struggled against sexism in male-dominated nationalist and solidarity organizations. At the same time, work to free Angela Davis and then Assata Shakur were among their highest priorities.

At the Liberation Day March in 1970, the Third World Women's Alliance, a Black feminist group led by Frances Beal that emerged out of the SNCC, took part in the demonstration with signs in support of Angela Davis. Frances Beal recalls, "We had signs reading 'Hands Off Angela Davis' and one of the leaders of NOW ran up to us and said angrily, 'Angela Davis has nothing to do with Women's Liberation.' "It has nothing to do with the kind of liberation you're talking about," retorted Beal, "but it has everything to do with the kind of liberation we're talking about."[59]

Both this scene and the white feminists' dismissal of the rebellion at Attica speak to an expansive consciousness on the part of Black women and a few white antiracist women in the early 1970s. Even within male-dominated organizations, where rank-and-file women did not work closely together across race, white women identified Black women as leaders and those to whom they held themselves accountable. By the time white women of the next generation—those coming of age politically in the late 1970s and early 1980s—were introduced to feminism, the explosion of art, activism, and scholarship of women of color provided multiple arenas for white women to learn about race and racism.

This essay first appeared in Becky Thompson, *A Promise and a Way of Life*. (Univ. of Minnesota Press, 2001).

NOTES

[1] Chela Sandoval, "Feminism and Racism: A Report on the 1981 National Women's Studies Association Conference," in *Making Face, Making Soul: Haciendo Caras. Creative and Critical Perspectives by Women of Color*, ed. Gloria Anzaldúa (San Francisco: Aunt Lute Press, 1990): 55.

2 Chela Sandoval, "Oppositional Consciousness in the Postmodern World: United States Third World Feminism, Semiotics, and the Methodology of the Oppressed" (Ph.D. diss., University of California–Santa Cruz, 1994).

3 The term "women of color" (which includes but is not limited to Native American, Asian, African American, Arab, and Latina women) is used for political rasons to underscore unity among women who have historically been colonized, enslaved, and exploited in the United States. The term "Third World" stresses similarities between oppression of women of color in the United States and of women in Third World countries.

4 Angela Davis, *The Angela Y Davis Reader,* ed. Joy James (Malden, MA: Blackwell, 1998): 15, 314.

5 Sherna Berger Gluck, "Whose Feminism, Whose History? Reflections on Excavating the History of (the) U.S. Women's Movement(s)," in *Community Activism and Feminist Politics: Organizing across Race, Class, and Gender,* ed. Nancy A. Naples (New York: Routledge, 1998), 38–39.

6 Miya Iwataki, "The Asian Women's Movement: A Retrospective," *East Wind* (Spring/Summer 1983): 35–41; Gluck, "Whose Feminism, Whose History?" 39–41.

7 Iwataki, "The Asian Women's Movement": 35–41.

8 Sonia Shah, "Presenting the Blue Goddess: Toward a National Pan-Asian Feminist Agenda," in *The State of Asian America: Activism and Resistance in the 1990s,* ed. Karin Aguilar-San Juan (Boston: South End Press, 1994): 147–58.

9 Iwataki, "The Asian Women's Movement": 41.

10 M. Annette Jaimes with Theresa Halsey, "American Indian Women: At the Center of Indigenous Resistance in Contemporary North America," in *The State of Native America: Genocide, Colonization, and Resistance,* ed. M. Annette Jaimes. (Boston: South End Press, 1992): 328–329.

11 Stephanie Autumn, "This Air, This Land, This Water—If We Don't Start Organizing Now, We'll Lose It," *Big Mama Rag* 11, no. 4 (April 1983): 4, 5.

12 For an insightful analysis of the multidimensionality of Black nationalism of the late 1960s and early 1970s, see "Black Nationalism: The '60s and the '90s," in Davis, *The Angela Y. Davis Reader:* 289–96.

13 Deborah Gray White, *Too Heavy a Load: Black Women in Defense of Themselves* (New York: Norton, 1999): 242.

14 Ibid.: 242–53.

15 Combahee River Collective, "The Combahee River Collective Statement," in *Home Girls: A Black Feminist Anthology,* ed. Barbara Smith (New York: Kitchen Table/Women of Color Press, 1983): 275.

16 In Black womanist theology emerging during this period, the concept of epistemological privilege paralleled this principle. The epistemological privilege is the right and responsibility of those in marginalized positions to name the strategies of resistance and change. See Katie C. Cannon, *Black Womanist Ethics* (Atlanta: Scholars Press, 1988).

17 Barbara Smith, "The Boston Murders," in *Life Notes: Personal Writing by Contemporary Black Women,* ed. Patricia Bell-Scott (New York: Norton, 1994): 315.

18 Ibid: 318–19

19 Anna Julia Cooper, "The Status of Women in America," 44–49 and Claudia Jones, "An End to the Neglect of the Problems of the Negro Woman!" 108–23; both in *Words of Fire: An Anthology of African-American Feminist Thought,* ed. Beverly Guy-Sheftall (New York: New Press, 1995).

[20] Davis, *The Angela Y Davis Reader:* 313.

[21] Barbara Smith, "Racism and Women's Studies," in *All the Women Are White, All the Blacks Are Men, but Some of Us Are Brave: Black Women's Studies,* ed. Gloria T. Hull et al. (Old Westbury, NY: Feminist Press, 1982): 49.

[22] Patricia Hill Collins, "Feminism in the Twentieth Century," in *Black Women in America: An Historical Encyclopedia,* ed. Darlene Clark Hine (New York: Carlson Publishing, 1993): 418, quoted in Vicki Crawford, "African American Women in the Twenty-First Century: The Continuing Challenge," in *The American Woman, 1999–2000,* ed. Cynthia B. Costello et al. (New York: Norton, 1998): 119.

[23] Alice Walker, *In Search of Our Mother's Gardens: Womanist Prose* (San Diego: Harcourt Brace Jovanovich, 1983).

[24] Patricia Zavella, "The Problematic Relationship of Feminism and Chicana Studies," *Women's Studies* 17 (1989): 29; *Chicana Critical Issues,* Mujeres Activas en Letras y Cambio Social, ed., (Berkeley: Third Woman Press, 1993).

[25] Chela Sandoval, "U.S. Third World Feminism: The Theory and Method of Oppositional Consciousness in the Postmodern World," *Genders* 10 (Spring 1991): 5; Gloria Anzaldúa, "La Consciencia de la Mestiza: Towards a New Consciousness," in Anzaldúa, *Making Face, Making Soul,* 377–89; Maxine Hong Kingston, *The Woman Warrior* (New York: Vintage Books, 1977) and Audre Lorde, *Sister Outsider* (New York: Crossing Press, 1984).

[26] Elizabeth Martinez, "History Makes Us, We Make History," in *The Feminist Memoir Project: Voices from Women's Liberation,* ed. Rachel Blau DuPlessis and Ann Snitow (New York: Three Rivers Press, 1998): 118.

[27] Celestine Ware, *Woman Power: The Movement for Women's Liberation* (New York: Tower, 1970). See also Katie King, *Theory in Its Feminist Travels: Conversations in U.S. Women's Movements* (Bloomington: University of Indiana Press, 1994): 126–30, 132–33, 177.

[28] Beatriz Pesquera and Denise A. Segura, "There Is No Going Back: Chicanas and Feminism," in *Chicana Critical Issues*: 97.

[29] Davis, *The Angela Y Davis Reader:* 291.

[30] Activist organizations of women of color in the 1970s and 1980s included the National Conference of Puerto Rican Women (NaCOPRW, founded in 1972); the Mexican American Women's National Association (MANA, 1974); the Organization of Pan Asian American Women (1976); OHOYO, a national network of American Indian and Alaska Native Women (early 1980s); the National Institute of Women of Color (1981); the National Coalition of One Hundred Black Women (1970); and the Coalition of Labor Union Women (CLUW, 1974). For an excellent multiracial chronicle of second-wave feminist organizations, see Leslie R. Wolfe and Jennifer Tucker, "Feminism Lives: Building a Multiracial Women's Movement in the United States," in *The Challenge of Local Feminisms: Women's Movement in Global Perspective,* ed. Amrita Basu (Boulder, CO: Westview, 1995): 435–62.

[31] Toni Cade, ed., *The Black Woman: An Anthology* (New York: Signet, 1970) and Ntozake Shange, *For Colored Girls Who Have Considered Suicide / When the Rainbow Is Enuf* (New York: Macmillan, 1977); Kingston, *The Woman Warrior; Conditions: Five, the Black Women's Issue,* ed. Lorraine Bethel and Barbara Smith, 1979; and Audre Lorde, *The Cancer Journals* (Argyle, NY: Spinsters Ink, 1980).

[32] Davis, *The Angela Y. Davis Reader:* 313.

[33] Ibid., and *This Bridge Called My Back: Writings by Radical Women of Color,* 2nd Ed., ed., Cherríe Moraga and Gloria Anzaldúa (New York: Kitchen Table/Women of Color Press, 1983).

[34] Gaye Williams, "Anzaldúa and Moraga: Building Bridges," *Sojourner: The Women's Forum* 7, no.2 (October 1981): 14.

[35] Cherríe Moraga, "Refugees of a World on Fire: Foreword to the Second Edition," in *This Bridge Called My Back.*

[36] Paula Gunn Allen, review of Moraga and Anzaldúa, *This Bridge Called My Back, Conditions: Eight,* 1982: 124.

[37] Paula Gunn Allen, review of Moraga and Anzaldúa, in *This Bridge Called My Back: Writings by Radical Women of Color,* ed., Cherríe Moraga and Gloria Anzaldúa (New York: Kitchen Table/Women of Color Press, 1983): 124.

[38] Merle Woo, "Letter to Ma," in *This Bridge Called My Back:* 140–47.

[39] Mitsuye Yamada, "Asian American Women and Feminism," in *This Bridge Called My Back:* 75.

[40] Gloria Anzaldúa, "Speaking in Tongues," in *This Bridge Called My Back:* 170, 172.

[41] Jane Mansbridge, "What Is the Feminist Movement?" in *Feminist Organizations: Harvest of the New Women's Movement,* ed. Myra Marx Ferree and Patricia Yancey Martin (Philadelphia: Temple University Press, 1995): 32.

[42] Gluck, "Whose Feminism, Whose History?" 32.

[43] Beth Brant, ed. *A Gathering of Spirit: Writing and Art by North American Indian Women* (Rockland, ME: Sinister Wisdom Books, 1984); Smith, *Home Girls;* and Moraga and Anzaldúa, *This Bridge Called My Back.*

[44] Cherríe Moraga, preface to *This Bridge Called My Back:* xiv.

[45] Judith Moschkovich, "—But I Know You, American Woman," in *This Bridge Called My Back:* 80.

[46] Adrienne Rich, "Notes Toward a Politics of Location," *Blood, Bread, and Poetry* (New York: Norton, 1986): 210–32.

[47] Sandoval, "Feminism and Racism": 59.

[48] James Green, "The Making of Mel King's Rainbow Coalition: Political Changes in Boston, 1963–1983," *Radical America,* double issue: 17, no. 6 (1983) and 18, no. 1(1984): 18–20.

[49] Margaret Cerullo et al., "An Interview with Jess Ewing: The Bus Stops Here. Organizing Boston School Bus Drivers," *Radical America* 17, no.5 (1983): 9.

[50] NWRO, which was founded in 1966, was Black-led and multiracial (85 percent African American, 5 percent Hispanic). Although NWRO did not explicitly call itself a feminist organization, founder Johnnie Tillmon considered women's liberation "a matter of survival" for poor Black women. See Diane K. Lewis, "A Response to Inequality: Black Women, Racism, and Sexism," in *The Signs Reader: Women, Gender, and Scholarship,* ed. Elizabeth Abel and Emily Abel (Chicago: University of Chicago Press, 1983): 189; White, *Too Heavy a Load,* 212–42; Guida West, *The National Welfare Rights Movement: The Social Protest of Poor Women* (New York: Praeger, 1981); and Vicki Crawford, "African American Women in the Twenty-First Century: The Continuing Challenge," in *The American Woman, 1999–2000,* ed. Cynthia B. Costello et al. (New York: Norton, 1998): 114–17.

[51] Ruth Frankenberg, *White Women, Race Matters: The Social Construction of Whiteness* (Minneapolis: University of Minnesota Press, 1993): 14.

[52] Barbara Smith, "'Feisty Characters' and 'Other People's Causes': Memories of White Racism and US. Feminism," in DuPlessis and Snitow, *The Feminist Memoir Project,* 480.

[53] Ellen Willis, foreword to *Daring to Be Bad: Radical Feminism in America* by Alice Echols (Minneapolis: University of Minnesota Press, 1989): vii.

[54] Smith, "'Feisty Characters'": 480.

[55] Ibid.

[56] Accounting for race and class disrupts the orthodoxy about stages of early second-wave feminism in other ways as well. For example, Nancy MacLean shows that viewing feminism from the perspective of working-class women "chips away at the orthodoxy" about the post–World War II years as a nadir in feminism, since working-class women made headway in union organizing and pay equity during that period. Nancy MacLean, "The Hidden History of Affirmative Action: Working Women's Struggles in the 1970s and the Gender of Class," *Feminist Studies* 25, no. I (Spring 1999): 43–78.

[57] Smith, "'Feisty Characters'": 480.

[58] Verta Taylor and Nancy Whittier, "The New Feminist Movement," in *Feminist Frontiers IV,* ed. Laurel Richardson et al. (New York: McGraw-Hill, 1997): 553.

[59] From Charlayne Hunter, "Many Blacks Wary of 'Women's Liberation' Movement," *New York Times* (November 17, 1970): 60, quoted in Paula Giddings, *When and Where I Enter: The Impact of Black Women on Race and Sex in America* (New York: Bantam Books, 1984): 305.

Strategies from the Field: Organizing as an Asian American Feminist

JULIANA PEGUES

Talking on the phone to a friend of mine, another Asian American woman who has worked in both broad leftist political spaces and identity-based circles, I tell her about this essay. That I am attempting to articulate my frustrations with the tried and tired models for organizing. I ask her what she thinks, for any comments she has.

"Aiyah!"

I wait for her to finish, then realize she is done. "Is that it? Aiyah?"

"That's it," she responds. "What more is there to say?"

To be honest, I know how she feels. As a feminist and bisexual woman who has participated in identity-based organizations and the white-dominated leftist movement, I am frustrated with the difficulty of organizing with both.

Many of us on the margins have experienced the racism, classism, sexism, and homophobia in white-male-dominated leftist organizations. On the other hand, we've also encountered a lack of political analysis among those with whom we share ethnic, gender, and sexual identities. How then should Asian American feminists build organizations? Whom do we choose to work with? Where is our place in a movement and how do we uniquely affect how movements are shaped?

Aiyah! indeed.

Limitations of the Left

I am sitting on the floor of the local anarchist center, my back resting on an old plaid couch someone has donated, every other piece of mismatched furniture and most of the available floor space occupied by other activists. The door to the storefront remains open, and the occasional flapping of the screen door provides the only breeze on an otherwise hot and humid summer day. I'm sure most of us would rather be outside basking in the sun, but our political commitment compels us to sit—wilt, really—surrounded by the mild mildew smell in this old office space. We are here for a "community meeting on racism," called in response to vandalism of our storefront by local Black teenagers, who most likely perceive our center as a white establishment in their community of color.

"Maybe we should call the police?" volunteers Marcus, a young red-haired punk. He must be new to the scene.

"No way!" "No cops!" A chorus of voices shoots him down.

"They are expressing their righteous anger in a racist society," Tom, seasoned

anarchist and de facto leader in this supposedly leaderless space, says.

"Right on!" "Right on!" A few clenched fists fly.

"Yes," says Dave, "it is understandable that they feel threatened after four hundred years of oppression."

The group listens as one white male after another expounds on the evils of racism, interrupted only by occasional words from a white woman.

I look over at Juanita, the only other person of color in this motley crew of rag-tag revolutionaries, and roll my eyes. My Chicana sister returns the sentiment with a half-hearted smile and a wink, but her expression soon returns to a serious frown as the discussion continues.

"But we're not the enemy," says Tammy, Tom's lover. "Maybe we can talk to them."

"Talk to them?" questions Dave. "We can't really. What could we say? As white people, it's really our job to understand them. We really can't say anything to them."

"Precisely," adds Tom.

"Yeah, what can we do? We're all white," says Rick.

"Ahem," Juanita pointedly clears her throat, and few activists miss her glare.

"Well, mostly white," says Tom.

"Exactly," Dave nods towards Juanita.

"Yes," Joyce joins in. "What can we do? We're mostly white."

My eyes glaze over. Snippets of the continuing discussion drift past me.

"I feel so bad.… I try so hard not to be racist.…" "I think we have to overcome our whiteness, be traitors to our race.…" "Isn't there a Black man in the socialist youth group at the university? We should ask him.…" "I really have worked on my racism.…" "I think these African American youth will change once they see we are really down with them.…" "I feel sooo bad.…"

As their voices drone on, my gut churns and I feel a rising red heat, a slow burning sensation that spreads throughout my body; I notice that my fingers are shaking. Still, I say nothing.

"Well, what do you think, Juliana? What do you think, Juanita?" Rapid-fire questions that give no space for answers.

"I don't know," Juanita spits out, her black eyes shooting fire. "Maybe you should figure it out yourselves."

Juanita quickly dismissed, all eyes turn to me. I swallow, pause. Swallow again. "Well, it seems to me that you aren't treating this like a real issue, you aren't treating these Black teenagers like real.…"

"I know exactly what you are saying," Tom jumps in. "We need to walk our talk, get to know what their issues are."

"What is that Malcolm X quote?" asks Dave.

"Oh, I know which one you are talking about," Rick responds. "I can't remember exactly what he says, but I know which one you are talking about."

And so it continues.

A few months later, I bump into Marcus, red hair now bleached blonde, sporting a new "Question Authority" button on his black-hooded sweatshirt.

"Hey Juliana," he says. At least he didn't call me Juanita. "How come you don't come to meetings any more? I'm on the core collective now and we could really use your energy."

"Yeah, sure," I mutter, turning to walk away.

"Hey," he adds, "if you see Juanita, bring her with you. We sure could use her righteous anger."

As I quickly depart he calls out, "On with the revolution!"

As a young, mixed-heritage Chinese American woman, Taipei-born and Alaska-raised, I organized my first protest on a small liberal arts campus in southern California against U.S. troops in Honduras. I came to academia from my quickly rising working-to-middle-class family. Somewhat a punk and somewhat a hippie, I participated in peace, women's, and environmental causes. These activities invigorated my spirit and I found I was not paying as much attention to my schoolwork. I dropped out and moved to Seattle, where I lived in my first women's collective household and worked in a vegetarian restaurant. The Emerald City is where I became hooked on politics and started identifying as a radical. The large protests were thrilling, and I met students, workers, squatters, and artists. Everyone was political and came with some leftist bent. An eager sponge, I listened and learned.

My political environment exposed and analyzed societal institutions, helping me make sense of my life and experiences. I became enraged with injustice and inspired by struggle. I encountered people who spoke critically about the U.S. government and its policies—people intent on eradicating oppression and creating a new world. I believed in this new world and wanted to be part of it. In the company of self-identified revolutionary anarchists and radical socialists, I found friends and allies, a community.

Unfortunately, it didn't last forever. While becoming confident as a politically aware person, I became increasingly confused about my own place in the struggle, particularly around my racial identity. During those years I was politically active in cities on both coasts and in the Midwest, but I met only a handful of other Asian American activists. Although there are and were many Asian American activists in the United States, there were few in the circles I was involved with.

The groups I worked with adamantly espoused antiracist and antisexist rhetoric, but time and time again refused to accept internal criticism from women and people of color, and leadership from anyone but a white male was unheard of. My growing awareness of these dynamics led me into direct conflict with the white male leadership in leftist circles. When I angrily challenged a comrade who claimed that all Asian Americans were well-off and therefore not concerned with political matters, he scolded me for being "disruptive." My anger was either ignored or deemed overly sensitive.

After being hired by a peace and justice nonprofit organization, I was first introduced to the board by the hiring committee, with my assets as an Asian American glowingly highlighted. The three-hour board meeting proceeded with a lengthy discussion of a recent antiracism workshop the all-white board had attended. Several members of the board complained resentfully that the workshop was an unnecessary waste of time, while others chided them for thinking this, carefully mentioning all the Black friends they had. Just as one member was guiltily recalling ignorant perceptions she used to have, I cut in to say that I thought the conversation was not really appropriate at a board meeting without specific direction and facilitation, and especially in front of a person of color. The discussion ended, but not before several people responded, incredibly, that they weren't aware I was a person of color. After the board meeting, I was approached by many board members who wanted to continue their individual thoughts on race relations, explaining how they weren't really racist. Two board members wanted to give me a hug. With no other person of color available at the time for a reality check, I actually wondered if I had done something wrong.

Another time, I was invited to speak to a group of students about anti-Asian immigrant-bashing. Afterwards, I was complimented by their professor, a European American socialist feminist, on how lucky they were to find an Asian American woman like me, since it is so hard to find smart Asian American speakers with a political analysis.

Coming out as a queer woman further separated me from the white male world. I could no longer hear the passionate words of white activists without irony and cynicism creeping in. I left the Left bitter and disillusioned, hurt and angry.

My story is not unusual; many of us have experienced this type of marginalization working within the U.S. Left. The current political landscape includes trade unions that scapegoat workers from other countries and immigrants within our borders, communist groups with political manifestos calling homosexuality an aberration in a decadent bourgeois society, and a socialist organization that claims a white member who raped a working-class Black teenage girl was "framed" and was actually a political prisoner.

The organizations I participated in and interacted with were unable to comprehend being majority white in an honest way. Many nearly white groups are unwilling to be exclusively white, but in reality they cannot accommodate the agendas of people of color. People of color are invited in or recruited to escape accusations an all-white group would be subject to from communities of color. But the reality is that in many cases these groups act as all-white groups internally, and white perspectives and standards are the norm.

In addition to the inability of majority white leftist groups to deal with race internally, stereotypes of Asian Americans are embedded in Left ideology as well. "We should not underestimate our invisibility either in U.S. politics in general, or on the left," cautions writer and activist Karin Aguilar–San Juan. "Myths about Asian Americans belittle the damage done by the discrimination we face, obscure the complexity of our experience, and make our contributions to the struggle against racism invisible."[1] This invisibility keeps us isolated, feeding into the belief that Asian American activists are few and far between, reinforcing the notion among white leftists that we are apolitical or conservative. Time and time again, white activists have expressed to me how surprising it is to meet an Asian American activist.

Noel Ignatiev, cofounder and editor of *Race Traitor*—a self-proclaimed "journal of the new abolitionism" that publishes articles and promotes dialogue about white people defying whiteness—was interviewed in the revolutionary anarchist newspaper *The Blast*. (The interview was reprinted in the *Utne Reader*.[2]) When asked why he referred to race relations in terms of Black and white people, Ignatiev replied that the term "people of color" wasn't useful, using Chinese Americans to prove his point. "Chinese are people of color and in the past they suffered fierce oppression in this country, and still suffer the effects of prejudice, but would anyone argue that Chinese in America today constitute an oppressed race? They have been defined as an ethnic group, indeed the 'model minority.'" That this long-time radical activist and antiracist scholar can make such a claim is frightening. His comment illustrates the obliviousness of white antiracists to the persistent and virulent oppression Chinese Americans, and all Asian Americans, face today.

Ignatiev's comments also emphasize a prevalent notion on the Left that race is a Black/white issue. When race is seen in Black-and-white terms, Asian American activists remain invisible, and our issues are again ignored. "The Black cause was the most important," Mai, a young Vietnamese American activist, complained of the antiracist group she was involved in. The group consistently balked at taking action against racism directed at non-Black people of color, including police harassment of Native Americans. "They didn't want to pursue it; they wanted to pursue Black issues." While Mai was one of the only people of color actively involved for over a year, this group of committed white antiracists continued to downplay the Asian American issues she worked on outside of the group.

Asian American women also have to contend with stereotypical images of Asian women as exotic. Before coming out, I was subjected to continuous male fascination with my heritage and more compliments about my appearance than about my viewpoints. One white leftist friend referred to me as his "little Mao." Asian American women are considered a safe bet for leftist groups; we boost their proportions of people of color, yet are expected to be cute, well-behaved, hard-working, and obedient. As Nisei poet Mitsuye Yamada writes,

> I am weary of starting from scratch each time I speak or write, as if there were no history behind us, of hearing that among women of color, Asian women are the least political, or the least oppressed, or the most polite. It is too bad not many people remember that one of the two persons in Seattle who stood up to contest the constitutionality of the Evacuation Order in 1942 was a young Japanese American woman.[3]

These and other barriers seem designed to ensure the participation of only a few people of color in majority white leftist organizations, leaving many radical Asian American women isolated from political communities and organizing.[4]

Ineffectiveness of Identity Politics

I am sitting in Shau Wen's living room, surrounded by plates with bits of Singapore rice noodles, Gai-lan with oyster sauce, rice, and kimchi starting to harden, chopsticks fallen into the half-eaten remains. Papers are strewn about, a few even crumpled and tossed into a convenient corner. Images of women smiling, playing, and kissing adorn the walls, along with a promotional poster for the movie The Joy Luck Club. *From her perch atop a bookshelf, Shau Wen's cat Sappho, a fat grey tabby with green eyes, surveys the dozen or so Asian and Pacific Islander lesbian and bisexual women sitting in a semblance of a circle.*

We have been meeting together, this local group, for over a year, organizing educational and visibility actions. Frequently we meet socially for official and unofficial potlucks and mahjong games. But no one is playing now. We are organizing a regional retreat for Asian and Pacific Islander lesbian and bisexual (APLB) women. Hour three of our retreat planning meeting finds us discussing the financial aid policy.

"No, I will not change my mind," Shau Wen states. "Any woman who wants financial aid should have it." Many nodding heads support this statement.

"I think it is a good idea," Nancy softly joins in, "but we have to have some

sort of guidelines. I get really mad that college students always get financial aid. What about working-class women? Women in college have a lot of privilege."

"That's really too harsh," says Meena. "My father was college-educated, but coming here as an immigrant, he never had it easy, and he worked menial jobs for the rest of his life."

"Can we get back to making a decision?" Me-Kyung asks. "I really need to leave soon."

"Okay," says Alice, "the way I see it, we need to come to a consensus on general guidelines, then set up a committee to do it."

"That's what I said half an hour ago," blurts May Lee. "No one ever listens to what I say." She gets up and moves next to her girlfriend Lisa.

Trinh clears her throat and shifts in her chair. "I'm sorry we didn't listen to you earlier, May Lee. But let's go ahead and set up guidelines, okay?"

"So it should be need-based, right?" I join in. "And could we just let the APLBs registering ask for the amount they need?"

"And then a committee could make final decisions if we have limited funds," adds Alice.

"I think that's a really good idea," Pramilla backs it up. "Are we ready to ask for a consensus?"

"I want to be on the committee," Nancy joins in.

"Me too, then," Shau Wen states. "Any woman who wants financial aid should have it."

"Shau Wen," Nancy sighs, "that's too idealistic."

I look around the room to see that half of the women are sitting at the edges of their seats, ready to jump, while the other half looks ready to fall asleep. Me-Kyung barely covers a yawn and May Lee is busy picking fuzz out of the carpet.

"I am wondering," says Trinh, "what women who haven't spoken think. Me-Kyung? May Lee? June? Lisa?" May Lee shrugs, June just nods.

Me-Kyung looks at her watch and adds, "I just would like to make a decision soon. I am really tired and we have been going at this for hours."

Lisa starts fidgeting. "I have something to say. It's really been bothering me but this conversation has been taking us too long. I think we are just babying other APLBs. We're giving women enough notice. If they can't earn the registration— and it is just not that expensive—maybe they shouldn't come. We are wasting way too much time on this."

June is now nodding more vigorously. "I wasn't going to say anything because there is always this PC air in this group, but I agree with Lisa."

"We are not a welfare service," Lisa emphatically adds.

"I cannot believe you said that." Shau Wen is pursing her lips. "That is so classist."

June rolls her eyes and Lisa throws her pen across the room. As it slides down the beige wallpaper, Trinh looks at Shau Wen and says under her breath, "Classist? You're the college professor."

"What about women who can't save?" Nancy raises her voice. "Single mothers? Poor rural women? Disabled women?"

"Hey, unless they come rolling up in a wheelchair," says June, "I don't think they are that disabled. I think they can save the money."

I sit among those stunned to silence. Breathing hard, breathing angry. The well-worn fabric of community quickly unraveling.

"Can we table this?" asks Me-Kyung.

After my departure from leftist communities to find more supportive spaces, I scooted to the opposite end of the movement spectrum. I joined a women-of-color discussion group and went to Asian cultural association meetings. I became very active in Asian and Pacific Islander Lesbian and Bisexual organizing. I immediately found what was missing in leftist circles: recognition as an Asian American queer woman, and validation of, and sensitivity to, my experiences. This new community was extremely affirming, and I was accepted unconditionally. At local, national, and global levels, from Minneapolis radio interviews and readings to the thrill of marching with other Asian queers from around the world at Stonewall 25, I met other queer Asian women with energy and passion who cared about this world we live in.

I thought that because we were all Asian American, women, and queer, we would have the same political views on ending oppression. Coming from my experience with the Left, I assumed that there were avenues for political organizing, within both my new APLB family and the larger queer community. This was not the case. When I verbally confronted an out Nazi marching in Gay Pride, I was stopped by Pride "marshals" who informed me that anyone who is gay has a right to march, even with a swastika. At a lesbians-of-color meeting an Asian American woman repeatedly used the term "poor white trash." When challenged on the offensiveness of such a term, she launched into stereotypical descriptions of poor whites to "show" why they are more racist/sexist/homophobic than rich white people. Lambda Legal Defense and Education Fund, a national law organization that champions gay and lesbian rights, used the racist Broadway play *Miss Saigon* as a benefit fundraiser, even after meeting with a coalition group mobilized by Asian and Pacific Islander queers who opposed the play's imperialist content.

These disturbing examples point to the underlying paradoxes of organizing based on identity.[5] In a society in which O.J. Simpson is seen as an African American hero by certain communities while African American political prisoner Mumia Abu-Jamal rots behind prison bars, we need to look at the dangers of identity-reductionist thinking. Addressing Asian American activists, Aguilar-San Juan warns, "We must take care not to subsume ourselves solely in efforts to build Asian American pride. Reducing race to a matter of identity, rather than expanding our experience of racism into a critique of U.S. society, is detrimental to our movement."[6]

By their very nature, identity-based organizations must remain apolitical in order to provide space for those with the shared identity, including right-wing Asian Republicans, lesbians who seek only their own visibility, and prolife activists in women's organizations. When political differences develop and tensions erupt, members often just leave, and the group fades away. Alternatively, endless amounts of time are spent discussing and rediscussing certain issues, and consensus between those with fundamentally different beliefs and convictions is never reached.

I was an active member of a lesbians-of-color organization in which incidents of cross-racial hostility occurred. With these left unchallenged, gossip and ignorance grew. When interethnic issues were finally discussed and various resources presented (a facilitator experienced with cross-racial relations, additional group discussions, and literature), it was very easy for those unwilling to change to resist or ignore them. Though there were several other factors that led to the group's eventual demise (control issues, different friendship circles, and burnout), racial hostility was one of the most salient ones. Similarly, I witnessed the destruction of a consensus-based APLB group that could not agree on issues related to feminism and class, and that folded after several all-day attempts at reconciliation.

Amie, an activist involved in APLB and Korean adoptee support groups, concludes, "It doesn't work if people aren't committed to each other. And how can I be committed to people who aren't serious about social change?"

Organizing Strategies for Radical Asian American Women

To build movements in a consistent and far-reaching way we must look at new models. We must think more strategically. As Asian American feminists and activists, we have valuable skills and experience. Many of us have been marginalized in broad political circles and frustrated in identity-based groups. Our analysis is critical in building new strategies and envisioning new movements.

Many believe that political and identity-based spaces are mutually exclusive, to the extent that each group usually defines the other as its antithesis. More useful, however, is viewing each model as exclusive but with positive aspects worth incorporating. Identity-based community organizing and an explicit political agenda can successfully complement each other, as evidenced by several labor organizing activities in the 1980s and 1990s.

In the United States during the 1980s, a number of community-based labor organizations formed to address the needs of Asian American workers. Significantly, the majority of this organizing occurred outside of the white male-led AFL-CIO. Groups such as Asian Immigrant Women Advocates (AIWA) and the Chinese Progressive Association (CPA) organized not around the traditional trade-unionist model of shop organizing, but rather on the basis of ethnic identity.[7]

In Boston in 1985, Chinese women workers, in conjunction with CPA and a coalition of students and community members, waged an eighteen-month struggle for job retraining and replacement after the closure of a large garment factory left three hundred and fifty workers out of a job. Their eventual victory solidified a leadership base of Chinese immigrant women who went on to form the CPA's Workers' Center, an emerging activist organization in which Asian immigrant workers are decision-makers.

AIWA was founded in 1983. Its membership consists of women in the San Francisco–Oakland Bay Area and Santa Clara's Silicon Valley. As part of its ongoing activities, AIWA offers workplace literacy classes for immigrant women to learn English while simultaneously learning about their rights as workers, immigrants, and women. In 1992, AIWA launched the Garment Workers' Justice Campaign, which effectively organized national support among workers, students, and community activists to secure corporate responsibility towards Asian immigrant women sweatshop workers. Their success in organizing a four-year-long national boycott against designer Jessica McClintock not only secured gains for the exploited sweatshop workers, but also developed leadership among Asian immigrant women and inspired a growing number of young Asian American activists.

These groups are usually viewed as marginal to both the organized U.S. labor movement and Asian American identity movements. But they have established a track record of organizing success precisely because, as marginal groups, they have organized for themselves, setting a progressive social agenda that is at the same time community-based. Asian American feminist and radical activists can look to Asian American community-based labor organizing for genuine leadership in a movement for social change. We can also look to the experience of older groups, including the Combahee River Collective, a Black feminist group that met in Boston in the 1970s and 1980s, and Out of Control, a lesbian committee that supports women political prisoners, which formed in the early 1980s and is still active today.

Unbound Feet is an important example of an attempt to build a group on identity and political vision, and should be studied both for its contributions to Asian American feminism and also for its eventual failure to successfully integrate identity, artistic creation, and political organizing. A collective of six Chinese and Korean American women writers, Unbound Feet formed in 1979 to perform their work, connecting writing and feminism. According to their original statement of purpose:

> As writers and cultural workers, we believe in the power of words as a tool for radical social change....We do not believe in isolating political struggles...but believe that real equality can only come about by all oppressed groups working together.[8]

A year and a half later the group had dissolved over disagreements as to whether it should focus on artistic expression of identity or on more direct political activism. Some members of the group felt bullied into political action, deeming it "time-consuming." "We already spend too little time on our art." Others stated,

> Today we have a split, not over petty issues or personal differences.... We will take political stands, particularly when issues affect us as women, as Asian Americans, as lesbians, as radicals, and as multi-issue feminists.[9]

To successfully form issue-based identity groups, we must clearly define whom we are willing to work with, both in terms of identity and political beliefs, proactively designating our own space. At a very basic level, this means taking personal responsibility to determine priorities and, with others, doing outreach, coming to group consensus over shared identity and political beliefs, and making a commitment to express this to other communities. Creating loose affinity groups would allow for both a sense of community belonging and a sense of purpose.

With affinity groups established, identity-based organizations can then be useful for networking and finding like-minded individuals. While recognizing the limitations of identity-based spaces, I believe that they provide necessary support and a logical place for affinity groups to reach out to political allies.

Established affinity groups can also work with leftist groups, regardless of the leadership of such groups. Affinity groups working with other political groups can control their level of involvement in leftist coalitions. Coalitions are vital to larger movement organizing, and affinity groups with expressed political agendas allow for solidarity with others in bottom-up, grassroots mobilizations.

This is, of course, just a blueprint for a possible organizing strategy, and there are still many issues to address. Should affinity groups have open memberships or be exclusive collectives? Which issues should they choose to take on and how?

Still, this vision of a radical Asian women's movement has already begun to take shape. It begins when a young Asian American who learns of Yuri Kochiyama's activism tells me, "just to hear about her is a total inspiration," and moves to the day she not only meets Yuri Kochiyama but is involved in political actions at her side. It begins with an APLB marching at Gay Pride with a sign that reads, "Gay white soldiers in Asia? Not my Liberation!" and ends with the absence of all soldiers, gay or straight, from any imperialist army. It begins with protesting with my Asian American sisters at a local boutique that exploits immigrant seamstresses and becomes a rallying cry for the rights of all workers around the world. It begins here, with all our joy and pain in politics and identity, and carries us to the day Asian American women are active and vital in a grassroots political movement for sweeping social change.

I would like to acknowledge the Asian American women activists I interviewed, and note that they requested their full names not be used. I would like to thank Joanna Kadi for her revision suggestions and general support in writing this essay. I would also like to thank Sonia Shah from South End Press for her insight and assistance in editing the original essay.

This piece first appeared in *Dragon Ladies: Asian American Feminists Breathe Fire* (Cambridge, MA: South End Press, 1997).

NOTES

[1] Karin Aguilar-San Juan, "Linking the Issues: From Identity to Activism," *The State of Asian America: Activism and Resistance in the 1990's*, Karin Aguilar-San Juan, ed. (Boston: South End Press, 1994), 1–15.

[2] "Treason to Whiteness Is Loyalty to Humanity: An Interview with Noel Ignatiev of *Race Traitor* Magazine," *Utne Reader* (Nov/Dec 1994), 82–86. Reprinted from *The Blast* (June/July 1994).

[3] Mitsuye Yamada, "Asian Pacific American Women and Feminism," in *This Bridge Called My Back,* Moraga and Anzaldúa, eds. (New York: Kitchen Table/Women of Color Press, 1983), 71–75.

[4] For discussion on the external and internal factors leading to Asian American exclusion from the feminist movement, see Esther Ngan-Ling Chow, "The Feminist Movement: Where Are All the Asian American Women?" *Making Waves: An Anthology of Writing By and About Asian American Women,* Asian Women United, ed. (Boston: Beacon Press, 1989), 362–377.

[5] For further analysis on contradictions within identity-based organizing see John Anner,

"Introduction," *Beyond Identity Politics: Emerging Social Justice Movements in Communities of Color,* John Anner, ed. (Boston: South End Press), 5–13.

[6] Aguilar-San Juan, 8.

[7] For further discussion of Asian American labor-based organizing within contemporary Asian American activism see Glenn Omatsu, "The 'Four Prisons' and the Movements for Liberation: Asian American Activism from the 1960's to the 1990's," *The State of Asian America: Activism and Resistance in the 1990's,* Karin Aguilar-San Juan, ed. (Boston: South End Press, 1994), 19–69.

[8] Kitty Tsui, Nellie Wong, and Merle Woo, "The Struggle of Unbound Feet," pamphlet, 1981.

[9] Ibid.

¡La Mujer Luchando, El Mundo Transformando! Mexican Immigrant Women Workers

MIRIAM CHING YOON LOUIE

At their Día de Los Muertos [Day of the Dead] celebration on November 1, 1994, *las mujeres* [the women] look gaunt but on a spiritual high. The women are members of Fuerza Unida, the organization they created with their own hands and hearts when Levi Strauss & Co. laid them off and ran away to Costa Rica in 1990. They have trekked all the way from San Antonio with sleeping bags to haunt Levi's plaza and corporate headquarters in San Francisco, California.

So that CEO Robert Haas will hear their cries for corporate responsibility loud and clear, the women shout at the tops of their lungs, *¡No tenemos hambre de comida; tenemos hambre de justicia!* [We're not hungry for food; we're hungry for justice!]. The women gently break their twenty-one-day hunger strike, savoring the miracle of *pan dulce* [sweet rolls] and steaming cups of coffee carted in by their many supporters. Their *comadre* [girlfriend] Puerto Rican activist Luz Guerra calls these *huelgistas de hambre* [hunger strikers] *las nuevas revolucionarias* [the new revolutionaries], who picked up where Emiliano Zapata, Pancho Villa, the *soldaderas* and *adelitas* [women soldiers and companions] of the 1910 Mexican Revolution left off.

Throwing back their heads in laughter, they clap and tap their feet as Chicano *poeta/músico/activista* Arnoldo García serenades them with his new rendition of a traditional Mexican song:

> *La Fuerza Unida*
> *En los frentes de liberación*
> *de este pueblo de trabajadores*
> *Existen mujeres fuertes y valientes*
> *Existen mujeres que saben luchar*
> *En ciudades y campos se forman*
> *dando fuerza y visión a los pueblos*
> *Son trabajadoras radientes de luchas*
> *Son trabajadoras de justicia y paz*
> *Su cultura y trabajo respeten*
> *Con la fuerza de su dignidad*
> *Son las costureras pidiendo justicia*
> *Son las costureras que saben luchar*
> *Son las desplazadas de la Levis*
> *Luchadoras del gran movimiento*

Son las costureras de la Fuerza Unida
Son las costureras de liberación[1] In the liberation fronts
of working people
There are women who are strong and valiant
There are women who know how to struggle
They are women developing
In the city and the countryside
Giving strength and vision to the people
They are working class women luminous with struggle
They are working class women for justice and peace
Respect their culture and work
With the force of their dignity
They are garment workers demanding justice
They are garment workers who know how to struggle
They are the women displaced by Levis
The strugglers of the great movement
They are the seamstresses of La Fuerza Unida
They are the seamstresses of liberation.

As Mexico's former dictator Porfirio Díaz lamented, "Poor little Mexico, so far from God, so close to the United States."[2] Mexico's fateful proximity to the developing "Colossus of the North"[3] has long shaped the destiny of its working people and the national, race, and class formation of the United States. Ever since the United States annexed half of Mexico's territory by seizing Texas in 1836 and launching the Mexican-American War (1845-1848), Mexican workers have served as a giant labor reserve and shock absorber for the bumps and potholes of U.S. economic development.[4]

Sharing a two-thousand-mile border with its powerful neighbor to the north, Mexico is the homeland of an estimated 40 percent of U.S. immigrants.[5] Migration to the United States also serves as a safety net for Mexico's economic and political system, yielding remittances of at least $6 billion a year, one of the largest sources of Mexico's foreign exchange, along with the oil, tourism, and *maquiladora* industries.[6]

Chicana labor historian Vicki Ruiz says that *Mexicanas* crossed the border as "farm worker mothers, railroad wives, and miners' daughters" to join male relatives recruited by those burgeoning industries during the spate of post-Civil War U.S. industrial expansion.[7] Especially since the 1920s, Mexican immigrant women and U.S.-born Chicanas have emerged as the backbone of many of the lowest-paying, most back-breaking jobs in Texas, California, New Mexico, Colorado, Arizona, and Illinois, such as the agribusiness, cannery, pecan-shelling, food-processing, garment, and domestic service industries. Mexicana labor migration has also increased to the U.S. Northwest, Midwest, East, and South.[8] By the end of 1996 there were 9.6 million Latinas in the United States, including 5.7 million women of Mexican origin, 1.1 million Puerto Rican women, 485 thousand Cuban women, and another 2.3 million women of Latin American descent.[9] Latinas continue to have the highest concentrations of workers in "blue-collar" operative jobs and the lowest in management and professions among all races of women.[10]

The rise in export-oriented production for transnational corporations along the U.S.-Mexico border since the 1960s and other aspects of economic restructuring have accelerated Mexicanas' internal and cross-border labor migration. Many of today's *nuevas revolucionarias* [new revolutionaries] started working on the global assembly line as young women in northern Mexico for foreign transnational corporations. Some women worked on the U.S. side as "commuters" before they moved across the border with their families. Their stories reveal the length, complexity, and interpenetration of the U.S. and Mexican economies, labor markets, histories, cultures, and race relations.

The women talk about the devastating impact of globalization, including massive layoffs and the spread of sweatshops on both sides of the border. *Las mujeres* [the women] recount what drove them to join and lead movements for economic, racial, and gender justice, as well as the challenges they faced within their families and communities to assert their basic human rights. The women featured in this article play leadership roles in La Mujer Obrera [The Woman Worker] in El Paso, Texas, Fuerza Unida [United Force] in San Antonio, Texas, and the Thai and Latino Workers Organizing Committee of the Retailers Accountability Campaign in Los Angeles, California.

Growing up Female and Poor

Mexican women and girls were traditionally expected to do all the cooking, cleaning, and serving for their husbands, brothers, and sons. For girls from poor families, shouldering these domestic responsibilities proved doubly difficult because they also performed farm, sweatshop, or domestic service work simultaneously. Refugio "Cuca" Arrieta, the only daughter of farm-worker parents in Ciudad Jiménes, Chihuahua, reluctantly left school early:

I stayed home because I had to take care of my younger brothers. I went to school and finished no more than the first, second, and third grade. At the nearby *ranchitos* [little farms] we learned how to read and write. Before starting school I had already learned how to read and write. I taught myself.[11]

Petra Mata, a former seamstress for Levi's whose mother died shortly after childbirth, recalls the heavy housework she did as the only daughter:

> Aiyeee, let me tell you! It was very hard. In those times in Mexico, I was raised with the ideal that you have to learn to do everything—cook, make tortillas, wash your clothes, and clean the house—just the way they wanted you to. My grandparents were very strict. I always had to ask their permission and then let them tell me what to do. I was not a free woman. Life was hard for me. I didn't have much of a childhood; I started working when I was twelve or thirteen years old.[12]

Neoliberalism and Creeping Maquiladorization

These women came of age during a period of major change in the relationship between the Mexican and U.S. economies. Like Puerto Rico, Hong Kong, South Korea, Taiwan, Malaysia, Singapore, and the Philippines, northern Mexico served as one of the first stations of the global assembly line tapping young women's labor. In 1965 the Mexican government initiated the Border Industrialization Program (BIP) that set up export plants, called *maquiladoras* or *maquilas*, which were either the direct subsidiaries or subcontractors of transnational corporations. Mexican government incentives to U.S. and other foreign investors included low wages and high productivity; infrastructure; proximity to U.S. markets, facilities, and lifestyles; tariff loopholes; and pliant, progovernment unions.[13]

Many of the women worked in electronics and garment maquiladoras before crossing the border to work in U.S. plants. María Antonia Flores describes her coworkers in the Juárez electronics plant where she worked as *puras jovenas* [all young women], while the supervisors were *puros varones* [all male]. Describing her quarter-century-long sewing career in Mexico, Celeste Jiménez ticks off the names of famous U.S. manufacturers who hopped over the border to take advantage of cheap wages:

> I sewed for twenty-four years when I lived in Chihuahua in big-name factories like Billy the Kid, Levi Strauss, and Lee maquiladoras. Everyone was down there. Here a company might sell under the brand name of Lee; there in Mexico it would be called Blanca García.[14]

Many of the women worked in the maquilas because of the unstable economic status of male family members—where men are either absent, unemployed, or earning well below the "family wage," i.e., the wage sufficient to support a family. Marta Martínez, a laid-off Levi's worker first learned to sew from her mom:

I was born in Mexico City in 1959. My mom was a seamstress who ran a little workshop about this size[she points to Fuerza Unida's small sewing coop production area]. Once in a while she was able to get a contract and work for a *maquiladora*. Dad worked as a *campesino* [farm worker]. I had four sisters and three brothers. I'm in the middle. But I was able to finish twelve years of school so I got to be a teacher.... In 1983, I worked for the Castro company on this side, making baby clothes. It wasn't hard to learn. I already knew from my mom how to use an industrial machine.[15]

Transnational exploitation of women's labor was part of a broader set of policies that critical opposition movements in the Third World have dubbed "neoliberalism," i.e., the new version of the British Liberal Party's program of laissez faire capitalism espoused by the rising European and U.S. colonial powers during the late eighteenth and nineteenth centuries. The Western powers, Japan, and international financial institutions like the World Bank and International Monetary Fund have aggressively promoted neoliberal policies since the 1970s.[16] Mexico served as an early testing ground for such standard neoliberal policies as erection of free trade zones; commercialization of agriculture; currency devaluation; deregulation; privatization; outsourcing; cuts in wages and social programs; suppression of workers', women's, and indigenous people's rights; free trade; militarization; and promotion of neo-conservative ideology.

Neoliberalism intersects with gender and national oppression. Third World women constitute the majority of migrants seeking jobs as maids, vendors, maquila operatives, and service industry workers. Women also pay the highest price for cuts in education, health, and housing programs, food and energy subsidies, and increases in their unpaid labor.[17]

The human costs of Mexico's neoliberal program and extended economic crisis are evident in the 60 percent drop in real minimum wages between 1982 and 1988 and the 30 percent drop in internal consumption of basic grains during the 1980s.[18] In 1986, some 62 percent of the economically active population of Mexico earned sub-minimum wages.[19] In 1994, the World Bank estimated that 38 percent of the total population of Mexico lived in absolute poverty. Two out of five households had no water supply, three out of five had no drainage, and one in three had no electricity.[20]

The deepening of the economic crisis in Mexico, especially under the International Monetary Fund's pressure to devaluate the peso in 1976, 1982, and 1994, forced many women to work in both the formal and informal economies to survive and meet their child-rearing and household responsibilities.[21] María Antonia Flores was forced to work two jobs after her husband abandoned the family, leaving her with three children to support. She had no choice but to leave her children home alone, *solitos,* to look after themselves. Refugio Arrieta straddled the formal and informal economies because her job in an auto-parts assembly maquiladora failed to bring in sufficient income. To compensate for the shortfall, she worked longer hours at her maquila job and "moonlighted" elsewhere:

> We made chassis for cars and for the headlights. I worked lots! I worked twelve hours more or less because they paid us so little that if you worked more, you got more money. I did this because the schools in Mexico don't provide everything. You have to buy the books, notebooks, *todos, todos* [everything]. And I had five kids. It's very expensive. I also worked out of my house and sold ceramics. I did many things to get more money for my kids.[22]

In the three decades following its humble beginnings in the mid-1960s, the maquila sector swelled to more than two thousand plants employing an estimated 776 thousand people, over 10 percent of Mexico's labor force.[23] In 1985, maquiladoras overtook tourism as the largest source of foreign exchange. In 1996, this sector trailed only petroleum-related industries in economic importance and accounted for over US $29 billion in export earnings annually.[24] The maquila system has also penetrated the interior of the country, as in the case of Guadalajara's electronics assembly industry and Tehuacán's jeans production zones.[25] Although the proportion of male maquila workers has increased since 1983, especially in auto transport equipment assembly, almost 70 percent of the workers continue to be women.[26]

As part of a delegation of labor and human rights activists, this author met some of Mexico's newest proletarians—young indigenous women migrant workers from the Sierra Negra to Tehuacán, a town famous for its refreshing mineral water springs in the state of Puebla, just southeast of Mexico City. Standing packed like cattle in the backs of the trucks each morning, the women headed for jobs sewing for name-brand manufacturers like VF Corporation (producing Lee brand clothing), The GAP, Sun Apparel (producing brands such as Polo, Arizona, and Express), Cherokee, Ditto Apparel of California, Levi's, Guess? and others. The workers told U.S. delegation members that their wages averaged US $30 to $50 a week for twelve-hour work days, six days a week. Some workers reported having to do *veladas* [all-nighters] once or twice a week. Employees often stayed longer without pay if they did not finish high production goals.

Girls as young as twelve and thirteen worked in the factories. Workers were searched when they left for lunch and again at the end of the day, to check that they weren't stealing materials. Women were routinely given urine tests when hired and those found to be pregnant were promptly fired, in violation of Mexican labor law. Although the workers had organized an independent union several years earlier, Tehuacán's Human Rights Commission members told us that it had collapsed after one of its leaders was assassinated.[27]

Carmen Valadez and Reyna Montero, long-time activists in the women's and social-justice movements, helped found Casa de La Mujer Factor X in 1977, a workers' center in Tijuana that organizes around women's workplace, reproductive, and health rights, and against domestic violence. Valadez and Montero say that the low wages and dangerous working conditions characteristic of the maquiladoras on the Mexico-U.S. border are being "extended to all areas of the country and to Central America and the Caribbean. NAFTA represents nothing but the 'maquiladorization' of the region."[28]

Elizabeth "Beti" Robles Ortega, who began working in the maquilas at the age of fourteen and was blacklisted after participating in independent union organizing drives on Mexico's northern border, now works as an organizer for the Servicio, Desarrollo y Paz, AC (SEDEPAC) [Service, Development and Peace organization]. Robles described the erosion of workers' rights and women's health under NAFTA:

> NAFTA has led to an increase in the work force, as foreign industry has grown. They are reforming labor laws and our constitution to favor even more foreign investment, which is unfair against our labor rights. For example, they are now trying to take away from us free organization which was guaranteed by Mexican law. Because foreign capital is investing in Mexico and is dominating, we must have guarantees. The government is just there with its hands held out; it's always had them out but now even more shamelessly.... Ecological problems are increasing. A majority of women are coming down with cancer— skin and breast cancer, leukemia, and lung and heart problems. There are daily deaths of worker women. You can see and feel the contamination of the water and the air. As soon as you arrive and start breathing the air in Acuña and Piedras Negras [border cities between the states of Coahuila and Texas], you sense the heavy air, making you feel like vomiting.[29]

Like Casa de La Mujer Factor X in Tijuana, and the women workers' centers and cooperatives whose work the Frente Auténtico del Trabajo [Authentic Work Front] (FAT) has prioritized especially since 1992, SEDEPAC also participates in national networks of Mexican women workers such as the Red de Trabajadores en Las Maquilas [Workers' Network in the Maquilas], which meets annually in different cities in the northern border region, as well as in binational networks like the Southwest Network for Environmental and Economic Justice.[30]

Maquiladorization Accelerates Migration

Many of the Mexicanas migrated to the United States in a two-stage process, similar to that of many of the Asian women workers. Migration to the northern border region offered women proximity to family members working on the other side, and after the initiation of the Border Industrialization Program in 1965, potential employment opportunities as well. Patricia Fernández-Kelly has suggested that by recruiting mainly young female workers, the border maquiladora program ended up drawing even more migrants to the border, yet failed to reduce male farm workers' unemployment caused by termination of the Bracero Program as the Mexican government had originally planned. Many migrants to the northern border eventually cross into the United States.[31]

For example, La Mujer Obrera organizer Irma Montoya Barajas was born in the central Mexican state of Aguascalientes. At age ten she moved with her parents to Juárez in northern Mexico, where her father found work as a carpenter while her mother took care of her nine brothers and sisters. Similarly, María Antonia Flores was born in the central state of Zacatecas, but moved with her family to Juárez when she was eight years old. There her parents found odd jobs working in maquilas, restaurants, and as food vendors. Petra Mata of Fuerza Unida traces her roots to Nuevo Laredo, Tamaulipas, across from Laredo, Texas. But she and her parents were actually born in the little village of Bustamante, Nuevo León. They moved when they could no longer survive through farming, and Petra's grandfather and father, like many Mexican and Chinese immigrant men, got jobs working for the railroad.

Over time Mexican migration networks have become more regionally diverse. María Antonia Flores explains that while many workers migrate from areas adjacent to the border, "people come here from almost all of the states in the south of Mexico to find work due to the economic problems throughout the nation and precisely because of the pull of all the maquiladoras located on the border."

> So every day people arrive at the maquilas from the south looking for work and trying to better their struggle to survive. But they find *nada, nada* [nothing]. Around here many people come from Coahuila, Durango, Zacatecas, and Chihuahua, but over there in Tijuana, there are also people from Chiapas, Oaxaca, San Luis Potosí, that is to say almost all of the states.[31]

Alberta "Beti" Cariño Trujillo, a dedicated organizer for the human rights commission in Tehuacán, Puebla, originally comes from the southern coastal state of Oaxaca. With her mother and siblings, Cariño struggled to survive in Oaxaca while her father worked as a migrant laborer picking oranges up in California.

Cariño is anxious to make contact with U.S. immigrant and workers' rights groups to develop an information network. She and her coworkers teach a night school for garment workers and their children in Tehuacán. The human-rights workers are concentrating on the fight for better wages and working conditions locally, and against toxic-waste dumping and water contamination by the maquilas, lack of child care and educational opportunities, domestic and street violence, unwanted pregnancies, and high stress levels, especially among single mothers. They also want to provide accurate information about what life is like for immigrant workers in the United States to dispel any illusions potential migrants might have.[33]

Indeed, the information "grapevine" extends into the farthest corners of Mexico. In the *colonia* [newly built, poorly served, suburban settlement] of Nezahuacoyotl on the outskirts of Mexico City, members of a local poor women's group shared their knowledge of the United States during a visit from international participants of a November 1989 garment workers' conference in Mexico City. Many of the women were themselves internal migrants to the world's largest city and they proudly told conference delegates of a free breakfast and milk program they developed so that poor children would not go to school on empty stomachs.

A Chicana activist's description of her work with immigrants in Los Angeles unleashed an animated exchange with the Mexicana colonia organizers. "Chicago is a bad place for Mexican workers." "Don't go to Fresno, they already have too many Mexicans; you can't find a job any more." "Orange County is very conservative and does not like Mexicans." "Go to Washington to pick apples. My cousin got a job there, and she likes it so much, she's going to send for her two daughters."[34] Perhaps some of such Mexicana organizers contributed their experience to the United Farm Workers Union efforts in the 1990s to organize Mexican immigrants in Washington's apple orchards.[35]

When the Border Was Just a Bridge Between Neighborhoods

The wide variety in the immigration and citizenship status of the women and their family members reflects the permeability of a border that workers of Mexican descent have criss-crossed since U.S. annexation in 1848. After centuries of relatively free movement within the region, only in 1924 did the U.S. government create the Border Patrol and the notion of the "illegal alien," thus transforming Mexican workers into potential fugitives of the law unless they could secure official permits. Yet employers escaped responsibility and often used the fear of deportation to lower the wages of undocumented workers.[36]

The period from World War I until the Great Depression marked the first big wave of migration, when the U.S. government launched a contract-labor program for male migrant workers, the predecessor of the Bracero Program.[37] Mexican government recruitment efforts initially targeted men from the central western states of Michoacán, Jalísco, and Guanajuato. These workers served as the links of migration chains stretching between rural Mexican communities to specific U.S. farms and towns.[38] Over time, tributaries from all the Mexican states contributed to the flow of Mexican workers across the border.

The elder relatives of many of the women interviewed for this book had worked in the United States, especially as farm workers, railroad workers, and miners. Some had been born in the United States or had become U.S. citizens at other times in their lives, yet continued to migrate across the border in both directions. For example, Celeste Jiménez was born in the northern state of Chihuahua in 1939. Yet she explains:

> My father was born in Candelario, Texas, and my mom in Sierra Blanca. I'm 100 percent Mexican. My father worked raising cattle and my mom was a housewife. There were ten children, eight girls and two boys. I was born in Mexico. I'm the third oldest among the kids. My dad was a U.S. citizen. My mom was a Mexican citizen. She was born in California but lived in Chihuahua most of her life. My mom's parents came here [to the U.S.] in 1942. In 1964, my mom and dad came here too, but they didn't work any more because they were getting too old. In 1982, I came here directly from Chihuahua. I'm a permanent legal resident.[39]

Similarly, María del Carmen Domínguez describes the peripatetic wanderings of her farm-worker father and how her mother moved closer to the border, anchoring the family:

> My father was born in California and lived and worked in Mexico many, many years. He also worked in El Paso, Texas and traveled to Los Angeles to work in the fields with machines and doing other jobs. My mother was born in Chihuahua, Mexico. She bore and raised four children. She stayed in Ciudad Juárez most of her life.[40]

Although Carmen "Chitlan" Ibarra Lopéz was born in Chihuahua, where her father worked as a miner and her mother as a homemaker, she traces her cross-border roots to her grandparents' generation:

> I became a naturalized U.S. citizen through my mother because my mother was born in the U.S. She was born in the U.S. but she went

back to live in Mexico. What I heard was that during the Mexican Revolution [1910-1920] my grandparents came to live in California. They went to Wasco. They were farm workers. They picked cotton. My mother and her brothers and sisters were born in Wasco. Me and my sister lived with one of mom's sisters for a while.[41]

Following the trail of Mexican migrant chili workers, long-time Juárez residents Alicia and Carlos Marentes packed up their belongings and crossed the international bridge separating Juárez and El Paso in 1971. After serving a stint in the Texas Farm Workers Union, they helped found the Border Agricultural Workers Union in El Paso in 1984. After a decade of struggle, the union opened a beautiful center in 1995. This shelter acts as an oasis for chili workers who are hired through a humiliating human-auction system to toil twelve-hour days in Texas and New Mexico under a haze of toxic pesticides at temperatures that alternate between scorching and freezing. Women and undocumented workers get paid the lowest of the low, averaging a scant $5,300 a year, while even male workers with documents earn only $6,000.

Alicia coordinates classes where women learn to make handicrafts that they can sell during the dead season when they can find no work in the fields. Her friendly face clouds with sadness as she reminisces. "So many of the campesinos Carlos and I started working with back in 1980 have already passed away because of their hard lives. We have lost whole generations of farm workers." Carlos says that workers must become visible within the broader society if they are to improve their lives. Yet the anti-immigrant backlash is dehumanizing and criminalizing these workers. He shakes his head, saying, "I remember when the border was nothing more than a bridge you crossed from a poor neighborhood to a richer one. That was before they started enacting all the anti-immigration legislation, rounding up immigrants, and militarizing the border."[42]

Ironically, and some insist intentionally, cross-border movement of people is increasingly restricted precisely during an unprecedented flow of capital, trade, goods, services, information, and culture, especially since the enactment of the North American Free Trade Agreement (NAFTA) in 1994. According to immigrant rights and environmental justice activist Arnoldo García, NAFTA has proven a total disaster for Mexican workers, farmers, and small business people and spurred more migration:

> During NAFTA's first year and a half, the U.S. trade deficit with Mexico grew by a whopping $4 billion and some eighty thousand U.S. jobs were lost. Mexican workers' wages declined 40 to 50 percent, ravaging their buying power. While the cost of living has risen by 80 percent in Mexico, salaries only increased by a mere 30 percent.

Mexico's inflation rate runs over 51 percent; 2.3 million Mexican people have lost jobs and the peso has been severely devalued—from 3.1 pesos to the dollar in January 1994 to 7.6 pesos in March 1996. Over twenty thousand small and medium businesses have gone belly-up in the face of increased multinational competition. And NAFTA's much touted labor and environmental side agreements have proven to be weak and ineffective.[43]

The Clinton administration doubled the budget of the INS after enacting NAFTA. The 1996 "Illegal Immigration Reform and Immigrant Responsibility Act" then mandated hiring another thousand border patrol agents. According to the Urban Institute, only four out of ten individuals who are in the U.S. illegally crossed the southern border, while the other six entered with legal visas as visitors, students, or temporary employees who failed to leave when their visas expired. These immigrants have documents and have been in contact with the INS. Only about one-third of the undocumented population is from Mexico. Yet 85 percent of all the resources of the INS, including the Border Patrol, are trained on the border with Mexico—reflecting both racist backlash against Mexican workers and the INS's evidently unquenchable thirst for money and military hardware.[44]

Mexico's extended economic crises prompted a major demographic shakeup in migration to the United States. These new stresses forced workers from large industrial urban centers without previous traditions of U.S. migration; more people from the urban and middle classes; and more women, children, and elderly people to risk crossing the border. Political scientist and immigration expert Wayne Cornelius dubbed this new, more heterogeneous pool of migrants *los migrantes de la crisis* [the crisis migrants].[45] Commenting on the utility of the border to politicians and employers, La Mujer Obrera [The Woman Worker] organizer Carmen Ibarra Lopéz reflects:

> It's very hard for us as Mexican workers to understand the line on the border. I think that's why nobody has really, really put attention on the border's workers because it's a very different situation. It's like another world when you come through El Paso. I think the kinds of problems we are seeing workers come in with are not just because of the lack of good opportunities, but also because of a lot of discrimination. When I say discrimination, it's because we have a lot of members who under the amnesty law have a perfect right to come to the U.S. and become citizens.[46]

The Feminization of Migration

Women do not always migrate or stay home based on male family members' unchallenged decisions, but sometimes play the principal role in initiating migration. In her insightful study of the immigration of undocumented Mexican workers, sociology professor Pierrette Hondagneu-Sotelo warns that contrary to popular stereotypes, extensive research on Chicano and U.S.-based Mexican families suggests that not all families are characterized by uniformly extreme patriarchy. Although sexism persists, she says that urbanization and women's growing role as income earners have begun to erode male dominance to varying degrees, and that traditional social relations and cultural resources neither disappear nor stay the same but are being constantly reshaped through the processes of migration and resettlement.[47]

Indeed, women made decisions to cross the border under a variety of circumstances, including invitations from their partners, other relatives, and friends. Some initiated the move themselves. For example, María del Carmen Domínguez decided to move from Juárez to El Paso because she got tired of commuting to work:

> I came to El Paso in 1972 because I needed to work to support my family. At that time I had two children. Eight years later I had another child that is my baby right now who's eighteen years old. I came to work in the factories. I was fifteen years old when I was pregnant with my first boy and I got married when I was seventeen, almost eighteen years old. I met my husband through friends and the family. He worked in the construction of houses and putting up fences. When I was living in Juárez, I worked for two years in El Paso, crossing the bridges every day from Mexico. That was too hard so we decided to come to live in El Paso and I stayed here. During the time I was crossing the bridges, I was coming to work in a garment factory.[48]

Petra Mata also began working in the United States as a cross-border commuter. She started working as a maid when she was twelve or thirteen years old after the tragic death of her mother and subsequent abandonment by her father. Although she worked hard and scrubbed floors on her hands and knees, she only made $10 a week. She recalls, "During the five years I worked for the same family, the highest pay I ever got was $16 a week." Later Petra moved to the United States permanently after she got married. She and her husband took up their friends' invitation to come, first as undocumented immigrants. Later Petra and her husband got U.S. citizenship to "have a voice, a right to vote."[49]

Lucrecia Tamayo, a garment worker and leader in the Thai and Latino Workers Organizing Committee of the Retailer Accountability Campaign, decided to make the big move from Acapulco, Guerrero to Los Angeles after her marriage failed. During her "stop-over" in Tijuana, that famous "travelers' advisory and transit center," she secured the means to make the crossing and picked up information on possible job leads in Los Angeles, the metropolis with the second-largest Mexican population in the world, after Mexico City. Lucrecia relied on a female relative, the well-developed migrant "underground railroad," and a waiting job market:

> I got married in Mexico, but the person I married was treating me bad, so I moved here fifteen years ago in 1982. I came by myself (laughs). I came by *el cerro* [through the mountains], with a *coyote*. Oh, it was scary! There were so many people, I was in the front with the driver, and over there, a mountain of people. And the driver was very nervous about running into Immigration. I only had one sister who was living here.
>
> I came to the United States because after [my former husband] left, I had a little girl to take care of. It wasn't my parents' obligation to raise her. So I had to find a new life. I came straight to Los Angeles. I lived with my sister for about a year. About six months after coming here, I started working in garment. When I was in Tijuana I heard about this kind of job by word of mouth. The people who came back to Mexico told us all about how life is here, about the kinds of work you can get. If you don't know about it, they teach you.[50]

Working *al Otro Lado* [on the Other Side]

Until recently, women who crossed the border were frequently able to land jobs in *El Norte* [the North], often performing work similar to what they had done in Mexico. Arriving in such well-established Mexican immigrant communities as El Paso, San Antonio, and Los Angeles, the women found jobs fairly quickly, in some cases even before they settled permanently in the United States. They heard about work through family members, friends, and neighbors. Women changed jobs as they got adjusted to U.S. working conditions and "learned the ropes."

After moving from Juárez to El Paso with her husband, Irma Montoya of La Mujer Obrera got a job working as an electronics assembler and inspector at a plant that made thermometers:

> My cousin's husband told me about the job. I worked there from 1987 until they laid us off in 1995. I made good money there, $6.30 an hour, and the working conditions were good, too. But in 1995 they shut us down and moved to Mexico. There were about four hundred

of us who lost our jobs. My husband lost his job after working for twenty years making Tony Lamas boots. Now he can only find work as a janitor.[51]

María del Carmen Domínguez heard about jobs through the grapevine. After commuting from Juárez, she changed to better jobs as she gained more experience and learned what was available:

I worked for fifteen years in garment factories. The first one was Rudy's Sportswear where I worked for almost five years. I worked for one year at Emily Joe and almost nine years at CMT Industries as a seamstress.

My friends told me about the job in the first factory. I think I got paid minimum wage there. In the last one I got paid more, sometimes up to $5.50 or $6 an hour because it was by the quota. At the other factories I was paid by the hour. I didn't get paid for overtime. In the last factory, at CMT, we got some benefits, like vacations and some holidays.

The first shop I worked at was so small. It expanded, but then they had a problem about wages and their contracts and it went bankrupt. The second one was a small factory, but it was too ugly! I didn't like it, so I quit (laughs).[52]

Tina Mendoza of Fuerza Unida started working in Mexico as a secretary when she was sixteen years old. After she came to the United States, it took her some time to adjust and find the right job:

At first I did not like it here. I come from a family that is very close so I felt really alone here. After I made friends I got used to the life here. First I got a job working with chemicals that they put on animals [insecticides] for about two years. After that I got a job working as a cook, frying chicken. Then I got a job at a maquiladora factory. After that I started working at Levi's. I stayed for eight years until they laid us off.[53]

Like many U.S.-born Chicanas who work in low-waged industries alongside Mexican immigrant women,[54] Viola Casares, a third-generation Chicana, started out doing farm work. Her father had picked cotton in Lubbock, Texas, and worked in Arizona. Over her husband's objections, she eventually landed a sewing job:

In a year [after getting married at eighteen] I got pregnant, then had my first daughter, Sandra. After six months, I went back to work in the fields. We went to Michigan and picked strawberries and tomatoes. When I was pregnant I used to get morning sickness at my job packing onions.... My husband was real macho and jealous and would not let me work. I was supposed to stay home. The kids were grown and going to school…. Because of his jealousy I stayed home for a while. But the children really needed extra things….

I [started] work[ing] for Farah making pants for a couple of months. Then it was the same thing again with my husband. He [began] harassing me until I quit. But I really needed to work. He had started drinking. I began working at Levi's in 1980. I thought I was finally going to have a secure job. I told myself that I had to work and that I was not going to let him stop me again. With work I could make a better home and get things for the kids…. At Levi's I thought it would be okay, that I would be able to work and support us until I could retire some time. But all of a sudden we lost our jobs. I was so worried—"Wow, what are we going to do?" It's so hard being a single mother.[55]

Wages, working conditions, and benefits tended to be better at the larger factories than at the smaller shops. For example, even though the Farah Manufacturing Company in El Paso was the target of a major struggle and national boycott (1972–1974) by the Amalgamated Clothing and Textile Workers Union, because it was a large factory of some four thousand workers, wages and working conditions were better than what women had experienced in Mexico or in smaller U.S. shops.[56] Carmen Ibarra López learned about job openings at Farah through her younger sister.

It was good pay at the time. The minimum wage I think was $1.60 an hour. I got paid by the hour. We worked in very good conditions, especially because the Farah on Gateway was in a new building.

I was there when the strike began. I just remember I didn't pay too much attention. First of all, in Mexico everything was different. I just remember one day at noon, at lunch time, I saw the workers walking out. And I was trying to find out about it and asked, "What's going on?" But we didn't have too much information about it even though I worked inside. Probably they had a workers' or union committee to lead the strike, but I don't know. That's why it's not until now that I realize how unions work. I think it was just because the unions select a few workers, but they don't give out as much information as other organizations do, like La Mujer Obrera does. Yes, that is what you need, a lot of information.[57]

Despite low wages and less than optimal working conditions, many of the women expressed satisfaction with being able to work outside their homes and contribute to their families' well-being. They were proud of their skills and job performance and enjoyed the friendships and camaraderie they developed with their coworkers. Refugio Arrieta worked in a variety of restaurants and garment factories in El Paso:

> The garment factories were small, maybe about a hundred people. It's small to me. I worked at Tex-Mex International. They made jeans. I worked as a seamstress, an operator. They paid us the minimum by the hour. Sometimes we worked overtime. There were no benefits there. Sometimes I worked forty hours a week, sometimes fifty hours when I put in overtime. At the last one it was twenty hours because that's how it was before they closed. I worked at Tex-Mex four years. We were all friends there (laughs). It was like we were all schoolmates.[58]

María del Carmen Domínguez's close relations with coworkers deepened as they banded together to confront the boss on failure to pay holiday leave as promised:

> The CMT factory was large and busy. I was working very well. It was comfortable for me, and I liked it a lot. When I was working there I think there were about 250 workers. Right now they have maybe a thousand workers. They sew garments like tuxedos. It's more skilled work. Devon was one of the labels. I don't remember the others. We also sewed vests. I think you get paid more money for sewing men's clothes…. I was the organizer in my area and we had ten women and I controlled it (laughs). Yes, *ellas* [they] would say "I love you." And I would say, "I love you, too." We were all partners. Yeah. I love to help the people. And I would fight, fight, fight in CMT, every day (laughs). Yes, that's a long time to fight![59]

Since she's now a highly skilled and vivacious organizer, one can easily imagine Petra Mata as a highly competent and outgoing worker before she lost her job at Levi's:

> I did the hard, more difficult operations, like sewing the pockets on the sides of the coat. For three and a half years I sewed this way before they put me on utility so I could do any operation. Then they made me a trainer to teach the new people. I liked working with the girls and helping out. Finally they made me a supervisor for eight years. I was very happy with my job because I got to work closely with my coworkers.[60]

NAFTA the SHAFTA

Like the Hong Kong and Korean workers whom transnational corporations dumped during the second stage of globalization, hundreds of thousands of U.S. manufacturing workers, many of them women of color, also found themselves out on the street as their jobs ran away to Mexico, Central America, the Caribbean, and Asia. After the Border Industrialization Program had begun in 1965, the Reagan administration launched the Caribbean Basin Initiative in 1983 during the height of U.S. military adventures in Central America. U.S. military intervention in and capital export to the region accelerated the migration of workers, including Salvadoran, Guatemalan, Honduran, Nicaraguan, Dominican, and Haitian women who subsequently found jobs working in the garment industry in Los Angeles, New York, and Miami.

Prior to the enactment of NAFTA in 1994, U.S.-based companies utilized Item 807 of the US Tariff Code, which specified that tariffs applied only to the value-added portion of products assembled abroad. If U.S. apparel firms cut their garments at home and had them sewn offshore, they only had to pay tariff on the labor value added by sewing—which could be very small, given the low wages of Third World women workers. Item 807 was principally used to exploit seamstresses in Mexico, Central America, and the Caribbean because of the region's proximity and the political clout the United States has exercised in the hemisphere since the days of the Monroe Doctrine. Thus, government trade policies effectively encouraged corporations to take jobs overseas to bolster U.S. foreign policy objectives.[61] In 1960, 2 percent of apparel was imported; in 1980, 30 percent; and in 2000, 60 percent. Conversely, the number of U.S. manufacturing jobs plummeted. While apparel employment peaked in 1970 with 1,363,800 jobs, by 1999 the figure had fallen to 696 thousand.[62]

In 1990, Levi's, whose brand-name jeans, together with Coca-Cola and McDonald's hamburgers, have become practically synonymous with the "American way of life" around the world, closed its San Antonio plant and moved to Costa Rica where workers earned in a day what the average San Antonio seamstress had made in half an hour. The San Antonio factory was Levi's largest U.S. manufacturing facility at the time. Overnight some 1,150 mainly Mexican-American women suddenly lost their jobs. Fuerza Unida, the fight-back organization the laid-off San Antonio workers founded in 1990, asserts that "we were early victims of NAFTA." With direct experience in the consequences of "free trade" policies, Fuerza Unida actively organized against the passage of NAFTA, sporting "AFTA NAFTA the SHAFTA!" and "Levi's, button your fly, your greed is showing!" picket signs. Between 1981 and 1990 the company had already closed fifty-eight plants, laying off 10,400 people.[63] But the San Antonio workers were the first to organize a sustained fight-back demanding corporate responsibility.

Under Republican and Democratic administrations alike, beginning with Reagan's, corporation-friendly politicians extolled the virtues of globalization and free trade policies while maintaining a conspicuous silence on the devastating impact of these policies on workers and their communities. The San Antonio workers' painful testimony gave voice to the economic and psychological trauma workers go through every single time a plant closes or a company "downsizes."[64] Denied useful retraining and other assistance, the former Levi's workers lost not only their jobs, but also their cars, homes, and peace of mind. Viola Casares says she will never forget the moment Levi's company representatives announced the plant closure:

> In less than fifteen minutes, the men in suits ruined our whole lives. As long as I live, I'll never forget how the white man in the suit said they had to shut us down to stay competitive. The funny thing is that no one said anything. We stood there like mummies. I heard some people fainted. They didn't even tell us in Spanish, just in English. We didn't want to lose our jobs. Nothing can replace a job with dignity.[65]

Petra Mata says she experienced the trauma twice, first at a secret preparation session management convened for supervisors, and again on the plant floor with the rest of the workers. Staff were told to keep the company's plans secret pending a general announcement to all the workers. Petra recalls:

> At 7:30 A.M., *boom!* They called for a general meeting in the middle of the plant. A guy got up on one of the tables and announced it. *¡Híjole!* That was something that we'll never forget for the rest of our lives, like it just happened yesterday. When everybody heard the announcement we started screaming, hugging each other, crying and asking, "Why? Why? Why?" But they have never answered. They never told us why. There was no reason to shut us down really. We made good quality clothes and high quotas every week. In May 1989 we got the $200 Miracle Bonus because we made such high production levels....
>
> A lot of people went crazy because they didn't know how they were going to live without a job. When you lose your job you feel like nothing but trash, a remnant, a machine to be thrown out. They take away your dignity. You get scared. How are you going to pay for the car, the house, the kids to eat and go to school? *¡Híjole!* After so many years of working for Levi's, overnight we had nothing.[66]

Levi's now sends work to some seven hundred sewing and finishing sub-contractors in fifty countries. From 1997 to 1999, Levi's closed twenty-nine of its manufacturing and finishing plants in North America, slashing some 18,500 employees—nearly half its remaining work force.[67] Levi's also sacked workers in Belgium and France. Over the protests of human-rights groups. the company announced plans to restart production in China.[68] CEO Robert Haas told the *San Francisco Chronicle* that most of the work from the closed plants would be moved to contractors elsewhere in the Americas, most likely to Mexico and the Caribbean.[69]

In another example of what "Made in America" now means, in March 2000, Levi's, Calvin Klein, Brooks Brothers, Abercrombie & Fitch, Talbots, and Woolrich were added to a class-action lawsuit alleging violations of garment workers' rights in Saipan, the Marianna Islands, a U.S. "trust" in the Western Pacific where over thirteen thousand garment workers typically work twelve-hour days for $3.10 or less an hour, seven days a week, often without overtime pay. The $1 billion-a-year industry in Saipan relies on "guest workers," mostly from China and the Philippines, many of whom must pay a cash bond up to $5,000 for a one-year contract to work.[70]

El Paso has been also been devastated by plant closures. The Labor Department said some ten thousand workers in El Paso had lost their jobs because of NAFTA by 1998, the most anywhere in the United States.[71] For example, Levi's, which had been El Paso's largest private employer, closed three of its six plants, laying off some fourteen hundred workers in 1997.[72] On August 29, 1997, the Greater Texas Finishing Corporation, a division of Sun Apparel, Inc., closed its El Paso operations to send production to Mexico, including the Tehuacán free trade zone. At the time Sun Apparel's largest contracted label was Ralph Lauren's Polo brand. Some two hundred laid-off workers included veterans who had served the company for more than eighteen years. In a statement calling for support, the laid-off workers said, "Most of us were let go with little more than a good-bye and directions to the NAFTA training and unemployment offices to join the more than seven thousand other workers in El Paso who have lost their jobs to NAFTA and have been unable to get new jobs."[73]

La Mujer Obrera (LMO) is a Mexicana/Chicana women workers' organi-zation founded by garment workers and Chicana/o movement organizers in El Paso in 1981. LMO fought hard against the passage of NAFTA, having had first-hand experience with maquiladorization enacted under the "twin-city" arrangement between El Paso and Juárez during the Border Industrialization Program. Since NAFTA's passage LMO has organized the thousands of workers laid off by NAFTA. LMO says that of the twenty thousand displaced workers in El Paso by 2000, 97 percent were Latino; two-thirds, women; one third, single mothers; 50 percent, between thirty and forty-five years of age, with the majority of the rest over forty-five years old; and four thousand were in job training programs.[74] After a running battle with state and federal agencies, NAFTA-displaced workers won a $3 million extension in government-funded training for laid-off workers in addition to the original $4.2 million allocated. But María del Carmen Domínguez says that workers in El Paso remain in a profound state of crisis:

> The economic crisis is the big, big problem right now. The women come to La Mujer Obrera because of unemployment. The factories are closing left and right now, and more of the women are becoming single parents. Problems within the families are rising because of this situation. It's hard when women don't have the money to pay the utilities, the rent, or food. When they are confronted with the denial of public services—no welfare, no food stamps.[75]

While workers in large and medium-sized plants lost their jobs to globalization, like their Chinese counterparts, Mexican immigrant women working in small sweatshops also reported declining wages and working conditions. Los Angeles, the apparel-manufacturing center of the Untied States, employed some 122,500 employees in April 1998.[76] Lucrecia Tamayo, an undocumented worker from Mexico, describes her experience working in Los Angeles sweatshops:

> The first day I started working I felt like I was working the whole twenty-four hours! *O sea* [that is to say], ever since I worked in this country I have worked over twelve hours a day, from 7 A.M. to 8 P.M. at night, without Sundays off, *siempre, siempre trabajando* [always, always working]. I earned $100 a week, working from 7 A.M. to 8 P.M. every day. I worked in four factories over a fifteen-year period. In the first place I worked there were about thirty people, in another about sixty.
>
> I worked six years in the El Monte shop…. There were about twenty Latinos working there, with Thai workers in another room…. We were paid by the piece, so the pay varied. Sometimes I made about $260 a week. Oh, that owner! I used to only get off twice a year, like for a two-hour break if I had to take my child to the doctor. In the case of emergencies, I had to ask my sister to take my child or else the owner would start screaming at me.[77]

Joining the Movement

Much of the education and leadership training the women received took place "on the job." The women talked about how much their participation in the movement had changed them. They learned how to analyze working conditions and social problems, who was responsible for these conditions, and what workers could do to get justice. They learned to speak truth to power, whether this was to government representatives, corporate management, the media, unions, or coethnic gatekeepers. They built relations with different kinds of sectors and groups and organized a wide variety of educational activities and actions. Their activism expanded their world view beyond that of their immediate families to seeing themselves as part of peoples' movements fighting for justice.

The women joined the movement through a variety of routes. Some women sought out workers' centers when they experienced a particular grievance at work. María del Carmen Domínguez just showed up at La Mujer Obrera with over a hundred coworkers one day. People packed into the tiny office, soon spilling out into the street. Workers complained that the boss was trying to cheat them out of holiday pay promised in the personnel policy. La Mujer Obrera provided an infrastructure of support for the workers during their wildcat strike and negotiations with management. Through this process the organization gained new leaders and members, including Domínguez. She recalls:

> We won! They had to give us back pay for our holidays and vacations, yes, for everything, for all the workers. I knew about La Mujer Obrera before the strike because their organizers used to come to the factory, outside the doors, and bring leaflets. So when we had problems (laughs and snaps her fingers), we remembered them.[78]

For a long time Domínguez felt angry that she had not known the law and what women workers could do to defend their rights. Through her participation in the movement, she developed her skills, leadership, and awareness:

> When I stayed at work in the factory, I was only thinking of myself and how am I going to support my family—nothing more, nothing less. And I served my husband and my son, my girl. But when I started working with La Mujer Obrera I thought, "I need more respect for myself. We need more respect for ourselves" (laughs). *Pero* [but] this also meant big changes for my husband, too (laughs)! But he supported me so much through many, many years. He died three years ago.
>
> I also learned so much about how to use the computer and communicate with other people because the kind of communication you

need to work in an organization is different from in a factory. I learned about the law and I learned how to organize classes with people, whether they were men or women like me. I learned how to develop curriculum and citizenship materials in Spanish. I made a book, yeah![79]

Domínguez also cherishes her friendships with women worker organizers from communities across the United States and overseas:

I did a lot of traveling for the organization. This is very good because now I know more about where and how we are living in the United States. I got the opportunity to meet with other women, worker women, which is very important to me. Projects like the Lucy Parsons Initiative [a collaborative of Mexican, Chinese, and Dominican women leaders from workers' centers supported by the Funding Exchange] are very good. I love it! And I got to know different organizations, who is doing what kind of work, and who are the women representing these groups.

I have also gone to international meetings.... I represented La Mujer Obrera in 1989, after there was the big temblor [earthquake] in Mexico. We participated in a giant march. It was very good with so many women in the streets. We worked with the September 19th Garment Workers Union.[80]

In other instances, women first came into contact with the workers' centers through family members, friends, and recruitment into specific programs and activities organized by the centers. Carmen Ibarra López learned about La Mujer Obrera from her aunt Esperanza Rodríguez, a veteran seamstress who labored thirty-seven years in the garment industry and continues to work as a janitor:

She invited me to come to the meetings so I started coming. I began doing a lot of volunteer work, and I was a member of the board of directors and of the Comité de Lucha. Finally Cecilia [the group's former director] asked me to work here.... When I started out, I just gave away flyers and La Mujer Obrera's newspaper. I participated in meetings, and when no one from La Mujer Obrera could attend a meeting, I was in charge of going. And also I helped in ordinary ways, cleaning, mopping, doing the bathroom. I don't mind doing it. I still do it because I like the workers to come and see this place clean.[81]

The confidence and skills women gained while standing up for their rights at work spilled over into other jobs. Ibarra adds:

I remember, about six years ago, Larry, the boss, sent his daughter to talk to us. She said that Larry was having a lot of problems paying his IRS bills. She asked us in the name of Larry if we wanted to support him. So we asked how he wanted us to support him. And she said if we could work eight hours but he was going to just pay us for seven hours. By that time I had just become a member of La Mujer Obrera and I said, "No way! I'm not going to do it. Why?" She said, "Well, *es que* [it's that] he doesn't want to close the factory. You can keep your job." But I said, "No way!" So a few of us said no, but the rest said yes. But even with that he shut down in March 1991.[82]

Irma Montoya came to a special summer camp that La Mujer Obrera organized for NAFTA-displaced workers after the electronics plant where she worked fled to Mexico. Montoya stayed on and became an organizer. One day when she went to testify to state and federal legislators about the impact of NAFTA and workers' need for quality job training and placement, her picture appeared in the *New York Times*.[83]

Refugio Arrieta first became involved with La Mujer when she came to attend English classes:

I came to classes one or two days a week for two hours each, and I ended up staying. Some of my friends from the factory also came here to attend the classes. We worked a lot to help out. We have demonstrations, we have meetings with the politicians. I am the president of *la mesa directiva* [the board of directors] here. I received the La Mujer Obrera Award.[84]

In some cases, the organizations conducted systematic political education to consolidate a core of women worker leaders. María Antonia Flores, María del Carmen Domínguez, and Eustolia Olivas were trained as the initial worker leadership core of La Mujer Obrera. Flores recalls:

On some occasions Cecilia gave the training, at other times Guillermo, people who came from different parts of the city, and political teachers, including from Mexico. [Cecilia Rodríguez and Guillermo Domínguez Glenn helped launch La Mujer Obrera and the Centro Obrero—Center for Workers—in El Paso.] They gave classes in politics and everything related to study, from Paolo Freire's methods to the political economy of Mexico. Trainings lasted two or three weeks, a month, three months, or sometimes daily when the teachers were here. What we got first from study we later put into practice.[85]

If one meets Flores today, it is hard to imagine her as the person she describes before her involvement in the movement:

I have learned so much here. I used to be shy. I hardly spoke. I was a submissive housewife. I had all the characteristics of a Mexican woman who was only made for marriage. But once we came here to this organization, we all learned something. For working class women it's harder to develop ourselves as leaders. I did not have these experiences in mind when I first came here. At least I did not know what it meant to be part of an organization. I got my liberation after being suppressed for fifteen years and limited to the house and home labor. I came out in the world. Before that I did not even know that such a thing as women's oppression even existed; one just thinks its normal.

When you are just sitting there listening to your husband, you think it's perfectly natural that you have no rights as a woman, as a person. Your rights are violated and you don't know it. When you go out into the outside world, you find another reality. I think that's what has made me so protective of this organization.[86]

"I Don't Want Other People to Go Through What We Went Through"

The government raid on the El Monte sweatshop on August 2, 1995, marked a turning point in Lucrecia Tamayo's life. She transformed from being a frightened worker to the campaign nerve center, who relishes speaking out and going to demonstrations against big-name retailers that profited from her labor:

The second of August woke me up. It was like I was a blind woman before that. I like going to the actions and demonstrations. Before when the owners screamed at me, I got real small. I wondered what I had done wrong to make them so mad. Now I know we have rights.

I have had two jobs since the raids at El Monte. Because of the publicity around our case, the owner knows who I am. The owner would call at six in the morning telling you whether or not you could come in. I didn't like it. There is no written contract. Everything is just done by his word. I was only getting paid $80 a week. But since I started working there I wrote down the hours I worked and how many pieces I sewed, like I learned to do. After a year, I took my calculations to KIWA [Korean Immigrant Workers Advocates]. Paul [Lee, a KIWA organizer] went with me to talk to the owner and they paid what they owed me soon after.

I'm the information source for our group of workers. If a problem comes up, I call everyone up to let them know what's going on. Ever since the raid on the El Monte shop, I have kept track of all the paperwork and keep workers informed. I no longer have any fear. My only fear is Immigration. But the rest, no. I do not want other workers to suffer. I don't want other people to go through what we went through. This experience opened up my eyes. It made me conscious. It gave me the motivation to speak up and fight against the owners. My husband thinks I'm crazy. I always ask Paul, "When are we going to have the next demonstration?" I like to yell and scream at the retailers in the stores that made so much money off of us.[87]

"This Is the Best School You Could Have"

Fuerza Unida allowed laid-off Levi's workers to channel their anger and sense of betrayal, while building on the friendships and ties they had relished in their jobs. A combination of curiosity and revenge first attracted Viola Casares to Fuerza Unida:

I remember when people were passing out information. I was curious and wanted to find out what they wanted to tell us. Because of my curiosity, I started going to the meetings. At first there were twenty-five to thirty ladies who started meeting at a small church hall. We began talking about how we have to do something. We needed to get more information about what is really going on. We needed to find out what the company was going to give us. We needed to do something because of the awful way they shut down the plant. I got interested. I was angry about what they did to us without warning. At first I just wanted to get back at them. I started as a volunteer, then became a board member, then a cocoordinator.[88]

Casares expanded her vision and network of friends through her involvement with Fuerza Unida:

I've done a lot of traveling and met wonderful people. I've learned that I am not the only one who has had problems. This experience has opened up my mind and views. For example, because of lack of information and education and the way I was raised by my family, I used to think that being gay, being homosexual, was a sin. But I don't believe that any more. We are all human beings.... I learned from my broken marriage, my job, and Fuerza Unida. I have a second chance to pass on what the movement taught me. I never thought I could have done the things that I have. Losing my job opened my eyes. I used to work and live in my own little world. We were taught to just look out for our own family and to compete with other people. Levi's taught us to compete against other workers to be part of their machine. Fuerza Unida taught us that we are part of a bigger family, that we should care about our sisters.[89]

Marta Martínez ran into problems making her way through the company rehiring and government job training programs after the layoffs but stuck with Fuerza Unida through thick and thin:

> I've been with Fuerza Unida from the beginning. They offered some of us work at the other plants. I worked there for three months. I had to quit because they treated us so bad. Even the other workers there were mad at us. They said we were stealing their jobs. The supervisors accused us of being lazy, saying that's why the plant shut down and moved out. They were very rude to those of us who came in from the old plant. I went through the ESL, GED, and job-training classes. The training mainly helped the people who could speak English. But they didn't really help people find jobs. With Fuerza Unida, I worked on the protests, the hunger strikes, everything.[90]

Similarly, Tina Mendoza put her energy into Fuerza Unida after the Levi's layoffs:

> I've been working with Fuerza Unida for eight years. The first two years I just went to meetings, but after that I started coming to the office regularly to help out. We work on everything. We never say we can't do it. Our biggest problem is with English. We do all these things so that Fuerza Unida can live on, so our struggle can continue, so that we can serve as an example to women about what is possible. We work to build pride that we are women. I have learned a lot here. I met so many different people and learned about what they do, about different struggles. For me I feel great pride to be a part of this struggle.
>
> At first I was afraid and ashamed to go the demonstrations. I tried my best to\cover my face so that I would not be seen. Now when I go, I scream as loud as I can. I do not cover my face. Fuerza Unida injects you with a lot of energy. *Ojala* [I hope to God/Allah] that we will continue to move ahead.[91]

Fuerza Unida members later reached out to low-waged workers in other plants and industries. Obdulia "Obi" Segura first came to Fuerza Unida after hearing about the food bank available for unemployed workers and low-income families in need:

> I try to help out at Fuerza Unida, doing whatever kind of work I can. I started coming here about two and a half years ago, first because I heard about the food bank. Now I help with sweeping, office work, and whatever needs to be done. Even though the women have their own families and homes to take care of, they all give a lot to the work of Fuerza Unida, to help other people in need. There are women in

this world who will not do anything for anyone else, who are very ego-tistical. But that is not the way of Fuerza Unida. Petra and Viola do everything they can to help the people, to build cooperation. That is the character of working with Fuerza Unida. Here we are always ready to help, to love each other, to work together. This is what moves me to volunteer here in whatever way I can.[92]

Petra Mata, who had already picked up many leadership skills as a daughter, wife, mother, and seamstress, got baptized in the fire of fighting the world's largest garment manufacturer:

I learned so much at Fuerza Unida. This is the best school you could have, working with people, listening, chairing meetings—all the things you have to understand to carry out the struggle. Here we are not just individuals. We go to support and participate in all struggles in the movement. We work with Asian, Filipino, African American, Mexican, white. We are part of the same vision, the same movement. In the past when Levi's said, "Blah blah blah," we said, "Yes sir." Now we ask, "Why? Wait a minute. I don't like it." They should do what's right, or fair at least. Companies cannot do without workers, it should be half and half, fifty-fifty, not just 100 percent going to one side. That's what we learned through Fuerza Unida.[93]

"Sometimes God Knocks Us Around a Little Bit"

For some of the women, showing compassion, solidarity, and faith in the face of hardships is sustained by deeply held religious beliefs. Viola Casares says she tells Petra Mata, "I think sometimes God knocks us around a little bit to make us think and to remind us to be thankful for what we have." Casares reaffirmed her faith during a visit to maquiladoras in Honduras with a U.S. delegation hosted by the Mennonite Church:

Sometimes when I get discouraged I pray for God to give me a sign to let me know if what I am doing is right. One day we were scheduled to visit different maquilas, including a place called Interfashion. No one knew what we would find there. But when we got there, the first thing we saw when we walked through the door was women sewing Levi's and Dockers label pants. God had given me a big sign to see that what we were doing was right. He showed us exactly what was going on in the factories our jobs had run away to. It was a miracle!

We saw just what Levi's was doing to our sisters in Central America. We saw that their chairs and working conditions were really uncomfortable and that they got paid so much less, with no benefits.

The place looked just like a prison and workers were treated like prisoners. I saw that with my own eyes. It made me really angry. That company just cares about profits.[94]

Similarly, Carmen Ibarra López of La Mujer Obrera explains: "All the time I like to do my job with *fé* [faith]. Yes, I have a lot of faith in God—period. I feel very, very respectful of all the religions. I do my job because I have faith in God."[95]

Bringing Home the Fight for Women's Rights

Work, migration, and activism are all threads that run through the women's histories. But as working-class women, they also endured distinct challenges as daughters, lovers, wives, mothers, sisters, and grandmothers. With their participation in movements seeking to overturn oppressive class, gender, and racial practices have come changes in their views of gender and family roles.

Viola Casares complained that her husband had run around with *sus mujeres de la cantina* [his women of the bars], while projecting his jealousy on to her. He refused to let her work outside the home despite their poverty. Casares swears that 1990 was absolutely the worst year in her life. During that dark time, she lost not only her job of nine years, but also her marriage. She finally separated from her husband, who had become a jealous alcoholic and broken her nose during a beating. The stress from the loss of her job and marriage, combined with her declining health, put Casares in the hospital:

I told him, "If you want to get back together it's got to be fifty-fifty, not 90 percent going to your side." But by that time his drinking had gotten really bad. We never got a divorce although we were separated for six years. He didn't want to give me a divorce. He'd come and stay for a couple of weeks. Our oldest daughter loved him dearly. He was such a strong man with his macho image. When we were living together he would run around with other women. I was a good wife and faithful, but I told him, "One of these days, I'm going to leave." He would come back and cry. He had his regrets. I think a lot of it was because of his drinking. I've lost a lot of uncles and cousins to drinking. His father used to drink. My husband died from drinking when he was only forty-six years old. I guess that's why I loved, hated, and pitied this man all at the same time. He lived in his own way. Maybe he did not know how to show love because he was not shown love since his father also drank a lot and ran around with women.[96]

Casares managed to climb out of the well of depression by channeling her energy into taking care of her children and grandchildren and building Fuerza Unida as a support center for women like herself. She explains:

I'm glad that I became part of Fuerza Unida. It's really changed my life. What I went through with the plant closure and my marriage prepared me for the work I am doing right now, even for the death of my husband and coping with the loss of my job. I think that if I didn't have this organization, I would be completely lost now. Fuerza Unida made us strong women, strong mothers. I like to be independent. I told my husband when he tried to come back, "You have to want the new Viola, not the old Viola that only stayed home."[97]

The barriers women had to surmount because of their gender status were made doubly difficult because of economic hardships they faced as working-class women. The women worry about their children, grandchildren, parents, and siblings. A number had experienced the loss of family to substance abuse and violence. The workers' centers acted as a women's support network. Remedios García tried to manage her stress and loss by staying active:

It's been almost seven years that my oldest son was murdered. That affected me greatly. Since that time I've gone from illness to illness to illness (starts crying). I haven't been able to recuperate. It's been seven years or more that I've stayed like this. Aieee! He was out with his friends. When the telephone rang that night and I thought it must be an emergency as soon as I heard it. Aieee! The doctor said I must not always think about this and move on to do other things. But it's my son, I told him. So a lot of problems have come from this. I started having problems with my husband, with a lot of things, because it affected me personally. But, nevertheless, one has to go on living. I can't recuperate so that's why I've been like this, do you understand? I feel a lot of guilt, that I didn't spend enough time with my son. I've had one complication after another. For this it is good to have a lot of friends and continue working.... I have my mama, my children, and people who need me. And they have me.[98]

Many of the women met their partners, had children, and started working outside the home when they were teenagers. They described a range of positive and negative experiences with partners. A number of the women had separated from their first husbands. Despite her high levels of skills, Elena Alvarez is suppressed by a jealous husband who will not permit her to work for pay. She can only leave the house with his permission, even though their household is in dire financial condition.

Carmen Ibarra López experienced a serious bout of depression when her first marriage did not work out, so she started going to beautician school and worked as a manicurist for many years before she returned to the garment industry. Still in the "honeymoon" phase of her new marriage, Carmen is crossing her fingers and says that she is praying that God will give her "a second chance."[99]

Tina Mendoza says her husband has been very supportive of her involvement with Fuerza Unida. She just tries to make sure she has his meals ready and makes sufficient time for her family:

> I no longer have babies at home. My children are grown. My husband supports my work with Fuerza Unida. He wants me to be useful, not just staying home watching TV. I make sure I get my husband's meals ready and make his life easier. I try to spend as much time with the family as possible. He's a second-level supervisor after working for the city for over twenty-five years. Where he works is unionized. Before the union came in, there used to be lots of discrimination against Mexicans. But thanks to the union, minorities have been able to raise their positions.[100]

Petra Mata also says her husband has been very supportive of her work at Fuerza Unida. Indeed, he has continued to work at two low-paying jobs to support the family, especially when funding runs out and she and her coco-ordinator, Viola Casares, stop getting paid. She says that sometimes his friend rib him when they see her speaking at some demonstration on TV, but she says, "at least he can see what I'm doing."[101]

María del Carmen Domínguez takes pride in her scrapper stance towards her father, brothers, and schoolmates while growing up, as well as in her children's strength:

> My family made it possible for me to organize the strike at the factory and work here (laughs). I started out fighting with my father. I fought in school. I fought with my husband (laughs). ¡Aiiyaiiyaii! Yes, because I am very strong! Come on! With the boys at school I played baseball (laughs). First I wanted to bat, to pitch.... My daughter has some of the same personality as me. Well, I think, no, not only my daughter, but my boys, too, yeah. My daughter is a very, very fighting woman (laughs). Yes, but she is also crying, fighting, crying.[102]

Carmen Ibarra López is both critical of her own upbringing as well as proud to break the mold in raising her daughter and son:

> You know, I was born and grew up in a culture where the women didn't have a voice. So I said I'm not going to do the same with my

children. I want to teach them to be different. I'm not the kind of a person who wants to do the same thing that my family does, did with me. No, I'm not. Especially with my daughter. You know my son is the oldest, and my daughter is the youngest. I taught my son how to clean house, wash dishes, and all kinds of tasks because I said, "Your sister is not going to be your maid. She is just going to be your sister and a human being." So they both respect each other very much. They are not just brother and a sister but very, very good and close friends. Yes, I don't want to keep doing the same thing that my family did. No, no way![103]

Through participation in their organizations and *el movimiento,* the women gained new skills and awareness, underwent major transformations, provided leadership to communities under siege, built working friendships with Asian immigrant women and other low-waged workers across the globe, and won victories.

During a protest at Levi's posh glass, steel, and brick corporate headquarters in San Francisco, to the surprise, consternation, then chagrin of management, *las mujeres* suddenly chained themselves to the front door. Calmly awaiting the arrival of police paddy wagons, over the bullhorn they issued a friendly, Texas home-style invitation to their upcoming benefit dance with Dr. Loco's Rockin' Jalapeño Band. *Las mujeres luchando* [the women in struggle] inspire stanzas in the band's catchy *cumbia* rhythm, "El Picket Sign" (1992):

> From San Anto to San Francisco Fuerza Unida has been saying
> *Desde San Anto hasta San Francisco Fuerza Unida anda diciendo*
> Don't buy Dockers or Levi's jeans and stop the Free Trade Agreement
> *¡Boicot Dockers y Levi's jeans y alto al libre comercio!*
>
> *El* picket sign, *el* picket sign
> *¡Que Viva La Mujer Obrera!*
> *El* picket sign, *el* picket sign
> *¡Queremos* [We want] Justice for Janitors!
> *El* picket sign, *el* picket sign
> We say *¡Chale* [too crazy] *con* Coors!
> *El* picket sign, *el* picket sign
> *¡Porque la unión es La Fuerza!* [Because the union is the Force][104]

María Antonia Flores, director of La Mujer Obrera and popular educator, tells the following story:

I was born in 1954 in Zacatecas, Mexico. My family moved to Ciudad Juárez in 1962. I have eight sisters and brothers, and I am the oldest. In Juárez my parents worked in maquilas, restaurants, [and] as vendors selling food.

I studied through middle school, then a year to be a secretary, and in a school for teachers. I was an adult literacy teacher while I was studying to become a teacher, but I didn't finish and get a diploma. I worked for two years as an educator, and later two years in a maquila.

The maquila was a rather large electronics factory called Centra Labs Components; about four hundred people worked there. I was nineteen years old then. For that period of time the pay was good—minimum wage, and one could earn seven hundred pesos, but it was very hard work. I started work at three in the afternoon, left at 11 P.M., and we worked Saturdays. I don't know the name, but we also used a paste, mixed like a dough to cover the capacitors, and it smelled really bad. We attached different components between the two edges so the current could pass through. Then we carried the capacitors and dipped them in alcohol or acetone. That work gave you a lot of headaches because sometimes when we handled such tiny capacitors, we had to use a big lens to see the small pieces well enough to grab them. After a while they changed me to a department where I worked at a machine that cut the capacitor wires, squared them, and sent them to be packaged in boxes for shipping. The majority of workers were almost *puras jovensitas* [all young women]; the supervisors were *puros varones* [all male].

I got married when I was eighteen, almost nineteen, on August 21, 1971. My daughter Paula was born August 18, 1972, a year after I got married. My son Gerardo was born in July 1973, my other daughter in February 1977, and my youngest son in July 1988. Now I have five grandchildren, four girls and one boy [laughs]. They're from my two daughters.

My husband and I came to the U.S. from Juárez to El Paso in 1974 because his parents had residency here, and we lived with them for two years. Then he left the house and us to live with his mama until 1985, when I moved out of my in-laws' house. Already he had gone running around with other women. I was separated from him, almost since 1977. We got to know each other because he lived near me and came to a *fiesta* [party] at my house. He used to work as a factory operative in El Paso.

I came here when I was about twenty-two, twenty-three years old. During the first years I was only a housewife, not doing anything but taking care of the family, the in-laws. But afterwards I started to work in small factory workshops, cleaning offices, doing home care for adults. I got special training to take care of a sick person who could not move. I was with this person for two years and after that I worked at a factory for another year. Then I returned to cleaning offices and from 1986 to 1990 I did both jobs. During the day I worked in the factory, and at night and weekends I cleaned offices (groans).

Aiiee! I never got any sleep! The garment factory was so difficult. I left my children home *solitos* [alone]. They went to school and we didn't see each other because I didn't get home from work until one or two in the morning.

The first factory where I worked was named Emily Joe. Later I worked at CMT and at other small shops, Elias Lavalla. The last one I worked at was Eddy Wad. With the first job I still didn't have my papers because my husband left me while he ran around with his friends and sweet young things. But because he was always working in these different industries he knew about jobs and told me where to go. On other jobs I had my own references, people that I worked with and knew. I always came with good recommendations. I found the last job because the factory was near where I lived.

After I got off from the factory I started coming to La Mujer Obrera. I volunteered because I enjoyed it. In March or April of 1985 a friend of mine who was a neighbor first brought me for a women's meeting on topics given by Cecilia [Rodríguez, La Mujer Obrera's cofounder], workshops on the oppression of la mujer, and planning for a festival for children. During those days I only participated in small meetings and visited, not as a member. In 1986 I became a member, worked on committees, then as part of the leadership. After a year they started to organize special workshops to train me and two other *compañeras,* María del Carmen [Domínguez] and Eustolia [Olivas] as the first three organizers trained to advance the organization.

Since about 1988 we began to develop more activities and a bit stronger membership. We started the first cooperative food project through a committee organized by María del Carmen. She also created the newspaper for educational work. It was about eight pages long and came out every month. María del Carmen developed all the educational material, leaflets and brochures, and gave classes. I was a teacher, yes, from my past training in Mexico.

There were big problems in the factories during this period so we leafleted them in 1988, 1990, 1991. We had over a thousand members, with educational meetings four times a week. Fifty workers came to every meeting. It was so busy! We were running La Cooperativa [the food cooperative] and also La Clínica [free workers' health clinic]. Fifteen to twenty people helped us operate our educational program and the coop. There was a *huelga* [strike] in November. That's when we had all the problems with the union, the divisions.

I was in charge of political education. In 1995 and 1996 we also moved into economic development. I prepared the curriculum based on what we were planning, for the workers, volunteers, and people who came from outside El Paso. We even had a volunteer from Spain. We made presentations according to the needs of the group, whether it was religious, progressive, or more conservative. We conducted political education in our Escuela Popular [People's School]. The courses lasted three months, two hours a week, with one hour in English or citizenship, and then one hour on economics, politics, and social issues. We made murals, drawings, and leaflets to reinforce the learning process. We do more murals and *dinámicas* [skits] and show videos. We developed plans for the Comité de Lucha and when the people developed as stronger leaders, they took on more responsibility for planning.

We have to design the curriculum so that everyone can understand. We do not rely much on writing because a lot of our people do not know how to read. Doing murals together is so people don't go to sleep like in church; they're so colorful. Workers come here tired and hungry so we have to capture their interest and keep them engaged. When people first come, we start with very basic stories and simple questions. If they go on to the second level, we cover more political economy and advanced topics. We talk about what money is, what transnational corporations are, why factories are closing, and neoliberalism. We draw pictures of the transnational corporations and their activities around the world and ask, What does this have to do with us? We talk about what is happening to people in Chiapas and what that poor people's struggle has to do with workers in this community.

I love doing educational work! We started before the big garment factories started closing, while the women were still working. Then the different corporations began setting up twin plants along the border in the 1970s here in Juárez and El Paso; later the biggest factories started to leave. Through our relations with workers in Canada we learned more about the disasters workers went through in Canada and the United States. We made many trips and shared stories with other workers. One of the most beautiful of all experiences is when workers support each other. Different people from La Mujer Obrera participate in these exchanges. It sets a good base of information. But the governments still passed NAFTA.

We started working [in solidarity] with the [independent Mexican labor union federation] Frente Auténtico del Trabajo [FAT], founded in 1960.[105] The FAT works in four sectors. First, it works in the workers' sector, which now has various national level unions, like the unions of iron and steel, farm, textile, and shoemaker workers, from northern Mexico to the southwest part of the central valley. Second, the cooperative sector organizes savings, credit, consumers', and producers' cooperatives, including a glass factory that the workers won after a strike. Third, people living in the colonias developed similar consumer cooperatives; in the urban sector colonia residents organize around all kinds of questions, like water, electricity, and sewage. Finally, the campesino sector is conducting a survey of the people in the countryside to estimate the results of the harvest so they don't get exploited by some company. They work with the *ejidotarios* [owners of communal land]. The fundamental goal is to improve the conditions of life of all the people.

Our groups are organizing independently because we belong to no political party or government, and the workers themselves are the ones who feel this [is important].... The FAT had to develop completely independently from the unions [that are] working in collaboration with the government. We are based in self-determination where workers are the ones who decide what we want and who is going to represent us. The situation in Mexico is very different from that of U.S. AFL-CIO unions; the CTM [Confederación de Trabajadores Mexicanos] is part of the official government and ruling party. The government's physical repression can't stop the workers, but does place many obstacles before them. For example, when workers really start organizing, the first thing they [the Mexican government] do is fire everyone [in the union]. Or the government labor commissions give false counts of the election votes. They bring in people to vote who really don't work there. Through these same laws and government bodies that are supposed to protect the workers, the administration carries out many tricks.

Since around 1963 they started to establish maquiladoras along the border and added many more in the 1980s and 1990s. So it became necessary for the FAT to establish a workers' center on the border,

Centro de Estudios y Taller Laboral [Labor Workshop and Study Center] to train women maquiladora workers about everything related to their labor rights to defend themselves, whether at the individual or collective level. Especially here in the United States where there is no understanding of what an independent union or organization is, we want workers to know how things could be different.

In general people who work in the maquilas have no previous experience in these kinds of jobs. Some maquiladoras require that workers have completed primary school, but in others, many do not know how to read and write. Workers receive no study or training because all the work in the maquiladoras is very easy and routine, so one needs only a certain amount of manual aptitude. They contract mostly young people, from sixteen to thirty-five years old, depending on the factory. If the work involves a lot of tiny pieces, they greatly prefer women's labor; when the work is a little more heavy, they contract more men. The ratio is about 60 percent women and 40 percent men. About 50 percent of the workers in Juárez are not from here, but from all the other states of the republic. Some 55 percent of the women also have children, averaging one or two. People often cannot secure the necessities of life. There are not enough child care centers to accommodate so many people. Many times parents have to leave their children by themselves.

Most of the factories are transnational, headquartered in the United States, Canada, and Japan, [and more recently, subcontractors from South Korea and Taiwan] with also some Mexican-owned maquilas. The average pay is $4 a day (exclaims). Yes, that's what it is! That includes bonuses for productivity, good attendance, punctuality, so that workers will work even harder to survive. They give some prizes, but the pay offered is so low because it benefits them to keep us needy. Many maquilas have people who worked ten, twelve years doing the same thing, but have not been trained to do anything else. At La Mujer Obrera we have classes twice a week. We try not to lose hold of our education program, or we will have no power. We need to motivate the workers so they can struggle for their rights. Before NAFTA passed we helped organize a big march on the bridge between here and Mexico and had problems with the police. It was very cold! We stayed in the plaza all night together with so many groups, including from Canada and Mexico.

Now the education we do is on the results of the crisis, the disaster, the unemployment, the people out in the streets, the treating of workers like they didn't exist. Workers are invisible in Mexico, here, and whatever part of the world. But how can workers become more visible and take on this problem? The problem we are having with NAFTA is not just a local one affecting El Paso; it is also the worldwide problem of neoliberalism. We have to educate workers, both immigrants and nonimmigrants. We must understand the roots of the problems. We need to know not just that we don't have work, but why we don't have work.

Women are not the only ones who come for help, but yes, the working woman is the one who is in the worst need. You can hear it in our name, La Mujer Obrera [The Woman Worker]; it comes out in our methods of organizing, initiatives, development of women's leadership. La Mujer Obrera is a name people know so women come here directly to see how we can support them. When a woman comes with her needs, we should be ready to help her, whether she stays or not, because she is unprotected. But we also want women to participate in this organization because it is in our interest to strengthen the group to promote the development of women. We don't want to continue to be used as objects, like furniture, right?!

We have been through so many experiences that were good, strong, and brave. One of the most important things for us as leaders of this organization is to have the support of our families. One way they do this is by accepting our schedules, since there is no fixed routine. If a husband or children opposes our activities, we would have to leave our work only half done. Working together with women through hard times like the hunger strike or the organizing of Camp Dignity [a popular-education, two-week summer camp LMO organized for NAFTA-displaced workers and their families] have been great learning experiences. [There] we saw how far each of us as an organizer could go and how the organization could grow. We have the experiences of building relationships among workers to better express themselves and communicate with others.

Now I can say what I want, what I expect, what I do or do not want done in the organization, in the family, for myself. But if you're only inside your home, you don't learn anything. Development is very important. Lots of good and bad things happen as one goes through life. The negative ones affect your health and psyche so we must be prepared to know how to get the strength to face problems and whatever lies ahead. If I know that my health could affect the organization, then I have to think not only of myself, but also of the group, of my coworkers. I think that once one joins an organization, one is not completely free because one has to think about the organization, the family, and the self. So you turn into many parts and you are not alone. You have to think about how you are going to respond to these different parts of your life because you cannot abandon them.

Our priorities for workers are in three areas: the economic, political, and ideological. In the future, I hope that we will reach our goal of having an economic base from which we can live and support the community and ourselves, so workers will be able to take care of their families. I hope that we will achieve the best for the workers, the dreams we've always had about creating a bilingual school and cultural plaza, which would be the greatest, most fabulous thing. Our political priority is to strengthen the workers to confront the bureaucrats to make them implement workers' rights. We must be conscious of what is happening so we can defend ourselves. We know what kind of politics we want and that we must exert efforts so that the voices of the community will be heard. Ideologically I will continue to uphold my ideals for the organization and my family to build a better future. If the conditions of the community improve, then my family's condition will also improve. If the community's conditions do not improve, then my family will continue to live in the same poor situation they are in now. Without this organization we cannot have a better future for our children or our grandchildren. We have to keep fighting all three fights. If we are conscious of our goals, we won't lose our way, our vision. Any woman who is a real leader has to be in the forefront of continuing to struggle to better our conditions.

The following account comes from Petra Mata, former Levi's garment worker, Fuerza Unida organizer, and miracle maker.

I was born on May 31, 1946 in a little town called Bustamente, Nuevo León, Mexico. My parents worked as farmers. When there was no more money in farming, they moved. My mother died at the very early age of twenty-eight years old, when I was only five. She had a baby in this small town they say is only a *rancho* [village]. The hospital services were very poor, no doctors, nobody. In those days women had their babies at home. I think they did not take care of my mom very well, so she developed problems.

My little sister, the baby that my mom bore, died. A few days later my mom died, too. That left us five kids, my four brothers and myself. I was in the middle. When my mother died, my father felt lost. He couldn't stand that my mother had died, so he left us. After that, my grandfather moved me and my brothers to Nuevo Laredo. He took care of us kids until we got married.

It was sad for me. I made a lot of sacrifices and suffered when I was young because my ma died. I don't think anybody cares about you the way your mother does because you are born from her. That's what I tell my kids now, "You only have one mother in your life." I didn't have a mother (eyes water). But in a way, my grandparents did something good for me because now I can live with dignity. When I was young I had to respect myself. I was always praying that I would not do something that was going to degrade me. I always tell my girls, "Respect yourself no matter what. You've got to have respect to receive respect."

After years and years my father came back and we accepted him. But I don't have the kind of love for him I would like to have because he never lived with us when we were little, when we needed him. When I got married I had all this sadness stored up in my heart that I had to let go of, that used to bother me. But now I have my family and a wonderful husband. He helps me a lot. I've got my four kids. My daughter turned twenty-seven in August. My oldest boy is twenty-six, my small boy is twenty-two, and my girl is seventeen.

I met my [future] husband in *el mercado* [the market] in Nuevo Laredo when I was fifteen. Then I left to work in the United States for three or four years. We knew this family in Laredo, Texas very well . They asked my aunt if I could work for them. I worked in their house for two straight years without going to see my family. I had to clean the floors on my hands and knees and wash windows and change everything every month.

When I was seventeen, I was able to go home to Nuevo Laredo on the weekends, then come back to work by Monday. I went back and forth like that. I cleaned the house because I just went to six years of school in Mexico. At that time there was no opportunity to go to school or college. So I had to *¡Híjole!* work as a maid and serve them. They had two kids, and I had to put them to bed every night, give them their clothes, prepare them for school, make breakfast, and do all the housework. There was a wife, but of course I was the maid (laughs)! I only made $10 a week.

I went back to Nuevo Laredo to the same place where I had worked and started talking with my [future] husband. One time, when I was getting off from work, I called his house and asked, "What are you going to do today?" He said, "Well, nothing." I said, "Well, I'm going to go to the movies. Do you want to go with me?" He said right away, "Yeah!" My sister-in-law told me, "The day you called, we were all ready to go out, but he got so excited because he was going to go with you." So I'm the one who took the first step (laughs). But it was only for that one day that he was just like a little chicklet with me. We have a very good relationship. We got married when I was twenty-three years old and Domingo was twenty-seven.

Three months later we came to the United States. All the kids were born here. I remember the first days were very bad because it was very cold. We didn't even have blankets to cover ourselves and the house didn't have any windows. Oooh! Then little by little we saved and began buying things. We are still in this house now.

After my third child was born I started working in a tortilla factory, counting tortillas on the night shift and taking care of my kids during the day. Then I moved to a restaurant where I was in charge of the kitchen and they paid me a very, very low wage, about $60 or $70 a week. I was hired three years and worked 6 A.M. to 4 P.M. every day, even Saturdays, making tortillas and everything. I was unsatisfied and felt like this was not all I could do.

People said that they were hiring at the Levi's factory on Zarzamora Street. The pay was very good. I said, "Well, wow! I would like to do this!" and decided to apply. I went one morning and took the test. I didn't even get back home before I already got a call. They told me to come in for an interview. So I went right away, and they hired me in 1976.

When I started working there, they were paying by levels A to D, with D getting higher pay—which I qualified for. The layoff happened on January 16, 1990. The Friday before the Martin Luther King holiday, they told us that all the supervisors and trainers had to go downtown for a meeting. We suspected something was wrong because we had heard a lot of rumors. Usually at Christmas they gave us a $500 bonus, but not that year. We found out later that they decreased our hours because they were planning to shut us down. Nobody got the benefit of a pay increase based on forty hours because we were working less hours.

We [supervisors] went downtown to a very fancy hotel on Tuesday. Everyone sat down around tables in a big room. Then all of a sudden we saw a lot of people coming with folders. We thought, "What's going on?" Finally, the person from Levi's started to speak and said that they were planning to shut us down because Levi's had to be competitive in the market. Everything turned black. We started screaming and saying "Why?"

They already had the package ready, knew who we were, and took us to different, individual rooms. Then they start explaining, "This is what you're going to get." I was very sad. I started crying. They told us, "Yeah, yeah, calm down. I know how you feel, I know." Ahhh! I told her (eyes water), "How in the hell do you know how I feel?" I mean I loved my job. After the fourteen years I worked for this company, they just turn us out like this. Our jobs are over. "You're going to tell me you know how I feel? You still have a job!"

We came back and went outside. We hugged each other and said, "What are we going to do?" "Ahhh!" "I just bought my car." "I just got my credit card to buy Christmas gifts." A lot of people were buying houses, then lost them. They lost their cars. I had two cars at the time. We lost everything because we couldn't pay no more, *sabes* [you know]? When they turned us away they said, "Oh, we want you to cooperate with us. We want you to help us to work with the people tomorrow." Everybody went back and said, "Oh no! You want us to help you when you are doing this to us?"

They had a lot of advisors [who] told us, "You poor lady, you're going to be all right." They gave some money to the city to provide services, but those services did not help Levi's workers directly, but instead went to the whole city with close to ten thousand people out of jobs. They [also] mishandled that money by renting a big office and buying a lot of things. We didn't get anything. About 1,150 workers were displaced.

When Levi's closed, it was a disaster for most of the families. My husband has had to work at two jobs since they shut us down. In the evening he's a cook at the Marriott Hotel and in the morning he's working with vegetables in a lot of grocery stores. Before I lost my job I sent one of my kids to college. My two older kids had everything that they needed, not what they wanted, but at least what they needed. The ones who suffered most were the small ones. They remember that we could buy five pairs of pants, one for each day. When I lost my job my small boy said, "Mom, how come we can only buy two pants, one to use today and the other one tomorrow?" He asked, "Why did Junior have this and I cannot?" It was hard for them to understand.

About two months before they shut us down, they started reducing personnel. They paid us whatever they wanted. Workers didn't know how to calculate their pay. So we started comparing. "How much do you have?" "How much did you get?" And they said, "Well, look I got less than you and I was working more years." That's when we started to get together, decided to form Fuerza Unida, and declared the boycott against Levi's.

At first we didn't have any office. We did all of the work from Rubén's house. Rubén [Solís of the Southwest Public Workers Union] was the one who helped us start to put together Fuerza Unida. The first day they made the shut-down announcement, Rubén was there protesting in front of the plant. We got a lawyer right away. We had meetings and formed the Concilio [board of directors]. The workers got involved, and we decided to put together our demands. Then we got a very little place at the Esperanza Peace and Justice Center on South Flores Street.

For six months we got unemployment benefits, $200 every two weeks. After that ran out, we felt very bad. We put more and more attention and time into Fuerza Unida. We put aside our personal and family problems. We used to cry *noches* [nights] to see the people with no food. We started having trainings and participating in conferences—locally, nationally, internationally. We moved again to 3946 South Zarzamora and stayed for almost two years until we moved over here [to 710 New Laredo Highway] where the rent is cheaper. We're low on income. The owner is a very good, cooperative man.

Viola, Irene [Reyna], and I were the cocoordinators at that time.... For the first year or two the people worked for free, nominated by the board. First, there was Frances Estrella, Raquelina, and another lady whose name I don't remember, and Margie Castro, who volunteered so much. A lot of girls got involved and put in a lot of time. Then they decided to make Fuerza Unida a nonprofit organization with papers and everything, and get a grant to pay full-time coordinators. They nominated Viola and Irene, and, because I was putting in my time volunteering, me in February 1992. We worked as a team, Viola, Irene, and myself. Irene had to leave when we ran out of money. I wish we had resources to hire technical assistance. We need someone to sit down and use the computer. Then we could move more quickly, with our sewing cooperative, food bank, and everything.

Every several weeks, we went to San Francisco to organize the campaign at Levi's corporate headquarters. We had to leave our families. It was good but hard. We needed to walk so far and learn to be good leaders to head the campaign. We have learned that if we want to do something, we just need to develop our own goals. I have a lot of friends who do not know what they can do. They see themselves as a wife and mother, washing dishes, cooking dinner, or making clothes only for their own families. A lot of women are heads of households; not enough attention is paid to the problems they face. San Antonio is very poor. Sometimes women fall deep down into that depression they must learn to cross so they can get to the other side. We also need to be motivated by other issues and aware of other people's problems to make changes. We tell women that if someone is trying to abuse you, you must speak up.

Of course, we learned these things. When we started picketing and going to protests, I held the poster up to cover my face. I was afraid. Now if people don't call me, I call them. If you are denied opportunities, you have to look for and create opportunities.

My two oldest [children] got married when I lost my job. I missed them a lot. With the two small ones I did not spend too much time at home. My son is very independent, but my little girl has always wanted to be with me. If I go to town and work late, she comes here to help me. It's hard for me to decide how many hours to work a day. You plan your day, but something comes up, people come in the door. Most of the time my family supports me. My husband's friends say, "Hey, I saw your wife on TV."

People come here to cry if they want to cry, complain if they want to complain, laugh if they want to laugh, and get recommendations and advice about what to do. We started a food bank two years ago, after the Levi's layoffs, to help people during emergencies with groceries. We didn't have many resources. We suffered and made sacrifices. We know what many people who are out of work need—flour, oil, rice, juices, canned goods, beans, crackers, laundry detergent, bread, tortillas. We pay twelve cents a pound to the food bank and give the bags away for free. People come to volunteer and sew in exchange.

We have a good group of volunteers working closely with us. The group is mixed between ex-Levi's and other workers. Our sewing coop sells ready-made items such as bedspreads, tablecloths, curtains, and aprons. We bought sewing machines after many fundraising events. We really need two more commercial machines with a single needle. We also need a new truck to pick up the materials for the sewing coop and the food coop.

When sales are good, we try to give volunteers a little something for their gas expenses. Through our Lotería Mexicana [bingo] everyone can take something home. Everyone brings something in and we cook and eat together. Anyone who comes here goes away with something. When women get frustrated we tell them, "Hey, come over here!" They leave with a piece of material, bingo prize, advice, and friendship to make them feel good. We are trying to expand the work of the organization. Our dream is to make pants. Now we are making miracles.

We never knew we were going to be around this long. When we met with La Mujer Obrera years ago, we asked, "How could you survive so long?" They told us, "You have to think about and plan how you are going to survive that long." We have survived this long. Six years from now, I would like to see a stronger, more established organization that can keep going boom, boom, boom! We need technical assistance to stabilize the organization. I want to see Fuerza Unida do not only local, but more global projects together with other women.

When we first came here my husband and I were undocumented. Then my husband got his citizenship. About two years ago I made myself a citizen, too, because I felt that it was not right for me to be in this struggle when I didn't have a voice, a right to vote. I got to be somebody in the United States. I want to continue to work for our people to have a better life. I want to teach my grandchildren to go to school and college, to be good citizens, and participate in making decisions.

My health bothers me. I want to talk more with the people, to sew, to pray, and get the power to sit down for a while. But God knows what he's doing. Maybe he uses my health to make me slow down and take a rest. My husband and kids are in good shape. My husband works at two jobs. He does not go out to drink. He talks to me. He helps me clean house, wash, and cook. What else could I want? I only want to see Fuerza Unida become an established organization working especially for gender equality.

This essay first appeared in *Sweatshop Warriors: Immigrant Women Workers' Take on the Global Factory* (Cambridge, MA: South End Press, 2001).

© 2001 by Miriam Ching Yoon Louie. Reprinted by permission of South End Press.

NOTES

[1] Traditional music with lyrics adapted by Arnoldo García (1994).

[2] Porfirio Díaz ruled Mexico with an iron hand from 1877 until the 1910 Mexican Revolution.

[3] José Marí, Cuba's beloved poet, writer, and leader who died May 19, 1895, fighting Spanish colonialism, coined this term and warned against U.S. designs on Latin America. See Emilio Roig de Leuchsenring, *Martí: Anti-Imperialist*. Havana: Book Institute, 1967.

[4] For example, while an estimated half-million people of Mexican origin, including U.S. citizens, were deported during the Great Depression, World War II brought Mexican workers back to the United States on a massive scale via the U.S. government-sponsored *bracero* (working arms) program, a contract labor project designed to address wartime labor shortages in agriculture. In 1954, during the post-Korean War recession, the Immigration and Naturalization Service (INS) implemented "Operation Wetback," which deported more than one million undocumented Mexican workers. At the same time nearly five million temporary labor contracts were issued to Mexican citizens between 1942 and 1964, while apprehensions of Mexican workers without documents also numbered more than five million. The bracero program ended in December 1964 due to strong opposition to abuses of migrant farm workers. See Pierrette Hondagneu-Sotelo, *Gender Transitions: Mexican Experiences of Immigration*. Los Angeles: University of California Press, 1994: 22–23; María Patricia Fernández-Kelly, *For We Are Sold, I and My People: Women and Industry in Mexico's Frontier*. Albany, NY: SUNY Press, 1983: 26. As of this writing, immigrant rights organizers feared that the George W. Bush administration will enact a new version of the bracero program to use guest migrant workers to work for one-year periods, making it difficult for them to organize without being deported, and forcing them to leave their families home in Mexico. (Author interview with Eunice Cho, National Network for Immigrant and Refugee Rights, February 26, 2001.)

[5] Michael Fix and Jeffrey S. Passel, *Immigration and Immigrants: Setting the Record Straight*. Washington, D.C.: Urban Institute,1994: 24–25.

[6] Pamela Falk, "Easing Up at the Border." *New York Times*, Feb. 15, 2001; Patrick J. McDonnel, "US Votes Could Sway Mexico's Next Elections." *Los Angeles Times*, Feb. 15, 1999.

[7] Vicki L. Ruíz, *From Out of the Shadows: Mexican Women in Twentieth Century America*. New York and Oxford: Oxford University Press, 1998: 7; Hondagneu-Sotelo: 20.

[8] By the 1920s many growers sought a more stable supply of immigrant workers, including Mexican women and children. See Hondagneu-Sotelo: 21–22. During the war years many Mexican and Chicana/o families migrated from Texas to California. As the population became increasingly urban, women moved from the fields into garment factories in the Southwest. See Teresa Amott and Julie Matthei, *Race, Gender, and Work: A Multicultural Economic History of Women in the United States*. Boston: South End, 1996: 79–80; Julie Kirk Blackwelder, *Now Hiring: The Feminization of Work in the United States, 1900–1995*. College Station: Texas A&M University Press, 1997: 71–72. For more on the role of Mexicana and Chicana labor, see feminist researchers including Patricia Zavella, *Women's Work & Chicano Families: Cannery Workers of the Santa Clara Valley*. Ithaca: Cornell University Press, 1987; Magdalena Mora and Adelaida R. Del Castillo, *Mexican Women in the United States: Struggles Past and Present*. Occasional Paper No. 2. Los Angeles: Chicano Studies Research Center Publications, University of California, 1980; Vicki L Ruíz, *Cannery Women/Cannery Lives: Mexican Women, Unionization, and the California Food Processing Industry, 1930–1950*. Albuquerque: University of New Mexico Press, 1987; Mary Romero, *Maid in the USA*. New York: Routledge, 1992; Fran Leeper Buss, ed., *Forged Under the Sun/Forjada Bajo el Sol: The Life of Maria Elena Lucas*. Ann Arbor: University of Michigan Press, 1993; Julie Kirk Blackwelder, *Women of the Depression: Caste and Culture in San Antonio, 1929–1939*. College Station: Texas A&M University Press, 1984; María Angelina Soldatenko, "Organizing Latina Garment Workers in Los Angeles," and Vicki L. Ruíz, "Las Obreras: The Politics of Work and Family," both in *Atzlan*, 20: 1 & 2, 1991. Margaret Rose, "From the Fields to the Picket Line: Huelga Women and the Boycott, 1965–1975." *Labor History*, 3, summer 1990; Margaret Rose, "'Woman Power Will Stop Those Grapes': Chicana Organizers and Middle-Class Female Supporters in the Farm Workers' Grape Boycott in Philadelphia, 1969–1970." *Journal of Women's History*, 7:4, winter 1995: 6–35; Roberto R. Calderón and Emilio Zamora, "Manuela Solis Sager & Emma Tenayuca: A Tribute," in Teresa Córdova, et al., eds., *Chicana*

Voices: Intersections of Class, Race & Gender. Albuquerque: University of New Mexico Press, 1990; Zaragosa Vargas, "Tejana radical: Emma Tenayuca and the San Antonio labor movement during the Great Depression." *Pacific Historical Review,* 66:4, Nov. 1997: 553–580; Emily Honig, "Women at Farah revisited: political mobilization and its aftermath among Chicana workers in El Paso, Texas, 1972–1992." *Feminist Studies,* 22:2, summer 1996: 425–453; M. Patricia Fernández-Kelly and Anna M. García, "Hispanic Women and Homework: Women in the Informal Economy in Miami and Los Angeles," in Eileen Boris and Cynthia R. Daniels, eds., *Homework.* Champaign: University of Illinois Press, 1989; M. Patricia Fernández-Kelly and Anna M. García, "Power Surrendered, Power Restored: The Politics of Work and Family among Hispanic Garment Workers in California and Florida," in Louise A. Tilly and Patricia Gurin, eds., *Women, Politics, and Change.* New York: Russell Sage Foundation,1992; M. Patricia Fernández-Kelly and Saskia Sassen, *A Collaborative Study of Hispanic Women in Garment and Electronic Industries: Executive Summary.* New York: Center for Latin American and Caribbean Studies, 1991.

[9] US Department of Labor, Women's Bureau, "Women of Hispanic Origin in the Labor Force." *Facts on Working Women.* Washington, D.C.: US Department of Labor, 1997. www2.dol.gov/dol/wb/public.wb_pubs/hisp97.htm.

[10] US Department of Labor, Women's Bureau: 6–7. According to US government statistics, leading occupations for "Hispanic Origin" women in 1996 were as cashiers, secretaries, sales, retail and personal service workers; janitors and cleaners; nursing aids, orderlies, and attendants; textile sewing machine operators, cleaners and servants in private households; and cooks. Segregation into lower-paying, secondary labor market jobs, layoffs and high unemployment, and lower educational attainment all combined to keep incomes low and poverty rates high for Mexicanas and Chicanas. The 1995 median incomes for full-time workers put Latinas at the bottom of the income scale, averaging $17,178. While Mexicanas and Chicanas earned only half as much as Anglo men, their male counterparts also made only 61 percent of white male earnings in 1990. Amott and Matthei: 91.

[11] Author interview with Refugio "Cuca" Arrieta, February 26, 1997.

[12] Author interview with Petra Mata, October 7, 1997.

[13] María Patricia Fernández-Kelly, *For We Are Sold, I and My People: Women and Industry in Mexico's Frontier.* Albany, NY: SUNY Press, 1983: 4 and 19–46. For more on the border economy, see Southwest Network for Environmental & Economic Justice, California Rural Legal Assistance Foundation, and Earth Island Institute, "The Border." *Race, Poverty & the Environment,* 6:4 and 7:1, summer and fall 1996.

[14] Author interview with Celeste Jiménez, February 26, 1997.

[15] Author interview with Marta Martínez, October 9, 1997.

[16] The neoliberal program was designed to address systemic problems of the 1970s, such as the falling rates of profit, global recession, oil crisis, slump in commodity prices and markets, and ballooning rates of foreign debt that international banks feared deeply indebted nations would be forced to default. See Elizabeth Martínez and Arnoldo García, "What is 'Neo-Liberalism'?" *Network News,* winter 1997: 4. Oakland: National Network for Immigrant and Refugee Rights; Jeanne Vickers, *Women and the World Economic Crisis.* London: Zed Books, 1991; Arnoldo García, "NAFTA and Neoliberalism: The Deepening Mexican Crisis." *Network News,* summer 1996: 6–7,14; "The Globalization of Asian Migrants." *Asian Migrant Forum,* Special Issue 11 (Nov. 1996). Hong Kong: Asian Migrant Center; Rubén Zamora, "Toward a Strategy of Resistance," *NACLA Report on the Americas,* 16:4, Feb. 1995: 6–21; National Commission for Democracy in Mexico, *The Zapatista Struggle.* El Paso: National Commission for Democracy in Mexico, 1997.

[17] See Pamela Sparr, ed., *Mortgaging Women's Lives: Feminist Critiques of Structural Adjustment.* London: Zed Books, 1994; Vickers, *Women and the World Economic Crisis*; Marcia Rivera, "The impact of economic globalization on women," in Eva Friedlander, ed., *Look at the World Through Women's Eyes: Plenary Speeches from the NGO Forum on Women, Beijing '95.* New York: Women, Ink, 1996; Estela Suárez Aguilar, "The impact of regional integration on women: The case of Mexico," in Friedlander, *Look at the World Through Women's Eyes.* Miriam Ching Louie and Linda Burnham, *Women's Education in the Global Economy: A Workbook.* Berkeley: Women of Color Resource Center, 2000.

[18] Lynn Stephen, *Women and Social Movements in Latin America: Power from Below.* Austin: University of Texas Press, 1997: 115.

[19] Sylvia Chant, *Women and Survival in Mexican Cities: Perspectives on Gender, Labour Markets and Low-Income Households.* Manchester: Manchester University Press, 1991, cited in Stephen, *Women and Social Movements in Latin America:* 115.

[20] Economic Intelligence Unit, *Mexico: Country Report, 1st Quarter 1994.* New York: Economic Intelligence Unit, 1994:13, cited in Stephen: 115.

[21] See Lourdes Benería and Martha Roldán, *The Crossroads of Class and Gender: Industrial Homework, Subcontracting, and Household Dynamics in Mexico City.* Chicago: University of Chicago Press, 1987. Stephen:111–157; and Ginger Thompson, "Mexico City Journal; Tortilla Rises: Must Belts Tighten?" *New York Times,* Jan. 4, 1999.

[22] Author interview with Refugio "Cuca" Arrieta, February 26, 1997.

[23] Human Rights Watch, 1996: 2.

[24] Fernández-Kelly, 1994: 263.

[25] Bustos and Palacio, eds., *El Trabajo Feminino en America Latina*:19; Miriam Ching Louie, "Life on the line." *New Internationalist,* 302, June 1998: 20–22.

[26] Fernández-Kelly, 1994: 265.

[27] Delegation meetings organized by National Interfaith Committee for Worker Justice and hosted by the Comisión para la Defensa de los Derechos Humanos del Valle de Tehuacán, Cetilizchicahualistli (Tehuacán Human Rights Commission), February 22-23, 1998. Author interviews with "María" and "Araceli," February 22, 1998. See Miriam Louie, "Life on the line." *New Internationalist,* 302, June 1998: 20–22.

[28] Author interview with Carmen Valadez and Reyna Montero, February 17, 1998 in Tijuana, Mexico. Author interview with Beatriz Alfaro, November 8, 1998. See also Carmen Valadez and Jaime Cota, "New Ways of Organizing for Women Workers in the Maquilas," in *Race, Poverty & the Environment,* 1996. Valadez and Montero explained that their group chose the feminist name, "Factor X," after the X chromosomes that distinguish females from males.

[29] Author interview with Elizabeth "Beti" Robles Ortega, July 10, 1998.

[30] Author interviews with Elizabeth Robles of SEDEPAC, July 10, 1998; Mathilde Arteaga of FAT, February 20, 1998; Carmen Valadez and Reyna Montero, February 17, 1998; and Beatríz Alfaro of Factor X, November 8, 1998.

[31] Fernández-Kelly, 1983: 62–63, 70–71. Between 1995 and 2000, for example, more than one million Mexicans moved to the northern border, largely in search of work in the maquila industry; Ginger Thompson, "Chasing Mexico's Dream Into Squalor." *New York Times,* February 11, 2001: A1.

[32] Author interview with María Antonia Flores, February 24, 1997.

[33] Delegation meeting organized by the National Interfaith Committee for Worker Justice with the Comisión para la Defensa de los Derechos Humanos del Valle de Tehuacán,

Cetilizchicahualistli (Tehuacán Human Rights Commission in Tehuacán), February 22, 1998.

[34] Miriam Ching Louie, "First International Exchange of Women Unionists." *off our backs,* 7:3, Mar. 1990: 18–19.

[35] Timothy Egan, "Teamsters and Ex-Rival Go After Apple Industry: All Out Drive to Expand Low-End Ranks." *New York Times,* Aug. 19, 1997: A10.

[36] Juan Gomez-Quiñones and David R. Maciel, "'What Goes Around, Comes Around': Political Practice and Cultural Response in the Internationalization of Mexican Labor, 1890–1997," in David R. Maciel and María Herrera-Sobek, eds., *Culture Across Borders: Mexican Immigration & Popular Culture.* Tucson: University of Arizona Press, 1998: 37–38.

[37] Hondagneu-Sotelo: 21.

[38] Alexander Monto, *The Roots of Mexican Labor Migration.* Westport: Praeger, 1994.

[39] Author interview with Celeste Jiménez, February 26, 1997.

[40] Author interview with María del Carmen Domínguez, February 24, 1997.

[41] Author interview with Carmen "Chitlan" Ibarra Lopéz, February 24, 1997.

[42] Author interview with Alicia and Carlos Marentes, February 25, 1997.

[43] Arnoldo García: 6.

[44] Fix and Passel: 25. For more on militarization of the border, see Tim Dunn and Jose Palafox, "Border Militarization and Beyond: The Widening War on Drugs." *borderlines* 66, vol 8, no 4 (April 2000); see also Michael Moore's spoof on the inconsistencies of US immigration policy, "Not on the Mayflower? Then Leave!" *Downsize This!* New York: Crown, 1996. 33–42.

[45] Wayne Cornelius, "Los Migrantes de la Crisis: The Changing Profile of Mexican Labor Migration to California in the 1980s." Paper presented at conference, Population and Work in Regional Settings, El Colegio de Michoacán, Zamora, Michoacán, Mexico, Nov. 1998, cited in Hondagneu-Sotelo: 31.

[46] Author interview with Carmen "Chitlan" Ibarra Lopéz, February 24, 1997. The 1986 Immigration Reform and Contract Act contained provisions for an amnesty-legalization program for undocumented immigrants who could prove continuous residence in the United States since January 1, 1982, and for those who could prove they had worked in US agriculture for 90 days during specific periods; Hondagnue-Sotelo: 26.

[47] Hondagneu-Sotelo: 2–20.

[48] Author interview with María del Carmen Domínguez, February 24, 1997.

[49] Author interview with Petra Mata, October 7, 1997.

[50] Author interview with Lucrecia Tamayo, March 3, 1997.

[51] Author interview with Irma Montoya Barajas, February 28, 1997.

[52] Author interview with María del Carmen Domínguez, February 24, 1997.

[53] Author interview with Ernestina "Tina" Mendoza, October 8, 1997.

[54] For more on second- and third- generation Chicanas' labor, see Romero, 1992; Patricia Zavella, *Women's Work & Chicano Families: Cannery Workers of the Santa Clara Valley.* Ithaca: Cornell University Press, 1987; and Ruiz, 1987 and 1998.

[55] Author interview with Viola Casares, October 7, 1997.

[56] See Laurie Coyle, Gail Hershatter, and Emily Honig, "Women at Farah: An Unfinished Story," in Mora and Del Castillo, *Mexican Women in the United States,* and Honig, "Women at Farah revisited."

[57] Author interview with Carmen "Chitlan" Ibarra Lopéz, February 24, 1997. For more on race and gender insensitivity and top-down leadership within the union during the Farah strike, see Coyle, Hershatter, and Honig.

[58] Author interview with Refugio "Cuca" Arrieta, February 26, 1997.

[59] Author interview with María del Carmen Domínguez, February 24, 1997.

[60] Author interview with Petra Mata, October 7, 1997.

[61] Edna Bonacich and David V. Walker, "The Role of US Apparel Manufacturers in the Globalization of the Industry in the Pacific Rim," in Bonacich, et al., eds., *Global Production: The Apparel Industry in the Pacific Rim*. Philadelphia: Temple University Press, 1994: 86–87.

[62] Sweatshop Watch, "The Globalization of Sweatshops." *Sweatshop Watch,* 6:2, summer 2000:1.

[63] Jeannie Kever, "A Thousand Lives." *San Antonio Light*, Special Series, Nov. 11–15, 1990.

[64] See Barry Bluestone and Bennett Harrison, *The Deindustrialization of America*. New York: Basic, 1982; Moore.

[65] Author interview with Viola Casares, October 7, 1997.

[66] Author interview with Petra Mata, October 7, 1997.

[67] Victoria Colliver, "Levi Strauss looking blue." *San Francisco Examiner*, May 5, 2000: B1; Karl Schoenberger, "S.F. jeans maker retools." *San Francisco Examiner*, June 25, 2000: C1, 8–9.

[68] Mark Landler, "Reversing Course, Levi Strauss Will Expand Its Output in China." *New York Times*, Apr. 9, 1998: Business section,1; Greg Frost, "Human rights groups assail Levi Strauss over China." *Reuters*, Apr. 10, 1998; Carol Emert, "Levi's Expanding in China." *San Francisco Chronicle*, Apr. 9, 1998: D1.

[69] Carol Emert, "Levi's to Slash US Plants: Competitors' foreign-made jeans blamed." *San Francisco Chronicle*, Feb. 23, 1999: A1.

[70] Sweatshop Watch, "Sweatshop Labor—Made in the USA." *Sweatshop Watch,* 4:1, spring 1998: 1–2. UNITE had initially requested that Levi's and Liz Claiborne not be included in the original suit.

[71] Sam Howe Verhovek, "Benefits of Free-Trade Bypass Texas Border Towns." *New York Times*, June 23, 1998.

[72] For information on the lawsuit filed by injured workers at Levi's plants in El Paso, see Wendy Tanaka, "Levi's sued over re-entry program: Injured workers say they're underpaid, ridiculed, harassed." *San Francisco Examiner*, Sept. 5, 1997.

[73] Greater Texas Workers Committee, "Greater Texas Workers Committee Needs Your Help!" (appeal) El Paso, 1997.

[74] La mujer Obrera, "Desastre causado por NAFTA-caused Disaster."(flyer) El Paso: La mujer Obrera, 2000.

[75] Author interview with María del Carmen Domínguez, February 24, 1997.

[76] Edna Bonacich and Richard Appelbaum, *Behind the Label: Inequality in the Los Angeles Apparel Industry*. Berkeley: University of California Press, 2000:16.

[77] Author interview with Lucrecia Tamayo, March 3, 1997.

[78] Author interview with María del Carmen Domínguez, February 24, 1997. After becoming an LMO organizer, Domínguez leafleted factory gates to inform workers of their rights during impending NAFTA closures.

[79] Author interview with María del Carmen Domínguez, February 24, 1997. See Centro de Trabajadores and La Mujer Obrera, *Escuela Popular Para Trabajadores Curriculum*. El Paso: Centro de Trabajadores and La Mujer Obrera, 1993.

[80] Author interview with María del Carmen Domínguez, February 24, 1997. The independent union adopted as its name the day in 1985 when angry workers launched the group as Mexico City sweatshop owners retrieved machines first, instead of injured seamstresses trapped under the earthquake's rubble.

[81] Author interview with Carmen "Chitlan" Ibarra Lopéz, February 24, 1997.

[82] Ibid.

[83] Verhovek.

[84] Author interview with Refugio "Cuca" Arrieta, February 26, 1997. LMO holds an annual awards dinner honoring outstanding women labor and community leaders.

[85] Author interview with María Antonia Flores, February 24, 1997. For discussion about popular education, see Paulo Freire, *Pedagogy of the Oppressed*. New York: Continuum, 1990; and Brenda Bell, John Gaventa, and John Peters, eds., *Myles Horton and Paulo Freire, We Make the Road by Walking: Conversations on Education and Social Change*. Philadelphia: Temple University Press, 1990.

[86] Author interview with María Antonia Flores, February 24, 1997.

[87] Author interview with Lucrecia Tamayo, March 3, 1997.

[88] Author interview with Viola Casares, October 7, 1997.

[89] Author interview with Viola Casares, October 7, 1997.

[90] Author interview with Marta Martínez, October 9, 1997.

[91] Author interview with Ernestina "Tina" Mendoza, October 8, 1997.

[92] Author interview with Obdulia "Obi" Segura, October 8, 1997.

[93] Author interview with Petra Mata, October 7, 1997.

[94] Author interview with Viola Casares, October 7, 1997.

[95] Author interview with Carmen "Chitlan" Ibarra Lopéz, February 24, 1997.

[96] Author interview with Viola Casares, October 7, 1997.

[97] Ibid.

[98] Author interview with Remedios García, February 26, 1997.

[99] Author interview with Carmen "Chitlan" Ibarra Lopéz, February 24, 1997.

[100] Author interview with Ernestina "Tina" Mendoza, October 8, 1997.

[101] Author interview with Petra Mata, October 7, 1997.

[102] Author interview with María del Carmen Domínguez, February 24, 1997.

[103] Author interview with Carmen "Chitlan" Ibarra Lopéz, February 24, 1997.

[104] Dr. Loco's Rockin' Jalapeño Band, 1992. Reprinted with permission.

[105] The FAT started organizing on the northern border at the General Electric plant in Júarez in 1993. On September 28, 1996, the FAT inaugurated its new center for maquila workers, the Centro de Estudios y Taller Laboral, A.C. (CETLA) [Labor Workshop and Study Center]. Author interview with Beatríz E. Lujan Uranga, CETLA organizer, Ciudad Júarez, February 25, 1997. Author interview with Mathilde Arteaga, in charge of national women's organization within the FAT, Mexico City, February 20, 1998. For more information on the FAT, see Dale Hathaway, *Allies across the Border: Mexico's "Authentic Labor Front" and Global Solidarity*. Cambridge, MA: South End, 2000.

Small Axe[1] at the Crossroads: A Reflection on African Sexualities and Human Rights

KAGENDO MURUNGI

My name is Kagendo Murungi and I am an African human rights advocate. I became engaged with formal human rights work in 1996, fresh out of graduate school, and in need of a work visa. Years before, as a women's studies major, I had been exposed to the intersectional analyses and creative expressions of lesbian feminists of color. As a feminist, I began to wonder whether human rights principles were being applied to the lives of continental Africans who loved people of the same gender and faced persecution for it. I wanted to know where this work was being done, whether it was part of the feminist movement, and how to become involved.

During my first semester in college, as I strolled through the bookstore one morning, I had been drawn to the bright orange of *Zami,*[2] and slipped it into my cart after briefly glancing at its back cover. I remember being impressed by the low wide stack of orange and marveling at the abundant visibility of a publication by a Black lesbian. My research began then and there.

As a young feminist African immigrant student coming of age in the late eighties and early nineties, I was exposed to pragmatic innovations in the application of rights frameworks to localized and transnational injustices, violations, and imbalances through my campus and community antiapartheid, anti-heterosexist, antiracist, feminist work.

The first image of an openly gay continental African I ever saw was of a smiling Simon Nkoli, the pioneering South African antiapartheid, progay-rights activist working against HIV/AIDS. My first encounter with the ramifications of visibly supporting human rights for all women without regard to their sexual orientation was in 1995, during the Fourth World Conference on Women in Beijing. For my participation in the lesbian human rights march, I was framed in a short but highly sensationalizing article in a national Kenyan daily as young, studying abroad, and surrounded by a sea of arm-waving white women (read: impressionable, too far from home for too long, whitewashed, Westernized, tokenized by a foreign colonial agenda, and confused). When I received a copy of the article from my father, I was too paralyzed by my own fear of the consequences to really consider what my parents' experience of shock, worry, anxiety, and concern must have been like at the time.

I wished then that I had emerged into a broadly recognized, obviously legitimate Pan-African, democratic, postcolonial liberation movement. I would come to understand more about the actual arena and my relative position to it in the months and years to come, through my work with human rights organizations to document the lived experiences of continental African LG (lesbian-gay) people and advocate on their behalf.

In hindsight, I have wondered how I could have somehow been more prepared for the complete damnation and stigma of dealing with sexual orientation, in any public way, as a continental African. There are few first-person descriptions of African lives in the transitions between isolation, shame, ridicule, threats, blackmail, violence, self-hatred, courage, hope, fear, activism, and love. I still search for a tangible sense of lived indigenous African same-gender loving experiences. I want to see detailed accounts, from Africans themselves, of their successful experiences navigating personal roles and community responsibilities. I want to see how people like myself have made the journey from these spaces to wholeness.

In the mid-nineties, the topic of homosexuality was introduced into the public domain in African countries at an unprecedented level. In the month prior to the Fourth World Conference on Women, President Mugabe of Zimbabwe became the first African head of state to publicly denounce and ostracize African homosexuals with such vehemence as to bring him infamy. I learned that Kenyan President Moi had responded to the international media frenzy surrounding the Beijing advocacy for lesbian rights as women's rights by ridiculing the women's rights movement, calling its agenda into question, and belittling its great strides and concrete achievements, especially in the decade since the Third World Conference on Women in Nairobi in 1985. I lamented later news about peripheral stigmatized communities and groupings in several African countries that had been pushed even further underground. Meanwhile, the vast majority of advocates for African women's rights kept any possible analytical proximity to these issues obscured, for fear of having their legitimate struggles as straight women undermined by association with lesbian issues. Open season on African homosexuals was officially underway.

Other African heads of state soon followed Mugabe and Moi's lead. Presidents Museveni of Uganda, Chiluba of Zambia, and Nujoma of Namibia (along with members of their administrations) have repeatedly weighed in with denigrations of homosexuality as "abnormal," "un-African," "anti-Christian," "opposed to African traditions," and "a disease of the decadent U.S. and West." They have increasingly called for the arrest of all known and suspected offenders. Heads of state seeking to police local women's movements, detract attention from pressing issues of national concern, and erode civil liberties—including the right to freedom of association via new restrictions on nongovernmental organization (NGO) registration—continue to take turns scapegoating African LG citizens and targeting organizations active on their behalf. State-led witch hunts via national newspapers have included orders for police to "arrest," "deport," and "imprison" homosexuals, amounting to calls on patriots to turn them in.

The expansion of civil society is not a priority for African states at this time. Mugabe, for one, has been vocal that lesbians and gays have no rights at all and his government made moves to criminalize cunnilingus among other things in the updated sexual offences act. This climate of hatred is limiting freedom of expression and association, decimating innocent lives through an increased sense of panic and heightened exposure to blackmail, threats, and violence against anyone viewed as displaying any external gender variant affect. The safety of continental African advocates for sexuality-related human rights has been extremely jeopardized. With the exception of South Africa, which provides constitutional protection from discrimination on the basis of sexual orientation in its bill of rights, African states for the most part criminalize same-sex relationships and consensual adult sexual contact through the retention of latent postcolonial penal codes.[3] Yet as South African activists and advocates continue to successfully legislate for precedent-setting cases to establish the horizontal application of the equality clause, there are already signs of the long battle ahead and deep struggle underway. At the 2001 World Conference Against Racism, in Durban, South Africa, the country's state representatives voted to bracket sexual orientation in the conference platform for action, signaling their lack of support for inclusion of the issue in the conference declaration.

In a couple of countries in the region, the introduction of legislation against intramarital rape has been coupled with new legislation against consensual adult same-sex acts between women.

The Making of an Activist

I was twenty-four years old when I formally began to do this type of work. The practical training period granted by my student visa, which permits a total of one year of off-campus, coursework-related employment, was due to expire within a matter of months. Following the emotional and political intensity of the women's conference in Beijing, I decided to engage with the substance of what was politically at stake in an issue that had impacted my life so dramatically. Accordingly, I accepted the offer of a full-time job with the International Gay and Lesbian Human Rights Commission (IGLHRC), where I would help create a regional program position including a focus on Africa. I practically stepped out of the classroom into the vast arena of international human rights. I set out to absorb as much knowledge as possible about international human rights protocols, conventions, and mechanisms; regional human rights bodies; relevant national constitutions and penal codes; allied nongovernmental organizations; and useful media outlets for the work.

My first cycle of involvement in working for sexuality-related human rights from a U.S. base exposed me to the daily rigors of working to legitimize human rights for "sexual minorities" in regions of the world where broad-based support for them is still in its infancy. I was transformed both personally and politically through my work alongside committed organizers, in which we supported and challenged each other in countless ways to expand our approaches to realizing sexuality-related human rights. The substance of my daily work included monitoring, confirming, and disseminating information about human rights violations; writing action alerts and press releases; liaising with governmental, nongovernmental, and intergovernmental organizations; and fielding information requests from media, policymakers, colleagues, and supporters.

I was fortunate to have been exposed, during my college years, to the importance of a gender perspective on human rights and its core concern with the invisibility of women's experiences in applying and developing mainstream human rights law and related United Nations mechanisms. In the historical development of human rights paradigms, women had never been conceptualized as legal subjects. The appropriate subjects of human rights law had been white, male, land-owning citizens of politically and economically independent Western nations, to whom alone the presumptions of universality and indivisibility of rights could possibly be applied. Most of the substantive norms of international human rights law had been defined in relation to individual men's experiences, and were stated in terms of discrete violations of rights in the public realm.

In order to address the equal status of women, advocates had begun undertaking conceptual shifts to explicitly and systematically address the respective socially constructed realities of women and men. The impact of culturally specific gender roles, particularly in the private sphere, had begun to be recognized as an impediment to women's full enjoyment of human rights as a condition of their equal status in society. The rights of all women to make individual sexual choices and to conceive children regardless of marital status, without the threat or reality of exposure to violence within the domestic sphere, were essential to their full enjoyment of rights to bodily integrity and health.

My involvement in the work taught me that these rights had direct implications for applying international human rights law and practice to the elimination of sexuality-related discrimination and injustice. I learned that issues of violence against women and women's reproductive freedom were inextricably linked to human rights issues related to sexuality, justice, and freedom. That African heads of state have most often addressed their antihomosexual, fundamentally antifeminist, inflammatory messages to local women's groups was no simple coincidence. Deteriorating socioeconomic conditions within African nation-states had turned African homosexuals into easy scapegoats in the face of expansions in civil society, growing movements for women's rights, constitutional reform, HIV/AIDS education and prevention, affordable drug and treatment access, postindependence land rights, and antihunger and prodemocracy movements.

I also learned that the success of work on African sexual rights should be reflected in a practical recognition of the multicentricity of issues and structures needing to be addressed. This should result in a constant structural transformation of the sites from which the work is being done as fresh analyses emerge from the work itself. In the face of the global drought of African-written publications on African same-gender desire, love, relationships, and communities, the application of human rights frameworks to the conditions of African homosexuals in independent African states necessitated linkages with African women's movements. My experiential understanding of the need for more accountable and effective applications of human rights law and practice to the lives and rights of African same-gender-loving people convinced me of the urgent need for multimedia documentation of best practices, or successful indigenous and diasporic strategies.

Working as an African immigrant on African lesbian and gay rights from a U.S.-based organization in the context of globalized economic inequities, prevailing patriarchal notions of indigenous statehood and citizenship and current resurgent fundamentalisms was an experience fraught with immense paradox. For some measure of self-protection at that time, I adapted by utilizing an alias for my professional work and seeking political asylum. Working for the implementation of human rights frameworks as a mobile, multiply located, indigenous African immigrant woman, crossing national borders, and dealing constantly with the immigration bureaucracies while speaking and acting from shifting locations, was purely exhausting and surreal. I was randomly faced with strange, harassing, and threatening phone calls and e-mails, along with the constant threat of blackmail. These tensions and perils of negotiating, juxtaposed with erasure and overexposure from within an obscured discourse, finally led to my taking a break.

I needed time to reflect on my personal and political experiences as a human rights agent. I craved channels through which to creatively claim more of my pan-African legacy. I yearned for a deeper exploration of the new dimensions of my life path. I sought more solid grounding in daily practical responsibilities for my health and to my loved ones. I left my human rights job and began searching for ways to more evenly balance my commitment to creative political work for socioeconomic justice.

With time and the patient support of friends and family, I began to understand that my isolated efforts to cope with the pressures of my experiences by fragmenting myself in practice and appearance had been based in illusion. Using my image in one place but not my name; speaking my name at one site but not my experiences; sharing my personal experience somewhere but not my full analysis anywhere—none of this had worked. Those partial identities and fractured narratives had not protected me. I had remained adrift in a hegemonic discourse on my rights, unprepared as yet to coherently contribute to shifting it. When I stopped working for the realization of identity-based civil and political human rights, it was because that daily work was failing to sustain me in basic ways. I needed the close proximity of people who shared more aspects of my daily experience. Thus, I relocated to the northeastern U.S., with its abundance of first-generation African immigrant communities. I sorely needed social and cultural infrastructural support for my whole black African self.

In downtown Manhattan and Brooklyn, I linked up with a group of pan-African performance artist friends who were creatively expressing themselves on issues of gender, sexuality, and nationality. They generously took me into their fold, and I joined them at rehearsals and discussions, primarily as an inquisitive voyeur into aspects of my own life. I attended social gatherings of pan-African friends of numerous sexualities and gendered realities, where we watched and critiqued gender-sexuality dimensions and stylistic devices in cinematic depictions of Africans; performed poetry; shared stories; flirted; danced; laughed; ate; and created community. There, so far away from "home," many of us unable to travel for long periods due to fluctuating immigration status, we bravely pieced our psyches together, contemplated wholeness, and created family. Witnessing my community's basic collective need for safety, trust, friendship, creative self-expression, and economic autonomy, and our individual contentions with that need, reaffirmed my sense of social and cultural human rights as primary to and indivisible from civil and political rights in this country as well as in our countries of origin.

This group of Northeastern artist-activists has initiated successful translocal initiatives (i.e., initiatives between localities rather than across national boundaries), which continue to be supported by the voluntary labor and generous donations of our translocal networks, along with assistance from progressive international philanthropic and human rights organizations. We are succeeding in mobilizing increasing funds in support of African political and sexual dissidents displaced due to their work on sexuality-related human rights. These courageous and resourceful men and women are survivors of harassment, detention, torture, and rape. The significance of our autonomous agency—our individual and collective choices as African communities—is evident, since our comrades often have no other immediate recourse to justice, even when their cases are already well documented by human rights organizations (whose missions nonetheless don't include the systematic release of emergency funds for sexual and political dissidents in need).

Linking the Past to the Future

Human rights discourses deployed in response to the current conditions of African all-sexual people too easily obscure the agency of these very subjects. The decontextualized visibility of African homosexuals, in the absence of sustained, autonomous educational efforts, limits our local and translocal organizing potential. While we remain exposed to all manner of personal policing, including the constant threat and reality of exposure and blackmail, we cannot afford to have our courageous life stories and initiatives erased, sidelined, or subsumed by the well-intentioned agendas of others. We must remain vigilantly conscious of our historical relationship to movements, both in the U.S. and in our countries of origin, that have had broader visions for social transformation.

Our historical legacy as African all-sexual[4] people includes victories over slavery, colonization, and apartheid; and centuries of experience with multipronged organizing for fundamental social, economic, and political transformation and freedom for all. Our conceptual approaches to organizing draw from the multilingual, interdependent, intertextual, intersectional strategies of pan-African, Black, and Third World feminist movements. It is essential that our progressive U.S.-based allies contextualize themselves relative to this country's history of genocidal war against indigenous peoples and enslavement of Africans, and recognize the centrality of white supremacist ideology to the maintenance of white structural privilege and U.S. capitalist expansion.

While current mainstream LGBT and human rights publications may provide some interesting and even useful perspectives on our lives and organizing, they too casually uphold white male structural privilege. These purported defenders of our existence and rights reveal their cynicism and myopia when they apply paternalistic packaging to African all-sexual experiences without explicit and systematic consideration of our complex autonomous agency in perilous circumstances. The survival of all-sexual

Africans working under life-threatening conditions in fragile coalitions urgently requires demonstrated recognition from our allies that the eradication of white supremacy and male supremacy goes hand in hand with the eradication of heterosexual supremacy.

Our daily material realities and political economies as migrants, along with our ideological convictions and political alliances as Africans, influence our social language, cultural expression, and pragmatic parameters as agents for change. In September, 1999, a tricontinental coalition of African, Black, and migrant LGBT people realized a timely cultural intervention at the first Africa-based International Lesbian and Gay Association (ILGA) Conference in Johannesburg, South Africa. With the support of the Astraea International Fund for Sexual Minorities (for whom I worked as a program consultant the following year), members of our New York-based African LGBT network, the Johannesburg-based Gay and Lesbian Organization of the Witwatersrand (GLOW), and Amsterdam-based Black and migrant LGBT group "Strange Fruit the Real" planned and created a cultural *free zone* dubbed "Unifying Links," which served as a clearinghouse for the experiences and needs of lesbian feminists of color attending the conference.

A group of us, hoping to inspire self-expression among global lesbians of color and our friends and allies, drafted and circulated a list of goals and strategies for our multimedia intervention and requested input and participation from our allies. Our explicitly antiracist and profeminist agenda prioritized self-empowerment, visibility, autonomous and equal participation on our own terms, the creation of space for networking and creative cultural self-representation, monitoring and documentation of the conference itself, and good old-fashioned fun. To this end, we secured and decorated a room in the conference hotel in which we screened independently produced videos reflecting our various communities, maintained tables and wall spaces where allies could display their organizational materials and creative works, and sustained a critical dialogue on issues arising at the conference as well as issues crucial to local and translocal organizing by lesbian feminists of color.

Africanizing Sexual Rights

As we know, many African states remained colonies of European countries during the drafting of the Universal Declaration of Human Rights, and only became party to it after gaining independence during the last half-century. This is the context of the on-going debate regarding questions of universality versus cultural relativism in the application of human rights frameworks. Global economic shifts of expanding capitalism in postcolonial African states keep them in unequal political relationships with Western industrialized nations, further complicating the application of human rights frameworks. These complexities, applied to the realization of sexuality-related human rights, require that we utilize interdisciplinary approaches that consciously explore the multiple dimensions of social oppression. Such approaches allow us to raise the following questions (among others):

How can we work collaboratively from a U.S. base with indigenous community-based organizations and individuals without usurping their territory and revictimizing them?

How can we utilize the human rights framework and its reliance on the identification of victimized individuals and groups (in this case lesbians, gays, bisexuals, transgendered people) while maintaining our critique of identity-based sexualities and the human rights framework itself?

How can we promote geographical equity and autonomy by contributing to the greater redistribution of economic resources?

How can we centralize issues of racist violence, xenophobia, and police brutality, anti-immigrant backlash, and racial profiling, all of which impact our daily lives, as part of a two-way information exchange?

How can we sustain autonomous networks and groups of pro-sexual rights and LGBT people of color as we maintain our employment in institutions with various agendas?

How do we access various sites and channels of communication to document and publicize our lived experiences and analyses?

The human rights questions in African sexuality-related issues must be related to practical, effective antiracist and anti-imperialist liberation politics. This requires conscious effort. One example of success in such efforts has been the application of feminist analyses to issues of women's agency and power in sexuality- and gender-related violence, resulting in the transformation of language by movements against sexual harassment and assault. The battered women's movement, in particular, has succeeded in changing the terminology from "victim" to "survivor" when referring to women who have been subjected to violence and abuse. Black feminist and Civil Rights movement analyses have also illuminated the discursive limitations and adverse collective psychic impact of referring to African Americans as a "minority group" rather than as members of "underrepresented," "underresourced," and "overexploited" communities. These sorts of discursive shifts necessarily disassociate conditions of social, economic, and political injustice from membership in particular ethnic groups or inhabitants of particular geographical locations.

The application of racial equality and the discursive empowerment of indigenous Africans, along with substantive measures to ensure gender equity, are inextricable from human rights approaches to sexual freedom. Only such multipronged approaches can hope to begin to surmount the obstacles of conservative cultural, religious, and political constraints on sexuality-related rights. Sexuality-related human rights are not merely an issue of sexual identity. Sexuality-related human rights practices, which require a public association with sexual orientation or membership in a "sexual minority group," must therefore be problematized. Failure to do so risks the loss of varied social, cultural, and economic dimensions in meeting challenges to the general realization of basic rights and fundamental freedoms.

In order to mobilize timely responses to the antihomosexual witch-hunts in our countries of origin, African all-sexual human rights workers based in the U.S. have found it strategically useful to develop ties with all-sexual organizers on the African continent and antiheterosexist allies throughout the world. There is an increasing demand for swift and coordinated resettlement assistance for political dissidents active in sexuality-related human rights work who are fleeing from their countries of origin. Integral to this is the need for the establishment and expansion of emergency funds for sexual and political dissidents and for indigenous organizers in the sexual rights arena.

If we are to destigmatize the defense of human rights for African homosexuals, we must first recognize that any African who does so publicly is immediately marked as a homosexual and directly subjected to social stigmatization. This is certainly true for Africans in Africa, but also for those of us in the diaspora. My three-year tenure as Africa/Middle East/Caribbean regional specialist at the International Gay and Lesbian Human Rights Commission made me the only "Kenyan lesbian" (as identified through Web searches) easily associated with lesbian and gay rights via internet searches, which contributed significantly to my duress at the time. This is clearly not helpful in sustaining an effective sexuality-related human rights movement. Ensuring African autonomy in self-identification is therefore crucial to this work, and requires the broad implementation of standards for security and the protection of confidentiality. These standards must include freedom in the selection of public identities, including the use of aliases as basic security prerogatives.

People-centered human rights advocacy work that protects freedom of expression should permit and encourage practitioners to frame and promote their work as they see fit. For example, when I returned to the IGLHRC as Program Officer for Africa and Southwest Asia, I elected to identify myself via a theoretical network (the Africa Southwest Asia Network) for purposes of identification with a collective rather than individual purpose. I also chose to identify myself as an African feminist as more practical and strategic than a public identification in terms of sexual identity in a limiting mainstream rights context. My work at IGLHRC evolved primarily into initiating locally directed applied research project partnerships combating violence against women ("curative rape") and between women (domestic violence), as well as fostering human rights and "personal growth" for women of various sexualities in Africa. To identify myself more strongly with African women's and gender rights activists, I have also at the time of writing succeeded in changing my professional title to "Africa Program Officer." Women's work for gender justice is a fine African tradition with which to ally myself as an African woman working from a U.S.-based gay and lesbian human rights organization.

Action networks have worked effectively as tools for postcolonial Third World feminist organizing for a few decades now. Issue-based and regional translocal networks empower collaborative work, while supporting the autonomy of the respective constituencies involved. They help mobilize political will and economic resources in urgent matters; expedite communications; and offer opportunities for social, cultural, and analytical support, among other things. In work on human rights issues related to African sexuality, region-identified action networks offer practical discursive and security platforms for promoting public identification with contentious issues. Political groups working on these issues are challenged to heightened creativity, in order to prevent the imposition of dangerous sexual identity labels that can mark particular subjects for discrimination and restricted mobility. Community strategies for action, such as identification and linkages with regional and issue-based networks, offer the advantages of depersonalized visibility and broader bases from which to advocate for justice.

We really need to conduct basic needs assessment surveys within indigenous and diasporic African all-sexual communities. Meanwhile, other documented needs include funding, technical support, strategies for overcoming language barriers, leadership development, human rights trainings, publications on similar lived experiences, multimedia production and distribution, speaker and performance venues, development and promotion of standards for the protection of intellectual property, "South-South" dialogues, and "Third World within–Third World without" dialogues.[5]

Bringing It All Back Home

My political methodology has been rooted in U.S.-based Black and Third World feminist principles and pan-African feminist strategies for translocal human rights work. My spirit has been sustained through creative expressions of community organizing and self-expression in my local neighborhoods. Being involved in aspects of video distribution and production along with poetry writing and performance have provided me with necessary sites for community interface and grounded inspiration. If sexuality-related human rights are to be equitably realized by Africans on the continent and in the diaspora, cultural agency is a basic necessity, along with autonomously documented knowledge and sustained material support of community-building initiatives.

My experiences have taught me that efforts to link human rights issues to our communal realities as human beings are about process and perception. Our familial processes impact on community perceptions and vice versa. We must always remain critically conscious of our complex and sometimes contradictory subjective positions in human rights advocacy. Human rights advocates are a diverse body of subjects, with varied perspectives based on their communal realities. In the development of appropriate methodology, effective human rights strategies must address both the experiential needs of the subjects under consideration and the content of specific rights. As new strategies are developed and implemented, the current climate of volatility in the sexuality-related African human rights arena necessitates particular sensitivity to the inclusion of African all-sexuals in decision-making positions. In this way, the benefits of deep analysis in consciously applied knowledge, along with those of content production and distribution, can be applied to expanded rights concepts and discourses.

Confronting the stigma, silence, and denial related to African homosexuality has challenged me to work to reverse the results of negative external identifications, incomplete self-definitions, fossilized attitudes, and static histories by naming what is connected and what matters to me. I returned to formal human rights work after three years of creative work for economic, social, and cultural pan-African human rights from a variety of geographical locations. I am blessed with a renewed sense of hope, a clearer vision of some next steps to implement, the close support of friends, and new daily rituals for self-care.

NOTES

[1] From a Bob Marley lyric:

> Why boasteth thyself, oh evil men,
> Playing smart and not being clever?
> I say you're working iniquity to achieve vanity, yeah,
> But the goodness of JAH JAH endureth forever.
> If you are the big tree,
> We are the small axe.
> Sharpened to cut you down,
> Ready to cut you down.

For the full text, see http://www.bobmarley.com/songs/songs.cgi?smallaxe.

[2] Audre Lorde, *Zami: A New Spelling of My Name.* Santa Cruz: Crossing Press, 1983.

[3] For information on sections of African legislation relating to sexuality, see the following Web sites:

http://www.iglhrc.org/news/factsheets/sodomy.html; http://www.iglhrc.org/news/factsheets/990604-antidis.html; http://www.polity.org.za/govdocs/constitution/saconst.html. The country that now criminalizes sexual acts between women as well as men is Botswana. The Sexual Offences Act amended in February of 1998 in Section 164 and 167 now uses gender-neutral language to criminalize "unnatural acts" and "gross indecency."

[4] "All-Sexual" is a term used in the Caribbean Forum of Lesbians, All-Sexuals & Gays (C-FLAG) network to indicate that it considers all-sexual behavior to be part of a sexual continuum in which classifications such as "gay," "lesbian," and "bisexual" often cannot be rigidly applied. The terms "men who have sex with men" and "women who have sex with women" are attempts to move around these rigid classifications. The term "all-sexual" refers not only to biological and sexual characteristics, but also to social attitudes related to them. "All-Sexuals" therefore refers to same-gender-loving persons whose actions are not in violation of the Universal Declaration of Human Rights, that is to say, whose actions are not abusive to minors and other persons who are in dependent circumstances or of diminished capacity, or otherwise in violation of the rights or personal dignity of any person. See http://www.jflag.org/misc/allsexual.htm.

[5] Third World Within (TWW) is a New York City-based network of People of Color organizations. Their purpose is to highlight "domestic" issues resulting from U.S. racism and economic restructuring, to educate and mobilize communities of color around these issues, and to work in solidarity with activists, organizers, and communities in the Third World and around the world to demand accountability from the U.S. government and international institutions for their role in developing and maintaining policies and institutions destructive to the Third World and Third World communities in the U.S.

Imagine

NELLIE WONG

Imagine if all the billions that companies pay their executives
     were used to improve education

Imagine if the millions spent on each Osprey
     were used to pay for health care for the poor

Imagine if all the money that Microsoft's lawyers spent on its defense
     were used to help Angolans get clean water

Imagine if Gov. Pataki of New York dramatically increased housing and
     other services for former residents of state mental institutions

Imagine if New York City's twenty-five thousand mentally ill prisoners
each year
     were released with their medications and a plan for housing
     and future treatment

Imagine if a disabled, nontraditional tradeswoman worked at a city utility
     that had preventative measures in the first place

Imagine if Mumia and the other thousands of political prisoners were freed
     and helped to work with youth in the inner cities

Imagine if Mark Garcia were not beaten to death by the SF Police
     and he were here, right now, talking to us

Imagine if the mayor of Philadelphia stopped making excuses as to why
     a dozen police officers beat up Thomas Jones for car-jacking

Imagine if New York City's police officers did not pump forty-one bullets
     into Amadou Diallo for pulling out his wallet

Imagine if the American Disabilities Act really worked for the poor,
     the mentally disabled, women, people of color, and immigrants

Imagine if Helen Keller hadn't pinpointed war, poverty and unsafe
    working conditions as the causes of disabling injuries
    and discrimination against the injured

Imagine if Latino immigrants didn't have to stand all day on Cesar
    Chavez waiting for someone to hire them so they could feed
    their families

Imagine if our for-profit system was dismantled and replaced by
    an economic system that put people over profits

Imagine if all forms of discrimination were eliminated and everyone
    had a right to free health care and education as they do in
    revolutionary Cuba

Imagine if everyone had a right to a living wage and full economic
    independence and the right to safe and healthy working conditions

Imagine if women had full control over our bodies and full
    reproductive rights for disabled women

Imagine if there were no more wars and the money was used for
    building schools, libraries, community and job-training centers

Imagine if every house, building, facility, airplane, train, bus, and van
    had access for people with disabilities

Imagine if drug addiction, alcoholism, and mental impairment
    were not treated as crimes but as illnesses to be treated with
    humane care

Imagine if community-based care were available to all of the disabled,
    the homeless, veterans, elders, youth, parolees, queers, people of
    color, and single mothers

Imagine if everyone truly had equal opportunity to develop
their creativity and highest human potential

Imagine if the profit motive was taken away from prostitution,
AIDS prevention, and housing the homeless

Imagine the disabled rights movement being seen and heard

Imagine the other side

Imagine socialism

Imagine feminism

Imagine revolution

Imagine

© 2001 by Nellie Wong.

Inside-Out and Upside-Down:
An Interview with Trailblazer Anne Braden

JUNE ROSTAN

June Rostan, director of the Southern Empowerment Project, talks about mul-
tiracial organizing with one of the South's amazing freedom fighters. This
interview was conducted in August 2000.

In 1954, when black people couldn't use most public facilities or buy homes
in segregated neighborhoods, Andrew and Charlotte Wade asked a white
couple, Anne and Carl Braden, to buy a house on their behalf in an all-white
area of Louisville, Kentucky. The Bradens bought the house, and the uproar
that followed changed all their lives. The house was bombed. No one was
hurt, but the perpetrators were never caught. Instead, the state charged Anne
and Carl with sedition—Carl was sentenced to fifteen years in prison and
served eight months. Anne wrote a book about this incident, *The Wall
Between,* in 1958. It was reissued by the University of Tennessee in 1999 and
2000 with a must-read, forty-page epilogue.[1] The bombing catapulted Anne
into the freedom movement, and since that time she has been at the heart of
anything that has to do with race and justice in the South.

Anne and Carl formed a lifetime partnership of social activism and were so
committed to self-determination and leadership for people of color that for
years they were regarded as pariahs by white liberals and castigated as communists. In the late forties and early fifties, they worked with civil rights and
labor groups in Louisville. In the 1960s, they staffed the extraordinary
Southern Conference Educational Fund (SCEF), and were central to the civil
rights movement. After SCEF broke up in the early 1970s, Anne helped
found the Southern Organizing Committee for Economic and Social Justice
(SOC). Seventy-six at the time of this interview, she was still working with
SOC and the Kentucky Alliance Against Racist and Political Repression in
Louisville. Anne has set the benchmark for white, antiracist organizing in the
South for more than fifty years.

You have an incredible ability to look at people who opposed you and Carl, to
understand where they are coming from and not be judgmental. How were you
able to do that?

I never did hate those people who opposed us in the fifties because I knew
that I could have been in their position. I was just lucky that I was able to
break out of being white in a racist society and privileged in a classist society.

The "open sesame" for my generation was race. Once we could under-stand what racism had done, then everything fell like a house of cards. It opened everything to question: economic injustice, foreign policy. If you don't understand white supremacy, then you do not understand the country. The first thing I had to realize was that the people I loved—my family, my friends, the people running Alabama—were wrong. But once you realized that, it was not hard to realize that the people running the national govern-ment were wrong too.

What did your generation learn from the civil rights movement of the fifties and sixties?

The sixties were so important because the country had to confront the issue of racism, which it was built on. When African Americans began to organize, they were the foundation. The foundation moved and the whole building shook. That is why people were able to organize against the war. That's why women were able to organize. All that happened because of the black movement.

I think our country was moving tentatively in the sixties toward turning its assumptions, policies, and values upside down. Southern whites of my generation who got involved in the civil rights movement turned our lives around. What we did is what this whole country needs to do: turn itself inside-out and upside-down and build a society that is not based on racism. You have to come to terms with this: That the society you live in is totally wrong and that it is destroying you as well as people of color. I have not overcome racism in myself. I have worked at it for fifty years but I still see life through white eyes.

How do we get other low-income and working-class white people to start working to overcome white supremacy?

If you want to get white people involved in the antiracist movement, the starting point is not to ask them to give up their privileges. That is not a good organizing approach. White people who are struggling economically or living in terrible poverty have a hard time seeing that they have white privilege.

A lot of white working-class people have been turned off to our movements because they have been put down. There is an assumption among white intellectuals who think they are liberals or antiracists that all working-class and poor whites are flaming racists. They may have been some of the people who joined the Klan, but I have met just as many flaming racists in the country-club set.

Why do you say that white people have to come to their understanding of racism, not just through an intellectual experience, but through something emotional?

Because racism goes so deep. The kind of emotional experience that can make a difference varies with different people. Some get there through personal relationships. I didn't meet just one person, I met a movement. A community has to go through a process of turning itself inside-out. I think of Birmingham—it's not perfect, but it's better than a lot of places in the South today. It went through the turmoil. White people in Birmingham in the sixties had to look at what the heck was going on. You had four little girls killed when the church was bombed; you had dogs and fire hoses turned on black protesters.

Do you think we can build multiracial social justice and organizing groups in the South?

The South is not black and white any more. We have growing Latino and Asian populations. And the Native Americans were always here, but we didn't know it until that movement surfaced visibly in the sixties. To build multiracial organizations in a racist society is virtually impossible. Impossible means it just takes a little longer. I tell people not to get discouraged if they try and fail, to try again.

I am part of two organizations that are really interracial, multi-ethnic, and definitely led by people of color. They are the Southern Organizing Committee for Economic and Social Justice (SOC) and the Kentucky Alliance Against Racism and Repression. We need more whites who are willing to take action and to serve in organizations with people of color in the leadership. Those of us who are white have to be careful that we aren't trying to dominate. We are so used to running things.

In the late forties when it was so repressive, the Southern Conference for Human Welfare (SCHW), which was started in 1938 as an economic justice group, reorganized into SCEF around a single issue: race. There were other issues, but Jim Crow segregation had to be dealt with first. SCEF was biracial from the beginning. Its outreach was to white Southerners. We wanted to get them involved in action on picket lines and going to jail, not just sitting around in human relations meetings. When the movement won the lunch counter battle and voting rights, SCEF began to shift back to more economic justice issues, as the black movement did. But then SCEF broke up in 1973. I came to the conclusion that the basic weakness in SCEF was that it became overwhelmingly white. We got this great influx of whites, after SNCC (the Student Non-Violent Coordinating Committee) told whites to go organize whites. SCEF became a battleground for white people to fight out their quarrels. The real purpose got lost.

I made up my mind then that I would never spend another minute of my life building something that was all or mostly white because it is not going to change anything. It is a waste of time.

We deliberately organized SOC as an interracial group. It has evolved into an organization that is clearly led by people of color.

What about groups that are made up of people of color only?

People of color need their own groups. African Americans and Latinos need their own separate groups. They need self-determination. They need to come together because they are oppressed. White people are not oppressed as white people. That is the difference.

Both the SCHW and SCEF, though interracial, were white-dominated. Yet I kept working to keep them going. I was so determined that we needed some kind of network in the South. I was willing to work for nothing and scrape by. I think SOC may be the only interracial group in the country that has evolved from a white-dominated group to a people of color-led group, and I am very proud of that. In the mid-eighties some strong African American leadership emerged and took over.

The whole history of the South has been littered with the ruins of movements that brought disenfranchised blacks and whites together and broke up on the shoals of racism. When the chips were down, whites always fled back to the security of their white skins. Principled black-white coalitions don't work unless there is a strong group in the black community first. The coalitions that fall apart are the white-dominated ones. Once the blacks are well organized and they have their own organizations, then the power relationships change.

What is SOC doing now?

Very exciting work on environmental justice with grassroots groups, primarily African American, all over the South. These are people who live on the fence lines, next to these industries and dumps. They are not civil rights veterans; they are new people. It's a whole new army. Some of these new leaders are becoming volunteer organizers. My husband used to say it will take fifty thousand organizers to organize the South. I don't care if we put all of our organizations together, we can't do it with just paid staff. Any social justice movement that made any difference had lots of people involved as volunteers.

Do you think it is important to keep bringing in new people?

That is the biggest weakness of our great progressive movement. We are reluctant to reach the people who are not involved. It's worst among whites who consider themselves antiracist. They don't want to talk to white people who are not involved. Most whites who come into anything interracial go through the stage of working mainly in black communities because it is more comfortable and exciting. That is what I did years ago.

In 1951, I wrote to William Patterson, head of the Civil Rights Congress, about what I was doing, including going to some of the black churches. He wrote me and said, "You don't need to be going to the black churches, Anne. They don't need you to tell them that they are oppressed. You need to be talking to the white churches." That changed my life right then.

That was when I really decided that my mission was to get out and talk to white people. That is why I was startled when all these white folks in SNCC got upset when they were told to go organize white people. Didn't they know that was what they ought to be doing?

My father, a working-class white man, said to me in the late sixties, "There's a revolution coming in this country and I don't have anything to lose from it." Then ten years later, his attitude was altogether different. He'd gotten this sense that blacks had asked for too much, that they had gone too far. What do you think happened to change his mind?

He did not come to that conclusion by himself. That was the propaganda that was being put out. The people in control knew what to do to keep control. This was what was being said in academic circles, in government, in the media, everywhere else. He heard that. He didn't think that up himself.

There was a campaign for the minds of white people and a campaign of repression against blacks. People don't understand the repression that happened in the late sixties. That movement did not just go away. It was destroyed by repression. They chopped off the black organizers.

It was irrevocably damaging to the country that the movement was blunted at that point. It really was merging the issues. It was taking on economic justice. The unfinished business of the civil rights movement was economic justice.

What is our hope for the future?

I think that there will be a new mass movement. I have been part of three mass movements in my life, times of great drama when things really explode: the upsurge of the fifties and sixties, the anti-Vietnam War movement, and the Jesse Jackson campaigns of the eighties. They were movements that really changed things.

At the first meeting of the Jackson delegates in 1984, there were four hundred people. People started talking about what was happening in their communities. There were white coal miners from Appalachia, Latinos from New Mexico, people from all over the country. To me, one of the political tragedies of the twentieth century is that the grassroots base of the Jackson movement collapsed after 1988. If it had kept going, we'd have a viable third force and an alternative to the two main parties.

Mass movements usually start from a specific struggle. The main thing you do, when you don't see the mass movement you have been hoping for, is work to build struggles around specific issues. We've spent lots of time in Louisville around the police brutality issue. We do the battles at our doorsteps, bringing new people in around specific issues. They are the building blocks. I don't know when this will explode into a movement. Nobody thought that Montgomery, cradle of the Confederacy, would be the place where the movement would break out in the 1950s.

For whites, none of this will change unless we deal with white supremacy. It's fine to sit and talk and get your heart in the right place, but it ain't going to have one bit of impact. Whites need to be visible and engaged. We have to break that solid white wall of resistance.

Do we talk about race or do we just bring people together to organize around common issues?

You have to attack the policies and practices of the society you live in. There are two different forms of attack: the common-ground issues and the frontal attack on white supremacist policies and practices. In any community, you need organizations that are doing both. Living-wage campaigns are common-ground issues. Race and economic justice in this country are so intertwined that you can hardly talk about any economic issue where racism and white supremacy are not also involved. You can deal with a common-ground issue and not only leave race out of it but also leave people of color out of it. And then you don't win. We need an organization in every community that makes a frontal attack on white supremacy. Those organizations need to involve white people and be led by people of color.

This article first appeared in *ColorLines* (Spring 2001).

© 2001 by *ColorLines*. Reprinted by permission of the publisher.

NOTE

[1] Anne Braden, *The Wall Between*. Knoxville: University of Tennessee Press, 1999.

Justice Journals–Palestine

SHARON JAFFE

September 2001

Today, the Shabbas preceeding Rosh Hashanah: a moment to pause, to appreciate the holiness of life in all its forms; a moment to pause before beginning the focus on my ancestors' stories, stories about learning from mistakes, stories about moving forward in life with a renewed awareness of innocence; a moment to pause before entering the formal practice of forgiveness, personal and communal; a moment just days after the horror of Tuesday. Tuesday, September 11. In my home city. People dead, hurt, grieving, terrorized, fearful, watchful, offering, with generosity, offering everything possible. What to call that horror. A *shoah*, a destruction? A *matsav*, a situation? An act of war? Which war? A war begun ten years ago when I wrote what would have been the epilogue to this collection of stories and thoughts? The Persian Gulf War? Next phase? A war begun long, long ago, a war between the haves and the have-nots? A war between capitalist imperialists and fundamentalists? Between fundamentalists and fundamentalists? A war between those who use power as a commodity to exert control and those whose powers generate community?

"War is not a path to peace." Words on a sign, blue words on a bright pink poster. The words smear in a light rain. It is Friday afternoon. Sixty people stand at an intersection in Minnesota at a vigil called by Minnesota Jews for a Just Peace. Our signs proliferate today. New Yorkers: "Our cries of grief are not a cry for war." Gandhi's message to the warmongers mixes with our usual "End the Israeli Occupation of Palestine." The light rain dampens the outer layer of my jacket. My insides are warm and dry. I am heartened by those of us standing in the rain. I am heartened by people walking by or slowing down in their cars and trucks; even city buses slow down, as people show their solidarity. Peace signs with fingers, horns honking loud, people grinning, people sticking their heads out the windows shouting at us *Yes, peace now!*

My face is wet from tears. I hug Polly, a cofounder of Women Against Military Madness. I hug Faadia, current chair of the American Arab Anti-Discrimination Committee. Lesbian feminists from twenty years ago, other activists from thirty-five, forty years ago punctuate the silence with chants that reverberate back through the antinuke, antiwar, civil rights movements: "The people united will never be defeated." I hug Michelle from the Anti-War Committee and I meet students from nearby colleges. I hug Soraya, who wears a black *chadour*. My face is wet from tears. I notice that Miriam didn't go out of town. She and her sister walk towards us. They wear bright red shirts over rain jackets. Bold white letters on the bright red spell out different messages on each shirt, they are a moving couplet: "I love Jews" on one, "I love Arabs" on the other.

At the vigil's end we huddle in the boulevard. After a few people speak, we form a circle. I realize no one wants to leave, not really. We have created a community, not only one united in grief for those killed in New York City or in D.C., or in Pennsylvania, but a community united to stand for life, all life. A community knowledgeable about the possibility of nuclear or biological or cultural destruction. A community grounded in the active labor of *love*. Love for a sustainable, just, equitable, affirming world. Yes, world. Big vision is needed at this moment. I ask those in the circle to follow me as I share a lesson gleaned from some American Indian and Pagan activists. I slowly wind the circle inward, a spiral dance, so each of us can look the other in the eyes, clasp hands, offer sanctuary, solace, gratitude, and appreciation.

That experience of community helps me finish writing this piece. I offer it to you, personally and collectively. One language in which I am fluent is the language of vigils, street theater, small and large political demonstrations. I recognize there are other languages, other stories. I come from traditions of people who love stories. Not for nothing are Jews stereotyped as people of the book. Not only do Jews love stories; feminists swap stories to map the present and the past, and to stand as guideposts for the future. Here are stories of activism. Outdated in some ways. In other ways, these tales of resistance hopefully will encourage other acts of resistance. These stories center around the years between the first Intifada and the Persian Gulf War. They echo backwards and they come forward. For me, those years dropped like an agate into a backwoods lake. The waves of change shift the shoreline, an intended, necessary change.

Blessed be, *b'shalom*.

Summer 1988

Today is a difficult day to stand downtown in front of the federal building holding a beautiful banner that reads "Israel: End the Occupation." In this heat sweat pours down my face. My shirt sticks to my skin. I worry if passers-by will avoid the vigil due to the large wet spots under my arms. The drought this summer in Minneapolis, worries about food and work, economy, and ecology all bear down upon me. I stand here with women who are Jews, Palestinians, and women who don't have such an obvious identity marker. When I call them secular Christian Americans they squirm, hesitate, and say, "I suppose so."

We're more comfortable with the term "white." Antiracism is another backdrop to the passion that brings us here. The vigil is strong; the heat strong; the alliance between women tenuous, a loose braid. We stand week after week for different reasons, for different visions, but we stand together.

We stand in a semicircle so we can hear each other while holding the banner for the public to view. Each week during the vigil women speak from the heart. This week we speak about the theme of home and homelessness. As we speak with each other, each woman has to strain to hear intimate words over the traffic noise, a nearby jackhammer, and the puzzled or hostile comments of people walking by.

I begin. I cook for residents in a transitional home for homeless women. These women recover from a terrible litany of violence: the specifics of woman-hating, racism, poverty, chemical dependency, satanic cult abuse, discrimination against people with a mental-health diagnosis…. Every day I cook for women who look to me as the mother in the kitchen. It's a hard job emotionally and concretely. I listen to and notice how much women need a stable, consistent, affirming presence. While peeling carrots I note the centrality of fear, how easy it is for fear to pattern their habits, to recreate in small and large ways the cycles of violence. I appreciate the difficulty in learning a life-affirming stance in a hostile, woman-hating culture. A switch in perspective is hard for anyone to maintain.

Staying within a budget of $1.50 per person per meal is difficult. We are dependent on charitable donations and government subsidies. Donations come from people or corporations that get rid of surplus. They don't ask what we need. I get choices: should I accept the donated apples the public won't eat because they've been sprayed with Alar? Government subsidies are a joke. This year there is no cheese. The government workers say it's because of the drought. I buy cheese for myself at the local coop. There is cheese, but not for poor people. The government, the economy, the dominant culture, none of it supports people I know, let alone celebrates people for being alive, creative, loved, and loving.

At the vigil a white woman tells of growing up in a small western Minnesota town. She came slowly to understand that her hometown, her cozy small town on the prairie, stood on what she came to call stolen land. Land stolen from neighbors she didn't know and wasn't supposed to know. She talks about her efforts to stay truthful. She learns about history, about Anishinabe people, about U.S. history. She reels off book titles. She says she begins to trust where this learning will lead.

Another white woman launches into the telling. She speaks about her work with the city. She researches zoning regulations and forecasts housing needs to city planners. As she speaks, she realizes that she herself is two paychecks away from living on the streets. She pours out her frustration with a city that tears up low-income housing for a sports stadium.

We listen to the city. It is hot. A Jewish woman tells briefly about being the daughter of a Holocaust survivor. Home to her is fragile. Since home can be taken away, her relationship to a specific land is negligible. Another Jewish woman speaks of growing up in St. Paul, where her grandparents settled in the 1870s. She grew up in her grandparents' home and identifies as a Midwestern American.

A Palestinian woman speaks of her home, a place where her family had lived for generations, centuries. Razed by Israeli Jews in the Israeli Defense Force. She speaks of pain and resistance. She remembers her home in Palestine; she does not recognize the political legitimacy of its current occupant. In this way she refuses to stay invisible, to be perceived as less than human. She says, "I wish it was beyond necessity to state my humanity and my dignity".

October 1982

On the day after Yom Kippur, 1982, I go to work at a restaurant in Philadelphia. A coworker asks me what I did yesterday, why I took a day off in the middle of the week. I tell her about Yom Kippur, the Day of Atonement. Judaism teaches that people make mistakes, both individual and collective. Atonement means forgiving and starting over with a commitment to make healthier choices, a return to at-one-ment—wholeness, holiness.

She seems interested so I continue. I sat behind a man who wore a *tallit,* a prayer shawl, with a picture painted on it, surrounded by Hebrew and Arabic lettering. All day I looked at a gold dome. The words, in English, printed underneath said Holy Temple, Dome of the Rock. Midday, the man gave a talk.[1] He spoke of how his heart was shaken by the recent massacres at Sabra and Shatilla, Palestinian refugee camps in Beruit. He read from a press release. It was from a group of Jewish lesbian feminists in New York, *Di Vilda Chayas,* the wild women.[2] They wrote that as Jews they could not support the Israeli involvement in the massacre. The women argued for solidarity with Israeli peace activists. The man requested that the community commit itself to acts for justice, to commit a next step, a tangible act. In the full sense of the word, I told my coworker, we had atoned. She replied sharply, "Yes, you Jews have plenty to atone for." I was silenced and shamed. Only later did my response take shape. In relation to Sabra and Shatilla, we, Americans and Jews, we are both implicated. Our government uses our taxes to send military aid to Israel. Don't we as Americans, all of us, need to atone?

In telling this story I have left out a fact. When my coworker said, "You

Jews have plenty to atone for," she spoke from her experience as an African American woman. She said, more fully, "You Jews have plenty to atone for, making money off my people." I, desperate for defense, pointed out the class difference between us, she being middle class and me working class. She turned away. When I told this story to a Jewish friend, she emphatically called the comment Jew hatred. She wouldn't hear about Jewish landlords in Black neighborhoods. She turned away when I started talking about our white privilege, both of us from mostly Eastern European Jewry.

November 1983

In 1983, the cruise missiles, which are nuclear first-strike missiles, were sent to Europe. Some of us in Minneapolis and St. Paul went to the federal court-house and performed a political ritual. We used rocks from the Mississippi River to dip in a bowl that held our own blood. As we dipped each rock we chanted, "The blood of the world is on our hands. The blood of Hiroshima. The blood of South Africa. The blood of South Philadelphia. The blood of Grenada.[3] The blood of the world is on our hands." Then we wove a web of justice around the pillars supporting the federal court building. White pillars, man-made, inflexible, unmoving pillars around which we wove, with bright colored yarn, a web of justice. For disturbing the peace we were sentenced to community service at Catholic Charities. Some women accepted while others refused. I asked, "Can I do community service at Jewish Family and Children's Service?"

The judge said, "No, the only legitimate place is Catholic Charities."

I replied, "That is anti-Semitic."

He cited me for contempt of court, and I went to jail for a week. I had two caseworkers. The first was a Russian woman whose Ukrainian family fled Stalin because they were Trotskyites. "Yes," she said, "so many ironies between us. Your family fled because mine tried to kill them during the pogroms. Now, Americans and Russians compete with horrible nuclear weapons. Here we are, jailer and jailed, both Americans." She introduced me to my second caseworker saying, "You'll test each other's strengths."

My second case worker was Hana, a Palestinian woman from Ramallah. Hana kept repeating, until it made some sense to her, "You're here because you faced discrimination as a Jew? In Israel, Jews discriminated against me. In Israel, Jews discriminate, oppress, beat, and murder." We talked for hours and hours. "Such passion we share," she said, "if only we had power; our passion could honor the land and our peoples."

Such possibilities we discussed. Why was she here in the U.S.? She ran a women's health clinic that the Israelis had shut down. She has since returned to Palestine and is now part of the Intifada every day, fighting on the land for her homeland. Intifada. The translation is imperfect. It is more than the uprising. It means a shaking off of dirt, of oppression, an act of cleansing.

December 1987

I want an immediate change. An immediate resolution to the pains and harm brought about by injustice and violence. People *can* unravel the parallel and intersecting forms of oppression. We *can* live according to need, desire, pleasure, integrity, harmony, and compassion.

There are many questions about how to bring about that simple vision. How to feed women who survive violence? How to take care of immediate needs while trying to change the systems? How to create and sustain homes within communities? How to reflect possibilities, respect, life? What would it be like to live without the experience or threat of the power elite and their interventions in our lives? Answering the tension between urgency and the slow pace of change shapes my life. We live in a transition time when individuals heal from, and resist, the powers that maintain pain, injustice, and violence. We live in a transition time when communities struggle to organize multifaceted resistance.

In my daily work I help break cycle of violences. I am grounded in the daily practice of resistance with women who are homeless and who are actively healing from violence against women. I know the healing takes many forms, the personal journeys aren't usually linear, nor is the collective journey necessarily a shared vision. Sometimes the personal and the collective criss-cross, sometimes they diverge, sometimes they mirror, and sometimes they urge each other onward.

The movement of women against violence against women provides clear pathways for personal healing and communal resistance. Whether the violence comes from rape, incest, battering, pornography, or prostitution, whether the violence is internalized or institutionalized, healing and resistance occur within a process feminists generally term "breaking the silence." The process is akin to the consciousness-raising sessions of the early phase in the second feminist wave.

Breaking silence means breaking the cycles of violence. Breaking silence means talking about and listening to women's stories. Stories about moving from fear to action, from violation to power, from individual isolation to participation in community. There is no one correct recipe for breaking the silence. The beauty of voices shapes sounds. There is no one song or story. Shelters, therapies, laws, children's books, feminist theory, the application of the lessons learned—we begin to know how to make our world.

I am also grounded in Judaism, in understanding my Jewish heritage, in knowing where I stand in relation to Jews and Judaism. *Tzit-tzit*. The long fringe hangs off the four corners of the tallit, the prayer shawl. The edge. The corner. The Hebrew word connects with a verb meaning the budding of a flower just about to blossom, to come out fully. Fully out, at the periphery, the tzit-tzit are necessary, central for the act of prayer. Fully out as a lesbian, on the edge of the lower middle class, the fringe, the flower child, at the periphery and central. It has taken me years to struggle with Judaism's sexist and homophobic tendencies. But because I am, in some ways, perceived as an outsider, because I care so much about Judaism, because I have experience of women acting against violence against women, I can hear a Palestinian woman ask me to at least, at least, approach the problem of a little strip of land and two peoples, two homeless peoples, who each want that land for their homeland.

February, 1988

Informed by my explicitly feminist work, I face the question asked of two homeless peoples and a little stretch of land each wants for their homeland. I came to argue against the Israeli occupation of Palestine and to argue for a climate of possibilities: a possibility for peace and justice in Palestine, Israel, and the U.S. How did I come to this? I imagined I was at a feminist meeting and let all the various communities within me speak out. What did I find? As a Jew I am implicated because Israel arrogantly presumes to act in my interest. As a working-class person I am outraged by the economic waste perpetuated by the U.S. in financing Israel for its own imperialistic needs and by Israel in financing the military instead of people's needs and by using Palestinian laborers for necessary jobs in an exploitative way.[4] As a lesbian feminist I answer Palestinian and Israeli women's calls for support. As a white person continually becoming aware of how racism operates in the U.S., I know that anti-Arab racism contributes to the Israeli occupation and the U.S. perception of that occupation. As an American I realize that this country's military and economic polices benefit from and stand at the core of the occupation.

From my imagined meeting, it was clear to me that another, real, meeting needed to be organized. I was lucky to be among those Jewish lesbian feminists tired of having solitary internal discussions. Several of us met, and so began a group called the Hannah Arendt Lesbian Peace Patrol. We took this name because we wanted our lesbian identity out front. We wanted to keep a sense of creativity, so we chose to be a patrol. "Patrol" literally means "to guide through water." We take Hannah Arendt as our guide. Hannah

Arendt (1906–75) was a German-Jewish political philosopher and the author of nine books, including *The Origins of Totalitarianism*.[5] In later life, Arendt was ostracized by the Jewish community because of her controversial analysis of the human capacity for evil. She thought that given certain political conditions, any people, including Jews, could be capable of acting as the oppressor.

At our first meeting we found that each of us had differing perspectives on Jewish identity and commitment to a Jewish state. We each came to Hannah Arendt with a different style of nudging change: Writing, street theater, community education, direct action. Another level of difference within our group comes from our varying connections to the U.S. Jewish community: a few secular Jews, one applicant to rabbinical school, one whose mom serves on the board of an East Coast Jewish Community Relations Council. How do we find common ground and appropriate actions? Our common ground is that each of us agrees that now, right now, if we take the risk to speak out, act up, write, whatever, then we can support Israeli and Palestinian feminist peace activists.

Through the years of working together we have found it crucial to be in contact with Israeli feminists and Palestinian activists. The information we get in "mainstream" media, whether American or Jewish, has a bias that is anti-Arab. Learning to compensate for this, we listen to alternative media and eyewitnesses, read writings by Palestinians, and subscribe to Palestinian news. This helps those of us in Hannah Arendt arrive at some shared assumptions.

Before I go into these assumptions I need to stress that Hannah Arendt didn't arrive at them like "Zap, this clicks." We had to help each other find a way through fear. Fear of not being Jewish enough. Fear that criticizing Israel gives fuel to the anti-Semites. Fear of not knowing enough, of being misinformed, of being wrong. Fear that we are alone in our fears. Fear of being invalidated, ignored, silenced. Fear that as American Jews, we have no right to comment on Israeli policy. Fear of self-righteousness, of being disowned. It was painful to acknowledge these fears. It was amazing to talk to many Jews and find the same fears kept us stuck in confusion, ambivalence, powerlessness. It was hard to come to terms with fear. Actually, we had support from Palestinian women who helped us distinguish between real and perceived fear.

How do we as Jews define safety in a world we perceive and experience as unsafe? The relation between the Holocaust and Israel inevitably comes up. It is not a simple cause/effect relation. I have heard an Israeli Holocaust survivor say, "I need all Israel, including the Occupied Territories, because nowhere else in this world is safe. So whatever I have to do to be safe is fine."

I heard another say, "I didn't survive in order to do to Palestinians what was done to me." The first stance assumes Israel exists in reparation for the Holocaust. This is an isolationist, protective, and self-destructive survival strategy. The second stance doesn't assume that the Holocaust necessitated the state of Israel. It says that neither protectionism nor patriotism brings safety. Safety comes by naming and dismantling the conditions that bring about all types of holocausts. In this way, Jews and Palestinians can find common ground on which to create states based on mutual respect.

Another, often overlooked factor in plowing through Jewish fear is the effect of assimilation. I think the assimilation of Jews into the dominant U.S. Christian culture functions to isolate, or derail, U.S. Jews from alliances and coalitions with other peoples who have experienced oppression. Since the mass arrival of Jews in the U.S. in the early twentieth century, most U.S. Jews have become well assimilated into the dominant culture in response to violent and subtle forms of anti-Semitism.[6]

Assimilating into an anti-Semitic culture, in my view, means denial is functioning as a survival strategy. If American Jews deny the major differences between Jewish and Christian cultures, and if we deny that the U.S. Jewish community can think for itself, instead of unilaterally supporting Israel's policies towards Palestinians, then some Jews can, indeed, stay in the relative safety that assimilation provides. This relative safety restricts the U.S. Jewish community. One of the consequences of this restriction is the silencing and disowning of Jews who move away from denial.

Alliances and coalitions with other oppressed communities in the U.S. can be generated by Jews. There are models in Jewish his/herstory. What about Jewish participation in the civil rights and labor movements? What about the Zionists like Martin Buber, who argued for a nonreligious, democratic state to include Jews and Palestinians?[7] I find possibilities when I talk with Palestinian women. We build a trusting, respectful alliance by becoming vulnerable to each other. This vulnerability, grounded in shared grief, gives me strength to face my fears and stand on solid common ground.

After those of us in Hannah Arendt explored these fears, we arrived at shared assumptions. Hannah Arendt's first assumption begins with recognizing that Palestinians have an existing government, the Palestine Authority,[8] which already provides health care, judicial and legal systems, public welfare, education, etc.

The next assumption is that Israel exists and Israel is necessary for Jewish people. We believe that the state of Israel is flawed, but not fatally flawed. The flaw is not inherent in the Jewish people, rather it echoes flaws within the U.S. Jewish people will argue over this, will argue over which flaws exist and why, but that is itself part of the process of repair. We note also that it isn't enough to just talk about flaws and healing; actual power imbalances of nationality, race, class, and gender among the people talking must also be taken into account.

A third assumption we acknowledge is the connection between the Israeli occupation and women's lives. Israeli feminists speak of their concern that violence against women, specifically battering, has risen as Israeli men spend more and more time "policing" the Occupied Territories. They also speak of a fear that because of Israel's militaristic posture, woman's role in Israeli society becomes that of breeder.[9]

Fourth, we perceive the Jewish community, including Israel, as analogous to a dysfunctional family system. In a dysfunctional family system every member participates in maintaining the dysfunction. In this case the dysfunctions include internalized anti-Semitism, assimilation of white Western European racism by U.S. Jews, and classism, nationalism, and women-hating. Jews who are struggling to recover from such abusive, oppressive, and entrenched systems are often discounted, invalidated, and silenced. For individual and collective well-being we need to cultivate alliances between Jewish, Palestinian, Israeli, and American feminists.

Our last working assumption regards Jew-hatred. We note anti-Jewish oppression can function to isolate Jews, to cause us to seek allies, or to do both. Anti-Jewish oppression does not explain away Israeli violence towards Palestinians. This assumption honors the human capacity to make useful distinctions, to stop ranking oppressions, and to affirm the human qualities of responsibility, creativity, and empowerment.

In my work with the Hannah Arendt lesbians, I find myself acting and breaking the silence. What inspires me is my work in a feminist world. We affirm many passionate endeavors to break silence, to end violence, and to nurture a wide-open heart, wild creativity, and outrage at the outrageous.

March 1988

Each Friday I produce a women's radio show. On many weeks I focus on Israel and Palestine. Before the Intifada began in December 1987, saying Israel-Palestine felt nerve-wracking for me, mostly because I felt ignorant and afraid to offend anyone. Since the Intifada, I have interviewed Palestinian women, eyewitnesses to the occupation, Israeli and American Jewish feminists, anyone who could educate me and the radio public about Palestine. I am no longer bothered by letter or calls saying I'm anti-Semitic. I try to be patient when people, usually Jews, tell me to say, "I'm for the Israeli peace movement," instead of "I'm a Palestinian solidarity activist." I am still bothered by people who say, "Oh, you're so courageous and brave to be so public!" Do something, I think, people are dying.

April 1988

At Israel's fortieth anniversary bash in Minnesota, some Jewish lesbians went to speak our despair. Not only that Israel's security is imperiled by Israel occupying Palestine; not only that Israel is as materialistic, militaristic, and macho as the U.S.; not only that too many American Jews support Israel unquestioningly; not only that Shamir/Peres/Sharon are Reagan/Bush; but also that we, we Jewish lesbians, are part of this community.

June 1988–March 1989

The codirector of the local Jewish Community Relations Council, a feminist, explains her silence, her compliance with the Israeli occupation, by putting her hand over her heart and saying "I am a Jew". I am a Jew also. We cannot hide by claiming only one identity. I am also a lesbian, a political activist, a cook from a working family. I want to yell, "Queers were murdered along with political activists, along with poor Jews, along with others in the camps!" I am afraid of being self-righteously hysterical.

Several months pass. We see each other at a demonstration against Meir Kahane, an Israeli-American racist who proposed transferring all Palestinians out of Israel. We stand on opposite sides of this street. I stand with peace activists and Palestinians. She stands with Jews. We both publicly disagree with Kahane. I cross the street to talk with her. She demands, "How can you stand there with people who chant, 'Hitler, Kahane, different name, same face'?"

I say, "Isn't there a kernel of truth in that? To Palestinians?" She sighs; I hesitate and continue, "That's what the Israeli occupation means. That's why there is the Intifada." I also look at her and say, "You are right; I'm not sure I'm rationalizing away possible anti-Semitism in that chant. But for me, I need to stand with the Palestinians." She says she'll think about it.

Not long after, a few Jewish lesbians from Hannah Arendt go to a high-class fashion-show fundraiser in Minneapolis, held to raise money for Israeli bonds. We dress in military garb and hold signs that say: "This is Israeli fashion." Few take our leaflets, which advertise the New Israel Fund, a progressive fund; most divert their eyes, and look down at the ground. Many well-dressed women angrily tell us that we don't know what we're doing. We're not real Jews. The gay/lesbian paper declines to print a report. They don't perceive this story as a lesbian/gay issue.

At the annual Twin Cities Take Back the Night event, two of us speak about Israel, Palestine, injustice, breaking silence, and healing. Several Jewish women express disapproval at us for "airing dirty laundry." Non-Jewish women expressed relief that Jews, not they, are saying something about Israeli injustices.

A month later the women's community erupts in a controversy. In a woman-only space, an Arab-American woman was to report on her two-month stay in Gaza. A Jewish woman on the collective that runs the space placed restrictions on the presentation. I say on the radio:

> It is racism to fly the banner of anti-Semitism to quiet those of us who stand in solidarity with Palestinians. Racist. I hate it. There is such a huge cost for disowning reality. It is a high cost for Jews to pay—to be the ones who exploit—the oppressors, the occupiers. This is a price I can't pay. Stop acting in my name. With my rage and grief I grow into my responsibility, my strength, my compassion and action. This is why Palestinian women help me to teach myself.

At a November Hannah Arendt meeting we compared notes about our families' relationships to Israel. My aunts looked towards Israel as a sign of reassurance and safety, but my mom disagreed. "Zionists aren't internationalists. Zionists gave in to the religious Jews when Israel became a nation-state. Zionists took money away from the effort to rescue people stranded during the war. Zionists are suspect; are we really any safer?" My aunts stood their ground, shifting their feet or stomping. They got the last word by telling my mom to get real and grow up.

Later that evening a friend called from another city. "I have to tell you this dream I had last night. A *bubie,* a grandmother, came to me and chided me loudly. She said, 'You worry so much that those who say Zionism is racism are anti-Semitic. You should worry more that there are Zionists who are racists. Can't you make sensible distinctions?'" This visitation was a breath of fresh air. I hope that bubie visits my dreams.

During the past year I have learned to peel back layers of racism towards Arab peoples, particularly Palestinians. Sometimes that racism appears as a neon word flashing before my eyes. I see the PLO representative to the U.N., and the label "terrorist" flashes in front of me. I wait until the neon dims, shake my head, and listen.

December 1988, Hanukkah

I had a vision to honor the Intifada, and it came to be. About a hundred people came together to light candles, to read the names, ages, and circumstances of deaths of Palestinians murdered during the first year of the Intifada. December 7 marked the anniversary. It was also Hanukkah, the sixth day. Many Jewish people told me I was anti-Semitic for scheduling this event on that day. At the planning meetings I was asked not to light the Hanukkah candles as that would dishonor the event. The request was made by a Christian woman. A Palestinian woman argued strongly for lighting the candles. At the event I lit the candles and talked about Hanukkah as a time for rededicating ourselves to freedom for Palestinians and Jews. Another Palestinian woman told me I touched her. It is only by us risking, she said, that peace and justice can grow.

February 1989

The Hannah Arendt Lesbian Peace Patrol took account of our despair. After a year of intensive activities on our part, the violence in occupied Palestine continues. We are used to it; we are numb. How do we effectively challenge the Israeli government, which needs moral and financial support from American Jews? In the pregnant silence after the question, yet another activity was birthed.

We stand vigil as Jewish women against the Israeli occupation at Shabbas services, outside local synagogues. We hold a banner that reads, "Israel: End the Occupation." It is the same banner that Jewish, Palestinian, and American women held during the past hot, hot summer. We face the synagogue. Before services we stand in silence, we wear black in solidarity with the Israeli Women In Black who stand vigil in Jerusalem, Haifa, Tel Aviv, and in many cities all over the globe. This is our prayer, our welcoming of Shabbas, the time of peace and reflection in our week. This is for all our people. All Jews are the children of Israel, and of Sarah, Rivka, Leah, and Rachael.

We are scared to do this. The male rabbis come out and paternalistically chastise us. "I didn't give you permission. You can't do this to Jews on the Shabbas. I agree with you politically but this isn't nice. Go study how to change institutions. You are compromising me. We have sponsored talks and dialogues. Fooey on you. Fooey." Afterwards, the emotional barrage dissipates. It is difficult for some of us to look at the congregants and not see Uncle Howie or Aunt Ethel. We wonder if we are betraying them, but we know this is our community and we need to speak out. They are defensive. They trivialize us. They want to render us as invisible as the Palestinians. They laugh at our name. *But we are them.*

We do this vigil because we are creative, empowered women. We know American Jews can affect Israel—it happened quickly regarding the law of return. When American Jews pressured Israeli Jews to overturn unjust Israeli legislation involving who gets to define who is a Jew, the law changed. We know talk is not enough. Palestinians are dying. Israeli soldiers act violently towards Arab people every day; they act violently towards Israeli women. This must stop. There are options for negotiation, for compromise, but the racism and the male glorification of violence block possibility. All the violence must stop.

We continue to stand at synagogues. There are a few women, and their numbers grow, who come to us and ask, "What are you doing?"

"We need to end the violence."

"Ah," they say. "Of course. Yes, stand here for me."

We invite them to join us.

"Not yet, soon. And maybe not this way. But soon. Soon."

April 1990

These words aren't fully cooked. I left something out about how the idea of one place as a homeland doesn't speak to me. I've been rooted, uprooted, transplanted, rerooted. I know other people stay rooted to a place, to their homeland. How do the rooted and the transient recognize and respect each other? The question pulls me away from Israel and Palestine. I live with a Salvadoran exile. I talk with Australian aborigines, Lakota women. Can we exchange ways of living the way women exchange recipes? Or, will a dominant power eat the conquered?

Transition time, food for thought. A time to sift through tradition, integrity, change, mix them up with sacred places and calendars, pour into various pans of communities, bake in the ovens of experience. Test it, try it, try it again.

Here's another story, one that has an obvious ingredient I've left out. I belong to a community rooted in time, so I tell a Jewish story, the story of Pesach, Passover, the holiday of freedom, of walking out from bondage, *mitzraim,* into the desert, the place where freedom begins. Each year this holiday retells, repeats, remembers the Exodus. For it is said, every person in every generation must regard herself as having been personally freed from bondage in mitzraim, the symbolic land of oppression. Each year the same story, but different. For it is said, whoever enlarges upon the telling of Exodus, those persons are praiseworthy. This year it takes three *sederim,* the ritual dinners of Passover, for me to fulfill Pesach.

At the first seder, we describe our individual mitzraims. I had finally gotten pregnant and then miscarried. Betrayed by my body, no longer home to a possible child, adrift, spinning with disappointment, I became distant from everyday. The next night, at the second seder, I am at work among women who are homeless. Mitzraim appears total, the bondage of many oppressions before us. Each woman speaks slowly, as if words could be one more thing snatched away. We tell the old story, walking out of mitzraim, stepping into the unknown, haltingly, unsure if we can provide for ourselves food, shelter, compassion. We move into the desert, hopeful that we can move towards freedom.

For a third and final seder I go to Tucson, to the desert itself. I need to find my strength. My friends invite me to the seder of the Tucson Women Against the Occupation. At the beginning I can barely hear the Hebrew changed to honor women silenced through the generations. *Brucha aht elilah, shekinah, elohaynu malkat ha'olam....* "Blessed is the spirit of freedom in whose honor we kindle the lights of this holiday, the season of freedom." We eat our way through the story. Matzah, bread of affliction, bread of liberation. Spring greens, bitter herbs, *charoset.* We invoke our mothers, our grandmothers, great-aunts by comparing recipes. We compile a cookbook for changing the world, for the various tastes of freedom.

During the meal women decide that to be Tucson Women Against the Occupation is not enough, *lo dayenu;* they need to be *for* some things. They make up slogans: Food not fists, Eating not meeting, Dessert not destruction. In this serious hilarity my voice, muted by powerlessness, opens up. We return to the storytelling, telling now of resistance. Resistance in Warsaw, resistance in Hebron. Resistance in East Jerusalem, resistance in West Jerusalem. The fourth cup of wine we dedicate to the future by naming our dreams. Dream of a world in which all Jews and all other peoples, and especially women, are free to be themselves. Dream of a world that honors creativity, honors the earth. Dream of a world blossoming, where grief runs its course, where work is play, and where dreams come true.

As I listen to these dreams my heart stretches. Home is this moment stretched to weave together these dreams, dreams from ancestors years ago, and the dreams offered by the two young girls who sit with us at the seder table. They ask to add their personal dreams. They want Jerusalem to be for both of them. They want to visit, they are enchanted with Jerusalem, city of dreams. One is a Palestinian and the other a Jew. The adults around the table are teary eyed. We end the seder by embracing their wish. We recite, in unison, a variation of a phrase that Jews have uttered for centuries, closing the seder, preparing for the one to come: Next year, may Jerusalem be at peace.

January 1991

After the U.S. military first started bombing Iraq, that very evening, five women got together. We put candles on a table to invoke the directions, the winds of change, and the passion of rage, the healing waters and enduring life; but we could not invoke the center, the place of change. It was empty, void. It took five women, strong, politically active, Jew, Wiccan, lesbian women, to merely light a candle.

I still worked at the transitional home that January. The women were scared. They were even scared that I had marched through city streets in large antiwar demonstrations. After one march, I stood alone in a fantastic wave of people at a rally. I heard the words, "Iraq bombed Israel, Tel Aviv." Shock, primal, like when I miscarried, shook through me. A friend caught me and held me sobbing. People around us hushed me, like they didn't feel the pain of Israel being bombed, or like hey, the Iraqis had already been bombed. My friend works with people with AIDS and she knows about holding friends during horrible realities.

The next night I went to services at an overflowing crowd of Jews like me, who needed to see other Jews alive. I heard the lesbian rabbi say words while the congregation nodded its agreement. The words, I can't remember, but the feeling was that the war was now justified, that the Palestinians sold out the peace movement, that those bastards deserved to die and let Israel live. Such alienation for me. I don't even want to remember. How can I be part of a people who think like this? Are we all going to suffer for such narrow-mindedness? I need Jews and I am growing again invisible, marginal, as my aunt's words ricochet around in my head: "You just don't know what reality is, grow up."

March 1991

All during the war I kept thinking about Europe's Middle Ages. I imagined the Middle Ages as a place and time when isolated but surviving communities wrestled with Rome. I became desperate for knowledge that other people and other generations had faced war and endured, even though I myself had lived through Vietnam, even though sometimes I feel as if I'm on the defensive front lines in the war against women. Throughout the Gulf War I paid attention to women older than I. Women older than I challenged me to shift perspective, to find the long view.

A white woman traveled to Washington, came back, reported about the peace drum. She told about the people in Lafayette Park, homeless activists, who beat a pulse on the peace drum. I went with some folk to our progressive senator's office to tell him, "Stop saying we support the troops. Why aren't you saying, Stop the war?" Before talking with the senator we prayed at a ceremony outside his office. While smudging sage a Native American woman was knocked down by a white security guard. This same woman spoke for her people to the senator: Stop the wars. It was crucial for me that women older than I sheltered me in some vital way.

I was envious of my housemates; two were in Mexico, one in Nicaragua. As they returned during or after the war it was obvious that I and many of us here in the U.S. had been emotionally, psychologically, and politically battered. The U.S. continues to consolidate power. There is a tight noose around peoples who resist or who want to survive. I think of five hundred years of collateral damage: Nissequoque, Ojibwe, Lakota, Maya, Grenada, Nicaragua, Guatemala, Vietnam, Cambodia. I think of women living on the streets.

I continue to organize but the contradictions and the damage from living in the U.S. during the Persian Gulf War burden me. I don't want to write any more. I don't want to learn about patience when I see pictures of the Kurds, the surrendered Iraqis' murdered bodies, women murdered everywhere. The pain is huge. I feel like a self-indulgent white girl. The privilege is that I used to think that there was a way out in my lifetime. I used to think I'd find people who would build a safe harbor from which, of course, we would organize to change the U.S. I need to prepare for a long-time, a lifetime of struggle against entrenched power over my body, my home, my peoples, my homelands.

I despair, for I fear that even women's raw outrage and power can not effectively challenge the power elite. Dare I hope to take the long view when there is so much horror?

I can tell you of listening to Dahlia, an Israeli feminist peace activist. This Israeli woman explained what it was like for her during the bombing, in a sealed room prepared for death with her friends, both Palestinian and Jew. Dahlia continues to organize with Palestinian women against the occupation of Palestine. During the war the Palestinians were under curfew. Food was desperately needed. Israeli peace groups brought food, which some Palestinians refused because they found the peace group's action to be patronizing and charitable. Other Palestinian women accepted food from Israeli feminist groups because of their consistent, principled, ongoing activities. I live with the stupidity of charitable nonprofits and patronizing peace groups. I need the strength of principled and visionary women. I can barely imagine the strength of women refusing food when hungry.

Dahlia also spoke about a women's international conference where Israeli and Palestinian women came to important agreements about how their peoples could share their one little strip of land. Someone at the conference made the comment that the issue of Soviet Jews immigrating to Israel and of Ethiopian Jews being airlifted from Ethiopia and taken to Israel obscures the underlying issue: a person should live where that person wants to. Deal with anti-Semitism where it is, deal with racism, class, ableism, any oppression where it is. All this moving people around to be safe is not only an illusion, it avoids disrupting the power elite in whose interest oppression functions in the first place.

July 2002

These stories continue. We are relentless. We are inventive. Hannah Arendt morphed into Minnesota Jews for a Just Peace. Each Friday we stand vigil in solidarity with the Israeli Women in Black. I ride the waves of change, as the entrenched violence threatens to overwhelm me. I trust ourselves to do what we can. That trust is my outrageous defiance. That trust is my lifeblood and the heartbeat of my community.

For centuries, under impossible conditions and with impossible choices, women resisted violence. Women survived, sustained themselves, their families, their communities. Women can figure out just and equitable allocations of resources. Women have the capacity to flourish. This legacy moves me to continue to find ways to not only work with other women to change the impossible, but also to bequeath to the next generation the contradictions and hope on which women take a stand. Let's sing, whisper, shout, and pray.

September 15 2001

These words are dedicated in memory of Sally Koplin, cofounder of the Hannah Arendt Lesbian Peace Patrol, cofounder of its current incarnation, Minnesota Jews for a Just Peace.

These words are dedicated to feminists who continue to celebrate even through the backlash against feminists and the reality of woman-hatred.

These words are dedicated to Polly Mann, cofounder of Women Against Military Madness, and to the bridges built between generations of peace-with-justice activists.

These words are dedicated to the people who stand vigil, or write letters to the editor, or who educate, or pray, or go to witness, or who do something, to counter the warmongers; people who seek peace with justice.

Thanks to Caroljean Coventree for her editorial skill and her Big Love!

NOTES

[1] Rabbi Arthur Waskow, director of the Shalom Center, http://www.shalomctr.org.

[2] *Di Vilde Chayes* was a group of Jewish lesbian feminists who denounced the massacres publicly. They included Adrienne Rich, Elly Bulkin, Irena Klepfisz, and Melanie Kaye/Kantrowitz.

[3] Grenada had just been invaded by the U.S.

[4] By 2002 Palestinian laborers have been replaced by Romanian and Filipina people. Israel instituted structural disadvantages to prevent Palestinians from entering both Israel and Israel's labor pool. Rabbis for Human Rights and B'Tselem, among other organizations, document discrimination and abuse, and advocate for workers' rights.

[5] Hannah Arendt, *The Origins of Totalitarianism.* New York: Harvest/HBJ Books, 1979. From here on, the name Hannah Arendt will refer to the Hannah Arendt Lesbian Peace Patrol. Also, most of this section appeared in the pilot edition of *Bridges, A Journal for Jewish Feminists and Our Friends,* edited by Clare Kinberg. Special appreciation to Melanie Kaye/Kantrowitz for her lucid teachings.

[6] See Matthew Lyon's essay, "Parasites and Pioneers," in this anthology.

[7] Buber, Martin, *On Zion: The History of An Idea.* New York: Schocken Books, 1973.

[8] The Palestinian Authority was named by the Palestinian Liberation Organization (PLO).

[9] New Profiles is an Israeli feminist organization that investigates and educates about the militarism of the Israeli society. The Web site is http://www.newprofiles.org. Another Israeli feminist organization is Bat Shalom, http://www.batshalom.org. This site features links to other Israeli and Palestinian feminist organizations.

Oberlin College Commencement Address, May 29, 1989

AUDRE LORDE

Hello. Before we say anything else, I would like to congratulate all of the parents and the families of these graduates who are here today. I know that having sat in your place twice for my son and my daughter, I know what it takes to have this day come to pass. And so, from my heart, I congratulate you. And to you, graduates, I also extend my best wishes, love, and my congratulations for the particular hard work I know each one of you has done to make this happen.

Most people do not remember their commencement addresses. And next year, when someone asks you who spoke at graduation, I really wonder what you are going to say? "I remember she was a middle-aged black woman." "I remember she had a nice mellifluous voice." "I remember she was a poet."

"But what did she say?"

After all, there are no new ideas. There are only new ways of making those ideas real and active throughout our lives. What you do not need here today, I think, is more rhetoric. I feel what you need are facts you don't ordinarily get to help you fashion those weapons for the war in which we are all engaged. It is a war for survival in the twenty-first century, the survival of this planet and all this planet's people.

I'm going to read you a short poem. It's a found poem, and a found poem is one of those poems that jumps out at you on a cereal box or out of a speech. And it does what any good poem should do, which is punch you in the mouth with a piece of the truth. So, the title of this poem is "Thanks to Jesse Jackson."

Thanks to Jesse Jackson

The U.S. and the U.S.S.R
are the two most powerful countries
in the world
but only one-eighth of the world's population.
African people are also one-eighth of this world's population.
Half of the world's population is Asian.
Half of that number is Chinese.

There are 22 nations in the Middle East.
So most people in this world
are Yellow, Black, Brown, Poor, Female
Non-Christian
and do not speak English.

By the year 2000
the 20 largest cities in this world
will have two things in common
none of them will be in Europe
none of them will be in the United States.

Those are the realities of a world into which you enter, and this is a rite of passage. I look into your faces, and you are all so beautiful. But I have stood in places like this, and I have seen beautiful before. And I must ask myself "Where are those faces now?" "How are they using that promise which I read?" And what makes you different?

Well, to begin with, you are different because you have asked me to come and speak with you out of my heart and with the urgency that fills my life and affects each one of you on this very special day. So when they ask you, who spoke at your commencement, remember this: I am an African Caribbean American, feminist, lesbian, warrior, poet, mother doing my work. And when they ask you, "What did she say?" tell them I asked you the most fundamental question of your lives: Who are you, and how are you using whatever power that lies within that self in the service of what you believe? How are you learning to use yourself in the service of what you believe?

You are inheriting a country that has grown hysterical with denial and with contradiction. Last month in space, five American men released a satellite that is now on its way to study the planet Venus, and the infant mortality in Washington, DC, the capital city of this nation, is higher than in the nation of Kuwait. We are citizens of the most powerful country in the world, and it is a country that stands upon the wrong side of every liberation struggle on Earth.

I want each one of you to reach down inside of yourselves, out of the power and the promise that is yours today, and I want you to feel what that means. And I want you to never lose that sense, five, ten years from now, wherever you are—singing, writing, digging ditches. Whatever you do, be conscious of who you are. It is a reality that haunts each of our lives. It is a truth that can help inform our dreams, our visions. This is not about altruism, this is about self-preservation—our survival.

A twenty-eight-year-old white woman is beaten and raped in Central Park. Eight Black boys are named, arrested, and accused. A seventeen-year-old white, mentally retarded girl is raped by five white boys in Jersey, and they still remain nameless, protected by a police department that questions and tests the victim. These are nightmares that affect each one of our lives. I pray for the body and soul of every one of those young people trapped in this compound tragedy of violence and social reprisal. None of us escapes the brutalization of the other. Using who you are, testifying with your life to what you believe is not altruism, it is self-preservation. Black children did not declare war upon this system, it is the system which has declared war upon Black children, both female and male.

Violence in our cities, in the cities across this nation, violence against women, escalates day by day. And that is a violence that cuts across every race, every class, every region. I look into your faces, and you give me hope. You are strong, you are intelligent, you are beautiful. Beauty and promise lie upon your faces like a haze. Please, I beg you, do not waste what you are feeling today. Translate that power, that beauty, into action, wherever you find yourself, wherever you choose to take your work up, or you will be participating in your own destruction.

Listen, I have no platitudes for you. Before most of you are thirty years old, 10 percent of you will be involved in the space race, and 10 percent of you will have lives that are touched by AIDS. This disease, which is now rivaling the Plague of the Dark Ages, is a disease said to have originated in Africa, spontaneously and inexplicably jumping from the green monkey to man. Yet in 1969, twenty years ago, a book published by the Monthly Review Press, entitled *A Survey of Chemical and Biological Warfare* (written by John Cookson and Judith Nottingham), discussed the green monkey disease as a fatal blood tissue, venereally transmitted virus that is an example of a whole new class of disease-causing organisms of biological warfare interest. Check it out; it's in your libraries. The book also discussed quite directly the possibilities of this virus being genetically manipulated to produce "new" organisms.

I have no platitudes for you. But I do have hope. That is the hope I read in your faces, in your wanting to do what must be done. Facing the realities of our lives is not a reason for despair. Remember this, despair is a tool of your enemies. That rumor, "You can't fight City Hall," is circulated by City Hall. Facing the realities of our lives gives us the motivation for action, it gives us the power to change. You are not powerless. What is happening here today is only a piece of your power. You know why the hard questions must be asked. Not out of altruism, but out of survival—self-preservation.

Each one of us sharing this place, in this moment is privileged. Each one of us is privileged. We have beds, and we do not go into them hungry. We are not part of those millions of homeless people roaming the streets of American today. Your privilege is not something to be turned away from, it is not a reason for guilt. It is a part of your power to be used in support of those things you believe. Because the greatest error of privilege is to absorb without use.

Become aware of who pays what for you to live the way you do. Remember, cheap labor is never cheap for the person who performs it. It is made cheap for the benefit of those who consume the products of that labor. South African coal is the cheapest coal in the world because of the Black coal miners who dig it out of the bowels around Pretoria for less than thirty cents a day. And it is that cheap South African coal that is putting miners in Kentucky and Virginia out of work and is breaking the coal-miner unions of this country. Check out the tags inside your clothes, in your shirts, on the back of your cassette recorders. Most of us here in this place would never be able to afford these commodities if it were not for the grossly underpaid labor of women of color around this world who slave to produce them. When you use your pocket radios, your computers, your cameras, be conscious that young women in Sri Lanka, in Thailand, Malaysia, are going blind assembling our electronics. When you go through your closets for clothes to wear, be aware that adolescents in the Phillippines and Jamaica are losing their health to the heat and dust of textile sweatshops sewing fine silks and cottons. Now understand, I am not saying go out in sack cloth and ashes. I'm not saying don't wear the clothes, don't use the electronics. I am saying be aware of who supports our technologies. Be aware that we have a responsibility to that "cheap labor" that makes our lifestyles possible. And that responsibility is not an altruistic one, it is one based, rooted in our own survival upon this planet.

The poorest one-fifth of this nation became 7 percent poorer in the last ten years, and the richest one-fifth of this nation became 11 percent richer. I ask you, how much of your lives are you willing to spend merely to protect your privileged position? Is that more than you are prepared to spend putting your dreams, your beliefs, the things you feel today, the hope for a better world into action? That is what creativity and empowerment are all about, how we use ourselves. The rest is destruction. And it will have to be one or the other.

Power doesn't hang uselessly in the universe. If we do not use whatever power we have—financial, economic, political, spiritual—it will be used. It will be used by our enemies against you, against me, and against our children.

It is not enough to say we believe in justice. The median income for Black and Latino families fell in the last three years; the median income of white families in the United States of America rose. We are eleven years away from a new century, and a leader of the Ku Klux Klan can still be elected to the Louisiana legislature as a member of the Republican party. Little fourteen-year-old Black boys in the seventh grade are still being lynched for dating a white girl. It is not enough to say we are against racism.

It is not enough to believe in everybody's right to her or his own sexual preference. Homophobic jokes are not just fraternity high jinks. Gay bashing is not just fooling around. It is hatred, it is deadly, and it has a response.

It is not enough to believe that anti-Semitism is wrong, when the vandalism of synagogues is increasing amid the home-grown fascism of hate groups like the Christian Identity and Tom Metzger's American Front. The current rise in jokes against Jewish women masks anti-Semitism as well as woman-hatred. So, what are you going to say the next time you hear a Jewish-American-princess joke?

Listen, we do not need to become each other in order to work together. But we do need to recognize each other, to recognize our differences as well as the sameness of our goals. And we recognize those differences because they can be used. They can be used as creative tools for change in which we all believe. Not for altruism—for self-preservation, survival.

Every day of our lives is practice in becoming the person you want to be. There are no instantaneous miracles. No angel is suddenly going to descend upon you, make you brave, courageous, true. It doesn't happen that way. It is every single day, the decisions we make that make us stronger. And every day that you sit back silent, refusing to investigate, to use however haltingly the power you feel, remember, terrible things are being done in our name.

Our federal taxes contribute $3 billion yearly in military and economic aid to Israel. Over $200 million of that money is spent fighting the uprising of Palestinian people who are trying to end the military occupation of their homeland. Israeli soldiers fire tear gas canisters, which are made in America, into Palestinian homes and hospitals, killing babies, the sick, the elderly. Thousands of Palestinians, some as young as twelve years old, are being detained without trial in barbed-wire detention camps. Even many Jews of conscience, citizens of Israel, opposing these acts have been arrested and detained. Encouraging your Congresspeople to press for a peaceful solution in the Middle East, for recognition of the rights of Palestinian people, is not altruism, it is survival.

In particular, my sisters and brothers, I urge you to remember, while we battle the many faces of racism in our lives as African Americans, remember also we are part of an international community of people of color, and people of the African diaspora all over the world are looking to us and asking us, How do we use the power we have? Or, are we allowing our power as citizens of this country to be used against them, our brothers and sisters in struggle for liberation around this world?

Apartheid is a disease spreading out from South Africa across the whole southern tip of the continent. This genocidal system is kept propped into place by the military and economic support of the United States of America, Israel, and Japan. Now, let me say here that I support the existence of the state of Israel as I support the existence of the United States of America, but this does not blind me for one moment to the grave injustices emanating from either, nor does it lessen my responsibility to speak wherever I am. Israel and South Africa are intimately entwined, politically, economically. There are no diamonds in Israel, yet diamonds are Israel's major source of income. And still, Black people slave in the diamond mines of South Africa also for less then thirty cents a day.

It is not enough to say we are against apartheid. Forty million of our tax dollars go as aid to the South Africa-backed UNITA forces that are suppressing an independent Angola. Our dollars pay for the land mines that are responsible for more than fifty thousand Angola children amputees. It appears that Washington is joining hands with South Africa to prevent the independence of the people of Namibia. My sisters and brothers, all of us, make no mistake: South Africa, Angola, Namibia—Southern African will be free. Southern Africa will be free; that is not negotiable. What is in question is what will our relationship be to it then? What will we have to say when our children look into our faces and ask us, "What were you doing while American-made bullets were murdering Black children in Soweto, in Lebanon, in Central America, in Vanuatu, around the world? What were you doing?"

In this country, children of all colors are dying of neglect. Since 1980, poverty has increased 30 percent among white children in America. Fifty percent of African American children, and 30 percent of Latino children grow up in poverty. That percentage is even higher for the indigenous people of this land, the American Indians. While the Magellan capsule speeds on its way through space toward the planet Venus, every minute that we're sitting here, thirty children on this planet die of starvation—every minute. And in each one of those minutes, almost $2 million are spent on war.

The white fathers have told us, "I think, therefore I am." It is the Black mother within each of us, within each one of us that poet inside whispers in our dreams, "I feel, therefore I can be free." I beg you, learn to use what you feel to move you toward the action you wish to accomplish. Change—

personal and political—does not come about in a day, it does not come about in a year, maybe will not even come about in our lifetimes. But it is our own day-to-day decisions, the way each one of us testifies with our lives to these things we believe that empower us. Power is relative, but it is real. And if you do not learn to use it, it will be used against us.

Change did not begin with you, it will not end with you, but what you do with your lives is an absolutely vital part of that chain. The testimony of your daily living is the missing remnant in the fabric of all our futures. Every Friday and every Friday for the last ten years, Women in Black gather opposite Prime Minister Shamir's house in Jerusalem. They hold up small posters that say, "End the Occupation." The numbers of these women have grown, in Haifa, in Jerusalem, in Tel Aviv. Despite being spat upon, despite being cursed as traitors, these women testify with enormous courage, with their lives to their belief in their country and in justice.

My friends, there will always be somebody looking into your face begging you to isolate one piece of yourself, one segment of your identity, hold it up and say, "Here, this is who I am." Resist it. We learn to use each other's difference as creative tools for change by learning how to acknowledge all of the conflicting parts within our selves and learning how to orchestrate them into action behind our beliefs wherever we are.

There are so many different parts to each of us, and there are so many of us. If we can envision the future we desire, then we can work to bring it into being. We need all the different pieces of ourselves to be strong, as we need each other and each other's battles.

So, that surge of power you feel inside of yourselves here today, it does not belong to me, it does not belong to the words out of my mouth, it doesn't even belong to your parents who you honor here today, nor to your professors, nor to those books. That power that you are feeling lives inside of you. It is yours. You own it. You will carry it out of this place. And whether you use it or whether you waste it, you are responsible for it. Good luck to you all. Together, in the conscious recognition of our differences, I have an absolute faith we can create that future I see reflected in your faces today. Congratulations. *A Luta Continua.*

V: SPEAKING (ABOUT) SILENCE

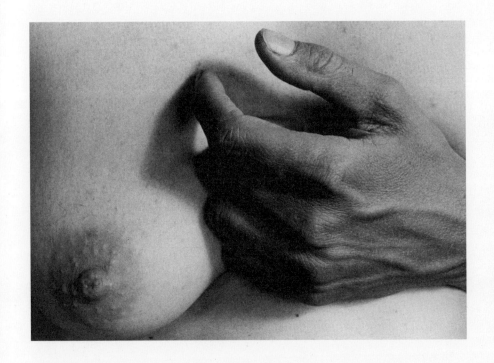

Speaking (About) Silence

JOANNA KADI

In 1988, I saw a call for an anthology to be edited by two women's studies professors who wanted to hear from feminist students about their grad-school experiences. Wow! Since I was spending my days creeping around academia's hallowed halls with my stomach in knots, I was immediately excited about the chance to write down and make sense of what was happening to me, and share it with other feminists. I wrote this article, and sent it off, with incredible fear and trepidation.

I wish now I'd saved that rejection letter. The opening paragraph said something vague and abstract about my piece not fitting, but the first sentence in the second paragraph is indelibly etched on my brain. "And also, we already have two pieces by minority writers." Ah, the sensitive, caring, respectful rejection letter! Not harmful at all to the terrified person attempting to find her voice!

Thankfully, someone pointed me in the direction of the editorial group for this anthology. And, years later, when EdgeWork Books wanted to publish this collection, I wondered if the piece should be printed. It's nothing like I would write now, either in tone or content. But I still like the piece and believe it has merit. So here it is.

If there is a hesitation with which I speak, it is because I am surrounded by spaces filled with my silences. If you want to hear me, you will listen to my silences as well as my words.

Who am I? A working-class Arab-Canadian radical queer woman. Who do I speak for? Myself. How do I spend my time? Doing political work and studying feminist ethics in graduate school. Was I ever meant to be in graduate school? No. Is there a connection between graduate school and silence? Definitely.

Listen. It's my second semester of graduate school. I am no longer staying awake half the night. The vast majority of the women in this room are white and upper-middle-class. The topic is Black Women's Literature. We read about African-American history, ethics, experiences; we spend classroom time analyzing these in terms of classism, racism, sexism. Or at least they do. The white, upper-middle-class women speak easily. They've been taught that the space into which they speak is their birthright. It's not mine. I am mostly silent, but there is much activity behind that silence: An inordinate desire to speak. Fear. Shaking hands. Sweat. An identification with the characters in the stories we read. Too much knowledge of how white, class-privileged women respond to working-class women of color speaking.

This is graduate school/This is a white, upper-middle-class space designed to keep people like me out. Or at least silent. The space is not built to fit me. I am a round peg in a square hole. I am all elbows and knees, a jerky, awkward adolescent who constantly trips and stumbles.

Listen. Here is a story about a four-month period of silence. I arrived at one of Canada's most prestigious universities in 1976. I arrived at one of Canada's most racist and classist universities in 1976. I had worked since age ten and saved every penny, because I understood education as one way out. My sister had worked since age ten and spent every penny on clothes, because she understood clothes as one way out. But that's another story.

I was nineteen. The university was old. My classmates never failed to inform me of this. "When did your parents graduate? When did your grandparents graduate?" I remained silent about my legacy of poverty, racism, illiteracy, factories, and a love of trade unions so fierce I could only produce stutters when the subject arose.

Listen. Depression hung over me like a thundercloud. In silence I went from class to class and received papers graded "C." In silence I did homework on Friday and Saturday nights. In silence I felt the dream of becoming a phys ed teacher slip through my fingers. In silence I shared a room with a white, upper-class woman who used one of my few cherished possessions – a pottery mug that was a going-away present from my favorite cousin, Mary Frances – as an ashtray. In silence I signed the withdrawal papers at the registrar's office. In silence I moved back with my abusive parents.

My stories of silence are of course political. Speech and silence are worthy of the most intense political analysis. Examine the spaces where speech happens, examine the spaces where silence is enforced. In many cases, speech is claimed by the oppressors: men, white people, middle- or upper-class people. In many cases, silence is left for the oppressed: women, people of color, working-class/poor people. Many times those of us in oppressed groups have rejected this and created our own spaces for speech. Many times we have had no choice but to remain in the space of silence.

My Uncle Pete remained in the space of silence. Who would have listened to him, an Arab born in poverty who died in poverty half a world away? Uncle Pete (really my great-uncle) was an important part of our extended family, and yet I heard only one authentic story about him. My dad told it several times, while Uncle Pete quietly chuckled in the background. "Oh, we'd drive into Tronno and go to the pool halls. Pete'd go up to the best-dressed guy and offer a big bet. The guy and his buddies'd take one look at him, and laugh, and agree to the bet." Having witnessed Uncle Pete's unbelievably non-flashy and unbelievably excellent pool playing, there could only be one humorously predictable punchline. "He'd take 'em to the cleaners every time," my dad finished this funny story/this political story. About strategies, intelligence, and survival. But Uncle Pete did not tell that story. Nor did he tell others. Racism and classism had taken many things from him, including his voice. And I wonder if the terrible weight of his unsaid words was released upon death.

I had a dream in which Uncle Pete just stood there, with his badly made glass eye, in clothes that bespoke poverty, in his less-then-five-foot stature that bespoke malnourishment at some early stage of life. He is silent. He stands there. I'm filled with an overwhelming sadness and a deep knowledge; he should not have looked like that. As if to corroborate this, Evelyn – my friend's grandmother – enters the dream. She stands there. At eighty-three, her hair is dyed and coiffed, her glasses are stylish, her clothes tailored. She looks younger than Uncle Pete did when he died. But that was fifteen years ago, and he was in his early seventies. You might guess that Evelyn lives with privileges Uncle Pete never dreamed of touching. I look at them, my sadness grows, my knowledge deepens, and I cry. For an eternity. For Uncle Pete and his silence that now cannot be broken; for myself and the strength to break silence. Then I wake up.

If there is a hesitation with which I speak, it is because I am surrounded by spaces filled with my silences. If you want to hear me, listen to my silences as well as my words.

Listen. Every space has its message. Every space lets you know who is welcome and who is not, every space lets you know whose words will be heard and whose will be swallowed up. Do you know this? The homes, restaurants, shops, schools, community centers, bowling alleys, bars, workplaces you frequent all contain messages. If you feel comfortable and speak easily, it's because those spaces have been set up for and by your own particular group of people. If it's a white, upper-middle-class space and you are a white, upper-middle-class person, your words will be welcome. Mine will freeze before they leave my throat. I will be aware of this. You will not.

Some feminists know this. Others do not. Often the ignorant ones – the ones who have chosen to ignore these facts – are white feminists with class privilege.[1] They have not had to understand. And that is one benefit of privilege.

I've heard many talks given by women of color from poor or working-class backgrounds who offer solid political analyses of racism, classism, and sexism. Predictably, I'm excited by these talks. Predictably, I'm disgusted by the insensitive, lengthy, and off-topic questions and comments raised by some of the white women in the audience. I've come to believe that these women are so secure in their privilege that they unthinkingly dominate the space where speech happens. A few months ago, after witnessing this once again, I came up with an idea. Maybe only women of color and/or working-class/poor women should be allowed to take part in the discussion after these speeches.

This idea interests me more and more. I've attended events in which feminists refuse to take questions from men. I believe there are at least two compelling reasons for doing this. First, it provides a space for women, for members of an oppressed group, to speak. There is an assurance that the space where speech happens cannot be once again taken over by members of an oppressor group. Second, it allows members of the oppressor group a chance to engage actively in a listening process that, at its best, is radical and transformative. I've seen this process work for women and men. I believe it would work for women of color and white women, for women separated along class lines. I'd like to try it.

Listen. I actually said this once, in graduate school, surrounded by white, upper-middle-class women who took their presence in this space as a fact unworthy of notice. One woman asked, with a slightly disbelieving tone, if it were true that some feminists refuse to take questions from men after they speak. I answered her, saying it is true and that I think it's a good idea. I explained why. Then I said quickly, because my shaking was becoming more pronounced, that I thought it would be valuable for us to apply this technique in a situation where working-class women of color spoke and others listened. The words went nowhere, or rather, they fell into a hole and disappeared.

Of course, if anyone really wants to hear working-class women of color, they will stop discussing how to attract women of color to their group and simply come to where we are. At Palestinian solidarity events, on picket lines, at welfare mothers' meetings.

I have a vision. A feminist event in the union hall, a speak-out on class oppression, working-class women talking, everyone else listening. Other times I envision a speak-out on race oppression; women of color have the floor and everyone else is listening.

Many days I cannot hold onto this vision. Some days I clasp it grimly, some days excitedly. After all, feminists have been critically aware of issues of speech and silence. Speak-outs on rape and abortion occurred because we made them happen. We knew that women speaking the truth about our lives would profoundly affect this culture. We helped each other find our voices and "heard each other into speech."[2] We took each story seriously. We wrote the words down and published them. This has been an incredible, radical act that has splintered patriarchal space and moved us into different planes of existence.

I have a deep love of and passion for the women's movement, which not only saved my life but gave me something to live for. It helped me find my voice. Feminists taught me how to talk. And surely a movement that accomplishes this can ensure that other kinds of oppression and pain are heard. A numerical minority of women in the feminist movement – white women with class privilege are a numerical minority when considering feminist movements here and around the world – must not be allowed to prevent this necessary shift.

And how to break silence around racism and classism? It must begin with stories of daily living. It is the (lack of) clothes, dreams, housing, schooling that I must discuss, not abstract, "universal" theories. Do you remember? Feminist work against male sexual violence did not begin with a theoretical analysis of rape as a tool of patriarchal oppression used to keep women in terror and in fear, to restrict our movements and to keep us bound to heterosexual relationships. The analysis followed the stories of individual women.

Listen. At age twenty-seven, I found myself in university again, in a women's studies program. A dream come true. So why did I continue to feel inadequate, stupid, and out of place? I had been a political activist for years and knew much of the analysis and theory presented. I had been in the work force and had taken care of myself. But. I sat in the back of the class and said nothing. I never expected to finish the program and earn the degree. I was suspicious when one professor supported and encouraged me.

It was a university/It was a white, upper-middle-class space. Designed to keep people like me out. Or at least silent. The space was not built to fit me. I was a round peg in a square hole. I was all elbows and knees, a jerky, awkward adolescent who constantly tripped and stumbled.

Listen. Many of the feminists in my classes embraced socialist feminism. They discussed Marxist theory with words I didn't understand while I remembered being taunted over my clothes. They shook their heads over union corruption while I longed to explain that the union came through for us, time and again, in ways that powerfully affected our daily lives. They pondered various graduate schools while I wondered gloomily to myself about work prospects and basic survival.

If there is a hesitation with which I speak, it is because I am surrounded by spaces filled with my silences. If you want to hear me, you must listen to my silences as well as my words.

My stories of silence are of course political. One way in which they are political is that they help me decode the tactics of an oppressor group. If any group is going to oppress another, the subordinate group must be silenced. This has many consequences. Members of the oppressed group cannot reach each other and organize revolts; they fall victim to the divide-and-conquer strategy. Further, when you are continually forced to swallow words, it damages you psychologically, spiritually, emotionally, physically. A weight accumulates. A burden hangs over you. You turn inward and become depressed. You swallow words, you swallow your own stories, and this is anti-thetical to what is meant to happen with words and stories. Words and stories are meant to be shared. Words and stories must be shared, or the person to whom they belong begins to wither.

I have felt this withering process. I have felt the weight of decades of unspoken words and stories gathering themselves, piling up, turning into dead weight. Weight, as in a heavy burden pushing you down. Dead, as in the opposite of alive. "Silence equals death," say the placards at every Gay and Lesbian Pride march.[3] And it does.

I have also felt the weight of decades of my ancestors' words and stories, because my stories of silence are of course historical. My people went to the grave with an abundance of untold stories. I have only fragments, from bits of conversation, from seeing photographs/not having photographs, from piecing things together. Things like where they lived, when they dropped out of school, who couldn't read, what kinds of illnesses they experienced. Other fragments came to me as gifts. One time the spirits of my two grandmothers hung over me excitedly as I wrote my statement of application to grad school. One time Uncle Pete visited me in a dream and left a powerful message. And so, when I begin to speak, I am not only speaking for myself. There are many untold stories of my ancestors attached to me that must be acknowledged.

Racism, classism, silence. When one group oppresses another, silence is always involved. Silence not only prohibits group action, it damages the psyches and spirits and bodies of the oppressed. It turns into dead weight.

If members of an oppressor group are committed to solidarity work and helping to remove these dead weights, one facet of that work involves listening. Listening actively, in a way that involves the body. Listening for a long time. If you want to know how racism and classism affected me, you'll first have to listen through my silence and then help me move beyond that to stories of "wrong" clothes, lack of dreams for the future, the perpetual desire to cover my mouth with my hand when I speak.

This is a story of silence around racism and classism. It could just as easily be a story around working-class people of color breaking silence, about a proud history of speech, action, and organizing against all odds. Because it is not, there is danger that once again we will be seen only as victims. I see the danger, but I must write this anyway. Because Audre Lorde was right: "Your silence will not protect you."[4] I trust this will be understood as part of my story, and only part.

If there is a hesitation with which I speak, it is because I am surrounded by spaces filled with my silence. If you want to hear me, listen to my silence as well as my words.

© 2001 by Joanna Kadi.

NOTES

1 Marilyn Frye brought this point to my attention. See "On Being White" in *The Politics of Reality*. Trumansburg, NY: The Crossing Press,1983: 118–121.

2 Nelle Morton, feminist theologian, created this phrase.

3 I was tempted to change the term "Gay and Lesbian Pride" to the more appropriate terms I now use — usually Queer Pride, sometimes GLBT Pride. But, embarrassing as it is to admit, that's not how I talked in 1988!

4 Audre Lorde, "The Transformation of Silence into Language and Action," in *Sister Outsider.* Trumansburg, NY: The Crossing Press, 1984: 41.

Stolen Memory

SHERI SCOTT

The author would like to say thank you—Miigwetch—to Sharon and Marlys, who helped her recover some stolen memory.

I've always had problems with memory. My early childhood is lost. Images float through my mind like driftwood on the open sea, no longer connected to their original source and body. And like driftwood, they're scattered, elusive. Once captured, they give only clues. The answer lies trapped beneath the surface, rotting, changing shape and form, creaking and groaning its hidden story, both its treasures and its tragedy submerged.

I take my thirty or so photographs. I line them up in what I assume is chronological order. I am trying to recapture my past, my self. Mostly, I try too hard, squint my eyes, burn holes into those unfamiliar images. Nothing comes to me, I feel crazed, unconnected even though I know those pictures are me. I'm lost in a space with no contact, no history to call my own.

To be a white American, we are asked to reject our past and live a fractured life. Memory is supposed to elude us. As Margaret Randall says in *This Is About Incest:*

> An oppressive system's most finely honed weapon against a people's self knowledge is the expert distortion of that people's collective memory. And so Vietnam becomes a page of glory, Three-Mile Island a nonevent, which then makes Chernobyl the first devastating nuclear accident in history.... Under patriarchy, in a commodity-oriented society...human movement falls into step in one giant game of follow-the-leader. When memory stood as the key to my absence and presence in the world, I looked at the ways in which our collective memory is manipulated—at times mutilated—in order that we forget who we are, what we have done, our feelings. And our strengths.[1]

And so we come to believe anything, to disbelieve everything. To forget and forget and forget.

I now see a little girl in a red dress. She is so sweet and soft, so curious and alive. Although she is not yet five, she knows terror and danger. She is vigilant for what she names the Feeling. It overtakes her, it spreads panic into her bones, it seizes her body with trembles, she feels that she will choke and gag. It can cause death, this Feeling. But this little girl has been trying to help me. She has kept memory alive, trying to stay sweet and soft, curious and alive in spite of it all.

I now know that she/I was raped. I know this only through feelings and nightmares, which I have come to accept as the truth despite a monstrous machine designed to convince all of us that feelings and perceptions are not to be trusted. I now know that the unspeakable is not only possible but happening around us every day. Nothing can surprise me any more; I believe that anything is possible. My search for memory will go on, relentless and ferocious. I am trying to re-fuse a fractured self. And from now on, I will fight for memory; I will never believe in forgetting.

Origins

I was born into a rural white world of extended family and watered-down Irish Catholic identity. My mother is the keeper of family memory. She, like so many second-generation children of working-class immigrants, knows little of her origins. She repaints her past—her father was a saint. (My aunt whispers to me that he was an alcoholic, a bootlegger, a failed farmer-turned-bartender, thoughtless and cruel.) Her father, the great patriarch. He suffered a stroke when I was four. After that we lived in his house. For seven years my mother bathed him, fed him, fixed his catheter, carried out his shit in a little white bedpan. He stayed in the living room paralyzed from the waist down, shouting nonsense syllables we couldn't understand. Long after he died, we still called it "Grandpa's room," and my mother would weep that she hadn't done enough for him. Her father, who had tried to keep her from being the first and only of his eight children to go to college, because education was wasted on a girl.

My own father says nothing. His mother died when he was thirteen. His father was a well-driller with eight children. We knew him as "Grandpa Charlie," who cooked rabbits for us when we went to visit on Sundays and had a large shot-glass collection. He died when I was thirteen.

I see pictures of four raggedly dressed children standing beside a wheelchair with an old man in pajamas. We hold up drinks for the camera, our "kiddie cocktails." The usual celebration of holidays, I assume. Memory, again, eludes me. My mother squirms at my questions, she doesn't really want to remember. I have no one to talk to. Both of my grandmothers died before I was born.

Why do I have to fight so hard to remember? What is this white amnesia that spreads through America like a horrible, rotting cancer? And why is it so hard for white feminists to recognize?

Openings

I remember the first time I meet her: her dark, teasing eyes, bold laugh. She hops into my rusty old Pinto, calls me a white girl, and we take off. We take off.

She is everything that I am not: large and dark-skinned, bold and friendly, angry and confident, a woman who works with her hands and whose people always have and always will belong to this land. She is also everything that I am: an outsider, filled with self-doubt and unexpressed rage, country-raised, and friend to trees, rocks, and birds.

She becomes my political comrade, lesbian mentor, harsh critic, dear friend. We weather feminist organizations, flirtations, personal crises, racism—everything that threatens to crack down and split two people apart.

My eyes open. I begin to see the world differently. A new landscape stretches before me, filled with dark-skinned people who don't come from anywhere but here. People whose parents had clothespins clamped to their tongues and wrenched out when they tried to speak their own language, whose sons and daughters were torn from them and sent off to boarding schools to be raped and beaten, people whose elders were quietly murdered with disease-infested government blankets, whose relations were ripped from holy ground and now lie trapped in cold museums, people whose most sacred cultural rituals were banned and despised (and white feminists now use these rituals freely with no knowledge of this pain, this cruelty). The theft goes on and on.

My only survival begins to come clear. I, too, know about survival. I am a woman in a world where no one cried out when my young body was violated. And I am a woman in a world where loving other women is cause for death, not celebration. But again, I learn: in some Indian lands, before the Europeans came, a lesbian woman was considered a blessing, with special gifts from a loving Creator. My heart is so filled with shame I cannot imagine this, but now I see the possibility and it begins to grow.

My heart opens. I weep for the cruelty and suffering. My heart opens. I cry out against the cruelty and suffering. My heart opens. I sing a song of joy to the stubbornness of Indian people for surviving, for the courage to be alive in spite of it all.

I know now that the survival of Indian people is not separate from my own, although in their struggle I must follow, and in mine I must lead. I walk down a busy street in the Indian part of town, on my way to a treaty rights organizing meeting. I remember the first time I meet her: we are on our way to Michigan. Some call it womyn's land but now I know a different story, of Potowatomi and Miami. Words from a Joy Harjo poem, "Anchorage" (dedicated to Audre Lorde), ring in my ears:

And I think of the 6th Avenue jail, of mostly Native
and Black men, where Henry told about being shot at
eight times outside a liquor store in L.A., but when
the car sped away he was surprised he was alive,

no bullet holes, man, and eight cartridges strewn
on the sidewalk
all around him.
Everyone laughed at the impossibility of it,
but also the truth. Because who would believe
the fantastic and terrible story of our survival
those who were never meant to survive?[2]

Deception

It continues to astonish me how utterly unfamiliar we are with the struggles of indigenous people in our very own backyards, while at the same time we are so well informed about the struggles of people thousands of miles away. As Paula Gunn Allen says, "America does not seem to remember that it derived its wealth, its values, its food, much of its medicine, and a large part of its 'dream' from Native America." She also describes an integral aspect of racism in white America: "In short, Indians think it is important to remember, while Americans believe it is important to forget."[3] As part of our struggle against patriarchy, feminists must not fall victim to historical amnesia. We know all too well how the distortion of history can make us feel crazy: Where are the women healers, the lesbians, the antiracist activists, the Native matriarchs, the anarchists, the leaders of slave labor and rebellions, the political prisoners, all of those women of all colors who brought us here with their wit and their wily ways? The powers that be want us to forget, and this forgetting is a powerful tool against us.

Many of us who enter into this feminist movement feel that we have just begun to overcome our powerlessness, to speak out, walk strongly, move boldly through our world. Then we are struck down with terror at the racism and ignorance roaring inside us. Our legacy in America is that we are both oppressed and oppressor, victim and victimizer, frightened and dulled by the burden of both of these roles. Yet we as white women who long for liberation must truthfully acknowledge our heritage of pain and violence and our training as oppressors.

As whites, we're supposed to reap the material benefits of a culture that needs people on the top and people on the bottom. We are trained to get our self-esteem from just such a system. If we haven't "made it," then something is wrong with us. But the reality is that whites, like people of color, have very different experiences within our society. Some of us are rich or upper-middle class, while others of us are lower-middle class or working class. Many of us, despite the propaganda, are poor. Only some of us have access to jobs, to the media, to academia, to health care, to food, and to housing. But if we don't have access to these things, we internalize shame around the message that if only we tried hard enough, we could make it. We learn to identify with women who have "made it," perhaps gotten voted into the legislature, have a business of their own. We are afraid to identify with women in jail (even if we are in jail with them) or with that woman we see yelling at her kids in the grocery line or with that group of women outside the welfare building. We assume (or hope) that we are better than them (or if we are polite, "different" from them).

If we do have access to class privileges, we assume (without thinking) that everyone does, or that we deserve these benefits because of our "hard work." We do deserve good things, but not at the expense of women we turn into "other." It's hard to let go of these old familiar notions and recognize that everyone, especially those whom we imagine are as different from us as anyone could be, is entitled to the same advantages that we have. It is not easy to struggle with these issues at a gut level because we are ingrained with so many damaging but seductive false notions. And even if we see the fallacy of these ideas in our heads, our hearts do not automatically follow. And our hearts are very important in this matter.

White privilege is real and takes many forms. White people can walk around in neighborhoods without being harassed by the police. We're not assumed to be stupid or dull on the one hand, and artistic or spiritual on the other. We're not assumed to be thieves or rapists. Institutionalized racism often takes the form of class privilege by keeping women and people of color in poverty. Charlotte Bunch talks about several common, but unhelpful, responses to criticism based on such privilege in her essay "Class and Feminism": "Middle- and upper-class women have tended to respond to class privilege in several limiting ways: 'What, me, oppressive? I'm just a powerless woman.'; downward mobility (voluntary poverty) and denial of class privilege; guilt and fear; romanticizing and patronizing the lower-class woman; and the all-too-often retreat into confusion." She goes on to bring up what most white women don't want to hear because it threatens the one thing we think we can control, our money and possessions: "Working-class women [and, I would add, women of color] also want us to use and share...privileges with them...they want us to share money, property, access to jobs, education, and skills."[4]

Reflections

As we learn about our heritage of causing pain and violence, we must also come to terms with our experience as victims in a cruel play, powerless in the face of a system that works so fiercely to keep us quiet and isolated. Women who have faced the truth recognize that we live in a world where we are despised and oppressed. As hard as this truth may be for some to accept, it brings the strength of connection, the understanding and clarity of an outsider who has survived. Such vision is clear and piercing. We need desperately to nurture the connections among us in the coming "third wave" of feminism, especially those connections that threaten to shake us to our core.

We are living a fractured life. We need to look at our own cultural grief and loss. We did not come to this country as "white," we came as Irish, Norwegian, Italian, French, Ashkenazi Jew, Polish, and so on. Most white people, like people of color, know of shame. Perhaps our grandparents spoke broken English (and we were made ashamed). Perhaps our parents are a little too loud in department stores (and we are made ashamed). Perhaps we get our gifts from Kmart or Walgreens or we don't get gifts at all (and we are made ashamed).

We feel the emptiness of this fractured life. We may want to lash out at others with a clear cultural identity. We feel jealousy and our own shame, inadequacy. When someone we are trained to see as "below" us exhibits something we don't have, we turn green with envy, bitterness fills our mouths and ugly words pour out.

We feel the emptiness of this fractured life. We often want to forget the part of ourselves that is connected to devastating crimes against other peoples. We are afraid of the truth of the history that brings us to the life we live today: We ripped people from their homelands in Africa, dragged them to this continent to enslave them, and treated them with unspeakable cruelty. We herded up indigenous people in this country, forced them onto small tracts of land, starved them, sterilized them, gave them diseases, outlawed their spirituality, and stole their children. These are truths and we know it, but as white women we must be ready to look at these truths squarely, to say "yes" to them and to look each other in the eye with a will and passion to say "never again."

We feel the emptiness of this fractured life. We want to fill up the hole in our souls that comes from our own cultural extinction. We become what my friend from India calls "culture vultures." We latch onto the spirituality of others (often Native Americans); we romanticize them and make them into less than human as we idolize them. (Remember that pedestal for white middle-class women?) But do we give anything in return for a people's beautiful, hard-won traditions? Do we know of the history of our people against theirs? Do we know anything of the suffering our people have caused by the outlawing of this spirituality we now suck up like vacuums? Do we give back land (if we are lucky enough to own it) so that Native spirituality will be able to continue? Do we redistribute our income to ensure the survival of Indian people? Do we participate in the struggle for treaty rights, sovereignty, and survival of Indian tribes?

Most of us do not. Some of us go to "undoing racism" workshops where we get in touch with our European heritage. But what does this undo? Some of our guilt for being white? Yes, we gain important self-understanding, but again it is white women who gain, while nothing, absolutely nothing, has been undone. Self-understanding not tied to specific and concrete action is once again a theft, because we've slipped by without hearing the anger of our sisters of color or facing our greatest fears. Rather than working for a world of true community, where cultural sharing is the norm (and where we know enough about our own culture to share) and where our connections fill us with joy, we fall into that horrible habit we have learned in a capitalist society—buy, buy, buy. We turn the spiritual into a commodity and get an instant fix. Or we live in fear of what we seem to want so desperately—real connection and community.

Connections

Every day in this country, American Indian people fight for their lives, their rights, their identities, their lands. From the Mohawks of the Northeast to the Lumbee of the South, from the Navajo and Hopi in the Southwest to the Ojibwe in the North, from the numerous tribal peoples in Washington to Indians flooding the urban areas in California.

Before the arrival of Columbus, there were an estimated five to eight million people living in what is now called the continental United States of America. Four hundred years later, only two hundred thousand of these original inhabitants remained.[5] What type of "civilization" arrived here, in this vast and abundant land, that would cause such a devastation of existing people? And how are we as white feminists bound up in this civilization's way of living and thinking?

During the 1800s, the U.S. government entered into land-use agreements called treaties with Indian nations. Although the circumstances of treaty history differ for each tribe, the underlying motive of the government was the same: the extermination of all American Indians and the acquisition of their lands. Horror stories abound of blankets riddled with infectious diseases, famous military "battles" that were actually massacres of Indian women and children, alcohol in abundant supply to ensure that Indian people could be easily taken advantage of. By 1871, the government had made treaties with most tribes and, despite spirited resistance, had carried out its policy of "removal" of Indian people to small tracts of land called reservations. Next came "assimilation" tactics, where Indian children were forced out of their homes into boarding schools, taught that Indians' values were evil, tortured for speaking their native tongue, and chastised by Christian missionaries for being Indian. Indian religious practices were banned and forced to be continued underground. Our ancestors had such greed that the little land accorded Indian people through treaties soon became the object of desire.

The ultimate blow to the Indian way of life came with the General Allotment Act (known as the Dawes Act) of 1887. Reservation land was broken up into small allotments to introduce individual "farming" to Indian people (whose cultural tradition is the opposite—collective and cooperative use of the land). These broken-up pieces of land were then easily acquired by whites through legal or illegal means. Today, many of the tribal lands look like checkerboards, with whites owning much of what was originally guaranteed for Indian use.

The official federal policy of relocation began during the 1950s. By this time, Indian traditions had been so undermined that the people on the reservation lived with alcoholism, poverty, unemployment, cultural shame, and despair. Our government encouraged Indian people to move to cities, luring them with the prospect of special programs for job training, housing, and social services. The government wanted Indian people to disappear quietly into urban ghettos so that fulfillment of our treaty obligations would no longer be necessary.

The Anishinabe people of the Northern Great Lakes (called Chippewa/Ojibwe by white settlers) resisted all of these pressures and endured. In their treaties with the United States, they had retained the right to hunt, fish, and gather on off-reservation lands but had long been kept from doing so by state authorities. In 1974, two brothers from the Lac Courte Oreilles band of Ojibwe decided to fish in an off-reservation lake. They were immediately arrested by wardens of the Wisconsin Department of Natural Resources. The following year, Lac Courte Oreilles filed a suit on behalf of their members to allow for hunting and fishing rights on off-reservation land. After a series of court cases, the judgment finally came in 1984—the Anishinabe people had reserved their right to use off-reservation resources and would be allowed to exercise those rights.

All hell broke loose in northern Wisconsin. Anti-Indian sentiment spread like a poisonous mushroom cloud. Bumper stickers and sports caps read "Save a Walleye—Spear an Indian" or "Save Two Deer—Shoot a Pregnant Squaw." The hate mongers began to organize. White parents and their children stood on boat landings and threw rocks as Indian people attempted to put their canoes into the quiet spring waters. Angry white men in powerboats roared past Indian spearfishers to tip them into the cold lakes. Groups like "Stop Treaty Abuse" (an anti-treaty organization) met with members of the Aryan Nation and crowed about how much they have in common. These groups are filled with people living a fractured life, people filled with envy, hostility, and shame. They are my sisters, brothers, husbands, cousins.

Money poured in from a carefully concealed source as a bounty went out for the head of the tribal member organizing much of the off-reservation activity. More ominous news: connections between legislators and the heads of mining corporations whose greed for underground copper, uranium, and other minerals knows no bounds. Poor and working-class whites in these economically depressed regions are being used as hate-filled pawns in the struggle for resources. The right-hand man of the state's governor just happens to be a former lobbyist from Exxon. (Perhaps he's your husband, my brother, her father.) The whole corporate world was now nervous—this latest court decision meant that Indian people may have legal ground to stop the industrial "march of progress" in the north woods.

Our state government rushed to protect "our" rights. In other words, white people must not lose control over land and resources. Three tribal councils negotiated with the Minnesota state government, two agreed to accept payments in exchange for their resources. When tribal councils in Wisconsin refused to accept similar payments and attempted to spearfish, the hatred around them escalated. Scenes of rock-throwing, threats, and racial violence spurred white supporters of treaty rights to organize. A group called Witness for Nonviolence offered to train members to support spearfishers and their families at boat landings, under the direction of Indian women who wished to remain nonconfrontational and nonviolent. Women and lesbians are at the forefront of organizing this movement to stand up to racist oppression. Connections between oppressions are finally being made.

As a member of the group standing witness, I think of how much I have learned. My life has been enriched beyond words by working together, listening, teasing, joking, and really seeing myself and other people for who they are. I have been frightened by my own ignorance, afraid to show it, to be wrong, to look stupid. But this is precisely what makes me a part of the community. Letting my guard down, asking questions when I don't know the answers, hearing the anger at my ignorance. And then just letting that anger be, not trying to "fix" it or make it better or gloss it over. Just be, between us. This is a space we will have to learn to move in. As Susan Griffin says, "We know in our hearts that there is much more than altruism in our rage, for example, at the oppression of a people with a darker skin. For within this rage at the oppressing of a 'dark' people is a knowledge of a dark and beautiful part of ourselves which has been silenced."[6] We must refuse to live as a fractured self.

In this next "wave" of feminism, if the voices of our American Indian sisters are not allowed to ring out loud and clear, we will fail miserably and tragically as a movement for social change. Our greatest challenge as white feminists is to learn that keeping quiet in order to listen is not the same as being speechless, that following women of color in leadership is not the same as being passive, that expressing outrage and anger is not the same as being abusive, and that encouraging ourselves and others to act, to confront the racism, homophobia, and sexism happening around us every day, is the strongest act of courage.

I am standing on the boat landing next to my lover and friends. Angry white men in camouflage gear, flicking cigarettes and shouting racist slogans into the crisp night air, press insistently against our backs, trying to reach past us to the Indian drumming circle. We stand firm, surprised at our strength, smiling in the midst of this hysterical feeling one gets when hatred is expressed so close and so unadorned. I remember the first time I met her. I smile, wondering at how I ended up here, standing cold and damp in the middle of the night, surrounded by people who hate and surrounding people who carry their identity with pride even as the obscenities about them fill the air. I tap my foot to the steady song of the drum and I, too, endure.

Postscript

This essay was written in 1990. Since then, the voices and waters of Northern Wisconsin have calmed. At dusk on quiet evenings, canoes darken the horizon on the distant lakes. Lights flicker above the water while their occupants watch carefully, with spears in hand, to take their share of the lake's bounty. Treaty rights have been reinforced, victories have been won. But the fight continues....

© 2001 by Sheri Scott.

NOTES

[1] Margaret Randall, *This Is About Incest*. Ithaca, New York: Firebrand Books, 1987.

[2] Joy Harjo, *She Had Some Horses*. New York: Thunder's Mouth Press, 1983.

[3] Paula Gunn Allen, *Sacred Hoop: Loving the Feminine in American Indian Traditions*. Boston: Beacon Press, 1986.

[4] Charlotte Bunch, "Class and Feminism" (1976), reprinted in *Passionate Politics: Feminist Theory in Action*. New York: St. Martin's Press, 1987.

[5] Russell Thornton, *American Indian Holocaust and Survival*. Norman: University of Oklahoma Press, 1987; Matthew C. Shipp, *American Indians: The First of this Land*. New York: Russell Sage Foundation, 1989.

[6] Susan Griffin, *Pornography and Silence: Culture's Revenge Against Nature*. New York: Harper & Row, 1981.

Bluebirdbluebirdthrumywindow

SONIA SANCHEZ

denn die einen sind im Dunkeln
(some there are who live in darkness)
und die andern sind im Licht
(while the others live in light)
und man sichet die im Licht
(we see those who live in daylight)
die im Dunkeln sieht man nicht
(those in darkness out of sight)

—Bertolt Brecht

And the Supreme Court said housing and welfare are not fundamental rights. The right to vote, marry and procreate are the only fundamental rights.
Question: What rights are considered fundamental?
Answer: Only those rights essential to our concept of ordered liberty.
Question: What do you mean? Make it plain, girl. Make it plain.
Answer: In other words, a democratic society without these rights would not be considered civilized. If you don't have 'em, you ain't civilized.
Isn't it lovely to be civilized?
You've seen her. You know you have. She sits on cardboard at Broad and Columbia in front of Zavelle's. Four coats layer her body. Towels are wrapped with a rope around her feet to keep them warm. A plastic bag full of her belongings stands in formation next to her. She's anywhere between forty and seventy years old. A gray Black woman of North Philadelphia. Sitting sharply. Watching the whirl of people pass by, she sits through winter, spring, summer, fall, and law students keeping time to memory.
You've seen her. You know you have. The old woman walking her ulcerated legs down Market Street; the old harridan mumbling pieces of a dead dream as she examines garbage can after garbage can.
"Hey there, girlie. Can you spare me a quarter? I ain't eaten in four days. C'mon now honey. Just one little quarter."
So you give her a quarter and keep on walking to your apartment. So you hand her the money that relieves you of her past present and future. Onward Christian country marching off as to war, with your cross behind you, going as before.

She was turning the corner of the rest room at Pennsylvania Station as I came out of the stall. It was 10:59 P.M., and I was waiting for the 11:59 P.M. to Philadelphia. She entered the bathroom, walking her swollen black feet, dragging her polkadot feet in blue house slippers. Her cape surrounded her like a shroud. She grunted herself down underneath one of the hand dryers.

I watched her out of the corner of my eyes as I washed and dried my hands. What did she remind me of? This cracked body full of ghosts. This beached black whale. This multilayered body gathering dust.

Whose mother are you? Whose daughter were you for so many years? What grandchild is standing still in your eyes? What is your name, old Black woman of bathrooms and streets?

She opened her dirty sheet of belongings and brought out an old plastic bowl. She looked up and signaled to me.

"Hey, you. There. Yeah. You. Miss. Could you put some water in this here bowl for me please? It's kinda hard for me to climb back up once I sits down here for the night."

I took the bowl and filled it with water. There was no hot water, only cold. I handed it to her, and she turned the bowl up to her mouth and drank some of the water. Then she began the slow act of taking off her slippers and socks. The socks numbered six. They were all old and dirty. But her feet. A leper's feet. Cracked. Ulcerated. Peeling with dirt and age.

She baptized one foot and then the other with water. Yes. Wash the "souls" of your feet, my sister. Baptize them in bathroom water. We're all holy here.

You've seen her. You know you have. Sitting in the lower chambers of the garage. Guarding the entering and exiting cars. Old Black goddess of our American civilization at its peak.

She sits still as a Siamese. Two shopping bags surround her like constant lovers. She sits on two blankets. A heavy quilt is wrapped around her body.

"Good morning, sister." I scream against the quiet. Her eyes. Closed. Open into narrow slits. Yellow sleep oozes out of her eyes. Then a smile of near-recognition. A smile of gratitude perhaps. Here I am, her smile announces, in the upper sanctum of Manhattan. A black Siamese for these modern monuments. Let those who would worship at my shrine come now or forever hold their peace. Hee. Hee. Hee.

She leans toward me and says, "Glorious morning, ain't it? You has something for yo' ole sister today? For yo' old mother?"

The blue and white morning stretches her wings across the dying city. I lean forward and give her five dollars. The money disappears under her blanket as she smiles a lightning smile. Her eyes open and for the first time I see the brown in her eyes. Brown-eyed woman. She looks me in the eye and says, "Don't never go to sleep on the world, girl. Whiles you sleeping the world scrambles on. Keep yo' eyes open all the time."

Then she closes her eyes and settles back into a sinister stillness. I stand waiting for more. After all, we have smiled at each other for years. I have placed five dollars regularly into her hand. I wait. She does not move, and finally I walk on down the street. What were you waiting for, girl? What more could she possibly say to you that you don't already know? Didn't you already know who and what she was from her voice, from her clothes? Hadn't you seen her for years on the streets and in the doorways of America? Didn't you recognize her?

I walk the long block to my apartment. It will be a long day. I feel exhausted already. Is it the New York air? My legs become uncoordinated. Is it the rhythm of the city that tires me so this morning? I must find a chair, or curb, a doorway to rest on. My legs are going every which way but up.

I find a doorway on Broadway. I lean. Close my eyes to catch my morning breath. Close my mouth to silence the screams moving upward like vomit.

She was once somebody's mama. I ain't playing the dozens. She was once someone's child toddling through the playgrounds of America in tune to bluebirdbluebird thru my window, bluebirdbluebird thru my window.

Where do the bluebirds go when they're all used up?

From the book, *homegirls and handgrenades* by Sonia Sanchez. NY: Thunder's Mouth Press, 1984. Reprinted permission of the publisher.

Emergency Poem

NELLIE WONG

This poem can't wait
impatient as a sore
busting loose on my skin
I'm using words
tizzy and skedaddle
as if on my last breath.
Riot, hunger, deprivation, despair
crowd together, proud conventioneers
hoist flags into my eyes.

Just hold it
you can't corral me in, run me
into the ground
just who do you think you are?

Warriors gather on the distant hillside
surrounded by trees you can't see
mountains drip warnings
maybe snow, avalanches
of memories of Chinese men
who died in the cold
blasting the mountainside
to build the railroad.

My foremothers in houses
loosening their Mandarin collars
spitting at their jailers
as if prostitution were a choice
as if their bodies were orchids
to be owned by men
profiting from women
who sell their bodies
to support their families.

Death hovers in shadows of prisons
for men to be hung
for stealing bread

Yet songs are sung
the International
when dissident poets and artists
faced death, singing
"It's the final struggle"
during the antirightist campaigns
in China, and I, a mere slip
of a girl, waited
on tables in Great China Restaurant

Ai yah, what is life
but rising, brushing my teeth,
answering phones, ordering supplies,
planning an information picket
of AFSCME clerical, service,
and patient technical-care workers

Meanwhile Karen's in pain
from breast cancer
the homeless now sing
in a stage musical
and Tammy and Jimmy hide out
in a Tennessee retreat
and Ralph Kramden's ensconced
in a bus forever, a symbol
of the working class
immortalized in
a graveyard of TV land.

Ding Ling is probably composing
another story about China's women
still fighting for their rights
and Grandpa Allen is plotting
a future for his unseen grandson
and the merry-go-round

whizzes by with horses and pigs
candles are lit in all-night vigils
for people dead or dying of AIDS
the Miskito and Rama Indians are meeting
the Contras are being killed
Nicaragua is sending help
to the Salvadoran rebels
and South Korea's exploding
with students and radicals
advocating
for democracy and free elections
while poems still are being written
in prisons in Chile, Nicaragua, El Salvador,
in America where folk songs
of Chinese immigrants
lift themselves from pages
of courtships and rituals
birth, death, marriage,
civil wars, pestilence, famine

And rage shouts
at the earth being raped
in India, Somalia, Ethiopia
evidenced in bloating stomachs
bones protruding from starving children
while rivers run red
and sun scorches land
and farmers still use sickles
to tend the earth

Yet voices sing and sing
and artists paint murals
and graffiti flowers
on New York subways
one lonely flower peeks out
between cracks of a sidewalk
shows its tender face
to the hot sun
nourishing the eyes

ravished with hunger
The fog moves in unison
its tempo quick as the dance steps
of Tong Wing as windows rattle
the store displays are blooming
with shorts and pants
of neon yellow and cotton-candy pink
reminding the living
that it's summer
in San Francisco

The wind is merciless
howls the earth's cry
demanding sacrifices
and death is dumped
in the garbage can

and the emergency continues
in song, in breath, in typing
the onslaught of images
filling the white page
and while poetry cannot hold
death back and while poetry lives
in tizzies and skedaddles
in steaming bowls of noodles
permeating the air with
the odor of sesame oil
and chili peppers, the broth slips
down the throat as we stretch
our muscular arms,
flexing our brains and visions
to make joy and struggle
the busiest inhabitants
on this our beloved earth.

This poem first appeared in *Dissident Song, A Contemporary Asian American Anthology* edited by Marilyn Chin and David Wong Louie (Santa Cruz, CA: Quarry West,1991).

Women Like Us

EDWIDGE DANTICAT

You remember thinking while braiding your hair that you look a lot like your mother. Your mother who looked like your grandmother and her grandmother before her. Your mother had two rules for living. *Always use your ten fingers,* which in her parlance meant that you should be the best little cook and house-keeper who ever lived.

Your mother's second rule went along with the first. Never have sex before marriage, and even after you marry, you shouldn't say you enjoy it, or your husband won't respect you.

And writing? Writing was as forbidden as dark rouge on the cheeks or a first date before eighteen. It was an act of indolence, something to be done in a corner when you could have been learning to cook.

Are there women who both cook and write? Kitchen poets, they call them. They slip phrases into their stew and wrap meaning around their pork before frying it. They make narrative dumplings and stuff their daughters' mouths so they say nothing more.

"What will she do? What will be her passion?" your aunts would ask when they came over to cook on great holidays, which called for cannon salutes back home but meant nothing at all here.

"Her passion is being quiet," your mother would say. "But then she's not being quiet. You hear this scraping from her. Krik? Krak! Pencil, paper. It sounds like someone crying."

Someone was crying. You and the writing demons in your head. You have nobody, nothing but this piece of paper, they told you. Only a notebook made out of discarded fish wrappers, panty-hose cardboard. They were the best con-fidantes for a lonely little girl.

When you write, it's like braiding your hair. Taking a handful of coarse unruly strands and attempting to bring them unity. Your fingers have still not perfected the task. Some of the braids are long, others are short. Some are thick, others are thin. Some are heavy. Others are light. Like the diverse women in your family. Those whose fables and metaphors, whose similes, and soliloquies, whose diction and *je ne sais quoi* daily slip into your survival soup, by way of their fingers.

You have always had your ten fingers. They curse you each time you force them around the contours of a pen. No, women like you don't write. They carve onion sculptures and potato statues. They sit in dark corners and braid their hair in new shapes and twists in order to control the stiffness, the unruli-ness, the rebelliousness.

You remember thinking while braiding your hair that you look a lot like your mother. You remember her silence when you laid your first notebook in front of her. Her disappointment when you told her that words would be your life's work, like the kitchen had always been hers. She was angry at you for not understanding. *And with what do you repay me? With scribbles on paper that are not worth the scratch of a pig's snout.* The sacrifices had been too great.

Writers don't leave any mark in the world. Not the world where we are from. In our world, writers are tortured and killed if they are men. Called lying whores, then raped and killed, if they are women. In our world, if you write, you are a politician, and we know what happens to politicians. They end up in a prison dungeon where their bodies are covered in scalding tar before they're forced to eat their own waste.

The family needs a nurse, not a prisoner. We need to forge ahead with our heads raised, not buried in scraps of throw-away paper. We do not want to bend over a dusty grave, wearing black hats, grieving for you. There are nine hundred and ninety-nine women who went before you and worked their fingers to coconut rind so you can stand here before me holding that torn old notebook that you cradle against your breast like your prettiest Sunday braids. I would rather you had spit in my face.

You remember thinking while braiding your hair that you look a lot like your mother and her mother before her. It was their whispers that pushed you, their murmurs over pots sizzling in your head. A thousand women urging you to speak through the blunt tip of your pencil. Kitchen poets, you call them. Ghosts like burnished branches on a flame tree. These women, they asked for your voice so that they could tell your mother in your place that yes, women like you do speak, even if they speak in a tongue that is hard to understand. Even if it's patois, dialect, Creole.

⚹⋲   ⚹⋲   ⚹⋲

The women in your family have never lost touch with one another. Death is a path we take to meet on the other side. What goddesses have joined, let no one cast asunder. With every step you take, there is an army of women watching over you. We are never any farther than the sweat on your brows or the dust on your toes. Though you walk through the valley of the shadow of death, fear no evil for we are always with you.

⚹⋲   ⚹⋲   ⚹⋲

When you were a little girl, you used to dream that you were lying among the dead and all the spirits were begging you to scream. And even now, you are still afraid to dream because you know that you will never be able to do what they say, as they say it, the old spirits that live in your blood.

Most of the women in your life had their heads down. They would wake up one morning to find their panties gone. It is not shame, however, that kept their heads down. They were singing, searching for meaning in the dust. And sometimes, they were talking to faces across the ages, faces like yours and mine.

You thought that if you didn't tell the stories, the sky would fall on your head. You often thought that without the trees, the sky would fall on your head. You learned in school that you have pencils and paper only because the trees gave themselves in unconditional sacrifice. There have been days when the sky was as close as your hair to falling on your head.

This fragile sky has terrified you your whole life. Silence terrifies you more than the pounding of a million pieces of steel chopping away at your flesh. Sometimes, you dream of hearing only the beating of your own heart, but this has never been the case. You have never been able to escape the pounding of a thousand other hearts that have outlived yours by thousands of years. And over the years when you have needed us, you have always cried "Krik?" and we have answered "Krak!" and it has shown us that you have not forgotten us.

><   ><   ><

You remember thinking while braiding your hair that you look a lot like your mother. Your mother, who looked like your grandmother and her grandmother before her. Your mother, she introduced you to the first echoes of the tongue that you now speak when at the end of the day she would braid your hair while you sat between her legs, scrubbing the kitchen pots. While your fingers worked away at the last shadows of her day's work, she would make your braids Sunday-pretty, even during the week.

When she was done she would ask you to name each braid after those nine hundred and ninety-nine women who were boiling in your blood, and since you had written them down and memorized them, the names would come rolling off your tongue. And this was your testament to the way that these women lived and died and lived again.

This essay first appeared in *Krik? Krak!* (NY: SoHo Press, 1995).
© 1991 by Edwidge Danticat. Reprinted by permission of SoHo Press.

Cornelia's Mother

ANGELA BOWEN

Cornelia's mother had headaches and lay on the couch in the living room with the shades pulled down, a wet washcloth over her forehead. I thought it was so romantic, just like white women in the movies who had fainting spells. Well, I guessed that made sense too, since she was more white than she was black, although of course I knew she was colored, just like us. Only not really like us.

It was 1950. Cornelia and I were eight years old, and had met in the schoolyard at the beginning of the school year. She was new here. I'd noticed her for the past couple of days standing by the end of the fence, just back from where we jumped rope at recess.

"Hi, you want to play jump-rope?"

"No, thanks." She shook her head quickly, but smiled a bit, showing a tiny dimple on her left cheek, just below where other people had dimples.

"You don't like to jump?" I asked.

"I'd rather just watch. I'm not very good at it."

"Well, neither am I. I just do it anyway."

"Oh, come on, I've been watching long enough to know better. You're just trying to make me feel good."

"Did it work?" She nodded. We laughed.

We were quiet, examining one another. Her eyes took in my dark brown complexion, broad nose, and full lips; my nappy hair with braids so tight they curled up at the ends, my ashy face and skinny legs, scuffed shoes and tumbledown socks. I wondered if the sash of my dress was torn. I played so roughly that the sash, tied in a bow in back, would often tear out from the seam at one side of the waist and hang down with the bow still tied, without my even noticing. Just as often, the hem would tear as I climbed over a fence and jumped to the ground.

As Cornelia's eyes passed over me, I was examining her too. She was exactly my height—we were both short for our age—but that's the closest she came to looking like me. She was the color of coffee ice cream, and just as smooth. Her hair, just a shade darker than straw, was parted in the middle and pulled straight back from a high, round forehead above inquisitive light brown eyes only a little darker than her hair. Two perfect thick braids reached barely below her shoulders, with a rust-colored bow sitting precisely above the end of each one.

"What grade are you in?" I asked.

"Third."

"I thought so. Well, how do you like Miss Bellamy?"

"How'd you know I have Miss Bellamy?"

"That's for me to know and you to find out," I teased, stepping back into the game to take my turn at the rope.

The next day at recess I spied Cornelia beside the fence and, ignoring the jump-rope crowd, moved over to join her. Her large brown eyes watched me steadily as I approached. For a fleeting moment I wished I didn't have to wear glasses. I actually liked them, but I'd heard people say I had such pretty eyes it's a shame I had to wear them. For the first time, I agreed. As I came closer, Cornelia's smile spread and the dimple appeared.

"I know how you knew I have Miss Bellamy," she announced. I grinned at her.

"Yeah, how?"

"Because there's only two third grades in the school, and you're in the other one."

"Give the girl a gold star," I said, standing tall and sweeping my arm toward her. We fell out laughing, because Miss Bellamy was famous for giving out those little gold stars.

"Have you gotten any of them on your papers yet?" I asked. She nodded, still smiling.

"Oh, the girl is smart, too," I said.

"What do you mean, *too*?" She asked softly. I suddenly became tongue-tied. What I'd meant was that she was smart as well as pretty, but of course I couldn't say it. Nobody talked that way in our neighborhood.

"So, where do you live?" I said instead. That afternoon, we walked to her house slowly, to make it last, before I ran the last two blocks home.

Cornelia was fun to be with. We'd march along three-legged, arms around waists, our middle legs so perfectly matched that we could gradually increase to a very fast run, then slow it down whenever we decided, without even saying a word or exchanging a glance. We made up word games with clues and codes that no one except ourselves knew the rules to—the kind you can play with only one person, because if you tried to include other people, the magic would disappear. One of our favorites was called *fast*. I'd start with a word like "sidewalk." She'd have to say a word beginning with the second letter, so she'd say "igloo"; then I'd say "door," she'd say "end"; and so on. But the rule was, you had to say each word faster than the one before, so sometimes we'd be saying words that didn't even make sense, shouting them faster and louder until we just fell out laughing.

The only trouble we had was with Cornelia's mother. She was sick a lot because she was so worried about Cornelia's father, who was overseas fighting "in the service," a phrase I had gradually come to realize was entirely different from the way Mama used "in service," as in, "Cousin Mary lives 'in service' at the Kaplans' out in Newton and only comes into town on Thursdays." A colored photograph of Cornelia's father sat in a gold frame on the table at the side of the couch, only inches from where the mother's feet rested when she was lying down with a headache. With her head propped on pillows, she could look directly into his face. He wore a brown soldier uniform with three gold stripes on his sleeve. A visored cap sat on top of hair that was the same light shade of gold-brown as Cornelia's. His eyes were darker than hers, but not by much, and he looked directly out at you with a serious but kind expression. His complexion too was a little darker than Cornelia's. The mother was paler than the both of them, but, except for her skin color and her smooth black hair and eyes, she could have been his sister.

She liked Cornelia to stay in the house, unlike the rest of the kids I usually played with, who could wander around freely in our Roxbury neighborhood. Cornelia and her mother lived in a five-room apartment on the second floor of a three-decker red-brick building right across the street from a park. Five rooms, for just one woman and a small child! We had seven rooms for a big family of eight. Theirs was sunny, quiet, spacious and extremely neat—an apartment where dishes never piled up in the sink. I'd never seen a roach there, but I just knew if one showed up, her mother would catch her breath in that little "Oh" kind of in-taking quiet gasp.

They were the kind who had dinner instead of supper, who ate meals all matched up with vegetables and potatoes and meat, and never ran out of food or had to have cereal for supper. They wore housecoats and slippers and had pajamas and nightgowns, not old shirts, to wear to bed. And of course, Cornelia would never wet the bed. In my house, besides wetting the bed, we also left clothes lying around and had to run from one room to another looking for our coats when it was time to go out. Sometimes we'd have to rob the bulb from one room to light another, leaving the first room in total darkness while we took care of whichever matter was more pressing elsewhere. We ran out of toilet paper and had to shout from behind the closed bathroom door for someone to bring a piece...or crumpled-up newspaper...or something!

The closed bathroom door also signified my only moments of privacy. In a family of seven children, with various sets of friends constantly coming and going, sitting and gabbing, eating, smoking, playing cards, arguing, listening to music and dancing, among other things, it took a bit of scheming just to find a quiet corner where I could read. My solution was to lock the door and sit on the laundry bag in the corner. But my solitude never lasted longer than ten minutes, and the last five of that was usually accompanied by impatient banging on the door and loud shouting. It seemed as if no one ever thought about going to the bathroom until I got in there. I'd keep reading while part of my mind measured the level of intensity in the voice outside the door, relinquishing my concentration and slamming the book shut only when the timbre of the voice matched the urgency of the message, *"Come out of there right now, right now, will you pleeeeeze??"*

I couldn't imagine Cornelia having to put up with such confusion. But then again, I didn't have to put up with anything near what Cornelia did if she wanted someone to come visit.

"Can you come play at my house tomorrow?"

"Sure I can. Right after school?"

"Wait, first I have to ask my mother, then I'll let you know."

"Well, why didn't you ask her first?"

"I don't know. It makes me nervous to ask, so just in case you couldn't come…"

"Why shouldn't I be able to come? You know I can come whenever I want to. It's just to play, it's not like staying over or something."

"Don't get mad, Aleta. My mother's not like yours. You know that."

"I'm not mad. Only dogs get mad."

Cornelia was silent. Then she said, "Okay, then, you're not mad, you're angry."

"Well, why does she have to make such a big commotion about everything, anyway?"

"How do I know? Do you think I like it?" Cornelia's face was starting to turn red. She was the only colored person I'd ever seen turn red when she got upset.

"Okay, okay," I said, "you can let me know what she says tomorrow. Just calm down, we don't want you to get apoplexy, do we?" I'd just discovered the word, and looked for occasions to use it. She smiled. Even though I sometimes lost patience with Cornelia's mother, part of me was fascinated by the way they lived. So neat. So orderly. The mother so carefully taking care of herself, lying back among the pillows on the couch.

Cornelia and I would play dolls or jacks quietly in her room or on the back porch—which had linoleum on the floor—and, if we laughed out loud, her mother would say in a whiny voice I had never heard from an adult, "Cornelia, please, dear, I have a headache."

"Sorry, Mother," Cornelia would say. I had only heard white kids in the movies say "Mother," instead of "Ma" or "Mama" or "Momma." If we let the porch door slam, it would be, "Cornelia, if you can't be quiet, your friend will have to go home. Mother is feeling ill." Ill. Nowhere outside of a book had I ever heard that word spoken aloud except for teachers who used it instead of "sick" when they sent you to the school nurse.

"All right, mother, we'll be quiet," Cornelia would say, looking pleadingly at me. I tried not to show what I was thinking, but sometimes it was beyond my control, and I would feel my eyes roll, totally on their own.

I never knew who else played with Cornelia, but I knew they'd have to have plenty of patience, which I believed I had. Besides, I did a lot of free, unsupervised kind of playing with other friends and with my brother Ralphie—roaming the city as we liked, sneaking on buses, playing jump-rope and dodgeball, climbing fences, stealing empty milk bottles from the crates in back of the corner store and reselling them to the proprietor. Cornelia didn't have my carefree type of life, so I could be generous.

But one thing I found it hard to be generous about was that Cornelia's mother never offered me anything to eat. It seemed as if they just didn't think about food. And since we hardly ever went outside to play, there was no way to swipe any goodies from the grocery or the drugstore—a form of fun I always had with anyone else I hung out with. Still, even if we had been able to go outside, something just told me I couldn't even suggest such a thing to Cornelia.

One other thing. I was a smart kid. I lived across the street from the library and spent a lot of time there. My library card was my most prized possession. On Saturdays, when my brother and sister and most of the other kids in my neighborhood went to the movies, I went to the library. You were allowed to take out only two books at a time, so I'd go early, pick up two books, rush home and read them, then double back before the library closed at five and pick up two more to get me through Sunday. I had also been class spelling champ every year since first grade. But Cornelia's mother assumed that she could spell over my head, as she did to Cornelia, who sometimes liked to pretend that she didn't understand, just so she could hear more.

Cornelia's mother's sister looked enough like her to be her twin and, whenever she visited, they were always smirking at each other while they spelled words about me being nice for coming from "such a family" and how it was good "training" for Cornelia to "share" her toys with me since I'd probably never have such an "opatunity" to play with such "high qwality" things otherwise. I never let on that I could spell such "complicated" words. They almost made me laugh, trying so hard to spell over my head that they were sometimes misspelling. But what made me the most angry was for them to think I couldn't even spell simple four-letter words.

One perfect spring afternoon, Cornelia's mother called us in from the back porch, where we were cutting out doll clothes. We came into the kitchen, where they sat listening to Stella Dallas on the radio and drinking tea from pearly china teacups that matched the pot. We had a set just like it in our dining room. The outsides were a soft greyish color, while the insides were a faint pink with rainbow colors swirling through. A line of gold ran around the rim of the cups and around the teapot, about two inches above the base. Our tea set sat behind the dusty glass doors of the china closet and only came out on rare occasions, like when Mama's women friends came for a club meeting, or on Thanksgiving when we kids were allowed to drink carefully out of them. Mama said the set had been a wedding present. Somehow it seemed right that Cornelia's mother and aunt would use theirs on a daily basis, just like it seemed right for us not to.

They asked us to run an errand. "Cornelia," said her mother, "would you and Aleta go down to the corner store for me? I need a few things for dinner."

The aunt chimed in. "Yes, this is a perfect time to go, while you have an extra pair of hands. Your mother doesn't feel well, and while I'm here I might as well prepare a good meal for the two of you." She was older than Cornelia's mother by four years, and seemed to like to show it.

The thing about going to the store for Cornelia's mother was, she didn't know the rules of the neighborhood. If you asked a child who wasn't yours to go to the store, you told them to spend a penny on candy—two cents if you didn't know them well or if they seldom did errands for you. If it was a child visiting, you simply gave them a snack or, if you didn't have anything suitable in the house, you asked them to bring back something you had included in your grocery list—cookies or an apple, maybe—then you presented it to them. Having had experience with Cornelia's mother, I knew better than to expect anything out of this trip. I would simply go along as a favor to my friend.

"Here, Cornelia," said the aunt, handing her a piece of paper. "Write this down." As she dictated the grocery list, I stood silently watching Cornelia write in her careful script. We did penmanship every day in school for twenty minutes—the Palmer Method, my teacher said—and I envied Cornelia's handwriting. Suddenly, the aunt said, "You take so long to form your letters. Here, give me the paper." She reached out and pulled it toward her, then snatched the pencil from Cornelia's fingers.

Watching my friend's face fall, I said in a snappy voice, "Are we in a hurry or something?" The aunt's hand paused as she turned her whole upper body sideways in her chair to look at me. Her eyes traveled slowly from my face to my feet and back up again. Then, looking me squarely in the eyes, she said, carefully spacing each word, "Well, *some* people like to have their dinner at a particular time every day, not just hap*haz*ardly whenever it happens. So, yes, we *would* like to get these groceries back here *rather* soon, if it's all right with *you!*

We took the list and went down the stairs. When we got outside, I said, "Whew, what a witch you've got for an aunt." I wanted to say something about her mother too, but you didn't talk about a person's mother unless you absolutely couldn't help it—and only if the other kid said it about their own mother first. Then you could agree with them. But only a teeny little bit. Cornelia said about her aunt, "Oh, she's all right most of the time. And she really likes you. She always says you're so smart, I should stick with you and I could learn something." I couldn't answer that with anything nice, so I just changed the subject.

When we got back to their building, I opened the door to the upstairs hall and turned to hold it open for Cornelia. She was struggling with the bag, so I said, "Here, I'll take it." Fair was fair, and, since we had forgotten to tell the man to pack the groceries into two bags, Cornelia had carried it all the way from the corner and up the outside steps. So I took it upstairs.

As we entered the apartment, the two sisters smiled slyly at one another. "Look," said the mother, "now Cornelia's got a M-A-I-D." Behind me, I heard my friend catch her breath. We stood in silence. The clock above the table ticked loudly, each second pushing time ever so slowly along. On either side of the clock, screened windows showed the light green of new spring leaves moving gently in the breeze. Yellow curtains with tiny raised brown dots drifted playfully up and down at the windows. As I turned to my friend, my eyes devoured in one glance the peaceful quiet of the kitchen with its polished red and brown tiled floor, spotless white sink and matching stove, where a shiny kettle emitted steam in a comforting, steady stream. At the brown, enamel-topped table with a red rim running around the edge, I saw the two sisters sitting catty-cornered, staring at us from wide, dark eyes.

"Bye, Cornelia," I choked out as I handed her the bag. For one moment, I looked into her loving brown eyes filled with tears, and wanted to reach out to hug her, but I could hear the sisters begin to snicker together behind us. I turned to the door. My hands were so sweaty I couldn't grip the knob to turn it. I knew Cornelia was willing me to look back at her but I couldn't raise my eyes. I could feel them all looking at my belt hanging off my dress, my drooping hem, tumbledown, unmatched socks, and run-over shoes. Besides, my nappy hair needed rebraiding and my lips were too big. Tears were swelling up at the back of my throat and my eyes were starting to burn.

My hand slipped round and round the knob until finally, with one mighty yank, I flung the door open and stumbled slowly down the stairs, gripping the rail to keep from falling as the hot tears rushed from my eyes. I heard

Cornelia's mother calling after me, "Aleta...Aleta? Don't you want to stay and play with Cornelia?" Then, to her sister, in an uncertain voice, "Do you think maybe she understood us?"

"Of course not," announced Cornelia's aunt in that know-it-all tone. Then, as I opened the door to the street, her voice trailed more faintly down the stairs, "Cornelia, did you understand what your mother just spelled?"

I never heard the answer. I never went back. Cornelia and I never played together again.

The Gift

SHARON DAY

I was walking toward the river
a river made by Kerr-McGee
little white fluffs from seagulls danced around the rocks
alongside empty cans of Miller Lite.
Before me lay a small Mishomis
imprinted with the markings of a small animal or fish.
I picked it up,
it was light tan in color and smooth on one side.

I carried it to the river
letting the water swirl over and around the small grandfather.
When I took it out of the water to look at it again
the light flowing from it
hurt my eyes.

I looked again.
I could see a beautiful river, so blue and crystal clear
I could see Ni Nokomis and Ni Mishomis
shining like twin orbs in the heavens.

Two hawks glided overhead,
the air was pure and fragrant
like medicine in my lungs.

I could hear drumming
  a water drum
    beating inside of me

People were singing songs
  ancient songs
    dancing a round dance

Yellow people, Red people, Black and White people
  Men, women, and children

Women dancing with women
Men dancing with men

People with no legs were dancing
People with no ears were singing
Loving themselves and each other.

The animals were talking…
"A-Ho! It is a beautiful sight."

My brother, the Makade Maingen came to me and said,
"Tell the people of this…
To sing
To dance
Take care of the earth, she is your mother. Be like the river,
like the stream, move in a sacred direction."

"Honor your loved ones,
The ones who came before you
the ones yet to come."

My tears fell like gentle rain as the light from the Mishomis faded. I
knew the small grandfather in my hand would be my first "Give-away"
of the day.

ED. NOTE:

"Ni" means my.

"Mishomis" means grandfather, and here a small fossilized rock.

"Nokomis" means grandmother or the moon.

Recitatif

TONI MORRISON

My mother danced all night and Roberta's was sick. That's why we were taken
to St. Bonny's. People want to put their arms around you when you tell them
you were in a shelter, but it really wasn't bad. No big long room with one
hundred beds like Bellevue. There were four to a room, and when Roberta and
me came, there was a shortage of state kids, so we were the only ones assigned
to 406 and could go from bed to bed if we wanted to. And we wanted to, too.
We changed beds every night and for the whole four months we were there we
never picked one out as our own permanent bed.

It didn't start out that way. The minute I walked in and the Big Bozo introduced us, I got sick to my stomach. It was one thing to be taken out of your
own bed early in the morning—it was something else to be stuck in a strange
place with a girl from a whole other race. And Mary, that's my mother, she
was right. Every now and then she would stop dancing long enough to tell
me something important and one of the things she said was that they never
washed their hair and they smelled funny. Roberta sure did. Smell funny, I
mean. So when the Big Bozo (nobody ever call her Mrs. Itkin, just like
nobody ever said St. Bonaventure)—when she said, "Twyla, this is Roberta.
Roberta, this is Twyla. Make each other welcome," I said, "My mother won't
like you putting me in here."

"Good," said Bozo. "Maybe then she'll come and take you home."

How's that for mean? If Roberta had laughed I would have killed her, but
she didn't. She just walked over to the window and stood with her back to us.

"Turn around," said the Bozo. "Don't be rude. Now Twyla. Now Roberta.
When you hear a loud buzzer, that's the call for dinner. Come down to the first
floor. Any fights and no movie." And then, just to make sure we knew what
we would be missing, *"The Wizard of Oz."*

Roberta must have thought I meant that my mother would be mad about
my being put in the shelter. Not about rooming with her, because as soon as
Bozo left she came over to me and said, "Is your mother sick too?"

"No," I said. "She just likes to dance all night."

"Oh," she nodded her head and I liked the way she understood things so
fast. So for the moment it didn't matter that we looked like salt and pepper
standing there and that's what the other kids called us sometimes. We were
eight years old and got Fs all the time. Me because I couldn't remember what
I read or what the teacher said. And Roberta because she couldn't read at all
and didn't even listen to the teacher. She wasn't good at anything except jacks,
at which she was a killer: *pow scoop pow scoop pow scoop.*

We didn't like each other all that much at first, but nobody else wanted to play with us because we weren't real orphans with beautiful dead parents in the sky. We were dumped. Even the New York City Puerto Ricans and the upstate Indians ignored us. All kinds of kids were in there, black ones, white ones, even two Koreans. The food was good, though. At least I thought so. Roberta hated it and left whole pieces of things on her plate: Spam, Salisbury steak—even Jell-o with fruit cocktail in it, and she didn't care if I ate what she wouldn't. Mary's idea of supper was popcorn and a can of Yoo-Hoo. Hot mashed potatoes and two weenies was like Thanksgiving for me.

It really wasn't bad, St. Bonny's. The big girls on the second floor pushed us around now and then. But that was all. They wore lipstick and eyebrow pencil and wobbled their knees while they watched TV. Fifteen, sixteen, even, some of them were. They were put-out girls, scared runaways most of them. Poor little girls who fought their uncles off but looked tough to us, and mean. God did they look mean. The staff tried to keep them separate from the younger children, but sometimes they caught us watching them in the orchard where they played radios and danced with each other. They'd light out after us and pull our hair or twist our arms. We were scared of them, Roberta and me, but neither of us wanted the other one to know it. So we got a good list of dirty names we could shout back when we ran from them through the orchard. I used to dream a lot and almost always the orchard was there. Two acres, four maybe, of these little apple trees. Hundred of them. Empty and crooked like beggar women when I first came to St. Bonny's but fat with flowers when I left. I don't know why I dreamt about that orchard so much. Nothing really happened there. Nothing all that important, I mean. Just the big girls dancing and playing the radio. Roberta and me watching. Maggie fell down there once. The kitchen woman with legs like parentheses. And the big girls laughed at her. We should have helped her up, I know, but we were scared of those girls with lipstick and eyebrow pencil. Maggie couldn't talk. The kids said she had her tongue cut out, but I think she was just born that way: mute. She was old and sandy-colored and she worked in the kitchen. I don't know if she was nice or not, I just remember her legs like parentheses and how she rocked when she walked. She worked from early in the morning till two o'clock, and if she was late, if she had too much cleaning and didn't get out till two-fifteen or so, she'd cut through the orchard so she wouldn't miss her bus and have to wait another hour. She wore this really stupid little hat—a kid's hat with ear flaps—and she wasn't much taller than we were. A really awful little hat. Even for a mute, it was dumb—dressing like a kid and never saying anything at all.

"But what about if somebody tries to kill her?" I used to wonder about that. "Or what if she wants to cry? Can she cry?"

"Sure," Roberta said. "But just tears. No sounds come out."

"She can't scream?"

"Nope. Nothing."

"Can she hear?"

"I guess."

"Let's call her," I said. And we did.

"Dummy! Dummy!" She never turned her head.

"Bow legs! Bow legs!" Nothing. She just rocked on, the chin straps of her baby-boy hat swaying from side to side. I think we were wrong. I think she could hear and didn't let on. And it shames me even now to think there was somebody in there after all who heard us call her those names and couldn't tell on us.

We got along all right, Roberta and me. Changed beds every night, got Fs in civics and communication skills and gym. The Bozo was disappointed in us, she said. Out of 130 of us state cases, 90 were under twelve. Almost all were real orphans with beautiful dead parents in the sky. We were the only ones dumped and the only ones with Fs in three classes including gym. So we got along—what with her leaving whole pieces of things on her plate and being nice about not asking questions.

I think it was the day before Maggie fell down that we found out our mothers were coming to visit us on the same Sunday. We had been at the shelter twenty-eight days (Roberta twenty-eight and a half) and this was their first visit with us. Our mothers would come at ten o'clock in time for chapel, then lunch with us in the teachers' lounge. I thought if my dancing mother met her sick mother it might be good for her. And Roberta thought her sick mother would get a big bang out of a dancing one. We got excited about it and curled each other's hair. After breakfast we sat on the bed watching the road from the window. Roberta's socks were still wet. She washed them the night before and put them on the radiator to dry. They hadn't, but she put them on anyway because their tops were so pretty—scalloped in pink. Each of us had a purple construction-paper basket that we had made in craft class. Mine had a yellow crayon rabbit on it. Roberta's had eggs with wiggly lines of color. Inside were cellophane grass and just the jelly beans because I'd eaten the two marshmallow eggs they gave us. The Big Bozo came herself to get us. Smiling she told us we looked very nice and to come downstairs. We were so surprised by the smile we'd never seen before, neither of us moved.

"Don't you want to see your mommies?"

I stood up first and spilled the jelly beans all over the floor. Bozo's smile disappeared while we scrambled to get the candy up off the floor and put it back in the grass.

She escorted us downstairs to the first floor, where the other girls were lining up to file into the chapel. A bunch of grown-ups stood to one side.

Viewers mostly. The old biddies who wanted servants and the fags who wanted company looking for children they might want to adopt. Once in a while a grandmother. Almost never anybody young or anybody whose face wouldn't scare you in the night. Because if any of the real orphans had young relatives they wouldn't be real orphans. I saw Mary right away. She had on those green slacks I hated and hated even more now because didn't she know we were going to chapel? And that fur jacket with the pocket linings so ripped she had to pull to get her hands out of them. But her face was pretty—like always, and she smiled and waved like she was the little girl looking for her mother—not me.

I walked slowly, trying not to drop the jelly beans and hoping the paper handle would hold. I had to use my last Chiclet because by the time I finished cutting everything out, all the Elmer's was gone. I am left-handed and the scissors never worked for me. It didn't matter, though; I might just as well have chewed the gum. Mary dropped to her knees and grabbed me, mashing the basket, the jelly beans, and the grass into her ratty fur jacket.

"Twyla, baby. Twyla, baby!"

I could have killed her. Already I heard the big girls in the orchard the next time saying, "Twyyyyyla, baby!" But I couldn't stay mad at Mary while she was smiling and hugging me and smelling of Lady Esther dusting powder. I wanted to stay buried in her fur all day.

To tell the truth I forgot about Roberta. Mary and I got in line for the traipse into chapel and I was feeling proud because she looked so beautiful even in those ugly green slacks that made her behind stick out. A pretty mother on earth is better than a beautiful dead one in the sky even if she did leave you all alone to go dancing.

I felt a tap on my shoulder, turned, and saw Roberta smiling. I smiled back, but not too much lest somebody think this visit was the biggest thing that ever happened in my life. Then Roberta said, "Mother, I want you to meet my roommate, Twyla. And that's Twyla's mother."

I looked up it seemed for miles. She was big. Bigger than any man and on her chest was the biggest cross I'd ever seen. I swear it was six inches long each way. And in the crook of her arm was the biggest Bible ever made.

Mary, simple-minded as ever, grinned and tried to yank her hand out of the pocket with the raggedy lining—to shake hands, I guess. Roberta's mother looked down at me and then looked down at Mary too. She didn't say anything, just grabbed Roberta with her Bible-free hand and stepped out of line, walking quickly to the rear of it. Mary was still grinning because she's not too swift when it comes to what's really going on. Then this light bulb goes off in her head and she says "That bitch!" really loud and us almost in the chapel now. Organ music whining; the Bonny Angels singing sweetly. Everybody in the world turned around to look. And Mary would have kept it up—kept calling names if I hadn't squeezed her hand as hard as I could. That helped a little, but she still twitched and crossed and uncrossed her legs all through service. Even groaned a couple of times. Why did I think she would come there and act right? Slacks. No hat like the grandmothers and viewers, and groaning all the while. When we stood for hymns she kept her mouth shut. Wouldn't even look at the words on the page. She actually reached in her purse for a mirror to check her lipstick. All I could think of was that she really needed to be killed. The sermon lasted a year, and I know the real orphans were looking smug again.

We were supposed to have lunch in the teachers' lounge, but Mary didn't bring anything, so we picked fur and cellophane grass off the mashed jelly beans and ate them. I could have killed her. I sneaked a look at Roberta. Her mother had brought chicken legs and ham sandwiches and oranges and a whole box of chocolate-covered grahams. Roberta drank milk from a Thermos while her mother read the Bible to her.

Things are not right. The wrong food is always with the wrong people Maybe that's why I got into waitress work later—to match up the right people with the right food. Roberta just let those chicken legs sit there, but she did bring a stack of grahams up to me later when the visit was over. I think she was sorry that her mother would not shake my mother's hand. And I liked that and I liked the fact that she didn't say a word about Mary groaning all the way through the service and not bringing any lunch.

Roberta left in May when the apple trees were heavy and white. On her last day we went to the orchard to watch the big girls smoke and dance by the radio. It didn't matter that they said, "Twyyyyyla, baby." We sat on the ground and breathed. Lady Esther. Apple blossoms. I still go soft when I smell one or the other. Roberta was going home. The big cross and the big Bible was coming to get her and she seemed sort of glad and sort of not. I thought I would die in that room of four beds without her and I knew Bozo had plans to move some other dumped kid in there with me. Roberta promised to write every day, which was really of sweet of her because she couldn't read a lick so how could she write anybody. I would have drawn pictures and sent them to her but she never gave me her address. Little by little she faded. Her wet socks with the pink scalloped tops and her big serious-looking eyes—that's all I could catch when I tried to bring her to mind.

I was working behind the counter at the Howard Johnson's on the Thruway just before the Kingston exit. Not a bad job. Kind of a long ride from Newburgh, but okay once I got there. Mine was the second night shift—

eleven to seven. Very light until a Greyhound checked in for breakfast around six-thirty. At that hour the sun was all the way clear of the hills behind the restaurant. The place looked better at night—more like shelter—but I loved it when the sun broke in, even if it did show all the cracks in the vinyl and the speckled floor looked dirty no matter what the mop boy did.

It was August and a bus crowd was just unloading. They would stand around a long while: going to the john, and looking at gifts and junk-for-sale machines, reluctant to sit down so soon. Even to eat. I was trying to fill the coffee pots and get them all situated on the electric burners when I saw her. She was sitting in a booth smoking a cigarette with two guys smothered in head and facial hair. Her own hair was so big and wild I could hardly see her face. But the eyes. I would know them anywhere. She had on a powder-blue halter and shorts outfit and earrings the size of bracelets. Talk about lipstick and eyebrow pencil. She made the big girls look like nuns. I couldn't get off the counter until seven o'clock, but I kept watching the booth in case they got up to leave before that. My replacement was on time for a change, so I counted and stacked my receipts as fast as I could and signed off. I walked over to the booth, smiling and wondering if she would remember me. Or even if she wanted to remember me. Maybe she didn't want to be reminded of St. Bonny's or to have anybody know she was ever there. I know I never talked about it to anybody.

I put my hands in my apron pockets and leaned against the back of the booth facing them.

"Roberta? Roberta Fisk?"

She looked up. "Yeah?"

"Twyla."

She squinted for a second and then said, "Wow."

"Remember me?"

"Sure. Hey. Wow."

"It's been a while," I said, and gave a smile to the two hairy guys.

"Yeah. Wow. You work here?"

"Yeah," I said. "I live in Newburgh."

"Newburgh? No kidding?" She laughed then a private laugh that included the guys but only the guys, and they laughed with her. What could I do but laugh too and wonder why I was standing there with my knees showing out from under that uniform. Without looking I could see the blue and white triangle on my head, my hair shapeless in a net, my ankles thick in white oxfords. Nothing could have been less sheer than my stockings. There was this silence that came down right after I laughed. A silence it was her turn to fill up. With introductions, maybe, to her boyfriends or an invitation to sit down and have a Coke. Instead, she lit a cigarette off the one she'd just finished and said, "We're on our way to the Coast. He's got an appointment with Hendrix." She gestured casually toward the boy next to her.

"Hendrix? Fantastic," I said. "Really fantastic. What's she doing now?"

Roberta coughed on her cigarette and the two guys rolled their eyes up at the ceiling.

"Hendrix. Jimi Hendrix, asshole. He's only the biggest—Oh, wow. Forget it."

I was dismissed without anyone saying goodbye, so I thought I would do it for her.

"How's your mother?" I asked. Her grin cracked her whole face. She swallowed. "Fine," she said. "How's yours?"

"Pretty as a picture," I said and turned away. The backs of my knees were damp. Howard Johnson's really was a dump in the sunlight.

✄   ✄   ✄

James is as comfortable as a house slipper. He liked my cooking and I liked his big loud family. They have lived in Newburgh all of their lives and talk about it the way people do who have always known a home. His grandmother is a porch swing older than his father and when they talk about streets and avenues and buildings they call them names they no longer have. They still call the A&P Rico's because it stands on property once a mom and pop store owned by Mr. Rico. And they call the new community college Town Hall because it once was. My mother-in-law puts up jelly and cucumbers and buys butter wrapped in cloth from a dairy. James and his father talk about fishing and baseball and I can see them all together on the Hudson in a raggedy skiff. Half the population of Newburgh is on welfare now, but to my husband's family it was still some upstate paradise of a time long past. A time of ice houses and vegetable wagons, coal furnaces and children weeding gardens. When our son was born my mother-in-law gave me the crib blanket that had been hers.

But the town they remembered had changed. Something quick was in the air. Magnificent old houses, so ruined they had become shelter for squatters and rent risks, were bought and renovated. Smart IBM people moved out of their suburbs back into the city and put shutters up and herb gardens in their backyards. A brochure came in the mail announcing the opening of a Food Emporium. Gourmet food it said—and listed items the rich IBM crowd would want. It was located in a new mall at the edge of town and I drove out to shop there one day—just to see. It was late in June. After the tulips were gone and the Queen Elizabeth roses were open everywhere. I trailed my cart along the aisle tossing in smoked oysters and Robert's sauce and things I knew would sit in my cupboard for years. Only when I found some Klondike ice cream bars did I feel less guilty about spending James's fireman's salary so foolishly. My father-in-law ate them with the same gusto little Joseph did.

Waiting in the check-out line I heard a voice say, "Twyla!"

The classical music piped over the aisle had affected me and the woman leaning toward me was dressed to kill. Diamonds on her hand, a smart white summer dress. "I'm Mrs. Benson," I said.

"Ho. Ho. The Big Bozo," she sang.

For a split second I didn't know what she was talking about. She had a bunch of asparagus and two cartons of fancy water.

"Roberta!"

"Right."

"For heaven's sake. Roberta."

"You look great," she said.

"So do you. Where are you? Here? In Newburgh?"

"Yes. Over in Annandale."

I was opening my mouth to say more when the cashier called my attention to her empty counter.

"Meet you outside." Roberta pointed her finger and went into the express line.

I placed the groceries and kept myself from glancing around to check Roberta's progress. I remembered Howard Johnson's and looking for a chance to speak only to be greeted with a stingy "wow." But she was waiting for me and her huge hair was sleek now, smooth around a small, nicely shaped head. Shoes, dress, everything lovely and summery and rich. I was dying to know what happened to her, how she got from Jimi Hendrix to Annandale, a neighborhood full of doctors and IBM executives. Easy, I thought. Everything is so easy for them. They think they own the world.

"How long," I asked her. "How long have you been here?"

"A year. I got married to a man who lives here. And you, you're married too, right? Benson, you said."

"Yeah. James Benson."

"And is he nice?"

"Oh, is he nice?"

"Well, is he?" Roberta's eyes were steady as though she really meant the question and wanted an answer.

"He's wonderful, Roberta. Wonderful."

"So you're happy."

"Very."

"That's good," she said and nodded her head. "I always hoped you'd be happy. Any kids? I know you have kids."

"One. A boy. How about you?"

"Four."

"Four?"

She laughed. "Step-kids. He's a widower."

"Oh."

"Got a minute? Let's have a coffee."

I thought about the Klondikes melting and the inconvenience of going all the way to my car and putting the bags in the trunk. Served me right for buying all that stuff I didn't need. Roberta was ahead of me.

"Put them in my car. It's right here."

And then I saw the dark blue limousine.

"You married a Chinaman?"

"No," she laughed. "He's the driver."

"Oh, my. If the Big Bozo could see you now."

We both giggled. Really giggled. Suddenly, in just a pulse beat, twenty years disappeared and all of it came rushing back. The big girls (whom we called gar girls—Roberta's misheard word for the evil stone faces described in a civics class) there dancing in the orchard, the ploppy mashed potatoes, the double weenies, the Spam with pineapple. We went into the coffee shop holding on to one another and I tried to think why we were glad to see each other this time and not before. Once, twelve years ago, we passed like strangers. A black girl and a white girl meeting in a Howard Johnson's on the road and having nothing to say. One in a blue and white triangle waitress hat—the other on her way to see Hendrix. Now we were behaving like sisters separated for much too long. Those four short months were nothing in time. Maybe it was the thing itself. Just being there, together. Two little girls who knew what nobody else in the world knew—how not to ask questions. How to believe what had to be believed. There was politeness in that reluctance and generosity as well. Is your mother sick too? No, she dances all night. Oh—and an understanding nod.

We sat in a booth by the window and fell into recollection like veterans.

"Did you ever learn to read?"

"Watch." She picked up the menu. "Special of the day. Cream of corn soup. Entrées. Two dots and a wiggly line. Quiche. Chef salad, scallops…"

I was laughing and applauding when the waitress came up.

"Remember the Easter baskets?"

"And how we tried to *introduce* them?"

"Your mother with that cross like two telephone poles."

"And yours with those tight slacks."

We laughed so loudly heads turned and made the laughter harder to suppress.

"What happened to the Jimi Hendrix date?"

Roberta made a blow-out sound with her lips.

"When he died I thought about you."

"Oh, you heard about him finally?"

"Finally. Come on, I was a small-town country waitress."

"And I was a small-town country dropout. God, were we wild. I still don't know how I got out of there alive."

"But you did."

"I did. I really did. Now I'm Mrs. Kenneth Norton."

"Sounds like a mouthful."

"It is."

"Servants and all?" Roberta held up two fingers.

"Ow! What does he do?"

"Computers and stuff. What do I know?"

"I don't remember a hell of a lot from those days, but Lord, St. Bonny's is as clear as daylight. Remember Maggie? The day she fell down and those gar girls laughed at her?"

Roberta looked up from her salad and stared at me.

"Maggie didn't fall," she said.

"Yes, she did. You remember."

"No, Twyla. They knocked her down. Those girls pushed her down and tore her clothes. In the orchard."

"I don't—that's not what happened."

"Sure it is. In the orchard. Remember how scared we were?"

"Wait a minute. I don't remember any of that."

"And Bozo was fired."

"You're crazy. She was there when I left. You left before me."

"I went back. You weren't there when they fired Bozo."

"What?"

"Twice. Once for a year when I was about ten, another for two months when I was fourteen. That's when I ran away."

"You ran away from St. Bonny's?"

"I had to. What do you want? Me dancing in that orchard?"

"Are you sure about Maggie?"

"Of course I'm sure. You've blocked it, Twyla. It happened. Those girls had behavior problems, you know."

"Didn't they, though. But why can't I remember the Maggie thing?"

"Believe me. It happened. And we were there."

"Who did you room with when you went back?" I asked her as if I would know her. The Maggie thing was troubling me.

"Creeps. They tickled themselves in the night."

My ears were itching and I wanted to go home suddenly. This was all very well but she couldn't just comb her hair, wash her face and pretend everything was hunky-dory. After the Howard Johnson's snub. And no apology. Nothing.

"Were you on dope or what that time at Howard Johnson's?" I tried to make my voice sound friendlier than I felt.

"Maybe, a little. I never did drugs much. Why?"

"I don't know; you acted sort of like you didn't want to know me then."

"Oh, Twyla, you know how it was in those days: black—white. You know how everything was."

But I didn't know. I thought it was just the opposite. Busloads of blacks and whites came into Howard Johnson's together. They roamed together then: students, musicians, lovers, protesters. You got to see everything at Howard Johnson's and blacks were very friendly with whites in those days. But sitting there with nothing on my plate but two hard tomato wedges wondering about the melting Klondikes it seemed childish remembering the slight. We went to her car, and with the help of the driver, got my stuff into my station wagon.

"We'll keep in touch this time," she said.

"Sure," I said. "Sure. Give me a call."

"I will," she said, and then just as I was sliding behind the wheel, she leaned into the window. "By the way. Your mother. Did she ever stop dancing?"

I shook my head. "No. Never."

Roberta nodded.

"And yours? Did she ever get well?"

She smiled a tiny sad smile. "No. She never did. Look, call me, okay?"

"Okay," I said, but I knew I wouldn't. Roberta had messed up my past somehow with that business about Maggie. I wouldn't forget a thing like that. Would I?

❧   ❧   ❧

Strife came to us that fall. At least that's what the paper called it. Strife. Racial strife. The word made me think of a bird—a big shrieking bird out of 1,000,000,000 B.C. Flapping its wings and cawing. Its eye with no lid always bearing down on you. All day it screeched and at night it slept on the rooftops. It woke you in the morning and from the *Today* show to the eleven o'clock news it kept you an awful company. I couldn't figure it out from one day to the next. I knew I was supposed to feel something strong, but I didn't know what, and James wasn't any help. Joseph was on the list of kids to be transferred from the junior high school to another one at some far-out-of-the-way place and I thought it was a good thing until I heard it was a bad thing. I mean I didn't know. All the schools seemed dumps to me, and the fact that one was nicer looking didn't hold much weight. But the papers were full of it and then the kids began to get jumpy. In August, mind you. Schools weren't even open yet. I thought Joseph might be frightened to go over there, but he didn't seem scared so I forgot about it, until I found myself driving along Hudson Drive out there by the school they were trying to integrate and saw a line of women marching. And who do you suppose was in line, big as life, holding a sign in front of her bigger than her mother's cross? "MOTHERS HAVE RIGHTS TOO!" it said.

I drove on, and then changed my mind. I circled the block, slowed down, and honked my horn.

Roberta looked over and when she saw me she waved. I didn't wave back, but I didn't move either. She handed her sign to another woman and come over to where I was parked.

"Hi."

"What are you doing?"

"Picketing. What's it look like?"

"What for?"

"What do you mean, 'What for?' They want to take my kids and send them out of the neighborhood. They don't want to go."

"So what if they go to another school? My boy's being bussed too, and I don't mind. Why should you?"

"It's not about us, Twyla. Me and you. It's about our kids."

"What's more *us* than that?"

"Well, it is a free country."

"Not yet, but it will be."

"What the hell does that mean? I'm not doing anything to you."

"You really think that?"

"I know it."

"I wonder what made me think you were different."

"I wonder what made me think you were different."

"Look at them," I said. "Just look. Who do they think they are? Swarming all over the place like they own it. And now they think they can decide were my child goes to school. Look at them, Roberta. They're Bozos."

Roberta turned around and looked at the women. Almost all of them were standing still now, wafting. Some were edging toward us. Roberta looked at me out of some refrigerator behind her eyes. "No, they're not. They're just mothers."

"And what am I? Swiss cheese?"

"I used to curl your hair."

"I hated your hands in my hair."

The women were moving. Our faces looked mean to them of course and they looked as though they could not wait to throw themselves in front of a police car, or better yet, into my car and drag me away by my ankles. Now they surrounded my car and gently, gently began to rock it. I swayed back and forth like a sideways yo-yo. Automatically I reached for Roberta, like the old days in the orchard when they saw us watching them and we had to get out of there, and if one of us fell the other pulled her up and if one of us was caught the other stayed to kick and scratch, and neither would leave the other behind. My arm shot out of the car window but no receiving hand was there. Roberta was looking at me sway from side to side in the car and her face was still. My purse slid from the car seat down under the dashboard. The four policemen who had been drinking Tab in their car finally got the message and strolled over, forcing their way through the women. Quietly, firmly they spoke. "Okay, ladies. Back in line or off the streets."

Some of them went away willingly; others had to be urged away from the car doors and the hood. Roberta didn't move. She was looking steadily at me. I was fumbling to turn on the ignition, which wouldn't catch because the gearshift was still in drive. The seats of the car were a mess because the swaying had thrown my grocery coupons all over it and my purse was sprawled on the floor.

"Maybe I am different now, Twyla. But you're not. You're the same little state kid who kicked a poor old black lady when she was down on the ground. You kicked a black lady and you have the nerve to call me a bigot."

The coupons were everywhere and the guts of my purse were bunched under the dashboard. What was she saying? Black? Maggie wasn't black.

"She wasn't black," I said.

"Like hell she wasn't, and you kicked her. We both did. You kicked a black lady who couldn't even scream."

"Liar!"

"You're the liar! Why don't you just go on home and leave us alone, huh?"

She turned away and I skidded away from the curb.

The next morning I went into the garage and cut the side out of the carton our portable TV had come in. It wasn't nearly big enough, but after a while I had a decent sign: red spraypainted letters on a white background—AND SO DO CHILDREN***. I meant just to go down to the school and tack it up somewhere so those cows on the picket line across the street could see it, but when I got there, some ten or so others had already assembled—protesting the cows across the street. Police permits and everything. I got in line and we strutted in time on our side while Roberta's group strutted on theirs. That first day we were all dignified, pretending the other side didn't exist. The second day there was name-calling and finger gestures. But that was about all. People changed signs from time to time, but Roberta never did and neither did I. Actually my sign didn't make sense without Roberta's. "And so do children what?" one of the women on my side asked me. "Have rights," I said, as though it was obvious.

Roberta didn't acknowledge my presence in any way and I got to thinking maybe she didn't know I was there. I began to pace myself in the line, jostling people one minute and lagging behind the next, so Roberta and I could reach the end of our respective lines at the same time and there would be a moment in our turn when we would face each other. Still, I couldn't tell whether she saw me and knew my sign was for her. The next day I went early before we were scheduled to assemble. I waited until she got there before I exposed my new creation. As soon as she hoisted her MOTHERS HAVE RIGHTS TOO I began to wave my new one, which said, HOW WOULD YOU KNOW? I know she saw that one, but I had gotten addicted now. My signs got crazier each day, and the women on my side decided that I was a kook. They couldn't make heads or tails out of my brilliant screaming posters.

I brought a painted sign in queenly red with huge black letters that said, IS YOUR MOTHER WELL? Roberta took her lunch break and didn't come back for the rest of the day or any day after. Two days later I stopped going too and couldn't have been missed because nobody understood my signs anyway.

It was a nasty six weeks. Classes were suspended and Joseph didn't go to anybody's school until October. The children—everybody's children—soon got bored with that extended vacation they thought was going to be so great. They looked at TV until their eyes flattened. I spent a couple of mornings tutoring my son, as the other mothers said we should. Twice I opened a text from last year that he had never turned in. Twice he yawned in my face. Other mothers organized living room sessions so the kids would keep up. None of the kids could concentrate so they drifted back to *The Price Is Right* and *The Brady Bunch*. When the school finally opened there were fights once or twice and some sirens roared through the streets every once in a while. There were a lot of photographers from Albany. And just when ABC was about to send up a news crew, the kids settled down like nothing in the world had happened. Joseph hung my HOW WOULD YOU KNOW? sign in his bedroom. I don't know what became of AND SO DO CHILDREN***. I think my father-in-law cleaned some fish on it. He was always puttering around in our garage. Each of his five children lived in Newburgh and he acted as though he had five extra homes.

I couldn't help looking for Roberta when Joseph graduated from high school, but I didn't see her. It didn't trouble me much what she had said to me in the car. I mean the kicking part. I know I didn't do that, I couldn't do that. But I was puzzled by her telling me Maggie was black. When I thought about it I actually couldn't be certain. She wasn't pitch-black, I knew, or I would have remembered that. What I remember was the kiddie hat, and the semicircle legs. I tried to reassure myself about the race thing for a long time until it dawned on me that the truth was already there, and Roberta knew it. I didn't kick her; I didn't join in with the gar girls and kick that lady, but I sure did want to. We watched and never tried to help her and never called for help. Maggie was my dancing mother. Deaf, I thought, and dumb. Nobody inside. Nobody who would hear you if you cried in the night. Nobody who could tell you anything important that you could use. Rocking, dancing, swaying as she walked. And when the gar girls pushed her down, and started roughhousing, I knew she wouldn't scream, couldn't—just like me—and I was glad about that.

                       ✖   ✖   ✖

We decided not to have a tree, because Christmas would be at my mother-in-law's house, so why have a tree at both places? Joseph was at SUNY New Paltz and we had to economize, we said. But at the last minute, I changed my mind. Nothing could be that bad. So I rushed around town looking for a tree, something small but wide. By the time I found a place, it was snowing and very late. I dawdled like it was the most important purchase in the world and the tree man was fed up with me. Finally I chose one and had it tied onto the trunk of the car. I drove away slowly because the sand trucks were not out yet and the streets could be murder at the beginning of a snowfall. Downtown the streets were wide and rather empty except for a cluster of people coming out of the Newburgh Hotel. The one hotel in town that wasn't built out of cardboard and Plexiglas. A party, probably. The men huddled in the snow were dressed in tails and the women had on furs. Shiny things glittered from underneath their coats. It made me tired to look at them. Tired, tired, tired. On the next corner was a small diner with loops and loops of paper bells in the window. I stopped the car and went in. Just for a cup of coffee and twenty minutes of peace before I went home and tried to finish everything before Christmas Eve.

"Twyla?"

There she was, in a silvery evening gown and dark fur coat. A man and another woman were with her, the man fumbling for change to put in the cigarette machine. The woman was humming and tapping on the counter with her fingernails. They all looked a little bit drunk.

"Well. It's you."

"How are you?"

I shrugged. "Pretty good. Frazzled. Christmas and all."

"Regular?" called the woman from the counter.

"Fine," Roberta called back and then, "Wait for me in the car."

She slipped into the booth beside me. "I have to tell you something, Twyla. I made up my mind if I ever saw you again, I'd tell you."

"I'd just as soon not hear anything, Roberta. It doesn't matter now, anyway."

"No," she said. "Not about that."

"Don't be long," said the woman. She carried two regulars to go and the man peeled his cigarette pack as they left.

"It's about St. Bonny's and Maggie."

"Oh, please."

"Listen to me. I really did think she was black. I didn't make that up. I really thought so. But now I can't be sure. I just remember her as old, so old. And because she couldn't talk—well, you know, I thought she was crazy. She'd been brought up in an institution like my mother was and like I thought I would be too. And you were right. We didn't kick her. It was the gar girls. Only them. But, well, I wanted to. I really wanted them to hurt her. I said we did it, too. You and me, but that's not true. And I don't want you to carry that around. It was just that I wanted to do it so bad that day— wanting to is doing it."

Her eyes were watery from the drinks she'd had, I guess. I know it's that way with me. One glass of wine and I start bawling over the littlest thing.

"We were kids, Roberta."

"Yeah. Yeah. I know, just kids."

"Eight."

"Eight."

"And lonely."

"Scared, too."

She wiped her cheeks with the heel of her hand and smiled. "Well, that's all I wanted to say."

I nodded and couldn't think of any way to fill the silence that went from the diner past the paper bells on out into the snow. It was heavy now. I thought I'd better wait for the sand trucks before starting home.

"Thanks, Roberta."

"Sure."

"Did I tell you? My mother, she never did stop dancing."

"Yes. You told me. And mine, she never got well." Roberta lifted her hands from the tabletop and covered her face with her palms. When she took them away she really was crying. "Oh shit, Twyla. Shit, shit, shit. What the hell happened to Maggie?"

This essay first appeared in *Confirmations: An Anthology of African American Women* edited by Amiri Baraka and Amina Baraka. (NY: Wm Morrow and Company). Reprinted by permission of International Creative Management, Inc.

Can a Tiger Climb Trees?

MI OK SONG BRUINING

October 20, 1997

One year ago
today,
I arrived here
in Korea.

The orange-colored trees
were decaying.
The river was muddy
& stagnant,
& the mountain became too steep
to climb.

I returned
after twelve long years
of running away
& running towards the yellow ghosts—
to plant my own tree,
forge a new river,
& climb up a different mountain.

Autumn—

I chopped down the trees,
drained the river,
fell down the mountain—

& returned
to the ancient & sorrowful soil
where I had been conceived.

Would I find what I was looking for?
Would I be found by someone

who was looking for me?

Winter—

I became a displaced parcel—
a product of my birth father's rage

towards his stunted & twisted trees,
& his failure to conquer the slippery mountain
while he drowned in the shallow river.

Now, today, one year later—
I have found
what I was looking for
& I was found by someone
who was looking for me.

Spring—

Learning about
my birth mother's own bare trees,
parched rivers
& barren mountains,

I now know the aching truth
of her own sorrows
in not being able
to grow her own trees,
cross rivers & climb mountains
with her only daughter.

I know now that I was sent away
to greener trees, cooler rivers,
& higher mountains.

Summer—

I love & hate this country—
for her majestic trees,

looming mountains
& icy rivers.

I have seen the yellow ghosts,
high up in the trees—
with the tiger
by the river
at the foot of the mountain.

As a foreigner, I am asked
what are the trees I can call my own,
how do I swim in the rivers,
& where are the mountains I climb?

Autumn—

As an outsider, I am naming
my own trees.
I am discovering
my own river,

to claim my own
mountain,
plant my own trees
& calling the yellow ghosts
home.

I am the tiger
crossing the river
& climbing
up the orange-colored tree
for a better view
of the yellow ghosts
on the mountain.

Omoni in Korea:
Finding My Birth Mother and Family

BY MI OK SONG BRUINING

November 1996. Seoul, South Korea. One crisp evening, I was sitting in one of my favorite cafes in *In-sa-dong,* my favorite neighborhood. I was with my friend Mihee. A Korean man walked into the cafe and Mihee introduced me to Mr. Choi, a reporter from the *Cho-sun Il-bo*—the largest and oldest newspaper in Korea. When he found out I was American, Mr. Choi asked me for a list of Korean adoptees in America, as he was writing an article about Korean adoptees in the United States and was going there. I gave him a list of about thirty Korean adoptees I knew of. Some of them I knew well and others I had never met. I asked him to write an article for me about my search for my birth mother in Korea.

I knew the only way I could find any information about my birth mother was with a newspaper article. I had no information about my birth family, and after three months in Korea I had not made any progress in searching for my birth family. Holt International Children's Services, Inc. is the adoption agency I was adopted through in 1966. I went to the Holt office several times to obtain my adoption records, but each time I was given different stories. All the information they provided me was conflicting and fabricated. The Holt social workers told me that my records were located at the orphanage and I would have to wait until the next week to obtain my files. The next time I went to the office, I was informed that my records had been burned in a fire. After complaining to my Korean friends who translated for me, I was finally given a one-page Xeroxed copy of my adoption record.

The social worker then told me that they had no information about my birth family, yet they knew that both of my birth parents had died in a car accident. I was baffled. How could Holt know that my birth family died in a car crash yet didn't have any information about them? It didn't make sense. When I spoke to other Korean adoptees I had met in Korea and asked them if they had checked with Holt about their birth families, they were also informed that their birth parents had amazingly died in car crashes as well. I became suspicious. These stories were far beyond coincidences of nature. Either Holt was hiding a systematic cover up, they were lying, or Korean birth parents in Korea were terrible drivers. I realize that people are notoriously bad drivers in Korea, yet could so many birth parents have died in car crashes? As far as I was concerned, Holt was useless to me—and more than that, detrimental to my finding out any tangible shred of information about my birth family. I didn't even know if my Korean first and last name were mine or given to me by the orphanage, as was customary with the thousands of Korean children who were "abandoned." I never believed I was abandoned either.

I never expected to find my birth mother. I didn't know whether she was alive, yet always felt she did not die in a horrible car accident. All I knew was that I had to try. All I hoped for was some information about a distant relative who might have known my birth mother years ago. I wanted to know whether the orphanage gave my Korean names to me. I wanted to know if Holt had fabricated my birthday as estimation of my age. I would have been thrilled to have met a distant cousin or in-law of a member of my birth family. Mr. Choi was reluctant to write an article about me because I had no information, yet I appealed to him that that was the reason I needed him to write an article about me in the newspaper. It was my last chance at trying to find my birth mother.

Upon Mr. Choi's return from the States back in Seoul, where he had met several of the Korean adoptees whose names I had given him, I begged him once again to write the article about my wanting to search for my birth mother. Two weeks later he agreed. The article was brief, with a newspaper photo of me holding my wooden statue—*Omoni*—"Mother." It was a sculpture carved and painted by my friend Yun Suk Nam. Mr. Choi wrote the article that evening, after I had I met him the second time in the same café; the next day, his article about me appeared in the newspaper.

The article appeared on Sunday, January 12, 1997. The next morning, the SBS-TV station contacted me. They interviewed me in the former *yog-wan* (cheap foreigner boarding room) I had lived in *In-sa-dong*. Mr. Choi's article described my former wretched living condition, my two bouts with acute bronchitis, and my struggles, my poverty, and failure at finding a teaching contract. After three months in Korea, I was very ill, exhausted, and penniless.

Media Response

The article also stated that I would be leaving Korea in a week to return to the States permanently. My three-month tourist visa would expire on January 20. More than forty phone calls came to Mr. Choi's office from Korean people who wanted to help me. They offered jobs, university teaching contracts, places to live, and inquired as to whether I was a missing relative. My friend Ahn Il Soon fielded most of the calls, then transferred them on to Lee Ok Young, with whom I was staying.

I was overwhelmed, shocked, and thrilled by the response. I never expected so many Korean people or anyone in the general public to respond to the article. I met one woman—a wealthy married woman with two adolescent children who were studying in private American schools, who offered me a free place to stay and a free roundtrip airline ticket, from Korea to America and back. I accepted graciously, not knowing when or how I would return. I later suspected that she was a birth mother years ago, yet she never admitted this, I was never was able to confirm this possibility and I never asked her.

According to Mr. Choi, this article generated one of the most enthusiastic responses an article of his had ever received. I was very moved by the reaction. My faith in humanity and belief in the human spirit were restored. I didn't feel alone and I didn't feel rejected anymore by Koreans. This alone was enough for me, even if I did return to the States without finding my birth mother or birth family. I felt that Mr. Choi and I had succeeded in raising people's awareness about the plight of Korean adoptees. There was greater understanding that Korean adoptees are now searching for their birth parents—attempting to embrace our lost cultures and forgotten pasts, and that we have never forgotten that we are Korean.

The day after the article appeared, I was busy being interviewed on television and having a job interview at Hong-ik University, the largest art school in Korea, where I accepted a contract to teach English. I then met the generous and kind Korean woman who had offered to pay for a roundtrip airline ticket to the States.

I returned back to Lee Ok Young's apartment, flabbergasted by all the media attention and excited that I could actually return to Korea and work full-time as a visiting professor teaching English.

A Phone Call from My Cousin

Late that evening, I received a phone call from a Korean man who claimed to be my cousin. He said he was the eldest son of my birth mother's younger brother. Would I be willing to meet him, his mother, and his aunt, who might be my birth mother, the next morning? Of course, I said yes, through Lee Ok Young's translations. We agreed to meet at 8:30 the next morning at Lee Ok Young's apartment. I slept very little. When Lee Ok Young asked me how I felt about all of this, I told her that I didn't expect anything until I met them the next morning, but I was nervous and excited. This was the moment I had been waiting for all of my life and I did not feel at all emotionally prepared.

Meeting My Birth Mother

They arrived the next morning, Tuesday, January 14th, at eight in the morning. (It seemed they too were anxious and so arrived early. Luckily, I was up and dressed already.) In walked two older women and a man who appeared to be slightly older than myself. I noticed the shorter, rounder woman immediately. She was my birth mother. She was crying—softly, not demonstratively. The other woman, my aunt, was staring at me the entire time—touching me, holding my hand, stroking my hair. My birth mother appeared to be in shock. Yes, I was her daughter. She was convinced. I showed her my childhood photos, my adoption records and whatever relevant information I could share with them. They looked at my hands and feet, at my ears, touched my arms and legs. They inspected me as if I was a piece of supermarket beef, wrapped in plastic and being purchased to grill for dinner. They intermittently squeezed, poked and prodded me in awe and amazement. Yes, I looked like my youngest brother. Yes, I had my father's eyes and my mother's mouth.

Lee Ok Young and the three intimate strangers in the room pored over and studied the documents and photos and commented in Korean—"Yes, that looks like so and so...yes, I see the resemblance, it is Mi Ok...she is the one"—as Lee Ok Young translated for me. I didn't understand most of what was being said and at one point, early in the meeting, after more than ten minutes of nonstop Korean, I became frustrated and walked out of the room. Everyone seemed astonished that I had gotten up and walked out. They had forgotten that I had been there all along. Lee Ok Young asked me what was wrong and I told that I knew nothing of what was being said and I didn't understand what was going on. I thought this meeting was about my birth mother and me and I was being ignored and left out. Lee Ok Young apologized.

After that tense moment, Lee Ok Young translated for me more. She often simplified what was being said because she could not find the English words to translate for me. I was grateful that she was trying and appreciative that this was difficult for her as well. The sadness, joy, shock, and amazement were palpable and felt by everyone in the room. My cousin told me that I had to meet the rest of the family. I told them I was returning to the States three days later—on Friday. Yes, they would see me off at the airport. In a flurry of phone calls to relatives, my schedule for the next three days was established.

My Birth Story

I found out from my birth mother and everyone who had their piece of the story why and how I was left to end up at the orphanage. I learned that my birth parents were married and raised three sons together. I had an older brother and two younger brothers. They lived in *Il-san* during the time I was living in the orphanage, less than five miles away. According to my birth mother and other relatives, when I was three months old, my birth mother had run away from my alcoholic birth father and my year-old brother. My birth father was drinking, unemployed and beating my birth mother repeatedly. She ran away to protect herself. I suspect that she went to her relatives in a rural area far from Seoul.

My birth father was then left alone with me, just an infant, and my brother. I was still being breast-fed. Panicked, my birth father brought me to his older sister so she could take care of me until my birth mother returned to the family. My aunt then took care of me for five months. She continued to breast feed me and named me Jin Ok. When I was eight months old, my aunt could no longer take care of me. She had a one-year-old son and she was just as poor as my birth parents were. In desperation, she and my birth father brought me to a childless couple in the neighborhood. This couple, known as Mr. and Mrs. Song, were slightly better off than my birth family. The Songs agreed to take care of me until my birth mother returned home.

About a month later, my birth mother returned. The next day, my birth parents and aunt went to look for the Songs. The Songs—and me with them—had disappeared. My birth mother told me she looked for me for months after that. She told me that all of her life, she never forgot me and always wondered what happened to me. Every day, she looked in newspapers, on television, and told anyone who would listen that her daughter was missing, asking if they had seen her daughter. The family still doesn't know what happened to the Songs because they were unable to locate them. My family doesn't know whether the Songs brought me to City Hall for the police to find me. What I do know is that I was processed at the police station, as were many thousands of children, then delivered to the Holt office, from which I was taken to the orphanage. None of my birth family members knew how to report me missing in Seoul, or how or where to even start looking for me. At that time, many families suffered similar tragedies. Missing children were common in Korea. Poverty was a typical and expected reality. No one paid much attention to what was happening to thousands of children who were displaced through violence, poverty, and eventually adoption.

According to my birth mother, I was wanted, and after my disappearance, she missed, mourned, and grieved for me her entire life. She always felt guilt, regret, sadness, pain, and despair. My birth family relatives describe how she was distraught for years after my disappearance.

I do not harbor any resentment towards the Songs either for losing me, bringing me to the police station, or for giving me to another family. They might have earned money they might have needed in the transaction. I do not seek retribution from them, or any form of reparation—although I would like to meet them to find out exactly what happened. Certainly, I have met my birth mother and know much more than I ever did before. That is enough for me.

My Many Names

Apparently, I arrived at the orphanage with the last name Song and the Holt staff named me Mi Ok—very similar to the name my aunt gave me, Jin Ok. My birth father's last name is Yum. My accurate birth name in Korean is Yum Jin Ok (family name first). My adoptive parents named me Anne, keeping my Korean first name, Mi Ok, as my middle name. Their last name is Bruining, so my full American and legal name is Anne Mi Ok Bruining. For years, I maintained my name as Anne Bruining, or Anne M. Bruining—rarely sharing my Korean middle name with any of my white American friends. For the first three months of my life, I was Yum Jin Ok. In the orphanage, for five years, I was Song Mi Ok. On January 19, 1966, while on the airplane flying from Seoul, South Korea to JFK International Airport, in New York, I was Song Mi Ok. Twenty hours later, after landing on American soil as the newly adopted daughter of Betty and Bud Bruining, I was abruptly Anne Mi Ok Bruining. My identity as Song Mi Ok was erased within minutes after being embraced by my new adoptive mother, Betty.

When I was thirty years old, in 1990, I reclaimed my Korean first name and dropped the usage of Anne, although I still maintain it as my legal name. My birth mother's last name is Park. I suppose I could have taken the last name of my birth father once I found out what it was, yet when I learned of how he abused my birth mother for years, I vowed never to acknowledge him by using his last name. I also learned that for years, my aunt blamed my birth mother for running away and abandoning me to my birth father. My aunt named me, so I will not acknowledge her and take back Jin Ok. However, my entire Korean and American names are as follows, in the order they were given to me. Yum Park Song Jin Ok Mi Ok Anne Bruining—seven names—four last names and three first names. I now use Mi Ok Song Bruining as my pen, social, and professional name.

My names were fiercely protected identities I carried for years inside myself. Mi Ok, my Korean name was a hidden, deep, dark secret I withheld from almost everyone for years until, at thirty, I no longer felt like Anne—my white adoptive family's Americanized member. I became proud of my Korean first and later, my last name, Song—feeling that it was all I had to call my own and it was the only connection I had to my Korean culture and identity as a Korean person. Despite the fact that I don't remember the Song family, and they may have abandoned me to the orphanage, I like the sound of the name, and I feel more connected to it than to my birth family's names. I was also Song during the time I was in the orphanage—five years—longer than I was with my birth family. I was thrilled when I learned how to write my Korean name in the Korean language. I could finally write in the language I had been born hearing and internalized in my soul. Though I will never be Jin Ok, or Yum, someday, I may incorporate Park into my name.

My Immediate Family

My birth father died in 1982 from the effects of chronic alcoholism. He might have been in his early fifties, although Korean ages are never clear with me. Because of the Lunar calendar and the fact that the first nine months of natal gestation is counted as part of a person's age, Koreans are a year older than Americans who were born in the same numerical year. My birth mother is twenty-three years older than I am. She was sixty years old in 1997. My older birth brother is one year older than I am. He has a wife whose age I don't know and two adolescent children—a daughter and a son, I guessed they were probably fifteen and thirteen respectively, when I met them. I barely know their names, much less their ages.

Holt was right. Someone in my birth family did die in a car crash: my youngest brother. He died in August 1996—six months before I found my birth family. I regret that I will never be able to meet my youngest brother. Apparently, he was a good human being. He left behind a wife and young daughter. My other younger brother is two or three years younger than I and has a wife and one or two children—at least one daughter. I have met my older birth brother several times; twice he has helped me move to new places in Korea and I have met my younger birth brother twice.

My Extended Family

I know that my birth mother has one younger brother. I met him and his family—a wife, two sons and two daughters, each with one or two children. These nieces and nephews I have met once or twice. I don't know if my mother has other siblings. My birth father has a few siblings, including the aunt who cared for me for five months. I met her three times. Each time she was drinking and smoking like a fiend.

According to those relatives willing to discuss this matter, my aunt felt guilty, yet blamed my birth mother for my disappearance. She started drinking excessively after I couldn't be found by my birth family. It is interesting how alcoholism runs its course through my family, down older generations to younger ones. My older brother also drinks excessively.

My mother blamed my father and aunt for losing me. My father blamed my mother and his sister for losing me. My aunt blamed my mother and father for losing me. Everyone blamed everyone else for the thirty-six years of regret, remorse, bitterness, guilt, and shame.

I just wished that my family would have stopped all the blaming and invested their emotional energy in searching more methodically for me. But this is not the Korean way. I don't like my aunt very much. The first time I met her—in a café in *In-sa-dong,* with my birth mother, my aunt hadn't seen my mother in thirty-six years. My aunt began hitting and yelling at my birth mother—screaming, "It's her fault for this!" My birth mother was cowering, humiliated that this older woman was yelling at her, disrupting the public place. Everyone turning and staring, looking horrified. I was mortified and asked Mr. Choi, who was there to write a follow-up article about the reunion, to tell this woman to please stop hitting my birth mother.

Family Dynamics

It was March 1997. At the beginning of getting to know my family, I agreed to meet my birth mother and relatives wherever they wanted. I asked my cousin—the man I met during our first meeting, to translate for me because he spoke the most English of my entire family. He had lived and studied in the Philippines for five years. I later found out that his wife spoke better English, but my cousin never allowed her to speak. I figured out that when I wanted to speak with her, I had to call her directly on the phone, or meet her individually with or without my birth mother. My cousin's wife was most helpful in gathering the documents I needed to obtain my work visa and gathering the documents, and took me to the hospital for the required physical check-up. After about the third meeting with the extended family and my birth mother, I discovered that my cousin was translating only what he felt was important that I know. He was either ignorant, arrogant, unwilling, or all these. When I realized this, I was livid. I realized that my cousin was censoring what I should have known from his own bias and prejudice, and he took it upon himself to either protect me, himself, or my birth family from whatever he considered uncomfortable, unimportant, or trivial. I demanded that he either translate everything that was being said or I would not visit him or my birth family anymore. He apologized. From this I learned that future meetings with my birth mother should include just her and a translator of my own recruiting. Although I hoped someday to meet with my birth mother alone after I learned more Korean, I didn't learn enough for her to be satisfied with my limited ability to speak and understand the Korean language. My birth mother never made attempts to learn English—not even the one-syllable word, "Hi." I was resentful of the fact that my birth mother expected me to learn Korean almost instantly. I was also resentful that she was resentful of the fact that I brought a translator with me for all of our meetings together.

Yes, But How Do I Feel?

Initially, after meeting my birth mother, I was in shock, stunned that we had found each other. I am thrilled that she is alive and well, healthy and stable in her life. I was relieved to hear that she had missed me, thought of me, and wondered about me all of these years. I noticed the sadness, regret, and remorse in her eyes, her voice, her face, how she carried herself and I felt bad for her. I told her I didn't blame her. Yet I know now on a subconscious level, I do blame her and I resent her for many things. I was content on seeing her face, being near her and able to feel her close to me. But I also felt a certain distance, like I was watching a film. I was in that film; it was starring me and my birth mother in the lead roles—yet I was not in the film. I watched myself in the role, going through the motions as though behind a glass window.

It was difficult to maintain communication with my birth mother. I tried to see her twice a month and attempted to call her on the phone once or twice a week during the almost two years I was teaching in Korea. I made every effort to get together with her when we both had available time and the translator could attend.

I went to her apartment once and met her second husband. She had been married to him for five years then. He didn't seem friendly toward me and appeared to be annoyed that I was there. According to my birth mother, he always asks about me, but I wonder if she was just trying to cover up for him. In the final three months I was in Korea, finishing up my teaching contract at *Hong-ik,* whenever I called, he would answer the phone. I asked him to leave a message for my birth mother. She never got those messages and never knew that I had called her. She complained to my friends that I had never called her. I was always frustrated and felt helpless to change the situation.

Perfection Also Missing

My birth mother seemed resigned to the fact that I will not live with her, not get married to a native Korean man, not have children in Korea, and not live in Korea forever. I will never give up my U.S. citizenship to become a Korean citizen and I will not be able to learn Korean in a matter of days or months. I know that she was as frustrated as I that we could not communicate with each other without the assistance of a translator. She repeatedly told my friends that she wished I would hurry up and learn Korean and she told me that she was patiently waiting for the day when I could speak to her in Korean alone.

In typical Korean mother fashion, my birth mother always asked about my health, was I eating, was I warm or comfortable where I was living, and was I sleeping—any mother's concern for her child's basic well-being. I always responded that I was fine. She didn't seem convinced and made a big display about how worried and concerned she was about me—also typical Korean mother behavior. I asked her the same questions she asked me: how her health was, was she eating, was she warm or comfortable where she was living and was she sleeping okay? She always chuckled and said she was fine, then her eyes would start to water—sadness.

When I told her that I was writing a book, she didn't seem to believe me. She never asked me about the book; in fact she never seemed the least interested in any of my activities, interests, goals, future, dreams, or hopes. She always told me I reminded her of my father. My mother said that my behavior and character are similar. I suspect that resemblance reminded her of the pain and anguish she had endured all the years they were married.

Whenever I asked for details—names, dates, events, and circumstances of my birth family, my mother seemed annoyed that I didn't remember what she had told me already. I also believe that she didn't want to speak of the past, yet this was a part of my past and history as well. Sometimes she seemed to have forgotten that I was not a part of her life for thirty-six years and that I have a few missing details of the history that we share. Of course, so much of what was actually discussed between my mother and me was lost in the translation.

I don't know exactly how my birth mother felt. My translator told me she was sad, but was unable to clarify what my birth mother was sad about. Yet, I noticed all of the gestures, the glances that conveyed her feelings by her body language. I could see she was uncomfortable. She wore her sorrow and despair on her heavy, sad expression. I wished I could have erased her angst, but I couldn't. I felt helpless in not being able to retrieve the *phantom* daughter she lost thirty-six years ago and I am regretful that I cannot be the daughter she wants me to be. I was not the typical Korean woman, married with husband, house, and children. I was not fluent in the Korean language and devoted to my family. I was not the perfect Korean daughter.

Every time my mother saw me, she was reminded of the loss and that she grieves and mourns that loss. That is what I saw in her body language, in her eyes, the expressions in her face, in the tears she wiped away, the wretchedness I feel and I felt her feelings, her emotions, everything she has carried around as a psychic burden for almost forty years.

The Aftermath—Almost Five Years Later: Bitterness and Hope

I have not addressed my own anger, resentment, and bitterness over the years of estrangement from my birth mother. She is not the *phantom* (birth) mother I was searching for. I am as disappointed in my mother as she is in me. My birth mother never asked about my life in America, my friends, my adoptive family, my education, my achievements, successes, or failures—ever. I always asked her if she wanted to know about my life. She always shook her head, no—she didn't want to know. I suspect it was because it was too painful to be reminded that she was not a part of my life for all those years in a foreign country she has never visited and I was not a part of her life in Korea for all of those years.

I also suspect that my Korean mother desperately wanted to pick up where we left off—when I was an infant. She wanted to mother me in the only way she knew how—as the mother of a small child she had left at three months old. I don't want that from her. I don't wish to be infantilized, taken care of or nurtured by her in a maternal way. What I was hoping for and still desire is for my birth mother to know who I am, what I do, why I do what I do, what my interests, passions, talents, flaws (although she had seen some of them already) and abilities are.

I have no need to impress my mother, but I did want to show her that I was capable, adult, grown up and not a baby to be coddled. I also suspect that my birth mother wished, desperately, to make up for all the lost years and I feel that is impossible. I don't want her to and I wanted her to stop trying. I wanted to try to tell her all of these things and I have through translation, but the message doesn't seem to transfer to the depths of her core being and I am frustrated. The cultural differences and the language barrier were too profound for me to help my mother understand what I wanted from her. I believe that I understood what she wanted from me. That saddens me tremendously.

I feel bonded to this woman who carried for me inside of her for nine months, gave birth to me and nursed me for three months. I feel a primal connection. The primal wound may have healed, but the psychic connection is still severed. Park Kwi Nam is my birth mother, but she will never be my *Mom*. Park Kwi Nam and I are intimate strangers—attached by blood, flesh, bone, and DNA, though that hasn't been medically proven or confirmed. I asked my birth mother if she wanted a DNA test to prove that I am her daughter. She said no, so I honored her wishes.

During the last three months I was in Korea, my mother refused to see me. I was able to call her and speak with her directly on the phone. She told me she was too busy to see me. In September, she had to cook food for her husband's family events. In October, she was busy preparing food for *Choo-sok*—the Korean version of Thanksgiving. I spent *Choo-sok* with my older birth brother and his family in *Il-san*. In November, my birth mother's mother died and she was busy visiting the cemetery to pay respects to her dead relatives and my ancestors, including my birth father. I was stunned when I heard that my maternal grandmother had died. I had always hoped that my birth mother would take me to visit her mother. Her mother knew that her daughter had found me, and my birth mother told me that her mother had wanted to meet me. I grieved with sadness of never being able to meet my grandmother. My birth mother never invited me to accompany her to the cemetery and I never suggested that I go with her. I was angry that she was always too busy to meet me, even for an hour.

I always knew it would be difficult if I ever met my birth mother. I knew that new issues would replace the old ones—that the process of learning, understanding, liking, loving one another would continue and probably continue for the rest of our lives. I am willing to work on this relationship with my birth mother, but I need her to meet me equally.

My birth brother asked me for my cellular phone when I left Korea, for his adolescent daughter. I gave it to him, asking that he put the account into his name. However, three months after I returned to the States, I found out that the telephone service had transferred more than $1,000 from my bank account in Korea to pay for the phone bill run up on my cellular phone. My brother had not changed the phone into his name. I felt betrayed and deceived. My friends in Korea have been unable to contact him. Almost five years later, it seems that my birth family has vanished as quickly as they came into my life back in January 1997.

I had hoped that my mother and my brother could come to the States to visit me. I know that I will return to Korea to visit my friends. I hope that I will be able to see my birth family also. However, I have no expectations of my birth family, just as I have no expectations of my adoptive family. I now have no expectations that they want to see me. I have no expectations that our relationship will be as I wish it to be. I have no expectations that we will be close as a family, as I originally hoped for.

I know it will take a lifetime to resolve my issues with my birth mother. At this time, as I write this while living in the States, I think about my birth mother in Korea. I wonder how she is doing. We have lost contact for almost four years. I have written several letters to her, had them translated into Korean, sent them on to her and never heard a word from her. I don't know if she ever received my letters. I have not been able to reach her with the phone number she gave me before I left Korea. I don't know where she is. My friends in Korea have attempted to contact her several times, also with no success.

Most people ask me about my reunion with my birth family. I tell them that it was not a reunion. A definition of a reunion is when an adult child has reunited with her or his birth family and maintained contact on a regular basis. Technically, a reunion can be as brief as a single get-together. A reunion is when the birth family is an integral part of the individual who was separated for years. My birth family is in Korea. I am here. It is organically impossible for me to maintain regular contact with my birth family in a way that I would prefer. For me, I do not believe that my series of meetings with my birth mother and a few meetings with my birth family constitutes a reunion.

The search for my birth family was successful. I met them and filled a hole that was in my life as an adoptee. I never expected that it would heal me completely. Yet, I also know that I am stronger, more resilient, and wiser from this experience. That is all I could have hoped for.

August 30, 2001

Remembering *This Bridge,*
Remembering Ourselves

M. JACQUI ALEXANDER

In March 2000, the Department of Gender and Women's Studies at Connecticut College organized an event to honor a multiracial group of women poets of distinction and to mark the twentieth anniversary of the publication of *This Bridge Called My Back*. Poets on Location was a way to bring back to memory an earlier historical moment when the vision of a pancultural radical feminist politics seemed more vigorous, more visible in the United States of North America. All six women had combined the search for beauty with the struggle for social justice in their life's work. We wrote in the program notes: "These women poets have scrutinized their lives, wrestled with their different inheritances of geography of place, race, class, sexuality, body, nationality, and belonging, and molded it all into sources of insight and wisdom. Among them they have lived 363 years, spanning continents, threading dreams, holding visions." Honored were Chrystos, Dionne Brand, Cherríe Moraga, Sonia Sanchez, Adrienne Rich, and Mitsuye Yamada, three of them original contributors to *This Bridge*. Audre Lorde, Toni Cade Bambara, and Pat Parker joined us in spirit. Donna Kate Rushin read "The Bridge Poem," and on the night of the honoring, nestled in between the overgrown stems of the most radiant sunflowers, she and Papusa Molina recalled the names of all thirty-two women who had put their pens, as Audre would have said it, in the full service of what they believed. The moment was electric: songs on drums; no land to light on; the heat of fire changing the shape of things; reminiscences of the desert and the promise of oasis; listening for something; dreaming of a common language; moving radiance to trace the truth of history. On that evening in March, a "terrible beauty" had soaked the cadence of playful flute and solemn drums, and a not-so-silent hunger of a crowd, determined to smell the taste of a past now brought present. Yearning, memory and desire. A powerful combination.

This recent commemoration is not my only memory of *This Bridge*. My earliest memory was planted fourteen years ago as I was giving birth to myself in the summer of 1986. I navigated the passage in the waters of *This Bridge*, *Homegirls*, *Cancer Journals* and *Sister Outsider*, yearning, without knowing, for the company of lesbian women to help me swim in those gray Maine waters on Greenings Island, which appear to be strangers to their turquoise blue green sisters thousands of miles away, but merely seven hours by plane. Unrelated on the surface only, for down in that abyss their currents reach for each other and fold, without the slightest tinge of resentment, into the same Atlantic, the rebellious waters of which provided the path for a more violent passage, many, many centuries, but not so many centuries ago. Secrets lie in the silted bottom of these waters. In that summer of a reluctant sun, incessant waves and what seems now like an interminably full moon, I remember how much I have forgotten of that daily awakening. Stark outlines remain to be sure, but the more tactile reminders have receded. There are no notes on the margins of my dissertation to indicate that as I wrote those slow pages heavy with the weight of the costs of medicine and the disproportionate brunt that workers bore at the hands of corporate and state managers, my heart was moving to a different rhythm. But I remember how my passion and love for a woman and a distant memory of a deep and necessary transgression folded into a joy I felt upon meeting the women in *Bridge* for the first time— women like me, I felt, bound in a collective desire to change the world. The experience of freedom in boundary crossing. I later went in search of *Zami*, but when these women "who work together as friends and lovers" announced a new spelling of their name in jet black letters on a thin blood-red spine snuggled under the section "Women of Color'" at New Words Bookstore in Cambridge, my fingers became tentative with a memory of the harsh sound of the word Zami in Trinidad, and the whispers about two women whom my furtive friends and I had climbed over a fence to see, on the way home, from the convent high school I attended.

I couldn't live Caribbean feminism on American soil and Caribbean soil had grown infertile to the manufacture of needs to its north. Caribbean people had docked one ship too many. Waved one goodbye too many to women recruited for the war in Britain or for work as domestics in Canada or the U.S. Grown one banana too many, thin and small—not Chiquita, not Dole—that would turn to manure before being eaten. Heard one demand too many to smile for tourists because they presumably provided one's bread and butter. I was not in Jamaica with Sistren as they documented the rage of women who worked in the sugar cane fields (in the play *Sweet Sugar Rage*), using theater to score the unequal vicissitudes of their lives. I would read much later CAFRA's inaugural discussions.[1] Nor had I joined the droves of women who left the Caribbean and the metropolis with equal discontent to build the revolution in Grenada. I was not in Boston in 1979, as the bodies of black women fell, one after the other, twelve in all, at least that time (the same year the People's Revolutionary Movement came to power in Grenada). Shedding blood that defied insistent rains and vowed to leave its mark on the harsh concrete, on the cluttered, winding, corners of dark alleys. Not in Pine Ridge, South Dakota as the "red blood full of those arrested, in flight, shot," flowed as Sioux and Lakota alike occupied Wounded Knee.[2] Or part of the "primary emergencies" confronting different women of color: living on the other side of structural inequities; of violence within the false safety of home; of the unnatural disaster of imposed invisibility; of passing across the lines of color, different shades of light and brown, wearing "exhausting camouflages"; and negotiating the pathologies of racism.[3] I had missed Nairobi completely, hidden away in the stacks in the basement of Widener Library, and was forced instead to go in search of my blood sisters at one of the many post-Nairobi reports back to the community, which the Boston Women's Health Book Collective had sponsored. It was there I met Angela Bowen for the first time, sister traveler come to sojourn only four blocks away from where I lived in Cambridgeport. We have walked these dusty tracks before. By the middle of the '80s, then, when at least 20,000 people had read *Bridge* and shared it with at least another 20,000 of their friends, I had only begun the journey, and then only in text. For me, *Bridge* was both anchor and promise in that I could begin to frame a lesbian-feminist-woman-of-color consciousness and at the same time move my living in a way that would provide the moorings for that consciousness. Neither anchor nor promise could have been imaginable without the women in *Bridge* who gave themselves permission to write, to speak in tongues.[4]

I was not a part of the sweat and fire that gave shape to a woman of color politic in this country in the '70s and '80s and this is why I want constantly to remember that I have been shaped by it. It is why I am indebted to the women who literally entered the fire for me, on my behalf. What I found compelling was plain ol' courage and determination of a bunch of different women, still tied to some kind of cultural inheritance, sometimes at a cost, sometimes isolated from it, at times yearning for it. They were my age, many younger than me, saying so much about so many different things, gesturing to me about a forgetting so deep that I had even forgotten what I had forgotten.[5] I had not known that a love letter could still be a love letter, to one's mother no less, and deal with betrayal and wounds. I read Merle Woo's "Letter to Ma" with my mouth open—and covered, of course. After all, I could not be caught staring at something, or someone, so impolitely, with my mouth opened. I couldn't imagine speaking in this way within my family, a family in which speech was such a scarce commodity and the trade in silence was the value. A system of silence, my uncle calls it. *How* do I come out to family? To all of my five brothers? No sister to tell. She closed her eyes for good nine days after she had opened them, when I was only four, and could barely see the eyelet bonnet that caressed her soft face in the coffin. To my mother? For years I would think that as a lesbian I had a cosmic duty to perfect my relationship with my mother. My father by then had died alone without telling me. Months afterwards, in one of those early hours before dawn, he visited me as a wraith, propped up on a walking stick. He saw my partner and me lying in bed, but said nothing. At least he knew. Later, I would see that my own hesitation about "coming out" in Trinidad was laced with the fears of a dutiful daughter's jeopardizing middle-class respectability. Anticolonial nationalism had taught us well about heterosexual loyalty, a need so great that it reneged on its promise of self-determination, delivering criminality instead of citizenship.⁶ And yet my father's death released a different desire: a different form of loving and a new kind of politic that I found first in *Bridge*.

In Barbara Cameron's "Gee you don't seem like an Indian from the Reservation," I saw reflected much of my first year undergraduate experience in this country, where for the first time in my life the majority of people around me were white. Accented, foreign, and seen as friendly in this pre-dominantly white environment, I had not yet known that I was being compared to black students ("African American" was not used then) and positioned in relation to the "unjustifiably angry" black American. I had not known until the slave auction, when white male students thought they could have fun by "hiring" white women as slaves for a day. And the campus exploded. In the midst of sit-ins and teach-ins, I was forced to confront the utter silence of white students who had previously befriended me, and the sudden shift to being a stranger. It was my most tactile experience of what I had only read about and seen on television that would begin to instill a *daily* awareness of seeing myself as black—and, equally important—to begin thinking about what white people were seeing/thinking as they saw me. I had not had to negotiate the daily assignment of racial superiority and inferiority or its most egregious costs as I grew up in Trinidad in the midst of an apparent black majority.⁷ It would take me six more years and a walk down the streets of Williamsburg, VA with my friend Beverly Mason to really understand how racism distorts and narrows the field and scope of vision. "Do you see how they look at us, Jacqui?" "No, No," I replied. "You don't see how they look at us!" "*No*," I insisted, not knowing even intuitively what I was supposed to have seen. At that time I had not felt double consciousness although I knew of its existence, mainly from Fanon's *Black Skins White Masks* that had implicated French colonialism in the psychic splitting so evident in Algeria and Martinique, and by extension other parts of the colonized world.⁸

Nor had I known that the texture of identities could be made into a theory of the flesh, as Cherríe Moraga outlined. It echoed consistently throughout the collection and in the Combahee River Collective Statement: "The most general statement of our politics at the present time would be that we are actively committed to struggling against racial, sexual, heterosexual, and class oppression, and see as our particular task the development of integrated analysis and practice based upon the fact that the major systems of oppression are interlocking. The synthesis of these oppressions creates the conditions of our lives."9 I had to work to understand this question of the conditions of our lives, how they are shaped daily through structures, and even how to use flesh-and-blood experiences to concretize a vision. I did not know how precisely the personal was political, since I had not yet begun to fully scrutinize much of what was personal. The mobilization of Black Power in the mid-1970s in the anglophone Caribbean spoke to our subordinate economic position in the world economy, foreign ownership of banks, for instance, that guaranteed jobs for whites, but much of the contextual history of slavery and colonization, how we came to be there and got to be who we were was largely missing from an educational system (nationalism notwithstanding) that tracked smart students to learn the history of imperial might—British history, U.S. of North America history and geography—nothing of Caribbean history. All of Dickens, Shakespeare, Chaucer. None of Jean Rhys, George Lamming, Louise Bennett, Ismith Khan. It gave no clues about the connections between the operation of systems and the behaviors of people, no clues about our social-sexual selves, or at least how we could be agents within them.

The processes of colonization in *Bridge* wore a face different from the ones I had been used to. Articulated by Chicanas, Puertoriqueñas, and Native women, it spoke to the internal colonies of the reservations; the barrios; the labor regimes of the cotton fields of Texas; the contentious inheritance of Malintzín, and the confusion between devotion and obedience usually cathected unto women in the secular sphere or otherwise collapsed into the religious figure of the Virgin Mary who had accompanied me throughout my thirteen years of Catholic school. I had longed to become a nun. Chrystos had learned to walk in the history of her people, had come to know there were "women locked in [her] joints."10 How does one know the stories and histories of one's people? Where does one learn them? Who were we? As Trinidadians we did not all come on the same ship as the national (ist) myth held. Some of us, Indian, had been captured/brought, under indenture, to work on plantations that had been evacuated after the "end" of slavery, with the broken promise of return to Calcutta, Bombay, Madras. A colonial betrayal that would be pushed under the surface in order to constantly test Indian loyalty to Trinidad, the home of forced adoption. Some Chinese, also smuggled/brought as contract laborers, also to work on sugar plantations.[11] Some black captured/sold from a geography so vast, the details would daunt memory and produce a forgetting so deep, we had forgotten that we had forgotten. Missing memory. Who are *my* people? How will I come to know the stories and histories of *my* people? With Chicanas and Puertoriqueñas, I shared a non- belonging to the U.S. Mirtha Quintinales was Cuban lesbian, a Caribbean lesbian. Like her, I did not belong in the U.S, and while I was not Cuban, there was a family link since my father's brother had left Tobago to search for home in Cuba, Oriente, where the roots of trees travel without the need of a compass to the deep forests of Mayombe, Kongo; to Dahomey, Da ha homey; and to New York. Trees remember and will whisper remembrances in your ear, if you stay still and listen.

Charting the Journey

It was this sensibility of a politicized nonbelonging, with its capacity to fuel an imperative about self-determination, that persisted in the sister companion to *Bridge, Charting the Journey*, that Black women in Britain had undertaken by navigating a different set of waters. Immigrant waters. Colonial waters. The material substance of the "idea" of Blackness, and the creation of a life in Britain, "of three to four million people and their descendants from former British colonies," worked as both scaffold and foundation to understand British imperialism both outside and within, as it created "strangers at home" in an "Alien Nation"[12] (not alien self). The borders of that nation had been made porous long ago, so when black women organized one of the campaigns, "We are here because you were there," they stood at the confluence of a set of historical forces that tied together a politics of dislocation and migration (which made ample room for solidarity with politics "at home" in Ireland, Palestine, Eritrea, Chile, Namibia, and El Salvador), a consistent critique of state practices, of Zionism, and systematically folded it into the praxis of what it meant to be black women in Britain.

In one sense the weaving of a transnational intention into *Charting the Journey* is but implicit in *Bridge. Charting* made room for a dialectic of intersecting forces, splintered, as they constituted both the local (several localities simultaneously) and the global, across inherited maps and also within them. The bridge, in its first incarnation, is an internal one, crossing into different experiences of colonization, to be sure, but it largely assumes that the very borders of American nation are intact, an assumption that is later dislodged and reimagined as a desire to be more explicitly international.[13] As Moraga stated in the preface to the second edition of *Bridge*, "The impetus to forge links with women of color from every region grows more and more urgent as the numbers of recently-immigrated people of color in the U.S. grows in enormous proportions." These metaphors of links, charts, journeys, bridges, and borders are neither idle nor incidental, however, as we come to terms with the different cartographies of feminist struggle in different parts of the world; our different histories; where they change course and how they diverge.[14] It seems crucial that we come to terms with, and engage, that confluence of the local and the global in order not to view the transnational as merely a theoretical option. That fact that our standard of living, our very survival here is based upon raw exploitation of working-class women, white, black, and third world in all parts of the world. Our hands are not clean.[15] We must also come to terms with that still largely unexamined, undisclosed faith in the *idea* of America, that no matter how unbearable it is here, it is better than being anywhere, elsewhere; that slippage between third world and third rate. We eat bananas. Buy flowers. Use salt to flavor our food. Drink sweetened coffee. Use tires for the cars we drive. Depend upon state-of-the-art electronics. Wear clothes, becoming of a kind of style that has called a premature end to modernity, to colonization. We travel. We consume and rely upon multiple choice to reify consumption. All of those things that give material weight to the *idea* of America, that conflate capitalism and democracy and demarcate "us" from "them." All of those things that give ideological weight to the *idea* of America, producing a constitutional fear of the erasure of the American nation as the borders of America become more permeable, a fear of the disappearance of the very (American) self.

What might it mean to see ourselves as "refugees of a world on fire." "What if we declared ourselves *perpetual* refugees in solidarity with all refugees?"[16] Not citizen. Not naturalized citizen. Not immigrant. Not undocumented. Not illegal alien. Not permanent resident. Not resident alien. But refugees fleeing some terrible atrocity far too threatening to engage, ejected out of the familiar into some unknown still to be revealed. Refugees forced to create out of the raw smithy of fire a shape different than our inheritance, with no blueprints, no guarantees. Some die in flight: Palestine. Afghanistan. Rwanda. Kongo. Bosnia. Haiti. Sierra Leone. Some live a different death: Silvia Baraldini. Leonard Peltier. Mumia Abu Jamal. Marilyn Jean Buck. Political Prisoners. And women and people of color shackled, in disproportionate numbers, at the height of their creativity, in a privatized system of imprisonment. Many undergo daily trials by fire: Women in Vieques, Puerto Rico who, since 1941, have lived with aerial bombardment and military maneuvers by the U.S Navy, and who now live with more carcinogens and cancers than their neighbors. Some die a different death: 46,000 of us, every single year, of breast cancer in the U.S. of North American;[17] the continuing deaths of African Americans from HIV/AIDS, in the face of reduced rates of infection in every other racial group; the stunning increase in HIV/AIDS-infected babies to whom immigrant women give birth. A preventable phenomenon![18] And a general globalized violence producing rapid dispersals of people, some 100 million, mostly women and children, seeking asylum. What are the different intolerables from which we desire to flee? And how do we distinguish between those sites to which we must return and those from which we must flee entirely? Those who cannot flee, no matter how intolerable the conditions? In order to wrestle with these questions we would need to adopt as daily practice ways of being and relating, modes of analyzing, strategies of organizing in which we constantly mobilize identification and solidarity, across all borders, as key elements in the repertoire of risks we need to take to see ourselves as part of one another, even in the context of difference.[19] We would need to disappear the idiocy of "us" and "them" and the cultural relativist underpinnings of that dichotomy, the belief that "it" could never happen to "us," so that our very consciousnesses come to be shaped by the multiple and not the singular: multiple histories and events, multiple geographies, multiple identifications.

And yet we must remember the character of fire, its paradoxical dimension: it provides sustenance and warmth, and it can destroy, it can kill. But the difference between those of us who fear fire and the "the welder" is her knowledge that she has to become intimate with this danger zone in order to recreate, to create anew; to enter the fire not figuratively or metaphorically, but actually, that is, in flesh and blood.[20] The difference between the welder and those who fear fire is the consciousness and attentiveness she brings to the process of entering fire, and it is this consciousness that cultivates the intelligence to discern, embrace, and live that important yet malleable relationship between destruction and sustenance. Fire can kill, but without it we *will* die. Can we see that a lotus can bloom in the furnace without losing its freshness?[21] We need to learn to make peace with contradiction and paradox, to see its operation in the uneven structures of our own lives, and learn to sense, taste, and understand paradox as the motor of things, which is what Marxian philosophy and political economy *and* the metaphysics of spiritual thought systems have in common. Dialectics of struggle. Paradoxes of the Divine. Still, we know that living contradiction is not easy in a culture that ideologically purveys a distaste for it and an apparent attachment to consensus.[22] But we know as well that living contradiction is necessary if we are to create the asylums of identification and solidarity with and for one another, without which our lives will surely wither.[23]

We Have Recognized Each Other Before

Who are we as women of color at this moment in history? Where is the political movement that calls itself a woman-of color-movement? Who mobilizes within it? On what terms? At the original writing women puzzled these questions even as they linked themselves to the emerging politic. Mirtha Quintanales got to the heart of the paradox of naming:

> Not all Third World women are "women of color"—if by this concept we mean exclusively "non-white…." And not all women of color are really Third world—if this term is only used in reference to underde-veloped…societies (especially those not allied with any superpower). Clearly then it would be difficult to justify referring to Japanese women, who are women of color, as Third World women. Yet if we extend the concept of Third World to include internally "colonized" racial and ethnic minority groups in this country, the crucial issue of social and institutional racism and its historic tie to slavery in the U.S. could get diluted, lost in the shuffle. The same thing would likely happen if we extended the meaning of "women of color" to include…women…who are victims of prejudice…but who nevertheless hold racial privileges and may even be racists.…Many of us who identify as "Third World" or "Women of Color," have grown up as, or are fast becoming "middle-class" and highly educated, and therefore more privileged than many of our white, poor and working-class sisters.[24]

Fractures of class and skin color, the different economic and cultural positions to which our countries of origin adhere in the capitalist hierarchy, all of these objective and lived conditions add considerable contention to this category woman-of-color. At this historical juncture, it is structurally larger and more internally differentiated than at the moment of its inception more than two decades ago. The ongoing fact of "immigration" and its transfor-mation of the complexion of racial politics, often jeopardizing relationships between indigenous and "immigrant" women, underscores the weight the identity woman-of-color is being called upon to bear. Yet, these are the very non-identical conditions, the objective conditions, what Avtah Brah calls the "entanglements of the genealogies of dispersal and those of staying put," that daily shape our consciousnesses *as* women of color, even as we negotiate the very different elements that constitute that consciousness.[25] As in all matters of racialization both our identity—our social, cultural, and historical location—and consciousness—the experiences, interpretations, and knowledge we use to explain that location—are constantly being contested.[26]

The challenge of the category woman-of-color and the question of whom the category can contain at this contemporary moment comes not only from the massive dislocations in women's labor that have by now become a permanent feature of capitalism. It comes as well in the destabilizing effects of the underside of capitalism that communities of color and white working-class communities disproportionately suffer. This is partly what makes it politically, emotionally, and spiritually necessary for women of color to return to their geographies of origin. Additionally, the movement that gave rise to *Bridge*, as well as *Bridge* itself, may well have helped to build a passing to the specificities of women's particular histories.[27] It would seem that at this moment many women of color have returned home, not necessarily to the homes they once vacated, but to a new temporality, a new urgency, to the cultures we had not fully known. This return is partially reflected in the growth of many culturally specific grassroots organizations, in aesthetic expression, as well as in more recent anthologies.[28]

Clearly a new moment has emerged, which has produced the need for a different kind of re-membering—the making of different selves. I shall not call it nationalism here, although I felt it as such as a Caribbean woman at the Black Women in the Academy Conference in 1994, when a small group of African American women asserted that they needed to sort out their own identity, on their own, before considering solidarity politics. To whom do I flee and where? I had made my home within African American community, among and with African American women. Now I am sensitive to the taste of exclusion, which as a girl I have sucked from birth. You see in my face neither sister, ally, nor friend. Only Stranger. Not even in my eyes can you read your yearning, nor mine. A loss so great, there is no safety in home. To whom do I flee and where? To whom do you flee? Where is my place in this new map of identity? Who are its cartographers? Have I not long since earned the right to belong? There is an urgent question I believe we must confront as women of color: How do we continue to be rooted in the particularities of our cultural homes and remain simultaneously committed to a collectivized politic of identification and solidarity, and its different historical complexions? There is a difference, for instance, between black consciousness, and its differentations, and woman-of-color consciousness. At the very least the latter requires collective fluency in our particular histories; an understanding of how different gendered racisms operate, their old institutionalized link to the histories of slavery here, as well as their newer manifestations that partly rely upon the "foreigness" of immigrants who have not been socialized into the racial/racist geographies of the U.S.;[29] and the conscious act of framing our analyses, our politics, our sensibilities, our being, through the chasms of those different, although overlapping, temporalities. We are not born women of color. We become women of color.[30] In order to *become* women of color, we would need to become fluent in each others' histories, to resist and unlearn an impulse to claim first oppression, most devastating oppression, one-of-a-kind oppression, defying-comparison oppression. We would have to unlearn an impulse that allows mythologies about each other to replace *knowing* about one another. We would need to cultivate a way of knowing in which we direct our social, cultural, psychic, and spiritually marked atention upon each other.[31] We cannot afford to cease yearning for each others' company.

The expression in 1994 at the Black Women in the Academy Conference was but a small episode in an ongoing choreography between African American and Caribbean people, oftentimes captured in fiction, all the time lived in the raucous seams of a predictable meeting, the ground for which was set at the time of that earlier Atlantic crossing. Predictable and more pronounced at this moment, four decades since the British, for instance, "announced" independence for certain parts of the anglophone Caribbean region. They buried their antipathy for the U.S without a single shot of the gun—a gentleman's agreement, the perfect foil—conceded their imperial role to America, setting the stage for global capital to operate more fully without regard for nations, their sovereignty, or their boundaries. In keeping with its logic, capital expelled large numbers of Caribbean women and men in successive waves, the majority of whom joined the ranks of an already disgruntled proletarian class on American soil, with its own peculiar brand of racial antipathies.[32]

Inscribed within these social relations are a set of tendentious claims that need to be named. Caribbean people have charged African Americans with a lack of political savvy under slavery; had African Americans been vigilant enough they would not have fallen prey to the psychic traumas of plantation slavery, they would not have believed themselves inferior. African Americans are charged further with the mistaken application of American plantation slavery and institutionalized racism to characterize the experiences of all black people. Further, the term African American is used in a way that contains and narrows the experience of blackness to the U.S. of North America with only tenuous solidarity with the black diaspora. Caribbeans believe that African Americans have been rejected by white Americans, yet have a deep desire to be recognized by them, seeking validation from the very group that has engineered its dismissal. The experience of racism notwithstanding, African Americans believe in America and in America's superiority to any other black third-world country. African Americans have squandered their economic chances and refused jobs that Caribbean people are more willing to take.

African Americans have charged Caribbean people with a willingness to participate in institutions that African Americans have systematically critiqued, thereby diluting claims of racism that African Americans have made. Caribbean people feel themselves superior to African Americans. Caribbean people refuse to understand that racism against African Americans has been formative of the entire structure of racism in the U.S.; they and other black people are better served by moving into that analysis and its attendant politics. When African Americans make it through everyone makes it through. A focus on difference is divisive. Caribbean people are reluctant to admit that they have benefited directly from the political struggles waged by African Americans. They allow themselves to be used in a set of wedge politics between white Americans and African Americans, aligning themselves with white structures of power (with white women in the academy, for instance) wresting economic gains and a level of legitimacy African Americans rarely enjoy.[33]

Not far beneath the surface of these expressions lies a mirror, refracting the twin companions of colonialism and slavery, their psychic and material legacies, the very historical antecedents that have made this contemporary meeting possible. Neither one or the other, but both, mutually aiding and abetting each other. The memory of slavery has receded in the lived experience of Caribbean people; colonization has greater force. The memory of colonization has receded in the lived experience of African American people; it is slavery that has carried historical weight. There is a cost to this polarized forgetting in the kinds of psychic distortions that both thought systems have produced: the hierarchies of inferiority and superiority and their internalizations; the internecine struggles in a gendered, racialized political economy of global capital with its intrepid mobilization of race, gender, and nation as it manages crisis after crisis in this late stage of its evolution. Racial polarization and contradictions is the face decolonization wears in the U.S at this moment.[34] As black people and people of color in this country, we are *all* living witnesses to the largely unfinished project of decolonization, some say a failed project, in the U.S, in Britain, the Caribbean, Asia, and Africa.

The failure of decolonization rests upon at least four axes. It entails a forgetting, on the part of some radical folk, that it is an unfinished project in which we are all still implicated; in other words, we still have work to do. Second, it entails the avid embrace (on the part of both third-world and first-world elites) of new structures of colonization, privatization and structural adjustment policies of NAFTA, the World Bank, and the IMF that make it almost impossible for the bulk of the population in the Third World, and for working-class and communities of color in metropolitan countries, to live with dignity. Third, a fierce denial on the part of the state and other institutions, including the academy, that its own contemporary practices of racialization have been shaped by a refusal to admit and confront its historical complicity in racism against indigenous people of color on these shores. Fourth, the fierce revival of ethno-nationalisms of different kinds. Part of our own unfinished work, therefore, is to remember the objective fact of these systems of power and their ability to graft themselvs onto the very minute interstices of our daily lives. It means that we are all defined in some relationship to them, in some relationship to hierarchy. Neither complicity (usually cathected unto someone else) nor vigilance (usually reserved for ourselves) is given to any of us *before* the fact of our living. They are learned in this complicated process of figuring out who we are and whom we wish to become. The far more difficult question we must collectively engage has to do with the political positions (in the widest sense) we come to practice, and not merely espouse, the mutual frameworks we adopt, as we live (both consciously and unconsciously) our daily lives.[35] No matter our countries of origin, decolonization is a project for *all*.

It is no longer tenable—it never really was—for Caribbean people to continue to seek immunity from racialized internalizations. Is it mere accident that it was Fanon who formulated *Black Skins White Masks?* Caribbean people of African descent may well have claimed a premature victory and comfort of a black majority, without having sufficiently wrestled with the racial inequalities in our own countries of origin, such as the position of Indians in Trinidad, which I came to understand as one of second-class citizenship only after experiencing racism in the U.S. This is perhaps why sometimes we continue to reenact within Caribbean organizations in the metropolis the same dominant repetitions that position us as most targeted vis-a-vis Indians and Chinese (now defined as Asians), whom we believe benefit more from the racial hierarchy in the U.S. than we do. Given the fact that this advanced capitalist colonial nation is constantly redrawing its own national borders, creating insiders and outsiders, African American claims for citizenship can no longer be undertaken as if the borders of the nation-state are fixed. Like neocolonial states, this U.S. of North America state is redrawing borders all the time and these gestures are becoming more transparent with the destabilizing effects within communities of color. Immigration policies are another face of racism.

Additionally, there are fissures of class, skin color, shades of yellow and brown, within our respective nation/communities: Linguistic and regional differences have created their own insiders and outsiders. So, at what historical moments does heterogeneity become homogeneity, that is, the moment to create an outside enemy? Neither African American nor Caribbean people created those earlier conditions of colonialism and Atlantic slavery.[36] Yet, we continue to live through them in a state of selective forgetting, setting up an artificial antipathy between them in their earlier incarnation, behaving now as if they have ceased to be first cousins.

We have recognized each other before. Blood flows—within individuals, within families, within neighborhoods—making a mockery of biology, of boundaries. One drop of blood is not sufficient to mark where one line begins and the other ends. Boundaries are never discrete. We have recognized each other before: in the streets of Harlem when we believed, along with six million black people worldwide, that Garvey's Black Star Line would sail clear to the continent above the objections of segments of the black middle class who believed that they had arrived by distancing themselves from Africa, refusing its proximity. Or in the heyday of PanAfricanism when, as Baldwin elegantly framed it, "we were concerned with the immensity and variety of the experience called [Black],"[37] both by virtue of the fact of slavery *and* colonization, but not only because of it. Neither of these movements were entirely free from exclusions, from sexism, from the contradictions and intrigue of class and color, or from xenophobia. But they kept alive an idea, which for all of its fractiousness, lent public visibility and legitimacy to our humanity. We have stood in the same lines, under the El in New York, year after year, in the period after the Second World War, some reports say, to be chosen for work as maids in white, wealthy households by the "Madames Jew and Gentile" alike.[38] We have recognized each other before. We agreed with Audre Lorde when she said that we are part of an international group of black women "taking care of business all over the world."[39] We have been neighbors, living in the raucous seams of deprivation. We have healed each other's sick, buried each other's dead. We have become familiar with the swollen face of grief that grows large in that stubborn space between love and loss.[40]

To be African American and exiled on the spot where one is born.[41] To be Caribbean and exiled on foreign soil, producing a longing so deep that the site of neglect is reminiscent of beauty. We have grown up metabolizing exile, feeding on its main by-products, alienation and separation.[42] We walk these foreign caves crouched in stealth searching for the bitter formations of betrayal and mistrust, seeking answers to who has betrayed whom. Crumpling expectations and desire unto half-written notes of paper, barely legible, that lie now in overstuffed baskets, never delivered. Hieroglyphic markings to an estranged lover.

Caribbean women ought to have come forward when African American women mobilized in defense of ourselves in the midst of the attack on Anita Hill as she brought charges of sexual misconduct against Clarence Thomas. I signed the petition along with hundreds of women, knowing I was not born on this soil. It was not the time to raise questions about the accuracy of social location. Our identity as Caribbean women was not the historical point to be made at that time. That ought to have been made later when Orlando Patterson claimed that had Thomas "harassed" Hill in Jamaica, it would not have been called sexual harassment. Caribbean women in the U.S. ought to have entered the debate then to say that Caribbean women in Jamaica and elsewhere in the Caribbean, both within and outside the context of feminist movement, had in fact culled a politic and language about sexual harassment and sexual violence in the region to counteract the very behaviors in which Thomas had engaged. Instead, silence worked on us like a vise, as we bought into the figment of ourselves Patterson had constructed, and indirectly supported his and Thomas's (mis)representations of Hill, in a larger context in which, as Kimberlé Crenshaw has shown, the scales against Hill had been tipped from the very start.[43]

What kinds of conversations do we as black women of the diaspora need to have that will end these "wasteful errors of recognition"? Do we know the terms of our different migrations? Each others' work histories? Our different yearnings? What is to be the relationship with Africa in the term African American? What is to be our different relationships with Africa? On this soil? New Orleans, New York? Or reincarnated in Cuba? Brazil? Haiti? Shall we continue to read Edwidge Danticat while Haiti remains, like the Pacific, on the rim of consciousness?[44] To which genealogy of PanAfrican feminism do we lay claim? Which legacy of PanAfrican lesbian feminism? These conversations may well have begun. If so, we need to continue them and meet each other eye-to-eye, black women born in this country, black women from different parts of the continent and from different linguistic cultural inheritances of the Caribbean, Latin America, and Asia, the Pacific who experience and define ourselves as black. For there is nothing that can replace the unborrowed truths that lie at the junction of the particularity of our experiences and our confrontation with history.[45]

"Are you sure, sweetheart, you want to be well?"[46]

Women of color. Who are we now, twenty years later? Have we lived differently? Loved differently? What has become of the thinking that linked the internal colonization of women of color born here with women of color who had experienced colonization elsewhere, and had either remained in their countries of origin or had become refugees—exiles on these shores? Where does one come to consciousness as a woman of color and live it, at this moment? Have we developed a new metaphysics of political struggle? Did *Bridge* get us there, as Toni Cade believed before she moved into timelessness, and probably still believes. Did it coax us into the habit of listening to each other and learning each other's ways of seeing and being?[47] Have we made the crossing? In what shape have we reached shore? In whose company? With what in hand? Do we remember why we made the crossing back then? Other crossings before and since? Or had a desire to do so? Who are we now, twenty years later? Why do we need to remember?

Remembering is different from looking back. We can look back sideways and not bring things into full view.[48] One can look back to a when, to some past perceived to be wholly retrievable in the present, or some mirage of it, a gesture of nostalgia that can gave rise to fascisms of different kinds. We live in a country that seems bent on inculcating a national will to amnesia, to excise certain pasts, particularly when a great wrong has been done. The recent calls for this American nation to move ahead in the wake of the presidential election of 2000 rest on forgetting. Forget intimidation at the polls and move on. Forget that citizenship is particular and does not guarantee everyone a vote. Forget that we face the state reconsolidation of conservatism as the fragile seams of democracy come apart. Forget that law and order can be invoked so that a court can act with supreme expediency and not supreme ethics. Forget that as media make the presidential election in the United States of North America *the* only news, Palestinians continue to struggle for a homeland and Haitians struggle for a democracy. Forget that in the midst of a "booming" economy, more people are hungry in New York than ten years ago. Forget that capitalism does not bring democracy. "Once a great wrong has been done, it never dies. People speak the words of peace, but their hearts do not forgive. Generations perform ceremonies of reconciliation, but there is no end."[49] And this is partly why the desire to forget does not rest only in one place.

At times forgetting stands in for never having known, or never having learned something, the difference between staying in tune with the source of our own wisdom and relying on borrowed substitutes, fleetingly fulfilling. As Audre Lorde says in the poem "Solstice," "we forgot to water the plantain shoots when our homes were full of borrowed meat and our stomachs with the gifts of strangers who laugh now as they pass us because our land is barren."[50] But plantain shoots are tricky because the young can choke out the mother, or the mother can choke out the children, as *my* mother has instructed me. How do we learn the antidote to barrenness? And it may be not so much that we had never known about keeping things fertile and watered, the ancient sources of wisdom, but that at times the forgetting is so deep that forgetting is itself part of what we have forgotten. What is so unbearable that we even forget that we have forgotten?

"The scent of memory (our own and that of strangers)" can become faint, as faint as the scent of dried roses, when things become unspeakable, unbearable, when the terms of belonging get reshuffled. This was the case in the white working-class community of Southall, London/Britain, where waves of South Asian immigration upset "origin stories" of white belonging, producing violence of different kinds.[51] The memory of the turbulent crossing, some of which still lies in the silted bottom of the deep, is a site of trauma and forgetting. "Traumatized memory" is what Elizabeth Alexander has called it. Such a memory of violence and violation begets will, a will to forget, to forget the innards of that violation. I remember Morrison's *Beloved*, who went to the depths of that silt. Her mother, Sethe, did not dare remember why she sent her there, and only could when it was safe to do so, when Paul D returned. "The last color she remembered was the pink chips in the headstone of her baby girl."[52] To trust and remember. Love inspires remembering. It caused "floods and floods of blocked memories" to break when Barbara Cameron returned to the reservation after an eight-year absence and rediscovered herself, "walking on the Lakota earth," looking at the "cragged faces of her grandparents."[53]

So much of how we remember is embodied: the scent of home; of fresh baked bread; of newly grated coconut stewed with spice (we never called it cinnamon), nutmeg and bay leaf from the tree (not from the bottle); when we see ourselves squinting our eyes, arms akimbo, frowning our faces, adopting the same intonation, especially when angry, or running from the rain in the same way that our mothers and grandmothers did. But violence can also become embodied, that violation of sex and spirit, which is why body work is healing work is justice work. Assimilation is another kind of violation that can be embodied, assimilating alienation, one's own as well as others.[54] We have to be sure we want to be well. "Are you sure, sweetheart, that you want to be well?" Minnie Ranson tests Velma Henry in the opening scene of *The Salt Eaters*, a necessary question, "just to caution folks," "…and not waste…time."[55] A question that makes conscious the yearning to be healed. Conscious and practiced. Conscious and embodied. "A revolution capable of healing our wounds."[56] Healing wounds by touch. Touching is part of the work of decolonization. It explains why Baby Suggs, holy, took her heart—she had nothing left to make her living with but with her heart—to the Clearing, "in the heat of every Saturday," to deliver the weekly sermon:

Here in this here place, we flesh; flesh that weeps, laughs; flesh that dances on bare feet in grass. Love it. Love it hard. O my people, they do not love your hands. Those they only use, tie, bind, chop off and leave empty. Love your hands! Love them. Raise them up and kiss them. Touch others with them, pat them together, stroke them on your face 'cause they don't love that either. *You* got to love it, *you*. Out yonder, hear me, they do not love your neck unnoosed and straight. So love your neck; put a hand on it, grace it, stroke it and hold it up.[57]

Practicing again and again the ways in which we want to be well.

Women don't want to forget in the pages of *Bridge*. Barbara Cameron "will not forget Buffalo Manhattan Hat and Mani."[58] "When some lonesome half-remembered place" is reawakened in a sweat, Valerio remembers a past, a time before, before colonization.[59] What brings us back to re-membrance is both individual and collective; both intentional and an act of surrender; both remembering desire and remembering *how* it works.[60] Daring to recognize each other again and again in a context that seems bent on making strangers of us all. Can we *intentionally* remember, all the time, as a way of never forgetting, all of us, building an archeology of living memory which has less to do with living in the past, invoking a past, or excising it, and more to do with our relationship to time and its purpose? There is a difference between remember *when*—the nostalgic yearning for some return—and a living memory that enables us to re-member what was contained in *Bridge* and what could not be contained within it or by it. What did it make possible? What else did we need? All are part of this living memory, of moments, of imaginings, that have never ended. And they will never end so long as we continue to dare yearning for each other. There is a writing exercise that Natalie Goldberg, author of the recent *Thunder and Lightning*, has popularized. For ten minutes, or some designated time, one is asked to write uninterruptedly "I remember," bringing to the present all things remembered. The exercise is then reversed with its supposed opposite: "I don't remember." As one writer negotiated this underbelly of recollections, she observed, "It scares me that I remember what I don't remember." [61]

For me, remembering *Bridge* is a way of remembering myself, for, even as I write, I am aware that memory is not a pure act of access. I had not imagined when I began "Remembering *This Bridge*," and named it after writing only three sentences, that it would require such excavation, such rememory of deep forgettings. Feeding hungry ghosts.[62] As I bemoaned the travails of this writing, my friend Chandan posed his version of the question with which Minnie Ranson confronted Vilma Henry: "What archaeologies have you undertaken, Jacqui?" "And I had promised myself," I continued without answering, "that I would begin to write in a different voice. But it is excruciating to keep that promise in the midst of impending deadlines." "You know, Jacqui," Chandan offered, "sometimes we can only authenticate our voice when we are up against a wall; if not, we are only an impostor in a new language, speaking in the name of populism." Authenticating voice comes through the rediscovery of the underbelly, literally unearthing and piecing together the fragmented members of existence.

Remembering the unrelenting vision of *Bridge* in the multiple ways that remembering occurs is crucial in these times. It is a generous vision that was gifted two decades ago. And I want to insist upon its generosity, for in the midst of uncovering the painful fault lines of homophobia, culture, and class fractures within different communities of belonging, and advancing critiques of racism within the women's movement, it did not relinquish a vision of interdependence, of interbeing. It was not a transcendent vision, but one that was rooted in transforming the dailiness of lived experience, the very ground upon which violence finds fodder. Vision can only be as effective and as sturdy as our determination to practice, emphasis on the practice. Novelist Toni Bambara and interviewer Kalamu Ya Salaam were discussing a call Toni made in the *Salt Eaters* through the Seven sisters, a multi-cultural, multi-media arts troupe, a call to unite our wrath, our vision, our powers:

"Kalamu: Do you think that fiction is the most effective way to do this?

Toni: No. The most effective way to do it, *is to do it!*" [63]

It is the daily practice that will bring about the necessary shifts in perception that make change possible. Vision helps us to remember *why* we do the work. Practice is the *how*; it makes the change and grounds the work. A reversal of the inherited relationship between theory and practice, between how we think and what we do. As Mab Segrest has argued, these components of what we do, who we are (ontology), how we know (epistemology) and how we act from within our interpretations of reality (metaphysics), are all part of *engaged action*. It is this that engages us at the deepest, spiritual level of meaning in our lives. It is how we constitute our humanity. [64]

El Mundo Zurdo and the Ample Space of the Erotic:

Moraga: If the gun and the cross have been used as instruments of oppression, we must learn to use them as instruments of liberation. [65]

Anzaldúa: And yet to act is not enough. Many of us are learning to sit perfectly still, to sense the presence of the Soul and commune with Her. We are beginning to realize that we are not wholly at the mercy of circum-stance.…We have come to realize we are not alone in our struggles, nor separate, nor autonomous, but that we…are connected and interdependent.[66]

Lorde: The dichotomy between the spiritual and the political is false resulting from an incomplete attention to our erotic knowledge, for the bridge which connects them is formed by the erotic, the sensual, those physical, emotional and psychic expressions of what is deepest and strongest and richest within each of us being shared: the passion of love in its deepest meaning.[67]

For three years now I have been participating in a set of ongoing meetings and discussions among a group of women and men—lesbian, gay, bisexual, transgendered, and heterosexual, of different nationalities and age, with different cultural and spiritual affinities, including those with close relation-ships to the institutionalized Christian church—to learn what sex and spirit—what sexuality and spirituality taken together—might tell us about who we are. Early in this work, we found that many "secular" activists were reluctant to come out spiritually. Some of that reluctance came from the his-torical ways in which the Judeo-Christian religion, in particular, operated as an instrument of colonization: enforcing heterosexuality and nuclear family as the moral norm; attempting to erase the connection between sexuality and land, in Hawai'i for instance; splitting apart the ontology of mind, body, and spirit into the particularities of (white) manliness, colonized "other," and (Christian) religion, respectively. A more contemporary religious Right had mobilized globally to advance an antihuman agenda, mistakenly attributing its authority to God. But this dominant mythologized collapse of spirituality into religion was also operating among us, another indication of the subtle internalization of dominance. We found that we had a great deal of practice coming out politically, but many were timid about coming out spiritually *as* (radical) political people. It seemed that in combining the two we were on the brink of committing heresy of a different kind.

There was another kind of shared internalization we identified as we moved to unite these powerful forces of sex and the spirit that belong together. As we grappled with the inherited division, we understood that it is sustained in part by an ideology that has steeped sex and sexuality in sin, shame, and general disavowal of the sacred. At the same time, this very ideology has attempted to contain all of what is of spirit and spiritual within the structure of religion, all with predictably devastating consequences. To this process of fragmentation we gave the name colonization, usually under-stood as a set of exploitative practices in political, ideological, and aesthetic terms, but also linked in minute ways to dualistic and hierarchical thinking: divisions among mind, body, spirit; between sacred and secular; male and female; heterosexual and homosexual; in class divisions; in divisions between the Erotic and the Divine. We saw its operation as well in creating mono-thinking—the mistaken notion that only one kind of justice work could lead to freedom. Presumably, organizing for a decent, just, living wage is not connected to anti-racist work, to anti-homophobia work, to organizing against the U.S. state in Vieques. Such thinking is always premised in negation, often translated into singular explanations for oppression. Breaking down these divisions and hierarchies, indeed making ourselves whole again, became the work that occupied us throughout our entire journey.

Since colonization has produced fragmentation and dismemberment at both the material and psychic levels, the work of decolonization has to make room for the deep yearning for wholeness, oftentimes expressed as a yearning to belong, a yearning that is both material and existential, both psychic and physical, which, when satisfied, can subvert and ultimately displace the pain of dismemberment. Anticolonial and Left liberation movements have not understood this sufficiently in their psychology of liberation, and as a result have not made ample political room for it. This yearning to belong is not to be confined only to membership or citizenship in community, political movement, nation, group, or belonging to a family, however constituted, although important. Indeed, we would not have come to the various political movements in which we have been engaged with the intense passion we have, had it not been for this yearning. With the help of Bernice Johnson Reagon we recognized in this yearning a desire to reproduce home in "coalitions": our political movements were being made to bear too much, too much of a longing for sameness as home, the limits of nationalism.[68] But we needed to wrestle with that desire for home a bit longer and examine a bit more closely the source of that yearning that we wanted to embed in the very metaphysics of political struggle, the very metaphysics of life. The source of that yearning is the deep knowing that we are in fact interdependent, neither separate nor autonomous. As human beings, we have a sacred connection to one another, and this is why enforced separations wreak havoc on our souls. There is great danger, then, in living lives of segregation. Racial segregation. Segregation in politics. Segregated frameworks. Segregated, compartmentalized selves. What we have devised as an oppositional politic has been necessary, but it will never sustain us, for while it may give us some temporary gains, (themselves becoming more ephemeral the greater the threat, which is not a reason not to fight), it can never ultimately feed that deep place within us: that space of the erotic, that space of the soul, that space of the Divine.[69]

"To sense the presence of the soul and commune with her," is what Gloria Anzaldúa has said is required in this job of excavation, this job of changing the self. It is a job. It requires work. It requires practice. It cannot be someone else's excavation that we easily appropriate as our own, use as our own. It cannot be done as spectator or ventriloquist. It requires the work of each and everyone one, to unearth this desire to belong to the self *in* community as part of a radical project, which is not to be confused with a preoccupation with the self. The one has to do with a radical self-possession, the other with self-preoccupation on which individualism thrives. Self-determination is both an individual and collective project.

There is an inevitability (which is not the same as passivity) in this movement toward wholeness, this work of spirit and the journey of the Soul in its vocation to reunite us with the Erotic and the Divine. Whether we want it or not, it will occur. The question is whether we dare to undertake this task of recognition intentionally, as self-reflexive human beings, open at the very core to a foundational truth: We are connected to the Divine through our connections with each other. Yet no one comes to consciousness alone, in isolation, only for oneself, or passively. It is here we need a verb, the verb *conscientize*, which Paulo Freire used to underscore the fact that shifts in consciousness happen through active processes of practice and reflection. Of necessity, they occur in community. We must constantly envision this as we devise ways to practice the building of communities (not sameness) over and over again. We can continue to hold on to a consciousness of our different locations, our understanding of the simultaneous ways in which dominance shapes our lives and, at the same time, water the erotic as that place of our Divine connection, which can in turn transform the ways we relate to one another.

Oftentimes when we have "failed" at solidarity work we retreat, struggling to convince ourselves that it is indeed the work we have been called upon to do. The fact of the matter is there *is* no other work but the work of creating and recreating ourselves within the context of community. Simply put, there is no other work. It took five hundred years, at least in this hemisphere, to solidify the division of things that belong together. But it need not take us five hundred more years to move ourselves out of this existential impasse. Spirit work does not conform to the dictates of human time. But it needs our courage, revolutionary patience, and intentional shifts in consciousness so that we can anchor the struggle for social justice within the ample space of the erotic.[70]

One of the earliest lessons we have all learned from feminism is that the personal is political, the insight that some of the most infinitesimal details of our lives are shaped by ideological and political forces much larger than our individual selves. In the midst of a pitched battle to transform the curriculum at the New School University where I taught five years ago, I came to appreciate another shade of this insight as the school's administration sought to make me *the* entire political struggle. It was with a great deal of help and a deep level of self-scrutiny that I came to understand how a single individual could ignite a political struggle, but ultimately had to be subsumed under it, simply be within it, if that struggle was to be successful. This interior work is indispensable in this journey to wholeness. In this conscious attention to the reknitting of sex and spirit we undertook in the task force,[71] and spiritual political work I have undertaken in my life, I have come to see that an inside change in the personal is not entirely complete if it remains at the level of a shift in ideas, or even in practice, although both are necessary. Desire is expressed most fundamentally where change takes place, at the root of our very souls, the base of the internal source of our power, the internal source of our yearning. Yearning and power we have been taught so much to fear. So when Gloria Anzaldúa asks us to commune with the Soul, or Audre Lorde urges us to find something that our Soul craves and do it, our first task is to become attentive to the desire of the Soul and to place ourselves in its service. It is a necessary and delicate undertaking in spirit-based politics, this joining of the sacred and secular, "to have," as Sharon Day imaged it, "the ethics of spirituality inform daily life." It requires intention, a revolutionary patience, courage, and above all, humility. Once this work begins, the temptation to cross narrow boundaries becomes irresistible; connections, once invisible, come into full view. And I am assured that when the practice begins to bear fruit, the yearning itself is transformed.

There is an old man who has etched himself into an ancient slab of rock deposited in a park at the end of my street in Harlem. His face comes into view only from afar, with distance, with perspective. Close up, he simply folds himself back into the stone, disappearing, pretending, perhaps, not to be there. When we do not see him does it mean he does not exist? Unlike the figures of Davis, Lee, and Jackson—patiently chiseled into the Mountain of Stone in Georgia, now pasted onto the tourist bus stationed opposite the park, figures that announce themselves from far and near—this old man works in stealth, through years of weather, bringing himself into my field of vision only by the angle of my gaze and the distance at which I stand. Although I have lived for seven years on this same street that presumably goes in one direction, a one-way street leading directly to this slab of stone, I had not seen him before now. And yet, he is there. The challenge for me is to see him in the present and to continue to know that he is there even when I cannot see. Rocks hold memory.

Land holds memory. This is why the land and live oak trees rooted in the Georgia Sea Islands of the Southern United States whisper in one's ear when we allow ourselves to listen. The Georgia Sea Islands. The Ibo of Nigeria were captured and brought to these islands. When they arrived and saw the conditions of their capture and homelessness, they turned around and walked to "wherever they was going that day." The place, bearing the name Ibo Landing, holds the memory of that moment, which still lives in the heart of every Gullah child and in the solid trunks of the live oaks. The live oaks will tell us these stories when we listen. And the mountains of Hawai'i will echo the ancient Kanaka Maoli belief that they are stewards of the land, eyes of the land, children of the land. Deep within their undulating folds that drape themselves with the ease of velvet around the opulent embrace of mist and cloud, we will feel the ancient power of land to heal. Ocean will reveal the secrets that lie at the bottom of its silted deep. She requires no name before her. Neither Pacific, Atlantic, Arctic, Southern, nor Indian. She is simply her watery translucent self, reaching, without need for a compass, for her sisters whomever and wherever they are. She will call you by your ancient name, and you would answer because you would not have forgotten. Water always remembers.

This essay is in honor of Cherríe Moraga and Gloria Anzaldúa, who bore the original vision. It is dedicated to Gloria Wekker. Much gratitude to AnaLouise Keating for her insights and for staying close throughout this process, and to AnaLouise and Gloria Anzaldúa for their gentleness. Angela Bowen, Gloria Joseph, Gail Lewis, Mab Segrest, Jerma Jackson, Linda Carty, and Gloria Wekker have all accompanied me throughout this process and have read different versions of this essay. I have relied upon them for the combination of their astute eyes, their commitment to sisterhood, their critical engagement, their desire to make our world intelligible in order to change it, and for their perpetual generosity and love.

A version of this essay was published in *This Bridge We Call Home: Radical Visions for Transformation,* Anna Louise Keating and Gloria Anzaldúa, eds. NY: Routledge, 2002.

NOTES

[1] See the videodocumentary, *Sweet Sugar Rage,* available from Sistren Theatre Collective, Kingston 5, Jamaica; See also, Sistren, with Honor Ford Smith, *Lionheart Gal: Life Stories of*

Jamaican Women. Toronto: Sister Vision Press, 1989. CAFRA stands for the Caribbean Association for Feminist Research and Action. Since its inception in 1986, the association has been explicit in its commitment to examine "the relations between men and women in capitalist and socialist societies; to use a framework inclusive of race, class and sex; and to demonstrate the ways in which exploitative relations between men and women are facilitated maintained and reproduced by exploitative capitalist relations, and how capitalism itself benefits in the process."

2 Chrystos, "I Walk in the History of my People," in *This Bridge Called My Back: Writings by Radical Women of Color,* ed., Cherríe Moraga and Gloria Anzaldúa (New York: Kitchen Table/Women of Color Press, 1983): 57. The occupation in South Dakota by the people of Pine Ridge and members of the American Indian Movement lasted for sixty-nine days in 1973. The conditions that led to the occupation still continue. Conversation with Sharon Day. See Dee Brown, *Bury My Heart at Wounded Knee: An Indian History of the American West.* New York: Henry Holt, 1991.

3 Mirtha Quintanales, "I paid very hard for my Immigrant Ignorance," in *Bridge:* 151; Mitsuye Yamada, "Invisibility is an Unnatural Disaster: Reflections of an Asian American Woman," in *Bridge:* 35; Rosario Morales, "We're all in the Same Boat," in *Bridge:* 92; Doris Davenport, "The Pathology of Racism: A Conversation with Third World Wimmin," in *Bridge:* 85.

4 Gloria Anzaldúa, "Speaking in Tongues: A Letter to 3rd World Women Writers," in *Bridge:* 173.

5 Neale Donald Walsch, *Communion with God.* New York: G.P. Putnam's Sons, 2000: 15.

6 See my argument in "Not Just (Any) *Body* can be a Citizen: The Politics of Law, Sexuality and Postcoloniality in Trinidad and Tobago and the Bahamas." *Feminist Review*, no. 48, 1994: 5–23.

7 Nationalist regimes in the Caribbean have constantly mobilized race in the name of popular nationalism, either to generate oneness on the one hand (in Jamaica, the national motto: "Out of Many One," or in Trinidad and Tobago: "Every creed and race has an equal place") or to mobilize majority status, an African majority at different moments in Trinidad and Tobago, or Indian majority status at different moments in Guyana.

8 DuBois's earlier analysis of double consciousness is pertinent in this context. These formulations lie at the heart of the concept of internalized oppression used within feminism. See W.E.B, DuBois, *The Souls of Black Folk.* New York: New American Library, 1969.

9 Combahee River Collective, "A Black feminist Statement," in *Bridge:* 210.

10 Chrystos, *Bridge*: 57.

11 See Pat Powell, *The Pagoda.* New York: Alfred Knopf, 1998, for a moving, complicated portrayal of Chinese migration to Jamaica and the different kinds of journeys it can signify.

12 Shabnam Grewal, et al., eds. *Charting the Journey. Writings by Black and Third World Women.* London: Sheba Feminist Publishers, 1988: 1–6.

13 The politics of black women in Britain have always been infused with a more systematic critique of state practices than has been the case with women of color in the United States. The claim for black women's citizenship was anchored on a subjectivity as colonials, hence the notion that the borders of British nation had never been fixed. Gail Lewis, one of the original editors of *Charting* (see previous note), believes that this is a new moment in which black women are posing questions of belonging in ways that are fundamentally challenging and changing the character of Britishness. There are a fruitful set of transatlantic conversations that black women in Britian and women of color in the United States need to have. See Gail Lewis, *Race, Gender, Social Welfare: Encounters in a Postcolonial Society.* Cambridge:

Polity Press, 2000 and Brah, below.

[14] See Mohanty Talpade, "Cartographies of Struggle," in *Third World Women and the Politics of Feminism,* Talpade et al., eds. Bloomington: University of Indiana Press,1991.

[15] Taken from the text of a song by Sweet Honey in the Rock, reproduced in Cynthia Enloe, *Bananas, Beaches and Bases: Making Feminist Sense of International Politics.* Berkeley: University of California Press, 1989.

[16] Moraga, preface to the second edition of *Bridge*; June Jordan, *Affirmative Acts: Political Essays.* New York: Doubleday Anchor Books, 1998: 94. There is an important distinction here between wealthy refugees who flee to protect privilege, for instance light skinned/white Cuban refugees who fled to Miami with the triumph of communism in Cuba; Asian Ugandans who were expelled by the 1972 edict of Idi Amin who had business interests in different parts of the world (See Avtar Brah, *Cartographies of Diaspora. Contesting Identities.* London/ New York: Routledge, 1996: 35); or the *comprador* classes of many Third World countries who flee to metropolitan countries partly out of a refusal to rebuild civil society in their own countries of origin. This latter insight came from Chandan Reddy in conversation. Also see Anannya Bhattacharjee, "The Public/Private Mirage: Mapping Homes and Undomesticating Violence Work in the South Asian Immigrant Community," in *Feminist Genealogies, Colonial Legacies, Democratic Futures*. M. Jacqui Alexander and Chandra Talpade Mohanty, eds. New York: Routledge, 1997.

[17] Jordan, *Affirmative Acts:* 159.

[18] See Cathy J. Cohen, *The Boundaries of Blackness: AIDS and the Breakdown of Black Politics.* Chicago: The University of Chicago Press, 1997: 123. I learned of these disturbing data and their implications in conversation with Barbara Herbert. They refer primarily to African and Brazilian women in Massachusetts. African American women who have had this disease since it became visible in 1981 continue to have disproportionate morbidity and mortality rates, even with the advent of new medications. Clearly the question of the kinds of political interventions we adopt to make breast cancer, HIV/AIDS, and other diseases central parts of our organizing, is urgent.

[19] Paolo Freire, *Pedagogy of the Oppressed.* New York: Continuum, 1970, 1994: 31.

[20] Moraga, *Bridge:* 219; Cheryl Clarke, 'Althea and Flaxie.'

[21] These lines are taken from Ngo An, an eleventh century Vietnamese Zen monk. The poem:

> *The jade burned on the mountain retains its natural color,*
> *The lotus, blooming in the furnace, does not lose its freshness.*

It is the epigraph of Thich Nhat Hanh's *Vietnam, Lotus in a Sea of Fire* (New York: Hill and Wang, 1967), in which he traces the history of Vietnamese Buddhism and its engagement in the conflagration called the Vietnam War. I thank Mab Segrest for this reference.

[22] Aurora Levins Morales, "…And even Fidel can't change that!" in *Bridge:* 53–56.

[23] Jordan, *Affirmative Acts:* 95.

[24] Quintanales, *Bridge:* 151.

[25] Brah, *Cartographies:* 242.

[26] For an exceptional analysis of dominant postmodernism's premature theoretical abandonment of the category of social location and identity, see Paula Moya, "Postmodernism, 'Realism' and the Politics of Identity: Cherríe Moraga and Chicana Feminism," in *Feminist Genealogies.*

[27] Cherríe Moraga, "A Tuna Bleeding in the Heat: A Chicana Codex of Changing Consciousness." Lecture delivered at the Center for Lesbian and Gay Studies, December, 2000. Moraga was the Center's recipient of the Kessler Award. Moraga also noted that her recent work has a stronger Chicano/a audience.

28 See for instance, Latina Feminist Collective, *Telling to Live: Latina Feminist Testimonios*. Duke University Press, 2000; Women of South Asian Descent Collective, *Our Feet Walk the Sky: Women of the South Asian Diaspora*. San Francisco: Aunt Lute, 1993; and Joanna Kadi, *Food for Our Grandmothers: Writings by Arab American and Arab Canadian Feminists*. Boston: South End press, 1994.

29 Brah, *Cartographies:* 154.

30 Alexander and Mohanty, "Introduction…" to *Feminist Genealogies:* xiii–xv.

31 Avtar Brah, "The Scent of Memory: Strangers, Our Own and Others." *Feminist Review*, no. 61, spring 6:31.

32 There are of course different class migrations that are in turn linked to the categories and quotas deployed by the Immigration and Naturalization Service. See Bhattacharjee, "The Public/Private Mirage…": 210, for a comparison with South Asian migration to the United States.

33 I have benefited enormously here from discussions with Andrée Nicola McLaughlin, founder of the Black Women's Cross-Cultural Institute; Gloria I. Joseph; Chandan Reddy; Tamara Jones; Gayatri Gopinath; Judith Halberstam, and Liza Fiol-Matta.

34 I thank Chandan Reddy for this point. This polarization is also reflected in a theoretical schism between postcolonial studies and ethnic studies. A larger analysis is warranted here which should also entail an analysis of hiring practices within the academy. Brah, "The Scent…": 13

35 Our understanding of this American social formation would benefit enormously from analyses that do not automatically imagine a democratic U.S state. Such a refusal would help to reduce the anomaly of positioning the state as democratic at home and intervention-ist abroad. See Jaimes Guerrero, "Civil Rights Versus Sovereignty," in *Feminist Genealogies*, for an understanding of how the American state negotiates a set of advanced capitalist *and* colonial relations, particularly in relation to Native peoples; Cathy Cohen, *The Boundaries of Blackness*, for an astute reading of the "advanced marginalization" of African American communities. See also Gail Lewis, *Race, Gender, Social Welfare: Encounters in a Postcolonial Society* (Cambridge: Polity Press, 2000), for an exceptional formulation of Britain as a post-colonial social formation.

36 The fact of African complicity in the Atlantic slave trade is a different point from the one I am making here.

37 Baldwin, "Princes and Powers," in *The Price of the Ticket. Collected Nonfiction 1948–1985*. New York: St. Martin's Press, 1985: 56. Of course Baldwin's conflation of PanAfricanism with royal manliness is not to be missed here.

38 Paule Marshall, *The Fisher King: A Novel*. New York: Scribner, 2000. There is an important argument that Joan Nestle has made about the need for white women to publicly recognize this history as one way to continue to move forward in solidarity politics. A closer analysis of the new racial composition of domestic labor needs to be undertaken.

39 Audre Lorde, *A Burst of Light: Essays*. Ithaca, NY: Firebrand Books, 1988: 109.

40 I recall here the shared mobilizations in New York City around the death of Galvin Cato, police brutalization of Abner Louima and the police shooting of Amadou Diallo.

41 Baldwin, "The American Dream and the American Negro," in *Price:* 404; Caryl Phillips, *The Atlantic Sound*. New York: Alfred Knopf, 2000: 252.

42 See this most important essay by Lorde, on which I lean very heavily: "Eye to Eye…" in *Sister Outsider. Essays and Speeches*. Trumansburg, NY: The Crossing Press, 1984: 145–175.

43 Kimberlé Crenshaw, "Whose Story Is It, Anyway? Feminist and Antiracist Appropriations of Anita Hill," in Toni Morrison, ed., *Race-ing Justice, En-gendering Power: Essays on Anita*

Hill, Clarence Thomas and the Construction of Social Reality. New York: Pantheon Books, 1992: 402.

[44] There is an exceptional PanAfrican tribute to Haiti that David Rudder, calypsonian from Trinidad, has penned. It is called, "Haiti I'm sorry." The last stanza goes as follows:

> *When there is anguish in Port-au-Prince*
> > *is still Africa crying*
> *We're outing fires in far away places*
> > *when our neighbors are just dying*
> *Dey say the middle passage is gone*
> > *so how come overcrowded boats still haunt our lives*
> *I refuse to believe that we the people*
> > *will forever turn our hearts and our eyes away*
> *Chorus: Haiti, I'm sorry, we misunderstood you*
> > *one day we'll turn our heads and look inside you*
> > *one day we'll turn our heads and restore your glory*

[45] Thich Nhat Hahn, *Fragrant Palm Leaves. Journals 1962–1966.* New York: Riverhead Books, (1966), 1999: 89.

[46] Toni Cade Bambara, *The Salt Eaters.* New York: Vintage Books, 1980: 1.

[47] *Bridge:* vii.

[48] Dionne Brand, *No Language is Neutral.* Toronto: Coach House Press, 1990. Brand is talking here about the sidelong glances Caribbean people give to slavery.

[49] Epigraph taken from the Tiv of West Africa, in Paule Marshall, *The Chosen Place, The Timeless People.* New York: Vintage Books, 1969.

[50] Audre Lorde, "Solstice," *The Black Unicorn.* New York: W.W. Norton, 1978: 117.

[51] Brah has simply done a brilliant analysis that plays on the title of an autobiographical account by a son, Lott, of his mother Jean's suicide in Southall. *(The Scent of Dried Roses* London: Penguin, 1997.) Brah reconstructs Lott's family genealogy in this white working-class community in the context of interviews that Brah herself had conducted earlier with Lott's contemporaries, and analyzes South Asian migration and the attendant violence against South Asians (which interrogate "origin stories" of belonging), in order to understand how Jean was implicated in her world and she in Jean's. It is a brilliant methodological piece demonstrating how to think about identification across difference.

[52] Toni Morrison, *Beloved.* New York: Penguin, 1987: 38.

[53] Barbara Cameron, "Gee, You don't seem like an Indian from the Reservation," in *Bridge:* 52.

[54] Isabel Fonseca, *Bury Me Standing: The Gypsies and their Journey.* New York: Vintage, 1995: 281.

[55] Bambara: 3–4.

[56] Aurora Levins Morales, "…And even Fidel," in *Bridge:* 56.

[57] Morrison: 89.

[58] Cameron, "Gee," in *Bridge:* 46–52.

[59] Anita Valerio, "It's in My Blood, My Face—My Mother's Voice, The Way I Sweat," in *Bridge:* 43.

60 Morrison: 20.

61 Natalie Goldberg, *Writing the Landscape of Your Mind, Natalie's Minnesota Workshop*, Writer's Audio Shop, Austin, Texas, 1994: Tape 1. Goldberg also discusses how the idea for the exercise, this writing at the place of what is seen and not seen, the space in between, comes out of her Zen practice. There is as well an implied point about memory and history; but it need not be made now.

62 Thich Nhat Hahn, *Touching Peace*. Berkeley, CA: Parallax Press, 1992.

63 *Bridge:* viii.

64 Mab Segrest, "Reflections on Theory from Practice: Reality as Transformation." Paper delivered at the 9th Annual Duke University Women's Studies Graduate Conference, October 1998.

65 Cherríe Moraga, *Loving in the War Years, Lo que nunca pasó por sus labios*. Cambridge, MA: South End Press, 2000: 57.

66 *Bridge:* iv.

67 Lorde, "Uses of the Erotic…," in *Sister Outsider:* 53–59.

68 Bernice Johnson Regon, "Coalition Politics: Turning the Century," in Barbara Smith, ed., *Homegirls: A Black Feminist Anthology*. New York: Kitchen Table/Women of Color Press, 1983.

69 Chela Sandoval's original formulation of an oppositional consciousness remains very important.

70 I borrow the term "revolutionary patience" from Gloria Joseph.

71 The taskforce was a group convened under the auspices of the United States Urban/Rural Mission, Project on Sexuality and Spirituality.

Grandmothers of a New World

BETH BRANT

This essay is edited from a speech delivered at the University of Illinois,
Champaign-Urbana for Women's History Month, March 1987.

Pocahontas and Nancy Ward hold a special fascination for me because of the
legends that have arisen around their names and lives. They are presented, by
white historians, as good friends of the whiteman, helping colonialists gain a
foot-hold in Indian Country. At the same time, some Natives have used the
word "traitor" to describe them. Deified and vilified. Somewhere outside
their legends the truth lies. As a poet, rather than a historian, I feel I have a
freedom of sorts to explore and imagine what those truths are.

According to history, Pocahontas was a favored daughter of
Wahunsonacock ("Powhatan"), chief of the Algonquin Confederacy in what
is now called Virginia. In 1607 or 1608 she saw her first whiteman, John
Smith, on a ship sailing into the harbor. She immediately became enamored
of his color and promptly fell in love with him. Wahunsonacock, being the
"savage" that he was, hated John Smith and, for no apparent reason, gave the
order to have him executed. Right before he was to be tomahawked,
Pocahontas threw herself on Smith, telling her father that he'd have to kill her
too. Since Pocahontas was willing to die for this particular whiteman, then
there must be something wonderful about all whitemen, so Wahunsonacock
spared not only Smith's life but the lives of the rest of his crew as well.

Smith eventually returned to England, leaving Pocahontas to pine away
until she met John Rolfe. Pocahontas must have thought that all white men
looked alike, or maybe she liked the name John, because she enthusiastically
fell in love with Rolfe and became a good christian. She also became a good
capitalist since she helped her husband grow rich in the tobacco trade, took
up wearing white women's clothing, had a son, went to England, where she
was a celebrity, and finally died happily there—her soul eternally saved.

Quite a story. Even Hollywood couldn't improve on this tale.

But I can.

Wahunsonacock had twenty children, ten of them daughters. Pocahontas
was a favored daughter, but more than that, she was a child in her father's
confidence. She understood only too well what the invasion of Europeans
meant for her people. I also must tell you that at the time she met John
Smith, she was twelve or thirteen—a woman by Native standards of the day.
Pocahontas was not just a good listener, she was listened to. When she spoke,

the Pamunkey people heard her and respected her voice. While not a true matriarchy, like the Mohawk of Molly Brant or the Cherokee of Nanye'hi (Nancy Ward), Pamunkey women held sway in the disposition of enemy warriors and in matters pertaining to war. John Smith's so-called rescue was, in fact, a mock execution—a traditional ritual often held after the capture of enemies. This ritual, in the eyes of John Smith, must have held all the trappings of a play, with Smith in the starring role. Pocahontas also played her part. She chose to adopt Smith as her brother since this was her right as a Pamunkey woman. Smith began writing letters home of how his life was saved by a genuine Indian princess, and of how he held the Algonquin Confederacy in the palm of his hand. Of course, this was nonsense.

Wahunsonacock and his daughter/confidante were not fools. They had a sophisticated view of the English and the other European nations who were clamoring to capture the "new" continent and claim it for their own. The continuation of their people was uppermost in the daughter's and father's minds. They thought to establish their Nation by making alliances with the British. Then, as now, survival was the most important thought on Native agendas. The art and practice of diplomacy was not a new concept to North American Native peoples. If we were as savage and warlike as the history books would like us to believe, there would not have been any of us left when the first whiteman staggered onto our lands. Pocahontas was probably the first ambassador to the British, just as La Malinche was to the Spanish. Not an easy task for anyone, let alone a thirteen-year-old woman who could not read, write, or speak the language of the intruders, and who most likely figured out early on that the British held little esteem for women—especially if they weren't white. Pocahontas saw as the alternative to genocide adopting John Smith as her brother.

History books speculate on whether Smith and Pocahontas were lovers. I doubt this is important, but "history," intent on romanticizing Pocahontas and Smith, seems to linger on this attachment. I think that "history" is a lie, written down to bolster the ego of the whiteman, to promulgate their status as macho and clever warriors, *and* the ludicrous idea that whiteman are irresistible to Native women. Boastful and self-involved, John Smith eventually left the Jamestown colony and went home to England. He hadn't made his fortune, but he was to make a mark in books to come through his lies about and distortions of Aboriginal peoples.

There are reports that Pocahontas and her father were greatly angered at Smith's leave-taking. Why? Did they see it as a withdrawal of agreement made between Great Britain and Algonquian Confederacy? Through Smith's adoption, they had woven a tenuous connection between the Nations. The

Algonquin Confederacy had lost few people to these British invaders. The confederacy was still strong in the eyes of other First Nations. They were not weakened by their relationship with the British, due to the diplomatic skills of Wahunsonacock and Pocahontas. The British had done fairly well in the colony. Natives taught them what to eat, how to eat, how to plant what they ate. It amazes me how Thanksgiving in the States is portrayed as whites and Natives happily sharing food in a gesture of friendship. The pilgrims had nothing to share. Suspicious and ignorant of new kinds of food, as well as Native peoples, it is a wonder to me that any of them survived at all. But we were generous—a generosity that became the beginning of the end of our cultures as we knew them. My eldest grandsons are righteously appalled when Thanksgiving is celebrated in their schools. "Teacher, the pilgrims were bad guys. They killed Indians!" Of course, "teacher" continues to perpetuate this mythical holiday as a story where the whiteman is the good guy, feeding the starving Natives! When *will* they get it right?

In Aboriginal languages there are no words for stingy or selfish, except to describe aberrant behavior requiring a shaman's intervention. Our generosity comes from the complex and sophisticated worldview of thousands of years of belief and practice. The concept of family is a wide and far-reaching part of our worldview. By adopting John Smith as her brother, Pocahontas was opening her home and family to him. Smith violated this honor and the meaning of family by leaving Jamestown without a proper goodbye and thank you. This violation brought humiliation to the family, clan, and Nation. As a result of Smith's behavior, Wahunsonacock and Pocahontas left the Jamestown settlement and went home, enjoining other Natives to follow them. Jamestown suffered heavy losses of life. They literally starved. Pocahontas was sent on various missions to other Nations by her father. Serving as a spokesperson for the Algonquin Confederacy, she arranged new trade agreements, cemented old friendships, built new ones. There is no doubt that Pocahontas was a skilled orator and politician. It sickens me that the story we learn in school is the racist and untrue depiction of her romance with John Smith, and her willingness to die for him

During her travels, Pocahontas took a Native husband. Of him, we can find no trace. She must not have had children, or they would have remained with their mother on her sojourns and her eventual return to her home and family. When Wahunsonacock and Pocahontas were ready to visit Jamestown again (to see what the whiteman was up to), they were taken prisoner. I imagine the settlers wanted to vent their anger on them for being deserted. It would never have occurred to the pilgrims that their own racism and stupidity had led to this "desertion" and ultimate loss of lives. Pocahontas and her father were not free to leave the colony, but could wander among the people and houses. They found a man who must have intrigued them to no end. He was a missionary and was teaching people to read and write. Reading was something the whiteman did, and because of it, he held a certain kind of power. Bargaining with the British, Pocahontas arranged for her father to be sent home and she would stay to learn more about the christian way. "History" says Pocahontas was an eager convert. I submit that her conversion to christianity was only half-hearted, but her conversion to literacy was carried out with powerful zeal.

I feel in my heart that Pocahontas was guided by divine power. Not a god in christian terms, but a communion with Creator. "Living with the spirits," as my father used to say. Pocahontas lived with and listened to these spirits. There is a term and philosophy that has been used for centuries—Manifest Destiny. It is a whiteman's term and logic implying that whites are superior and therefore, it is Nature's law that the white race hold dominion over all natural things. In other words, the whiteman is king and emperor over all—people, animals, plants, the very air. I propose that Pocahontas had her own destiny to fulfill—that of keeping her people alive. Would Wahunsonacock and his people have listened and learned so readily from Pocahontas if she had not already given evidence as being a person who "lived with the spirits"? Was Pocahontas a shaman, a seer, a holy woman? In some English translations of her name, it appears to come up as "getting joy from spirits." Name-giving in Native cultures is a serious event. Many signs and omens are consulted before giving a name and getting a name. In many Nations, it was the role of the *berdache,* or Two-Spirit, to bestow this honor. History will not tell us that Pocahontas was a holy woman, but there is a feeling inside me that tells me this is so. I know my feeling cannot be substantiated by an academic literature; but I am not a member of the academy, nor am I a scholar of institutions—I am a Mohawk woman storyteller who knows there were and are prophets among my people. Pocahontas was such a prophet who lived her prophecy.

Linda Hogan, a Chickasaw poet, has written to me about the "New People." These are people like her and me—the mixed-bloods. Did Pocahontas envision Nations of New People? Did she vision a New World? A world where people would say, "I am a human being of many races and Nations"? Is this the real destiny? Vine Deloria once said, "Blood quantums are not important; what really matters is who your grandparents were." These women I am writing about were our grandparents. They are our grandmothers in spirit, if not actual blood. This does not mean that I think every person who dwells on this continent is a spiritual Indian. That would be a dishonor to my ancestors. I emphatically believe that our culture and ritual belong to us—First Nations. A person does not become an Indian by participating in a sweat, or observing a Sun Dance, or even working on political issues that affect our Nations. One cannot choose to be Indigenous like one chooses new clothes or chooses a brand of toothpaste. One is not Indigenous because they believe in our values. But the prophecy of New People *can* mean the beginning of a different kind of discourse between nations and races.

While learning to read and write, Pocahontas met John Rolfe. The accounts come down through time that he greatly admired her. He may indeed have admired her. She was a powerful voice in the territory; she held great wealth of land; she knew the many secrets of growing tobacco, which Rolfe had come to realize could make him a rich man. Rolfe came from gentry stock, but he was fairly poor compared to others of his class. Why else would he have come to the continent, except in search of untold wealth, just waiting for him to take? "History" tells us that Rolfe was taken with Pocahontas because of her "regal bearing, her christian demeanor, her wisdom." All this may be true and perhaps love even entered into it. Did Pocahontas love John Rolfe? Maybe. Did the spirits tell her that Rolfe was a good choice to begin the prophecy? There were other whitemen waiting in the wings to know the favors of Pocahontas and her father, for one was not possible without the other. John Rolfe was a man easily handled by those who had more charisma and political savvy than he. And he was not ugly. The courtship began, but not without obstacles. The court of King James was adamant in discouraging contact between the races (although I doubt there was discouragement against rape and pillage). The issue of class was a barrier to the marriage. This is why we end up with the ridiculous legends of Pocahontas being a princess. John Smith had started the flame of this particular bonfire when he wrote home about having his life saved by a princess of the realm. John Rolfe added more fuel to the legend in his desire to be married. Thus Wahunsonacock is made a king and Pocahontas a princess. In reality, kings and princesses—royalty—did not exist and never have existed in our cultures.

Of a dowry there is no mention, but it would be fair to speculate that Rolfe received a parcel of land on which to experiment with tobacco. The smoking of tobacco was a great hit in England among the royals. King James was said to disapprove of the habit, but it doesn't appear that too many people paid attention to what he had to say. Queen Anne was addicted to the stuff and she and her ladies-in-waiting spent hours smoking tobacco and requesting more.

The myth of Pocahontas wants us to believe that after marrying Rolfe, she quickly became a lady of leisure, even acquiring the name of Rebecca. I find this choice of names intriguing and prophetic. In Pocahontas's quest for literacy, the Bible was the only tool she had at that time. Did she read the story of another ancient legend, Rebecca, who was told, "Be thou the mother of thousands of minions, and let thy seed possess the gate of those which hate them"? When Pocahontas found herself pregnant, did she feel the joy of having a child of prophecy? A child of mixed blood, who would learn to read and write as a matter of course while inheriting the wisdom, political skills, and rich culture of his mother?

To ensure that this child would come into the best of all worlds, Pocahontas surrounded herself with female relatives and her father. John Rolfe may have been alarmed that Lady Rebecca was choosing to have her child in what he considered a primitive and heathen manner, but, then again, maybe he wasn't. We do know that in 1615, Pocahontas gave birth to a son amidst the chanting and singing of her people. So much for Pocahontas's christian submissiveness. After the birth, the relatives stayed on. Unlike John Smith, Rolfe seemed to recognize the honor of being part of Pocahontas's family. When a non-Native becomes part of a Native household or family group, whether through marriage or companionship, the Native family takes over. This is assimilation of a kind that is never discussed or written about. The non-Native often has to put up small battles to hang on to a separate personality rather than the personality of the Native group.

I have seen this happen in my own family with my non-Native uncles, mother, and my lover. Soon they are talking like Natives, joking like Natives. The prevailing Native culture and worldview is assimilated by the non-Native. I suspect this process is not discussed because the dominant culture does not want to admit that another way of *seeing* may be a more integrated way of being in the world, as opposed to Manifest Destiny. Again, this process of assimilation is *not* becoming Indigenous. It is a recognition that every part of what constitutes life, *makes life*.

This integrity of life can be explained through the example of the Sun Dance of the Plains Indians. Each person entering the circle to dance has an objective. Whether he or she is dancing for, strength, for healing the body and/or mind, that purpose will be reflected on the community, for the good of the community. In Oklahoma a few years ago, a Vietnam veteran asked to participate in the Sun Dance while using his wheelchair. This had never been done, but a way was worked out where a guide would maneuver him through the rigorous ceremony. This was not an easy task for the veteran or guide. The Sun Dance can last for hours; it has been known to last for days until communion with Creator has taken place. Later, when the dance was done, the vet told a friend of mine that he was dancing to be forgiven for the "sins" (his word) he had committed in Vietnam. As he was dancing, he began to relive his experiences in Vietnam; he began dancing for his buddies, dancing for the Vietnamese people, he began dancing for peace and the end to racism, he began dancing for the spiritual health that would bring him home to his own people again. This story has everything to do with Pocahontas and her prophecy. While not belonging to the Plains worldview that produces a Sun Dance, Pocahontas was doing her own dance for the good of the community. Her community, because of the child she bore, was an enlarged one. And I am wondering if John Rolfe's idea of family and community was also enlarged.

Pocahontas and Rolfe were invited to England to be presented to the king and queen. The tobacco industry was a profitable one to the monarchy. They wanted to meet Pocahontas, the "princess" of the Indians. Natives were becoming the rage in England. Natives were "in." To this day, Natives remain an object of fascination to European people. Perhaps they are fascinated by the fact that we still exist after five hundred years of persistent genocide. North Americans are not much better—to them we are invisible, extinct, or relics of a past ("primitive") way of life.

The England of the 1600s was a primitive, filthy place and must have been a terrifying sight to Pocahontas and her relatives. For she did not travel to London with just her husband and son, she took many female relatives and her uncle, Uttamatamakin, a medicine man to her people. It has been recorded that while in London, Pocahontas and her Native relatives swam daily in the waters of the Thames. This was seen as a heathen aberration by the British, who were accustomed to taking baths once or twice a year. Some of Pocahontas's relatives became ill from the polluted waters and had to stop their "savage" habit of bathing daily.

Pocahontas met the king and queen. It is reported that they were impressed. We have no account that Pocahontas reciprocated the feeling. And this leads to another question—where are Pocahontas's writings? We know she could read and write in English; does it not seem likely that she kept a diary or journal of the events in which she was participating? Illness began making inroads into the health of the Native people. John Rolfe got permission to take them to the country, where the air and waters were cleaner. Thomas, the son, could play, and Pocahontas and her relatives could relax away from the rude stares and comments that followed them everywhere. Pocahontas also met up with her old acquaintance/brother, John Smith. He wrote in his diary that the princess seemed angry with him. He was probably quite angry himself. The reception accorded Pocahontas and Rolfe must have rankled him. The "princess" of his making was truly being treated as royalty.

Pocahontas fell ill. She had already lost some of her people to England's diseases and had spent her time in the country in mourning. Thomas was ill also, which must have sent his mother into a frenzy trying to get him away from a country that did nothing but kill her people. Rolfe and Pocahontas prepared to take their leave and go home. They set sail; but in Gravesend, in the county of Kent, the ship had to stop and Pocahontas was removed to receive medical care. Perhaps she had tuberculosis or small pox. Uttamatamakin performed healing rituals for her. This may have been enough to ease her mind and spirit, but British doctors came, and over the protestations of her relatives, applied leeches and gave her purges. This weakened her further. Pocahontas died and her last reported words were, "It is enough that the child liveth." John Rolfe, a weak man without Pocahontas's intervention, failed her in death, since he had her buried christian-style. Uttamatamakin was infuriated, and the anti-white feelings that had were held at bay during Wahunsonacock's tenure began stirring and set the scene for hard times to come in Virginia.

Why did Rolfe fail Pocahontas? It may be due to the fact that his son was still very sick and he wanted to leave for Virginia as soon as possible. Rolfe may have chosen the most politically expedient way to placate his British hosts. Pocahontas was no longer there to strengthen him. Or perhaps John Rolfe was always a fool, believing that the Brit way was the only way. Pocahontas's relatives were token christians as she was, and probably would have gone along with a christian burial *if* they also could send her to the Spirit World through Pamunkey ministrations. But Pocahontas was interred at Gravesend in full English dress and tradition; her body remains there to this day.

Wahunsonacock died within a short time after receiving news of his daughter's death. He longed to stay alive to take his grandson to live with him. He must have mourned and longed himself to death. His beloved daughter would never come home again. Her bones would nourish British land instead of her own. And the precious child Thomas, so important to Pocahontas's vision of a new world? He stayed in England and was reared by his father's uncle. John Rolfe went back to Virginia and died shortly after the Native uprising. This foolish, weak man who failed his wife's dream, failed all of us. As a teen, Thomas did return to Virginia and experienced the desire to see his mother's people and the place he first drew breath. He journeyed to the Pamunkey, which was considered enemy territory by the British. What happened to Thomas as he journeyed to the land and language of his birth? A few years later, he was a commissioned as a lieutenant in the colonial militia and took up duty as a colonist against the Native people. The so-called Peace of Pocahontas was at an end. Had his mother lived, would the outcome have been different? It is hard to speculate. La Malinche lived to see her son by Cortez take up arms against her people and his. The Pamunkey people and those of other many other Nations were on a path to extinction through the Europeans' greatest weapon—disease. It is estimated by Native historians that two-thirds of Indigenous North Americans were wiped out as by measles, chicken pox, tuberculosis, smallpox, and the common cold. Did Pocahontas see this in her vision?

It is ironic and horrible that Pocahontas became grandmother to an estimated two million people who lay claim to being her descendants. Ironic, because a Virginian who would recoil in horror at having a Black ancestor, points with pride to the Native blood in his body. Horrible, because the British did their job well—anointing Pocahontas a princess, while excising her Native blood. We are left with the legend of a woman made into an "incidental" Indian. There was nothing incidental about Pocahontas. She fought for her people and for the future of her people. She spoke in her own language even at the end. She brought her son into the world through Native womb and hands. Even her final words— "It is enough the child liveth"— speak volumes of her plan. The false European legend must end. Pocahontas's honor demands it.

><   ><   ><

Nancy Ward was also a woman committed to a vision. Her name Nanye'hi, "Spirit People" or "Spirit Path," describes communion with a dream that gave direction to her life and that of her people, the Cherokee Nation.

Nanye'hi became the wife of Kingfisher in 1750, and the stories about her begin at that time. While a mother of two young children, she went into battle with her husband to fight the Creek, traditional enemies of the Cherokee. The Cherokee nation was a true matriarchy, meaning the blood lines flowed through the mother. Clans of the mother became the clans of the children. Women influenced all political and family matters. Accompanying her mate into battle was not a new phenomenon to the Cherokee. While in what is now called Georgia, Nanye'hi took up the arms of her husband who lay dying, and continued to fight and rally the people around her. This inspiration led her people into ultimate victory over the Creek Nation. Stories began to circulate among the Cherokee about Nanye'hi's heroism. She was soon chosen to become a Beloved Woman of the Cherokee. Beloved Woman means just that; she was beloved by the people, but even more, was beloved by Creator and was a conduit through which Creator spoke.

It seems that only Indigenous could come up with this particular way of being and seeing. Most of us know some stories of christian saints who supposedly were in communication with a god, but Native peoples so cherish and personalize Creator and the sprits who make the mysteries that this Great Mystery chooses to speak through women's voices. This is not unique to the Cherokee. Across North America, one will hear the voices of women speaking from the spirits. Again, I think of christian women saints who had to be martyred and *die* before achieving that state of grace their religion told them they didn't have in life. How much more sensible to be in a state of grace as a living human.

When Nanye'hi became a Beloved Woman, the Cherokee were literally caught in the middle between France and England. Each European nation was panting and scheming for Cherokee land and it fell on Nanye'hi to negotiate with each nation while retaining and preserving the integrity and strength of her own Nation. Like Pocahontas, she was a diplomat of skillful means. She worked in close connection with her uncle, Attakullkulla, maintaining a balance of power. Imagine it—young woman, aging man, holding war at bay, gathering strength to withstand the onslaught they knew would eventually come. Because she maintained this balance and peace, Nanye'hi has been seen by some of her descendants as a traitor and lackey to the British. But this story is old and familiar. Take strong Nationalist women and turn them into pale myth. Make *our own people* believe the lies. This is what oppression is—the enforcement of amnesia—to make us forget the glory and story of our own history. These women called traitors, what was their treachery? Neither Pocahontas nor Nanye'hi handed over lands or people to the whiteman. For one thing, it would not have been in the Native consciousness to do so. Land was given by Creator. Neither woman give up secrets or culture. These women knew what was in their vision. These women lived with spirits.

In 1757, Nanye'hi married a white trader, Bryant Ward. She had a daughter, Elizabeth. Bryant Ward did not live with Nanye'hi and the Cherokee. Why? My own guess is that Nanye'hi did not want him to. She sent him away after her child was born. The words of Pocahontas come back to me—"It is enough the child liveth." Were these Nanye'hi's words also? Did she have a vision of a New People also?

In 1775, the Watauga Purchase took place. Twenty million acres of Cherokee land were "sold" to the British for two thousand pounds. There is no record of Nanye'hi's voice, but a woman who always counseled "never sell the land" must have been frightened and appalled at what she saw as a break in Cherokee tradition and culture. But already, whether because of her arrangement with Bryant Ward, or the adoption of white values by some of her people, Nanye'hi was losing her influence.

In 1776, a Cherokee faction led by Dragging Canoe and Old Abram set siege to the Watauga fort. They captured a white woman, Lydia Bean, and were going to burn her alive. It is said that Nanye'hi stepped to the fire and shouted, "No woman shall be burned at the stake while I am still Beloved Woman." This story has a familiar ring to it, but it is true. Cherokee men, after years of staving off the whiteman, were nevertheless learning from him. The very notion of murdering a woman, regardless of her being non-Cherokee, reflects how Native beliefs were being swept away by colonialism. In all the horror stories that have been told since we first laid eyes on the whiteman, I find this one the most telling—how Native attitudes toward women changed and became more and more like the oppressors'. This change was not everywhere, and not in everyone, but enough change to freeze the blood and enrage the heart. Nanye'hi must have felt similar horror. For if attitudes about women could go against Creator's wishes, what other terrors must follow? This is not to say that we Native peoples brought this destruction upon ourselves. Such a statement would be untrue. But this change in a religious worldview surely helped to lay us open to the self-doubt and self-loathing imposed by the "Manifest Destiny" that tore the material of our Nations.

After saving Lydia's life, Nanye'hi took this woman to live at Chote, Nanye'hi's ancestral home. History does not tell us how long they lived together, or what they talked of together. Did they talk of politics and raising children? Did they become lovers? One thing is known—Nanye'hi learned to make butter and cheese from the milk of the "whiteman's buffalo." She later used this knowledge to introduce dairying into the Cherokee Nation. But what of Lydia Bean? Did she learn of the spirits? Did she learn that woman's voices were the means to Creator? Did she become assimilated into the Native way of seeing and being? I want to know the answers to these questions because they are essential to the tenuous discussion that is taking place between Native and non-Native women. I am reminded of a time when Denise and I went to Tyendinaga for a visit. We stayed with one of my many great-aunts and cousins living there. One night we sat at the kitchen table, shelling beans. We sat for a few hours, five of us, doing women's work—making food for the family. There was a magic to that evening, probably because we were performing a simple and primal act of love—feeding those we love. Denise, always aware she is a white woman among the Mohawk, felt loved and filled to be part of this act. We Mohawk women felt the same. I think of that evening, especially when I am asked to speak or read in unfamiliar places. Lydia and Nanye'hi made food together—physically and spiritually. Surely this is a possibility for us. Pocahontas saw a new world, filled with new people. Can we be less visionary than she?

War intensified between the Cherokee and the emerging American nation. The Cherokee found themselves defeated at every turn, while Nanye'hi stood her ground and shouted for peace. In 1781, trying to negotiate a peace treaty, she cried, "Peace…Let it continue. This peace must last forever. Let your children be ours. Our children will be yours. Let your women hear our words." The idea that different races could belong to each other in family and love is the most radical of ideas. Did the white women hear Nanye'hi's words? It is doubtful. How could they have heard unless their men chose to tell them?

The year 1785 found Nanye'hi still living at Chote with her children and grandchildren. Elizabeth had married an Indian agent. Her two children by Kingfisher had married and produced children. She had also opened her home to orphans, of which there were many. Deep changes were occurring within the Cherokee Nation. In 1817 the last Cherokee Council meeting was held, and Nanye'hi was expected to speak and bring counsel. Old and ill, she sent her son Fivekiller to represent her and to read her written message. And here I have another question. Nanye'hi was a literate woman. *Where are her words?* As a Native woman it makes me weep to know that "history" has not deemed it worthwhile to note that Nanye'hi and Pocahontas could write and think and feel, and therefore must have put ideas and thought on paper. Nanye'hi and Lydia must have corresponded. Where are these precious documents I long to see? Were they lost? Were they thrown away like *we* have been thrown away? Were they burned—like the truth of their lives was burned out of history and memory?

Fivekiller read his mother's message to the people, words that have survived history:

> Your mothers, your sisters ask you not to part with any more of our land. We say you are our descendants and must listen to our request. Keep the land for our growing children for it was the good will of Creator to place us here. Keep your hands off of paper for it is our own country. If it was not, they (the whiteman) would not ask you to put your hands on paper. It would be impossible to remove us all for as soon as one child is raised, we have others in our arms. Therefore children, don't part with any more of our land but continue on it and enlarge your farms and cultivate and raise corn so we may never go hungry. Listen to the talks of your sisters. I have a great many grand-children and I wish them to dwell on the land.

Nanye'hi's words were a prophecy, especially about the impossibility of removing all the people from the land. Even during the forced removal of southeastern Nations to Oklahoma, known as the Trail of Tears, many Cherokee escaped and blended into other families and races. Nanye'hi died in 1818. She had lived a long life as compared to Pocahontas. When she died, there were no last words recorded, but her great-grandson said that a light rose from her body and fluttered like a bird around her body and her family in attendance; then flew in the direction of ancestral land. If Nanye'hi had spoken last words, I imagine they would have been Cherokee words she had spoken all her life—Don't sell our land. Let the women hear my words. Our cry is for peace.

My friend Awiakta, a Cherokee writer and champion of Nanye'hi, has told me of the historic reunion of the Cherokee Eastern and Western Councils in 1984 at the Red Clay Historical area in East Tennessee. "These are the same council grounds," Awiakta said, "where the last council met before the Removal and also where Nanye'hi came during her lifetime. (Her homesite and grave are in the vicinity.) The Cherokee had carried the Sacred Fire with them on the Trail of Tears. At the Reunion they brought brands of it back. On a hill, in a receptacle made of native stone, they relit the Sacred Fire which will burn eternally." Awiakta also said that twenty thousand people were there, the descendants of Nanye'hi's vision of a new world. Red and white, Red and Black, Red, white, and Black. all these glorious mixtures come together as family. "Let your children be ours; our children will be yours." How prophetic were those words!

What is history? Does it still lie in the domain of the whiteman who churns it out according to his politic? What is women's history? Is it still the history of white women who were privileged by their birth? Will history become something new—a story of all Nations—instead of the story of European conquest? I am a grandmother and I feel it is imperative that I tell the truthful story of the Americas. My grandsons will need this story to help them grow into good men—the kind of men our Nations deserve. My grandsons—so many kinds of blood flow in their veins. Among the four of them flows the blood of Mohawk, Irish, Scots, Polish, Cree, French, Norwegian, Cherokee—the blood of the future.

This piece first appeared in *Writing as Witness*. (Women's Press, 1994).

Jelly Beans

MERLE WOO

The harmony of a million languages—
Colors never before seen;
People with
Cultures so many so rich always changing
Each with a sense of place
Not ownership.

And also,
We began to see people
Becoming tangible and real,
Becoming their potential.

A thousand-fold of gender expressions—
A wild flourishing of sexualities—

The nuclear family unit had
Disappeared,
Because everyone had everything
Without ownership—
Males and females were equal
Children were no longer
Blue and pink incipient workers.

It didn't matter any more if you
Were mannish or womanish—

Why, you could be
Two spirits, three spirits, four—
Fluid, changing by choice
Or desire,
Merging
Interpenetration of sexualities—
And genders—
For some

Clearly male and female for others—
So many expressions
And speakings-out
We no longer laughed at
But admired
The chick who kept her dick—

The tomboy who grew up to be a man,
The tomboy who grew up to be a lesbian,
The tomboy who grew up to be a woman—

The girlboygirl who is still changing
The girlman who is trying to find
The boy he had lost.

We decided that gender expressions
Like racial expressions
Were like jelly beans—
One alone is pretty enough
But one among many
Multiflavored, multicolored
Jelly beans
Is
Ecstasy!

Nitassinan: The Hunter and the Peasant

WINONA LADUKE

There is a long-ago Cree and Innu story about Wesakejack and the Great Flood. It seems that, at that time, the people, the animals, and all of Creation were not behaving well. There was much arguing and fighting, and even children were doing what the grown-ups were doing. Badly.

Wesakejack found this to be true for all the relatives, whether they had four legs or two, and the Creator also observed this. That is why the Creator sent the Great Flood—to make things new again. And that flood did just that. Afterward, there was nothing left, except for a few animals and Wesakejack. All clean. And with the breath of Wesakejack and some earth collected by the humble muskrat, the earth was made new again.

Wesakejack's dilemma is the dilemma we face today. Who has the right to make the earth anew, and how is it made so? There is a transformation going on in the North—in the subarctic from Nitassinan to Eeyou Aski, to Anishinaabe Akiing, Anishinaabe Aski, and beyond.[1] The military, miners, and dam-builders are "developing" the land, leaving a path of destruction in their wake. There is, by and large, no historical or scientific precedent for understanding the consequences of their actions, either collectively or in isolation. They are performing a great technological and geological experiment.

From the North looking south one finds a curious history, a series of cultural interactions driven by strange motivations. People from the temperate climes, motivated by fear, a perception of entitlement, and greed, have attempted to conquer the Arctic and the subarctic. This "temperate colonialism" is what is occurring in Nitassinan, a region the size of France in northeastern Canada. The military, the miners, the electric companies, and the loggers—along with their associated cultural baggage, technological accoutrements, and garbage—have been jackhammering this region for the past forty years.

Nitassinan, which means "the land" in Innuaimun, is the wellspring of a culture and a way of life. On this peninsula spanning the Canadian provinces of Quebec and Labrador, almost twenty thousand Innuaimun-speaking Innu live. Their land is a land of mountains, thundering rivers, vast boreal forest, sweeping tundra, and Atlantic seashore. Their colonial name, Montagnais, means "mountain people" in French. They are also known to other Native people as Naskapi, or "those beyond the horizon." The majority of the Innu people live in eleven villages along the north shore of the St. Lawrence River in what is now Quebec. Over three thousand live in two villages in what is today Labrador. Their culture and language are much like those of their relatives, the Cree (Eeyou), Ojibwe (Anishinaabeg), and Mi'kmaq, all of whom are Algonkin speakers who maintain a northern harvesting and hunting culture.

Theirs is a rich land. The George River caribou herd of at least seven hundred thousand animals roams Nitassinan, and many of the raging rivers are full of Atlantic salmon. The land has provided well for the Innu, and it could continue to do so. But only if a delicate balance between the animal world and the human world, the world of rivers and the world of canoes, is maintained. And if the humans continue to please the Caribou Master, Katipenima.

Seventeenth-century colonists documented the Innu's comfortable standard of living, describing robes of bear, moose, beaver, and bear skins covering floors; infants diapered in sphagnum moss, wrapped in soft materials, or moss-filled bags; and a diverse diet of moose, caribou, bear, beaver, porcupine, hare, marten, snow goose, eel, sucker, salmon, and a wide variety of berries. They remarked on the egalitarian nature of Innu life, reporting no class system in the bush or competition between the sexes.[2]

Innu elder Philomene Mackenzie said in a 1997 interview that

> Women and men both hunt. They have always been equals. When a woman delivered a baby, the next day she was up and ready to move onto the next camp. Today, she stays in the hospital for a few days, and she takes all kinds of medications. Women have lost their strength by this way of living.

> Since I lived the Innu way, I know how to deliver a baby myself. I delivered a baby myself, three years ago, in a tent. If the culture had not been broken, there would still be midwives here. We'd still have our babies in the bush, we knew everything about how to cure illnesses, to have our babies, we knew how to use the medicines of the forest.[3]

Egalitarianism and collective process are still revered today. "A hunter's prestige came not from the meat and goods he acquired for his family, but from what he gave away and shared with others."[4]

Each spring and fall many of the Innu travel far into the bush to hunt and fish. Their knowledge of hunting, trapping, fishing, hide preparation, cooking, snowshoe making, and rituals has been passed down from generation to generation. Their seasonal migration into the bush for fishing, hunting, harvesting, and trapping can last up to eight months. It is the essence of being Innu.

Surviving sustainably in the subarctic is a challenge mastered by northern Indigenous peoples. The hunting-and-harvesting way of life requires immense diligence, physical strength, and a vital relationship to the Creator and spirits. Pimaatisiiwin, which translates as the "good life" or, alternatively, "continuous rebirth," is a term used to describe the Innu practice of continuous balance, a balance maintained in ceremony. According to Daniel Ashini, the chief land rights negotiator for the Innu, the Innu religion is

> based on a belief in animal masters and other forest spirits. When we hunt we must show respect for the animal masters. We place the bones of the caribou, bear, marten, mink, and other creatures in tree platforms so the dogs do not eat them. We do not overhunt or overtrap areas where animals are scarce. If we do not show respect in this way, the animal masters get angry and punish us by not giving us any animals at a later date. Our elders communicate with the animal masters through dreams, drumming, steam tent, and a form of divination called Matnikashaueu. A caribou or porcupine shoulder blade is placed in the fire until it is charred and cracked. We read the marks to discover the future location of game.

> Our hunting culture thrives in the bush. We do things that very few non-Innu know anything about. Non-natives think they know us because they see us in their stores and at their hockey rinks, but they don't realize that there is another side to us, a side that they would have trouble understanding unless they spent time with us in the bush.[5]

The Peasants and the Hunters

> A colonial situation is created, so to speak, the very instant a white man…appears in the midst of a tribe…so long as he is thought to be rich and powerful…[and has] in his most secret self a feeling of his own superiority.

> —Octavio Mannoni, Prospero and Caliban[6]

According to anthropologist and cartographer Hugh Brody,

> The modern empires that now vie with one another for material and cultural domination of the world emphasize their historical and social differences. The rhetoric of global politics is replete with insistence by one or another of the superpowers that their institutions and points of view are underpinned by distinctive history and culture. Yet all these nations have in common one factor that provides a profound cultural

unity—namely an agricultural heritage. The commonality of social and mental form may be traced even more specifically to peasant forms of agriculture. This foundation of so many societies means that ideas about land, property, religion, sexuality, children, patriarchy, and social control are also shared. Urban and suburban attitudes to hunters are still shaped by an agricultural and peasant history that bridges other ideological chasms....

Hunters do not share peasant and urban consciousness. Their ideas and institutions, their views about property, children, sexuality, and social control are radically unlike those founded in settled, originally agricultural societies. Peasant attachment to specific plots of land, the wish to have a large number of children in short periods of time, emphasis upon marriage, subordination of women to men, preoccupation with private ownership, and bodies of explicit law that are enforced by some form of police—all these notions and practices are deeply alien to most hunting societies.[7]

Colonists from the temperate climates could not understand the North, which they found frigid and barren, a vast untamed wilderness. Jacques Cartier, a French explorer who hit the shores of Nitassinan in 1534, reported the doings of the Innu with great disdain:

These men may very well and truely be called Wilde, because there is no poorer people in the world. For I think all that they had together, besides their boates and nets was not worth five souce. They go altogether naked save their privities, which are covered with a little skinne, and certain olde skinnes that they cast upon them.[8]

Strangely enough, these skewed, negative perceptions of the Innu continue despite three centuries of interaction with them. There is a continuing presumption—subtle as it may appear at times—that hunting cultures are primitive and outmoded. This presumption is evident in current discussions with the animal rights movement and the Department of Indian and Northern Affairs (DINA) in Canada, for example. At various times, anti-hunting and -trapping activists have callously called for northern hunting cultures to progress from their outmoded practices and away from the trapline, while DINA officials (until recently) heavily encouraged town wage-work (and dependency) over a bush lifestyle.

Often, the most sustainable economy and way of life in the northern ecosystems is based on hunting, not on agriculture or industrialism. The Innu's hunting economy and culture work with the land and allow the animals to remain on their own path.

If the vast ecosystem of the North rankled the European sensibilities, the religious practices of the Innu and other northern hunting cultures horrified them. Cultural practices central to the Innu, such as divination, recognizing animals as relatives, and holding feasts to honor spirits, became the focus of colonizing efforts. And so it was that the first of the Europeans to enter the interior of the region were priests, then soldiers and entrepreneurs.

Jesuit Father Paul Le Jeune recorded his experiences during the early winters he spent with Innu families on the south shore of the St. Lawrence River in 1633–34. He, like his religious brethren elsewhere in the world, was determined to change the Innu. In 1637, he attempted to encourage a group of Innu to settle and farm at his Sillery mission and created a prototype Canadian "Indian reserve." Like those that would follow, it failed, even though food, houses, and clothing were provided. The Innu preferred their own way of life and eventually moved back into the bush.

It was the Hudson Bay Company that unleashed the most economic strife in the North and is likely the largest single exploiter of the region. The Hudson Bay Company created what scholars generally regard as an economic serfdom in the region. Canadian historian Alan Cooke, among others, argues that, during the eighteenth century, the traders deliberately set out to destroy the economic independence of the Innu by making them dependent on goods they could obtain only from trading posts and by cheating the Innu and other Native people on their price for furs and other trade items.[9]

At the close of the Second World War, the federal government decided that the North could be exploited for its land and its raw materials. The fur trade had collapsed, and the Hudson Bay Company's unfair practices with the Innu had left them hungry, dependent, and in some cases in servitude.[10] The new players in the North would be the military, the mining companies, and those who would take the rivers themselves.

The Military and the Bombs

Militarism is a form of colonization which takes away from our lives. That future is without hope for us. But we will fight for our rights. I believe in non-violence and civil disobedience. I am ready to go to jail, to take blows or die for our cause, because I believe in the struggle for the freedom of my people. I don't want your sympathy, I want your support. Your strong and collective support against the oppression of your government. What we need is your resistance.

—Penote Ben Michel, January 31, 1987[11]

In the early morning at Nitassinan, the mist moves through the forest like an ancestor. The hunter walks carefully, yet still silences the animals. The animals watch as the hunter walks, acutely aware of each movement. The rustling of leaves and the sharp crack of a branch resonate against the quiet as the hunter walks. Something catches his eye, and he stoops to one knee to inspect a hoof print, the trail of a caribou.

As if from nowhere, the silence is shattered with an explosion of sound. A jet fighter screams seventy-five meters overhead, and the hunter presses his hands to his ears and throws himself to the ground. His head pounds, and he screams with pain. In a few seconds, the jet fighter is gone, but all the hunter can do is hear is his own heart beating and smell his own fear.

Monica Nui, Innu elder, tells a similar story.

> We were camping on the Kenamu River…we were overflown several times. What is the most scary is that the jets come in with no warning. They are very low, just above the trees, and the noise bangs inside your head for a long time after. In fact, you can see the treetops bending when they go over. If they pass over the tents, the tent canvas starts to shake, also. A little girl about five years old was so scared that she fainted. She had been playing near the lake, and she almost fell in. When this happened, they radioed another camp, and the other camp had been overflown as well. They had been making a fire outside the tents, and the coals from the fire had been scattered all over the ground. After the three jets went over, I could hear the ringing inside my head for at least a half hour.[12]

The sound of low-level flights overhead is the specter that returns day in and day out to the Innu, to the caribou, and to Nitassinan. Many of those flights are between seventy-five and one hundred meters above ground, with some in Labrador as low as thirty meters. Their purpose is to penetrate unnoticed into enemy territory by passing below radar screens. Who is the enemy in the forest? That is what the Innu ask. Why use offensive rather than defensive weapons?

In 1941, the Canadian military claimed Goose Bay, in the heart of Nitassinan, as its own. Determined to have an outlying station linking North America and Europe during the Second World War, the Goose Bay base was established as the closest link to the old country from the continent. In 1952, the U.S. Air Force signed a twenty-year lease to use the base as a refueling station for interceptor squadrons. Before that lease expired, the United States generously lent these installations to the British Royal Air Force and its Vulcan Bombers.

In the mid-1970s, European resistance to low-level flight training over densely populated areas was increasing. The physical and psychological impact of the flights had not gone unnoticed by others. West Germany and the other allies decided that it was better to fly somewhere other than their own backyards. They began to eye the vast territories of Nitassinan.

In 1980, NATO's military committee had sponsored a feasibility study on the construction of a fighter-plane training center in Goose Bay. Not to be outdone, then-Canadian Minister of Defense John Crosby announced in 1985 that the government would spend $93 million to modernize the existing base and encouraged new countries to join in the war games in the sky. Canadian government brochures and videos described the test area as "wilderness interior free of human habitation." Six countries—Belgium, Great Britain, West Germany, Netherlands, the United States, and Canada—joined in the flights over Nitassinan more intensely than ever.

By the mid-1980s, more than four thousand "training flights" were being carried out over the one-hundred-square-kilometer area. Between April and November 1989, there were eight thousand low-level flights: between thirty and fifty flights per day during the training season. But the worst was yet to come.

NATO's proposal would have increased the number of flights from eight thousand to one hundred thousand a year. And so it was that the Canadian government began a bidding war against Turkey for a NATO base on Nitassinan, in a long and protracted process.

The Innu believe that NATO's proposal would make their territory uninhabitable. There are some simple mechanics in their argument. The noise produced by a military aircraft flying at thirty to seventy-five meters is generally exactly at or above the human pain threshold of 110 decibels. The pounding of a jackhammer, for example, produces about 100 decibels of noise. Sonic booms created by military aircraft are in a different league. The sonic boom produces a constant shock wave, traveling along the ground like the wake of a boat over water. The power of the shock wave at close range can lift the water off the lake and tip a canoe and can drive animals insane: foxes have been known to eat their kits, geese to drop their eggs midflight, as a consequence of the sonic boom.[13]

Canadian journalist Robert Jobst describes the science: "The surface area affected by this shock wave is roughly one mile wide for every 1,000 feet of altitude between the aircraft and the ground. Therefore, a jet flying supersonically at 20,000 feet would produce a sonic boom 20 miles wide beneath it. Sonic booms are measured in pounds per square foot. The limit of human tolerance is less than two pounds per square foot. U.S. military aircraft produce sonic booms that average four to five pounds per square foot."[14]

The Innu had observed that caribou migration and social patterns were disturbed by the flights, that migratory birds seemed confused, and that the reproduction rates of the animals were low. But in 1990, the Canadian government concluded the opposite: that the construction of the NATO test base would not cause significant harm to the environment. The Innu testimony of massive disturbance and damage was dismissed as "unscientific," even though the Department of National Defense (DND) had already been forced to compensate people for the damage the flights had caused. The DND had paid more than $145,000 to property owners, including $45,000 to a New Brunswick farmer whose foxes ate their newborn kits and whose pregnant foxes aborted their fetuses, as a result of similar flights. The Innu experience, the Innu observations, and the Innu pain, however, still have not been seriously acknowledged by the Canadian government.

Daniel Ashini wonders why Canadians don't see the "inherent bias of a process where the federal government is establishing the terms for a review of its own program. It's like asking McDonald's to conduct a study on whether or not it makes good hamburgers. Of course they are going to say they make the best hamburgers in the world."[15]

Next, the Canadian Federal Ministry of Transport established standards by which to judge the impact of low-level flights, sonic booms, and other forms of "sonorous aggression" on a given community. By their rather complicated mathematical calculations, the "noise exposure level" of a single flight of an F-4 jet was found to be higher than that allowed in Canadian suburbia, hotels, or stadiums. The Ministry's study found that exposing a community to such sonorous stress would provoke "energetic and sustained complaints by individuals. In addition, organized action and a law suit could also be expected."[16] Yet the flights over Nitassinan continued.

Shutting Down the Runway

In 1987, Rose Gregoire, Innu mother of four, her sister, Elizabeth Penashue, and friend Francesca Snow were among some of the first Innu to protest on the runway. The daring resolve of this small "mother-led band of peace warriors" as *Toronto Now* magazine called them, were truly a formidable force. Said Snow, "We are not afraid of anything, even if I get shot. We struggle all the way, no matter what happens."[17]

There is an image I cannot get out of my mind. It is of an eighty-year-old couple shutting down the runway. They stand there as a five-hundred-ton jet careens toward them and takes off above their heads. That image symbolizes the intensity of the commitment of the Innu and the story of their resistance to the military.

In 1988, Father Jim Roche walked onto the bombing range on the base as part of a protest. "On that bombing range," he said. "I really felt for the first time what it meant to the Innu. There were all these bomb shells and craters, and it hit me that what was really happening here was preparation for war." Roche spent five months in jail for his protests with forty other Innu, a longer sentence than most, because he refused to sign a document stating he would not return to the runway. He told the judge, "We do not fear prison. There is no shame in being imprisoned for the pursuit of justice and the struggle for what we believe in."[18]

In 1989, Canadian authorities charged the Innu with trespassing on military land, and the Innu were hauled in front of a Newfoundland provincial court. On its face, the case was significantly biased against the Innu. The Canadian judicial system is foreign to the Innu's value system and way of life: English common law and Canadian law are not Innu laws. Plus, the court had an inherent interest in confirming the land title on which its jurisdiction is based. And the entire proceedings took place absent any simultaneous translation into Innuaimun. Finally, consider that to the Innu, the laws themselves make little sense.

But Judge James Iglioliorte agreed with the Innu claim that what the government called "military lands" were their own. The judgment acknowledged that the Innu had never signed a treaty or land-claims agreement, and the Canadian constitution states that aboriginal peoples cannot be deprived of their land except through just, equitable negotiations. According to Iglioliorte's written decision,

> We are not dealing with land which has been the subject of divestiture through treaties…provincial and federal statutes do not include as third parties or signatories any Innu people….All of the legal reasonings are based on the premise that somehow the Crown acquired magically by its own declaration of title to the fee a consequent fiduciary obligation to the original people. It is time this premise based on 17th-century reasoning be questioned in the light of 21st-century reality.

> In the end, the court ruled that the Innu could not be charged with trespassing on their own lands.[19]

After almost a decade of repeated Innu occupations of the runway, in May 1995, the Canadian Environmental Review Panel released the conclusions of its eight-year, $16-million study: *that the evidence of low-level flights' negative impacts on the environment and on the Innu was still inconclusive.* The panel recommended that the number of flights be doubled, a second bombing range be allowed, and the proposed avoidance program to avert flights over Innu and animals be essentially scrapped because there were too many sensitive areas to be practical.

And so the Innu stay on the runway, in a nonviolent campaign that may be the most persistent and longest-running in Canada's history. Entire communities have occupied the runways and fill the jails, as harsher and harsher sentences mount and the Innu enter their second decade of resistance to militarization.

"A lot of elders were taught that you never stand up against white people, you never challenge them," says Roche. "Since the protests started, that's been changing. They learned that they can fight back."[20]

The Liberation from Legal Colonialism

After the fear is quelled from your first arrest, the liberation of your mind from the legal colonialism begins. Facing down the white man's laws was indeed a process of unlearning oppression for the Innu.

It started with hunting. In the early 1970s, the Canadian government decided that the caribou of the Mealy Mountains needed a rest from hunting, and consequently the government banned Innu hunting in their traditional area for, they said, a few years. While American pilots stationed at the base had been known to make low passes over caribou to decapitate them for their antlers, it was deemed that the Innu shouldn't hunt from the same herd.[21] As the few years dragged on to fifteen, it became apparent to the Innu that Canada's laws didn't apply to all.

Finally, after their own ceremonies, prayers, and agreements with those they refer to as the Animal Masters, the Innu felt the herd had recovered enough in 1987 to allow for a limited hunt. And the meat-eaters were hungry for their relatives. Father Jim Roche tells what happened next. "I heard the older men talk about the pain of being treated as foreigners in their own land. They felt they had already lost so much…they were frustrated that they had to sneak around when they hunted caribou as though they were doing something wrong."[22]

And so they walked into the bush and took their animals. In April 1987, the Innu were charged with hunting violations. Ben Michel stood before the judge in Goose Bay to defend what the Innu were doing. "We are a hunting people," he declared. "It is this form of living which lies at the core of our identity as a people, which gives expressiveness to our language, which animates our social relationships, and which for thousands of years breathed life into our people. Without exception those who have categorized our hunting existence as primitive are those who have not tried to live it."[23]

Six years later, the Innu of another remote village, Davis Inlet, also liberated themselves from the white man's law, in a different way. The Canadian government historically had a provincial court in Davis Inlet. Many of the trials the court conducted were on charges that were eighteen months to two years old. Few Innu could speak English, and the translator brought in to address this spoke a different dialect. Then there was the transportation challenge. On each of the four days the court was in session, the court party would fly into town, arriving in the morning, and spend the night in Goose Bay, to the south. The community found this schedule offensive, especially since prior courts took up residence in the town. Finally, virtually every case involved substance abuse, a fact that Chief Katie Rich and others considered to be symptomatic of deeper problems that the community ought to address over the long term, outside the Canadian court system.

In December of 1993, the Davis Inlet Mushuau Innu finally took matters into their own hands. They shipped out the judge and began to recover themselves, eventually reconciling with the court.

On the afternoon of December 13, 1993, Chief Rich, accompanied by a group of women, delivered a note to Newfoundland provincial court judge Robert Hyslop, who was presiding over Innu-related cases on Innu land in Davis Inlet. It read,

> This letter is to inform you that you are to cease and desist immediately the operation of the court in the community of Davis Inlet and to withdraw yourselves immediately from this community. You are further advised that no future holding of the court in our courtroom will be permitted until further notice by order of the councilors and community members.

After some back and forth discussions, the court left town.

Dams

> Soon there will be no great and beautiful wild rivers left in Quebec, the entire territory will be crisscrossed with a network of powerlines, which like spiderwebs will spoil the beauty of our mountains and valleys.

> —Innu traditionalist

They called the great falls Patshetshunau—"steam rising." The white people called it Churchill Falls, named after a British guy who had never even seen them. Strange how that all works.

Larger than Niagara Falls, Patshetshunau seemed infinite. In 1895, the geologist A.P. Low visited the falls and wrote: "The noise of the falls has a stunning effect and although deadened because of its enclosed situation can be heard for more than ten miles away as a deep booming sound. The cloud of mist is also visible from any eminence within a radius of twenty miles."[24]

The Great Falls Patshetshunau are now silent. The long chute is dry, a result of the ambition of the Newfoundland and Labrador governments and the greed of Hydro-Quebec. In the 1960s, then-Premier of Newfoundland Joey Smallwood began a rather bizarre and co-dependent relationship with the province's wealthier cousin, Quebec, in an attempt to exploit the natural resources of Newfoundland (i.e., Nitassinan). First, he sold the idea of a hydro-electric power plant at Churchill Falls to a group of investors. His next obstacle was figuring out how to sell and distribute that hydro-electric power.

In what journalist R. John Hayes describes as a desperate move, "Smallwood signed over the right to sell most of the power to Hydro-Quebec at a fixed rate for forty years at a price of less than three-tenths of one cent per KWH. Hydro-Quebec has the option to renew the contract for another 25 years at only two-tenths of a cent per KWH. Newfoundland locked themselves in until the year 2044."[25]

Hydro-Quebec made a good chunk of change on the deal. The company has been able to sell the power at nine times its purchasing price. Not a bad deal. Newfoundland's revenues are estimated to be $70 million to $80 million per year. Hydro-Quebec's revenues were approximately $750 million in 1976 from the same dams. Hydro-Quebec turned around and invested that income into new dams from James Bay to any available river in its presumed domain.

What it left in Nitassinan was ecological disaster. Joey Smallwood will always be remembered for this. The so-called Churchill River is the largest river in the area, draining 29,900 square miles and providing an inland route for the Innu. Dammed before its monumental three-hundred-foot plunge, the river now squeezes through several shafts and tunnels, leaving a mere trickle for the lakes and rivers below. The Smallwood Reservoir floods 5,698 square miles of central Nitassinan and is half the size of Lake Ontario. Boastful politicians in the 1970s lauded it as the third-largest artificial body of water in the world.[26]

When man does the Creator's job, it usually doesn't turn out right. The black spruce forest that was drowned in the flooding died slowly. Natural processes of decay seemed to pull the heavy metals, particularly mercury, out of the soil. And in its dying breath the forest killed the water. By 1977, studies determined that mercury levels in the Smallwood Reservoir were elevated. Thirty-seven percent of the Innu surveyed had elevated mercury levels.[27] The provincial government issued a bulletin advising people to limit their fish consumption to one fish per week. Since then, there have been no new studies done, almost as if the provincial government hoped that in not documenting mercury problems in the reservoir, the problems would disappear.

The Innu hunting, harvesting, and burial grounds flooded by the Smallwood Reservoir were of little interest to the electric company. River habitats of the animals were destroyed, and dams set in motion a process that threatens much of the commercial salmon fishery of the region. Hydro-Quebec kept on making dams in Nitassinan, on the Manicouagan, Outardes, Betsiamites, and Magpie rivers. The utility sold the power to some industries that needed cheap power, then it turned to James Bay, in Cree country.

James Bay Dams

The settler's eyes see differently than the Native's. So it was that when Quebec Premier Bourassa looked to the north of Quebec, he saw a vast hydro-electric plant in the bud; for what he called a "tremendous waste" of resources crashed through gorges, and rivers meandered through vast forests, and finally made their way to the sea. The James Bay I complex was a result: the idea being to put 11,500 square kilometers of land behind the dams underwater and produce twelve thousand megawatts of electricity. Ultimately, the initial project, concentrated along the Eastmain and Rupert rivers, ruined the ecological balance of some 176,000 square kilometers of land, an area about two-thirds the size of the former West Germany.

The Cree, Inuit, and Innu of the northern villages whose land and lifeways were at stake did not hear about the project until the planning was well underway. The Native community, led largely by the Crees of James Bay, mounted an aggressive campaign to head off the project. After six months of testimony concerning the cultural and environmental impact of the project, in March of 1975, James Bay I was halted by a court injunction. A week later, the Quebec Court of Appeals overturned the lower-court ruling, largely on the premise that too much money had already been spent on the project to abort it. The "balance of convenience," according to Hydro-Quebec and the government, rested in favor of continued development. That argument has been the bane of many northern development projects. The resulting "James Bay and Northern Quebec Agreement," shoved down the throats of the Cree, Inuit, and Innu of northern Quebec, alleged to give the Cree and other Native people more power to determine the future of the North. That agreement has been continuously contested over the past two decades.

Within a decade of the completion of the La Grande Complex, signs of environmental disaster had become obvious. Massive flooding had once again leached methyl mercury from the soil, changing an inorganic mercury compound in the water into organic mercury. The result was mercury contamination in the reservoirs, with levels six or more times what was considered "safe." The most significant mercury contamination levels in North America—as pronounced as those found in Minimata, Japan, where thousands of people suffered severe neurological diseases—are now present in the waters of the La Grande Complex. To avoid its deadly impact, the Cree of the downstream villages had their hair tested for the presence of mercury and were advised not to eat fish from the dam complex.

Then there was the problem of the caribou and the water. The flow of water in the river has been radically altered from its natural path. At times, the flow may be increased or decreased by about twenty times the normal rate, according to the electrical demand at the end of the powerline. This situation carries obvious implications for fish, beaver, and other water-based creatures downstream. The Cree remember the picture of beavers, which in response to the dams built houses many stories high, and of dead animals floating in the toxic waters. In 1984 came the most deadly dam-release of water, precisely during the annual migration of the George's River caribou herd across the Canapiascau Reservoir. As a direct result, more than ten thousand caribou drowned. Hydro-Quebec officials refused to accept responsibility, callously calling the deaths "mainly an act of God."[28]

So it was that when Hydro-Quebec came forward with a set of proposals known as James Bay II in the late 1980s, they were met with resistance. Their proposed new projects would have destroyed four major river systems: the Great Whale, Lower Broadback, Nottaway, and Rupert, and would have also flooded Lake Bienville. Further, James Bay II would involve the total deforestation of some 922,040 square kilometers of land, an area the size of Maine, Vermont, and New York state combined. That $60 billion megaproject, according to National Audubon Society's Jan Beyea, "would make James Bay and some of Hudson's Bay uninhabitable for much of the wildlife now dependent on it." According to the society, if James Bay II were constructed, "in fifty years, [this entire] ecosystem will be lost."[29]

The Cree and Innu and their Native and environmental allies began an organizing campaign, this time not only in Quebec, but in the Northeast, thus breaking the political isolation on which environmentally racist proposals are so often based. The James Bay project would only go through if Vermont, New Hampshire, Maine, and New York bought the power. Hydro-Quebec required American contracts and money to mount the project in the first place, and so the northeastern United States was where the organizing needed to take place. The Cree and their allies—such as the Vermont Natural Resources Coalition, the newly formed No Thank You Hydro-Quebec, the Conservation Law Foundation, the Natural Resources Defense Council, the Student Environmental Action Committee, and many Native and human rights organizations—put the James Bay projects on the public agenda.

Consumer groups pointed out that conservation practices could save 30 percent of presently used electricity, not to mention millions of dollars, for the taxpayers and ecosystems. The issue is not whether or not to use nuclear, coal, or hydro, the issue is conservation. Jim Huggins, a longtime organizer for No Thank You Hydro-Quebec, took a broader stance. "We must live within our means. We don't believe that we, as Vermonters, should be partaking in human rights abuses, even if they happen outside our borders," he said.[30] The *New York Times* referred to the resistance as a "rag-tag band of organizers." Those organizers, however, were successful. A multitude of student organizers successfully secured the divestment of their universities' stocks and bonds in Hydro-Quebec. Consumer groups, environmentalists, human rights organizations, and the Native community challenged state public utilities commissions to justify the power purchases in light of economic, human rights, and environmental impacts. And organizers broke the isolation by going to the press, to stockholders meetings, and to the American public about the project. After battling a six-year resistance campaign, Hydro-Quebec backed down. In November of 1994, James Bay II proposals were put on ice.

The utility, however, had a backup plan. In 1993, at the height of James Bay resistance, the utility announced that in addition to the nineteen dams it had already built in Nitassinan, it would build another dam on the Sainte Marguerite River. That dam, with a price tag of $2 billion, would divert the Moisie River's two tributaries, the Pekans and the Carheil, and cut the river's flow by 40 percent at the confluence of the three rivers.

At the same time, Hydro-Quebec submitted new proposals to expand the Churchill Dam project again, in a combination of projects that environmentalists now refer to sarcastically as the Two Gorges Dam project. The new project is being called the second-largest construction project in the world, after the Three Gorges project in China.

The $12-billion, 3,100-megawatt complex would consist of dams at Muskrat and Gull Island Falls, an underwater transmission cable across the Strait of Belle Island to Newfoundland, and another high-voltage transmission line, carrying two thousand megawatts of power, to the United States. Proponents once again lauded the project as a "clean" source of hydro-electric power for the northeastern United States.[31]

"Even though oil prices had dropped, there was the expectation that oil and gas were going to be scarce and expensive," says energy economist Ian Goodman. "The utilities in the northeast U.S. were reluctant to build power plants. 'We'll sell you power, it'll be easy, and it'll be cheaper than building your own power plants,' that's what Hydro-Quebec said."[32]

A lot of utilities were interested. Many of the nuclear power plants in the region had come under fire, and some had been canceled.[33] In Vermont, "the utilities managed to get most of their contracts approved, as a fast forward." Not surprisingly, the contracts were by and large uneconomical. Vermont is "paying on the order of eight cents a kilowatt hour, and the price on the wholesale market is three cents a KWH," Goodman explains.[34] Other states canceled their contract negotiations after it became clear that Hydro-Quebec's offer wasn't a good deal. Vermont's Central Vermont Public Service and Green Mountain Power ended up holding the bag.

Goodman doesn't think any of Hydro-Quebec's new dams can provide electricity cheaply either, whether from the Nitassinan dams or the newly revived James Bay III project at Great Whale. But Hydro-Quebec is intent upon selling to the U.S. market and is hoping to have its entire scheme of new dams and power plants underwritten by American utilities.[35]

Since the Canadian fisheries collapsed, there is a driving political need for development in the region, says Goodman. The loss of fish stocks in Newfoundland and Labrador have left tens of thousands unemployed. Big dam projects bring jobs, and, as Goodman points out, by the time everyone figures out that the jobs don't last, the politicians who approved the projects are gone. "The benefits are up-front, the costs are long-term," says Goodman.[36]

In the year 2040, the colossal nuclear plants of the northeastern United States—Rowe, Seabrook, Indian Point, and Millestone—will be past their projected "lifespans." They will be either on the way to or in the process of "decommissioning." Hydro-Quebec will be ready. By that year, if they are able, Hydro-Quebec hopes to have dammed all the rivers in Quebec worth damming and most of those in Newfoundland and Labrador as well, positioning itself to become one of the largest energy brokers on the continent and possibly the world.[37] The utility's vision of the future hinges on an export market modeled after the rest of the provinces' plans for economic development—pillage natural resources, and sell them to the South, to the settlers.

In late 1996, Hydro-Quebec applied to the Federal Energy Regulatory Commission to secure unregulated exports to the United States. By mid-1997, the utility had signed five new contracts with U.S. utilities—Long Island Lighting Company, Montaup Electric Company, Boston Edison, United Illumination Company, and Central Maine Power Company—and had purchased controlling interests in Noverco, a natural gas interest with assets in Quebec and New England.

Given the current interest in environmentally safe products, Hydro-Quebec is marketing its higher-priced product as "green power." But hopefully, the "people that are interested in buying green power are not going to be interested in buying power with a high environmental and human rights price," such as Hydro-Quebec's, says Goodman. The reality is that the formula does not work and that, on a worldwide scale, people have found that mega-development projects usually entail various sorts of political injustices. "The politicians are slow in realizing the world is changing. Even in Quebec, there is beginning to be a realization that you're not going to get rich building dams," Goodman says.[38]

The Innu of the North Shore came out in strong opposition to these proposals in early 1998. Spokesman Guy Bellefleur denounced the proposals as "anti-democratic," since most were created during a state of emergency in response to the ice storm of the Winter of 1997–98.

> There exist already 15,000 megawatts of hydroelectric power from installations in Innu territory, and the reservoirs total approximately 4,500 square kilometers (excluding the 6,700 square kilometers in Smallwood). We have already paid too much. We were never consulted or even informed [when] the dam at Churchill Falls began, and we were never compensated for the damage from the flooding. Our people lost not only our lands and possessions when Mishikama was flooded to create the Smallwood Reservoir, but also a part of our history and identity as Innu. We will accept no more developments imposed from the outside. All discussions on the subject of development must include the Innu.[39]

In the decade ahead, this public policy debate and battle over Innu rivers will occur in the land, courts, and utilities of New England.

Voisey's Bay

There's only one road that transects Labrador, and it cuts it in half. That five-hundred-kilometer, unpaved road links "developments" of the white people's iron ore mines in western Labrador to the Churchill River hydro project and the Goose Bay military base. Driving it is sort of a road trip of ecologically destructive projects. Beyond the tree line is where there is life: caribou, wolf, bear, and Innu. This is where the pristine rivers run from the mountains to the sea and are filled with salmon and char that live and die relatively free of the poisons of the rest of the world. All of this life is threatened now, not only from the air, but in the land and water.

Emish is what the Innu call the place, after the Emish River, "the land inside." "Voisey" is what the white people call the land, after an English trader by that name who, like other white men before him whose names mark maps of Nitassinan and other Native territory, only passed through the area.

In November of 1994, Diamond Fields Resources announced their "discovery" in Emish of the richest nickel ore body in the world. Six months later, when the snow had subsided, hundreds of mining companies descended upon the land. More than fifty companies remain today, all with the approval of the government of Newfoundland and without the approval of the Innu.

The newly created Voisey's Bay Nickel Company has moved to the top of the pile, a company now owned by Sudbury, Ontario–based nickel giant INCO. They began exploring the area in early 1995, proposing to build roads, airstrips, and loading docks without any environmental assessment. Innu and Inuit went to the courts to stop what the company called "advanced exploration infrastructure," which could have occurred without an environmental assessment. Their claims initially rejected by the courts, the Innu blockaded the site in the summer of 1997, with some three hundred protesters stopping the company's work. The blockade continued until the court finally ruled in favor of the Innu and ordered a stop to further construction, pending the completion of an environmental review.

Voisey's Bay Nickel Company has big plans. They propose to extract an estimated one-hundred-fifty million tons of nickel, cobalt, and copper ore from a massive deposit located in what is now a fertile valley. According to the Friends of Nitassinan, a Vermont-based support group, approximately sixteen million tons of acid-generating waste rock will be discharged into presently pristine marine environments, and fifty-five million tons of waste rock will be spread over the land. The company, however, promises to "rehabilitate the site post-mining" to "approach predevelopment conditions." That is impossible. Studies by the Department of Natural Resources done in Wisconsin, for instance, indicate that there has never been a sulfuric ore mine in the history of ore mining that has been reclaimed. Rather, the ore will remain toxic for thousands of years. Mine wastes, or "tailings ponds," are pretty much an "ecological time bomb," the Innu contend, and the project remains a threat to the entire region's land and marine environment.

INCO is gambling on Voisey's Bay. With operations in twenty-three countries, INCO is the largest nickel producer in the world and sees Voisey's Bay as the cornerstone of its global expansion strategy. Some suggest it is a failed proposition from the start. In 1997, INCO, which operates the huge Sudbury, Ontario, complex, cut about five hundred jobs from its Sudbury and Thompson plants, and saw a huge drop in profits. The international nickel market is glutted in production, equated with falling prices, and the remotely situated Voisey's Bay project will likely be a costly addition to an already precarious investment portfolio.[40]

Ironically, Canada uses its big dam projects and hydro-electric power plants as proof of its commitment to stemming global warming. Yet it skirts the actual price of this resource-intensive development policy, particularly in Nitassinan. First, consider that because of the dam's resultant flooding, Newfoundland will allow clearcutting of trees in the water's path, then additional pulp and paper mill capacity will be added to accommodate the new boom in logging. Then consider that INCO's Sudbury smelter is presently the single largest source of acid rain-causing emissions in the Western world. The Voisey's Bay smelter, powered by the dams, will exceed the Sudbury smelter and will be located directly over the famed Grand Banks, once considered one of the world's richest fisheries. The Innu and their allies pledge to continue their resistance against the huge projects.

Davis Inlet: The Future for the Environmental Refugees

There is a term that has become increasingly common in this era: "environmentally displaced peoples." These are the refugees of industrialism's destruction. According to Julia Panourgia Clones, these displacements are

> the by-product of urban programs or of the construction of dams, highways, industrial estates, ports, agribusiness ventures, and so forth. It starts by taking away land, which is the main asset for family livelihood in poor countries, and, unless properly addressed by the states, it is certain to degenerate into processes of massive impoverishment and social disorganization.... In China, more than 10 million people were involuntarily resettled over a period of 30 years as a result of dam construction alone. In India, the aggregate numbers are of comparable magnitude, about 15.5 million people over the last four decades including displacement from reservoirs, urban sites, thermal plants, and mines.[41]

It happened two years in a row, eerie as this may be, on the same night. Well past midnight in late January 1992, with the outside temperature around minus-thirty-five degrees Celsius, four Innu teenagers intoxicated on solvents and gasoline fumes staggered and screamed their way down the littered dirt road of their village. Exactly one year later, the town policeman found six Innu teenagers sniffing gasoline in an unheated shed, shrieking that they wanted to die. The videotape of their torment was distributed nationally in Canada and brought subsequent national attention and media. It has only changed some things in Davis Inlet.[42]

The Innu call Davis Inlet Utshimassit, the place of the boss, the white man. It is aptly named. In 1967, the Canadian government forcibly relocated the Innu to this rocky island from their original lands inland. The Innu say that the provincial government and the Catholic priests moved them there so they would stop following the caribou and would live as the boss man would like them to. The reality is that the Innu of Davis Inlet are political and environmental refugees, forced out of their village by one bad development project after another. Their lives have been, by most measures, a living hell ever since. Before they moved to Davis Inlet, the Innu said that the "saltwater was no good." Now eighty-four-year-old James Pasteen will simply say, "Davis is an evil place, eating away at the young people." James prefers the caribou and the bush way of life to village life. According to journalist Gavin Scott, "self-destruction is virtually a civic preoccupation in Davis Inlet." When Bill Partridge, a former police officer from Halifax, Nova Scotia, arrived in Davis Inlet in the early 1990s, he found himself involved in four suicide interventions a month. "Every adult in the community has contemplated suicide," he says, "Every second person has attempted it in one form or another." Partridge found that 95 percent of the adult population suffered from alcoholism and estimates that more than 10 percent of the children sniff gasoline.

It is not surprising. The Canadian government had forced the formerly self-sufficient Innu into a village, ice-locked from the mainland for most of the year, and then starved them, physically and emotionally, by disrupting their day-to-day cultural practices. A century ago, French sociologist Emile Durkheim documented how such forced, rapid transitions cause profound social disruption.

Records indicate that only a handful of the Innu at Davis Inlet have any kind of work. Many simply wait for their welfare checks in their cramped houses. Up to twenty people may live in a single, unpainted, clapboard dwelling. There is no running water or sewage system, and seldom is there garbage pickup, even though the Innu were promised acceptable housing, running water, and fishing boats.

After the story about the four Innu children found stoned out of their minds in minus-thirty-five-degree-weather broke in the Canadian press, planeloads of federal and provincial public servants, preachers, television crews, and private and public agency workers descended on the village. "No government likes to be affiliated with that kind of horror," explained Leslie Anderson, then-director of major projects for the Department of Indian Affairs. So they turned on the public faucet, doubling public funding for Davis Inlet, which shot up from a little over $4 million to a little over $8 million, translating into $16,730 for each Innu adult and child. For the six children and a dozen other youngsters addicted to solvents, $1.7 million was appropriated for drug treatment.[43]

The Innu of Davis Inlet want to go home, to a home that suits them well. In late 1996, two years after the children's tragedy, the government finally signed an agreement with the Innu allowing them to leave Davis Inlet. All five hundred Innu were promised a traditional campsite on the mainland called Little Sango Pond, five miles away from Davis Inlet, but a different world. The relocation will cost the government $62 million, including the construction of schools, an airstrip, roads, housing, and other infrastructure.

Still, the Innu trust Katipenima, the Caribou Master, more than the Canadian government. The caribou can deliver more. That is clear after all these years. That is absolutely clear.

Ghost Dance
Two hundred seventy
Ghost Dancers
Died dreaming a world where the white man would drown
In a worldwide flood of their sins.

Where the earth,
Renewed
Would reclaim their
Cities and towns
Leaving only
The Ghost Dancers
Who lived by her laws.

History books tell us
The threat is gone.
The ghost dance
Died with the ancestors
Wovoka and his sacred dream
Destroyed.

Each time it rains
I go out to the sidewalk
Where tree roots have broken the concrete and listen to the water's
Whispering
"It is coming soon."

—Sara Little-Crow Russell (Anishinaabe)[44]

Bloodties

If the Innu constituted that 1 percent of the U.S. population that controls an estimated 50 percent of the country's wealth, they would certainly be left alone. Their lifestyle would be glamorized, the subject of tantalizing books, movies, and television series, their every move chronicled. Their land would be protected behind thick curtains of public policy, with tax write-offs for horse pastures.

If they were farmers, at least, close to that agrarian culture of temperate climates, they and other subarctic and Arctic peoples would at least be considered in public policy. Perhaps. However, they are neither. They are Innu, with a rich culture and history and a nuanced understanding of their ecosystem's land, water, and animals.

Out of sight, out of mind. The Innu are relentlessly jackhammered by those handmaidens of colonialism, neocolonialism and globalization. The military, mining, and energy capitalists always return. When they have every last river dammed, every last secret metal cached in Mother Earth carved out, every last bit of serenity shattered by a combustion engine, will they be happy? Can they contain themselves before they destroy the North altogether? Pimaatisiiwin. It is quite the time to reconcile the hunter and the peasant.

This essay first appeared in *All Our Relations: Native Struggles for Land and Life.* Cambridge, MA: South End Press, 1999.

NOTES

[1] These are the names for the land of the people who live there: to the west, it's Eeyou Aski (Cree), to the south, Anishinaabe Aski (Ojibwe).

[2] Marie Wadden, Nitassinan: *The Innu Struggle to Reclaim Their Homeland.* Vancouver: Douglas and McIntyre, 1991: 28.

[3] *On Indian Land,* September 1997: 14.

[4] Wadden: 29.

[5] Wadden: vii–ix.

[6] Hugh Brody, *The People's Land: Inuit, Whites and the Eastern Arctic.* Vancouver: Douglas and McIntyre, 1991 (1975).

[7] Hugh Brody, *Living Arctic: Hunters of the Canadian North.* London: Faber, 1987:13.

[8] Jacques Cartier, *Two Navigations to Newe France.* Norwood, NJ: W. J. Johnson, 1975.

[9] Alan Cooke, *The Exploration of Northern Canada, 500 to 1920: A Chronology.* Toronto: Arctic History Press, 1978.

[10] Brody, *The People's Land:* 31.

[11] Translation by Mark Drouin, from a speech at an organizers' conference, Montreal, January 31, 1987.

[12] Testimony in court, provided by Mennonite Central Committee, 1989.

[13] www.innu.ca

[14] Barbara Harsanyi, "NATO Flights Threat to Innu and Environment." *Between the Issues,* Oct–Dec 1989: 18–19.

[15] Friends of Nitassinan, "NATO's War on the Innu and the Earth." *Newsletter,* August 1996: 4.

[16] Ian Bailey, "Newfoundland Minister Rules out Armed Response to end Innu Standoff." *Canadian Press.*

[17] Winona LaDuke, "Occupation of Nitassinan." *Indigenous Woman,* 1(4), 1989:14.

[18] Kevin Cox, "Priest Local Hero to Natives." *Toronto Globe and Mail,* February 12, 1990: A3.

[19] Robert Jobst, "Thunder." *Gauntlet,* November 9, 1989: 12–13.

[20] Rick Bauman, "Innu Battle for Their Land." *Ottawa Citizen,* November 18, 1989: G3.

[21] Wadden: 93.

[22] Bauman: G3.

[23] Wadden: 95.

[24] Wadden: 48.

[25] R. John Hayes, "Innu Still Shut out of Power Deal." *Windspeaker,* December 1, 1996.

[26] Friends of Nitassinan, "Churchill Falls: One of the World's Great Cataracts." *Newsletter,* August 1996: 2.

[27] Drouin, March 19, 1989.

[28] Boyce Richardson, *Strangers Devour the Land.* Post Mills, VT: Chelsea Green, 1991: xi.

[29] Andrés Picard, "James Bay: A Power Play." *Toronto Globe and Mail,* April 13–17, 1990.

[30] Interview with Jim Huggins, March 11, 1989.

[31] Friends of Nitassinan, "Project Two Georges Churchill Dams to Be Announced." *Nitassinan News,* 4 (1), March 1998.

[32] Interview with Ian Goodman, January 16, 1998.

[33] For instance, Long Island Lighting Company's plants.

[34] In the northeast United States, the prices are between two and three cents per KWH. Goodman, January 16, 1998.

[35] Goodman not only believes that it's unlikely that they can bring the power in cheaply, but points out that "It takes seven years to build a dam, if you can sign a contract for a high price in a secure market that will guarantee your risk. They're going to build it on 'spec,' that's the situation now." Interview with Ian Goodman, January 16, 1998.

[36] Ibid.

[37] Andre Caille, head of Hydro-Quebec, announced the goal of making the utility one of the five major energy companies in North America, on par with Enron and Duke/Energy and other colossals. Tom Holzinger, "Letter from Quebec: Save Our Wild Rivers:HQ Proposes Eight New River Diversions to Feed U.S. Market." *Nitassinan News,* August 1997: 3.

[38] Interview with Ian Goodman, January 16, 1998.

[39] Friends of Nitassinan, *Nitassinan News,* March 1998.

[40] Friends of Nitassinan, "Victory at Emish: Innu and Inuit Blockade Construction." *Nitassinan News,* November, 1997: 3.

[41] Julia Panourgia Clones, in Lenora Foerstel, ed., *Creating Surplus Populations: The Effects of Military and Corporate Policies on Indigenous Peoples.* Washington, DC: Maisonneuve Press, 1996: 227.

[42] Moira Welsh, "Chief Finds 'Lack of Hope' in Davis Inlet." *Toronto Star,* February 2, 1993: A2.

[43] Michael Valpy, "Davis Inlet." *Toronto Globe and Mail.*

[44] Sara Little-Crow Russell, "Ghost Dance." *Nitaassinan News,* August 1997.

Caretakers of the Water

SHARON DAY

By December 1998, the Mdwakanton Mendota Dakota people and the Earth First folks had erected a camp around 54th Street in South Minneapolis to prevent the re-routing of Highway 55 by the Minnesota Highway Department. The re-route would cost many people their homes, destroy hundreds of trees, and place the Campcoldwater Spring, considered a sacred site by the Tribal people, in danger. The M'de people had been called to aid those resisting. We assisted the folks who were at the encampment in building a sweat lodge and held a sweat with them. Two weeks later, six hundred state troopers and Minneapolis police officers descended on the encampment, arrested the folks there, and destroyed the houses.

The Mdewakanton Mendota Dakota and Earth First people then moved to set up a new encampment near the four oak trees sacred to the Mendota people. This encampment was destroyed on December 11, 1999, along with the four oaks and hundreds of more trees. The road is being built. It runs two hundred feet from the Campcoldwater Spring. The Minnesota Chippewa Tribe had tried to get the legislature to designate the spring a cultural traditional property and sacred site, but the bill did not get a hearing in the Minnesota House of Representatives. In February 1999, many tribal people came and testified before the federal and state highway departments attesting to the importance of the spring to tribal people. We had a water ceremony at the spring and sang the water songs—but nothing changed the hearts of the bureaucrats.

February 9, 1999

To My Sisters....
As I sat and listened to the grandmothers,
I began to understand in a profound way
my feelings for this spring they call Camp Cold Water.
The grandmothers say
the women are the ones who care for the water.
In our ceremonies, women gather the water.
It is we who sing the songs
calling for blessings from the water spirit,
this life force that sustains us.
The grandmothers spoke of this water that flows through our bodies
nurturing us, even before we enter the world.

They spoke of the necessity to care for the water.
In the spiritual realm, there is a lake that is never-ending...
it has no beginning and no end...
this lake is shimmering, brilliant, blue water.
It is pure and clear, sacred.
Now I understand my desire to prevent this road from being built,
the heavy equipment used so close will destroy the limestone,
thus destroying this spring...
it is a sacred place...
this water bubbles up from the earth and is pure,
like medicine, as it makes it way through this fragile limestone
on its way to the surface of the land.
Native people have used this spring since the beginning of time for
medicine.
I wonder what would happen if all women of the world said "no
more."
If we said to the corporate destroyers,
to the farmers whose pesticides run off into the streams and rivers,
to the cities and municipalities, "no more"?
We will not allow you to continue to pollute our water,
the life blood of the earth mother.
I will say no more...
and I will continue to take women,
one by one if necessary,
to the Camp Cold Water Spring.
I watch them as we go.
I see the tears running silently down their faces
as they gaze at this wondrous spring.
There is no need for words...
The water spirit speaks to them.

Tuesday, July 24, 1999, 7 A.M.

I arrive at the location of Hiawatha and 46th. I meet my sister, Dorene.
We say hello to Linda Brown, Jim Anderson, and Lou. I inform them that I
do not plan on being arrested; I am there to support the protest. We send my
niece Arianna across the street to Bridgeman's to get coffee. Community
activists have been talking to the protestors and there are many state troopers
on site, along with Minneapolis police officers. One of the speakers tells the

folks assembled to join two lines to participate in the civil disobedience. Neither my sister nor I join this line.

Shortly, the people who are doing the civil disobedience link arms and begin to enter the street. I move up closer to observe. Immediately after the protestors take a seat on the ground and link arms, the state troopers begin to swarm around them. I move further into the street to observe. One state trooper with a leather glove on his right hand rushes to a young person seated on the street and proceeds to place this hand over the young person's face and nose. I move into the street, afraid for the safety of this young person and others. I move closer and tell the state trooper to stop. He looks up at me and says, "Fuck you, you're next." I move around the circle and see another trooper with his hand on Jim Anderson's neck. A press photographer with a scared look on her face is watching. I yell to her, "Take a picture of this," pointing at the state trooper. The next thing I know, I am thrown to the ground. I feel a hand pushing my head to the ground and a knee in my back. I do not resist. I am afraid of what else they will do. I feel them putting handcuffs on me, very tight. My shoulder hurts. They pick me up and move me into a grassy area on the west side of Hiawatha behind the snow fence they had erected. They leave me lying face down for a few minutes, then someone comes and sits me up. I look around and see Jim Anderson and several other men and women sitting there with cuffs on. I look across the street and see them bringing my sister and my niece over. They are both crying and cuffed as well.

3 P.M.

We have been booked and taken to the jail. We are told to stand by our beds. It is three o'clock and time for a bed check and quiet time. I stand by the portable bed they have assigned me to. Two prison officers come in and begin to ask each person their name. When they get to me, one of the officers asks my name. She looks at my neck and asks me, "What is that you have on?" I pull out my medicine pouch and say, "It is a medicine pouch. I am M'de." She says, "Give it to me." I say, "No, I can't do that." She says, "Yes, give it to me." I repeat that I cannot do that. The officer following her says, "Let's continue, we'll come back." So they continue on their rounds and then come back to me. The first officer again says to me, "Give me that." I say no, I cannot do that. An African-American woman across from me says, "Sister, give it to them. It will be easier." I say, "No. You do not understand. This is a medicine pouch; it contains my megis shell."

The officer says that for safety reasons, no one is allowed to wear anything around their neck. "You will have to go to segregation." I say, "Fine." She says, "Pick up your things and follow us." I do so. They take me to another pod and open a door. I go in and they close the door.

They bring me a food tray a couple of hours later and after a while take it away. I lay back down and go to sleep. The door opens and the same two officers, accompanied by a male officer, are standing at the door. The male officer asks me if I am dressed. I say I am, and sit up on the bed. He says, "Give us that thing on your neck." I say, "No, I cannot. What happened to religious freedom?" He says, "We have checked with the prison chaplain and he says there is no more significance to what you're wearing than a Lutheran wearing a cross. I say, "I am M'de, this is my life megis, I have worked hard for it, I am not supposed to take it off. If I were a priest would you ask me to remove a ceremonial object?"

He says, "Here it is contraband. Give it to us." I say, "No, I cannot do this." And I observe that they have canisters of some kind of spray in their hands. I ask them what are they doing with the spray and the male officer says, "If you don't give it to us, we will have to pepper spray you and then we will take it."

"Why spray me? I am not going to fight you or resist."

He says, "We have to spray you for our protection."

I say again, "I am not going to resist, but I am not going to give it to you."

He says, "Don't move." Two of them enter the room, one takes the medicine bag off my head and the other says, "Get up and stand against the wall and assume the position."

One of them frisks me once again, while I am spread-eagled against the wall. The other two are taking my bed apart. I am sobbing; they leave. I remain in segregation until 9 P.M., when they release me.

I ask the officer who was so set on taking it from me, "Can I have it back?"

She says, "We will give it to you when we are ready."

I say, "Will it be with my things downstairs?"

She repeats, "When we are ready to give it to you, you will get it back."

Downstairs in the holding cell, another male officer brings my medicine pouch in a plastic bag. He holds it out to me and says, "You can have it back if you promise not to put it on."

"Say what?"

"If you put it in your pocket, you can have it."

He takes it away and says, "You will get it when you get the rest of your things."

I was afraid they were going to "lose it." They did return it to me with my other personal items at discharge.

December 9, 1999

(This was an email I sent to people on my list.)

Today, about 4 o'clock, the chief of the Minnesota state troopers delivered this document to us at the four oaks. They say that when they come, they will not use chemical sprays on us, but those of us who passively resist will be carried out and arrested. We will be barred from the land around the trees and Campcoldwater Spring. I asked him how they can bar us from the spring. As it is, if we have a ceremony on Saturday or Sunday, we have to go and get the water on Friday, because they lock the spring from Friday until Monday morning. He said he would take care of it.

I asked him why he thinks the state troopers will act any differently than they did a year ago, or last summer. He said he can only give his word. He said they will come before the new year begins. We are trying to get an injunction based on the violation of civil rights regarding the public hearings on the re-route planning. I think they are going to act quickly and cut the trees before that is possible. My request to you is this: Offer tobacco everyday between now and January 1st. It doesn't look good. Migwetch.

December 11, 1999

It's December and no snow.
The ground has no cover
and neither do I.
This morning they came to cut the trees…
And so they did.
These four oaks that stood on sacred Mendota Dakota ground
were felled today. They began with the western tree and continued
counterclockwise.
I wonder if they knew what they were doing.
They will continue the destruction, the devastation
because they can.
Today hundreds of trees—small poplars, large ancient oaks
all fell under the bright orange earth movers
operated so efficiently by the Minnesota Department of Transportation
and guarded by the Minnesota State Highway Patrol and Minneapolis
Police Officers.
We sang songs for the trees, for ourselves, for the earth and water.
Many tears were shed today, there are many more to come.
It's not too late to save the spring Camp Coldwater, but can we?
The oaks are gone, and the spring is less than a mile away.

December 18, 1999

It is a Sacred Place
The spring that gurgles up through the limestone
before it enters the world.
Crystal clear, pure, sacred.
The Trees that stood so tall
planted in the cardinal directions were sacred.
They were wrapped in the colors of the M'de.
The fire that burned for over a year was sacred.
A fire tended with love and care.
The sweat lodge that was erected for cleansing
the mind, body and spirit was sacred.
There were ceremonies.
Pipe ceremonies, full moon ceremonies,
ceremonies where people made offerings for the trees,
the spring, the earth, and for us.
Now, they have cut the four oaks along with hundreds of others.
Felled them to the ground so quickly
we could hear the crack and crashing of the trees as they fell to the
earth.
We watched as the limbs and tree trunks were gobbled up by a
machine
that looked like a huge scary lawn mower.
The inner wood flew through the air
glistening as the shards reflected the rays of the bright afternoon sun.
We sang to comfort ourselves and the trees.
The Wind picked up, perhaps, from sorrow.
The temperature began to drop as the day wore on.
By the time we left our twelve-hour vigil
we were chilled to the bone
as much as from the destruction
as the cold.
It has been a week.
Already they are planning
new ways to destroy the spring.
The spring that has provided medicine to tribal peoples
since the beginning of time.
The spring guarded by Ogimaequay, Head Woman.
A water main will run two hundred feet from the spring.

Will it survive?

Will we survive?

Women are the caretakers of the water.

It is up to us to say "NO MORE."

It is a simple thing. Migwetch.

May 22, 2000

We are heading to the spring to get water for a sweat and for a Native women's teaching session coming up. An elder will be here, and we need the water for her to use in medicine. We drive up to the Bureau of Mine's road, where we are greeted with a sign that says, "Access to Campcoldwater Spring on 54th Street." That is almost a mile away, too far to walk and carry a five-gallon bottle of water and eight gallon-size jugs. My sister is parked in front of me. I get out of the car to confer with her. My grandson, Kirby, sitting in the car, looks at me, grins and shakes his head saying, "Oh, you two," as I walk to my sister's car. We decide to drive in. The only thing the security guards can do is escort us out. By the time they call the state troopers, we will be gone.

We drive on in, our cars going slowly over the dirt road and the big ruts the heavy equipment has made in the soft gravel that is the temporary road. Once at the spring, we both walk over to the water, place our tobacco and ask for blessings, and give thanks for the water. My niece and grandson carry the bottles to the spring. Funny after all this time, it is the first time they have actually seen the spring. My niece, Arianna, was arrested with my sister and me, last summer at a protest to save the trees and the water. Yet it is the first time she has actually seen and touched the water. This is also true for my grandson, who probably knows as much about the spring as anyone but has never actually been here. This is partly due to the limited access to the spring imposed by the feds. The feds only open the gates Monday through Friday, 9 A.M. to 2 P.M., when our children are in school. The feds say that it is too difficult to provide security beyond these hours. If we want water for ceremonies that occur on the weekends, we have to get the water some time during the week. Hmmm, what happened to religious freedom and the right of access to sacred sites and gather materials for our ceremonies?

We fill our water bottles with the water. It is a beautiful day, the sun is warm and feels good on our skin. It is quiet and peaceful. It is amazing to me that the highway will run only two hundred feet from here.

My grandson takes some tobacco and when Dorene is done filling the bottles, he jumps down to where the water tumbles out of the limestone. I watch him place his tobacco in the water, then drink from the spring. He is suffering from an intestinal problem and has stomach cramps. We carry the bottles back to the cars and Dorene calls to Kirby. "Come," she says. "Take your clothes off, I want to wash you in the water." He takes his shirt and tennis shoes off and sits by my sister on the edge of the pond. He screams as only an eleven-year-old boy can as she pours the ice-cold water over his head and stomach area. After he climbs out of the water, he says to me, "Grandma, cancel my doctor's appointment. I'll just drink the water like I did last winter."

My sister and I, along with the Dakota people and many others, have been working to save this spring for almost two years now. We have not prevented the re-routing of Highway 55. All we can do now is pray and hope those with the power will monitor the construction and keep the spring safe, as they say they will.

We leave, mission accomplished.

September 24, 2001

State legislation has passed in Minnesota to protect the flow of water to the spring. Chi Migwetch to our friend, State Representative Karen Clark. Still, red dye that was placed in the ground waters southwest of the spring where construction for the Light Rail Transit Station has dug into the bedrock has showed up in the spring.

I continue to take women to the spring. We use water for birthing ceremonies, cleansing sweats, and medicine. My young friend Tara and I sang water songs at the spring on November 11, 2000 and then brought the water to the hospital where my sister Dorene was ready to give birth. With this water, we sang Akilli into the world.

On June 21, the day we honor the spring equinox, we performed another water ceremony, with Tibetan monks, for the water and for ourselves. On the morning of September 11th, I drove to the spring, and while I was just minutes from the airport, I was alone with the silence except for the gurgling of the water. Once again, I offered my tobacco to the water spirits and prayed for peace and, most of all, for magic and miracles.

Niconidahnah (All my relations).

© 2001 by Sharon Day.

The Dying Road to a Nation
A prayer para un pueblo[1]

for CHR

CHERRÍE MORAGA

We, you and I, must remember everything. We must especially remember those things we never knew.

—Jimmie Durham, *A Certain Lack of Coherence*

catholic memory

I remember
when I was a little esquincle in the new mexico
mech(x)ico los angeles califas san gabriel lomas gangland
pero en el otro lado de los tracks
the missionary sisters taught me about chuy christ
and impure thoughts and que thoughts were igual
que'l real act and that was the catch–22 que te chinga every time
cuz someone tell you not to pensar en el pezón y pues
ya ves you already got the pinche picture en tu mente
millones de pechos all sofialoren and bustin'
outta pleasant peasant campesina cotton
al estilo italiano
y bueno…
all this thinking on what NOT to think
caused me to consider the question of thought
unadulterated, learned later
'bout buddhism and emptying the mind de toda la mierda
which I never been good at
only good at dying
cuz
that's where my nine-ten-eleven-&-twelve-year-old-thoughts
took me to knowing that dying was all there was inside
outside was puro sueño, tú sabes:
just whitedoctors putting sadistic dreams
of paganbabies&christianconquest

inside your cabeza-head
and this was pre-race-consciousness
pre-the-body-politik
pre-puberty casi
children's faces be a dream
their vacant laughter, their causa
to humiliate the fat nun with the fat open mouth
standing stupid and oblivious
in front of our sixty-two catholic school-girl desks,
mosca buzzing
in 'n' out
in 'n' out
it all be a dream before Martin Luther King's
I knew and kept waiting for some jesus
to save me from the word
the only word: death

susto

I was raised by a fierce fighter of a woman, who already in her mid-thirties having had the necessary round of babies and betrayals knew what she believed in: a God, surely, but a God far outside the "mystical body" of the Catholic Church as I had learned it. My mother is a Mexican Catholic of humble origins which, in short, means an Indian Catholic which she would never admit but demonstrates in her basic indifference toward Church dogma and basic faith in the saints in candles in a relentless rosary more like canto than christian prayer.[2]

My mother has faith. Faith that looked like an eighty-five-pound post-op woman in 1961 walking the streets of Montebello, Southern California dressed in the robe and rope of San Antonio de Padua. The seamstress had come to my Tía Eva's house. I remember her pulling out the yards of brown Franciscan-heavy cotton from a Woolworth's shopping bag. Followed by a tape measure which she wrapped around my mother's frail frame of bone and scar tissue. And with that, she custom-designed my mother's "ofrenda."

My mother had lived. And the garment was her thirty-day prayer of gratitude to the saint that had interceded in her behalf. After two surgeries and five weeks in the hospital, my mother survived what had been erroneously diagnosed as cancer which turned out to be an ulcer which required the removal of three-quarters of her stomach. My mother had survived when we thought she wouldn't when I prayed hopelessly, neurotically because there was no God I already knew, only fear, only a relentless scratching scratching scratching nervously tearing into the flesh of my inner arm in the effort to dig down to some ground, some land, some "where" whole and embraced by a mother's love.

She did return. But mothers, I had already learned, *could* die. And the world of the heart could end while the world continued indifferent around you. I am every woman who was once a little girl who has lost a mother, almost lost a mother, been betrayed by a father/a brother/an uncle who learned in a brutal unforgiving way that there is no childhood really, no innocence. There *is* no protection. Death teaches children this. So does incest and all those hushed abandonments. Your protector can die on you or disappear or not notice or not respond when you are in danger. You have to grow up too fast and be alone.

My only child learned this aloneness, spilling into the world three months too soon, weighing two and a half pounds. He knew. That no matter how surely his mother squeezed his toothpick-sized finger, I could not keep him on this planet.[3] That was between him and his God, which returns me to the subject of this reflection: death. Still the one word I understand for God.

I call God by the name of death because nothing other than death wields such unyielding power in my life. I am afraid of death, the loss of the body-life. I recognize this fear as I sit in meditation, rigidly holding onto the body of what I imagine to be myself. I am so afraid, my mind conjures many images in the vain attempt to secure the parameters of "self"— delusions of my importance and conversely my own pitifulness. And language language language which codifies raw being. All this, oh so preferable to the promise (threat) of the experience any real "god-ness," and the radical re-vision of meaning it requires in our lives. My preciously guarded "me" is a world I have known intimately since my earliest remembrance of an internal reflective life. It was that place in which I held my first private anguished conversations with Catholicism, and what I came to understand as prayer. It is infinitely lonely.

> Sometimes I just feel like my eyes are too open.
> It's like the more you see, the more you gotta be afraid of.
> —Lupe, *Shadow of a Man*[4]

siguen los sustos

At nineteen, I was sedated and had my wisdom teeth pulled out. Although I was a child of the sixties, the psychedelic drug culture arrived belatedly at my doorstep, so my oral-surgeon-sanctioned high came as the most unexpected pleasure...and the most beauteous dream. It was all shape and color and design. All movement, infinitely fascinating. While sedated I had, for the first time in my life, forgotten my "self" completely. I had disappeared. I missed no one, had no attachments to people, my name, my memory. I was a dream without a dreamer. When I came to, too soon, I found the dentist (a brutal butcher of a man) hacking away at the remains of the last impacted tooth. As consciousness returned to me, so did the pain. And an unspeakable fear. The fear that a drug could have that kind of power over me, that it could allow me to leave this planet and not care. That one *could* leave this planet and not care. I knew it was like that in death. That indifference. That ultimate aloneness. I panicked as the dentist put me under a second time and suffered a tortuous dream of entrapment. Still, I did extract some "wisdom" with the extraction of those impacted molars, or so I thought: the revelation of the impermanence of our earthly passions and attachments, which I speedily repressed.

In recent months, I have carried in my briefcase, like those mid-nineties San Diegan comet-crazed suicide-missionaries in Nikes,[5] everything that could identify me to an alien who reads Earth English: passport, certified birth certificate, hospital birth certificate with the "Angelina" crossed out and "Cher'rie" written over it with an apostrophe instead of an accent in the wrong place with the wrong last name of an adopted grandfather ("Lawrence") whom I never met. My son's life is in the briefcase, too: five-year-old with passport, social security number, birth certificate, baptismal record. Then there are pages and pages of "documents": "Power of Attorney," "Last Will & Testament," "Custody," and "Guardianship" clauses in the event of death (mine), etc.

I have been on the way to the bank's safe-deposit box for weeks now, never getting there, lugging the stuff around cuz home ain't safe enough, they say, in case of fire, they say, burglary, in the event of some unforeseen disaster...tragedy. But here in this briefcase, it all feels too heavy, too final, like I'm already planning my death and securing the key to the lock for my survivors to find. As my parents have done, putting *their* key in an overnight bag buried in the bottom of the back bedroom closet. Months ago, my sister and I each received in the mail a list of what the box contains, typed out on my father's Olympia manual. Am I waiting for my parents to die? To open up their safe-deposit box, not for some imagined inheritance of wealth, but for the inevitable coming to pass? The inevitable is just that.

I cry over every new arruga on the face of my mother, the ever-slowing steps of my father, straining up the stairs to my new home. I mourn the passage of time in their frail and failing bodies. I am afraid of doctors' exams in the women I love. I am afraid to miss any month of my son's growing up for sleepwalking. I sleepwalk anyway, fearfully.

My mother laments her imminent passing, cancels vacations and anniversary celebrations as her body continues to betray her. "My bones are showing," she says. "I can't take the trip. I look too ugly," meaning too old and I wonder how she imagined she would look at eighty-four. She is not ugly. She is a woman shrinking into her old age, growing in frailty and a rising anger against all that she cannot control: my sister's forty-seven-year-old independent motherhood; the heaviness of the cast-iron pots she once used to toss effortlessly onto the open flame of the stove; grandchildren foreign-blonde and too-often remote. I know she thinks about dying daily. She won't admit it when I (sort of) ask. She speaks only of the overnight bag on the closet floor in the back bedroom closet. She's got everything under control. My mom fighting for the life of her that dying, which no scratching can ward off. *She's gonna leave me after all.*

dying lessons

When a revered uncle died of lung cancer, a few years after my son's almost-death, I remembered the obvious: *We live to die.* Suddenly all decisions began to matter with an urgency I hadn't experienced before. All decisions were a matter of life and death. I know (and not unconsciously) that the death of that aging uncle became the stimulus for me to act on a lesbian divorce years in coming. I know that the same mantra—*if not now, when* —catapulted me into the arms and the family of a Mexican woman I had ignored (intentionally) for years—that inevitable return to my own.

I do believe in the dead and dying, their lessons. The lesson my premature son taught me upon his threatened birth, that we are not born new, but come from some place of return. That we re-live in death a memoryplace we have forgotten. I prayed for my son's life and got him long enough to learn the word "*quiero*" not just for leche, but love. Got him long enough to forget the promise of death I had birthed. Still three years after his birth, I am forced again to remember in this death of my father-close uncle. And then again, and again…and again. Until I am standing face-to-face with a death that looks very much like myself.

My comadre, Marsha, comes to me in dreams. I stand in a circle of women on Indígena land in Tejas. Marsha is impatient with the group, their shocked inaction upon the news of her violent death. She tells me, "Build me a dome," a round-house she means. To continue her work. There is no time to waste.

In September 1998, Marsha Gómez, artista-activista-madre-hermana, was murdered by the hand of her only son. Marsha Gómez was like me, mixed-blood. Off-seasons, she could be mistaken for Jewish or something else not quite white, but not necessarily always Choctaw, not siempre the darker side of Mexican. "Cajun and Hispanic" is what her blood sisters called themselves. But unlike her sisters and mine, Marsha was hundred-percent "colored girl" "red-skin" and kickin' butt. Thoroughly. And her thorough-courage frightened and compelled me because I knew Marsha was afraid, always a little, some place in her not quite convinced she belonged. But my god, that other world, a dead world. The white world from which she could not protect her son. And we are left with her legacy. With desperate fingers we try to unknot the noose of this tragedy, how to change that fate, steer our sons and daughters (our nation's children) away from hopelessness.

I am learning in hard ways. Daily. That we live in a violent and unforgiving world and all our acts of heartlessness return to us. I have also learned there is a time for heartlessness, for an unmoving warrior-stance. I have learned this the most palpably in relation to my son. For him I have committed unforgivable acts, denied motherhood to a woman who saw herself as his mother because she could not accompany us on the road I was to walk. I turned *away* from her and *toward* that disappearing Chicano tribe, in which without country or contract, I seek place, for myself and my son.

The rupture of what was an eight-year relationship was nothing less than a death consciously chosen, a brutal sacrifice for change. Sacrifice: not the interminable suffering proferred by Christianity, but sacrifice as understood within the pre-Columbian world: An ofrenda to the angry god that requires it. My spirit-gods, so incensed by my ignorance, my looking away from that soul-self for so long, required nothing less.

> Still
> when I turn on the cold-water faucet
> put the toothbrush
> under the winter-cold ribbon of water
> when I do what I do every day of my life
> I remember the ordinary
> life with her
> lost.

a change of heart

I do not re-write history. I tell the story for the first time.
The story of holding one's self apart, to hold oneself together.

A few years ago, my once-partner asked me as we severed our relationship for the last time, "Just answer me one thing, do you think you are an Indian?" She was very angry with me, angrier that I had run away with someone undeniably "Indian." Mexican Indian, yes. Indian via las montañas de México and naturalized Chicana in this country where most mestizos are required to lose their Indian identity through their American Mexicanism.

I was humiliated by the question. To not answer would have been to suggest (by my silence) that her question and her role as interrogator were somehow legitimate. To answer the question dignified its cultural arrogance. As I stood there speechless and ready to bolt out her front door, the worst accusations regarding my own "authenticity," ironically, were hurled by the hand of my own self-doubt. In my mind's heart, I heard her saying, "I know your hungriest places even if I couldn't feel them/fill them. Being hungry for a thing doesn't give you it. You ain't no Indian. You're a half-breed Mexican at best who, when you choose, can move effortlessly, we arm-in-arm as white women in the world."

I hold a great rage within me. A rage and shame against myself. How the whiteness of my skin and my habitual identification with it continues to seduce and betray me with its shifting disguises. Some place in me remained convinced I didn't have the right to *feel* so different from this whitewoman I loved because I didn't *look* so different. This was what she always told me. Most times without words. The question I am plagued with is why I believed her. Never totally. I was always the "lover-in-cultural-resistance" and she complained of it often, my basic sexual nationalism. Still, when the accusation of my own "racial" inauthenticity comes whirling out at me—"Do you think you are an Indian?"—I know that the question itself (and her felt entitlement to ask it) is *the* critical point of departure between us. I have to choose. There is no place for ambivalence, no place for immigrant-ethnic meanderings, no place for biracialized maybes. We part ways, choose different paths. For life. "Conscientização," I remember Paulo Freire's term.[6] "Conscientización" (in Spanish), a consciousness born of a body that has a shade, a language, a sex, a sexuality, a geography and a history. And that sometimes changes everything, including whom you love and lie with.

coming out

Twenty years ago, I wrote what I consider to be my first real work of "conscientización": the kind of writing that in the act itself strives to know and where the knowing will require change. Writing "La Güera,"[7] I was physically sick through the entire first draft, holding back the urge to vomit a personal history that tore at my guts. Driven by an exhausted self-censorship, the writing was for me a kind of "coming out" as a half-baked brown woman and a silent collaborator in whiteness. It was also a confession and a declaration of conscientización as a Chicana in a light-skinned body, drawn relentlessly toward women by bone fide lesbian desire. I would pay (was already paying) for that desire, but what most viscerally entangled my stomach in that web of knots was the unstated knowledge that I would also pay, more dangerously, for how Mexican that desire was.

Coming out is about choices and running out of them. As a young woman barely out of my teens, I came out twenty-five years ago because I was just plain tired of lonely. Having sex without a body in the arms of a man, I was not going to spend the rest of my life wanting, waiting. I made the move to return to women, knowing the world was wholly bent on my separation from them. What frightened me so in the writing of that essay (now nearly a generation ago) was that I discovered that that return required a return to my people (chicano/mexicano/indio) as well, *when the world was wholly bent on my separation from them.* The world had opened its door for me, light-skinned, college-educated, and born anglo-surnamed, and I was shutting that door in its face, as I would shut that door on that ex-lover's face twenty years later.

The latch clicks behind me. I walk down the hallway of her building for the last time. I think: *I am a traitor to my race* (if color is its measure*); that is what she resents in me.* There is nothing magnanimous in my betrayal of whiteness. It is about (again) plain tired of lonely. And a rage. A rage against a culture that I can only call enemy. One whose collective ego (ethnocentrism) kills spirits, lives, art. I cannot justify my actions beyond this. There is no compromise. It is finally a matter of life and death.

I don't know how much Indian I got in me. I don't know if it's called Yaqui, Seri, Apache, O'odham…or if the Indian people on my mother's side just gave it all up upon the conquest and were subsumed by Spanish culture which, combined with Indian people and Indian ways, became Mexican. So I do dignify the accusation with an answer, when I respond with what my "Ex" already knows, but refuses to believe matters. "I am Chicana. And yes, I imagine I have Indian in me." What else *is* there to say when it is impossible say all the rest, to speak of Return to one's people without our tongues tied by amerikanisms. I say, "return," and Amerika hears, "nostalgia," "romantic idealism," "escapism."

So I keep myself secret, preparing the ground
in the private dream of a more generous heart.

I think of this lost love daily. She whom I used—her accusations are correct—to postpone this look at the self. No mirror reflection there. Or maybe her mirror always made me feel dark in comparison and I liked the look and feel of that. I don't know. I loved her. Hard and true as I could and stayed in the closet of my strongest desires cause I didn't want to be left holding them alone.

"It was not a murder but a sacrifice." I remember Linda's words when I had told her that I felt like a murderer, leaving this eight-year loving so completely. "It was a sacrifice," she counseled. "For great change." (I think of Marsha.) And so it is. An offering up of the life I've known for something else, not there. I have become a criminal in a world whose values are the real crimes. I have chosen "nation" over prescribed Euro-American lesbian ethics about motherhood;[8] and I have lost friends and funds because of it. It was one of the hardest things to do in my life.

But this is harder yet...
this naked step I take into a clouded mirror
that is my woman, my self.

the return

"Que vale la vida[9] if we can't take each other back." That's all my new love, so long in the knowing, had to say to finally bring me to her. But how far back is Return? What radical action does Return require? What junctures of separation and connection, separation and connection do we encounter again and again on the neglected road of our mistakes and forgetfulness?

journal entry.

I feel very young, unremarkable, an ordinary student nada mas. I have to ask my beloved daily many things I have to ask her what the pain in this desert means, why do the women cry so awkwardly. I have to ask her how to enter the arbor, how to tie a prayer tie, wrap a sage stick, roll a cigarette of prayer tobacco. And I wonder how can she want me, baby that I am.

"Teach me how to pray," I say. She takes me by the hand, presses the copal between my fingertips, then releases the pebbles into the burning embers. And in the act, I am sent home to what I already learned at my mother's breast: faith. I turned to her for God. I break some taboo to write that. That God is found in bed, in the open face of consummated desire. That death is found there, too, limpio y sencillo. That the fear of death has a way of subsiding. In love. That's all. For a moment. All I prayed for was to find a woman with whom I could make familia, with whom I could wake up each morning with a shared purpose, a shared prayer, a shared practice. No mentiras, no illusions that death did not await us at every turn. How do we love on the dying road? What does that kind of spiritual practice look like?

I read Buddhism because it calms me down, but I don't feel the land under my feet on those pages. I am an earthworshipper and the earth's Indian in América, that's all; and mexicanismo (its indigenismo, its cultural nationalism) has saved me from the obscenity of American individualism. That's all.

"Do you think you are an Indian?" What I should have answered was that what is female and brown in me (is that Indian?) has been my Salvadora in the worst of times. This she-knowing in me, that darkness, has been my deepest prayer. A prayer against cruelties small and great. I do not speak of identity politics here. I speak of a living knowledge of "otherness" that inspires compassionate action. A knowledge that is the prayer assuming flesh.

Maybe my spiritual practice is nothing more than this writing. Maybe one wakes up every morning and really wakes up. Maybe that is the daily prayer. The "Give Us This Day Our Daily Breath." And the bread…something as simple as bread…the matter of a revolution. But the revolution begins at home. A cliché born of truth.

home truths

You want to change your life, I tell myself. You light a candle. You pray on it. Daily. All day long. Then you do the hard work of living the prayer.

Years ago, I made a prayer. Same prayer. Every day. Bring me family. And I knew in the praying, I was inviting the sons of lovers and brothers of nation and the children of every shade to return to me. It took them a long time to arrive, but now that the time has come, I know that the hardest work is in front of me. I do not have the same trouble loving women, but the men in my family—from the darkest to the palest—keep arriving at my doorstep and pleading entrance, most profoundly in the brown body of my son. Loving him is easy. Raising him is not. The others—his father, my partner's sons, my nephews, the students I have adopted as sons—require a heart-wrenching kind of work. They are missing their fathers, angry at their mothers. They want to return home, to make a different kind of man, brother, father, son. At times they mirror in their youth and self-important arrogance, what I could never assume as a woman and for which I still resent their fathers. I miss the mexicano brothers I never had, a whole generation of men who let my generation of women down in their refusal of feminism, in their looking away from the source of their "home sickness."

I could write harder words, I could write confession, how much we envy men and their freedom, how much we, lesbians, have built our lives apart from their murderous impulses. Has it all been written before? The history of Mexican women: the colonization that tried to make Guadalupes of us all, all-forgiving madres, and those of us who rebel, Chingadas; how our men have colluded in this 500-year-old mentira. But I remember Coatlicue, Aztec Goddess of Creation and Destruction, that buried knowledge of our female rage, our venganza, and our inherent power as Creators of Life to take life away. I remember that pre-memory when men openly admitted that they were awed by our diosas and us. And so they were less angry then, less brutal, less frightened and frightening. I remember…

> And then we give birth to sons,
> who become men.
> And we are unable to defend ourselves
> against this most intimate,
> most beloved
> of oppressors.

> . . . . .

> He used the tools of her art
> to murder her.
> This is not a metaphor.
> He bludgeoned his mother to death
> with the tools of her trade.

> She was a sculptor.

Marsha Gómez was murdered by her only son, that once-soft boy who saw in himself a woman's vulnerability and learned to despise it. This matricide is not a metaphor; it is an eruption of violence that speaks to the real incarcerated state of the mechicano familia: the wounded heart of our nation. There are those who will look away from this death as an aberration; but it is not an aberration. It is a gift, even in its violence—

because we cannot imagine it

because our minds can't conjure it

because she was so unworthy of it

because we see ourselves in it, we are forced to rethink everything about our lives, why we are standing on this road, at this hour, broken-hearted as we are.

I still want to believe that at some point Marsha made a decision toward life, that she offered up her body to save her son from himself, to save other women from the violence of his corazón inquieto, She was not the first woman he had assaulted. Maybe as mothers, there's a place in us where we all fear the retribution of our children: the anger from our sons never mothered enough in a motherless world of missing fathers. Maybe it's too easy to say that. Too easy to speak of genocide, matricide. But I know those responsible for Marsha Gómez's death have faces and do not have faces, that in my speechless shocked heart only one truth resounds: that her death was not an accident, but the result of a murderous political history still in the making.

None of us is immune to that history. I recognize myself in this sister-artist, in her aging body, in her son's rage she used as a weapon against herself. I've seen my own son's anger at only five years old. "Mom, the tears won't stop." He tells me con ojos lagrimosos. He slaps each of his own cheeks. "They just keep coming down. Make them stop. Por favor." I bring a tissue, the end of my shirttail, or maybe a sleeve to his moist puppy-nose, soaked lashes. He stops crying. For now. Did Marsha's son ask for anything more complicated than that? "Relieve me of myself, Mom, make the tears stop coming down." But what a mother may cure at five, twenty years later is not enough. It is never enough. We women can never cure our sons of the "manhood" imposed on them.

A few days following Marsha's death, I learned from friends that hours after the murder her son was seen on a nearby country road looking for the man who killed his mother. The bitter irony is that maybe this is la búsqueda that all our sons and brothers and fathers should undertake, that search for their murdered mestiza/india mothers, sisters, daughters, lovers. This is and this is not a metaphor. Feminism and Indigenism.[10] The only tools at my disposal to construct a son, a family, a people. I take hold of them, wield them as murderous weapons. There is no room for liberalism now.

All I know is that I awaken every morning remembering that there was a life before greed, before family as private property. Before competition, linear plotlines and Romance and Western Reason. Before and After Reason. I know there was a time where "two-spirit" people like Marsha, like me, like my mujer, held a place in some tribal circles without compromise to our being.[11] I am fighting for my son's life and how that life is shaped. I want to walk with him through my own opening heart to a different country, one we may still only inhabit within the walls of our home or inside the circle of those with whom we pray, or on a small square of dirt not yet stolen off from us. Pero es algo. It is something to try and build a nation by heart.

The rest is just questions. I could die tomorrow and the small world who reads my work will say, "Mira, see how she suffered the same questions her whole life. I wonder about the relationship between our lives and the manner of our deaths; about a relentless exhaustion that invites death. I wonder about small and mass deaths, about genocide and every individual life lost there.

home prayer

On the Day of the Dead, we put out food for our ancestors. Tequilita for my Tía Tencha, white roses for Marsha (her favorite), tamales, chocolate, water, black coffee with a tablespoon of sugar for Doña Domitila. Cigarettes for my Tío Bobby who died of lung cancer. Frijoles and pan. We pray.

I wonder if they come to visit, my relatives. Or if, upon death, they are relieved of us. Finally. I wonder if this offering is really for them or for us. I pray for the dead, that when they come to visit us in our sleeping and waking dreams, I pray them large enough to hold a piece that remembers us, but where their heart no longer aches, wants as we do so pitifully now. I pray that our spirits are something much grander than this pitiful longing and all the beauteous attachment we have to it. I am a llorona, my tears, at times, my most faithful companions. I cry Marsha away from this earth. I pray that with the release (the relief) of the body, her spirit is not encumbered by the ego through which her body thrived and suffered.

These prayers are my preguntas, I write this as if I were without faith, but when my María Cristina carries Marsha's spirit back into our home through the few small wordly tokens of Marsha's life (a piece of hair, an earring), I am altered by the spirit's presence.

I believe in the dead and the dying. Their lessons.

la lección

On the way across the Bay Bridge my son asks me, "Can God count to infinity?" I answer yes, since Rafael, newly acquainted with letters and numbers and long-time fascinated with superheroes, wants to understand the limits of power and numerical comprehension. He goes on. "Is God more powerful than Batman?"

I answer "Yes," again adding an expletive about the nature of the power to which I refer. Power of the heart, of the spirit, etcetera, etcetera, knowing on some level he just wants to know if God can kick Batman's butt. Now that would be a comfort, someone infinitely strong in charge of it all.

Since I know my son is thinking hero equals male, my feminism kicks in to remind him that God is both male and female—well really neither male nor female but all energies simultaneously. And my Indigenismo and Buddhism prompt me to remind my son of the presence of God in all things living, even things that can't punch back. *Yes, even rocks breathe I've seen them.*

My answers are pitiful as I try to separate in my mind truth from lie from myth and cuento. I teach myth's truth. I teach my son about a God person-ified somehow in his mind as a superhero because that's what he understands about power. It's the best I can get for now but only because I want him to know humility. I am a mother in search of a language to know awe in the face of beauty, art, the ongoing creativity of nature and its insistent survival, its flourishing in the face of death. Because whatever my religion is, it counters the solipsism of American greed and the egotism of "rugged individualism." Because I want him to know he is not the center of the universe, but that the universe resides within him as in the flower. I want to relieve him of the burden, but reinforce the responsibility, of knowing his interdependent place upon this planet and its consummate heavens.

He is one among many, as am I.

Superheroes and his male-identification firmly intact, my son is attracted for some of the same reasons to the image of Christ on the cross. But it is not Christ, the Hero, that draws my son in. But the Naked Christ. Christ, the Unjustly Scorned. Christ, the Martyr. At five years old, Rafael is also fasci-nated with child-imagined bondage and can often be found tied up with all manner of shoestring, curtain cord, or discarded packing twine. We joke that he may have inherited this need for restraint from his mother's cultural Catholicism or I suggest he is responding to a vague memory of his earliest months of premature life spent within confines of a doll-sized hospital isolette, his body tied to IV lines. Who knows? But undeniably this image of the bound Christ moves my son.

I don't have crucifixes in my house as a rule. As a rule Christ never answered a prayer I can remember. But my son discovers the one crucifix I've packed away, given to him by his grandmother when he was about two years old. I am sure my mother fully expected that I would nail the dying figure above my son' sleeping head the night that I received it. Well, I could neither display the Crucified Christ (a dream catcher hangs in its stead) nor toss it away, for the faith my mother had imbued it with in passing it on to my son. Upon spying the half-naked and bleeding figure, Rafael immedi-ately begins hammering me with questions about him. "Who hurt him like that?" "Why doesn't he have more clothes on?" "Did his mama know?" And in spite of my rejection of Catholicism at the age of eighteen, the Life, Death, and Resurrection of Christ is probably the best religious story I know. So, I tell him what I know and can live with. I refer to Jesus as a holy man and explain that people were jealous of him, that they wanted to stay cruel and greedy and he wanted change and peace in the world. I'm fumbling badly, I think, when he asked why they hung him on the cross to die. I don't remember my answer; but later, when he retells the story to a friend, I overhear him say…

"They killed Jesus because he knew God."

And I think, maybe my answers aren't so pitiful after all.

la ve p'atrás

Months later, I attend a Latino academic conference in New York City. I am speaking with the Critic about Nation. We are on-stage and I am trying to make a point. I turn my whole body away from the audience, a full 180 degrees. I look behind me. I am trying to illustrate the point with my body; I am trying to teach the teachers something about ourselves, about looking backward toward our Indian and Black mothers to find a future. An image stays in my mind: a Casta Painting by Miguel Cabrera of Eighteenth Century New Spain. It is a portrait of miscegenation. In the painting, the mixed-blood child sits on the lap of his Spanish father. The child's facial features and coloring are a delicate blend of European and Native. His mestiza/india mother stands next to the pair, This child is looking back, back at her, to his Indian antecedents, to his past and to the future he will choose. This is my own face looking back. Not all of us are compelled to return, but I am. And I want to take the others with me, I tell them so, "Qué vale la vida if we can't take each other back?"

A young man in the audience is outraged. He stands in the second row from the rear and accuses me of feigning shamanhood, playing "some kind of curandera" role. He is angry that he too is white enough to move forward effortlessly into americanmanhood and I am his mamá reeling him back in and backwards. Into darkness. *We were not always like this, stupid and forgetful.*

But there *is* nothing new. No theory, no computer program, no virtual nada that has anything more profound to teach us than what is found in the dark quietude of this ancestral prayer. This is "infinity," I want to tell my son, and as close to god as we can get.

> We, you and I, must remember everything.
> We must especially remember those things we never knew.
>
> —Jimmie Durham

My family is dying. My blood and heart relations are vanishing with each passing of seasons. I am next. I know. Always next. I pray only for the courage to remember what I may never have the chance to live. And in the remembering may I know and in the knowing may I teach.

It's the little bit I have to offer the exiled and forgotten I call my nation.

NOTES

[1] First presented at the Academy of American Religion Conference in Orlando, Florida in November 1998; subsequently presented in a revised version at the National Association for Chicana/Chicano Studies Conference in San Antonio, Texas on April 30, 1999; originally published in Cherríe Moraga, *Loving in the War Years: Lo que nunca paasó por sus labios.* (Expanded Second Edition). Cambridge, MA: South End Press, 2000.

[2] Although the incursion of Catholicism into the Américas was essential to the project of colonization, i.e., de-indianization, Mexican Catholicism among the poor and working class is less identified with the Church as institution than with rituals, prayer and ceremony that have, over the centuries, maintained a decidedly Native American cultural sensibility.

[3] In 1993 my son was born three months premature, weighing two and a half pounds. After three and a half months in the hospital and two surgeries, Rafael Angel recovered a healthy infancy, and now a growing boyhood. This journey is described in a memoir released in 1996, *Waiting in the Wings: Portrait of a Queer Motherhood.* (Ithaca, NY: Firebrand Press).

[4] *Shadow of a Man* is published in *Heroes and Saints and Other Plays.* Albuquerque: West End Press, 1994.

[5] On March 26, 1997, police found the 39 bodies of the Heaven's Gate religious cult at a mansion in the suburb of Rancho Santa Fe near San Diego, California. Timed with the celestial arrival of the Hale-Bopp comet, the group's leader, Marshall Herff Applewhite (whom members believed was Jesus Christ reincarnated), promised his devotees that a UFO—hidden behind the traveling Hale-Bopp comet—would transport the souls of Heaven's Gate members to heaven if the members joined Applewhite in death. When police discovered the mass suicide, all members were found dressed alike (black clothing and new Nike tennis shoes), each with five dollars and several quarters in their pockets; all were neatly laid out upon beds, and a purple cloth had been draped over each member's head and torso. At the side of each bed was a packet of identification papers and a packed suitcase— preparations for their journey aboard the waiting spaceship.

[6] The original Portuguese, "conscientização," refers to the awakening of a "critical consciousness." See Paulo Friere, *Pedagogy of the Oppressed,* Rev. ed. N.Y.: Continuum, 1993.

[7] Published in the first edition of *This Bridge Called My Back: Writings by Radical Women of Color,* Cherríe Moraga and Gloria Anzaldúa, eds. Watertown, MA: Persephone Press, 1981; current edition by Third Woman Press, Berkeley, CA, 2000.

[8] Co-parenting remains a complex and controversial issue among lesbian parents. Being unable to legally marry or reproduce biologically with our same-sex partner impacts politically and emotionally our (and our children's) experience of motherhood. In the effort to protect historically denied lesbian parental rights, lesbian rights advocates generally view the non-biological parent as having equal parental rights with the biological mother (with or without co-adoption of the child). I do not share this position, which precludes the integration of a race and class analysis. The Euro-American movement for lesbian parental rights has conveniently ignored the history of the institutionalized removal of children of color and poor children from their biological homes through the social "welfare" system, Indian

boarding schools, missionary conversions, slavery, and the courts. Such removals have often-times come at great cost to the cultural identity and the spiritual welfare of the child; and this history is not forgotten when the issue of mother-right and custody arises among working-class and poor lesbians and other lesbians of color, especially in the case of interra-cial lesbian relationships.

Related to this issue is the rising number of white lesbian and gay couples' adoptions of children of color. Regardless of my personal empathy for, and recognition of, the genuine affection and deep commitment white queer couples may bestow upon their children of color, politically I remain confused and alarmed by the growing phenomenon. Where are those kids' birth mothers? We know the answer: on drugs, in prison, in poverty. Further it's been my observation that while white middle-class lesbian couples have found a measure of success in being able to adopt babies of color, the same has not held true for lesbians of color. I believe our work as lesbian activists has failed to really take into account these kind of racial and economic inequities that separate mothers (lesbian and heterosexual) from children of color.

[9] (Translation) What's life worth…

[10] As Ward Churchill defines "indigenism," "[An indigenist is] one who not only takes the rights of indigenous peoples as the highest [political] priority…but who draws on the tradi-tions—bodies of knowledge and corresponding codes of value—evolved over many thousands of years by native peoples the world over." From *A Native Son: Selected Essays in Indigenism, 1985-1995.* Boston: South End Press, 1996: 509.

[11] The term "two-spirit" is used to refer to contemporary Native American/First Nation gay men, lesbians, transvestites, and transgender individuals, as well as to traditions of multiple gender categories and sexualities in tribal cultures. Some Xicanas who recognize themselves as Native have also begun to employ the term. For a diverse discussion on the subject, see *Two-Spirit People: Native American Gender Identity, Sexuality and Spirituality,* Sue-Ellen Jacobs, Wesley Thomas, and Sabine Lang, eds. Urbana and Chicago: University of Illinois Press, 1997.

The Lessons of Candomblé,
The Lessons of Life

VALDINA OLIVEIRA PINTO

*This essay was given as a public lecture at the Caribbean Cultural Center,
New York City, March 2001. It was translated by Rachel Harding.*

Bakulo bawonso, nkisi awonso vana nzila kwame kwa vova kwa bantu
*May all the ancestors and all the nkisis open the path for me to speak
to the people.*

I am asking permission of those present who are older than I, religious leaders
in the traditions of Pálo, of Lucumí, of Santería who are equivalent to what
we call in Bahia—*tatankisi, nenguankisi; iyalorixas, babalorixas; donés, dotés*. I
am asking permission from those who are older than I am that I may speak
to this group here.

I especially ask permission of Nganga Fu-Kiau Ka Bunseki—*vana nzila
kwame,* give me permission.

My birth certificate says that my name is Valdina Oliveira Pinto. But when
I was initiated in the Candomblé community I recovered an African name. I
received the *djina,* the ritual name, Zimewaanga. And I was initiated as a
makota. After my initiation, the *nkisi* to whom I was consecrated gave me the
role, the responsibility of *makota a ngunzo.*

I was initiated by the hand of Elizabeth Santos da Hora in the Tanuri
Junçara *terreiro,* whose ritual name is Kunderene. She was initiated by Mona
Lubidí who was initiated by two persons, Kambambi and Nlundi a
Mungongo, who were themselves initiated by Maria Genoveva de Bonfim,
whose ritual name was Twembe dia Nzambi. This is as far back as I can go in
reconstructing my Candomblé family tree. I know that Maria Genoveva,
who was better known as Maria Nené was initiated by Roberto Barros Lins,
but I don't know his African name.

When I was initiated, the first lesson I was taught was "Respect the elders,
respect the elders, respect the elders." I was also taught that one should be
awake to see the sunrise at dawn; to be alert and yet reserved when the sun is
in its midday position; to also be awake to see the sun go down at sunset; and,
if one has to be awake at the midnight hour to be in a position of reserve.

See glossary for definitions of foreign words and phrases and a description of Candomblé.

Touch the earth with your feet, which is to say, walk barefoot. Honor the sun by looking at the sun. Respect the woods when you have to go to the woods. Learn by observing and repeating—listening, listening, listening. Speaking sometimes very little or nothing at all. Feeling, feeling, feeling. This helped me a great deal—a lesson that was passed on silently. The lesson that the earth teaches, that the plants teach, that the water teaches, that the wind teaches, with no words.

When I was initiated in Candomblé in 1975, I was initiated as an adult. And in that time I was already a professional woman. I was a teacher in a primary school. I had read some books. When I entered into Candomblé, I saw that I had to relearn how to live. And when I began to learn in Candomblé, I realized that much of what I had already learned that was useful and was similar to Candomblé, no book, no teacher, no school had taught me. I had learned it from people. I had learned it as a child playing; running in the woods, playing with animals, animals that today I might even be afraid of. Because at that time it was my privilege to grow up in a neighborhood (Engenho Velho da Federação, the neighborhood where I was born, where I grew up and where I live today) where there was still a forest, there were woods, there was pure water. I would scoop up water from the spring and drink it.

I used to pick up leaves in the back yard. Or from the bush that was the fence between my house and the neighbor's house. And I would buy a little bit of *bambá*, a paste that we would use when we make palm oil at home. I would get the leaves and make play food, doll food, with my sister and my brothers. And when the food that my mother made was ready, I wasn't hungry any more because I satisfied my hunger with the play food, the dollhouse food.

I remember when I was a little girl, there was a midwife that all of us in the family called "grandmother." When sometimes we would be crying for some reason—because our mother had hit us or if we had fallen—one vivid memory that I have of this woman, who wasn't my blood grandmother but *was* my grandmother, was a song she used to sing to me as she would rock me when I was crying in order to calm me. It was only later that I realized the words to the song were African words, they were words from the Kikongo language. And the language of my grandmother Maria passed through my head, rocking and singing:

Tualembe Fumu
Tualembe Nganga
Tulembo Tulembo
Malanganga

It was only later when I began to study the Kikongo language that I realized these were Kikongo words. And I began to remember these things when I entered into Candomblé. I learned a lot of things in Candomblé. I have learned things from people who may not know how to read books, from people who don't know how to write, but who have a wisdom that does not exist in any book that has ever been written. I have learned lessons about the connections between the world that I touch, the world that I see, the world that I smell, and the other world that I can't touch, that I can't see, that I can't smell, but that I can perceive and feel. I have learned these lessons in the contact and interaction that I've had with people and from the contact that I've had with this our world, the land, the plants, the water, the wind.

When we enter Candomblé, we learn by singing and repeating the songs, and praying and repeating the prayers, listening, singing the songs wrong, singing over again, being corrected and continuing. But we also learn a great deal in silence. Because when you remain silent, you can hear the voice of the earth, the voice of the plants, the voice of the water, the voice of the air. The voice of our ancestors. We arrived here, we appeared here on the earth after all of this (the earth, the plants, the water, the air) was here already.

So when I think about ancestors, my *bakulu,* I think of those first people that ever lived, down to my great-great-great-great-great-grandparents. But I especially think about these other ancestors, my plant and earth and water ancestors, who were created and appeared long before the earliest human beings. And at the same time, what we call *nkisi* in our Angola candomblé community is precisely this energy, this force that is in the earth. It is not just minerals, it's something that I don't see. But it is there, the energy; it's my energy. *Nkisi*, for us, *is* this energy. If you look at a leaf, you can see the form, the color of the leaf. And if you take it to a laboratory you might even find its properties. But there is something that you don't see that is in the plant. And that is what gives each plant its particular function, its particular use. Sometimes we don't recognize the function of each plant and I think that may be because we haven't been in a situation where we needed to discover what that plant has to give us. But it's there.

An interesting thing—and I imagine this must happen to many people related to religions of African origin—sometimes I go into the woods, and I find some plants that I don't recognize. But I do recognize them. Something called them to my attention. Sometimes it is the smell. Sometimes I pass by and they touch me, I turn around and I see them, I feel them. Sometimes I may not know the name of the plant. But it is as if the plant were calling to me saying "Look, you need me. Look, I have something to give you." I pick up the plant and I take it to the *terreiro*. And I talk to the older people there, the people who know about plants. Sometimes they know the name, sometimes they don't know it either. But they look and they say, "Yes this is a saint's plant, an *nkisi's* plant, it is plant with a good energy, a plant that we can use safely." I thought to myself the other day, maybe this is the way the first people, the first men and the first women, or the first women and the first men, found plants and began to discover what they were good for— what you could eat, what you could make a tea out of, what you could make a syrup with to cure yourself.

More and more I recognize the necessity of learning this mute language of the earth, of the plants, of the water, of the waterfall, of lakes, of oceans, of the rains. But sometimes, I'm also able to hear this language, this voice, even in an environment when there is no waterfall running. Sometimes it is like we're in a stone forest; not natural stones but the stones that people have created. A concrete jungle. We're running here and there and having almost no time to think about these things. But I think that's because we have become accustomed to thinking that when someone talks about the environment they're talking only about plants, and water, and animals and not about human beings as well, who are also part of the environment.

We are in the midst of this. We are part of the environment. Because we have forgotten this we have caused a great deal of imbalance on this earth. We have distanced ourselves a great deal from each other. We've become more and more individualistic. And we've lost the understanding that we live, that we have to live and are only able to live, at the level of community.

And we've lost the way to exchange, to exchange ideas, to exchange things, ways of living, ways of thinking about the world. To recognize that there are some things that one person may have more of and another person may have less of but we can put it all together and share with each other. And we have made the world so cruel at times. When we always think in terms of superiority/inferiority, better/worse, developed/underdeveloped, civilized/uncivilized, primitive/savage. Who are the savages? Who are the primitives and who are the civilized people? Maybe our world today needs, really needs, to go back a ways and to get what we threw away and thought was not worthy, what we thought was savage, what we thought was primitive. We put in its place what we thought was civilized, which caused so many imbalances, so many injustices, so many inequalities and so much racism.

And that's why I say racism is an environmental issue, racism is an environmental problem. And we Black people, though our ancestors suffered so much, we still in many ways suffer the weight of prejudice, the weight of racism. But over these long centuries, wherever we were taken and according to the environments we were taken to, each group discovered how to recreate, figured out how to reconstruct, how to re-elaborate the greatness of that which was called "primitive" and "savage." And today it is in our hands to put the feeling of suffering aside a little bit and see and understand that we, all of us, all of the descendents of Africans taken from their motherland, all of us have a great deal to teach the world, and we must do it. That is our work.

Some doing it one way, some doing it another way, but we can do it in a very profound way, which is through our spirituality. Because our spirituality is not fragmented. Our spirituality must be in consonance with, joined with, everything in the world. It doesn't matter if it's in the form of Santéria, of Pálo, of Lucumí, of Umbanda, of Candomblé, of Black churches, or many many other names it might have. We have to do it. We have to get informed about our various ways and manners of spirituality and bring them together and act in the world. For a balanced world, for a just world, for a peaceful world. We owe this to the coming generations. Because all the suffering in the past wasn't in vain. We received a legacy. We must build on this legacy and give it to the world and show the world; and show those who don't know what this world can be, or indeed what it truly is. I believe this. Candomblé helps me to see the world like this. My ancestors, my *bakulu*, they left this for us. And they have taught me everyday. Thank you.

GLOSSARY

Candomblé: an Afro-Brazilian religion centered on the cultivation of spiritual energies or divinities *(nkisis, orishas, voduns)* for the benefit of individual devotees, the ritual community, and the larger world. Based in a variety of West and Central African religious traditions, Candomblé was created by enslaved Africans and their descendants in eighteenth- and nineteenth-century Brazil. The religion is part of the larger complex of Afro-Atlantic religions, which includes Cuban Santeria, Haitian Vodou, Surinamese Winti, and the folk Christianity of the African American south.

babalorixá: supreme male leader in Yoruba Candomblé tradition; high priest

bakulu: ancestors

doné: supreme female leader in Ewe-Fon (Jeje) Candomblé tradition; high priestess

doté: supreme male leader in Ewe-Fon (Jeje) Candomblé tradition: high priest

iyalorixá: supreme female leader in Yoruba Candomblé tradition; high priestess

nkisi: spiritual energy; divinity (equivalent to Yoruba *orisha*)

nengua nkisi: supreme female leader in Kongo-Angola Candomblé tradition; high priestess

tata nkisi: supreme male leader in Kongo-Angola Candomblé tradition; high priest

makota: female ritual elder in Kongo-Angola Candomblé tradition.

makota a ngunzo: female ritual elder responsible for secret rites and initiations.

terreiro: Candomblé ritual community; sacred space; temple

Editors

M. Jacqui Alexander is a teacher, scholar, activist, and writer. Formerly she taught at Connecticut College, New London, Connecticut where she held the Fuller-Maathai Chair. With Chandra Talpade Mohanty, Alexander coedited *Feminist Genealogies, Colonial Legacies, Democratic Futures* (Routledge, 1997). Her collection of essays, *Pedagogies of Crossing,* is forthcoming from Duke University Press.

Lisa Albrecht is an activist educator and writer. She is associate professor and Morse-Minnesota Alumni Association Distinguished Professor of Teaching in the General College of the University of Minnesota, where she teaches undergraduate courses in writing. Albrecht is affiliated with the departments of women's studies, rhetoric, and American studies, the Center for Advanced Feminist Studies, the Center for Interdisciplinary Studies of Writing, and the Gay, Lesbian, Bisexual, and Transgender Programs Office. With Rose Brewer, she coedited *Bridges of Power: Women's Multicultural Alliances* (New Society, 1990). From 1986–1991, Albrecht was the managing editor of *Evergreen Chronicles: A Journal of Gay, Lesbian, Bisexual and Transgender Cultures and Arts.* Currently she is working on a memoir, *Lessons of My Life.*

Albrecht is cofounder of the Freire Center: A Popular Education Center for Democratic Social Change. In partnership with various neighborhood and activist groups, the Freire Center brings people together to discuss problems of injustice and how to work for social transformation. She is also on the board of directors of Project South: Institute for the Elimination of Poverty and Genocide in Atlanta, Georgia. In her spare time, Albrecht says, "I play percussion and tell jokes in the Tsatkelehs, Minnesota's only all-grrrl Klezmer band, and live happily with Pat Rouse, my partner of nine years, and our two cats."

Sharon M. Day is Ojibwe and a citizen of the Bois Forte Band of Chippewa Indians. She lives in St. Paul, Minnesota with her grandson Kirby, her dog Max, and six assorted feathered friends. Her daughters, Suzanne and Melissa, and the rest of her grandchildren all live nearby. Day is the executive director and cofounder of the Indigenous People's Task Force (formerly the Minnesota American Indian AIDS Task Force), whose mission is to improve the health and education of indigenous peoples. She is an artist, musician, and director of the Ogitchidag Gikinooamaagad Players, an adolescent theater group that has performed eight plays in twenty-seven states since 1990. She is the recipient of the Resourceful Women Award and the Gisela

Konopka Award for her work with youth. The mayors of St. Paul and Minneapolis and the Governor of Minnesota have named a day in her honor.

Day says: "Everything is part of a creative process, whether it is carving wood, sketching a shield, making a drum, or developing a school or a housing complex. It is through our connection to the spirit that dreams, the lyrics and melody to a song, poetry and prose, and the vision for creating change come to us."

Mab Segrest is a writer, organizer, and teacher who lives in Durham, North Carolina, where she received a Ph.D. from Duke University. For over twenty years as a social justice activist, Segrest has worked between and across genres and political movements as an essayist, organizer, poet, teacher, journalist, antiracist, and lesbian. She was a founding coordinator of North Carolinians against Racist and Religious Violence. Her book, *Memoir of a Race Traitor* (South End Press), narrates this groundbreaking work and was named an "Outstanding Book on Human Rights in North America." From 1992 to 2000, Segrest worked as coordinator of the United States Urban-Rural Mission, a program of the World Council of Churches. Her book *Born to Belonging* will be published by Rutgers University Press in 2002. Mab Segrest teaches at Connecticut College.

Contributors

Dorothy Abbott is the former assistant director of the National Endowment for the Arts' literature program and the editor of seven literary anthologies, including *The Signet Class Book of Southern Short Stories* (Penguin USA). She has published articles and reviews in more than fifty publications, including *The Village Voice, Southern Exposure, St. Petersburg Times*, and *Women's Review of Books*. Abbott's radio productions and commentaries have been heard on National Public Radio and Pacifica stations across the country. Her work has been reviewed in *The New York Times Book Review* and by Doris Grumbach on National Public Radio. Abbott is a multimedia producer and cultural activist, specializing in radio and print media with an emphasis on social justice and women's culture. In 2000 she founded the Women's Radio Fund in order to forge links between women in radio and their allies: funders, a worldwide audience, strategic partners, and the global women's movement. Forthcoming from Dorothy Abbott: a radio documentary on women in the civil rights/freedom movement and a collection of essays, *Facing Love Clearly*. Abbott was a major force in bringing this book to life.

Gloria Anzaldúa is a Chicana *patlache* (queer) feminist writer. Her *Entrevistas/Interview*, edited by AnaLouise Keating, won the Susan Koppelmann Award and *Borderlands/La Frontera* was chosen as one of the hundred Best Books of the Century by both *Hungry Mind Review* and *Utne Reader*. Her bilingual children's picture books, *Friends from the Other Side* and *Prietita and the Ghost Woman* are Smithsonian Notable Books and received the Americas Honor Award. In addition, her book *Making Face, Making Soul/Haciendo Caras* won the Lambda Lesbian Small Book Press Award. *This Bridge Called My Back*, coedited with Cherríe Moraga, won the Before Columbus Foundation American Book Award. Anzaldúa is co-winner of the American Studies Association 2001 Bode-Pearson Prize and has received an NEA Fiction Award, the Lesbian Rights Award, and the Sappho Award of Distinction. Anzaldúa has been profiled in *Ms.* Magazine; *Utne Reader* has chosen her as a "visionary."

Deborah Barndt teaches in the department of environmental studies at York University-Toronto in the areas of critical education for social change, cultural production, and women and development. She is a mother, popular educator, photographer, and author of several books. Barndt has many years of experience working with migrant and immigrant women in Canada and in Central America. She has worked in social justice and popular education programs in Latin America, Canada, and the United States.

Angela Bowen is a professor of women's studies at California State University, Long Beach, where she also teaches English literature. In her previous two incarnations, she was first a dancer, choreographer, and founder and director of a cultural-arts center; then a political activist and national public speaker. In 1987 Bowen began writing a group of short stories. "Cornelia's Mother," her first-born (and special favorite), has eight siblings. Bowen says: "Thanks to the Money for Women: Barbara Deming Memorial Fund for a 1989 grant, which enabled the completion of 'Cornelia's Mother' and several other stories within the waiting-to-be-finished collection."

Beth Brant is a Bay of Quinte Mohawk from the Tyendinaga Mohawk Territory in Ontario. She is the editor of the groundbreaking collection *A Gathering of Spirit: Writing and Art by Native American* (1989). Brant is the author of *Mohawk Trail* (1985) and *Food & Spirits* (1991). In 1983 and 1986 she received the Michigan Council for the Arts Creative Artist grant and in 1989, the Ontario Arts Council awarded her a grant. Brant was also a 1991 recipient of a literature fellowship from the National Endowment for the Arts.

Mi Ok Song Bruining was born in Seoul, South Korea in 1960, the year of the rat. At five years old, she was adopted by a white family who lived in New Jersey. After attending art school in Virginia, Bruining earned a BA from Vermont College and an MSW from Smith College School for Social Work. She has practiced social work for more than ten years, but identifies as a poet, writer, artist, and activist. In 1996, Bruining returned to Korea to live and work until 1998, when she returned to Cambridge, Massachusetts. Bruining has had numerous poems published and has conducted more than eighty speaking engagements on international adoption. She lives as a leaping lesbian with her cat, Iona, and drives a 1978 VW bus named Lulu. Bruining produces hand-made greeting cards and posters celebrating women feminism, multiculturalism, diversity, cats, children, and landscapes.

Linda Burnham cofounded the Women of Color Resource Center and currently serves as its executive director. WCRC, now in its tenth year, is a nonprofit education, community action, and resource center committed to developing a strong, institutional foundation for social change activism by and on behalf of women of color. Burnham's most recent publications include *Women's Education in the Global Economy* (coauthored with Miriam Louie) and *Working Hard, Staying Poor*, a study of the impact of welfare reform on poor women and their families. The dynamic, often perilous intersections of race, class, and gender—and the organizing women of color undertake to resist marginalization and oppression—are the subjects of Burnham's lifelong inquiry and activism.

Chrystos writes: "I'm a Menominee Two Spirit Warrior for justice, a visual and print artist, performing internationally. Self-educated, I am more well read than the majority of college professors I meet. My lesbian-feminist publishers stole my royalties and destroyed my books, only one is still available: *Fugitive Colors* from Cleveland State University Poetry Center. I fight daily to overcome bitterness and despair, to make the art which is my sustenance. I passionately love women, as I have since 1965. I pray that testosterone poisoning will not destroy our earth."

Edwidge Danticat   was born in Haiti in 1969 and came to the United States when she was twelve years old. She graduated from Barnard College and received her MFA from Brown University. Her first novel, *Breath, Eyes, Memory,* was published when she was twenty-five. The following year she was nominated for the National Book Award for her story collection, *Krik? Krak!* Danticat is a recipient of a Lila Wallace-Reader's Digest Foundation grant and was named one of the twenty "Best Young American Novelists" by *Granta* in 1996. She lives in New York.

Angela Y. Davis   first came to national attention in 1969, when she was removed from her teaching position at the University of California-Los Angeles because of her membership in the Communist Party. In 1970, she was placed on the FBI's Ten Most Wanted List and was the subject of an intense police search, culminating in one of the most publicized trials in recent history. After a sixteen-month incarceration, Davis was acquitted. In 1998, she helped organize a national conference at UC-Berkeley on prison issues, "Critical Resistance: Beyond the Prison Industrial Complex," which is the focus of her current scholarship and activism. Her most recent publications include *The Angela Davis Reader* and *Blues Legacies and Black Feminism.*

El Comité de Mujeres Puertorriqueñas–Miriam Lopez Perez   was composed of Alixa Borrero, Marigna Camacho, Elba Crespo, Annette Diaz, Dorotea Manuela, and Milagros Padilla. They write: "We organized in 1987 to confront racism and to educate others regarding our reality in both the United States and Puerto Rico. This work was accomplished via many different activities and along different fronts. We ended our collective work as a comité in 1992 following the trial of Yvonne Melendez Carrion. We had completed important historical work and decided to take an extended hiatus from organized activities. Our commitment to defending women's rights and to our national independence struggle continues. We will always respond to injustice and oppression and will join in other organized efforts to achieve these goals and perhaps reorganize one day as the comité. We are grateful to all those individuals and organizations who supported our work."

Carmen Suarez, who updated "In the Belly of the Beast: Puertorriqueñas Challenging Colonialism," was born in Puerto Rico. She has dedicated most of her life to women's health care in the United States. "It was in Minnesota," she says, "among the Ojibway community, that I felt the closest to home." Suarez, now retired in Puerto Rico, is still trying to right the wrongs and fight the windmills.

Denise Giardina grew up in a coal camp in McDowell County, West Virginia. She received a BA in history from West Virginia Wesleyan College and an M.Div. from Virginia Theological (Episcopal) in Alexandria, Virginia. Giardina has written five novels: *Good King Harry* (1984), *Storming Heaven* (1987), *The Unquiet Earth* (1992), *Saints and Villains* (1998) and *Fallam's Secret* (forthcoming, 2003). Her books have won many awards, including an American Book Award from the Before Columbus Foundation and the Lillian Smith Award. Giardina lives in Charleston, West Virginia, and teaches at West Virginia State College.

Janice Gould is an enrolled member of the Koyangk'auwi Maidu tribe. She is the author of two collections of poetry, *Beneath My Heart* (1990) and *Earthquake Weather* (1996), and co-editor of *Speaking to Me Words* (forthcoming), a collection of essays on American Indian poetry. Gould has received writing grants and awards from the National Endowment for the Arts and the Astraea Foundation, and her writing has been published in a number of journals and anthologies. She received her Ph.D. in English from the University of New Mexico and is currently the Hallie Ford Chair in Creative Writing at Willamette University in Salem, Oregon.

Suheir Hammad is the author of *Born Palestinian, Born Black,* and *Drops of This Story*. Her work has appeared in anthologies and journals, and she is currently a member of Def Poetry Jam ensemble. Hammad writes: "My work has traveled farther than I have, but I hope to catch up soon."

Rachel E. Harding is Director of the Veterans of Hope Project, an interdisciplinary initiative on religion, culture and participatory democracy based at the Iliff School of Theology in Denver, Colorado. She earned a Ph.D. in Latin American History from the University of Colorado in 1997. She is author of *A Refuge in Thunder: Candomblé and Alternative Spaces of Blackness* (Indiana University Press, 2000), a history of the nineteenth century development of Candomblé, an Afro-Brazilian religion. Her essay, "'What Part of the River You're In': African American Women in Devotion to Òsun," is published in *Òsun Across the Waters: A Yoruba Goddess in Africa and the Americas* (Indiana University Press, 2001). Harding is also a poet and has published work in *Callaloo, Chelsea, Feminist Studies, The International Review of African American Art, Hambone,* and in several anthologies. For this anthology she translated the essay, "The Lessons of Candomblé, The Lessons of Life," by Valdina Oliveira Pinto.

Suzan Shown Harjo is Cheyenne and Hodulgee Muscogee. She has reshaped federal Indian policy since 1975 and has helped Native Peoples to recover more than one million acres of land. Harjo has developed the most important Native cultural laws in the modern era, including the 1996 Executive Order of Indian Sacred Sites, the 1990 Native American Graves Protection and Repatriation Act, the 1989 National Museum of the American Indian Act, and the 1978 American Indian Religious Freedom Act.

Sharon Jaffe says, "I believe in creativity, community, and the necessary involvement in a legacy to bequeath the struggles for justice, equality, and liberation to a vibrant and alive ecosystem."

Joanna Kadi is a musician, poet, and writer. She is the author of *Thinking Class: Sketches from a Cultural Worker* (1996) and the editor of *Food for Our Grandmothers: Writings by Arab-American and Arab-Canadian Feminists* (1994), both published by South End Press. Kadi plays *derbeke* (Arabic hand drum), *jembe* (West African standing drum), fiddle, and piano. She has performed her music in venues ranging from community centers to art museums to concert halls to outdoor benefits. Her home is in rural Wisconsin.

Winona LaDuke lives on the White Earth Reservation in Minnesota and is an enrolled member of the Mississippi Band of Anishinaabeg. She is the program director of the Honor the Earth Fund and founding director of the White Earth Land Recovery Project. In 1994, LaDuke was named by *Time* magazine as one of America's fifty most promising leaders under forty years of age. In the 1996 and 2000 presidential campaigns she served as Ralph Nader's running mate on the Green Party ticket, and in 1997, with the Indigo Girls, was named a *Ms.* Woman of the Year. She is the author of many articles and a novel, *Last Standing Woman* (1997). Her nonfiction debut, *All Our Relations: Native Struggles for Land and Life*, was published in 1999 by South End Press.

Barbara Lee was first elected to the House of Representatives for the Ninth District of California in a 1998 special election to fill the seat of retiring Congressman Ron Dellums. She is currently the vice chair of the Progressive Caucus, chair of the Congressional Black Caucus (CBC) Task Force on Global HIV/AIDS, Democratic Regional Whip for Region 2 (Northern California, American Samoa, Guam, and Hawai'i), and a member of the CBC Minority Business Task Force. Congresswoman Lee went to Washington, D.C. after serving in the California State Assembly from 1990 to 1996 and the California State Senate from 1996 to 1998.

Audre Lorde was born in 1934, in New York City, of parents who migrated from Grenada, West Indies. She graduated from Hunter High School, then attended Hunter College where she received her BA degree and two years later a masters degree in library science from Columbia University. She received an NEA grant in 1968, became poet-in-residence at Tougaloo College near Jackson, Mississippi, and published her first volume of poetry, *The First Cities.* In 1978 Lorde became a professor of English, first at John Jay College of Criminal Justice in New York and later at Hunter College. She published nine volumes of poetry and five works of prose, including *From a Land Where Other People Live, The Cancer Journals,* and the 1989 American Book Award winner *A Burst of Light.* In October, 1990, her work and life were celebrated by more than a thousand women attending the "I Am Your Sister" conference in Boston. She was the recipient of many distinguished honors and awards including the Walt Whitman Citation of Merit, and the Manhattan Borough President's Award for Excellence in the Arts, and she was named the New York State Poet, 1991–1993. Audre Lorde, an acclaimed social activist and cancer survivor, succumbed to the disease in November 1992, on the island of St. Croix, West Indies.

Miriam Ching Yoon Louie has devoted more than three decades to empowering women of color, immigrant women workers, and grassroots Asian communities. Her book *Sweatshop Warriors: Immigrant Women Workers Take on the Global Economy* (South End Press, 2001) features the stories of Chinese, Mexican, and Korean women grassroots leaders in "bleeding-edge" antisweatshop and anticorporate movements for justice. She cowrote *Women's Education in the Global Economy,* a popular education workbook. Louie serves on the board of the Women of Color Resource Center, which she helped found in 1990. She was WCRC's "Beijing and Beyond" project coordinator and cofacilitated international roundtables of migrant workers' centers and of racial and ethnic minority women at the 1995 U.N. World Conference of Women Forum in China.

Matthew Nemiroff Lyons is a fourth-generation socialist and atheist Jew who grew up in Ithaca, New York. His work as an independent historian has focused on systems of oppression and social movements. Lyons is coauthor, with Chip Berlet, of *Right-Wing Populism in America: Too Close for Comfort* and author of *The Grassroots Network: Radical Nonviolence in the Federal Republic of Germany, 1972–1985.* He currently lives in Philadelphia and works as an archivist at the Historical Society of Pennsylvania.

Judith McDaniel is a writer, teacher, and activist who has published many books and articles on peace and justice issues. She lives in Tucson, Arizona, and is deputy director of the Southern Arizona AIDS Foundation. Before coming to SAAF, Judith was the director of the Peacebuiding Unit of the American Friends Service Committee in Philadelphia, PA. Judith has been an activist in the lesbian and gay movement since the 1970s. She co-founded Spinsters Ink, a lesbian/feminist press, in 1978, and wrote and published *The Lesbian Couples Guide* (HarperCollins, 1995). During the 1980s, she worked with Sanctuary Movement in upstate New York and visited Tucson for the first time in 1985–86 during the trial of the Sanctuary workers there. It was during this trip that she went to Big Mountain and began to connect issues of security in many different contexts. Her book about those experiences, *Sanctuary: A Journey,* was published in 1986. *Taking Risks*, her most recent book of poems, was published in 2001 by Tucson's Rising Tide Press. She is currently writing the biography of peace and civil rights activist Barbara Deming.

Marcie McIntire is a traditional artist who is frequently asked to furnish her pedigree papers for American Indian art shows, museums, and galleries. She is currently involved with reviving and revitalizing Ojibwe art objects that have nonreligious purposes and are within living memory. She is a member of the Grand Portage Band of Chippewa Indians, with whom she currently resides.

Cherríe Moraga is a poet, playwright, and essayist, and the coeditor of *This Bridge Called My Back: Writings by Radical Women of Color.* Her plays have been anthologized in numerous collections and are also published in a three-volume series of collected works published by West End Press (Albuquerque), including her most recent work, *Watsonville: Some Place Not Here.* Her collected nonfiction writings include: *The Last Generation* (South End Press); a memoir, *Waiting in the Wings: Portrait of a Queer Motherhood* (Firebrand Books); and a new, expanded edition of the now-classic *Loving in the War Years*, republished by South End Press in 2000. Moraga is a recipient of the National Endowment for the Arts Theatre Playwrights' Fellowship and is the Artist-in-Residence in the Departments of Drama and Spanish & Portuguese at Stanford University.

Mary Moran was born in the upper peninsula of Michigan during the winter of 1946. She is of Metis and Irish heritage. Moran has been writing and contributing her work to anthologies for more than twenty years.

Toni Morrison was born Chloe Anthony Wofford in Lorain, Ohio in 1931. She earned her MA at Cornell University in New York in 1955. Morrison taught at the State University of New York and edited books for Random House, including those by black authors Toni Cade Bambara and Gayl Jones. In 1984 she was appointed to an Albert Schweitzer chair at the University of New York at Albany. Morrison's widely acclaimed books include *Sula* (winner of the National Book Critics Award), *Song of Solomon*, and *Beloved*, which won the 1988 Pulitzer Prize. In 1993, Morrison was awarded the Nobel Prize for Literature. She is Robert F. Goheen Professor, Council of the Humanities at Princeton University.

Kagendo Murungi, a Kenyan by birth, is committed to applying African feminist principles to human rights advocacy on gender and sexual rights. She is a founding member of "Uhuru: Africans for Justice," a Diasporic African initiative whose mission is to support indigenous African sexual rights organizing. She is also Africa program officer at the International Gay & Lesbian Human Rights Commission (IGLHRC), a position she helped institute in 1997. Murungi served for several years on the Astraea Lesbian Action Fund's international grants panel, and has worked in independent partnership with artists and activists in various locales to develop and produce independent video festivals and other sites for creative cultural agency. She is currently collaborating with gender and sexual rights activists in Cape Town to develop an applied research project on the impact of gender-based violence and HIV/AIDS on lesbian, bisexual, and all-sexual women in South Africa.

Orayb Aref Najjar was born in Jerusalem, Palestine, in 1947. She is associate professor of journalism at the department of communication at Northern Illinois University and the author of articles and book chapters on media law as well as on women. Her book *Portraits of Palestinian Women* was published by the University of Utah Press in 1992. Many of Najjar's articles have been anthologized, including: "Freedom of the Press in Jordan 1927–1998" in *Mass Media and Society in the Middle East: Impact for Political and Social Development* (2001) and "Can This Image Be Saved: Arab Americans and the Media" in *Islam and the West in Mass Media: Fragmented Images in a Globalizing World* (2000), both edited by Kai Hafez and published by Hampton Press.

Debbie Nathan is the author of *Women and Other Aliens: Essays from the U.S.-Mexico Border* (Cinco Puntos Press), and coauthor with Michael Snedeker of *Satan's Silence: Ritual Abuse and the Making of a Modern American Witch Hunt* (Basic Books). She has published work about women, politics, culture, and the U.S.-Mexico border in *The Village Voice, Ms., The Nation, The Progressive, Texas Observer, Pacific News Service, Women's Review of Books, The Atlantic Monthly*, and other venues. A native of Texas, Nathan has spent most of her life there. While living in El Paso in the 1980s and 1990s, she was an activist for immigrants' civil rights and women's issues. She currently lives in New York City.

Berta I. Perea is an anthropologist and history teacher at Westinghouse High School in Brooklyn, New York. She has been a visiting assistant professor of social science at Medgar Evers College, CUNY and has worked as a research consultant at many other institutions. In Bogota, Columbia she served as director of the Center for Afrocolombian Studies and Social Research. Perea has lectured in Europe and the United States about her research on Afro-Colombian women and work, the Afro-Colombian family, and the folkloric tradition. Her writing has appeared in several books and international journals in Spain, Zimbabwe, Colombia, and the United States.

Juliana Pegues is an activist, writer, and performer living in Minneapolis. After a decade-long hiatus, she is finishing her undergraduate degree in comparative ethnic studies at the University of Minnesota. When she is not trying to breathe life into academic papers, Pegues helps organize events for Guerrilla Wordfare, a community-building project for people of color based on the vision that creative expression of our experiences and struggles is a beautiful and powerful thing.

Rosalind P. Petchesky teaches political science and women's studies at Hunter College and the Graduate Center of the City University of New York, where she is a distinguished professor. Petchesky's books and articles have for many years helped to define feminist visions of reproductive and sexual rights, more recently in the context of globalization. Her new book, *Global Prescriptions: Gendering Health and Human Rights,* will be published by Zed Books, London, in mid-2003. She was founder of the International Reproductive Rights Research Action Group and has been active in transnational women's groups working to bring gender, race, and class perspectives to United Nations processes. Petchesky is a MacArthur Fellow and a trained kick boxer.

Valdina Oliveira Pinto is the Makota a Ngunzo (senior female ritual elder) in the Tanuri Junçara Candomblé community in Salvador, Bahia, Brazil. She has been initiated for twenty-seven years and is a respected authority on cosmology in the Kongo-Angola Candomblé tradition. She is also an educator and environmental rights activist and has created a widely acclaimed environmental and citizenship education project for marginalized youth in Bahia drawing on models of teaching and learning from Candomblé communities. Ms. Pinto lectures frequently on environmental philosophy in Afro-Brazilian religion; anti-racism and environmental justice; and healing in Candomblé.

Grace Poore is a feminist lesbian writer and award-winning video-maker whose work deals with ending violence against women and girl children. As part of this work she focuses on the dynamics of cross-racial hostilities and redefining the concepts of home and community for South Asians in diaspora. She has worked for the United Nations Special Rapporteur On Violence Against Women in Sri Lanka as well as the US-based National Coalition Against Domestic Violence where she did crisis advocacy on the national battered women's hotline and edited the organization's quarterly journal. Her writing has appeared in journals such as *Meridians, Sinister Wisdom, Conditions,* and *Trikone.* She has also published in anthologies such as *Our Feet Walk the Sky, Patchwork Shawl: Chronicles of South Asian Women in America,* and *The Very Inside.* She is currently working on a cross-cultural video-book project to raise awareness about preventing the perpetration of incest. Poore was born and raised in Malaysia and is currently based in Maryland. She used to write and publish under the pseudonym, V.K. Aruna.

June Rostan grew up in Valdese, North Carolina. In college she was involved in student rights and anti-Vietnam War organizing. She spent two years in Italy working with immigrant workers and in the women's movement. For more than twenty-five years, she has worked as an organizer, popular educator, researcher, and occasional writer with unions, women coal miners, and education and training organizations. Since 1987, Rostan has been the director of the Southern Empowerment Project, an organization that does training in community organizing and fundraising with an antiracist focus. Recently the SEP has begun organizing and leadership development with new Latino immigrants.

Sonia Sanchez was born Wilsonia Driver in 1934, in Birmingham, Alabama. She received a BA from Hunter College in 1955. Her first two collections of poetry, *Home Coming* (1969) and *We a BaddDDD People* (1970), reflect a militant stance inspired, in part, by the example of Malcolm X. Sanchez has taught at several universities, including San Francisco State College, the University of Pittsburgh, Rutgers, Amherst, the University of Pennsylvania, and Temple University in Philadelphia. Her publications include the play *Uh Huh: But How Do It Free Us?* (1975) and *homegirls & handgrenades* (1984), which received an American Book Award from the Before Columbus Foundation. She continues to teach and write in Philadelphia.

Sheri Scott lives in North Carolina, but enjoys frequent road trips to the lovely lands up North with her partner, Leigh, and their dog, Chase. She sends out a special *miigwech* ("thank you" in Ojibway) to Sharon Day and Marlys Whiteagle, from whom she has learned so much.

Mary TallMountain (1918–1994) was a Native Alaskan poet and storyteller who lived for most of her adult life in San Francisco. She authored eight collections of poems and stories, including *Light on the Tent Wall* (1990) and *Listen to the Night* (1994). In 1989 she was a featured poet in Bill Moyers's PBS series "The Power of the Word." TallMountain was born in Nulato, a small Native village less than a hundred miles from the Arctic Circle. Her mother was Koyukon Athabaskan and her father was a Scots/Irishman from California, stationed in Alaska during World War I. Much of her writing was inspired by the tragedy and loss of being taken from her family in early life and by her deep spiritual connection with her homeland, her family, and her Native culture. An archival collection of Mary TallMountain's work is housed at the Rasmuson Library at the University of Alaska in Fairbanks. Her unpublished novel, *Doyon*, is being prepared for publication.

Becky Thompson is the author of *A Promise and a Way of Life: White Antiracist Activism* (2001); *Mothering without a Compass: White Mother's Love, Black Son's Courage* (2000); *A Hunger So Wide and So Deep: A Multiracial View of Women's Eating Problems* (1994); and co-editor with Sangeeta Tyagi of *Names We Call Home: Autobiography on Racial Identity* and *Beyond a Dream Deferred: Multicultural Education and the Politics of Excellence* (1993), which received the Gustavus Myers Award for Outstanding Book on Human Rights in America. She is an associate professor of sociology at Simmons College in Boston, where she teaches African American studies, women's studies, and sociology. For 2002–2003, she will be a visiting associate professor of African and African American studies at Duke University.

Edén Torres makes her living as an assistant professor of women's studies and Chicano studies at the University of Minnesota. She writes: "I make my life through family, friends, food, music, and poetry."

Haunani-Kay Trask is a member of Ka Lahui Hawai'i, a Native Hawaiian initiative for self-government. She received her Ph.D. in political science from the University of Wisconsin–Madison. Her publications include numerous articles, a book of political analysis, *Eros and Power: The Promise of Feminist Theory* (1986), and *From a Native Daughter: Colonialism and Sovereignty in Hawai'i* (1993), which Alice Walker calls "a masterpiece." An accomplished poet, Trask published the much-acclaimed *Light in the Crevice Never Seen* (1994). Her second book of poetry, *Night Is a Sharkskin Drum,* was published by the University of Hawai'i Press in 2002. She served as the executive producer and scriptwriter for the documentary film *Act of War: The Overthrow of the Hawaiian Kingdom.* Currently Trask is professor of Hawaiian Studies at the University of Hawai'i at Manoa.

Nellie Wong was born in Oakland, California, the first U.S.-born daughter of immigrants from Toishan, China. Wong is the Bay Area organizer for the Freedom Socialist Party and is also active in Radical Women, a socialist feminist organization. She has worked as a secretary and administrative assistant for the majority of her working life. She is now retired after working as a senior affirmative action analyst at the University of California, San Francisco for fifteen years. She is a delegate to the San Francisco Labor Council, representing her union, University Professional and Technical Employees (UPTE), Communications Workers of America (CWA) 9119. She is the author of three collections of poetry with a fourth manuscript, *Broad Shoulders*, awaiting publication.

Merle Woo is a socialist-feminist educator and writer who currently teaches in the women's studies department at San Jose State University. For twenty years Woo has been a leader in Radical Women and the Freedom Socialist Party. During the 1980s, she won an unfair labor practice, a civil suit, and a union arbitration against the University of California for violation of her free-speech rights and multidiscrimination based on race, sex, sexuality, and political ideology. At San Francisco State University during the 1990s, Woo fought alongside other progressive faculty and students to maintain a lesbian, women of color, and community focus in women's studies.

Mitsuye Yamada is founder and coordinator of Multicultural Women Writers and adjunct associate professor in the Asian-American Studies Department at University of California, Irvine. She is an active member of Interfaith Prisoners of Conscience, an organization that works to support and free political prisoners in the United States. She was formerly a board member of Amnesty International USA and continues to serve on the Committee on International Development, which promotes and funds development of human-rights work in Third World countries. Shaped by her concentration-camp experiences during World War II, Yamada's activities as a writer, educator, and political activist are interrelated with each other by human-rights, peace, and gender issues. Her most recent publication, *Camp Notes and Other Writings*, is a newly combined edition of her first two books and was published by Rutgers University Press in 1998.

The Girl Who Went and Saw and Came Back

a novel by Kim Chernin

From the author of *In My Mother's House* and *The Hungry Self* comes an experimental novel about the mysteries of identity, the page-turning story of a woman's desperate search for her lost girlhood friend, an abused and troubled child whom she repeatedly finds and loses again in the course of a lifetime. "A rare depth of psychological understanding, and one of the most beautifully etched and engaging central characters in modern fiction." (Lillian B. Rubin).

ISBN 1-931223-00-9 | $24.95 | 5.5 x 7.5
296 pages | Hardcover

Moon of the Swaying Buds

a spiritual autobiography
by Gail Sher

Recounts what it felt like to be a woman involved in the beginnings of Zen in the United States. Sher was ordained by Shunryu Suzuki, the man credited with bringing Soto Zen practice to the West. Her story, of the interior life that led her to enter and then leave a Zen monastery, is told in *haibun*, a traditional Japanese prose/poetry form that evokes rather than describes the feeling of a journey.

ISBN 1-931223-03-3 | $26.95 | 5.5 x 7.5
432 pages | Hardcover

Where They Left You for Dead/Halfway Home

poetry by Margaret Randall

Two poetry collections in one, from the renowned writer, photographer, and teacher. Poems in the first series emerge from the experience of loving someone who suffers chronic pain. The second series addresses the experience of aging. Neither collection is dark, because Randall finds joy in living throughout.

ISBN 1-931223-06-8 | $16.95 | 5.5 x 7.5
112 pages | Hardcover

Seduction: A Portrait of Anais Nin

a study by Margot Beth Duxler

A friend of Nin's in the last decade of her life, Dr. Duxler sees compelling evidence in Nin's early diaries of the young girl's ability to "seduce the father", in an effort to "seduce" into being a self worthy of love. A highly original discussion, casting new light on Nin's life and on her entire body of work, and successfully combining literary analysis, psychoanalysis, and biography.

ISBN 1-931223-02-5 | $24.95 | 5.5 x 7.5
256 pages | Hardcover

The Fortune Catcher

a novel by Susanne Pari

A young Iranian-American woman, daughter of a Moslem father and Jewish mother, is swept into the violent aftermath of the 1979 Islamic Revolution. A journey of ethnic identity and feminist philosophy.

ISBN 1-931223-08-4 | $16.95 | 6 x 9
528 pages | Paperback

Praise for *The Fortune Catcher*
"An exciting literary debut and a riveting love story, woven with intrigue and psychological complexity. The writing is sensual, the characters are memorable, and the story is intelligently structured so that the reader floats easily between two worlds. This is the work of a first-rate storyteller." (Amy Tan)

Charlie's Exit

a novel by Tobey Hiller

A mystery novel of identity and event in which we encounter the transforming power of the search for truth. A woman's house burns to the ground, and she disappears. We learn about these events in vivid snatches, as different characters in the story speculate, remember, imagine, or report on what they saw. The voices include the moving diary of a pioneer woman, Charlie's ancestor, who, like Charlie, is travelling into a new world.

ISBN 1-931223-01-7 | $22.95 | 5.5 x 7.5
224 pages | Hardcover

Love's Learning Place: Truth as Aphrodisiac in Women's Long-Term Relationships

a study by Renate Stendhal

In our culture, we all need to learn to make love, and the surprising key to keeping sex alive in long-term relationships, Stendhal explains, is truth. She persuades us that this can indeed be done, illustrating her thoughts with humorous and poignant vignettes of couples with whom she has worked over the years.

ISBN 1-931223-04-1 | $16.95
5.5 x 7.5 | 128 pages | Hardcover

The Grasshopper's Secret

a magical tale by Renate Stendhal

For the child in every adult and the wisdom in every child. A feisty thirteen-year-old girl in Los Angeles resents an orphaned German boy arriving in her family. But when Zelda chances upon the secret of Kidcou's grasshopper, she is taken on a magical journey, witnesses the dramatic story of Kidcou's life in Europe, and begins to understand her own mission. A story about the magic in daily life, the meeting of different cultures, and the power of understanding and compassion.

ISBN 1-931223-05-X | $23.95 | 5.5 x 7.5
272 pages | Hardcover